Reserved Words

and	array	begin	case
const	div	do	downto
else	end	file	for
forward	function	goto	if
in	label	mod	nil
not	of	or	packed
procedure	program	record	repeat
set	then	to	type
until	var	while	with

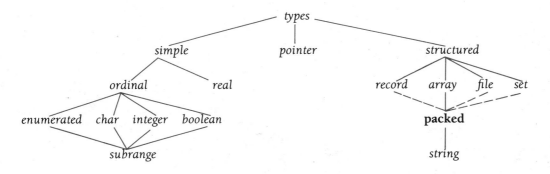

Operator Precedence

not

* / div mod and

+ − or

= <> < <= > >= in

Required Types

real	integer	char	boolean	text

Required Functions

abs (x)	sqr (x)	sqrt (x)	sin (x)	Arithmetic
cos (x)	arctan (x)	ln (x)	exp (x)	
trunc (x)	round (x)			Transfer
ord (x)	chr (x)	succ (x)	pred (x)	Ordinal
odd (x)	eoln (f)	eof (f)		boolean

Required Procedures

read	readln	write	writeln	Input and Output
rewrite (f)	reset (f)	put (f)	get (f)	File Handling
page (f)				
new (p)	dispose (p)			Dynamic Allocation
pack	unpack			Transfer

(model program inside back cover)

Condensed Pascal

Condensed Pascal

by Doug Cooper
University of California, Berkeley

W.W. Norton & Company
New York and London

Condensed Pascal was designed and typeset by Doug Cooper.

PART ONE: PASCAL

PART TWO: PROGRAMMING

PART THREE: REFERENCE

ADDITIONAL APPENDICES

Preface

Welcome to *Condensed Pascal*, the book that answers the question 'Why isn't there a programming text like *Oh! Pascal!* for students who *don't* panic when they sit down at a computer?'

Condensed Pascal is really two books in one volume—a compressed and revised *Oh! Pascal!*, and the complete *Standard Pascal User Reference Manual*. *Condensed Pascal* is primarily aimed at students who have some high school or home computing experience; however, a reasonable level of enthusiasm for learning to program will serve just as well. Although the introduction of elementary, Pascal-specific material is hastened, I've kept *Oh! Pascal!'s* emphasis on program development and problem solving, as well as its chapter-by-chapter antibugging advice and review sections.

While *Condensed Pascal* maintains the virtues (and most of the advanced topics) of *Oh! Pascal!*, it has shed its predecessor's leisurely pace and studiously technophobic discussion. The examples and exercises are now intentionally drawn from math and science. Where *Oh! Pascal!* lay between the 'general programming' and 'programming for CS majors' courses, *Condensed Pascal* heads for the middle ground between 'programming for majors' and 'programming for scientists and engineers.' My focus is still on programming, rather than coding, but almost every substantive program is new, and all the exercises have been rewritten from scratch.

In overview, *Condensed Pascal's* three main parts are:

Pascal: introductory Pascal programming, covered more quickly than in *Oh! Pascal!* 2, and relying on examples that better students will find more interesting (and exercises they will find more challenging).

Programming: more difficult Pascal and general programming issues—software engineering, recursion, advanced pointer applications, correctness, algorithms—most of the new material introduced throughout *Oh! Pascal!* 2, collected into standalone chapters.

Reference: a rigorous explanation of Pascal, based on the BNF, that allows a formal introduction to the language for CS majors. It describes the historical development of the language, and gives the reasoning behind many obscure restrictions and requirements of the ISO/ANSI standard.

The main changes from the second edition of *Oh! Pascal!* were accomplished by:

- *Condensing* basic material: many elementary discussions and digressions have been edited out, repetitive examples and simple Self-Checks have been merged or deleted, long introductions and build-ups have been pruned, and all humor has given way to wit, which is shorter. Over two hundred pages of the original text have been deleted.

- *Reordering* the text: as described above, Pascal and basic programming are presented in Part One, while advanced material (recursion, pointer applications) and most of the language-independent programming discussion (analysis, correctness, software engineering) are reserved for Part Two. A variety of internal ordering changes (e.g. **case** is now the last statement) and shortening of chapters make it easier to pick and choose from the book.

- *Revising* example programs and exercises: there are many, many new long and short examples—Fourier sums, chemical reactions, vector and matrix analysis, polynomials, etc.—and hundreds of new exercises. Some examples and problems dip into specialized topics, but overall, no particular background is required beyond high school math and science, and a healthy curiousity.

- *Adding* the *Standard Pascal User Reference Manual* as Part Three. This book (available separately from the same publisher) is a widely-cited formal reference to ISO/ANSI Pascal. In *Condensed Pascal*, it provides a bottom-up definition of Pascal, built on the BNF, that is correct, comprehensive, and comprehensible, and makes the text a worthwhile investment for any student, CS major or not, who will continue programming after this course.

I assume that in assigning the text, most instructors will work through chapters 1—11 more or less in order, and require other chapters as meets their needs. Some particular side trips you may find appealing are:

Part One: Pascal	*Part Two: Programming*	*Part Three: Reference*
1 basic tools		
2 subprograms		A1 formal notation
3 **for** statement	13 analysis of algorithms	A6 blocks, scope, activations
3-2 arrays (optional)	15 software engineering	
4 **if** statement	12 defensive programming	
5 **while/repeat**	16-1 loop recursion	
5-2 text processing		A5 textfile I/O
6 **case**, enumerations	14 program correctness	
7 arrays	16-2 recursion with arrays	A9-5 conformant array parameters
8 records	18 introduction to algorithms	
9 files		
10 sets		A11 structured types
11 pointers	17 advanced pointer applications	A12 pointer types

Condensed Pascal begins its introduction to programming and Pascal at ground zero. Although students who have had some experience in coding BASIC or Pascal may find the earlier chapters easier going, no language-specific knowledge is assumed. Thus, while *Condensed Pascal* can be used in any CS major or 'science-sequence' college-level course in Pascal programming, it is also perfectly suitable for the sort of motivated students who are attracted by the ETS Advanced Placement course.

Part Three (Reference) will, I think, be especially interesting to students who want to get a feel for programming language design. It teaches almost nothing about programming, but almost everything about Pascal. To help make it easier to use, Part Three is extensively cross-indexed via marginal notes. I've also attached 'cross reference' sections to each chapter in Part One; they contain specific cross-references, and explain some of the differences between classroom and formal terminology. Those who do have programming experience can attempt to read through the Reference directly, and rely on the Pascal introduction in Part One solely for its extended examples.

As usual, I've done the typesetting, and have been able to minimize the disruptive effects of printing long programs on short pages. All examples have been tested from the original typesetting source, and output has not been 'cooked.' Supplements to *Condensed Pascal* are available from the publisher, and include a teacher's manual with answers or hints to the exercises. An earlier manual, *Teaching Introductory Programming (with Oh! Pascal!)*, contains a great deal of material on organizing and running introductory programming courses in general, along with nearly 600 quiz/exam type exercises.

I would like to thank Richard Crandall of Reed College (author of the fine *Pascal Applications for the Sciences*), as well as Doug Kidder and Dave Blackman of Berkeley for their assistance, particularly with the exercises. Naturally, I must bear all responsibility for any lingering errors or lack of clarity. Special thanks also go to my editor at W.W. Norton, Jim Jordan, for his continued support and encouragement even when I announced (in the middle of his vacation) that this 'easy' book would miss our publication deadline by six months.

I hope that you enjoy working with *Condensed Pascal*, and I welcome letters with comments or suggestions. If you write to point out an error, incidentally, please include the printing number (the lowest number at the bottom of the reverse of the title page), since known errors are reset and corrected in each printing (once or twice yearly). I'd appreciate a self-addressed, stamped envelope with your note.

Doug Cooper
Computer Science Division
University of California
Berkeley, Ca. 94720
(dbcooper@BERKELEY.EDU)

This book is dedicated, with affection,
*   to all undergraduate Computer Science majors,*
In the hope that
*   (by its clarity—and brevity),*
They will gain enough free time
*   to read a novel or two,*
That weren't required for any class.

Hardware / Software
Programming Languages
Algorithms and Problem Solving
Program Style

Introduction

COMPUTER SYSTEMS HAVE TWO SIDES: hardware and software. Neither side is of much use without the other, and programs depend on both. A very simple picture of a computer system shows why:

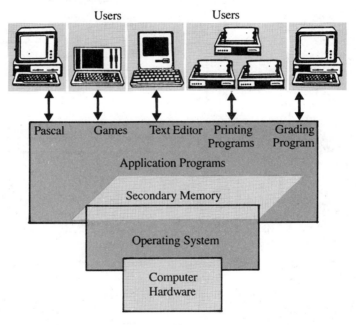

Even the simplest tasks rely on both hardware (in gray) and software (in red). We obviously need hardware—a terminal, at the very least—to enter data, but software is required to link the terminal and computer together. We need hardware to print a stored file, but must depend on software to transfer letters, one at a time, from the computer to the printer. We need hardware to carry out calculations, but we've got to have software that prepares the figures for computation. Before we start to study Pascal and programming, then, let's take a quick tour of the hardware and software that make up a computer system. I'll start with hardware.

Hardware   Computer hardware can be divided into three groups of electronics. The *CPU*, or central processing unit, runs programs, performs calculations, and manages the operation of the other parts. *Memory*, the second essential component, organizes and stores information, from data a program could need microseconds hence to database information that might not be used for years. Finally, *I/O*, or input/output, devices are necessary for communication between a computer and its human users, or other electronic devices.

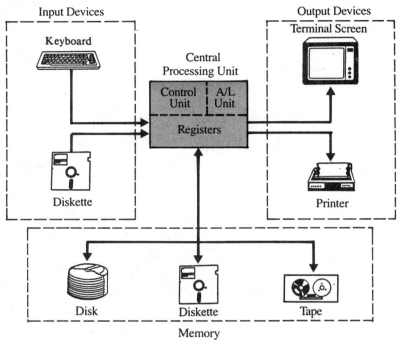

On closer examination, the CPU breaks down into three simpler components as well. First are the *execution registers* that hold program instructions during execution. Typically, only the current instruction is stored, so, from the viewpoint of the execution registers, there is no difference between big programs and little ones, or hard programs and easy ones. The execution registers are also in charge of keeping track of current information—values that are in the process of being changed, currently active locations in memory, and the like.

Determining the effect of each program step is largely the province of the *ALU*, or arithmetic and logic unit: the CPU's decision-maker. Its primary task is to make small comparisons (are these values equal? which is greater?) that, when taken in great number, seem to be reasoned choices. To support its decision-making capability, the ALU also carries out elementary arithmetic operations like addition and subtraction. Again, each small step may be insignificant in itself, but they can eventually add up to give the computer the illusion of sophisticated mathematical ability.

The execution registers and ALU work hand-in-hand, with the registers posing the questions and the ALU supplying the answers. The last CPU component, the *CU*, or control unit, keeps them in touch with each other, and also

the CPU

execution registers

the ALU

control unit

with the rest of the computer. In effect, the control unit serves as the machine's traffic controller.

Give and take between the execution registers, ALU, and control unit largely determine the power of a CPU. One major contributing factor is the speed at which the control unit can transfer information between the ALU and registers. A second is the amount of time required for the ALU to actually make a computation. A third is the amount of overlap that can occur—expensive systems have additional execution registers and ALU's that let work begin on a new program step before the old one is completely finished. A final power-enhancement mechanism, found only in the most advanced computers, lets operations take place in parallel—several program steps are carried out simultaneously.

computer power

The CPU stands poised to carry out single program steps. To do useful work, though, it must interact with the other computer components. *Memory* is the most important. It's usually divided into two varieties—*main* or *primary* memory and *secondary* memory. Main memory comes with the computer; it's built in, but can usually be increased by purchase of additional boards or chips. Simply stated, main memory stores running programs and the information they currently use. It is directly in the service of the CPU, which means that the CPU (which is very fast) can go to and from main memory to get new program steps, and to store or retrieve data. Main memory is usually one of the more expensive hardware components, so computers typically have just enough to meet the requirements of the largest programs they're liable to encounter.

memory

main memory

Secondary memory holds programs and information that are not currently being used. Floppy disks are widely used to provide secondary memory for personal computers. Typically, a floppy stores the instructions for (and has room for the results of) a single program. The computer user has to physically insert the disk in order to transfer its contents to main memory, and run the program it holds.

secondary memory

Secondary memory for bigger, shared, computers is generally made from large, rigid disks that are permanently mounted alongside the computer. Each user has a share of this common secondary storage. Multi-user computers automatically carry out any transfers between secondary and main memory for the benefit of the computer user.

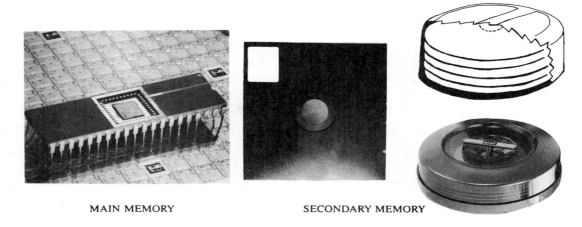

MAIN MEMORY   **SECONDARY MEMORY**

I/O (for input and output) devices are the third major component of computer hardware. I/O devices are specialized machines for communication between computer and people, or other computers. Without I/O devices, we'd have no way to store programs, or to supply data when they ran, or to receive results when they were through. An output device, like a printer, can be used to get the results of running a program, or to inspect data stored in another computer component—say, the main memory. Input devices serve a complementary purpose; we use them to supply the CPU (or memory, through the CPU) with new information.

I/O devices

Network connections are a relatively new addition to the I/O family. They allow extremely high-speed communication between different computer systems. Networks are most commonly used to let computer systems share access to certain components, like printers or terminals. However, experimental networks let one computer's CPU interact with the memory of an entirely different machine, or give two remote users the illusion of being on the same system.

networks

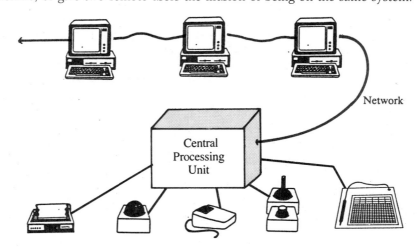

comparing computers

We can compare hardware in several ways. CPU speed is a convenient reference point because, regardless of the computer's price or its programmer's ability, programs are almost invariably executed one step at a time. Since a computer's actual computing is completed in the interaction between its control unit, execution registers, and ALU, the time a single step takes provides a reasonable basis of comparison for two computers that will run the same kind of programs.

We can also compare computers by the size, or potential size, of primary memory. This can be important, because some programs may require very large amounts of primary memory to run effectively, or to run at all. Finally, we can compare computers on the basis of peripheral equipment, including include secondary memory as well as input and output devices.

Each of these measures has its uses. However, we generally find that head-to-head comparisons of CPU speed, memory size, and peripherals are best applied to smaller computers intended for personal use. For larger computers that will probably be shared between a number of users, though, these measurements are often too simple. The prospective purchaser must try to determine just how harmoniously the separate hardware components work together. Ultimately, this will often turn out to depend on our next topic—software.

Software

Computer software falls into two major categories: applications programs, and operating systems. *Applications programs* are specific; each program does a job when (and only when) a computer user requests it. The *operating system*, in contrast, is a general piece of software that runs continuously to govern the operation of the computer's hardware and software resources. In effect, computer users interact directly with applications programs, while the operating system usually helps out indirectly on their behalf.

An operating system is necessary because applications programs usually need more than just raw computational power. Consider an applications program—say, a spreadsheet, or even a game. It will undoubtedly require the services of different input and output devices. It may be stored with other programs in the computer's secondary memory, and have to be retrieved before it can be run. It might even need hardware that's currently being used by another programmer.

operating system

This is where operating system software comes in: to control and coordinate the operation of computer hardware for the benefit of individual users and their programs. A computer that just runs one program—like the microprocessor found in a toaster or carburetor—doesn't really need an operating system. But when programs or users must share resources, and use the computer in a variety of ways, an operating system is needed to maintain order.

controlling access

What are some of the practical problems that an operating system deals with? On shared computers, the operating system *controls computer access*. When you enter a password to log on, you do so at the operating system's request. The operating system organizes users; it, rather than you, is responsible for keeping stored programs and information that belongs to dozens or hundreds of computer users separate and retrievable.

allocating resources

The operating system also *allocates independent resources*. Suppose that several computer users want to use a single printer. Each user might independently request that some stored information be printed; it is the operating system's job to form a waiting list that handles requests in turn.

sharing resources

Not all resources are independent, so the operating system must *schedule shared resources* as well. Although a printer can only handle one job at a time, faster resources (like the CPU) can be shared between users. The result of resource sharing is that each system user gets the illusion that she is working on her own personal computer. Behind the scenes, though, the operating system must work furiously to ensure that individual users' programs don't get mixed up as each takes its turn at using the CPU and main memory.

managing the environment

Finally, from our point of view as computer programmers, the operating system's main job is *managing the programming environment*. It supplies the tools we need to write programs, then arranges for the programs to run. This brings us to our next topic—programming languages.

Programming Languages

There's an old story about an untutored bumpkin who overheard some students talking about the stars. Although the concepts they discussed were strange, he felt he could understand how astronomers used telescopes to measure the distance from the earth to the celestial bodies. It even seemed reasonable that they could predict the stars' relative positions and motions. What totally puzzled him, though, was how the devil they were able to find out the stars' *names!*

Computer languages often inspire the same respectful awe, but their evolution from one generation to the next is hardly mysterious. Let's look at the first three generations of programming languages: low-level machine languages, intermediate assembly languages, and, finally, high-level languages like Pascal.

instruction sets

The lowest-level codes belong to a built-in instruction set that's not much more sophisticated than the operations available on programmable hand calculators. There are instructions for doing simple arithmetic, of course, and for saving partial results. A variety of instructions are used to compare values, and to decide what to do next. A special set of instructions manages storage and retrieval of data and program steps from memory.

machine language

A machine language is defined by numbering the instruction set. Eight-digit binary values allow 256 different instructions, starting with 00000000 and ending with 11111111. A machine language program is nothing but a long series of eight-digit numbers.

assembly language

Machine language programming is easy, but it's incredibly tedious. A bright idea was practically inevitable: Why not write a machine language program that could recognize short sequences of English letters, and would automatically translate the English into the proper machine language instructions? Such programs were called assemblers; they understood assembly language, and were soon found on every computer.

Assembly language programming is a bit more palatable. An assembly language program is a sequence of brief commands, usually accompanied by references to one or two memory locations. For instance, the assembly language command **ADD R2, R4** means 'add the contents of memory location R2 to memory location R4, and save the sum in R4.' Assembly language programs can be extremely efficient, which is why control programs for systems with relatively limited CPU or memory resources (like video games) are usually written in assembler.

But assembly language hardly exhausted the limits of human ingenuity. Why be limited to three-letter words? When memory space or CPU speed were not at a premium, programmers wanted to express themselves in relatively English sentences, rather than in the computer-oriented terms of machine and assembly languages. The response was obvious: more complicated programs, called *interpreters* and *compilers*, that translated increasingly sophisticated sequences of letters—high-level languages—into a form the computer could understand. In time, optimizing versions equaled or even surpassed assembler efficiency.

interpreters, compilers

High-level languages, like FORTRAN, BASIC, and Pascal, are consciously designed to help solve problems, and to free the programmer from having to memorize instructions, or keep track of numbered memory locations. In contrast, low-level machine and assembly languages were expressly intended to operate computers. High-level language programmers give commands in a language that resembles a terse English, using phrases that are liable to be found in the statement of a solution—**if** a condition is met **then** we take an action or **else** do something different.

high-level languages

Pascal was developed in the early '70s by the Swiss computer scientist Niklaus Wirth, who named his new language after the 17th century mathematician and religious zealot Blaise Pascal. Wirth designed Pascal with two main goals:

Pascal

1.   To provide a teaching language that would bring out concepts common to all languages, while avoiding inconsistencies and unnecessary detail.

2.   To define a truly standard language that would be cheap and easy to implement on any computer.

In a sense, Pascal is a *lingua franca*, or common tongue, of programming. It's easy to learn, and provides an excellent foundation for learning other languages. People who know Pascal can master BASIC in an afternoon, and pick up FORTRAN in a week or two.

Is Pascal the ultimate programming language? No. Almost before the ink was dry on the original standard, implementors were figuring out ways to extend Pascal, both to make up for perceived shortcomings (like Pascal's lack of string types), and to take advantage of improved hardware (that made features like graphics available cheaply). Many of these extensions are quite beneficial;

nevertheless, our focus is primarily on learning programming, rather than coding, and the less idiosyncratic Standard Pascal is easier to deal with than the extended versions.*

newer languages

An eventual successor to Pascal may be Modula-2, which was also developed by Wirth. Fortunately, the first term's worth of Modula-2 is almost exactly like Pascal. Modula-2 contains some additional features that make it attractive for later programming courses, particularly those that involve writing large programs to translate languages (the compiler course) or to control computers (the operating systems course). Within a few years, Modula-2 may become a language widely used for undergraduate coursework (and *Oh My! Modula-2!* will probably appear on the shelves!).

Another potential Pascal successor, the Ada programming language, was commissioned by the U.S. Department of Defense. The DoD hoped to create a language that would be more reliable for the control of weapons systems, as well as less expensive to program in, than FORTRAN and others. At the time of this writing it is not clear that either goal has been met, nor that the language will be widely used outside of defense contractors' programming shops.

the fourth generation

There are also successors to the entire range of high-level, third generation languages. We might think of the development of programming languages in the following manner: machine and assembly languages are *operations* languages, closely tied to actual machine events. High-level languages, in turn, can be called *implementation* languages, which draw on lower-level codes to actually implement some particular problem's solution. The fourth generation of programming languages can be characterized as *applications* languages, intended to solve a general range of problems (say, implementing a data base) without burdening the programmer with the actual implementation details. She describes what she wants, but doesn't have to provide a step-by-step plan for getting there.

Algorithms and Problem Solving

We, however, are still humble third-generation programmers, and before we can write a program we have to develop its *algorithm*. An algorithm is an outline of the steps that solving a problem will require. It's usually detailed enough to be the basis of a computer program, but it isn't written in a computer language. Instead, the algorithm is expressed in English. A good programmer will be able to implement, or realize, the algorithm in almost any programming language.

what are algorithms?

Is a recipe an algorithm? If it were, a Pascal textbook would consist of chapter after chapter of standard programs. A recipe is a highly restricted algorithm at best, because it only solves one specific instance of a problem—how to bake a chocolate fudge cake, say, rather than how to bake a cake in general. Algorithms tend to be less special-purpose; an algorithm is a set of rules to follow to solve a certain kind of problem, rather than one particular example of it.

* To be honest, I feel like a fuddy-duddy in making such a statement—I fear that in a year or two people will be lumping me with those who claim that freshmen should really learn to program in assembler!

Suppose that we want to divide one fraction by another. If we knew the particular fractions involved we might be tempted to supply a recipe, rather than a broader algorithm. For instance, 1/4 divided by 1/2 can be solved by applying the specific rule 'divide the denominators,' which gives a correct answer: 1/(4/2), or 1/2. However, this is just a special case! The general algorithm we should follow—exchange the numerator and denominator of one fraction, then multiply the two fractions—is an algorithm that solves *all* fraction divisions.

dividing fractions

Computer algorithms usually include some details that take machine limitations into account. For instance, if we were going to add two numbers by hand we'd just specify one step—add the numbers. A computer algorithm has extra operations for the computer's benefit:

> *get the numbers*
> *add them up*
> *print the answer*

exchanging numbers

What about exchanging two numbers, a job we might have to do in a program that divided fractions? It's tempting to say that our algorithm is:

> *get the numerator and denominator*
> *give the numerator the value of the denominator*
> *give the denominator the value of the numerator*

Can you spot the error? Both variables (the numerator and denominator) will end up representing the original denominator, because we didn't save the value of the original numerator. A computer algorithm has to take this step explicitly:

> *get the numerator and denominator*
> *save the numerator*
> *give the numerator the denominator's value*
> *give the denominator the saved value*

problem solving

Now, a considerable amount of the work that goes into teaching programming deals with problem solving in general, rather than the details of a particular programming language per se. One of the most interesting aspects of teaching is the realization that relatively little effort goes into the development of new algorithms. This doesn't mean that all the good algorithms have already been devised, but, rather, that the great majority of problems can be solved with a fairly small subset of computing techniques.

top-down design

Certain modes of problem solving seem to work best when a program is the desired solution. Chief among these is the *top-down* approach—breaking a problem into its component parts before working on the low-level details. There are several reasons for the top-down design's popularity. First of all, even Pascal programs are written in low-level terms that require huge amounts of detail. The top-down approach—describing the problem, then parts of the prob-

stepwise refinement

lem, then parts of those parts, etc.—forces us to plan a programming strategy in plain English before diving into actual coding. The problem restatement or decomposition aspect of top-down design is sometimes called *stepwise refinement*. I'll discuss it in detail in Chapter 2.

A second desirable feature of the top-down approach is that dividing a big problem into subproblems is tantamount to breaking a big program into subprograms. In consequence, each one can be written and tested separately, and presumably more easily. It doesn't require much reflection to realize that this implies a third advantage of top-down design—it may reveal subproblems that have already been solved by existing programs. In Chapter 12 we'll see that building software with parts from a 'toolbox' of code is an extremely effective approach to programming.

public library project

Let's look at an example of the top-down method. Suppose that a public library wishes to computerize its operations—a fairly ambitious programming project. The first step in cutting it down to size is a top-down decomposition or restatement of the problem. However, we can just as easily call this a top-down description of the program's main subroutines:

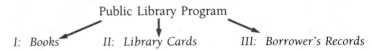

Public Library Program

I: *Books*   II: *Library Cards*   III: *Borrower's Records*

If anything is left out, we can always backtrack to this step of the refinement. Let's go a stage further, and restate each of the first level's entries:

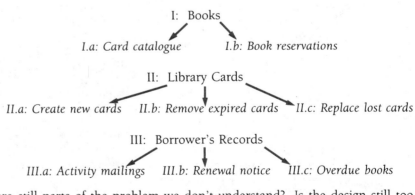

I: Books

I.a: *Card catalogue*   I.b: *Book reservations*

II: Library Cards

II.a: *Create new cards*   II.b: *Remove expired cards*   II.c: *Replace lost cards*

III: Borrower's Records

III.a: *Activity mailings*   III.b: *Renewal notice*   III.c: *Overdue books*

Are there still parts of the problem we don't understand? Is the design still too abstract for a programmer to encode? Let's add more detail:

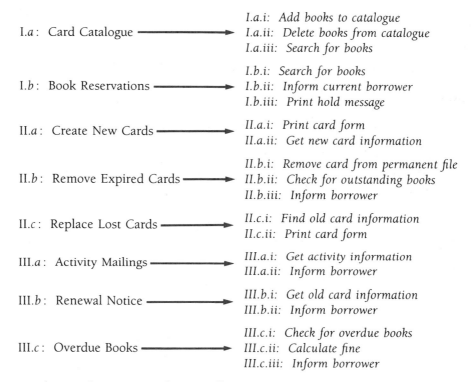

I.a: Card Catalogue ⟶
- I.a.i: *Add books to catalogue*
- I.a.ii: *Delete books from catalogue*
- I.a.iii: *Search for books*

I.b: Book Reservations ⟶
- I.b.i: *Search for books*
- I.b.ii: *Inform current borrower*
- I.b.iii: *Print hold message*

II.a: Create New Cards ⟶
- II.a.i: *Print card form*
- II.a.ii: *Get new card information*

II.b: Remove Expired Cards ⟶
- II.b.i: *Remove card from permanent file*
- II.b.ii: *Check for outstanding books*
- II.b.iii: *Inform borrower*

II.c: Replace Lost Cards ⟶
- II.c.i: *Find old card information*
- II.c.ii: *Print card form*

III.a: Activity Mailings ⟶
- III.a.i: *Get activity information*
- III.a.ii: *Inform borrower*

III.b: Renewal Notice ⟶
- III.b.i: *Get old card information*
- III.b.ii: *Inform borrower*

III.c: Overdue Books ⟶
- III.c.i: *Check for overdue books*
- III.c.ii: *Calculate fine*
- III.c.iii: *Inform borrower*

The top-down approach pays off as we get down to subproblems that are obviously easy enough to solve directly—*print card form*. We can also recognize that some of the technical details—*calculate fine*—aren't important to the overall structure of the program, and can be delayed. As an extra bonus, we find that some program segments (like the *inform borrower* parts) may be similar enough to be written once, then shared. Overall, the main subprograms are largely laid out by name, and can be coded and tested separately.

Program Style

Once we've figured out how to solve a problem, and have an algorithm in head or in hand, it's time to get down to business and write a program. Now, programming is a field that has undergone drastic changes in the past few decades. In the early days of computing, programs were of relatively limited concern for two reasons. First, hardware was incredibly expensive—a computer's cost far outweighed the salaries paid to its dutiful programmers.

Second, the general applicability of software was thought of as being quite limited. As a result, even though a great deal of attention might be paid to individual programs as they were written—programmers prided themselves on knowing undocumented processor features that might save a few bytes of memory or milliseconds of running time—once entered, programs were seldom encountered again. Most programs were custom jobs, and few were too large for a single programmer to handle completely.

hardware vs. software cost

Nowadays, though, the human costs of computer operation are far greater than those of the mechanical components. It is the production of software, rather than the purchase of hardware, that is relatively expensive. Moreover, as the cost of producing software grows, the desire to save money or development time by reusing, adapting, or modifying existing software becomes increasingly attractive. Studies in the last decade consistently show that considerably more time and effort goes into patching and improving *existing* programs than is devoted to writing new ones.

software engineering

The raw size of programs has, in itself, led to difficulties that were unknown when programs were crammed into a meager 64K. As a result, interest has focused on methods of writing programs that not only work, but can also be understood by others. The new field of *software engineering*—the study of producing programs—is one of the hottest areas in computing today.

program style

Now, this text is not intended to serve as a primer on software engineering, although I will devote a complete chapter to it in Part Two. However, we can expect to encounter a consistent attention to an important subcategory called program *style*. What are some of the characteristics of stylish Pascal?

- *clarity*: The program is readable, and the operation of its constituent parts can be easily summarized and understood. Identifiers are meaningful, and constants are defined when possible.
- *structure*: The program is written in a manner that takes advantage of Pascal's features—it isn't a FORTRAN or BASIC program that happens to be written in Pascal. It uses statements and data types appropriately.
- *documentation*: The program is well-commented—a program reader doesn't have to mentally simulate computer operation in order to understand what the program does.
- *robustness*: The program will not fall apart when it's confronted with an easily-anticipated user error. It rejects faulty input and lets the user try again, or fails gracefully, letting the user know what went wrong.
- *modularity*: The program is built of relatively independent parts that can be tested or improved individually. A modest change in requirements will not require a complete program rewrite.
- *portability*: The program doesn't rely on local system pecularities or undocumented features—it will run on every Standard Pascal system.

A well-written program doesn't just outwit the computer. It's put together in a way that someone who may have to read it two or ten years hence can understand. It implements the detailed sequence of steps that a computer requires, without losing or confusing a human reader who deals in concepts. Programming problems are divergent—they usually have many solutions. Let's hope (for the sake of those who may one day have to read *your* code) that you learn the difference between good solutions and bad ones.

1

The Basic Programming Tools

The first chapter introduces the basic tools of programming in Pascal. Our initial lessons involve data—using variables to represent values, writing expressions to manipulate them, and making assignments that save results. We'll learn about Pascal's standard functions and its input and output procedures, and get a feel for the basic form of Pascal programs.

Out of necessity, this chapter contains a considerable amount of detail. This may temporarily discomfit readers who are eager to open consulting firms, but even whiz kids should try to work from a solid foundation. Above all, resist seeing the language as a hodgepodge of detail; try to understand Pascal as it fits together, rather than as an arbitrary collection of separate facts. Don't be afraid to question the language designer's wisdom ('Why'd he do it that way?'), or my method of explanation. Pascal was largely designed as a teaching language, and as students you're the final arbiters of its success or failure. Good luck!

Programming For Output 1-1

BEHOLD A COMPLETE Pascal program.

```
program FirstRun (output);

    {This is our first program.}
begin
    writeln ('Hello. I love you.')
end.
```

FirstRun is a rather friendly program whose output you can probably figure out already. We'll begin to study Pascal by reconstructing it from scratch.

The first step, not surprisingly, is to indicate that what we're writing is a program. The first word of every Pascal program is the reserved word:

reserved words

program

I'll always print reserved words, which can't be redefined, in **boldface type**.

identifiers

Next, we need to name our program. A Pascal identifier, or name, must begin with a letter, and then may contain any series of digits or letters, as long as it doesn't have the same spelling as a reserved word. This makes *R2D2* and *Top40* legal identifiers, but invalidates names like *then* (a reserved word) and *2Bor02B* (which starts with a digit). I'll print identifiers in *italic*.

syntax charts

The wary reader will anticipate having to remember quite a few rules for Pascal program construction. I'll help by supplying syntax charts when appropriate. The chart of an identifier is:

identifier

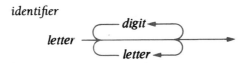

As long as we start on the left and follow the arrows, we'll have an identifier that satisfies Pascal's rules: it must start with a letter and can be followed by as many letters or digits as we wish. All syntax charts are collected in Appendix E.

program heading

A program's heading, or first line, ends with abbreviated instructions to the operating system. It must know in advance if we intend to get data from the program's user—*input*—or to deliver results to her—*output*. Since this particular program only has output, the heading is completed with:

program *FirstRun* (*output*);

A semicolon ends the heading. If it had input as well, we would write:

program *FeedBack* (*input, output*);

comments

Explanations of a program's operation are called comments. They go between curly brackets like these: { }, because the compiler ignores anything written between curly brackets when it translates a Pascal program into machine language.

> As far as program operation is concerned, comments are unnecessary. In practice, they're used in *every* program as explanatory notes to ourselves, or to other people reading the program (just as I highlight exceptionally important points in boxes like this).

alternative comments

Some keyboards may not include curly brackets (also called braces), so Pascal allows alternate symbols as synonyms—'(*' is the same as '{', and '*)' has the same meaning as '}'. A comment can go on the same line as Pascal code, or it can extend over several lines, as long as a left comment bracket appears at the beginning, and a right comment bracket turns up at the end.

```
{              Program FirstRun
                      by
               Rachel Jetaime                    }
program FirstRun (output);       (*This is also a comment.*)
```

statement part

Since *FirstRun* won't make decisions or computations that would require storing values in variables, we can get right to work on the program's statement part. It starts with the reserved word **begin**, and contains a series of instructions, called statements, for the computer to execute, or carry out.

> **program** *FirstRun* (*output*) ;
>
> {This is our first program.}
>
> **begin**

standard procedures

The first statements we'll use are the standard procedures—essentially built-in commands—for printing output. Procedure *writeln* (pronounced 'write line') works like this:

> *writeln* ('Everything between the quote marks will get printed.')

using *writeln*

Any text, or words, that *writeln* prints go between single quote marks. They may not contain a carriage return.

Program *FirstRun* commences amiably (perhaps *too* amiably) by printing 'Hello. I love you.' After this output statement, all that's missing from our program is the reserved word **end**, followed by a period.

> **program** *FirstRun* (*output*) ;
>
> {This is our first program.}
>
> **begin**
>   *writeln* ('Hello. I love you.')
> **end.**

Program *FirstRun* is complete—on paper. Actually running the program generally involves using a few of the computer's applications programs. We typically face a three-step process:

1. *Editing*. First, the Pascal program (like the one we just wrote) is stored in a computer file.

2. *Compilation*. Second, the file is read, but not changed in any way, by a compiler or interpreter. It translates our stored Pascal program into a machine-oriented version the computer can run, and usually saves this version in a new file. The compiler or interpreter will spot, and complain about, many kinds of errors in our original program. These must be fixed (by a return to step 1) before the program can be compiled.

steps for running
programs

3. *Execution*. Third, a command is given to execute the machine-oriented version of our original Pascal program. This step is sometimes joined with step 2.

The exact editor, compiler, and program execution commands you give aren't specified by Pascal, and will depend on your particular computer system. When *FirstRun* is executed, its output will be:

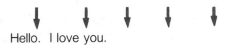

Hello. I love you.

(I use downward arrows (↓ ↓) to mean 'The program's output would look like this.' The funny typeface is used for printing program output.)

more statements
Let's try a more complicated example with additional output. Now, the *writeln* procedure prints a carriage return after printing its text message, so each line of output is on a separate line. Another standard procedure, *write*, prints without going to the next line. This means that the output of two or more *write* procedures can wind up on a single line. Eventually, when a *writeln* is encoun-
write vs. writeln
tered, it prints its own output message (if there is one), and then a carriage return. If there's no partial line or new output, the *writeln* prints a blank line.

In program *SeveralLines*, below, notice the semicolons (;) between the *write* and *writeln* statements. In Pascal, semicolons are used as statement separators. They belong between any two statements or parts of a program.

program *SeveralLines* (*output*);

{Demonstrates the statement separator with procedures *write* and *writeln*.}

separating statements
begin
    write ('A fine ');   {These lines are printed ... }
    write ('romance, ');
    writeln ('with no kisses.');   { ... on the same output line.}
    writeln;   {These put two blank lines in the output,}
    writeln;   {since there's no earlier output or new output.}
    write ('A fine romance, ');
    writeln ('my friend, this is!')
end.

A fine romance, with no kisses.

A fine romance, my friend, this is!

Not all Pascal systems immediately print the output of a *write*. Some collect the partial line internally, without printing, until a *writeln* is encountered. As a result, it may actually be impossible to print anything without a carriage return (through *writeln*) at the end of the line.

printing single quotes
'How do I print a carriage return?' is always one of the first questions to ask when you learn a new programming language. 'How do I print a quote mark?' is another. In Pascal, the single quote, or apostrophe, is itself quoted by being entered twice:

writeln ('You wouldn''t, I couldn''t, and she won''t!');

You wouldn't, I couldn't, and she won't!

Variables and Types

Programs that contain only *writeln* statements can be amusing, but they aren't overwhelmingly useful. Variables—value holders—are the key to more interesting work. Consider program *FeedBack*, below. One variable (*Number*) holds a value entered by the program user; the other (*Sum*) is assigned, or given, twice *Number's* value. Finally, a *writeln* is used in a new way—without single quote marks—to print the variable's value.

variable demonstration program

```
program FeedBack (input, output);
     {Reads the value of a variable, performs a calculation,
            saves the new value, and then prints it.}
var Number, Sum : integer;
     {This declares two variables that can store numerical values.}
begin
     writeln ('What is your favorite number?');
          {After printing this message, the computer waits for the program
            user to enter a value, or reads it from a data file.}
     readln (Number);  {This input statement gets Number's value.}
     Sum := Number + Number;  {This assignment gives Sum a value.}
     write ('Twice that number is');
     writeln (Sum)
end.
```

What is your favorite number?
47
Twice that number is   94

(I'll always show program input **like this**.) We'll discuss input and assignments in a few pages.

Pascal variables are more versatile than memory keys of a hand calculator—for instance, they can hold non-numeric values—but they are also *declaring variables* more strictly regulated. When a variable is declared the *type*, or category, of values it will store is specified. It is a program error to try to store a value of the wrong type in a variable.

Four basic types are predefined in Pascal—the standard simple types *the standard simple* *integer, char, boolean*, and *real*. *integer* values are the counting numbers: *types* −2,−1, 0, 1, 2, and so on. Type *char* contains all available single characters—letters, digits, punctuation, etc. *real* values are decimals and positive or negative powers of 10: −3.55, 0.0, 187E−02, 35.997E+11. Finally, *boolean* (boo'-lee-an) variables can have either of two values—*false* or *true*.

Variables get their names and types in the variable declaration part of a Pascal program; after the heading, and before the statement part. It begins with the reserved word **var**, then each identifier is listed along with its type.

variable declaration
part

```
var AptNumber: integer;
    ShoeSize: real;
    FirstInitial: char;
    OutToLunch: boolean;
```

The syntax chart of a variable declaration part looks like this:

variable declaration

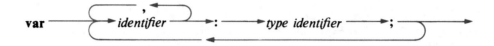

According to the chart, we can declare any number of variables, in any order, as long as a semicolon separates the variables of each type. This is also a legal variable declaration:

```
var TVchannel: integer;          {One integer variable.}
    GPA, BattingAverage: real;
    Pagenumber, age: integer;    {Another integer variable.}
```

integer, char, and *boolean* are called *ordinal* types. I'll use this term when I want to exclude type *real* from the other simple types, but the distinction isn't critical now. However, it is important to understand floating-point, or scientific, notation. To express very large or small Pascal *real* numbers, the letter 'E' stands for 'times 10 to the power of.' A *real* given as a power of 10 need not contain a decimal point, but if it has one, there must always be a digit—even a zero—to the left of the decimal. Thus, the fraction ½ can be shown as 0.5, or 5E–1, or even 0.005E1, but never as an unadorned .5.

floating-point notation

Why does Pascal use types? Basically, to protect the programmer from the computer. Since values are stored internally as binary numbers, computers would be perfectly content to add *integers* to characters, or to subtract *true* from 45.378. Errors of this sort (for example, where a programmer forgot that she was using a variable to store characters, and instead treated the stored value as a number), used to cause serious errors in large programs. Pascal's type separation provides a scorecard that helps prevent such nonsensical activity. If the compiler spots a problem, it prints an error message that points out the imminent type clash. The mistake must be fixed before the program is run.

why have types?

type clashes

Naturally, type checking goes on during program execution as well, to detect improper input or assignment. There is only one exception to strict type checking: *integer* values are automatically converted to *reals* if assigned to *real* variables. Aside from this exception, the type rule is inviolable. When it's broken, the program ignominiously crashes—stops running.

crashing

Pascal programs are considered to be free format. This means that the position of words in a program is generally unimportant, as long as they are in the right order, and no words or words and numbers, are run together (like **pro-**

program format
gram*FirstRun*). We can make a declaration that has minimal spacing (just one blank to keep **var** from running into *GPA*):

> **var** *GPA,BattingAverage* :*real* ;*Pagenumber,age,TVchannel* :*integer* ;

Or, we can put in a zillion unnecessary spaces:

> **var**   *GPA*   ,   *BattingAverage*
> :   *real*   ;   *Pagenumber*
> ,*age*   ,*TVchannel* :   *integer* ;

When you write programs, try to approximate the format of programs shown in this book. Above all, *be consistent* .

Assignment Statements

An expression is generally a sequence of values and the operators used to combine or modify them. The assignment statement—the most frequently used statement in programming—saves the outcome of this effort. In Pascal, assignment takes the form:

> *variable identifier* := *the value represented by an expression* ;

The *assignment operator* (:=) changes the value of a variable within a program; to give it a starting value, or to alter its current value. In an assignment statement, the expression on the right-hand side of the assignment operator is evaluated. Then the result, or computed value, is given to the variable on the
evaluating expressions left-hand side. To avoid confusion with the plain equals‧sign, we're best off reading the assignment operator as 'gets.' For example, this assignment:

> *LuckyNumber* := 7+5 ;

would be read: 'the variable *LuckyNumber* gets assigned the result of adding 7 and 5,' or, more tersely, '*LuckyNumber* gets 7 plus 5.'

> A variable must be *initialized* , or given a starting value, before it can appear in an expression. The variable is *undefined* until it is initialized.

> *Age* := 17 ; {Once *Age* is initialized . . . }
> *LuckyNumber* := 2 ∗ *Age* ; { . . . it can appear in an expression.}

initializing variables
Reading a new value (we'll see how, soon) is an alternate way to initialize a variable. But one method or the other must be used, since an uninitialized variable is like an unmade-up motel room—you can never be sure of what you'll find.

Naturally, you should be sure that assignments involve values and variables of the same types. If *Age* is an *integer* variable, and *Fraction* is of type *real* , then these are valid assignments:

$$Age := 16; \qquad Fraction := 16.5; \qquad \text{\{legal assignments\}}$$

numerical assignments These assignments contain type clashes between *Age*, 16.5, and *Fraction*:

$$Age := 16.5; \qquad Age := Fraction; \qquad \text{\{illegal assignments\}}$$

Assignments to *char* variables pose a special problem. When a character character assignments is used as a value of type *char*, it must be enclosed within single quote marks:

$$Initial := 'E'; \qquad SeventhDigitCharacter := '6';$$

This avoids confusion between the letter 'E' and a variable named *E*, or between the character '6' and the *integer* value 6. Note that a *char* variable can only represent a single *char* value—an assignment like 'RMS' would be in error.

The *integer* and *real* Operators

The *integer* and *real* operators are rules for combining operand values into new expressions. The *real* arithmetic operators are:

Real Operators

real operators

+	addition	*Price + Surcharge*
−	subtraction	*Tuition − Scholarship*
*	multiplication	32.87 * 6.5E−02
/	division	*Spoils* / 2.0

integer division The *integer* operators are the same except that the slash has been replaced by two special operators for *integer* division—**div**, and **mod**. The first, **div**, gives us the quotient of a division without any remainder, as though the quotient had been rounded toward zero. **mod** does just the opposite. It ignores the 'whole' part of the quotient, and provides only the remainder. Although **div** and **mod** are reserved words in Pascal, they're thought of as symbols that represent operations, just like + and −.

9 **div** 5 *is* 1	24 **div** 9 *is* 2	−9 **div** 5 *is* −1
9 **mod** 5 *is* 4	24 **mod** 9 *is* 6	9 **mod** 24 *is* 9

Since they're *integer* operators, **div** and **mod** may only be used with *integer*-valued operands. We can't use *real* operands with **div** and **mod** even when it seems perfectly reasonable. The expressions 4 **div** 2.0 and 1E+02 **mod** 50 are both invalid, because 2.0 and 1E+02 are *real* values.

Integer Operators

integer operators

+	addition	*FamilySize* + 2
−	subtraction	*ShoppingDays* − 1
*	multiplication	*Fine* * *DaysLate*
div	'whole number' division	10 **div** 3 (is 3)
mod	'remainder' division	10 **mod** 3 (is 1)

mixed expressions

> If an expression contains both *reals* and *integers* (or only *reals*), then the result of evaluating the expression will be of type *real*. The result of any expression that uses the *real* division operator (/) is also of type *real*.

In Pascal, as in ordinary arithmetic, we can combine small expressions into a chain of operations. As long as the type rules are obeyed, expressions can be as complicated as you like. However, a problem of operator precedence

operator precedence

arises: what part of the expression is evaluated first? Pascal's solution is to define a hierarchy, or ordering, of different operations. Expressions that contain more than one operator from a given level of the hierarchy are evaluated from left to right. Parentheses can change the order of evaluation, or make it clearer.

The arithmetic operations have two precedence levels—addition and sub-

operator hierarchy

traction have less precedence than the other operations. This means that:

*	/	**div**	**mod**	these operations are completed...
+	–			...before these operations.

When an expression contains more than a single operator from any one level, we do the multiplications and divisions first, then perform the lower level additions or subtractions.

5.5–3.375/1.125	is 5.5–3.0	is 2.5
5*3+14 **mod** 4	is 15+2	is 17
4.5/1.125–3.325*6.5	is 4.0–21.6125	is –17.6125
7–6*2–33 **div** 4–3	is 7–12–8–3	is –16

parentheses

Parentheses change this order of evaluation, because a subexpression within parentheses gets evaluated before the rest of the expression. When we *nest* parentheses—use multiple levels of parentheses—calculations are done from the inside out.

(5+3)*(8–2)	*is equivalent to* 8*6
(6/3)*(2–4)	*is the same as* 2.0*(–2)
2.5*(1.25+0.25)	*is like* 2.5*1.5
(8 **mod** (2 * (5 – 4)))	*is like* 8 **mod** 2

The Standard Functions

The final component of expressions are the standard functions. Like function keys built into a pocket calculator, they save us from the death of a thousand cuts—a single *call*, or invocation, computes what might otherwise require a long series of program calculations. Pascal's standard functions are:

arithmetic

sqr	*sqrt*		{Square and square root}
sin	*cos*	*arctan*	{Standard trigonometric functions}
exp	*ln*		{Exponential and natural log functions}
abs	*round*	*trunc*	{Absolute value, rounding, and truncation}

ordering	*succ*	*pred*	{Successor and predecessor of ordinal values}
	ord	*chr*	{Ordinal position, and *char* value in a given position}
boolean	*odd*		{Is an *integer* odd?}
	eoln	*eof*	{Are we at the end of an input line or file?}

function calls

> A function call usually has two parts—the name of the function, followed by the function's *argument* in parentheses. The *result* of a function is the value the call represents. Its Pascal type is the function's *result-type*.

function terminology

To spout all these new terms at once, I'll say that a function (call it '*f* '), takes an argument (that I'll call '*x* '). The value the function call represents is the result of evaluating the expression $f(x)$, and has the function's result-type.

The first group of functions take numerical values as arguments.

arithmetic functions

sqr (*x*), *sqrt* (*x*)   Represents the square, or square root, of *x*, which may be either *real* or *integer*.

sin (*x*), *cos* (*x*)   Sine and cosine functions. They represent the sine and cosine of the argument *x* (given in radians), respectively.

arctan (*x*)   Arctangent function. Represents the inverse tangent of *x*; the *real* result is in radians.

ln (*x*)   Natural log function. Represents the log (to the base *e*) of its *integer* or *real* argument *x*. The argument must be greater than 0.

exp (*x*)   Exponential function. Represents *e* (the base of the natural log system), raised to the *real* or *integer* power *x* (i.e. e^x).

Function *sqr* has the same result-type as its argument, but *sqrt* is always *real*:

$$sqr\ (3.0)\ is\ 9.0000000000E+00 \qquad sqr\ (3)\ is\ 9$$
$$sqrt\ (4.0)\ is\ 2.0000000000E+00 \qquad sqrt\ (4)\ is\ 2.0000000000E+00$$

figuring exponents

The natural logarithm functions have *real* results whether their arguments are *real* or *integer*. Between them, *ln* and *exp* help overcome a Pascal shortcoming that often annoys programmers—the lack of a specific *exponentiation* operator (there's no predefined function for raising a number (call it *a*) to some power (call it *n*) as in a^n). This formula:

$$a^n = exp\ (n * ln\ (a))$$

is subject to the following restriction: the base, *a*, must be a positive *real* or *integer* value, as required by the definition of *ln*.

The final arithmetic functions do jobs that are trivial on paper, but require some specialization in the computer.

abs (*x*) Absolute value. This function gives the absolute value | *x* | of its *integer* or *real* argument *x*. The result type of the function matches the type of its argument.

$$abs\,(-10)\text{ is }10 \qquad abs\,(-3.5)\text{ is }3.5000000000E+00$$

trunc (*x*) The truncating function represents the 'whole' part of its *real* argument *x* as an *integer*. Any portion of the argument that is a fraction less than 1 is truncated—cut off. In effect, the argument is rounded to the nearest *integer* toward zero.

$$trunc\,(4.8)\text{ is }4 \qquad trunc\,(-3.9)\text{ is }-3 \qquad trunc\,(0.22573E+02)\text{ is }22$$

transfer functions

round (*x*) The rounding function represents its *real* argument, *x*, rounded to the nearest *integer* according to this rule:

If *x* is positive, rounding is *up* for fractions including and greater than .5, and *down* for fractions less than .5.

If *x* is negative, the result is rounded *down*—away from zero—when the fractional part is greater than or equal to .5, and *up*—toward zero— otherwise. This makes *round* (–*x*) equal to –*round* (*x*).

$$round\,(1.6)\text{ is }2 \qquad round\,(1.5)\text{ is }2$$
$$round\,(-2.6)\text{ is }-3 \qquad round\,(-1.5)\text{ is }-2$$

Functions like *round* and *trunc* are *transfer functions* that let a value of one type be treated as though it had another. This is sometimes necessary to make calculations obey Pascal's strict type rules.

ordering functions

Lest you start to think that computing is all numbers, I hasten to introduce four functions—*pred, succ, ord*, and *chr*—used to juggle other values. I'll relate the ordinal functions to *char* values for now, and find more applications in the discussion of enumerated ordinal types in Chapter 6. A bit of background is necessary.

collating sequence

Each computer's *character set*—all the letters, numerals, punctuation it can input or output, plus some—are in a certain fixed order, called the *collating sequence*.

control characters

The most common character set-up is the ASCII* (ask'-ee) character set, of 95 printable characters, as well as many 'control', or special characters, that cannot be printed and are used internally by the computer. The standard order of the printable characters is:

```
! " # $ % & ' ( ) * + - , . / 0 1 2 3 4 5 6 7 8 9 : ; < = > ? @
A B C D E F G H I J K L M N O P Q R S T U V W X Y Z [ \ ] ∧ _
a b c d e f g h i j k l m n o p q r s t u v w x y z { | } ~
```

* That's the American Standard Code for Information Interchange.

The very first character is a space. A similar character set, EBCDIC, is used on IBM computers. Although most of the characters are the same as those in the ASCII set, their order is considerably different. Neither the upper nor lower-case letters are entirely contiguous (j doesn't immediately follow i, for instance), but the gaps in each set of letters are the same (j is the same distance from i as J is from I).

The ordering functions (except *chr*) may take arguments of any ordinal type, but I'll confine these examples to arguments of type *char*.

relative ordering functions　　*pred* (*x*), *succ* (*x*)　　The *predecessor* and *successor* functions represent the value that comes immediately before, or after, the argument *x*.

ord (*x*)　　The *ordinal position* function represents the 'place number' of a value within its entire type. If its argument is a *char* value, *ord* (*x*) represents *x*'s position within the computer's collating sequence.

positional functions　　*chr* (*x*)　　The *character position* function represents the *char* value in a particular ordinal position. Its argument must be an *integer* value.

$$\begin{array}{ll}
pred\,(\text{'d'})\ is\ \text{'c'} & pred\,(\text{'6'})\ is\ \text{'5'} \\
succ\,(\text{'y'})\ is\ \text{'z'} & succ\,(\text{'3'})\ is\ \text{'4'} \\
ord\,(\text{'A'})\ is\ 65 & ord\,(\text{'0'})\ is\ 48 \\
chr\,(67)\ is\ \text{'C'} & chr\,(57)\ is\ \text{'9'}
\end{array}$$

The examples used throughout this text reflect ASCII character ordering. Numbers may seem high because non-printing characters precede the visible ones. Incidentally, the initial value in an ordinal sequence is the 'zeroth' value—not the first.

It's apparent from inspection that *ord* and *chr* are transfer functions (just as *trunc* and *round* are), and may be inverse functions as well. This is useful, because sometimes we'll want to treat *integer* input as though it were a string of characters instead of a number. Suppose we try a simple example. Assume that **converting digits to numbers** the value of a *char* variable *InputCharacter* is '0', '1', '2', '3', '4', '5', '6', '7', '8', or '9'. How can we convert *InputCharacter* to the *integer* it represents? The obvious assignment is tempting:

　　　　ConvertedToInteger := *ord* (*InputCharacter*) ; {Tempting, but incorrect.}

But were we to inspect different collating sequences, we'd find that the numeral '5' is unlikely to have an ordinal value of five. However, the Pascal Standard requires that all digit characters be contiguous. Thus, this assignment solves our problem:

　　　　ConvertedToInteger := *ord* (*InputCharacter*) − *ord* ('0') ;

A test case or two (in particular, '0' and '9'), should convince you that the new assignment does just what we want it to. The trick of testing only the outside cases is called *boundary condition* testing. We assume that if an algorithm **boundary conditions** works for the highest and lowest numbers, it is well-behaved and will work for all the in-between numbers too.

The last group of standard functions have *boolean* results. They indicate whether some situation is *true* or *false*. For example, the function call *odd* (*Number*) represents the *boolean* value *true* or *false*, depending on whether the variable *Number* represents an odd or an even *integer*.

boolean functions

The other two functions are used when we're reading input into a program—*eoln* stands for 'end of line', and *eof* means 'end of file'. For example, if we weren't sure how much data a program was supposed to get, we could tell the computer to keep reading input until either *eoln* or *eof* was *true*, i.e., until it was at the end of an input line, or had exhausted the entire 'file' of input data. We'll start to use *boolean* values with the **if** statement in Chapter 4, and learn about *eof* and *eoln* with **while** loops in Chapter 5.

: . . . . : . . . : . . . . : . . . . : . . . . . : . . . . . . : . . . . . : . . . . : . . . . . : . . . : . . . . : . . . : . . . . :

Self-Check
Questions

Q. Match the variables with the expressions they may represent. Which values may not be given to *any* variable? Assume we've made this declaration:

> **var** *IntegerValue* : *integer* ; *Letter* : *char* ; *RealValue* : *real* ;

a) 7	*b*) 0.0	*c*) T	*d*) .3519
e) –52	*f*) 0	*g*) 5.E+22	*h*) ;
i) .9E–3	*j*) 35.2E–17	*k*) –18E+6.0	*l*) dd
m) –667.3	*n*) 1,387	*o*) –7	*p*) –12E–7

A. *IntegerValue* may be 7, –52, 0, or –7.
Letter may be '7', 'T', '0', or ';' .
RealValue may be 7, 0.0, –52, 0, 35.2E–17, –667.3, –7, or –12E–7.
The values .3519, 5.E+22, .9E–3, –18E+6.0, dd, and 1,387 aren't legal Pascal, and can't be given to any variables at all.

Q. Write these mathematical expressions using Pascal function calls. Assume that *PI* equals π.

> a) $8^{9.4}$ b) e^0 c) *sine* 45°   d) *cosine* $3.0672^{2\pi}$
>
> e) $\ln \dfrac{1+a}{1-a}$ f) $\dfrac{e^x}{2}$ g) $\ln \left(\dfrac{\pi}{2}\right)$ h) $\dfrac{e^u - e^{-u}}{2}$

A. Answers:

> a) *exp* (9.4*ln (8))   b) 1 (any number to the zero power is 1)
> c) *sin* (PI /4)   d) *cos* (*exp* (2*PI *ln (3.0672)))
> e) *ln* ((1+a)/(1–a))   f) *exp* (x)/2
> g) *ln* (3.141592654/2)   h) (*exp* (u)–*exp* (–u))/2

: . . . . : . . . : . . . : . . . : . . . : . . . . . : . . . . . : . . . . : . . . . : . . . . : . . . : . . . : . . . : . . . :

Input, Output, and Constants
1-2

VARIABLES, ASSIGNMENTS, AND EXPRESSIONS WERE probably a snap. Unfortunately, the tedious part of learning most programming languages involves the details of input and output, and Pascal is no exception. This section goes over many fine points of Pascal's I/O procedures (so that important details don't get buried elsewhere). You should use it to clarify problems, but please don't try to memorize everything at once.

Now, you'll recall from our discussion of output that two procedures, *write* and *writeln*, share responsibility for printing partial and full lines of output. Two more standard procedures, *read* and *readln* (pronounced 'read line'), play the same part for program input. When a program encounters a *read* or *readln*, it stops to get input for the variable or variables given between parentheses. For example:

program *Interactive* (*input, output*);

    {Demonstrates interactive program input and output.}

interactive I/O demonstration program

  var *Number* : *integer*;
  begin
    writeln ('Please enter your IQ.'); {Prompt for input.}
    readln (*Number*);
    write ('You wish! You probably can''t even count to:'); {Label the output.}
    writeln (*Number*)   {Print the value of *Number*.}
  end.

↓   ↓   ↓   ↓   ↓

Please enter your IQ.
237
You wish! You probably can't even count to: 237

By itself, a Pascal program will not announce that it is waiting for input. The programmer must include a *writeln*, with text, that prompts the user to enter a value. Thus, program *Interactive's* request 'Please enter your IQ.' is essential for successful operation. Without it, the user wouldn't know that she was supposed to enter a number, and the computer (unable to complete the *readln*) couldn't move on to subsequent statements.

prompting for data

In chart form *read* and *readln* look like this:

read and readln

read and *readln* differ in the way they deal with extra values on a line of input. *readln* discards any extra values left on a line of input. When used without any variables in parentheses, *readln* removes the entire line. *read*, in contrast, leaves remaining values, even if a carriage return is the only value left.

read vs. readln

To mentally picture this, imagine that input comes in the old-fashioned way—from a stack of punched cards placed in the computer's input hopper. Each card is equivalent to a line of input, and ends with a special character equivalent to a carriage return. *readln* always ejects the current card (and gets the next) as part of its action. *read*, in contrast, leaves the current card in the hopper as long as possible, until even the 'end-of-card' value has been read. Only then will the current card be ejected, and the next one obtained.

Let's look at some examples. I'll declare some *char* variables:

var *C1, C2, C3, C4, C5, C6: char*;

return is read as a blank

and assume that each input statement below gets the sample input shown. A carriage return ends the input—it is *always* read as a blank.

Sample input to each statement: **ABCDE**

Statement	*Last value read*	*Value about to be read*
1. *read* (*C1*);	**A**	**B**
2. *read* (*C1*); *read* (*C2*);	**B**	**C**
3. *read* (*C1,C2,C3*);	**C**	**D**
4. *read* (*C1, C2, C3, C4, C5*);	**E**	*blank* (*the return*)
5. *read* (*C1, C2, C3, C4, C5, C6*);	*blank*	*start of next line*
6. *read*;	*illegal—read must actually get values*	
7. *readln*;	*none*	*start of next line*
8. *readln* (*C1*);	**A**	*start of next line*
9. *readln* (*C1,C2,C3*);	**C**	*start of next line*
10. *readln* (*C1, C2, C3, C4, C5*);	**E**	*start of next line*

If you compare the effects of statements 1 and 8, and 3 and 9, you'll see that although they both obtain the same values, the *readlns* remove the rest of the line as well. Statement 5 mimics statement 7 because it reads all input values *including* the carriage return that ends the line.

In practice, we will almost invariably use *readln* for ordinary input. We don't use *read* because it doesn't automatically get rid of the carriage return that ends each line—and could be inadvertently read as a space character later (as in statement 4).

The exact meaning of *start of next line* depends on how input is being provided. The example program, *Interactive*, assumed that input was being typed into a keyboard during program execution. This is called *interactive* program operation because the user and computer interact with each other. Interactive programs usually have only one line of input (entered in response to the most recent prompt) waiting at any time.

interactive programs

Not all programs run interactively, though. Those that don't are sometimes called *batch-oriented* programs. They get their input from stored *data files*, rather than from the terminal keyboard. The computer may require this sort of data entry, or it may just be more convenient to use a data file than to type input interactively. In either case, all program input is prepared in

data-file programs

advance, so we can actually say what value is about to be read.

A special rule must be observed whether input is being supplied interactively or via data file.

> The Golden Rule of Input
>
> Always make sure that there's enough input.

If a program expects to read in eight characters or numbers, there had better be at least eight values waiting to be read in. If an interactive program is given too few values, it will hang without informing the user that more input is expected. A program that tries to read past the end of its data file comes to a worse fate—it will crash.

Numerical Input and Output

So much for character I/O. The input and output of numerical values is more complicated.

> Spaces and carriage returns *separate* numbers. Any non-numerical character *ends* a number.

In our earlier examples of *char* input, spaces (and, implicitly, carriage returns) were characters in their own right. When we read in *integer* or *real* values, though, spaces and carriage returns are ignored except as value separators. If it is seeking to read a number, the computer will skip over spaces (or carriage returns) as though they aren't there.

For example, suppose that *First* and *Second* are *integer* variables. The statement: *readln (First, Second)* treats the three inputs below identically, even though the first separates the numbers by a single space, the second by many spaces, and the third by many spaces and a carriage return.

a) **53 174**
b) **53**   **174**
c) **53**
                            174

where do numbers end?

Concern about where a numerical value ends develops when character and numerical values are intermingled. After a number is read, what value is *about* to be read? It's the character that ended the number—a space, letter, or punctuation mark. We can't just say it's a non-digit because of *real* input, which may include a period or letter 'E' as part of a number in floating-point notation. For example, if we assume these declarations:

var *C1, C2* : *char* ; *N1, N2* : *integer* ;

and this input to each statement:

123 A45B

we can develop the following table. A blank is shown as an underline:

		C1	C2	N1	N2	About to be read
a)	read (C1);	'1'				'2', or **23**
b)	read (C1, N1);	'1'		23		'_'
c)	read (C1, C2, N1);	'1'	'2'	3		'_'
d)	read (N1, C1);	'_'		123		'A'
e)	read (N1, C1, C2, N2);	'_'	'A'	123	45	'B'
f)	read (N1, N2);			123		crash! N2 can't be 'A'
g)	read (N1, C1, N2);	'_'		123		crash! N2 can't be 'A'

Although I've carefully separated them to avoid confusion in earlier examples, numerical output can be intermingled with ordinary text output. Commas separate variables from each other and from text.

program *Planetary (input, output)*;

{Demonstrates simple input and output.}

var *Year, Moons* : *integer*;

simple I/O
demonstration
program

begin
    writeln ('When was Neptune discovered? How many moons does it have?');
    readln (Year, Moons);
    writeln ('Neptune was discovered in', *Year*, ' and has', *Moons*, ' moons.')
end. {*Planetary*}

↓   ↓   ↓   ↓   ↓

When was Neptune discovered? How many moons does it have?
1846   2
Neptune was discovered in   1846 and has   2 moons.

Note that the numbers seem to be misprinted; in contrast to the text output, the numbers are preceded by blank space. When they're printed by a Pascal program, *integer* and *real* values are aligned with the right margin of a space known as a printing field, mainly to make it easy to print columns of figures.
printing fields
The width of the column is the number's *field width*. In the example below, the values of the *integer* variables *a*, *b*, *c*, etc. vary, but they are always printed in 10-space fields.

writeln (a, b, c);
writeln (d, e, f);
writeln (g, h, i);

↓   ↓   ↓   ↓   ↓

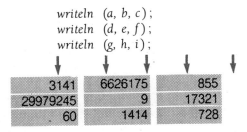

3141	6626175	855
29979245	9	17321
60	1414	728

Unfortunately, solving the column problem causes another. If the *default* field width (usually eight or ten spaces) is too big, extra space is left when an *integer* is printed in the midst of text output. You can change the default width by following the value being output with a colon, and the *integer* number of spaces in the field. As this example shows, field widths can be specified for the output of text as well as variables.

writeln ('WOW':10, 'MOM':10, 'WOW':10);
writeln ('In', Year:1, ', Columbus sailed the ocean blue.');
writeln ('In', Year:5, ', Columbus sailed the ocean blue.');
writeln ('In', Year, ', Columbus sailed the ocean blue.');

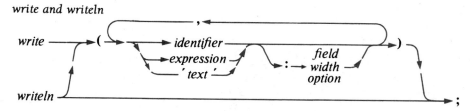

WOW   MOM   WOW

In1492, Columbus sailed the ocean blue.
In 1492, Columbus sailed the ocean blue.
In   1492, Columbus sailed the ocean blue.

If the new field width is greater than the number of characters in the value, blanks are printed on the left. For safety, a field that is too small for an *integer* or text value will automatically expand to accommodate the entire value. As a result, programmers often give a field width of one when they want *integer* values printed in the smallest possible space. The final digit of shortened *real* values is rounded.

The syntax chart for *write* and *writeln* shows the field width option:

write and writeln

```
                                    ,
                         ┌─────────←──────────┐
write ──────→ ( ──→──┬──→ identifier ────────┬──────→ ) ──┐
              │      ├──→ expression ─┘      └─ : ─→ field ┤
              │      └──── ' text ' ──┘              width │
              │                                     option │
              │                                            ↓
writeln ──────┘─────────────────────────────────────────────→ ;
```

write and *writeln* give *real* values one additional privilege: *fixed-point* notation. Recall that in floating-point notation, the decimal always 'floats' to a position just to the right of the *real's* first digit, and a positive or negative exponent compensates for the floating decimal point. Fixed-point notation, in contrast, fixes the decimal point between the 'ones' and 'tenths' columns of the *real* value. There is no exponent. For example:

Fixed-point	Floating-point
1.0	1.0E+00
10.0	1.00E+01
100.0	1.000E+02

real accuracy

When they're output, *real* values may be given a second 'argument' after their field width. It specifies the exact number of decimal places (the *real's decimal accuracy*) that should appear. Thus, in the example below, the field width accorded each expression (100/8) is always ten spaces. However, the result values printed have progressively greater (and therefore better) decimal accuracy: 1, 2, and 5 places.

writeln (100/8:10:1, 100/8:10:2, 100/8:10:5)

field width and decimal accuracy

Field width —

| 12.5 | 12.50 | 12.50000 |

— *Decimal accuracy*

Programs that handle money are obvious candidates for fixed-point notation. A program like *SalesTax*, below, needs neither the sometime convenience, nor the extreme accuracy, of floating-point arithmetic (what would you make of a price tag that read $3.9899E+02?). Note the use of constants in setting the field widths. Their definition is described afterward.

program *SalesTax* (*input, output*);

    {Asks for a price and amount tendered. Computes sales tax and change.}

const *TAXRATE* = 0.065;   {The local tax rate—6.5%.}
    FIELD = 5;
    DECIMALS = 2;   {Print output to two decimal places.}

decimal accuracy demonstration program

var *Price, AmountTendered, Tax, SalesPrice, Change*: *real*;

begin
    writeln ('Please enter the price.');
    readln (*Price*);
    Tax := *TAXRATE* *Price*;
    SalesPrice := *Price*+*Tax*;
    writeln ('The sales price is $', *SalesPrice*:FIELD:DECIMALS);
    writeln ('What do you need change for?');
    readln (*AmountTendered*);
    Change := *AmountTendered*–*SalesPrice*;
    writeln ('Your change is $', *Change*:FIELD:DECIMALS)
end. {*SalesTax*}

Please enter the price.
15.75
The sales price is $16.77
What do you need change for?
20.00
Your change is $ 3.23

Constants

Identifiers that are *mnemonic* (nih-mahn´-ick)—easy to remember—make programs easier to read, write, and understand. Mnemonic names can be given to particular values by defining them as *constants*. Once it has been defined, a constant's value *cannot* be changed during the course of a program. The syntax chart of a constant definition is:

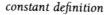

constant definition

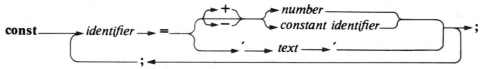

Constant definitions come just after the program heading:

> *program heading*;
> *constant definitions*;
> *variable declarations*;
> *statement part*;

text constants

A special kind of constant—a text constant—represents an entire string of characters. It must be enclosed by single quotes. In the examples below, notice that I capitalize all constant identifiers as a matter of programming style, to make constants instantly distinguishable from variables.

> **const** *PLANCK* = 6.63E–34 ;   {The constant's type isn't given.}
>   *LASTLETTER* = 'Z' ;
>   *THISYEAR* = 1986 ;
>   *TRUELOVE* = 'Nicole' ;
>   *FIVEBLANKS* = '   ' ;

Although text constants cannot be assigned to variables of type *char* (because they all include two or more character values), we can print the values of text constants with output statements.

> *writeln* ('I wish ', *TRUELOVE*, ' would call me up!') ;
>   ↓   ↓   ↓   ↓   ↓

I wish Nicole would call me up!

MAXINT

The constant *MAXINT*, which represents the maximum *integer* the compiler allows, is predefined in every Pascal installation.

An important restriction on constant definitions is that they be specific values, or previously defined constants. A constant declaration can't contain variables or arithmetic operations. This means that the value of a constant can't depend on program execution. These:

> **const** *HALF* = 1/2 ;
>   *ROOT* = *sqrt* (4) ;   {Illegal constant definitions.}
>   *RATE* = *InputRate* ;

are all illegal definitions. They require that a value be computed, or supplied by a variable identifier (like *InputRate*).

Using constants is a matter of programming style. No program needs defined constants in order to work, but programs often require constants in order to be good programs. Suppose that a 2000-line program calculates property taxes like clockwork for a few years, and then—horrors! the tax rate changes. Must we search the entire program to update every instance of the old tax rate? Not if we had made the definition:

why use constants?

const *TAXRATE* = 0.003 ;

Changing the value of the constant *TAXRATE* updates the whole program. Could *TAXRATE* have been declared as a variable? Yes, but that would open the possibility of accidentally changing its value within the program. It's also misleading to call *TAXRATE* a variable instead of a constant, because declaring something as a variable implies that its value will change frequently, or be obtained from the program's user.

for style

A second style motivation for constants is less obvious. Writing a program is a little like writing an instruction booklet. Just including all the facts isn't enough—they have to be presented in a manner that even a casual reader can follow. Now, comments provide a running commentary, called *documentation*, that explains what's happening in a program. Defined constants go further. Like mnemonic variable identifiers, they help make a program *self-documenting*. This statement doesn't say much:

as documentation

$a := b-5$;

Better variable names, and a comment, help it out:

Speed2 := *Speed1* –5 ;
    {Find true speed by subtracting the fixed speedometer error.}

But mnemonic identifiers and a defined constant manage no-hands commenting—they document *without* additional comments, and are the best of all.

CorrectedSpeed := *IndicatedSpeed*–*SPEEDOMETERERROR* ;

I'll continue this discussion of program 'antibugging' techniques in Chapter 12.

Chapter Notes
1-3

FINDING (AND FIXING) THE BUGS, or mistakes, that creep into programs is called *debugging*. Bugs aren't inevitable, but they often occur in computer programs because men and women don't think in the literal way that machines operate. People have a remarkable, automatic, ability to fix mistakes that is miles beyond anything computers can do.

What is wrong with
with this sentence?

Bugs fall into two general categories. *Syntax* bugs are 'grammatical' Pascal errors, while *semantic* bugs cause mistakes in the effect of programs. Syntax errors are found and fixed with the least effort, since the compiler usually

compilation bugs

detects them automatically as it prepares a program to run. For example, some words invariably occur in pairs—every **begin** must be matched by an **end** later in the program. A compiler that cannot find a closing **end** prints an error message to point out the problem:

"END" EXPECTED – – END OF PROGRAM NOT FOUND

Punctuation bugs are caught in a similar manner. For instance, the semicolon is Pascal's statement separator, so the compiler expects to find a semicolon before every statement, and may even temporarily insert one if we've forgotten. As before, a compiler message keeps the programmer posted.

Now, an unexpected side-effect of temporary compile-time fixes is that a real error early in the program may cause the computer to diagnose many

spurious bugs

apparent, but non-existent, mistakes further on (which can be very intimidating). Consider the sequence of statements below. If you can decipher this mess, you'll see that the misspelled **begn** makes the compiler treat the entire program as a long **var** declaration. The bug throws the compiler out of kilter, and we get a long string of error messages.

```
PROGRAM ERRORPRONE (INPUT, OUTPUT);
VAR DATA:  INTEGER;
BEGN
        ↑INSERTED ","
      WRITELN  ('PLEASE ENTER A NUMBER.');
                    ↑INSERTED ":"
                     ↑INVALID TYPE IDENTIFIER
      READLN  (DATA);
                  ↑INSERTED ":"
      WRITELN  (DATA);
                  ↑INSERTED ":"
      "DATA" IS DEFINED MORE THAN ONCE IN THIS BLOCK
        ↑MALFORMED VARIABLE DECLARATION
    END.
    ↑UNEXPECTED "END" – – END OF PROGRAM NOT FOUND
```

When you're debugging a program, read the error messages first. Then, get a *listing*, or hard-copy printout, of the program and try to find the actual

get a listing

mistakes. When a short program produces a long series of error messages, look for a simple reason—a misspelled word, or misused feature. Don't despair. As you gain more experience, you'll become adept at separating the real bugs from spurious ones.

run-time bugs

Some syntax-type bugs may not manifest themselves until the program is in operation—they are *run-time* errors, and will cause program crashes. For example:

ABNORMAL TERMINATION – –
IMPROPER DATA FOUND AT INTEGER READ, LINE 32

Apparently, program line 32 was a *read* or *readln* statement that tried to get the value of an *integer* variable. The program user entered a value of the wrong type (perhaps it was *char* or *real*) and the program crashed. The clear implication is that it's crucial to ask for appropriate input.

Some syntax problems that border on the semantic come from local system features or shortcomings. Three particular points: First, although the Pascal Standard requires that all characters in an identifier be significant, a compiler may have a shorter limit. If the limit is eight characters, then these two identifiers will seem identical:

local variations

NapoleonBonaparte   *NapoleonJones*

Second, case of letters in identifiers is supposed to be irrelevant. The identifiers below are identical in Standard Pascal, so that a program written on a computer with upper- and lower-case characters works equally well on a machine with only upper-case. However, this rule is ignored in many implementations of Pascal, which will treat these examples as completely different:

highnumber   *HIGHNUMBER*   *HighNumber*

Third, some systems may extend Pascal by letting non-letters appear within an identifier to improve readability (*TIME_TO_LEAVE*). Programmers often become so used to this extension that they forget to delete the illegal characters when programs are transferred to less obliging systems.

Pascal's strict type checking can cause bug problems at first. As noted earlier, a variable may never represent a value of the wrong type. Similarly, operators and functions are usually restricted to operands or arguments of some particular type. Many type problems are picayune; for example, the expression 4.0 **div** 2 is illegal because both operands of **div** must be *integer*. Steer clear of these minor problems by remembering:

1.   If **div** or **mod** are used in an expression, all of the values in the expression must be *integer*.

2.   If / or any *real* values are used in an expression, the result of the expression will be a *real* value.

types of expressions

3.   The value a function call represents sometimes belongs to a different type than the function's argument. (We'll see how, and why, in a few pages.)

4.   The types of a variable, and a value assigned to it, must be identical.

As I pointed out earlier, the fourth rule is a bit inconsistent. An *integer* value may be assigned to a *real* variable, but the opposite is not allowed. An ounce of prevention—using arithmetic values of the proper type rather than relying on Pascal's laxness—is worth a lot of program debugging.

Undefined values might or might not provoke type problems. An attempt to find the square root of a negative number, say, will invariably cause a program crash, but certain other undefined values won't always cause such drastic results. If we request the character that comes before the first character, *pred* (*chr* (0)), it may turn out to be the *last* character in the computer's character set. This means that we can't always rely on a run-time error to stop a program for us.

Important
to
Remember

- Expressions represent values. The simplest expressions are constant or variable identifiers, numbers, and characters. More complicated expressions can be stated as a sequence of operators and operands. A result is obtained by evaluating the expression.

- A variable must be initialized before it can appear in an expression, and is undefined before then.

- The standard simple types are *integer, real, char*, and *boolean*. All except *real* are also known as ordinal types.

- Variables can only be assigned values of the same type. The exception is *real* variables, which can be assigned *integer* values.

- When an expression contains both *real* and *integer* operands (e.g. $1.0 + 1$) the expression's result type is *real*.

- A call of one of the standard functions usually consists of the function's name, followed by an argument value in parentheses.

- The computer's character set is in a particular collating sequence that will vary from system to system.

- Translate a digit character to the number that it represents with: *ord* (*TheDigitChar*)−*ord* ('0'). Compute *a* to the *n*th power with: *exp* (*n*∗*ln* (*a*))

- To help make programs self-documenting, identifiers should be mnemonic, and give an indication of the variable or constant's purpose.

- The carriage return is read as a space. When reading *integer* or *real* values, multiple spaces and carriage returns are ignored. The value about to be read is the character that ended the number.

- Interactive programs must always prompt for input.

- A compile-time, or syntax, error will be recognized by the compiler, but must be fixed by the programmer. A run-time error will cause a program crash. Semantic errors cause bugs that show up as incorrect results.

- Pascal programs are free format, but they should be written with indenting and spacing that makes them easy to read.

- Give unto variables only values of the same type.
- Finally, remember that a program should be as easy for a human being to read and understand as it is for a computer to execute.

Cross Reference

Part Three of this book, the *Standard Pascal User Reference Manual*, describes Pascal in the formal terms used by the official ISO/ANSI standard. Let me suggest that you begin by reading *Axi—Axiii* for some historical background on Pascal and the standardization process. The next few pages are also crucial—A1 explains the Standard's precise notion of an error, while A2—A3 describes the BNF, or Backus-Naur Formalism, used in most programming language definitions. After that . . .

- By convention, terms that have a specially defined meaning in the Standard are hyphenated—'program-heading,' or 'variable-declaration.' Their BNF definitions are collected in Appendix C, and there is a special index to their appearance in the Standard in Appendix D.
- The basic symbols that make up Pascal programs, including numbers, reserved words, identifiers, and comments, are called tokens. They're described in A3—A7.
- Constant definitions are described in A65—A66, while variable declarations follow in A67—A68.
- Statements are introduced on A8, and the assignment statement is defined on A9.
- The program heading is described briefly on A47, and more formally in A130—A131.
- Input, and the differences between *read* and *readln*, are first discussed in A48—A50.
- Output, and distinctions between *write* and *writeln*, are first described in A52—A54. The discussion of output formats continues through A57.
- The formal description of arithmetic expressions is fairly complicated. *real* and *integer* values are discussed in A31—A33, along with the effects of the arithmetic operators. A40—A43 defines the construction of arithmetic expressions in more technical terms.
- The required functions are discussed in A35—A38.
- The values of type *char* are described in A34—A35.

Exercises

1-1 Since 1961, the standard meter's length has been fixed at precisely 1,650,763.73 wavelengths of a particular orange-red line of krypton-86. When the standard meter was first defined, though, it was intended to equal 1 ten-millionth of the distance between the North or South pole, and the equator. As it happens, a nautical mile is defined to be the distance equal to one minute of arc over the same range. If there are 60 minutes in each degree, and 90 degrees between the equator and a pole, how long, in kilometers, is a nautical mile?

1-2   *Bode's Law*, ascribed to J.E. Bode (1747–1826), is an empirically-derived rule that describes the distance from most of the bodies in the solar system to the Sun. It is:

Distance of n th planet = $(4 + 3 \times 2^{n-2}) / 10$ astronomical units

with the exception that Mercury has no $3 \times 2^{n-2}$ term. One astronomical unit is about 93,000,000 miles. How well does Bode's Law predict the actual distances shown below? How do you account for a certain missing planet (at $n = 5$)?

Mercury	0.39	Mars	1.52	Uranus	19.18
Venus	0.72	Jupiter	5.20	Neptune	30.07
Earth	1.0	Saturn	9.54	Pluto	39.67

1-3   How strong is the attractive force that holds a positive sodium ion (cation) and a negative chlorine ion (anion) together to form a single salt molecule? This force, known as a *coulombic attraction* F_c, is defined as:

$$F_c = - \frac{k_0 (Z_1 q) (Z_2 q)}{a_0^2}$$

where k_0 is a proportionality constant (9×10^9 Vm/C), Z_i is the valence of the ions ($+1$ and -1 in NaCl), and q is the charge of a single electron (0.16×10^{-18} C). Finally, a_0 is the sum of the ionic radii, 0.278 nanometers in this case.

   Now, how strong is the ionic force that holds a salt molecule together?

1-4   Molecules of polyethylene provide the standard example of long molecule chains, since a single molecule may have 500—1000 'mers' of ethylene, C_2H_4 (hence the names *poly*ethylene and *poly*mer). But how long, exactly, is such a molecule?

   Suppose the length of a single C—C bond is 0.154 nanometers. The length of such bonds in a straight row is easy enough to multiply out. However, the calculation must take into account the fact that carbon atoms do not line up in neat lines! Each atom is offset from its neighbor by 54.75°, which means that the distance between two carbons is only 0.154 $sin\,54.75°$ nanometers. (Actually, the situation is even worse—the bonds can 'kink' in space as well, but I'm willing to ignore this.)

   Given a 750—mer chain, with 2 carbon atoms per mer, how long is a polyethylene molecule? (Note: to use Pascal's *sin* function, you'll have to convert degrees to radians—1°=π/180 radians.)

1-5   The energy of a photon, E, is defined as:

$$E = \frac{hc}{\lambda} \qquad h = Planck's\ constant = 6.63 \times 10^{-34}\ joule-sec$$

The speed of light is 0.2998×10^9 meters/second. The wavelength, λ, of ultraviolet light varies from 1 to roughly 400 nanometers,

   Now (to digress to the purely physical), the strength of a carbon—carbon bond, like those that hold polymers like polyethylene together, is about 2.2×10^{-17} joules. How does this compare to the energy of a UV photon? Is it a good idea to expose polyethylene to ultraviolet light? What do you think the result might be?

1-6   Aluminum foil is practically pure aluminum. Suppose that one sunny Wednesday you pay $5.15 (plus 0.065% tax) for a roll of aluminum foil that is 200 feet long, 12 inches wide, and 3 mils thick. Consider further that the density of aluminum is 2.70 grams/cm^3, and that the atomic mass of aluminum is 26.9815 atomic mass units, where one such unit is 1.66×10^{-24} grams. Bear in mind that Avogadro's number, 6.02×10^{23}, is the number of 1—amu particles in a mass of 1 gram. Don't forget that there are 28.34

grams in one ounce, 39.37 inches in a meter, 1,000 mils in an inch, and that Wednesday is 3%-off day.

Now, tell me how much an atom of aluminum costs on Fridays.

1-7   The *refractive index*, n, of a material is defined to be:

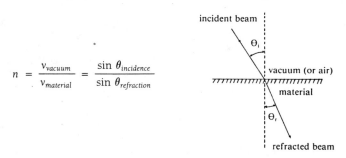

$$ n = \frac{v_{vacuum}}{v_{material}} = \frac{\sin \theta_{incidence}}{\sin \theta_{refraction}} $$

where v is the speed of light in a vacuum (close to its speed in air), 0.2998×10^9 meters/second.

1.   Suppose that a light beam strikes a water surface ($n = 1.33$) at an angle of 18°. What is the angle of refraction?

2.   Cerenkov radiation occurs when a particle's speed exceeds the speed of light in a given medium. How fast would a particle have to travel in water to cause the blue glow of Cerenkov radiation? (This is a really incredible property that underlies the search for neutrinos—huge underground tanks of water are surrounded by suitable 'glow' detectors).

1-8   The fraction of light reflected at the interface between two materials is its *reflectance*. For a light source perpendicular to an interface, reflectance is related to the refractive index n, defined above, by *Fresnel's formula*:

$$ Reflectance = \left[\frac{n-1}{n+1} \right]^2 $$

Suppose the n of a chlorinated swimming pool is 1.42. Is it really true that lounging poolside (so as to cop those reflected rays) will improve your tan? At best, what percentage of sunshine will reflect from the water?

1-9   Why doesn't light escape from a fiber-optic cable? It turns out that, to pass through the boundary between a high-refraction medium (like the silica glass that fibers are drawn from) and a lower-refraction medium (like air), light must strike at the interface an angle less than $\theta_{critical}$ from perpendicular. This critical angle is breached when $\frac{\sin \theta_{critical}}{\sin 90°} = \frac{1}{n}$.

Suppose that the refractive index for silica glass is 1.458. What is the critical angle for escape?

1-10   Most of you who have traveled at near-light speeds are, of course, familiar with a variety of peculiar phenomena: rulers shrink, clocks slow down, and mass increases. This is responsible for a variety of the changes that occur when you begin to work Sunday evening on a 10-page paper due 8AM Monday—the accelerating effects of intense concentration cause dawn to hasten, your paper to malinger at 8 pages, and you to gain weight. In general, the relation that governs change is:

$$ new\ measurement = \frac{time\ at\ rest}{\sqrt{1 - v^2/c^2}} \quad or \quad \frac{mass\ at\ rest}{\sqrt{1 - v^2/c^2}} \quad or \quad length\ at\ rest \times \sqrt{1 - v^2/c^2} $$

where v is the (accelerated) velocity and c is the velocity of light.

1.   How fast must a yardstick travel in order to shrink by 10%?

2.   How much time would a clock traveling at 150,000 miles/second appear to lose?

3.   Suppose you were to move at 90% of the speed of light. How much would your mass increase?

1-11   Three professors of Classics were arguing over their coffee—or, more precisely, about their coffee. Apparently, three temperatures were available: boiling, 50°, and room temperature (which happens to be 20°). The professors all agreed that the room temperature cup wouldn't cool any further, but they disagreed about how long it would take the other cups to cool one degree apiece.

'It makes no difference—a degree's a degree,' claimed the professor of Greek, who had many degrees herself. 'Stuff and nonsense,' retorted her colleague, the Latin specialist. 'The boiling one is twice as hot, so it cools twice as quickly.' 'Hold your tongue,' snapped the third professor. 'What's important is the difference from room temperature—the hot one will shed one degree 8/3 times faster.'

The engineering student who was serving coffee (and failing all three Classics courses) knew that the real answer was proportional to the black body (coffee, in this case) temperature[4], less the room temperature[4], with all temperatures in degrees Kelvin (Celsius plus 273), of each cup. Having grown to appreciate the Socratic method, though, she didn't speak up.

Well, how much faster *does* the hotter cup cool off 1 degree? In other words (ignoring convection and conduction), solve:

$$\frac{Hot\ coffee_{kelvin}{}^4 - room\ temperature_{kelvin}{}^4}{warm\ coffee_{kelvin}{}^4 - room\ temperature_{kelvin}{}^4}$$

1-12   A physics professor who hoped to teach her students creative methods of problem solving gave each a barometer, and the task of measuring the height of an office building. Most of the students came up with clever, innovative approaches: dropping the barometer from the top of the building and timing its fall, boiling the barometer at the top of the building and checking the water temperature, giving the barometer to the building superintendant in exchange for a glimpse at the blueprints, and so on.

Naturally, there's a dullard in every crowd. One student actually checked the pressure at ground level (30.28 inches of mercury), and on the roof (30.16 inches), then wrote a program that applied the formula:

$$height\ in\ feet\ =\ 25,000\ \ln \frac{ground\ pressure}{roof\ pressure}$$

How tall is the building? Write a general-purpose program to find the answer for any two pressures.

1-13   The resistance of a piece of wire is:

$$resistance\ =\ \rho \times \frac{length}{area}\ ,\qquad where\ \rho\ =\ 1.56 \times 10^{-8}\ \Omega-meters,\ for\ copper$$

Suppose that a copper wire one millimeter in diameter is wrapped tightly around a cylindrical form three centimeters in diameter and fifty-seven centimeters long. Counting to the nearest full turn, how long is the wire, and what is its total resistance?

1-14   10 seconds remain on the Super Bowl clock when a horrible accident befalls a broadcaster stationed high overhead in the Goodyear blimp. Just as play begins, the broadcaster drops his hairpiece. Suppose that the game is being played at Mile-High stadium in Denver, so air resistance is negligible. If the blimp is hovering at 1,350 feet over the line of scrimmage, and the descent time is given by:

$$time = \sqrt{\frac{twice\ the\ height}{32.174ft/sec^2}}$$

is it possible that the hairpiece will be mistaken for a penalty flag before the game ends?

1-15   The relative centrifugal field F_g, popularly known as the *G-force*, of a spinning centrifuge, can be computed as:

$$F_g = \frac{4\pi^2\ revolutions/min^2 arm\ radius}{60\ sec/min^2 \times 9.81\ meters/sec^2}$$

where the arm radius is given in meters.

Suppose that NASA decides to use a record player to test the effects of increased G-force on ants. Will the relative centrifugal field be greater on the rim of a 45 rpm record (traveling at 45 rpm) or an LP (turning at 33 1/3 rpm)? (If you do not have records to measure you are spending too much time on CS homework.)

1-16   When a roadbed is properly banked a driver is in no danger of skidding—as long as she travels neither much faster nor slower than the posted speed. The proper angle of banking for a given radius and velocity is given by:

$$\tan\theta = \frac{velocity^2}{radius} \times 32 feet/sec^2$$

Suppose a road is posted for 40 MPH. At what angle θ should a 400 foot curve be banked?

1-17   The surface area of a person, in square meters, can be roughly calculated as $7.184^{-3} \times Weight_{kg}^{0.452} \times Height_{cm}^{0.725}$.

Suppose that the sun worshipper of problem 1-8 covers herself with 0.05 mm of suntan lotion. Write a program that she can use to find out how much lotion she will require in all.

2

Procedures and Functions

People, like chimpanzees, racoons, and other higher species, think rather well of themselves for using tools. It is no surprise, then, to find that most programming efforts in Pascal (and other higher languages) aim at creating new implements. The tools we can build into programs are called *subprograms*; in Pascal, subprograms are divided into *procedures* and *functions*. Procedure calls stand in for actions, while function calls compute and represent values. I'll start by showing how subprograms in general help program design by encouraging the use of *top-down design* and *stepwise refinement*.

Section 2-2 deals with the mechanics of creating new subprograms—their declaration, the use of *parameters*, and problems with conflict between identifiers. Like Chapter 1, this section contains many details that should be learned through practice, rather than by rote memorization. You might want to go directly from here to Chapter 12, which continues the discussion of subprograms in avoiding bugs and designing large programs.

If you're eager to start useful programming, Chapter 2 may seem like an unnecessary delay. Take my word for it—although the techniques it teaches aren't essential until your programs start to get big, they are far easier to learn while your programs are still small.

Top-Down Design and Stepwise Refinement 2-1

MANUALS THAT JUST DESCRIBE A PROGRAMMING language's syntax usually deal with subprograms last, because many details depend on knowing everything else about the language. Programming texts, though, usually introduce procedures and functions early because of their importance for problem solving. Two related techniques, called stepwise refinement and top-down design, rely heavily on your ability to write a program as a collection of smaller subprograms.

> Breaking a problem down into precisely stated subproblems is part of the *top-down* method of writing programs. It's called *stepwise refinement*.

stepwise refinement

In stepwise refinement, a problem is stated as a collection of obvious subproblems. We hope that some of them will be easy enough to encode in Pascal. If not, the problem is restated in parts. Each subproblem is decomposed, or restated as a collection of even more elemental subproblems.

Outline of a Problem

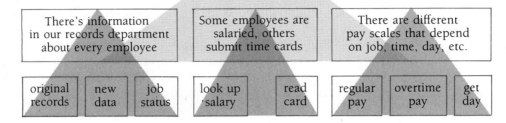

The refinement proceeds from the general to the particular; from the abstract statement of a problem to a precise specification that may even include specific coding suggestions. If a subproblem is particularly truculent, the refinement step may need to be repeated several times. 'Stepwise refinement' is a stilted and unnatural phrase—'relentless massage' might be better. Still, it accurately describes what we're doing—refining a problem, one step at a time, into its most basic description. Its best consequence is that . . .

> In exploring a problem through stepwise refinement, a program's algorithm is considered at all levels well before the details of its Pascal coding are dealt with.

top-down design

Top-down design describes a methodology for working on programs, rather than problems. Top-down programming starts with the big decisions that have to be made in writing a program's main procedures. Eventually, we work our way down to the small choices that are faced in implementing small procedures and functions. Major coding decisions are made first, and lesser ones are delayed for as long as possible.

Outline of a Program

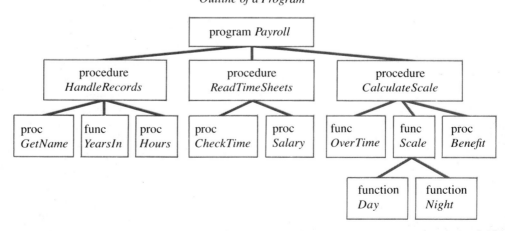

Once again we're going from the general to the particular. We design a program's main subprograms first. Small procedures and functions that are used in the main subprograms aren't considered until they're ready to be called.

Stepwise refinement, then, is a term we usually reserve for working on problems, while top-down design is more broadly applied to describe our approach to programming. In the long run, we'll see that top-down design is also concerned with methods of scheduling, debugging, testing, and modifying code.

why use them? There are several reasons why stepwise refinement and top-down design are important programming methods. Most obvious is the combined strategy's divide and conquer aspect. A formidable programming problem may turn out to be a combination of easily solved subproblems—in like a lion, and out like four or five lambs. Even if a crucial procedure is beyond our abilities at present, we can still work on the program because we've made independent subdivisions in the problem. As a result, the final program is modular. It's composed of separate pieces that can be written and tested by themselves, and then eventually merged together.

When the separate pieces are ultimately joined, procedures and functions help make programs easier to understand. Even relatively simple programs are usually broken into sequences of procedure calls like this:

```
begin
    GetInput (arguments ... );
    ProcessTheData (arguments ... );
    PrintResults (arguments ... )
end.
```

transparency because procedure calls make the program's inner operations *transparent*. We know *what* the program does, but we can ignore *how* it does it. The detailed code of the procedure doesn't obscure our view of the program—it's invisible unless we go looking for it.

thinking in English Stepwise refinement and top-down design also let a programmer plan most of a program without actually writing in Pascal. It's easier to think in English than in any sort of computerese, and tackling a problem from the top puts off the nitty-gritty of encoding for as long as possible. Outlining a program in terms of its procedures (and procedures and functions *within* procedures) provides a transitional phase between words and code.

pseudocode A more detailed intermediate version is often presented as *pseudocode*; a sort of Pascal that doesn't adhere religiously to Pascal's syntax requirements. Pseudocode is so convenient that it has all but replaced flowcharting (diagramming a program with boxes and arrows) as a tool for program planning. I'll use pseudocode extensively when we begin to work with the **for** statement.

finding the seams In real-life programming projects, the ability to find the seams of a problem or program is the earmark of a good programming manager. If several people are to work on a single program effectively, each must have a clearly delineated task. Each individual has to know exactly how her piece of the program interacts with the whole. Stepwise refinement and top-down design slice a problem up in a natural, intuitive manner.

Here are two outlines: one demonstrates stepwise refinement as an approach to programming problems, and the other shows how procedures are part of top-down program design. Notice how smoothly they merge together— the plan for breaking down a problem goes hand-in-hand with the guide for building a program.

Stepwise Refinement of a Problem

1. State the problem simply, decomposing it into its logical subproblems.

2. If you can immediately figure out how to encode all of the subproblems, you're done. These will be the major procedures of your program. If the subproblems are too complex...

3. Refine the subproblems into smaller, more basic subproblems. Their solutions are written as procedures or functions within procedures.

Top-Down Design and Procedures

1. Write the statement part of the main program first. In a program of any size, this will mainly consist of procedure calls. Each procedure should solve one part of the original problem.

2. The main program's statement part should be simple enough for a non-programmer to read and understand, yet detailed enough to give a programmer an idea of how the program works.

3. If a procedure is particularly complicated, or does more than one job, it should probably be broken down into sub-procedures.

length of subprograms

Remember that a procedure isn't a rug for sweeping code under! One page (or screenful) of code is enough for any human to try to read and understand. If the procedure is longer, *try to break it down*.

Programming with Subprograms 2-2

PASCAL HAS TWO SORTS OF SUBPROGRAMS—*functions*, and *procedures*. As I've just argued, subprograms make main programs easier to read and understand, because a single name can take the place of a long or complex code segment. An interested human browser, no less than the compiler, is referred to an area set aside for the detailed code of the subprogram's *declaration*. At execution time, the subprogram's name acts as a *call*, or invocation, of the specialized code.

A procedure call is a statement; it represents a sequence of actions. Here's the code of a simple procedure that reads two numbers and prints their sum.

procedure *AddInput*;
{Read two numbers, then print their sum.}
var *First, Second*: *integer*; {local variable declarations}
begin
    readln (First, Second);
    writeln (First + Second)
end; {*AddInput*}

a typical procedure

A function call is an expression; it represents a value. The short example below is given two numbers when it's called, but represents, rather than printing, their sum.

function *Add* (*First, Second*: *integer*): *integer*;
{Represents the sum of its arguments.}
begin
    Add := First + Second {assign the function its value}
end; {*Add*}

a typical function

Thus, a procedure call is a statement all by itself—like a call of *writeln*. A function call, in contrast, is generally just part of a statement—like, say, *sqr*(*x*), it has a value that's used to create a longer expression.

Subprograms are declared one at a time, after program variables, but before the statement part:

program outline

program heading
constant definitions
variable declarations
procedure and function declarations
statements

Everything that a subprogram requires, but that isn't used elsewhere in the program, can be created within the confines of the subprogram declaration. Except for the heading, program and subprogram outlines are almost identical— subprograms can include constant definitions, as well as declarations of variables and even nested subprograms. These are called *local* definitions and declarations; they exist only during a call of the subprogram. Letting subprograms contain all the definitions and declarations they need helps make them *modular*, or self-contained.

nesting definitions

local identifiers are temporary

modularity

As a concept, subprograms are simple, and even programmable calculators usually support 'gosub' calls. In high-level languages like Pascal, though, subprograms are complicated by a need for *communication*—between subprograms, or between a subprogram and the program it's part of. On various occasions, procedures and functions...

parameters

1.   may need to get values from the main program—they may need 'value input,' just as *sqrt* needs a value to compute the square root of, or a *write* procedure needs an output value to print; or they,

2.   may have to return values to the main program—they may have 'value output' that involves changing the value of main program variables.

We can arrange for the transfer of values between the main program and its subprograms by declaring *parameters* in the procedure or function heading.

value parameters

> A *value parameter* is a local variable, used only in the subprogram, whose starting value is given by an argument in the subprogram call. Changing the value parameter has no effect on its argument.

variable parameters

> A *variable parameter* is an alternate name, meaningful only in the subprogram, for the variable that's supplied as its argument in the subprogram call. Changing the variable parameter *does* affect its argument, since they're the exact same variable.

Any expression can be the argument of a value parameter. Only a variable, though, can be a variable parameter's argument. As you might imagine, there has to be exactly one value or variable parameter declared in the subprogram heading for every argument in the subprogram call.

Function calls (as described in Chapter 1) have generally needed arguments for value parameters. We haven't encountered any variable parameters yet, but it's easy to imagine a situation that requires them. Suppose that we want to read two values, then have a procedure exchange them. A call would look like this:

```
readln (First, Second);    {get the values}
Switch (First, Second);    {exchange them}
writeln (First, Second);   {print them in reversed order}
```

When *Switch* is called, the arguments *First* and *Second* must be variables—they couldn't be plain numbers or constants. Inside *Switch*, variables *First* and *Second* are given alternate names—the identifiers of the variable parameters. Exchanging the values of these variable parameters is exactly like exchanging the values of the argument variables. The actual code of *Switch* might be:

a variable parameter
example

```
procedure Switch (var Local1, Local2: integer);
   {Swap the values of two variable parameters.}
   var Temporary: integer;
begin
   Temporary := Local1;
   Local1 := Local2;
   Local2 := Temporary
end;  {Switch}
```

Procedure *Switch* is overkill for a program that only has to swap the values of a single pair of variables. However, since *Switch* can be called with *any* two variables as arguments, it's useful in a program that makes many exchanges.

Scope of Identifiers

Once we start defining identifiers in different locations, a problem arises. Let's consider the simplest case—a procedure with local constants and variables, but no parameters. You shouldn't have any trouble following program *Music*, below. Notice that the main program and its procedure *Tune* have like-named identifiers—the constant *SCALE* and the variable *JohnnyOneNote*:

identifier scope demonstration program

```
program Music (output);
      {Illustrates procedure declaration, and the scope of identifiers.}
   const SCALE = 'Bass clef ';  {This is a text constant.}
   var JohnnyOneNote: char;
   procedure Tune;  {Note the identically named local identifiers.}
      const SCALE = 'Treble clef ';
      var JohnnyOneNote: char;
      begin
         JohnnyOneNote := 'A';
         writeln (SCALE, JohnnyOneNote)
      end;  {Tune}
   begin  {Music}
      JohnnyOneNote := 'D';
      writeln (SCALE, JohnnyOneNote);
      Tune;
      writeln (SCALE, JohnnyOneNote)
   end.  {Music}
```

↓   ↓   ↓   ↓   ↓

Bass clef D
Treble clef A
Bass clef D

scope

> The word *scope* describes the realm of meaning of an identifier that names a constant, variable, or subprogram. The scope of an identifier is the portion of a program—called a *block*—in which it continues to represent a particular value or action.

local precedence

In program *Music* the identifiers *SCALE* and *JohnnyOneNote* are used twice. But when they appear within procedure *Tune*, only the local definitions are recognized. Thus, the assignment of 'A' to the local *JohnnyOneNote* has no effect on the value of the global variable with the same name. The local identifier is said to take *precedence* over a like-named, but relatively global, identifier.

The illustration below provides a more general example of *block structure*. Each block, consisting of a definition part, declaration part, and statement part, is shown as a box. The scope of a global constant is the entire program—the

block structure   largest block. A local identifier's scope is limited to the block it's declared in—
'its' subprogram, and other subprograms declared within that subprogram. As
far as the internal subprograms are concerned, an outer local identifier might as
well be global. Not all languages have a block structure like Pascal's; some have
only local identifiers, some only globals, and some don't allow subprogram
declarations at all.

```
program A
procedure B
   function D
      begin {D}
         . .

      end; {D}
   begin {B}
      . .

   end; {B}
procedure C
   procedure E
      begin {E}
         . .

      end; {E}
   function F
      begin {F}
         . .

      end; {F}
   begin {C}
      . .

   end; {C}
begin {A}
   . .

end. {A}
```

| program A |
| procedure B |
| function D |
| procedure C |
| procedure E |
| function F |

Identifiers defined in: *Their scope is blocks:*

program A	A, B, C, D, E, F
procedure B	B, D
procedure C	C, E, F
function D	D
procedure E	E
function F	F

     Suppose there isn't any ambiguity in definitions. Can an identifier defined
in the main program be used in a procedure or function? The answer is yes.
Typically, we will only take advantage of this when a subprogram uses a main-
main-program   program constant. This is one reason that constant identifiers are usually
constants   capitalized—so that they immediately stand out to the program reader.

A more interesting question is whether or not we can make an assignment directly to a global variable from within a subprogram.

side effects

> Technically, nothing in Pascal prohibits making a direct assignment to a global variable from within a procedure or function. However, this sort of assignment is known as a *side-effect*. It is strongly discouraged; side-effects lead to some of the most difficult-to-find bugs in programming.

Like variable and constant identifiers, procedure and function identifiers follow the rules of scope. Once a procedure or function has been declared, its name has meaning in other parts of the program. These include:

1.   The main program's statement part.

subprogram scope

2.   The statement parts of subprograms declared after the procedure or function we're concerned with.

3.   The statement part of the procedure or function itself.

Usually we'll invoke procedures or functions from the main program, or from subprograms declared later on. The third case, in which a subprogram calls itself, won't concern us until we explore recursion in Chapter 16. At that time, we'll also see how a **forward** declaration lets two subprograms call each other.

> In general, subprograms are declared in an order that makes sense to the program reader. They can be called in any sequence, for any number of times. There is only one rule to follow—a subprogram must be declared before it can be called.

Procedures and Parameters

The syntax of a procedure declaration is like a program's, with two small exceptions:

1.   The heading uses the reserved word **procedure** rather than **program**.

2.   The procedure definition ends with a semicolon, and not a period.

The heading is also the place where value and variable parameters are declared. The syntax chart of a procedure heading is:

procedure heading

procedure ⟶ *identifier* ⟶ (⟶ *parameter list* ⟶) ⟶ ;

The *parameter list* syntax is:

parameter list

local definitions	After the heading, a procedure block (or body) contains definition, declaration, and statement parts, just like a main program. When constants or variables are created in subprograms, they're known as *local* definitions, as opposed to the *global* definitions of the main program. The potential problem of using the same identifier twice, once globally, and once locally, is resolved as I described earlier—the local definition takes precedence.

We'll usually find that the action a subprogram takes depends, somehow, on a value or variable provided when the subprogram is invoked. Value and variable parameters let values or variables be 'passed' to the subprogram. Parameter declarations are like plain variable declarations, except:

syntax of parameters

1.   The parameter list goes between parentheses.

2.   **var** only precedes declarations of variable parameters.

value parameters

The headings below declare only value parameters, because **var** doesn't appear in the parameter list. Since they only have value parameters, we can assume that procedures *ShowInterval* and *Debugging* need arguments that vary from call to call, but don't change any global variables.

> **procedure** *ShowInterval* (*Argument*: *real*;   *UpperBound, LowerBound*: *integer*);
>
> **procedure** *Debugging* (*CompleteTest, Antibugging*: *boolean*;
>   *Message*: *char*;   {This is a good place for comments.}
>   *Value1, Value2*: *integer*);

variable parameters

The next pair of headings only contain variable parameters, because **var** appears before every group of identifiers. Since every parameter is a variable parameter, it's a safe assumption that *AdjustTerms* and *Increment* will somehow change the values of their arguments.

> **procedure** *AdjustTerms* (**var** *FirstTerm, SecondTerm*: *real*);
>
> **procedure** *Increment* (**var** *Initial, Monogram*: *char*;
>   **var** *From, Until*: *integer*);

mixed headings

Finally, these headings are mixed. A distinct declaration, with its own type, is needed to separate value and variable parameter declarations. In all these examples, *Huey* and *Dewey* are variable parameters, while *Louie* is a value parameter. In terms of the kinds of parameters created, each heading is identical—the arguments to *Huey* and *Dewey* will be changed in the procedure, while the value of *Louie* will just be used. However, each procedure gets its arguments in a different order.

> **procedure** *Able* (**var** *Huey, Dewey*: *integer*;   *Louie*: *integer*);
>
> **procedure** *Baker* (*Louie*: *integer*;   **var** *Huey, Dewey*: *integer*);
>
> **procedure** *Charlie* (**var** *Huey*: *integer*;   *Louie*: *integer*;   **var** *Dewey*: *integer*);

Let's consider an example. Program *ParameterCrazy*, below, contains nothing but procedures and calls. It's interesting because the global variables *First* and *Second* are neither assigned to, nor inspected, in the main program— procedures do all the work. Nevertheless, the variables must be declared in the main program since they are repeatedly used as arguments to value and variable parameters. Since *First* and *Second* are used as arguments, the information they carry is shared between *GetTheNumbers, SwitchThem* , and *PrintTheResults* .

```
program ParameterCrazy (input, output);
    {Reverses two input integers.}

var First, Second: integer;

procedure GetTheNumbers (var Primero, Segundo: integer);
    {Reads values for the variable parameters Primero and Segundo.}
    begin
        writeln  ('Please enter two integers.');
        readln (Primero, Segundo)
    end; {GetTheNumbers}

procedure SwitchThem (var Premier, Deuxieme: integer);
    {Swaps the values of two variable parameters.}
    var Temporary: integer;
    begin
        Temporary := Premier;
        Premier := Deuxieme;
        Deuxieme := Temporary
    end; {SwitchThem}

procedure PrintTheResults (Primo, Secondo: integer);
    {Prints its value parameters.}
    const PRINTSPACE = 1;          {Provide the minimum output field.}
    begin
        write ('In reversed order, the numbers are ');
        writeln (Primo:PRINTSPACE, ' and ', Secondo:PRINTSPACE, '.')
    end; {PrintTheResults}

begin {The main program, ParameterCrazy}
    GetTheNumbers (First, Second);
    SwitchThem (First, Second);
    PrintTheResults (First, Second)
end. {ParameterCrazy}
```

parameter passing
example program

↓   ↓   ↓   ↓   ↓

Please enter two integers.
27   −935
In reversed order, the numbers are 935 and 27.

When I wrote *ParameterCrazy* I carefully used unique identifiers throughout, at the expense of practically exhausting my knowledge of Romance languages. To really understand parameters, though, you should be able to follow examples that involve identifier scope and name precedence as well. Program *SummerBummer*, below, demonstrates the relative independence of global variables, and local variables and value parameters. Its procedure, *SumSquares*, relies on value parameters that are initialized as part of the call. However, changes to the local *First, Second*, and *Sum* don't affect their like-named global counterparts.

value parameter
example program

```
program SummerBummer (output);
    {Demonstrates value parameters.}

var First, Second, Sum: integer;

procedure SumSquares (First, Second: integer);
    {Squares, and sums, its value parameters.}
    var Sum: integer;
    begin
        First := sqr (First);    {Are these three assignments local or global?}
        Second := sqr (Second);
        Sum := First + Second;
        writeln (First, Second, Sum)
    end;  {SumSquares}

begin
    First := 2;
    Second := 3;
    Sum := First + Second;
    writeln (First, Second, Sum);
    SumSquares (First, Second);
    writeln (First, Second, Sum)
end.  {SummerBummer}
```

```
    2        3        5
    4        9       13
    2        3        5
```

Note that *SumSquares* could be called with any two arguments that represent *integer* values—numbers, function calls, expressions, variables, etc. Any similarity between names would be purely coincidental.

value parameter
arguments

```
SumSquares (5, 9);
SumSquares (3 + 2, 9 mod 8);
SumSquares (First, Second);
SumSquares (Second, First);
SumSquares (sqr (3), SomeValue);
```

Variable parameters are needed when a procedure has 'output'—when it's expected to modify a main-program variable. Recall my original example of a procedure that exchanges the values of two variables from the calling program. We don't know what variables to exchange; indeed, the pair may change with every call.

If we arrange for the variables that accompany the call to be temporarily renamed with variable parameters, though, there's no problem in making the switch. Since the variable parameter names become temporary aliases for their arguments, switching the variable parameters is the same thing as switching the arguments themselves. An assignment to a variable parameter is just like an assignment to its argument. Suppose we declare this procedure:

procedure *Double* **(var** *Parameter* : *real*) ;
    {Demonstrates a variable parameter.}
    begin
      Parameter := *Parameter* * 2.0
    end ; {*Double*}

Imagine that *Income* is a variable of type *real*. The call: *Double* (*Income*) ; is is exactly equivalent to the main-program assignment:

    Income := *Income* * 2.0 ;

A final example uses both kinds of parameters. I'll write a procedure like *SumSquares*, but instead of printing the computed value, I'll use a variable parameter to return the sum of the squares of the value parameters to the main program.

procedure *FindSquareSum* (*First, Second* : *integer* ; **var** *Sum* : *integer*) ;
    {Uses value parameters to help compute a variable parameter.}
    begin
      First := *sqr* (*First*) ; {These assignments are local...}
      Second := *sqr* (*Second*) ;
      Sum := *First* + *Second* ; {...but this one has a global effect.}
    end ; {*FindSquareSum*}

In this procedure, assignments to *First* and *Second* last only for the duration of the call, but the assignment to *Sum* has a permanent effect. The variable supplied as the third argument to a call of *FindSquareSum* will have its value altered within the procedure. The first two arguments can be any *integer*-valued expressions, but the third argument must always be an *integer* variable:

    FindSquareSum (5, 9, *Answer*) ;
    FindSquareSum (3 + 2, 9 **mod** 8, *Result*) ;
    FindSquareSum (*First, FIXED, Sum*) ;
    FindSquareSum (*Second, First, Total*) ;
    FindSquareSum (*sqr* (3), *SomeValue, Solution*) ;

I'll close with a summary of the rules that pertain to arguments and parameters. First, there must always be the same number of arguments in a procedure call as there are parameters in the procedure heading, so that a one-to-one correspondence between arguments and parameters is maintained.

arguments and parameters

Second, a value parameter's argument can be any value that could ordinarily be assigned to the value parameter, in any valid form for an expression. The argument is evaluated at the beginning of the procedure call, and initializes the value parameter.

Finally, a variable parameter's argument must be a variable. Furthermore, the variable parameter and its argument must have the exact same type. This rule comes as no surprise, since the variable parameter merely renames its argument.

Functions

Pascal functions compute and represent values. The appearance of a function's name in a program signals the computer to suspend regular program operations while it executes the function subprogram's code. After the function's value has been determined, the program picks up from where it left off. For instance, a call of function *Distance* (with its arguments *SpeedometerReading* and *Elapsed-Time*) is used here to supply a value for the variable *AmountTraveled*:

$$AmountTraveled := Distance\ (SpeedometerReading,\ ElapsedTime)\ ;$$

Naturally, a function must be declared before it can be used. In the declaration of *Distance*, below, note the specification of the function's type, and the assignment of its value.

> **function** *Distance (Rate : integer ; Time : real) : real ;*
>   {Calculates *Distance* given *Rate* and *Time*.}
> **begin**
>   *Distance := Rate ∗ Time*   {This statement assigns the function its value.}
> **end** ; {*Distance* }

The syntax chart of a function heading is:

function heading

Function declarations are intermingled with procedure declarations at the end of a program or subprogram's declaration part. As I've pointed out before, a function (unlike a procedure) represents a value. This has two consequences. First, since the function represents a value, we have to specify its type. Second, the function has to contain an assignment that actually gives it the value.

special function rules

function type

A function call may represent any simple type of value, ordinal or *real*. The function's *result type* is specified at the end of the function heading—a colon is followed by the type identifier.

My example function *Distance* was of type *real*. Having set the stage by giving the function a type, we have to assign it a value.

assigning function
values

The statement part of a function must contain an assignment that gives the function its value. This assignment can only take place within the function itself.

In *Distance* this assignment formed the function's entire statement part. Functions may be very complicated, of course; but a function's last action is to give itself a value.

We'll almost invariably find that functions use one or more value parameters to compute a value—a value that the function then represents. Some typical function headings are:

> **function** *Cube* (*Number* : *real*) : *real*;
>
> **function** *Decode* (*Letter* : *char*; *CodeKey* : *integer*) : *char*;
>
> **function** *Highest* (*First, Second, Third* : *integer*) : *integer*;
>
> **function** *NoArguments* : *integer*;

In each case the heading ends with a colon and the function's type.

arguments and
parameters
As with procedure calls, there must be a one-to-one correspondence between the arguments of a function *call*, and the parameters of a function *declaration*. Thus, any given function will always be called with the same number of arguments.

(Function heading—value parameters)

function *Yield* (*Investment* : *integer*; *Interest* : *real*; *Days* : *integer*) : *real*;

Income := *Yield* (1000, 0.097, 365);

(Function call—arguments)

Variable parameters are seldom declared in function headings, because the avowed purpose of a function is to compute and return a *single* value. If a function has variable parameters, it will wind up returning more than just one value. This creates a situation that can confuse an unwary program rewriter.

If a subprogram is supposed to calculate more than one value for the main program, write it as a procedure.

I'll demonstrate functions with a few examples that are standard in some other computer languages (and even some Pascal implementations). A reciprocal function is found on most hand calculators:

```
function Reciprocal (Number: integer): real;
    {Represents the reciprocal of Number.}
    begin
        Reciprocal := 1/Number
    end; {Reciprocal}
```

reciprocals

Exponentiation is a must in Pascal:

```
function Power (Base, Exponent: real): real;
    {Raises Base to the Exponent power.}
    begin
        Power := exp (Exponent * ln (Base))
    end; {Power}
```

exponentiation

A tangent function—also missing from Pascal—is equally easy to create. We make use of the fact that tangent ϕ = (sine ϕ / cosine ϕ) in writing function *RadianTan*.

```
function RadianTan (AngleInRadians: real): real;
    {Represents the tangent of its argument.}
    begin
        RadianTan := sin (AngleInRadians)/cos (AngleInRadians)
    end; {RadianTan}
```

tangents

RadianTan's value parameter, *AngleInRadians*, clearly documents the fact that *RadianTan's* argument should be supplied in radians, rather than degrees. Unfortunately, the most familiar measurement of angles works the other way around; in degrees, rather than in radians. We can modify *RadianTan* to work with a degree-valued argument by including a radian conversion function within the declaration of *RadianTan*.

```
function Tan (AngleInDegrees: real): real;
    {Represents the tangent of its degree-valued argument.}
    var Angle: real;        {This variable is local to tan.}
    function ConvertToRadians (Angle: real): real;
        const PI = 3.14159265358979; {1° = π/180 radians}
        begin
            ConvertToRadians := Angle *(PI/180)
        end; {ConvertToRadians}
    begin
        Angle := ConvertToRadians (AngleInDegrees);
        Tan := sin (Angle)/cos (Angle)
    end; {Tan}
```

radian conversion

The operation of *Tan* can be checked by including it in a *driver* program that does nothing but call *Tan* with different arguments. This ploy lets us test the function in an environment that isn't cluttered with extraneous function or procedure declarations. There are small mathematical inconsistencies in *TestFunctions'* output because of inaccuracies in the computer's arithmetic.

driver programs

```
program TestFunctions (input, output);
   {A driver program that tests function Tan.}
function Tan (AngleInDegrees: real): real;
   · · .    {As declared above.}
begin
   writeln ('The tangent of 0.0 degrees is ', Tan (0.0));
   writeln ('The tangent of 45.0 degrees is ', Tan (45.0));
   writeln ('The tangent of 60.0 degrees is ', Tan (60.0));
   writeln ('The tangent of 120.0 degrees is ', Tan (120.0));
   writeln ('The tangent of 135.0 degrees is ', Tan (135.0))
end. {TestFunctions}
```

function driver
program

↓   ↓   ↓   ↓   ↓   ↓

```
The tangent of 0.0 degrees is   0.00000000000000E+00
The tangent of 45.0 degrees is  9.99999999999998E-01
The tangent of 60.0 degrees is  1.73205080756887E+00
The tangent of 120.0 degrees is -1.73205080756889E+00
The tangent of 135.0 degrees is -1.00000000000000E+00
```

A final example implements a collection of the functions and procedures used in simple analytic geometry. It was originally written, in a somewhat less ornate form, by an overachieving advisee of mine who was trying to demonstrate her qualifications for skipping Berkeley's pre-calculus course (and her excuse for skipping the placement exam). Program *Geometry* prompts for a starting position (call it A), and an angle of rotation about the origin. It locates the newly-defined point (call it B), then computes the magnitude of the line AB, its midpoint, the line's Y-axis intercept, and so on. For each of the subprograms in *Geometry*, note both the choice of procedure *vs.* function, and of value *vs.* variable parameter. Do you agree that this is one of the rare programs for which extremely simple variable identifiers are suitably mnemonic?

problem: analytic
geometry

```
program Geometry (input, output);
  {Performs an impressive sequence of operations with Cartesian coordinates.}
var Ax, Ay, Bx, By, RotationAngle, Slope: real;
procedure ConvertToRadians (var Angle: real);
  {Converts its degree-valued argument to radians.}
  const PI = 3.14159265358979;
  begin
    Angle := Angle * (PI / 180)
  end;  {ConvertToRadians}
function Magnitude (x, y: real): real;
  {Represents the magnitude of the line from point x,y to the origin.}
  begin
    Magnitude := sqrt (sqr (x) + sqr (y))
  end;  {Magnitude}
procedure Rotate (var NewX, NewY: real; x, y, Angle: real);
  {Locates the coordinates that result from rotating point x, y by Angle.}
  begin
    NewX := x * cos (Angle) - y * sin (Angle);
    NewY := y * cos (Angle) + x * sin (Angle)
  end;  {Rotate}
function Mid (Left, Right: real): real;
  {Computes the midpoint, along one axis, between Left and Right.}
  begin
    Mid := (Left + Right) / 2
  end;  {Mid}
function Intercept (Slope, x, y: real): real;
  {Finds the y-intercept using the slope-intercept equation of the line.}
  begin
    Intercept := y - (Slope * x)
  end;  {Intercept}
```

analytic geometry
program

```
begin
    writeln ('Enter the x,y coordinates of point A.');
    readln (Ax, Ay);
    writeln ('Give the angle of rotation in degrees.');
    readln (RotationAngle);
    ConvertToRadians (RotationAngle);
    Rotate (Bx, By, Ax, Ay, RotationAngle);
    writeln ('The coordinates of point B are ', Bx:5:2, By:5:2);
    writeln ('A and B are both ', Magnitude(Ax,Ay):5:2, ' from the origin.');
    writeln ('The length of line AB is ', Magnitude(Ax - Bx, Ay - By):5:2);
    Slope := (Ay - By) / (Ax - Bx);
    writeln ('The slope of AB is ', Slope:5:2);
    writeln ('The coordinates of the midpoint are ',
            Mid(Ax, Bx):5:2, Mid(Ay, By):5:2);
    writeln ('AB intercepts the Y axis at ', Intercept(Slope, Ax, Ay):5:2);
    {How necessary is this next complicated call?}
    writeln ('A line perpendicular to AB intercepts the Y axis at ',
            Intercept(-1/Slope, Mid(Ax, Bx), Mid(Ay, By)):5:2);
    writeln ('Distance from midpoint to origin is ',
            Magnitude(Mid(Ax,Bx), Mid(Ay,By)):5:2)
end.   {Geometry}
```

↓   ↓   ↓   ↓   ↓

```
Enter the x,y coordinates of point A.
4.0   5.0
Give the angle of rotation in degrees.
120.0
The coordinates of point B are -6.33 0.96
A and B are both  6.40 from the origin.
The length of line AB is 11.09
The slope of AB is  0.39
The coordinates of the midpoint are -1.17 2.98
AB intercepts the Y axis at  3.44
A line perpendicular to AB intercepts the Y axis at  0.00
Distance from midpoint to origin is  3.20
```

Self-Check Questions

Q. The following procedure declaration contains an error that should be easy to spot. What is it?

```
procedure Wrong (A: integer; var B: integer);
    var A: integer; B: real;        etc.
```

A. Declared parameters share the scope of local variables. Procedure *Wrong* tries to use two identifiers (*A* and *B*) in equally local places. Whether the parameters and local variables are of identical or different types is irrelevant. It's as incorrect a pair of declarations as this would be:

> **var** *A*: *integer*; *A*: *real*;

Q. What will the output of this program be?

> **program** *Confusion* (*input, output*);
>   {Comments? Nope—that would be telling.}
>   **var** *A, B, C, D: integer*;
>   **procedure** *Confuse* (*C,A*: *integer*; **var** *D*: *integer*);
>   **var** *B*: *integer*;
>   **begin**
>   *A* := 5;   *B* := 6;   *C* := 7;   *D* := 8;
>   *writeln* (*A,B,C,D*)
>   **end**; {*Confuse*}
>   **begin**
>   *A* := 1;   *B* := 2;   *C* := 3;   *D* := 4;
>   *writeln* (*A,B,C,D*);
>   *Confuse* (*B,A,D*);
>   *writeln* (*A,B,C,D*)
>   **end**. {*Confusion*}

A. This intentionally muddled program deliberately tries to confuse value parameters, variable parameters, and local variables. Its output is:

1	2	3	4
5	6	7	8
1	2	3	8

Chapter Notes 2-3

OF ALL THE PASCAL I'VE PRESENTED SO FAR, only subprograms might help prevent more trouble than they cause. Their syntax follows that of main programs closely, so you'll usually have plenty of reference models at hand. Bugs associated with parameters often result from confusing value parameters and variable parameters.

> If a subprogram only *uses* a value, declare a value parameter.
> If a subprogram *changes* or *returns* a value, use a variable parameter.

order of arguments

There has to be a one-to-one correspondence between parameters and arguments, and they have to be correctly ordered. A misordered procedure call might produce the error message:

EXPRESSION GIVEN (VARIABLE REQUIRED) FOR VARIABLE PARAMETER

Passing a defined constant as the argument of a variable parameter would provoke an identical message, since a constant's value can't be changed.

type of arguments   Like other Pascal variables, value and variable parameters belong to some
particular type. Their arguments must be of appropriate types for a procedure
or function call to be valid. If they're not, there are more error messages...

ARGUMENT TYPE NOT IDENTICAL TO TYPE OF VARIABLE PARAMETER
EXPRESSION TYPE CLASHES WITH TYPE OF VALUE PARAMETER

function bugs   Most errors that occur in function declaration result from oversight. There
are two main rules to remember. First, specify the function's type at the end of
the function heading. It can have any simple type, either ordinal or *real*.
Second, don't forget to assign the function its value. An omitted assignment
might not be spotted by the compiler, since the assignment isn't specified as a
syntax rule. Unfortunately, the missing assignment is sometimes equally hard
for the programmer to find—it's such an obvious bug that we tend to overlook it.

accidental recursion   A serious problem is the accidental creation of a recursive function or procedure call—a subprogram that calls itself. The appearance of a subprogram's
name serves as a call or invocation of that subprogram. Function *Double*,
below, inadvertently invokes itself during its own execution.

> **function** *Double* (*Argument*: *integer*): *integer*;
>   {Incorrect example that contains a recursive call.}
> **begin**
>   *Double := Double (Argument) * 2*
> **end**; {*Double*}

What is the value of *Double (Argument)* on the right hand side of the assignment? The computer will try to call the function to find out. That call leads to
another, and another, and another. Where does it all end? Find out when we
discuss recursion in Chapter 16.

A similar example is only spotted through an error message that complains
about a shortage of arguments to the function:

> **function** *Increment* (*Argument*: *integer*): *integer*;
>   {Incorrect example that contains a recursive call.}
> **begin**
>   ·.·
>   *Increment := Increment + 1*;   etc.

The error message is:

```
Increment := Increment + 1;
          ↑ NOT ENOUGH ARGUMENTS TO "INCREMENT"
```

order problems

A final error in subprogram declarations comes when subprograms are inadvertently declared in the wrong order. It may be a rude shock to get an error message about an undefined procedure when a listing shows, perfectly clearly, that the procedure *has* been defined. However, it must be defined before it is called, or the compiler will not be aware of its existence.

Let's leave syntax problems, and turn our attention to a more programming-oriented aspect of using subprograms. The most common error in procedure usage is quite serious, even though the program it's found in may execute perfectly well. Can you spot it?

```
begin {main program}
    RunProgram        {procedure call}
end. {main program}
```

The error is using a procedure at all! Does it make the program any easier to read? No, because it doesn't break down the program's action. Does it make the program any easier to write? Again, no, because we're just substituting a long, complicated procedure for a long, complicated program. The example above is merely a sham subprogram that doesn't take advantage of the procedure's benefits.

Important to Remember

- Local variables are declared in procedures or functions. They do not exist between calls of the subprogram, and must be reinitialized on every call.

- A parameter is declared in a procedure or function heading; an argument is part of the subprogram call.

- A value parameter is a local variable whose starting value is supplied, as an argument, during a subprogram call. Changing the value parameter has no effect on its argument.

- A variable parameter is a local identifier, known in the subprogram, that is an alternative name for a variable supplied as an argument in the subprogram call. Thus, changing the variable parameter also changes the argument variable.

- If a subprogram uses a value *from* the main program, pass it to a value parameter. If a subprogram computes or changes a value *for* the main program, pass it to a variable parameter.

- The argument of a value parameter can be any value with the same type. A variable parameter's argument has to be a variable, though. There must always be an argument for every parameter, and a parameter for every argument.

- A block is the body of a program, procedure, or function—its definitions, declarations, and statements. Identifiers created within the block are said to be local, while those defined in a outside block are relatively global.

- The scope of an identifier is the area of a program in which it's recognized. If a local and global identifier have the same name, the local identifier's definition takes precedence.

- Constants should be capitalized so that they can be easily recognized if they are used within an enclosed subprogram. However, variables should never be used this way, because that would create side effects—use value or variable parameters instead.

- Stepwise refinement is the problem-solving strategy of repeatedly restating a problem in terms of smaller, simpler, subproblems. Top-down design is a programming strategy that involves delaying detailed coding decisions for as long as possible.

Cross Reference

- Blocks are formally defined in A58—A59. A59—A63 continues the discussion of identifier scope, and explains a variety of obscure special cases.

- Value and variable parameters are described in A79—A83. This discussion becomes rather difficult when parameters of other than simple types become involved, so you may want to refer back to this section later.

- Procedure statements, or calls, are first mentioned on A12. Procedures are fully discussed in A73—A75, while A76—A78 covers functions. Recursive subprogram calls are mentioned there—read Chapter 16 if they pique your interest.

- The formal description of restrictions on parameters and their arguments refers frequently to the discussion of assignment compatibility in A10—A11. However, the distinctions drawn there are not particularly important until we extend type definitions in Chapter 6.

Exercises

2-1   The image of a procedure or function as a black box that magically computes an answer isn't far from the truth. The choice of one such box over another may depend on an issue as small as the form of its arguments.
   Suppose that we have two representations of triangles:

1.   as three pairs of points $(X_a, Y_a, X_b, Y_b, X_c, Y_c)$ that mark the triangle's vertices;

2   as a triple (a, b, c) that represents the length of the triangle's sides.

Write and test black boxes that compute the area of a triangle using different formulae. Some that may be helpful are:

$$area = \frac{(X_a Y_b - Y_a X_b) + (X_b Y_c - Y_b X_c) + (X_c Y_a - Y_c X_a)}{2}$$

$$area = \sqrt{(a+b+c)(a+b)(a+c)(b+c)} \qquad (Heron's\ formula)$$

Can you figure out how to call the Heron's formula subprogram using the vertex arguments?

2-2   Journey with me now to the wilds of New Mathico, where the sun rises on the x–axis, and most everything can be described by an equation.
   A cowgirl is riding the range one day when she finds herself, hot and thirsty, at some point x, y. The position of the nearest river can be described by the point-slope equation $y = mx+b$. How far is she from the river? Write a program that asks for her position and the river's equation, then prints the distance.

2-3   Resistors can be connected in parallel, in series, or in a combination of the two. The total resistance of resistors in series is just the sum of the individual resistances, while parallel resistance is the reciprocal of the sum of the reciprocals:

$$R_{series} = R_1 + R_2 + \cdots + R_n$$

$$\frac{1}{R_{parallel}} = \frac{1}{R_1} + \frac{1}{R_2} + \cdots + \frac{1}{R_n}$$

Write functions that compute parallel and series resistance, and put them in a program that finds the resistance of a given circuit. Assume that the circuit will consist of two resistors in series, followed by three in parallel, followed by two more in parallel. You will find that computation is the easy aspect of this program—the tough part is defining your input formats.

2-4   The distance in nautical miles between two points whose latitude and longitude are known can be computed with:

$$Distance = 60 \times \cos^{-1}(\sin(Lat_1) \sin(Lat_2) + \cos(Lat_1) \cos(Lat_2) \cos(Long_2 - Long_1))$$

(Southern latitudes or eastern longitudes should be treated as negative values.)

Write a program that finds the distance between Peoria, Illinois, (lat. 40° 38′ 54″N, long. 89° 41′ 23″W) and Dubuque, Iowa (lat. 42° 30′ 2″N, long. 90° 38′ 59″W). Since there aren't too many navigable passages thereabouts, convert nautical miles to kilometers (one nautical mile, the distance of one minute of latitude, is about 1.852 kilometers). Note that you will have to convert the degrees, minutes, and seconds of geographical coordinates to radians to use Pascal's trigonometric functions. You will also be pleased to write a cos^{-1} function that relies on the identity:

$$\cos^{-1}x = \frac{\pi}{2} - \tan^{-1}\frac{x}{\sqrt{1-x^2}}$$

2-5   Pascal's *ln* function uses e as its base; $ln(u)$ equals the power that e must be raised to in order to equal u. On occasion, though, other logarithmic bases (particularly base 2, and base 10 of common logarithms) are useful. In general, we can say that:

$$\log_a u = \frac{\ln u}{\ln a}$$

Write a function that returns the log of a number given any arbitrary base a.

2-6   We can write Pascal functions to explore certain aspects of standard calculus. Suppose we have a function $f(x)$. The function's derivative, $f'(x)$, gives the rate of change of the original f. Thus, if $f(x) = 5x$, then the derivative $f'(x)$ is 5, since any change in x causes a fivefold alteration in $f(x)$.

One way of computing the derivative of a function at a particular point is to compute the value:

$$f(x) = \frac{f(x+\epsilon) - f(x)}{\epsilon}$$

where ϵ represents some very small value (say, 1E–06). Smaller and smaller values of ϵ yield progressively better approximations to the theoretical derivative (which involves the concept of ϵ going to zero).

Armed with these ideas, write a program that performs Pascal calculus by computing values of derivatives. Naturally, you'll have to implement various functions to test. Some results to check are:

$f(x)$	$f'(x)$
$5x$	5
$sqr(x)$	$2x$
$sin(x)$	$cos(x)$
$ln(x)$	$1/x$

2-7   Although most people compute an arithmetic mean when they want to average two numbers, there are actually a variety of different conceptions of 'average.' Given x and y, we can define several means:

arithmetic mean A: Satisfies $2*A = x + y$
geometric mean G: Satisfies $G^2 = x * y$
harmonic mean H: Satisfies $1/H$ = arithmetic mean of $1/x$ and $1/y$

Write a program that implements the three means as different subprograms. Try to find out, for various positive x and y input values, how the means tend to be ordered. In particular, is one of the means always greater than the others?

2-8   As noted in the text, Pascal does not support exponentiation directly, so we must write our own function to compute powers. Fortunately, we know that:

$$x^y = exp(y*ln(x))$$

for positive *real* values of x and any *real* value of y.

Write a power function, and use it in a program that asks for x and y, then computes x^y. Verify that:

1.   any positive x to the zero power is 1;

2. x to the -1 is the reciprocal of x;

3.   2.718281828 to the 0.69314718 is approximately equal to 2;

4.   2 to the power 16 is 65536.

2-9   The octal number system is a base-8 system whose digits are 0, 1, 2, 3, 4, 5, 6, and 7. As in the decimal system, each digit represents a value between 0, and the system's base less one. When digits are joined to form numbers, each digit's position is also significant—the three-digit octal number XYZ equals 8^2 (or 64) times the decimal value of X, plus 8^1 (or 8) times Y, plus 8^0 (or 1) Z.

Write a program that asks for a three-digit octal number and prints its decimal equivalent. Test it on special cases like:

Octal	Decimal
100	64
111	73
777	511

2-10   Write a program that asks for two values of x that are constrained so that:

$-1 < x1, x2 < 1$

Then, find the points directly above these that lie on the unit circle:

$x^2 + y^2 = 1$

Print the interior angle, in radians, of the wedge-shaped sector defined by the upper pair of points and the origin.

2-11   Atwood's machine is a fiendish device invented by George Atwood (1746-1807) for the specific purpose of bringing misery to physics students. It consists of two unequal weights, attached by a massless string that is slung over a frictionless pulley.

We can compute the tension in the string by the following formula:

$$Tension = 2m_1 \frac{m_2}{m_1+m_2} g$$

where g is the acceleration due to gravity, 9.8 meters/sec^2, and m_1 and m_2 give masses in kilograms. Write a program that computes the tension for any two masses. Be sure to define constants where appropriate. To show off, write additional functions that compute the acceleration and velocity of the two masses after a time t.

2-12   Unlike the indefinite shelf life of a Hostess Twinkie, the life of any particular unstable—i.e. radioactive—atom is impossible to predict. Nevertheless, we can say that, on average, half the atoms of a given sample will decay with a particular time period called the *half-life*. This rate of decay follows an exponential curve given by:

$$undecayed \ fraction = e^{-\lambda t}$$

where t is time, and

$$\lambda = \frac{\ln 2}{T}$$

where T is the substance's half life. Write a program that asks the user to supply the half-life of a particular substance, and its starting mass. Compute the undecayed mass that remains after half the half-life, twice the half-life, and 100 times the half-life.

2-13   A *cycloid* is the name of a curve that describes the path of a point on the rim of a rolling wheel:

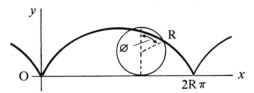

The parametric equations that give the position of the point on the rim in relation to θ are:

$$x = R(\theta - sin\theta)$$
$$y = R(1 - cos\theta)$$

Suppose a tall bicyclist (with 27" wheels) is tooling along the road when a spoke, at angle θ from vertical, suddenly snaps. What are the x, y coordinates of the spoke's connection to the rim? How much further will the bike travel before the connection point is located at the bottom of the wheel? Finally, suppose that the forks holding the wheel are positioned at an angle ϕ from vertical. How far will the bicycle go before the spoke becomes entangled in the forks?

2-14   A traveling salesperson travels between five cities. Suppose that the x, y coordinates of each city are supplied as input to a program. What is the total distance the salesperson travels? What is the direct distance between the first and last cities on her route?

2-15   A *rational transformation* is a function of the general form:

$$R(x,a,b,c,d) = \frac{(ax+b)}{(cx+d)}$$

where x is a *real* variable and $a, b, c,$ and d are *real* constants. Write a program that verifies that the transformation:

$$R(x,d,-b,-c,a)$$

is the inverse of the first function. In other words, show for various x values that:

$$R(R(x,a,b,c,d),d,-b,-c,a) = x$$

2-16   Two functions of interest in various branches of theoretical physics (and bicycling) are the hyperbolic functions:

$$\tanh x = \frac{e^x - e^{-x}}{e^x + e^{-x}} \qquad\qquad \text{sech } x = \frac{2}{e^x + e^{-x}}$$

Write a program that verifies these facts and relations:

1.   The derivative of $\tanh(x)$ is $sech^2(x)$,

2. $\tanh(x)$ approaches ±1 as x approaches $\pm\infty$,

3. $sech(x)$ is shaped somewhat like a single pulse, with a bulge over the origin,

4. $\tanh^2(x) + sech^2(x) = 1$

This last fact is interesting because it reveals two functions that have a 'sine-cosine relationship' in the sense of adding in quadrature to unity, but have two completely different shapes (a long sloping curve and a pulse).

3

The **for**
Statement

In their original definition and explanation of Pascal, Kathleen Jensen and Niklaus Wirth pointed out that...

> 'Essential to a computer program is action...a program must do something with its data—even if that action is the choice of doing nothing!'*

Like most languages, Pascal includes a variety of control statements (**for**, **while**, **if**, and so on) that govern the execution of simple statements (like assignments and procedure calls). I introduce the **for** statement first because it's simplest. We'll have a chance to practice some Pascal details (parameters from Chapter 2, and *nested, compound*, and *empty* statements) before delving into *boolean* expressions in Chapter 4. I'll also start using pseudocode before coding as a matter of course. In case you find all this too elementary, section 3-2 contains an (optional) introduction to a data type—the array—that is essential for scientific programming, and is often used in conjunction with the **for** statement.

Program Actions
3-1

THE FOR STATEMENT IS PASCAL'S basic loop. Its form is:

> **for** *counter variable* := *initial value* **to** *final value* **do**
>   *action* ;

The reserved word **downto** in place of **to** reverses the counting process. In chart form, the **for** statement is:

for statement

for⟶ *variable-identifier* ⟶ : = ⟶ *expression* ⟶ { **to** / **downto** } ⟶ *expression* ⟶ **do**
    ⟶ *statement* ⟶

Program *ShowFor*, below, shows a couple of **for** statements in action.

---

* Kathleen Jensen and Niklaus Wirth, *Pascal User Manual and Report*, Springer-Verlag 1974.

program *ShowFor* (*output*);
    {Demonstrates the **for** loop.}

var *LoopCount*: *integer*;
      CounterCharacter: *char*;

for demonstration
program

begin
    writeln ('This program shows what a for loop does.');
    for *LoopCount* := 1 **to** 5 **do**
        write ('Loop ', *LoopCount*:1, ', ');
    writeln;
    for *CounterCharacter* := 'Z' **downto** 'A' **do**
        write (*CounterCharacter*);
    writeln
end. {*ShowFor*}

↓   ↓   ↓   ↓   ↓   ↓

This program shows what a for loop does.
Loop 1, Loop 2, Loop 3, Loop 4, Loop 5,
ZYXWVUTSRQPONMLKJIHGFEDCBA

The two **for** statements' actions (both *write* calls) are shaded. The **for** statements themselves, though, differ in two ways. Obviously, one counts up (with **to**) while the other counts down (with **downto**). But also notice that the values used for counting are quite different—we count up by *integer* values, and down with *chars*.

Pascal uses a rather clever mechanism to control counting. Instead of giving the exact number of times we want the action to occur, we state expressions that give the initial and final values of a local variable.

> The variable that controls a **for** statement is called the *counter variable*. It can belong to any ordinal type, but must be locally declared.

the counter variable

When a **for** statement is entered, its counter variable is assigned the initial value. The counter variable is *incremented*, or increased to the next higher value, each time the **for** statement's action is carried out. When the counter variable represents the final value, the loop iterates one last time, and the program moves on to the next statement. In the **downto** form, counting is reversed. In either case, no action is taken if the difference between the initial and final values is less than zero.

This round-about method of tracking iterations lets the counter variable belong to any of Pascal's ordinal (counting) types. In *ShowFor*, the first counter variable was an *integer*, and its value increased by 1 on each circuit of the **for** loop. The initial value was 1, the final value was 5, and the action was repeated:

$$(final\ value\ -\ initial\ value)\ +\ 1$$

times—in other words, five times. But suppose we want to 'count' by characters? *ShowFor's* second **for** loop used a *char*-valued counter variable to progress, character by character, from 'Z' down to 'A.' I'll return to some special rules governing the counter variable soon.

First, though, let's see how to devise more sophisticated actions. The **for** loops of *ShowFor* were somewhat pathetic examples because they only controlled single *writes*. However, control statements can regulate a variety of actions. The most primitive program action is an inaction, or empty statement.

> A semicolon can indicate an *empty* or null statement.

empty statements

The semicolon itself isn't the empty statement—you should recall that it's Pascal's statement separator. In practice, though, the compiler assumes that every semicolon was preceded by a statement, even if no action was supplied. This formal inaction is occasionally required to meet special-case syntax requirements, but more frequently it is just an inadvertant semantic programming error. Although we would never intentionally write a **for** loop like this:

```
{A loop that controls an empty statement.}
for Counter :=1 to 5 do ;
```

the statement above has perfectly legal Pascal syntax. The **for** statement does nothing five times.

nested statements

A control statement can include other control statements as well. The internal statement is said to be *nested* inside the outer statement, and is treated as a single statement. For example:

```
for Outer := 1 to 3 do
    for Inner := 1 to 2 do
        write ('Hip, ');
writeln ('Hooray!')
```

Hip, Hip, Hip, Hip, Hip, Hip, Hooray!

compound statements

Now, an empty statement and a nested control statement are both technically single actions. Suppose that we want a **for** statement to control a sequence of unrelated actions, though; e.g. to repeat two separate *writelns*. The separate statements must be grouped into a single action by putting them between a **begin** and an **end**. This forms a *compound statement*; it lets a **for** statement control the repetition of two or more distinct statements. In chart form, we have:

compound statement

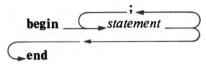

The **begin** and **end** are like statement parentheses that mark the boundaries of an action. Although statements within the compound statement must be separated by semicolons, the compound statement's **end** doesn't have to be preceded by a semicolon. For example:

> **for** *Outer* := 1 **to** 3 **do begin**
>   *writeln* ('Hip, Hip, '); {These are grouped as a single action.}
>   *writeln* ('Hooray!')
> **end**;

↓   ↓   ↓   ↓   ↓

Hip, Hip,
Hooray!
Hip, Hip,
Hooray!
Hip, Hip,
Hooray!

I'll close with some details about the counter variable before moving on to practical programming examples. Five rules govern possible values of the counter variable. First, the counter variable, initial value, and final value must *real* **counters are** all belong to the same ordinal type. They may not be of type *real*, because it **forbidden** makes no sense to talk of incrementing a *real* value—there is no next *real*.

the counter is local   Second, the counter variable must be locally declared. This means that a global variable can't be used as a counter variable within a subprogram (recall that this would be an undesirable side-effect in any case).

evaluating the bounds   Third, the expressions that give the counter variable's initial and final values are evaluated when the statement is first entered. Consequently, the number of times the loop iterates cannot be modified by the loop's action. Assignments to variables that represent the initial and final values will not affect the counter variable or its limits.

assigning the counter   Fourth, it's an error to make an assignment to the counter variable from within the loop's action. The counter variable, like any other variable, represents a value within the action of the **for** statement. But although it may be *used* within the **for** loop's action, it may not be *changed* there. Thus, the documentation implicit in the control statement's first line—that it will repeat for a certain number of times—cannot be undermined or invalidated by changing values from *within* the loop.

Fifth and finally, the value of the counter variable is undefined on exit from the **for** statement. In effect, the variable is in the pristine condition it held when it was first declared. It must be reinitialized before being used in an expression.

Procedure *AddNumbers*, below, demonstrates most of this section's ideas. The algorithm isn't difficult; a number is read, then added to a running sum.

```
procedure AddNumbers (Several: integer; var Sum: integer);
    {Read and add a sequence of Several numbers.}
    var Count, Current: integer;
    begin
        Sum := 0;
        for Count := 1 to Several do begin
            readln (Current);
            Sum := Sum + Current
        end {for}
    end; {AddNumbers}
```

Be sure you understand the reasons behind the different variable declarations. *Several*, which supplies the **for** loop's upper limit, must come from the main program. It is used, but not permanently changed, so it's passed as a value parameter. Assignments to *Sum*, in contrast, are expected to be reflected in a main program variable, so it's a variable parameter. Since *Count* is the **for** counter variable, it must be declared as a local variable. Finally, note that *Current* is declared locally because it's only used with the current procedure.

Focus On Programming: Pseudocode and **for**

Some might sneer at the lowly **for** statement, but it can solve some interesting problems. I'll work a few examples that range from the trivial (printing lines of characters) to the sublime (adding Fourier sums). As a quick warmup, let's get more practice with procedures and parameters.

The first example, program *Bars*, uses two value parameters. Its subprogram *DrawBar* is a 'utility' procedure that draws a line of characters with a **for** statement. (It might later be used in a bar-graphing program.) The length of the bar, and the character used to draw it, are arguments to each call of *DrawBar*. They provide starting values for the value parameters *Length* and *Bar-Character*.

problem: drawing
bars

bar-drawing program

```
program Bars (output);
   {Draws three rows of characters using the for statement.}
const DOLLARSIGN = '$';
var Income: integer;
    Symbol: char;
procedure DrawBar (Length: integer; BarCharacter: char);
   {Prints BarCharacter exactly Length times.}
   var Counter: integer;
   begin
      for Counter := 1 to Length do
         write (BarCharacter);
      writeln
   end; {DrawBar}
begin
   Income := 20;
   Symbol := '#';
   DrawBar (12, 'X');
   DrawBar (3*5, Symbol);
   DrawBar (Income, DOLLARSIGN)
end. {Bars}
```

```
XXXXXXXXXXXX
###############
$$$$$$$$$$$$$$$$$$$$
```

When *DrawBar* is called, it's given two arguments—the values of *Length* and *BarCharacter*. Since they go to value parameters, they can be expressions of any sort, as long as each has the correct type. Incidentally, the declaration of *Counter* within *DrawBar* isn't just good programming practice. It's required by the regulation that **for** loop counter variables be locally declared.

A second easy warmup will give us some exercise with nested and compound statements.

problem:
multiplication tables

Write a program that prints a 'times' table. Have it show all multiples, from $1 \times N$ to $N \times N$, of any number.

It's probably been some time since you've had to rely on such a table for help with multiplication! A pseudocode restatement of the problem will help clarify the eventual Pascal program:

get the limit N;

first refinement

print every multiple from 1 to N^2

Print every multiple might be clear as an English-language instruction, but it's far too abstract to be the basis of Pascal. A second refinement is necessary:

second refinement

> *get the limit N*;
> **for** *every number from 1 to N*
>   *print all multiples of that number*;

Now, what should the output look like? An ordinary table with labeled rows and columns, as in a math book, would hold a product at each intersection. As computer output, we can imagine that the table is printed by marching from column to column, one row at a time. My third pseudocode refinement contains one added feature—duplicate products are suppressed. Can you see how? Note that I use indenting to imply that compound statements are grouping actions together.

third refinement

> *get the limit N*;
> *label the columns*;
> **for** *every Row from 1 to N*
>   *label the row*;
>   **for** *every Column from 1 to the current Row value*
>   *print all multiples of that number*;

Program *TimesTable* is shown below. Pay special attention to its use of compound statements to control the actual printing of each line.

multiplication table
program

```
program TimesTable (input, output);
   {Prints a multiplication table of Limit values.}

var Limit, Row, Column: integer;

begin
   writeln ('Enter the upper limit for this times table.');
   readln (Limit);
      {Label the columns of the table.}
   write ('    ');
   for Column := 1 to Limit do
      write (Column:3);
   writeln;
      {Print the table.}
   for Row := 1 to Limit do begin
      write (Row:3);
      for Column := 1 to Row do
         write (Row*Column:3);
      writeln
   end   {the outer for loop}
end.   {TimesTable}                              {output follows}
```

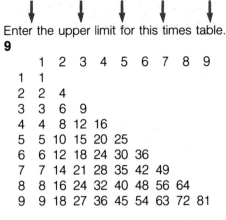

Enter the upper limit for this times table.
9

```
       1  2  3  4  5  6  7  8  9
 1     1
 2     2  4
 3     3  6  9
 4     4  8 12 16
 5     5 10 15 20 25
 6     6 12 18 24 30 36
 7     7 14 21 28 35 42 49
 8     8 16 24 32 40 48 56 64
 9     9 18 27 36 45 54 63 72 81
```

Our next problem is more complicated—we'll find Fibonacci numbers. This series begins 0, 1, then each subsequent number is the sum of the previous two. I'll state the problem like this:

*problem: finding
Fibonaccis*

Imagine that the values in the Fibonacci sequence are numbered. Write a program that lets a user request the *m*th through *n*th Fibonacci numbers.

The first step of a pseudocode refinement is just a problem restatement:

first refinement

skip the first m−1 Fibonacci numbers;
print the mth through nth Fibonacci numbers;

Converting the pseudocode into a more Pascal-like form requires a second refinement step. It's not hard, though, to see the **for** statements lurking even in the first refinement:

second refinement

for *the first m−1 Fibonacci numbers*
    get the next Fibonacci number;
for *the mth through nth Fibonacci numbers*
    get the next Fibonacci number;
    print it;

It looks like *get the next Fibonacci number* will require yet another refinement step. What is the current Fibonacci number? It's the sum of the previous two. This means that if we remember the *last* Fibonacci, and know the current one, we can always generate the next number. I'll propose the pseudocode algorithm shown below. It's a lot like our old friend procedure *Switch*; it gives two variables new values, but has to use their present values in the process.

*generating each
Fibonacci*

let a temporary variable get the sum of Last and Current;
Last gets the present value of Current;
Current gets the present value of Temporary;

Should this pseudocode for finding a Fibonacci be implemented as a procedure, or as a function? Well, if all we wanted was the next Fibonacci number, a function would be appropriate. After all, a function should be used when we want a subprogram to calculate and return a single value.

procedure or function?

In this case, though, we want to maintain the ability to figure out subsequent Fibonacci numbers as well. This means that we have to return two values—the last Fibonacci, as well as the newest. Since the subprogram will change two values, a procedure with two variable parameters is right for usus.

One more detail will require our attention before we can translate our pseudocode into Pascal. Will our algorithm find the first Fibonacci in the series? No. Since it has to start with 0, 1, the first Fibonacci our procedure computes will be the third. We'll have to remember this when we write the **for** loop that skips the first $m-1$ Fibonacci numbers.

Fibonacci program

```pascal
program PrintFibonaccis (input, output);
    {Prints the m th through n th Fibonacci numbers.}

var Counter, FirstFib, LastFib,  {will represent m and n }
    CurrentFibonacci, NextFibonacci: integer;

procedure GetNextFibonacci (var Last, Current: integer);
    {Generates the next Fibonacci number.}
var Temporary: integer;
begin
    Temporary := Last + Current;
    Last := Current;
    Current := Temporary
end;  {GetNextFibonacci }

begin
    writeln ('This program finds the mth through nth Fibonacci');
    writeln ('numbers. Enter m and n. Be sure m is at least 3.');
    readln (FirstFib, LastFib);
    writeln ('Fibonaccis ', FirstFib:1, ' through ', LastFib:1, ' are:');
    CurrentFibonacci := 0;  {Initialize the sequence.}
    NextFibonacci := 1;
    for Counter := 3 to FirstFib-1 do
        GetNextFibonacci (CurrentFibonacci, NextFibonacci);
    for Counter := FirstFib to LastFib do begin
        GetNextFibonacci (CurrentFibonacci, NextFibonacci);
        write (NextFibonacci)
    end;  {for}
    writeln
end.  {PrintFibonaccis }
```

↓   ↓   ↓   ↓   ↓   ↓

This program finds the mth through nth Fibonacci
numbers. Enter m and n. Be sure m is at least 3.
10   14
Fibonaccis 10 through 14 are:
          34   55   89   144   233

Fourier sums

Our final **for** loop problem takes advantage of the same pseudocoding techniques. About a century ago, the mathematician Francois Fourier invented a truly neat method of analyzing periodic wave forms. He showed that any regular wave could be represented as the sum of simultaneous sine waves, as long as they had appropriate amplitudes, frequencies, and phases. Of particular interest was the fact that these characteristics could be related in an extremely simple way to some starting frequency.

For example, the square wave (left, below), can be expressed as a coinciding collection of sine waves (center). When they are summed (right, below), they begin to assume the square wave's regular appearance. Were we able to sum an infinite number of terms, we'd recreate the square wave.

adding sine waves

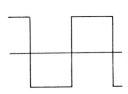

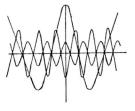

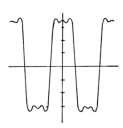

a perfect square wave   *three sine waves*   *the sine waves' sum*

By Fourier's definition, a square wave is the sum of the sequence of sine waves whose relative frequencies are the odd-numbered multiples of the starting frequency, and whose relative amplitudes are the reciprocals of the frequencies, which can be shown as:

$$f(t) = \frac{4}{\pi} \sum_{n=1,3,5\cdots} \frac{\sin(2n\pi t)}{n}$$

problem: generating
square waves

An ideal square wave with amplitude 1 oscillates between the values 1 and −1, depending on the exact instant we choose to look at the wave. Write a program that shows how we approach this ideal by summing the sequence for larger and larger numbers of terms.

This kind of problem cries out for **for** loops: to vary the time at which we sample the wave's current amplitude, to sum the terms of any particular sequence, and to run the series of experiments in which we add 'larger and larger' numbers of terms.

Pseudocode helps prevent the loops from becoming impossibly complicated. For example, the Fourier expansion of a square wave says that at time *t* the wave's amplitude is:

amplitude at t = $(4/\pi)$ $(\sin(2\pi t) + \sin(6\pi t)/3 + \sin(10\pi t)/5 + \ldots)$

A pseudocode that computes the wave's amplitude at one point is:

first refinement

initialize a sum variable;
for *the proper number of terms*
 add the current term's value to the running sum;

Since the problem requires sampling at a variety of times, the pseudocode can be expanded:

second refinement

for *a variety of time values*
 initialize a sum variable;
 for *the proper number of terms*
  add the current term's value to the running sum;
 print the wave's value at present time t;

This pseudocode solves the problem for some given number of terms. However, we are required to run the experiment multiple times. Another pseudocode loop outlines the program—now a triply-nested **for** loop:

third refinement

for *a series of experiments*
 for *a variety of time values*
  initialize a sum variable;
  for *the proper number of terms*
   add the current term's value to the running sum;
  print the wave's value at present time t;

The completed program is shown below. Although I won't dwell on it, I've gone to considerable trouble to make its output both sensible and readable. First, I've avoided taking readings at time points that are atypical—note the use of the constant *OFFSET* to miss time 0.0 (where the so-called *Gibbs phenomenom* would cause peculiar results). I also obtain a greater variety of readings by using an oddly-valued *INCREMENT* to avoid complementary values on either side of time 0.5. The number of terms added (in a total of ten experiments) ranges from 1 through 100 by the simple expedient of using the square of a counter variable, rather than the counter itself. Finally, although it's easy to scan each column and see that the readings approach 1, or −1, as the case may be, I've included a final column ('relative error') that sums the inaccuracies in each row.

```
program SquareWave (input, output);
  {Computes square wave signal using Fourier sum.}
const PI = 3.1415926535897932;
      OFFSET = 0.05;  {Try varying these figures.  Does the}
      INCREMENT = 0.1005;  {square wave always form so neatly?}
var Term, Frequency, NumberOfTerms, Trial, Interval: integer;
    CurrentTime, Signal, Error, Temp: real;
begin
    writeln ('                              Time of each sample',
                                            Relative error');
    write ('Terms ');  {The number of terms summed in each experiment.}
    for Interval := 0 to 9 do  {Print the heading.}
        write (Interval * INCREMENT + OFFSET:5:3, ' ');
    writeln;
    for Trial := 1 to 10 do begin  {We'll run 10 experiments.}
        Error := 0.0;  {This will sum the 'errors' in each trial.}
        NumberOfTerms := sqr (Trial);
        write (NumberOfTerms:4, ' ');
        for Interval := 0 to 9 do begin  {We'll sample at 10 time intervals.}
          Signal := 0;
          CurrentTime := (Interval * INCREMENT) + OFFSET;
          for Term := 1 to NumberOfTerms do begin
            Frequency := (2 * Term) - 1;  {Finally, the actual summing.}
            Signal := Signal +
                        sin (2 * Frequency * CurrentTime * PI) / Frequency
          end;  {the current Term's summing loop}
          Temp := (4/PI) * Signal;
          write (Temp:5:3, ' ');
          Error := Error + abs (1 - abs (Temp))  {Deviation from ideal value.}
        end;  {the Interval, or current sample, loop}
        writeln (Error:8:5)
    end  {the current Trial's loop}
end.  {SquareWave}
```

square wave
generating program

Time of each sample										Relative error
Terms 0.050	0.151	0.251	0.352	0.452	0.553	0.653	0.754	0.854	0.955	
1 0.393	1.032	1.273	1.023	0.378	−0.412	−1.044	−1.273	−1.011	−0.359	3.11333
4 1.139	0.965	0.922	0.956	1.122	−1.156	−0.977	−0.923	−0.945	−1.097	0.82659
9 0.922	1.013	1.035	1.022	0.940	−0.907	−1.001	−1.033	−1.032	−0.969	0.39760
16 1.055	0.991	0.981	1.000	1.065	−1.031	−0.981	−0.985	−1.012	−1.065	0.29060
25 1.041	1.016	1.012	1.014	1.033	−1.029	−1.009	−1.006	−1.005	−1.004	0.16836
36 1.024	0.994	0.992	1.004	1.028	−0.996	−0.989	−1.000	−1.011	−1.004	0.09904
49 0.983	1.000	1.005	1.008	1.007	−0.987	−0.992	−0.996	−1.003	−1.022	0.08567
64 1.013	1.001	0.997	0.994	0.989	−1.003	−1.005	−1.005	−1.002	−0.993	0.05665
81 0.990	1.004	1.002	0.995	0.998	−1.012	−0.999	−0.996	−1.003	−1.009	0.05153
100 0.990	0.997	0.999	1.001	1.009	−1.010	−1.003	−1.001	−0.999	−0.991	0.04891

Self-Check Questions

Q. What will happen if you give program *PrintFibonaccis* a value of *n* that's less than *m*? A value smaller than 3 for *m*?
A. Neither input will cause a program error, although we might not get useful output. If a **for** statement's initial value is greater than its final value, the loop simply won't take any action. As a result, an *n* smaller than *m* won't print any Fibonacci numbers. An *m* less than 3 will simply give us incorrect output, since the smallest Fibonacci the program can print (under any circumstances) is the third in the series.

Arrays: Vectors and Matrices (Optional) 3-2

IN CHAPTER 1 WE LEARNED HOW TO declare simple variables—variables that store single values of Pascal's standard simple types. In this optional section, we'll take an advance look at a *structured* variable type—the **array**—that some instructors like to introduce along with the **for** statement. This section can be skipped without harm, because its contents won't be referred to again until Chapter 7. It deals mainly with using arrays for vector and matrix operations.

The simple variables we have used so far have shared a characteristic so obvious that it's hardly borne mentioning: each variable has referred to a single value only. We can, however, declare variables that store more than one value. These are known as *structured*, rather than simple, variables. Array variables are the most commonly used form of structured variables. For example:

array demonstration program

```
program ArrayUser  (input, output);
      {Reads in 10 values, then prints them in reverse order.}
const LIMIT = 10;
type TenValues = array [1..LIMIT] of integer;
var i: integer;          {the for loop's counter variable.}
    Hold: TenValues;
begin
    writeln ('This program will read ten integers, then print');
    writeln ('them in reverse.  Please enter ten numbers.');
    for i := 1 to LIMIT do          {Get the values.}
        read (Hold [i]);
    for i := LIMIT downto 1 do          {Now print them in reverse order.}
        write (Hold [i]:3);
    writeln
end.  {ArrayUser}
```

↓   ↓   ↓   ↓   ↓   ↓

This program will read ten integers, then print them in reverse. Please enter ten numbers.
8 17 22 5 93 66 18 41 59 74
74 59 41 18 66 93 5 22 17 8

In program *ArrayUser*, above, *Hold* is an array variable that can hold ten different values. According to the shaded code, *Hold* temporarily saves input values before they're printed again. Notice in particular the line of code that begins with the word **type**. This line customizes the array variable (*Hold*, of type *TenValues*) by limiting it to storing ten values, all of type *integer*.

type *TenValues* = **array** [1..*LIMIT*] **of** *integer*;
var *Hold*: *TenValues*;

More formally, an array is said to have *elements*, which are its stored values. In Pascal, an array can have almost any number of elements, but they must all be of the same Pascal type. For instance, we might have an array that holds *integer* or *char* values. However, we can't create an array that sometimes holds one type, and sometimes another. *Hold*, above, is an array of *integers*.

array elements

The *size* of the array is the number of elements that it contains. An array's size is given in an interesting way that recalls the method used to state the number of times a **for** statement is intended to loop. Instead of explicitly stating the size of the array, we give the *bounds* of the *subscript* that we'll use to refer to individual array elements. In effect, each element is numbered with a subscript (much like a mathematical subscript). The bounds give the starting and ending values of this 'numbering,' which might be 1 through 10 (as above), but could just as easily run from 'A' through 'J.' *Hold*, above, is subscripted by the integers 1 through 10, and has a size of ten.

subscripting

Finally, we *reference*, or access, a particular array element by putting its individual subscript between square brackets. In *ArrayUser* the **for** loop's counter variable *i* served as the subscript. Thus, within the loop, *Hold*[*i*] referred first to *Hold*[1], then *Hold*[2], *Hold*[3], and so on. Any representation of a subscript value is all right, as long as it falls within the range established by the bounds of the array's type definition.

Now, when we've declared ordinary variables thus far, a **var** declaration has been sufficient. This is because the standard simple types *integer, real, char*, and *boolean* are predefined in every Pascal system. Arrays are different, though. Before an array's type identifier can be used in a variable declaration, it must be defined in a *type definition*. As a rule, we have to define the array type before we can declare an array variable. The *type definition part* of a program or subprogram comes just before the variable declaration part, and begins with the reserved word **type**.

type definition part

The definition of an array type contains three necessary pieces of information: the type's identifier, the array's subscripts, and the type of its elements. The example below defines an array type that is particularly useful for representing values in scientific or mathematical applications—a vector.

basic vector definition

const *LENGTH* = 10; {The number of elements in the vector.}

type *Vector* = **array** [1..*LENGTH*] **of** *integer*;

Note the use of the defined constant *LENGTH* in setting the subscript. It will be convenient later as the upper bound of a **for** loop.

Let's consider a series of examples that describe the most common vector operations. The easiest is vector magnitude:

problem: vector magnitude

The magnitude of a vector $|\mathbf{v}|$ is defined as the square root of the sum of the squares of its elements. Write a function that represents the magnitude of an argument of type *Vector*.

Imagine the problem as one of reading and summing the squares of a sequence of *integers* that were *not* stored in an array. In pseudocode:

a non-array refinement

> *initialize a Total variable to* 0;
> **for** *the proper number of times*
>   *read a number*;
>   *add its square to the running total*;
> *print the square root of Total*;

When we compute a vector's magnitude, though, the numbers will have already been input and stored in an array. Instead of reading numbers entered by a program user, we want to step through array elements.

the array refinement

> *initialize a Total variable to* 0;
> **for** *the proper number of elements*
>   *add the square of the current element's stored value to Total*;
> *print the square root of Total*;

Thus, the **for** loop's counter variable serves to subscript the current array element. The completed function is:

vector magnitude function

> **function** *Magnitude* (*Full1*: *Vector*): *real*;
>   {Compute the magnitude of *Full1*.}
>   **var** i: *integer*;
>   *Total*: *real*;
>   **begin**
>   *Total* := 0.0;
>   **for** i := 1 **to** *LENGTH* **do**
>   *Total* := *Total* + *sqr* (*Full1* [i]);
>   *Magnitude* := *sqrt* (*Total*)
>   **end**; {*Magnitude*}

problem: dot product

The dot product of two equal-length vectors $\mathbf{V} \cdot \mathbf{W}$ is the sum of the products of the corresponding elements of the vectors. Compute the dot product of two variables of type *Vector*.

Once more we are computing a scalar, rather than vector, value, so a function is suited to representing the results. As before, we can use a **for** loop to visit each element of the vectors. As function *DotProduct*, below, shows, there's no need to develop a separate counter variable for each vector array.

function *DotProduct* (*Full1, Full2* : *Vector*) : *integer* ;
    {Computes the dot product of *Full1* and *Full2*.}
    var *i, Sum* : *integer* ;
    begin

dot product function

Sum := 0 ;
for *i* := 1 **to** *LENGTH* **do**
   Sum := *Sum* + (*Full1* [i] ∗ *Full2* [i])

end ; {*DotProduct*}

problem: cross product

The cross product of two vectors **V** × **W** produces a new vector. It can't be represented by a function, because functions can only have scalar (or in Pascal terms, simple) values. Suppose we define this type:

type *CrossVector* = **array** [1..3] of *real* ;

Procedure *CrossProduct*, below, computes the cross product of its value parameter arguments *Vec1* and *Vec2*. The result is assigned to the variable parameter *Vec3*. Be sure you understand why I use both varieties of parameter—had I made *Vec3* a value parameter, the effect of the assignments would be lost on return to the main program. Note that, in a simple case like this, using a **for** loop would probably greatly confuse, rather than simplify, the operation.

vector cross product procedure

procedure *CrossProduct* (*Vec1, Vec2* : *CrossVector* ; **var** *Vec3* : *CrossVector*) ;
    {Computes the cross or vector product of *Vec1* and *Vec2*.}
    begin

Vec3 [1] := (*Vec1* [2] ∗ *Vec2* [3]) − (*Vec1* [3] ∗ *Vec2* [2]) ;
Vec3 [2] := (*Vec1* [3] ∗ *Vec2* [1]) − (*Vec1* [1] ∗ *Vec2* [3]) ;
Vec3 [3] := (*Vec1* [1] ∗ *Vec2* [2]) − (*Vec1* [2] ∗ *Vec2* [1])

end ; {*CrossProduct*}

You might check the operation of this procedure by seeing if the magnitude of *Vec3* equals the product of the magnitudes of *Vec1* and *Vec2*. Will the *Magnitude* function we wrote above be suitable for the test, or does it require a small modification?

array parameter types

> When arrays are passed to subprograms, each parameter must have the exact same type as its argument.

Even though arrays of type *CrossVector* have only three elements, and thus are smaller than the ten-element *Vector*-type arrays, *Vec1, Vec2*, and *Vec3* could not be arguments of *Magnitude*—they have the wrong type. This could be quite a pain in the neck if we were collecting these subprograms in a *library* or *package* of vector analysis routines.

routine libraries

One common solution is to make *LENGTH* (the constant used to define the array's length) as long as the longest potential vector will require. Additional constants can be passed to subprograms, as necessary, to explicitly provide the useful length of the current vectors. I'll use this approach for the next sequence of examples, which involve two-dimensional arrays or *matrices*. Consider this definition:

const *MAXROW* = 15; {The lengths of the matrix's rows and columns.}
      MAXCOLUMN = 25;

type *Matrix* = **array** [1..*MAXROW*, 1..*MAXCOLUMN*] **of** *integer*;

var *Table*: *Matrix*;

a matrix type
definition

Type *Matrix* defines a variable that is a *MAXROW* by *MAXCOLUMN* array of *integer* values—375 in all. Since the type is defined with two sets of bounds, accessing any particular element requires two subscripts, almost as though we were providing Cartesian coordinates. The first subscript specifies the row, and the second gives the column. For example:

Table [1, 1] := 1.0; {Initialize the upper left element.}
Table [1, *MAXCOLUMN*] := 1.0; {Initialize the upper right element.}
Table [*MAXROW*, 1] := 1.0; {Initialize the lower left element.}
Table [*MAXROW*, *MAXCOLUMN*] := 1.0; {Initialize the lower right element.}

Obviously the subscripts must be in the proper order. The element *Table* [*MAXCOLUMN*, *MAXROW*] doesn't exist; not because of the English meaning of the constant identifiers (as it happens, there is a *MAXROW*th column), but because of their values (there isn't a *MAXCOLUMN*th row).

problem: initializing a
matrix

As noted above, I defined type *Matrix* to be as large as my largest application. I won't necessarily use every element in every application. For example, suppose that I want to initialize *N* rows of *M* columns; in effect, the upper left corner of the array. Imagine yourself handing out papers in a classroom, seat by seat, one row at a time. In pseudocode we have:

refinement

    for *each of N rows*
        for *each of M columns*
            read the current element's value;

A completed procedure is supplied values for *N* and *M* via the parameters *Rows* and *Cols*:

matrix initialization
procedure

    procedure *ReadMatrix* (*Rows, Cols*: *integer*; **var** *Table*: *Matrix*);
        {Reads the values of a *Rows* by *Cols* array.}
    var *i, j*: *integer*; {The subscript/for loop counter variables.}
    begin
        for *i* := 1 **to** *Rows* **do**
            for *j* := 1 **to** *Cols* **do**
                read (*Table* [*i, j*])
    end; {*ReadMatrix*}

problem: transposing
a matrix
As with vectors, there are a number of basic matrix operations. A matrix is *transposed* by interchanging its rows and columns. Thus, the first row and first column are exchanged, the second row and second column, and so on. An alternate, and perhaps more practical, way of viewing transposition is to see that, for every row i and column j, elements *Table* $[i,j]$ and *Table* $[j,i]$ are exchanged.

Procedure *Transpose*, below, should be studied for the common errors it avoids. First, using a temporary variable to carry out the two-element switch is necessary to avoid inadvertantly giving both elements the same value. Second, careful choice of **for** loop bounds prevents the even more treacherous error of switching every element of the matrix not once, but twice—which would leave the array in its original condition.

matrix transpose
procedure

```
procedure Transpose  (Rows, Cols: integer; var Table: Matrix);
    {Transpose a Rows by Cols array.}
    var i, j: integer;  {The subscript/for loop counter variables.}
        Temp: real;  {Holding variable for the current element.}
    begin
        for i := 1 to Rows-1 do  {We can skip some elements because...}
            for j := i +1 to Cols do begin  {...we stay right of the diagonal.}
                Temp := Table [i, j];
                Table [i, j] := Table [j, i];
                Table [j, i] := Temp
            end
    end;  {Transpose}
```

problem: matrix
multiplication
A final example calculates the product of two matrices. For two matrices to be multiplied, the number of columns in the first matrix, and the number of rows in the second matrix, must be the same. Now, the product of an n by m matrix (call it A) and an m by p matrix (call it B) is an n by p matrix (that we'll call C). Each i,j element of the result matrix, C, is the dot product of the i th row of A—a vector—and the j th column of B—also a vector.

It would seem that the problem of matrix multiplication might be easily solved by slicing each matrix, then relying on a function we defined earlier:

refinement

```
for each of n rows
    for each of p rows
        C [i, j] gets DotProduct (A [i], B [j]);
```

However, Pascal's type checking stymies this approach. If you reread the definition of function *DotProduct* you'll see that its parameters are of type *Vector*. Although $A[i]$ and $B[j])$ are both vectors in the mathematical sense of the word, neither of them has *any* named Pascal type. Although it is possible to define the *Matrix* type in a manner that allows slicing, we will not consider this technique until the full discussion of arrays in Chapter 7.

Fortunately, the computation of the dot product isn't overly complicated, and so it's just carried out in place in procedure *Multiply*, below. Note that since the matrices need not have the same dimensions, this is an ideal demonstration of the value of defining type *Matrix* with a maximal number of rows and columns.

procedure *Multiply* (*RowsA, ColsA, RowsB, ColsB*: *integer*;

A, B: *Matrix*; var C: *Matrix*);

{Multiply matrices *A* and *B* into *C*. *RowsA* and *ColsB* must be identical.}

matrix multiplication procedure

var *i, j, k*: *integer*; {*k* helps compute the dot product.}

Sum: *real*; {Holding variable for the current element.}

begin

    for *i* := 1 **to** *RowsA* −1 **do**

        for *j* := 1 **to** *ColsB* **do begin**

            Sum := 0.0 ;

            for *k* := 1 **to** *ColsA* **do**

                Sum := *Sum* + (*A* [*i, k*] * *B* [*k, j*]);

            C [*i, j*] := *Sum*

        end

    end; {*Multiply*}

Chapter Notes 3-3

THE VARIETY OF STATEMENTS INTRODUCED in Chapter 3 will, inevitably, be accompanied by a host of syntactic and semantic bugs. Let's begin by reviewing some of the rules associated with **for** statements.

As I pointed out in 3–1, it is an error to try to change the value of a **for** loop's counter variable from within the loop. In effect, the counter variable is *read-only*; it may be inspected, but not modified. The **for** loop below attempts to print only odd numbers by 'secretly' incrementing *Counter* within the loop. The assignment is an error because the counter variable can only be changed before or after the **for** statement.

counter variable bugs

for *Counter* := *LowOdd* **to** *HighOdd* **do begin**

    writeln (*Counter*);

    Counter := *Counter* + 1   {Invalid assignment}

end; {**for**}

Another sort of attempt at modifying **for** loops is simply ineffective. Since the expressions that form the initial and final value values of the **for** loop's counter variable are evaluated before the loop is entered, changes to variables that might form these expressions have no effect on the loop. For example, this segment:

```
Lower := 1;
Upper := 3;
for Counter := Lower to Upper do begin
    Lower := 0;
    Upper := 1000;  {These have no effect on the counter variable.}
    writeln ('Hello.')
end;  {for}
```

prints 'Hello' only three times, instead of one thousand and one times.

Semicolons and compound statements bring their own problems. This example, for instance, is perfectly reasonable Pascal:

```
begin ; ;
    begin ; ;
        writeln ('Hi there.') ; ; begin end; begin end
    end ; ;
end ;
```

empty statement bugs

But this innocently misplaced semicolon causes a calamity:

```
for Counter := 1 to 5 do ;
    DoSomething;
```

The statement is supposed to call procedure *DoSomething* five times. Unfortunately, the semicolon right after the **do** forms an empty statement. This empty statement happens (for lack of a better word) five times, and the procedure is only called once.

compound statement
bugs

The most common compound statement bug occurs when an **end** is forgotten. As far as the compiler is concerned, the last **end** in the program is the closing bracket of a compound statement or subprogram written *within* the program. Thus, the missing **end** bug is easy for the compiler to detect, but is hard to pinpoint. Commenting the ends helps:

```
for Counter := 1 to Limit do begin
    . . .
end;  {Limit for}
```

Another technique is to indent, and make **end**s line up under the control statements they close (as I do in this text). This works best when procedures and functions are relatively short—no more than a page or so.

Don't forget that program format has absolutely no effect on semantics. The general style of indenting I've used should be adhered to because it simplifies the job of checking code. The two samples shown below are deliberately misleading. Their appearance says one thing, but their output tells a different story.

```
program ThreeCheers (input, output);
var Cheers: integer;
begin
    for Cheers := 1 to 3 do
        writeln ('Hip hip, hooray!');      {This looks like a compound}
    writeln ('Congratulations.')           {statement, but it isn't.}
end. {ThreeCheers}
```

compound statement
bugs

If run, program *ThreeCheers* would print 'Hip, hip, hooray!' three times, and 'Congratulations' only once. *Congratulations*, below, provides both plaudits three times.

```
program Congratulations (input, output);
var Cheers: integer;
begin
    for Cheers := 1 to 3 do begin
        writeln ('Hip hip, hooray!');       {This doesn't look like a}
        writeln ('Congratulations.')        {compound statement, but it is.}
    end
end. {Congratulations}
```

Moral: Code is hard enough to read even *with* indenting. Don't make it unnecessarily difficult.

Important to Remember

- A **for** loop's counter variable, initial value, and final value must all have the same Pascal type.
- The counter variable must be locally declared.
- It's an error to assign to the counter variable from within the loop.
- The expressions that give the counter variable's initial and final values are evaluated when the loop is first entered. Changing them won't change the number of times the loop iterates.
- The counter variable is undefined when the loop is exited.
- Beware of inadvertantly creating empty statements by misplacing semicolons.
- Similarly, beware of leaving statements out in the cold by not including them in compound statements.

Cross Reference

Although the **for** statement is simple in concept, it turns out to have been somewhat difficult to nail down formally. Problems developed from attempts to control assignments to the counter variable (formally known as the 'control-variable')—rules that were easy to draft on paper were too difficult to actually implement. It's interesting to read through five different versions of the same rule!

• The **for** statement is discussed in A26—A29, along with all the details regarding its counter variable and bounds. A27 points out some of the difficulties involved in formally defining the **for** statement rules, and introduces the notion of *threatening* statements.

• The empty statement is defined in A15—A16.

• The compound statement is defined in A16—A17.

• The array type is discussed extensively in A112—A121, but I would advise waiting until you've completed Chapter 7 before tackling it.

Exercises

3-1 Write a program that finds the sum of the first *n* integral squares:

$$1^2 + 2^2 + 3^2 + 4^2 + \ldots + n^2$$

Compare this to the identity for the sum: $\dfrac{n(n+1)(2n+1)}{6}$

Similarly, sum the first *n* integral cubes:

$$1^3 + 2^3 + 3^3 + 4^3 + \ldots + n^3$$

and compare your result to: $\dfrac{n^2(n+1)^2}{4}$

Finally, sum the first *n* odd numbers:

$$1 + 3 + 5 + \ldots + Odd_n$$

and compare that to n^2.

3-2 Let us journey again to New Mathico, where the skies are seldom cloudy, and most everything can be described by an equation.

New Mathico cowgirls, like ranchhands everywhere, have an inexhaustible supply of chores to do. One day Sagebrush Sue's boss said to her:

'Sue, do you know that $y=sin\ X$ fence where the dogies are getting out? I'd like you to replace the barbed wire from 0 to 2π. Pick up your supplies in town.'

'How am I supposed to know how much barbed wire to get?' grumbled Sue to her bunkmate, Mesquite Mary. 'Don't complain,' came Mary's reply. 'Last week I went to work on that goldurn $y=cosecant\ X$ fence, and just out to π, too, but it doesn't look like I'll ever get done!'

Write a program that solves Sue's problem. (Hint: break the curve into very small segments, and treat each as the hypotenuse of a triangle.) How much barbed wire should she get?

3-3 Imagine that you have a deck of 52 cards sitting just at the edge of a table. Starting from the top, slide cards out so they hang over the edge. How far can the outer edge of the top card extend?

Clearly, the top card can be slid out just about one-half card length without falling off. If the top card has been slid out, the card below it can be pushed out too—as much as one-third of its length. Then, the third card can, as it happens, be slid out one-fourth of its length. All the while the top card is riding out a bit further each time.

A little thought reveals that the theoretical reach of the tip of the first card, measured in units of one card length, is given by the series:

$$Tip\ distance = \frac{1}{2} + \frac{1}{3} + \frac{1}{4} + \cdots + \frac{1}{n}$$

Does this series converge or diverge? How far can the top card on a 52-card deck extend? How about a 1000-card deck? An n-card deck?

3-4   In 1730, James Stirling published his *Methodus Differentialis*, which included an approximation for $n!$, or n *factorial* $(n*(n-1)*(n-2)*\ldots*1)$. Two versions of his formula are:

$$n! \approx \sqrt{2\pi n}\ \left[\frac{n}{e}\right]^n \qquad\qquad n! \approx \sqrt{2\pi n}\ \left[\frac{n}{e}\right]^n \left[1 + \frac{1}{12n}\right]$$

Write a program that implements both versions of Stirling's formula, along with a rote method of calculating factorial. Print a table of exact values, along with the relative errors of each approximation. (Note: factorial grows extremely rapidly, so you may wish to rely on *real* rather than *integer* values.)

3-5   A number of series have been designed over the centuries with the prescient intention of providing examples for the **for** loop. Write programs that confirm these basic limits.

1. $e = 1 + (1/1) + (1/2!) + (1/3!) \ldots$

2. $e^x = 1 + x + (x^2/2!) + (x^3/3!) + \ldots$

3. $sin(x) = x - (x^3/3!) + (x^5/5!) - (x^7/7!) + \ldots$

4. $cos(x) = 1 - (x^2/2!) + (x^4/4!) - (x^6/6!) + \ldots$

5. $\pi/4 = 1 - (1/3) + (1/5) - (1/7) + \ldots$

For additional, far hairier examples, look up the method of computation of Euler and Bernoulli numbers in any math reference book.

3-6   Oddly enough, the sum of the first n natural logs of whole numbers:

$$ln(1) + ln(2) + \ldots + ln(n)$$

approximates the compound logarithm $n(ln(n))$, not to mention the quantity $ln(n!)$. Verify, by printing out the sum and the compound log for various n values, that this is reasonable.

3-7   In Chapter 2 I defined a power function for raising values to *real* powers. A simple **for** loop, though, can raise numbers to *integer* powers, since x^y is just $x*x*x\ldots$

1.   Write a program that uses a **for** loop to raise a *real* to an arbitrary *integer* power. Thus, the assignment $Product := Product * Number$ will be carried out $Power$ times.

2.   Write a more efficient version of the same program. This time, use the assignment $Product := Product * sqr(Number)$.

3.   Finally, write a yet faster version that relies on the assignment $Product := Product * Product$.

For parts 2 and 3, will additional **for** loops will be required? Beware of nesting **for** loops, though—nesting won't gain any advantage in speed.

3-8   In Chapter 2's exercises we used Pascal to approximate a function's derivative at a single point. The **for** loop expands our capabilities—now we can do integration! More accurately, if we have a continuous function $f(x)$, we can write a program that computes the area bounded by $x=A$ on the left, $x=B$ on the right, the X-axis below, and the curve $f(x)$ on top. As before, you need not know any calculus either to do or to understand the calculation.

Since $f(x)$ is a curved line, our approach is to divide the total area into many small rectangles, side-by-side, then add the areas of each rectangle. Suppose we divide the area into n small rectangles. Then:

a)   the length of the base of each rectangle $= (B-A)/n$

b)   the approximate position of the j-th rectangle $= A + (j*base)$

c)   the height of the j-th rectangle $= f(A+j*base)$

where f is the function we're integrating. Clearly, the larger n is—and the smaller each rectangle's base is—the better our approximation of the total area will be.

Write a procedure that integrates the continuous function of your choice, between limits A and B supplied by the user. Put the procedure in a loop that lets the user provide several different n values. Test the program on these celebrated integrals:

1)   The area under $f(x) = x^2$ from $x=0$ to $x=1$. The exact result is area $= 1/3$.

2)   The area under $f(x) = sin(x)$ from $x=0$ to $x=\pi$. The exact result is 2.

3)   The area under $f(x) = e^{-x}$ from $x=0$ to $x=\infty$. The exact result is 1.

Can you improve your program's accuracy, or reduce the size of n, by taking the area of trapezoids instead of rectangles? Does it involve much more work?

3-9   All thrifty students are familiar with the notion of compounding interest. Say that you invest a dollar amount of principal P at 5 per cent interest, compounded 12 times per year. After one year, you'll have:

$$amount = P \left[1 + \frac{0.05}{12} \right]^{12}$$

Now, suppose that we insist (since, after all, banks do have computers) that interest be compounded more and more frequently. In other words, suppose we invested at some rate of interest i:

$$amount = P \left[1 + \frac{i}{n} \right]^{n}$$

but made the value of n quite large—compounding weekly, daily, and hourly. What will your actual rate of return be after one year if the nominal annual interest rate is 5%? 24%? Why might you expect this return at the Napier National Bank? Would yet more frequent compounding be advantageous?

3-10   An elegant test for prime numbers, attributed to John Wilson (1741–1793), but actually devised by Leibnitz in 1682, says that P is a prime if and only if the number $(P-1)!$ **mod** P is equal to $P-1$. For example, let $P = 5$. Then, $4! = 4*3*2*1 = 24$, and 24 **mod** $5 = 4$, so 5 is prime.

Write a program to perform Wilson's test on an *integer*-valued P. Note that the danger of overflow from a large *integer* factorial (with value greater than *MAXINT*) can be sidestepped by reducing the partial factorial **mod** P at each step of the computation. This yields the same result as taking the entire factorial **mod** P. Unfortunately, this test is slow and is not practical for very large primes.

3-11   Two computer science students are giving a party. Being computer science students, they send out n invitations, and immediately begin to worry about how many guests will show up, and whether or not the guests will get along.

The first student says: 'Wouldn't it be horrible if only Jane and Sue showed up— they hate each other!' Fortunately, the second student was able to point out that *Combo* (n, p)—the number of different combinations of n things taken p at a time—is:

$$Combo(n,p) = \frac{n!}{p!(n-p)!}$$

Thus, the likelihood of Jane and Sue being the only attendees at a two-person party was only one in $Combo(n,2)$.

Nevertheless, the second student imagined a long series of impending social disasters. 'But so many of our friends are disagreeable! One doesn't even get along with herself! Somehow, I'm sure that no matter what size the group is, there's some combination of incompatible people! And if *everybody* shows up, *I'll* freak out! I wonder how likely it is that, for a p-person party (choosing from n potential partygoers), only the p people who can't stand each other will show up?'

'That's easy,' said the first student. 'The odds are only $\frac{n}{2^n}$.' Was she right? Write a program that finds out by summing calls of $Combo(n,1)$ through $Combo(n,n)$.

3-12   The *geometric mean* of a series of positive numbers $x_1, x_2, \cdots x_n$ is defined as the nth root of their product. Three professors of Romance Languages are discussing the implications of this. The Italian professor is heard to claim that if n is large the geometric mean of the first n positive integers $(1..n)$ should be $n/2$, since that is the average value. The Spanish specialist says that the higher integers should predominate (after all, they're bigger), and that the geometric mean should approach n itself as n goes to infinity. 'No, no,' says the French instructor, who thinks that lower integers should predominate (since they are more numerous) and the mean should approach $n^{1/2}$.

By performing a numerical investigation, guess the correct behavior of the geometric mean of $1,2,3,\ldots,n$ for n up to 30; and show how all three distinguished faculty are wrong.

3-13   The Fourier sum discussed in Chapter 3 is only one of many such sums. Write a program that helps you determine the shape of the wave described by:

$$S(t) = \sum_{n=1,3,5,\cdots} \frac{\cos(nt)}{n^2}$$

Although this wave is far from square, its derivative is a square wave similar to that of the earlier example.

3-14   The 'Catenary' is a fascinating curve whose name is derived from the Latin *catenus*, which means chain. The curve was described by Jacob Bernoulli in 1690 with the equation:

$$y = a\cosh(x/a)$$

a gives the height of the curve's low point, and *cosh* is the hyperbolic cosine function:

$$\cosh x = \frac{e^x + e^{-x}}{2}$$

Write a program that allows input of an a value, then computes and prints a range of y values. What does the Catenary curve describe? (A piece of graph paper, a length of thread, and two push-pins will all be helpful in working this problem.)

3-15   An important function in mathematics, called the ζ (*zeta*) function, was invented by the great Riemann in the 19th century, and is used to this day in deep analyses. The function is defined as an infinite sum of reciprocal powers:

$$\zeta(n) = \frac{1}{1^n} + \frac{1}{2^n} + \frac{1}{3^n} + \frac{1}{4^n} + \cdots$$

Two particular closed expressions for the infinite sum are:

$$\zeta(2) = \frac{\pi^2}{6} \qquad\qquad \zeta(4) = \frac{\pi^4}{90}$$

A computer science student who has just learned about the **for** statement resolves to find a closed expression for $\zeta(3)$ by summing several hundred terms of the sequence, then comparing the sum to π^3/b for every b from 7 through 89. Write such a program, then tell me what b value comes closest to equaling the zeta function.

(Unfortunately, to this day, nobody knows an expression for $\zeta(3)$ or, in fact, for any $\zeta(n)$ when n is odd. Indeed, some have attempted to prove that $\zeta(3)$ is not of the form π^a/b for any integers a, b.)

3-16   A biologist who is studying pollination wants to know, on average, how often a bee lands on a particular type of flower. Now, she could simply count the total number of bee landings, then divide by the number of hours of observation. However, the biologist is also interested in developing a theory about the bees' circadian, or day-to-day, rhythms. Thus, she also wants to track hourly changes in their activity.

From the biologist's point of view, a useful program will print:

1.   the number of observed landings per hour;

2.   the percentage change relative to the previous and subsequent hours;

3.   the current hour's landings in comparison to the hourly average thus far.

Assuming 24 hour's worth of input data, write a program to help out the biologist.

Hint: if the current average (of j terms, or number of hours of observation) is called *Average*, then a new term x will yield a new *Average* (of all $j+1$ terms) of:

$$Average_{new} = \frac{(Average_{old}*j + x)}{(j+1)}$$

3-17   Write a program that asks for a positive *integer*, then writes out its binary representation. You may assume the input number does not exceed 32767 (which is fifteen consecutive 1's). For example, if you enter 14, output should be 000000000001110; while 17 should yield 000000000010001. You might note that the far left-hand digit of the binary representation is given by: *input value* **div** c, where c is initialized to 2^{15}. If both the input value and c are progressively reduced by a power of two on each iteration, the value of each binary digit can be found.

3-18   A computer science student who has taken up tennis cannot help but notice that the head of her racquet (the special beginner's oversize model) has the shape of an ellipse. Being a cat lover, she begins to wonder how long a piece of catgut will be required to string the oversize racquet.

Suppose that the racquet's dimensions are as shown below:

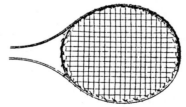 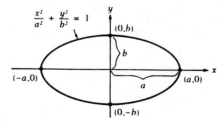

We can define an ellipse mathematically as:

$$\frac{x^2}{a^2} + \frac{y^2}{b^2} = 1, \quad \text{thus} \quad y = \pm\sqrt{b^2 - \frac{x^2}{a^2}}, \quad x = \pm\sqrt{a^2 - \frac{y^2}{b^2}}$$

Suppose that there are no vertical strings in the first or last inch along the x-axis, and no horizontal strings in the top or bottom inch along the y-axis. In all, there are 19 vertical strings, and 16 horizontal strings. If you allow an extra inch per string (for 'turnaround'), what is the total length of the gut used to string the racquet?

Additional exercises that use arrays may be found following Chapter 7, on page 201.

4

The **if** Statement

Mathematics, so they say, is the art of computation without calculation. Once you start to use *boolean* expressions, your programs can aspire to equally lofty heights. Chapters 4 and 5 introduce *boolean* values, along with the conditional statements Pascal uses to make decisions—to compute, rather than merely calculate. Conditional statements let the programmer announce, in an English-like manner, the terms that must be met if a program action is to be taken or repeated. This chapter describes the **if** statement, which is almost identical to its BASIC and FORTRAN counterparts.

Some instructors introduce this relatively simple statement earlier in the course. I hold back, not because the **if** statement is complicated, but because proper use of the *boolean* expressions used to give conditions can be—and I hate to encourage bad habits. Consider this chapter an extended introduction to the full range of *boolean* operators and expressions—I'll try to state some problems that are hard enough to make your patience worthwhile!

boolean Expressions 4-1

LIKE ALL EXPRESSIONS, *BOOLEAN* EXPRESSIONS represent values. The simplest examples are the constants of the ordinal type *boolean*:

> *false*   *true*

The *odd* (x) function also represents a *boolean* value—*false* if its *integer* argument x is even, and *true* if it's odd. We can state longer *boolean* expressions by using the *relational* operators.*

Math	Pascal	English
=	=	*equal to*
<	<	*less than*
≤	<=	*less than or equal to*
>	>	*greater than*
≥	>=	*greater than or equal to*
≠	<>	*not equal to*

relational operators

* One other relational operator, **in**, is discussed in Chapter 6.

Pascal uses the fact that equalities and inequalities always make an assertion (claim) that has to be either true or false. This makes them *boolean* -valued
expressions. For example, these are either *true* or *false*:

$$LowerLimit > 5 \qquad ApplicantsAge <= 65$$

They assert that a variable named *LowerLimit* has an *integer* or *real* value
greater than 5, and that the value of *ApplicantsAge* is less than or equal to 65.
Since character sets are ordered, these *boolean* expressions, which confirm or
deny the alphabetical ordering or equality of two *char* variables, are just as plausible as their more numerical counterparts:

$$Finished = 'Y' \qquad 'X' <> chr\ (63) \qquad SecondLetter >= FirstLetter$$

> The operands of the relational operators (the values that are being com-
> pared) must be of the same type.

As a minor exception, *reals* may be compared to each other, and to
integers. However, the vagaries of computer arithmetic can make comparisons
unreliable if they depend on precise *real* representations. (For example, the
real value 3.0*(10.0/3.0) might equal 9.99999999... instead of 10.0.)

It's important to recognize that the relational operators can't be used in a
manner that's very common in mathematics—to show multiple inequalities. The
mathematical phrase $5 < X < 10$ has no meaning in a Pascal program. We'll
soon see how to express such relations in Pascal; this particular example is
correctly written as $(5 < X)$ **and** $(X < 10)$.

Constants and variables can also be used to represent *boolean* values.
Note that these definitions are not *boolean* expressions, even though '=' is a
relational operator under other circumstances.

> **const** *THISPROGRAMWORKS = false*;
> *TESTING = true*;

Assignments to *boolean* variables are like all other assignment statements:
an expression is evaluated, and its result value is given to the variable. Given
these variables:

> **var** *Balance*: *real*;
> *Heir, Broke*: *boolean*;
> *Temperature*: *integer*;
> *ActivateDebuggingProcedures, NotDivisibleBy2*: *boolean*;

we can make the assignments shown below. The constants of type *boolean*
(*false* and *true*), user-defined *boolean* constants (like *TESTING*), and *boolean*
variables may all appear on the right-hand side of the assignment.

Heir := *true* ;
ActivateDebuggingProcedures := *TESTING* ;
Broke := *Balance* <=0 ;
NotDivisibleBy2 := *odd* (*Temperature*) ;
Broke := *Heir* ;

In practice, the constants *true* and *false* are seldom used in stating relations. Here's why: Suppose that *Willy* and *Nilly* are *boolean* variables. What will the value of *Willy* be after assignment 1, below, if *Nilly* is *true*? *false*? Is there anything wrong with assignment 2 syntactically? From the viewpoint of conciseness or clarity?

Willy := *Nilly* = *false* ;   {Assignment 1}
Willy := *Nilly* = *true* ;   {Assignment 2}

The first assignment statement gives *Willy* the opposite value of *Nilly*. If *Nilly* equals *true*, *Willy* becomes *false*, and if *Nilly* represents *false*, *Willy* takes on the value *true*. (Soon, we'll use the **not** operator to make the same assignment as: *Willy* := **not** *Nilly*.) The second assignment statement has correct Pascal syntax, but is redundant. It should have been written as:

Willy := *Nilly* ;

because the expression *Nilly*=*true* is identical to the value of *Nilly*.

The **if** Statement

Now that we've seen the basic *boolean* expressions, let's use a control statement that requires them. The **if** statement lets a program choose between taking two alternative actions. Its general form is:

if *boolean expression*
    then *action*
    else *alternative action*

The statement's syntax chart shows an option (omitting the **else**) that I won't get to for a few pages.

if statement

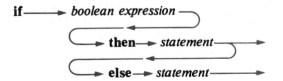

When an **if** statement is entered, its *boolean* expression is evaluated. If it's *true*, the **then** action is carried out, and the alternative **else** action is

how it works

skipped. If the *boolean* expression represents the value *false*, the **then** action is jumped over, and the **else** action is executed instead. In either case, only one of the two actions is taken. For example:

program *SquareRoot* (*input*, *output*) ;
    {Computes square roots. Error-checks input using **if**.}
var *RootExists* : *boolean* ;
    Argument, *Answer* : *real* ;

if demonstration
program

begin
    writeln ('Please enter a number.') ;
    readln (*Argument*) ;
    RootExists := *Argument* >= 0 ;
    write ('The square root of ', *Argument* :2:2) ;
    if *RootExists* **then begin**
        Answer := *sqrt* (*Argument*) ;
        writeln (' is', *Answer* :2:2)
    end {**then** part}
    else begin
        writeln (' is imaginary.') ;
        writeln ('Try using the complex number program in Chapter 8, instead.')
    end ; {**else** part}
    writeln ('Thanks for using this program.')
end. {*SquareRoot*}

↓   ↓   ↓   ↓   ↓

Please enter a number.
−24.6
The square root of −24.60 is imaginary.
Try using the complex number program in Chapter 8, instead.
Thanks for using this program.

In this application, the **if** statement is used to *error-check* its input. Without this check, program *SquareRoot* would crash if given negative input.

robustness

Using **if** statements to error-check input helps make programs *robust*—less sensitive to user errors or misuse. They end gracefully instead of crashing.

When an **if** statement's alternative actions are just single statements (like assignments or procedure calls) the **begin** and **end** of compound statements can be omitted, as in program *GuessFactor*, on the next page.

factor-guessing
program

```
program GuessFactor (input, output);
   {Determines if one integer factors another.}
var First, Second : integer;
begin
   writeln ('Enter two positive integers.');
   readln (First, Second);
   write (First, ' is');
   if (Second mod First) = 0
      then writeln (' a factor of', Second)
      else writeln (' not a factor of', Second)
end. {GuessFactor}
```

↓   ↓   ↓   ↓   ↓

```
Enter two positive integers.
187 1888887
          187 is a factor of     1888887
```

But in either case, **if** statements should be formatted in a way that highlights their alternative actions. However...

> *Syntax determines semantics.* Spacing and indentation are for the benefit of human program readers—not the compiler.

an **else** rule

A picayune syntax rule independent of format is extremely important: the reserved word **else** is *never* preceded by a semicolon. I'll return to this small, but crucial, detail in the Chapter Notes.

Incidentally, **if** statements aren't necessarily required where they might seem essential. Can you rewrite this **if** statement as an assignment?

```
if Response = 'Q'
   then Finished := true
   else Finished := false;
```

The rewrite requires an insight obvious enough to overlook—relations have *boolean* values:

```
Finished := Response = 'Q'; {the rewritten if statement}
```

Omitting the **else** Part

We'll frequently want a program to decide whether or not to execute a single action, rather than choose between two alternative actions. Pascal provides a convenient variation: the **else** portion of an **if** statement can be omitted entirely.

Unfortunately, an abbreviated **if** statement that nests an **if** complete with its **else** clause can appear ambiguous at first sight. An unindented example shows the problem. With which **if** statement is the **else** action, *statement2*, associated?

> **if** *B1*
> **then if** *B2*
> **then** *statement1*
> **else** *statement2*
> *statement3*

> In Pascal, an **else** is always the alternative of the *nearest* prior **then** action.

Thus, *statement2* is executed if *B1* is *true*, and *B2* is *false*. Procedure *TwoDwarves*, below, shows the effect of the nesting rule.

> **procedure** *TwoDwarves* (*Sleepy, Grumpy*: *boolean*);
> > **begin**
> > > **if** *Sleepy* **then**
> > > > **if** *Grumpy*
> > > > > **then** *writeln* (´I´´m grumpy and sleepy.´)
> > > > > **else** *writeln* (´I may be sleepy, but I´´m not grumpy.´);
> > > *writeln* (´I hope you´´re satisfied.´)
> > **end**;

This association can be changed by hiding the inner **then** within a compound statement.

> **procedure** *TwoMoreDwarves* (*Sneezy, Dopey*: *boolean*);
> > **begin**
> > > **if** *Sneezy* **then** **begin**
> > > > **if** *Dopey* **then** *writeln* (´I´´m sneezy and dopey.´)
> > > **end**
> > > **else** *writeln* (´I´´m not sneezy, but I might be dopey.´);
> > > *writeln* (´Bother me again and I´´ll bite your leg.´)
> > **end**;

Using **if** statements to make single choices and either/or decisions hardly requires subtlety—there is no need to devote much thought to the 'best' way of arranging the choice or decision. However, some algorithms may require a distinction between a series of independent decisions, and a sequence of mutually exclusive choices. For example, consider this deceptively simple problem:

Write a change-making program that accepts as input a price and amount of money tendered, then prints the minimum number and type of coins required for change.

Who hasn't made change? First, you count out the dollars, then the half-dollars, and so on through the pennies. Aside from the detail of correctly ordering the coins, the change-making algorithm of program *ChangeMaker* isn't going to be a great advance in either computer science or mathematics.

Stylish programming, though, poses the challenge of imitating the fine steps a human change-maker takes almost automatically. A real-life clerk would inform the customer if she were shortchanged, and so should our program. A person doesn't think about pluralizing words, but we'll have to teach the computer to add an 's' to plural coin names. A human wouldn't bother announcing the coins that she *wasn't* returning as change, and neither should *ChangeMaker*. We'll have to develop a pseudocode outline that avoids useless or misleading work:

> *find out the price and amount tendered*;
> *decide if there's enough money*;

first refinement

> **if** *there's no change*
>   **then** *say thanks*
>   **else**
>   **if** *there are dollars in the change, return them*;
>   **if** *there are half-dollars in the change, return them*;
> $\cdots$
>   **if** *there are pennies in the change, return them*;

ChangeMaker should also be as well-written as possible. Its output should be clear. It should be robust, and able to deal with the 'unexpected' situations I just mentioned. It should be self-documenting where possible, but comments should be added to clarify less-than-obvious features. It should take advantage of procedures to minimize the length and complexity of its code.

Finally, it should use statements—even the humble **if** statement—correctly. Read the code of program *ChangeMaker*, below. The **if** statements in the main program of *ChangeMaker* are basically independent of each other. Since the statements are in series, each statement's *boolean* expression is evaluated regardless of the previous statement's effect.

mutual exclusion

In contrast, the **if** statements in procedure *ComputeChange* are nested, or arranged in a manner that short-circuits the process. Since the tests are mutually exclusive, once a *boolean* condition is met the remaining tests can be skipped.

program *ChangeMaker (input, output)*;
{Computes minimum coinage for making change. Data file oriented.}

change-making program

const *DOLLAR* = 100;
    HALFDOLLAR = 50;
    QUARTER = 25;
    DIME = 10;
    NICKEL = 5;
    PENNY = 1;

```
var Price, Tendered : real ;   {Amounts are input as real dollar amounts ...}
    Change : integer ;          { ... but are dealt with as pennies in the program.}
    MoneyIsDue : boolean ;

procedure ComputeChange (Unit : integer ;  var Change : integer ) ;
    {Prints number of coins.  Reduces Change by that many Units .}
    var Pieces : integer ;
    begin
        Pieces := Change div Unit ;
        Change := Change mod (Pieces *Unit ) ;
        write (Pieces :1 ) ;
        if Unit = DOLLAR  {Pick the proper action.}
            then write (' dollar')
            else if Unit = HALFDOLLAR
                then write (' fifty-cent piece')
                else if Unit = QUARTER
                    then write (' quarter')
                    else if Unit = DIME
                        then write (' dime')
                        else if Unit = NICKEL
                            then write (' nickel')
                            else if Unit = PENNY
                                then write (' cent') ;
        if Pieces >1  {Take care of multiple coins.}
            then writeln ('s')
            else writeln
    end ;  {ComputeChange }

begin  {ChangeMaker }
    writeln ('What''s the price?  How much did you get?') ;
    readln (Price, Tendered ) ;
    MoneyIsDue := Price >Tendered ;
        {Express the potential change in pennies.}
    Change := abs (trunc (100*(Price−Tendered ))) ;
    if Price = Tendered
        then writeln ('Thanks!')
        else begin
        if MoneyIsDue
            then writeln ('Too little!  You''re short by')
            else writeln ('Your change is exactly') ;
        if Change >=100 then ComputeChange (DOLLAR,Change ) ;
        if Change >=50 then ComputeChange (HALFDOLLAR,Change ) ;
        if Change >=25 then ComputeChange (QUARTER,Change ) ;
        if Change >=10 then ComputeChange (DIME,Change ) ;
        if Change >=5 then ComputeChange (NICKEL,Change ) ;
        if Change >=1 then ComputeChange (PENNY,Change )
        end  {else}
end.  {ChangeMaker }
```

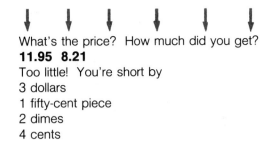

What's the price? How much did you get?
11.95 8.21
Too little! You're short by
3 dollars
1 fifty-cent piece
2 dimes
4 cents

Let's consider the short-circuit technique in the reverse application—arranged to end testing when a condition *fails*. This application is common when we want to minimize the testing of large amounts of data. The Quirky Quark Mystery is an entertaining statement of the problem.

problem: Quirky Quarks

Three physicists have succeeded in accomplishing the unlikely—they have isolated a collection of unbound quarks. The first physicist is investigating the up and down properties of these elementary particles, so she takes all the up and down quarks—exactly 1/3, plus 1, of the total collection. The second physicist (who works with charmed and strange quarks) also takes a share—it turns out that exactly 1/3, plus 1, of the remaining quarks have either charm or strangeness. Finally the third physicist, interested in truth and beauty (the remaining quark properties), finds that 1/3, plus 1, of the dwindling pile of quarks are suited for her work.

Unfortunately for current quantum theories, there are still a few quarks remaining. The physicists, now very excited at the prospect of thinking up funny names for new quark properties, divide the remainder into three equal portions—except for one remaining quark, which spontaneously dissociates.

The problem I pose is this: Each of the four three-way divisions left one extra odd quark. How many quarks could the physicists have isolated? Assume that there were no more than 500 to begin with.

We can solve the quirky quark mystery by mimicking the action of the physicists—testing each number between 1 and 500 to see if it, after the repeated divisions and subtractions, still leaves a remainder of 1. In pseudocode we have:

refinement

> **for** *every potential solution from 1 through 500*
>   **if** *the first physicist's division leaves a remainder of 1* **then**
>   **if** *the second physicist's division leaves a remainder of 1* **then**
>   **if** *the third physicist's division leaves a remainder of 1* **then**
>   **if** *the final division leaves a remainder of 1* **then**
>   *we've got a possible answer*

Picture what will happen when a program based on this pseudocode runs. Suppose our trial number passes the first division. If it fails the second division, the third and final trials are not made. Nesting the statements abbreviates the loop. Only numbers that pass each test will be considered in subsequent tests, and only numbers that pass every **if** test will be printed as solutions.

quirky quark program

```
program Quarks (output);
    {Demonstrates nested if statements.}

var TrialNumber, DividedNumber: integer;

begin
    for TrialNumber := 1 to 500 do
        if (TrialNumber mod 3) = 1 then begin   {First physicist.}
            DividedNumber := 2*(TrialNumber div 3);
            if (DividedNumber mod 3) = 1 then begin   {Second physicist.}
                DividedNumber := 2*(DividedNumber div 3);
                if (DividedNumber mod 3) = 1 then begin   {Third physicist.}
                    DividedNumber := 2*(DividedNumber div 3);
                    if (DividedNumber mod 3) = 1 then
                        writeln (TrialNumber:3, ' is a solution.')
                end
            end
        end
end.  {Quarks}
```

$$\downarrow \quad \downarrow \quad \downarrow \quad \downarrow \quad \downarrow$$

```
 79 is a solution.
160 is a solution.
241 is a solution.
322 is a solution.
403 is a solution.
484 is a solution.
```

Sophisticated *boolean* Tests

Three 'word-symbols'—**and**, **or**, and **not**—are the *boolean* operators. Just as the word-symbol **div** takes *integer* operands to form an *integer*-valued expression, the *boolean* operators use *boolean* operands to create *boolean*-valued expressions. *boolean* operators can combine tests that would otherwise require a series of **if** statements. The first, **and**, joins two conditions.

the **and** operator

> If we have two *boolean* values (call them *Condition* and *Decision*), the expression:
>
> > *Condition* **and** *Decision*
>
> is evaluated as *true* if both *Condition* and *Decision* are *true*. If either or both of them are *false*, the entire expression is *false*.

and can appear in any *boolean* expression. It can help set the condition of an **if** statement:

> **if** (*Value* >=5) **and** (*Value* <=10) **then**
>   *writeln* ('The value is between 5 and 10, inclusive.');

or appear on the right-hand side of an assignment:

> *Capital* := (*Letter* >='A') **and** (*Letter* <='Z');

For example, program *StrangeProperties*, below, finds every four-digit number that has these peculiar simultaneous features: each number is a perfect square, each number's first pair of digits is odd, each number's second pair of digits is odd, and the two pairs, when added, are also a perfect square. Notice how the *boolean* function *Perfect* is used to take a detailed bit of code (that decides if an *integer* is a perfect square) out of a *boolean* expression that's complicated enough as it is.

> **program** *StrangeProperties* (*input, output*);
>   {Looks for numbers with peculiar properties.}
>
> **var** *i, First, Last*: *integer;*

strange number program

>   **function** *Perfect* (*Candidate*: *integer*): *boolean*;
>   {*true* if *Candidate* is a perfect square.}
>   **begin**
>   *Perfect* := (*sqr* (*round* (*sqrt* (*Candidate*))) = *Candidate*)
>   **end**;
>
> **begin**
>   **for** *i* := 1001 **to** 9999 **do begin**
>   *First* := *i* **div** 100; {compute the pair values}
>   *Last* := *i* **mod** 100;
>   **if** *Perfect* (*i*) **and** (*odd* (*First*) **and** *odd* (*Last*)) **and** *Perfect* (*First* + *Last*)
>   **then** *writeln* (*i, First* + *Last*)
>   **end**
> **end**. {*StrangeProperties*}

↓	↓	↓	↓	↓

1521	36
7569	144
7921	100

The second operator, **or**, yields a result of *true* if one or the other (or both) of its operands has the value *true*. This English sentence: *If I do well on the midterm, or ace the final, then I'll pass*, is a perfect example of 'or'ing' two *boolean* values:

> **if** (*I do well on the midterm*) **or** (*I ace the final*) **then**
>   *I'll pass*

The **or** operator is less restrictive than **and** is. The expression:

   Condition **or** *Decision*

is *true* if either *Condition* or *Decision*, or both of them, are *true*. It's only *false* if *Condition* and *Decision* are both *false*.

For example, this program segment:

   if (*PurchasePrice* <= *BankBalance*) **or** *CreditIsGood* **then begin**
      writeln ('Who should I make the check out to?') ;   etc.

lets a check be written if there's enough money in the bank to cover the purchase (*PurchasePrice* <= *BankBalance*), or if the value of the *boolean* variable *CreditIsGood* is *true*. Naturally, it's all right for both conditions to be *true*, too.
   The third *boolean* operator, **not**, reverses a *boolean* condition.

The **not** operator's result is the opposite of its operand. Thus,

   not *Condition*

represents *true* if *Condition* is *false*, and *false* otherwise.

   if not *odd* (*InputValue*) **then**
      writeln (*InputValue*, 'couldn''t possibly be prime.') ;

As you've seen in the examples, I'll generally use parentheses within *boolean* expressions. As a basic rule, equalities and inequalities must be parenthesized when **not, and** or **or** appear in an expression. Parentheses *must* be used in these examples:.

   not (*Key* = 'T')
   (*Voltage* = 110) **and** (*Amperage* < 10)
   (*Limit* < 5) **or** (*Limit* >= 10)
   (*Temperature* > 80) **and** *Sunny*

Operator precedence is the reason. All of the *boolean* operators have higher precedence than the relational operators, so $A > B$ **or** $C > D$ is misinterpreted by the computer as $A >$ (B **or** C) $> D$, which is meaningless (unless A, B, C, and D are *boolean* expressions—in Pascal, *false* is 'less than' *true*).
   Parentheses may also be required to circumvent the regular precedence of the *boolean* operators.

The order of precedence in the *boolean* operator hierarchy is: **not, and, or**. **not** has the most precedence, while **or** has least.

Suppose we want an action to take place if *Condition* and *Decision* are both *false*. This statement:

> **if not** *Condition* **and not** *Decision* **then**   etc.

does the job. These expressions:

> **not** *Condition* **and** *Decision*
> **not** *Condition* **or** *Decision*

always use parentheses

might sound good in English, but their effect in Pascal is unexpected—only *Condition* is being **not**ed. In fact, I'll give the unusual advice that you forget about the relative *boolean* operator precedences entirely. When **not**, **and**, or **or** appear in *boolean* expressions, it's good programming practice to use parentheses as internal documentation, even if they don't affect the expressions' value. This expression uses the smallest legal number of parentheses—zero:

> **if not** *Hot* **and** *Humid* **or** *Raining* **then**   etc.

But this version is self-documenting and unambiguous:

> **if** ((**not** *Hot*) **and** *Humid*) **or** *Raining* **then**   etc.

distributive laws

Let me make a few closing comments about *boolean* expressions before our next programming example. If *boolean* operator precedence makes an expression long enough to be unwieldy or confusing, it can usually be rewritten by following the *distributive* laws, as shown below. Assume that p, q, and r are *boolean*-valued expressions or variables:

> $(p$ **or** $r)$ **and** $(q$ **or** $r) = (p$ **and** $q)$ **or** r
> $(p$ **and** $r)$ **or** $(q$ **and** $r) = (p$ **or** $q)$ **and** r

De Morgan's laws

A similar set of relations is known as *De Morgan's* laws:

> $(\textbf{not}\ p)$ **and** $(\textbf{not}\ q) = \textbf{not}\ (p$ **or** $q)$
> $(\textbf{not}\ p)$ **or** $(\textbf{not}\ q) = \textbf{not}\ (p$ **and** $q)$

boolean expressions may seem hard to evaluate at first, but looking at them one term at a time helps bring them into perspective. The effect of the *boolean* operators can be summarized in this *truth table*:

> **not** *true* is *false*
> **not** *false* is *true*

truth tables

true **and** *true* is *true*	*true* **or** *true* is *true*
true **and** *false* is *false*	*true* **or** *false* is *true*
false **and** *false* is *false*	*false* **or** *false* is *false*

Now, sometimes we'll know that an expression will be *false* even before each subexpression is evaluated, as in this program segment:

> **if** (Denominator <>0) **and** ((Numerator /Denominator)>Fraction) **then**
>   *writeln* ('We have a lucky winner!') ;

An output statement is executed if *Denominator* doesn't equal zero, and if the quotient of *Numerator* and *Denominator* exceeds *Fraction*. Well, if *Denominator* does equal zero, the entire expression will be *false*, because both operands of **and** must be *true* for the expression to be *true*. Unfortunately, the computer doesn't think ahead—it usually tries to evaluate the expression by carrying out the division.

<table>
<tr><td>full evaluation</td><td>In Pascal, we must assume that *boolean* expressions are always completely evaluated.</td></tr>
</table>

Since division by zero is an affront to all thinking women, men, and computers, a run-time error occurs and the program crashes. The segment should be rewritten to make the two evaluations explicitly consecutive, and not inadvertently simultaneous.

<table>
<tr><td>avoiding division by
zero</td><td>

```
if (Denominator <> 0) then
    if (Numerator/Denominator) > Fraction then
        writeln ('We have a lucky winner!');
```

</td></tr>
</table>

I'll close with a programming problem that exercises the **if** statement, as well as *boolean* expressions, in various forms.

<table>
<tr><td>problem: pool table
simulation</td><td>Write a program that simulates the travel of a ball on a pool table. Let the user enter the ball's starting position and direction, as well as the distance the ball should travel. Report back on the number of table rails hit, along with the number of times the ball crosses its original position. Error check as necessary.</td></tr>
</table>

Computer simulations, unlike real life events, must take place in small, discrete increments. The heart of our program will be a **for** loop that breaks the ball's total travel into a sequence of tiny steps. In each increment, while time stands frozen, the **if** statement goes to work. If we cross the original starting position a return should be counted, and if we've hit a rail the ball must carom off at the proper angle. A first refinement is:

<table>
<tr><td>first refinement</td><td>

```
get the starting position;
get the starting angle;
get the distance to travel;
for the proper number of times
    if a rail has been hit, change direction;
    if we're in the original starting area, count it;
print the results;
```

</td></tr>
</table>

<table>
<tr><td>making it realistic</td><td>Now, one of the major challenges of devising computer simulations is to remember the details that flesh out real life happenings, and to anticipate the minor problems that might give the simulation absurd results. An obvious step is to error-check the original ball placement—to make sure it's on the table:</td></tr>
</table>

if *starting X and Y components aren't within the table bounds*
  reposition X and/or Y;

A more subtle flaw might result from treating the pool ball as a hard-to-hit point, rather than as a relatively large sphere, when we check crossings of the original starting area. Fortunately, we have recourse to the geometric definition of a circle: $r^2 = x^2 + y^2$. A crossing has occurred if our current position is less than *sqr (the ball's radius)* of the starting position.

state variables

One major problem remains. Our method of simulation is to repeatedly move a tiny bit, take our bearings, then increase counts or change directions as necessary. But suppose it takes more than one incremental move to completely pass through the ball's original starting position? As presently outlined, the program will count a 'hit' again and again until we leave the area (in fact, it starts counting crossings as soon as the program starts). We can solve this problem with a *boolean state* variable, *InTheArea*, that begins as *true*, then is 'switched' on and off:

a *boolean* switch

InTheArea := true;
 . . .
if *we find ourselves in the starting area*
  then if *we're* **not** *InTheArea to begin with*
    then *increase the count*;
      InTheArea := true
  else *InTheArea := false*;

We only count an additional crossing if we weren't in the starting area to begin with. Thus, the crossing is only counted when we first enter the area—not while we pass through it. Notice that this sequence involves nested **if** statements, so special attention will have to be paid to the proper association of the closing **else**.

The completed program is shown below. I've used official sizes for the table and ball. My starting position is the normal break spot, and you may wish to trace the path laid by the particular angle I've chosen. As you will see, there are still simplifications incorporated into the program (for instance, the ball is treated as a point when it hits a rail).

Although I treat speed as constant, the program is written in a manner that will let you model friction more accurately after you learn about conditional loops in Chapter 5, or implement the program on a graphics terminal if your Pascal system allows. You may also want to improve the program so that it checks—and stops for—the ball rolling into one of the corner or side pockets.

pool table simulation
program

```
program PoolTable (input, output);
{Tracks a cue ball on a pool table.  Counts returns to the start, and rails hit.}
const PI = 3.1415926535897932;
      DT = 0.1;                    {used to compute the incremental moves.}
      SPEED = 1;
      RADIUS = 1.125;              {an official 2.25″ ball.}
      LEFTRAIL = 0.0;              {an official 4′ by 8′ table.}
      TOPRAIL = 96.0;             {I assume that the origin is at the}
      RIGHTRAIL = 48.0;           {lower-left corner of the table, and that a}
      BOTTOMRAIL = 0.0;           {0-degree shot goes straight up the Y axis.}
var XPos, YPos, XStart, YStart, XVel, YVel, StartingAngle, Distance: real;
    Strikes, Banks, Increments: integer;
    InTheArea: boolean;
procedure Reposition (var XStart, YStart: real);
  {Corrects starting positions if necessary.}
  begin
    if XStart < LEFTRAIL
      then XStart := LEFTRAIL
      else if XStart > RIGHTRAIL
        then XStart := RIGHTRAIL;
    if YStart < BOTTOMRAIL
      then YStart := BOTTOMRAIL
      else if YStart > TOPRAIL
        then YStart := TOPRAIL
  end; {Reposition}
procedure Rebound (var VelocityComponent: real; var Banks: integer);
  {Reverses one of the ball's velocity components and counts banking.}
  begin
    VelocityComponent := −VelocityComponent;
    Banks := Banks + 1
  end; {Rebound }
function ItCrosses (XPos, YPos, XStart, YStart: real): boolean;
  {true if the ball has grazed against its starting position.}
  begin
    ItCrosses := (sqr (XPos−XStart)+sqr (YPos−YStart))<=sqr (RADIUS)
  end; {ItCrosses }
```

```
begin  {PoolTable }
    writeln ('What are your starting coordinates?');
    readln (XStart, YStart);
    if ((XStart < BOTTOMRAIL) or (XStart > RIGHTRAIL)) or
            ((YStart < BOTTOMRAIL) or (YStart > TOPRAIL)) then
        Reposition (XStart, YStart);
    XPos := XStart;
    YPos := YStart;
    writeln ('Enter starting angle in degrees, and travel distance in feet.');
    readln (StartingAngle, Distance);
    StartingAngle := PI * StartingAngle / 180; {Convert to radians}
    XVel := SPEED * sin (StartingAngle);
    YVel := SPEED * cos (StartingAngle);
    Strikes := 0;
    Banks := 0;
    InTheArea := true;  {Since we're starting there!}
    for Increments := 1 to round ((Distance * 12) / (SPEED * DT)) do begin
        if (XPos < LEFTRAIL) or (XPos > RIGHTRAIL) then
            Rebound (XVel, Banks);
        if (YPos > TOPRAIL) or (YPos < BOTTOMRAIL) then
            Rebound (YVel, Banks);
        XPos := XPos + (XVel * DT);
        YPos := YPos + (YVel * DT);
        if ItCrosses (XPos, YPos, XStart, YStart)
            then begin  {Why must this be a compound statement?}
                if not InTheArea then begin
                    InTheArea := true;
                    Strikes := Strikes + 1
                end
            end {ItCrosses then part}
            else InTheArea := false
    end;
    writeln (XStart:4:3, ', ', YStart:4:3, ' was hit ',
            Strikes:1, ' times, with ', Banks:1, ' banks.')
end.  {PoolTable }
```

↓   ↓   ↓   ↓   ↓

What are your starting coordinates?
25.0   25.0
Enter starting angle in degrees, and travel distance in feet.
9.45   100.0
25.000, 25.000 was hit 2 times, with 16 banks.

:········:········:········:········:········:········:········:········:········:····:

Q. Write each of these relations or conditions as a *boolean* expression.

a) *ConditionMet* is *true*
b) 50≤*Time*≤100
c) *Letter* is 'V' or *Goals* is less than 4
d) *A* 27, *B* > 6, *C* ≠ 13, and *Char* isn't 'T'
e) *A* 27, *B* > 6, *C* ≠ 13, and *Char* isn't 'T', or,
    on the other hand, 50≤*Time*≤100
f) *State* is neither *High* nor *Low*.

A. Note the necessary use of parentheses around relational expressions.

a) *ConditionMet*
b) (*Time* >=50) **and** (*Time* <=100)
c) (*Letter* ='V') **or** (*Goals* <4)
d) (*A* <27) **and** (*B* >6) **and** (*C* <>13) **and** (*Char* <>'T')
e) ((*A* <27) **and** (*B* >6) **and** (*C* <>13) **and** (*Char* <>'T'))
    or ((*Time* >=50) **and** (*Time* <=100))
f) (*State* <>*High*) **and** (*State* <>*Low*)

:········:········:········:········:········:········:········:········:········:····:

Chapter Notes
4-2

**compound statement
bugs**

MOST AUTOMOBILE ACCIDENTS HAPPEN close to home, because that's where people do most of their driving. By the same token, the **if** statement probably tends to generate more than its fair share of bugs, because it appears in just about every program.

A common bug, at first, is to forget to bracket multiple actions with the **begin** and **end** of a compound statement. Errors like this are usually due to carelessness. The action of a statement may have originally been just one statement or procedure call. If the program is modified, and additional actions are added, it's easy to overlook the need for a **begin** and **end**. Defensive programming helps obviate the problem—many programmers write *every* action as a compound statement. Reading an unnecessary **begin**, **end** pair doesn't cost the computer anything, and it may save lots of trouble later on.

Another small bug that's extremely hard to find is caused by a misplaced semicolon. For example, in the segment below, *GetMoreData* is called whether *ReadingData* is *true* or *false*. Can you see why?

> **if** *ReadingData* **then** ;
>   *GetMoreData* ;
> *NextStatement* ;   etc.

empty statement bugs

Reformatting the segment would make the bug stand out—the compiler thinks that the **if** statement controls an empty statement. This is a *semantic* error. The segment is syntactically correct, and will compile, but its effect is unintended.

Preceding an **else** with a semicolon, in contrast, is strictly a syntax error. The semicolon's effect is to dissociate an **if** statement's **else** and **then** parts. The compiler will complain about the sudden appearance of the reserved word **else**.

boolean bugs

A common *boolean* error occurs if you forget that **and** and **or** don't literally mean 'and' and 'or.' This assignment is meaningless in Pascal:

RightAnswer := *Response* = ('A' **or** 'B');

because **or** is a *boolean* operator, and is only used to compare *boolean* values. The statement is rewritten correctly as:

RightAnswer := (*Response* = 'A') **or** (*Response* = 'B');

Errors also occur in translation from English to Pascal. For example, the English phrase 'neither *A* nor *B*' translates into Pascal as (**not** *A* **and not** *B*), rather than (**not** *A* **or not** *B*)

keep *booleans* simple

Using **not** in complex *boolean* expressions can also be tricky (but always, as Mr. Spock would say, perfectly logical). It's particularly important to keep track of parentheses. These two expressions are not identical in meaning:

not (*Hot* **and** *Tired*)   (**not** *Hot*) **and** (**not** *Tired*)

although they appear to be rather similar. This expression:

not (*Hot*) **or not** (*Tired*)

states the same as the left-hand expression above. You can appreciate that there are often a variety of ways to express identical conditions, some considerably more obscure than others. Any expression that's difficult to decipher should be rewritten by using parentheses, the Distributive laws, or De Morgan's laws.

A final common bug is to mistakenly assume that two **if** statements with opposite conditions are always the same as an **if** statement with an **else** alternative. Can you name the circumstances that would make this program segment:

if *BitCount* <0 **then** *Twiddle* (*BitCount*) ;
if *BitCount* >=0 **then** *Twaddle* (*BitCount*) ;

order matters

differ in effect from this one:

if *BitCount* <0
    then *Twiddle* (*BitCount*)
    else *Twaddle* (*BitCount*) ;

Suppose that *Twiddle* modifies the value of its argument *BitCount*, and makes it equal to or greater than zero. In the first program segment, both *Twiddle* and *Twaddle* might be called. In the second segment, only one procedure is—never both—no matter what *Twiddle* does to *BitCount*.

**Important
to
Remember**

- The constants of type *boolean* are *false, true*, in that order. *boolean* expressions are always fully evaluated in Standard Pascal.

- Equalities and inequalities must be parenthesized when **not**, **and**, and **or** appear in an expression (because of the low precedence of the relational operators). The precedence of operators found in *boolean* expressions is:

not	*most precedence*
and	
or	
<, >, <=, >=, =, <>, **in**	*least precedence*

- An **else** is always the alternative action of the nearest prior **then** action. Put the entire nearest prior **if** statement (with **then** part) in a **begin** ... **end** to suppress this association.

- When **if** statements follow each other, each one's *boolean* expression is evaluated—the statements are independent. If the **if** statements are nested instead, the evaluation may be short circuited—statements nested more deeply will be skipped once a test is failed.

- Robustness—for now, the ability to withstand errors that can be anticipated—is a desirable program quality. **if** statements should be used, when possible, to do error-checking on the 'reasonableness' of program values.

Cross Reference

- The **if** statement is discussed in A17—A20; you'll find a familiar example on the effect of potentially ambiguous nesting.

- Type *boolean* is defined in A33—A34, along with the *boolean* operators. The construction of *boolean* implication, equivalence, and exclusive **or**ing is described on A34.

- The standard *boolean* functions *odd, eoln*, and *eof* are first discussed on A38. (We'll encounter *eoln* and *eof* in section 5-2.)

- A44—A46 contain additional comments about the relational and *boolean* operators.

- Evaluation of expressions, with particular reference to the full evaluation of *boolean* expressions, is described in A39—A40.

- Finally, the output representation of *boolean* values is discussed on A55.

Exercises

4-1   Write a *boolean* function that returns an affirmative result if its *integer* argument is a perfect square. Hint: a single assignment (that includes a few calls of standard functions) will do the job. Test your function on a program that lets you know which numbers between 543,210 and 555,555 are perfect squares. (You may have to choose smaller bounds—say, 23,456 and 24,567—on some computers.)

4-2   A traveler starts out at the origin and walks according to a chain of direction characters, e.g. **NNEWSEWNEE** ...   Each character corresponds to one of four compass directions, and implies a one-unit step.

Let a program user supply the total number of steps to be taken, along with the sequence of characters. What is the traveler's final *x, y* position? Verify that the 'parity' of the final point equals the parity of the number of steps, in other words, that *x+y* is even if an even number of steps have been taken, and vice versa. For a more difficult and interesting problem, let the user enter relative directions **F** (forward), **B** (backward), **L** (left), and **R** (right).

4-3   One limitation of Pascal's **or** operator is that it's unable to differentiate between a single *true* operand and two *true* operands. But suppose that we want an action to be carried out if A is *true*, or B is *true*, but absolutely not if both of them are *true*. This condition is called an *exclusive or*; some languages, but not Pascal, include a special operator, **XOR**, to state it. Write a *boolean* function that takes two *boolean* arguments, and can take the place of **XOR**.

4-4   How many integers between 1 and 10000 inclusive are divisible by 3 but not by 7? What are some of them? Write a program that prints every hundredth integer that meets the requirements, along with a count of the total.

4-5   Write a program that determines how many numbers between 1 and 10000, inclusive, are divisible by 3 and 5, but not by 7. A little thought will reveal that there should be roughly (10000–(10000/7))/(3∗5) such numbers.

4-6   Many, many interesting programming problems can be devised by considering the relations between a number and its digits or divisors. For instance, have you ever paused to reflect that 145 equals 1!+4!+5! exactly? I thought not. (What other number besides 1, 2, and 145 has this property?)

A *perfect* number equals the sum of its *integer* divisors excluding itself; thus, 6 is perfect because it equals 1+2+3. If the sum of the divisors is less than the number, the number is said to be *deficient*, while if its divisors form a sum greater than the number, it is *abundant*.

1.   Which three numbers below 1000 are perfect?

2.   What odd number below 1000 is abundant? Which seven odd numbers below 5,000?

3.   What are the relative proportions of deficient, abundant, and perfect numbers?

4-7   Write a program that reads a list of *real* values, and determines if the list is in ascending order, descending order, or if all the values are the same.

4-8   It's easy to write a swap procedure that exchanges the values of two variables. With the **if** statement at our disposal, we can use a two-variable swap to order any sequence of numbers or letters.

Suppose that you write a procedure that orders two *real* values. Write a program that reads three *real* numbers, then stores and prints them in ascending order (with just one *writeln*), using only **if** statements and calls of your ordering procedure.

How many **if** statements, at most, are required to sort 5 numbers in this manner?

4-9   An exercise similar to the problem above lets us sort an arbitrarily long list of numbers. We can compensate for not declaring an arbitrarily long series of variables by running the program repeatedly.

Using a swap procedure, an **if** statement, and a **for** loop, write programs that sort an input sequence in two ways. Assume the program's input starts:

10   4   1   11   13   6   2   20   9   7

In a *fixed pair* sort, input is read two numbers at a time. The numbers are sorted, and both are printed. A fixed pair sort of the numbers above would yield:

4   10   1   11   6   13   2   20   7   9

In an *overlapping pair* sort, after getting the first number, the program reads just one number at a time. Again, number pairs are sorted, but only the smaller is printed. The larger is saved for comparison with the next input value. An overlapping pair sort of the original input would give:

4   1   10   11   6   2   13   9   7   20

Suppose that you wanted to use these programs to sort a list of numbers. It is clear that you might have to enter the input list repeatedly. But will the fixed pair sort ever order the list? Can it be modified to do the job? How about the overlapping pair sort? What kind of input sequence would take the longest time to sort in each case? How many runs would be required in this 'worst case?'

4-10   Write a program that reads two words of three characters each—six input characters in all—then prints the words in alphabetical order. Be sure to test your program on relatively difficult cases, like cad and cat. Note that there are several ways to do this; one clever method relies on treating the characters as digits in two base-26 numbers.

4-11   A paddlewheel captain has been whiling away long, lonely trips up the mighty Mississippi by taking a correspondence course in mathematics. When she encounters the mathematical description of the *prolate cycloid*:

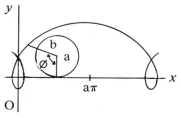

she recognizes that if the main body of the waterwheel can be assumed to ride along the water's surface, the tip of a paddle follows the path described by:

$$x = a\,\phi - b\,\sin\,\phi$$
$$y = a - b\,\cos\,\phi$$

She decides to determine the amount of time a paddle spends in the water by modeling it as a prolate cycloid.

Write a program to help her out. Break one full revolution of the wheel into 1,000 parts. For what fraction of a revolution is the tip of a paddle submerged?

4-12   Return with me once more to the high country of New Mathico, where most everything can be described with an equation. A cowgirl, once again, has spent a dusty day rounding up stray dogies. With foresight she has brought along a canteen, so that when quitting time arrives she is ready to head back to the bunkhouse.

Her horse, though, would prefer to stop at the river on the way back to the corral. As it happens, the closest river is the $f(x) = -32$ Creek. The cowgirl is presently at x, y coordinates (5,7), while the bunkhouse is located at (103, 17).

Assume that the horse always travels in a straight line. Write a program that simulates a trip via every plausible *integer*-valued point along the river (i.e. between $x = 5$ and 103), and finds the point that minimizes total distance traveled. What are the angles of travel toward the river, and back to the bunkhouse, at this point?

4-13   Historically, computational exercises that have posed problems of finding the best location for smelters, bridges, grain depots, and so on have required the student to find a point that minimizes the distance to a number of outlying towns.

Suppose, though, that we are trying to find a location for a nuclear waste dump. 'Not near me!' comes the cry from each city. We face the problem of *maximizing* a distance.

Write a program that reads x, y coordinates for five cities. For convenience, it's all right to assume that their locations form a rough pentagon in a 100×100 plane. By finding the largest and smallest x and y points, define the smallest rectangle that confines all the cities. Within this rectangle, what is the least objectionable location for the dump? In other words, what point has the greatest average distance to the five cities? Will everybody be happy with this kind of site planning? (You may assume that computations to the nearest x, y intersection are close enough.)

4-14   'All roads lead to Rome,' goes the ancient saying, but are roads through a single hub the shortest way of connecting a number of outlying cities?

The illustration shows two alternative means of connecting four points. Each approach reduces the distance between two particular pair of cities, but neither method minimizes the total length of the city-to-city connections.

Let your four outlying cities appear on the corners of any convenient rectangle. Write a program that finds two centrally-located 'crossroad' or intersection points (not necessarily at $90°$) that minimize total road length. Two cities will connect to each crossroad, and the crossroads will connect to each other. Are these points unique, or is there more than one such pair? What is similar about the angles of intersection with each of the crossroads? (Hint: split the total area in two, then use a doubly-nested **for** loop to investigate all possible pairs of points. Don't forget to check points along the border as well.)

4-15   Here is a problem that is easy to state and sounds easy to solve, but is really quite tricky, and requires careful use of the **if** statement. Write a program that accepts as input the x, y coordinates of a point in the plane, then prints, in degrees, the angle from the x-axis (with vertex at the origin) that corresponds to this point. Difficulties that must be overcome include:

1.   The function arctan is typically defined only for angles between $-\pi/2$ and $+\pi/2$, and you need to handle the full range 0 to 2π.

2.   When x approaches 0, the argument y/x approaches $\pm\infty$, and will cause a program crash.

4-16   Write a program that asks for input of n *integer* values, and one y value, then counts the number of contiguous (next to each other) numbers that differ by no more than y. For instance, with $n = 10$ and $y = 2$, this input:

8   5   2   4   2   10   8   5   3   4

should yield as output the answer 5.

4-17   Let's improve our skills at integration by using a counting method. Consider the function:

$$f(x) = \frac{1}{1+x^2}$$

Suppose that we want to approximate the area under the function's curve between points A and B, where $A = 0$ and $B = 1$. Let's look at, say, N points that are equally distributed throughout a unit square with corners at $(0,0)$, $(1,0)$, $(1,1)$, and $(0,1)$. The area under the curve will be approximately:

(*number of points under the curve*) / N

Write a program that looks at a 100-by-100 grid of points in the unit square and by test-ing each point, verifies the theoretical area $\pi/4$ for the given function.

4-18   Anybody who has ever listened to her little sister's fourth grade orchestra is keenly aware of the musical phenomenon of *beat* notes.

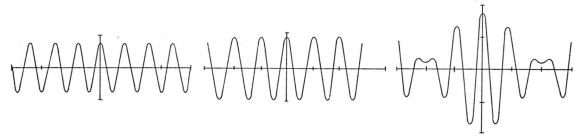

one sine wave   another sine wave   their sum

When two sine waves are close to each other in frequency, their high and low points will tend to join (when they are in phase), or cancel (when they are out of phase). The result is a throbbing beat note that is rather jarring to the ear, and appears each time the waves sum to a local maximum value. The beat note's speed is determined by the relative frequencies of the waves; when they are close, the beat appears infrequently, and vice versa.

The formula of a sine wave is:

$$f\,(time)\;=\;amplitude\;\left(\sin\left[\frac{\omega}{2\pi}time+\phi\right]\right)$$

where the *amplitude* is the sound's intensity, ω is the note's frequency in Hertz, and ϕ is the phase angle; in effect, the starting point of the sound wave. For our purposes, ampli-tude and phase angle can be held constant and ignored.

Write a program that simulates two simultaneous sine waves, for *time* increments of 1/5,000 second, over a period of three seconds. As noted, a beat appears when the two sine waves sum to a local maximum, which means that a single 'largest' value should appear several times over the course of your simulation. Now, rerun the simulation, but time the appearance of the maximum. What is the time between beat notes? Assume starting frequencies of 400 Hz and 402 Hz.

4-19   Although a home computer may be a waste of money in the hands of the unini-tiated, the canny programmer can use her computer to reap unexpected savings. For example, although birthday candles invariably come 24 to the box, one is only 24 once. On other years, the extra candles are usually thrown to the waxworms and lost forever.

Now, if one were to save the extras instead, a single box of candles would last through the sixth birthday, and still leave three extras. Suppose that you light one candle on your first birthday cake, two on your second, and so on. Write a program that tells you, in advance, on what birthdays you will have to buy a new box, or boxes, of candles. Let the user enter her own life expectancy. (For a fancier version, let the user enter an arbitrary starting birthday as well.) How many candles will be left for the next genera-tion?

4-20   Optics is a beautiful topic that often links physical concepts that seem entirely disparate. For example, consider refraction, the behavior of light when it crosses the boundary between two different media. Suppose that a light beam passes from air to glass. In x, y coordinates, let $y > 0$ define the region of air, while $y \leq 0$ defines the region of glass

Assume the light ray starts at the point $(-1,1)$, and winds up at the point $(1,-1)$. Since refraction will cause the light ray to bend at the air-glass interface, we can assume that the ray will cross the x axis—and move from air to glass—at some point other than $x = 0$.

Now, according to the law of refraction discovered by Willebrord Snell (1591-1626), the angle of refraction at the boundary of two materials is inversely proportional to their optical densities:

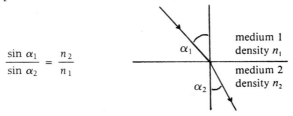

$$\frac{\sin \alpha_1}{\sin \alpha_2} = \frac{n_2}{n_1}$$

For the sake of a more interesting problem, we'll use heavy air ($n_1 = 1.5$) and leaded glass ($n_2 = 2.25$).

However, the mathematician Pierre de Fermat stated an alternative point of view. *Fermat's Principle* requires that light always travels between two points in the least amount of time. Assume that:

$$\textit{the speed of light in a medium} = \frac{\textit{speed of light in vacuum}}{\textit{optical density}}$$

Write a program that assumes a ray of light is straight from $(-1,1)$ to some interface point $(x,0)$, then straight again from $(x,0)$ to $(1,-1)$. Seek out the x for which transit time is a minimum, then compare your findings with the predictions of Snell's Law.

4-21   The pool table simulation we discussed in this chapter relied on the fact that a billiard ball's travel is entirely predictable. Let's consider a different simulation that is interesting because it relies on random elements. You'll find the code of a function that can be used to generate random numbers supplied on page 116.

Write a program that simulates a traffic intersection, and determines the timing of red and green lights that interferes least with the flow of traffic. Assume that:

1.   traveling along Pascal Avenue, from 5 to 22 cars arrive at the intersection every 15 seconds;

2.   traveling along Fortran Way, some 10 to 30 cars reach the intersection each 15 seconds;

3.   the Pascal Avenue cars each take 0.9 seconds to cross the intersection;

4.   on Fortran Way, which has been optimized, cars take 0.4 seconds to cross the intersection;

5.   a car making a left turn prevents 3 cars behind it from crossing the intersection, but fortunately, only 1 car in 20 turns left.

6.   the entire red/green cycle takes 90 seconds. Ignore the yellow light.

Assume that the signals can be switched in 5 second intervals; i.e. red 5 seconds and green 85, red 10 seconds and green 80, etc. Run the simulation three times for each setting (using different seeds), for twelve minutes each. What setting inflicts the least total waiting time on the motorists?

5

The **while** and **repeat** Statements

The loop is the bridle used to harness computer speed. A single statement lays down a condition that might not be satisfied for thousands, or millions, of repeated program steps. We've already seen the **for** loop at work, but its applications are limited in a fundamental way—we have to know, in advance, exactly how many iterations are required. Although we might use a **for** to see if the numbers between some lower and upper bounds have a property, it's not easily used to find the first *n* numbers with the same property—we don't know how many numbers will have to be inspected overall.

The conditional loops **repeat** and **while** come to the rescue. Each one uses a *boolean* condition (like *NumbersFound = n*) as a test for continued looping. Section 5-1 considers a variety of loop applications that tend to involve numbers. I'll focus on three standout algorithms devised over a span of 2,000 years—Newton's method for computing square roots, Euclid's algorithm for finding greatest common divisors, and Pollard's 'rho' method of factoring. Section 5-2, in turn, deals with the subcategory of loop programs that involve text processing. It introduces the *boolean* functions *eoln* and *eof*, along with the *file window*.

repeat and **while** 5-1

LIKE MOST CONTROL STATEMENTS, the **repeat** uses a *boolean* expression to control the execution of an action.

> The **repeat** statement's action takes place, then its *exit condition* (a *boolean* expression) is evaluated. The loop's action is repeated until the exit condition is met.

looping and terminating

If the expression that represents the exit condition is *false*, the exit condition is *not* met, and the loop's action is iterated (repeated). If the expression is *true*, the exit condition *is* met. The loop is terminated and the program moves on. In outline form, the **repeat** statement is:

> **repeat**
>   *action*
> **until** *boolean expression*;   {the exit condition}

The statement's syntax chart is:

repeat statement

Note that compound statements are unnecessary with **repeat** loops, since the words **repeat** and **until** delimit the loop's first and last statements. Furthermore, the enclosed sequence of statements is an unbreakable unit. If the **repeat** loop's exit condition suddenly becomes *true* while we're in the midst of executing the loop's action, we're not snatched out of the loop. The exit condition is evaluated only after the entire loop action has been completely carried out.

exit only at the loop end

Conditional loops are ideal when the number of iterations required can't be known in advance. Let's consider a classic application:

The equation $y^2 - y = x$ isn't terribly exciting, and were we English majors, we'd probably invoke the quadratic formula and be done with it. However, I can restate it as a *pervasive root* in the following form:

problem: pervasive roots

$$y = \sqrt{x + \sqrt{x + \sqrt{x + \sqrt{x + \cdots}}}}$$

Compute the value of the pervasive square root of a given number to the limit of your computer's accuracy. Determine how many steps were required to reach that limit.

Clearly, we could continue computing the value *sqrt* (x) indefinitely. However, computer arithmetic ultimately provides a limiting factor—in effect, the root of the last increment becomes too small to influence the computer's *real* representation of the sum. In program *Pervasive*, below, the pervasive root is effectively calculated from the inside out. The **repeat** loop's exit condition is met when an additional calculation makes no difference in our result.

```
program Pervasive (input, output);
   {Computes a pervasive square root to the limit of real accuracy.}
var Number, Current, Last: real;
   Count: integer;
```

pervasive roots
program

```
begin
   writeln ('Enter a number.');
   readln (Number);
   Count := 1;
   Current := sqrt (Number);
   repeat
      Last := Current;
      Current := sqrt (Number + Last);
      Count := Count + 1
   until Current = Last;
   writeln ('The root took ', Count:1, ' steps to converge on ', Current)
end.   {Pervasive}
```

```
Enter a number.
20.0
The root took 18 steps to converge on  5.00000000000000e+00
```

while statement

The **while** statement is also a conditional loop, but its condition is checked prior to entering the loop, instead of on exit. The loop's action is not executed at all if the entry condition is not met.

> In the first part of the **while** statement, a condition is stated as a *boolean* expression. It determines whether or not the loop will be entered (because it's an *entry condition*), and when the loop will terminate (because it implies an exit condition—the opposite of the entry condition—as well).

entry, exit conditions

In a sense, the entry condition serves as an **if** statement—a *boolean* expression must be *true* for the statement to be entered. But since the **while** is a loop statement, the expression is evaluated again after the action is completed. If it's still *true*, the action gets repeated. If the entry condition has become *false*, the action is skipped entirely, and the program moves on.

```
while boolean expression do   {the entry condition}
   action;
```

In chart form, the **while** statement is:

while statement

Procedure *LongDivision*, below, uses a **while** statement to simulate the effect of the **div** and **mod** operators. It employs a simple brute-force algorithm—repeated subtraction. However, since the dividend may be smaller than the divisor, it's possible that no subtractions will be required. Thus, a **while** loop (whose action may be skipped) is superior to a **repeat** loop (whose action always occurs at least once) in this application.

long division procedure

```
procedure LongDivision (Dividend, Divisor : integer ;
                              var Wholes, Remainder : integer ) ;
    {Simulates div and mod using only addition.}
    begin
        Wholes := 0 ;
        Remainder := Dividend ;
        while (Remainder–Divisor )>=0 do begin
            Remainder := Remainder–Divisor ;
            Wholes := Wholes +1
        end  {while}
    end ;  {LongDivision }
```

Whatever the action of a **repeat** or **while** loop is, a fundamental rule must be respected—the loop must end eventually. Therefore, the entry or exit condition has to contain a variable whose value is changed by the loop's action. Consider procedure *CheckInput*, below, which increases a program's robustness by letting the user correct improperly entered data. We don't know when (or even if) an appropriate value will be entered. We *do* know, though, that the exit condition can conceivably be met, and that the crucial variable, *Value*, is reinitialized on each iteration.

the condition must change

improving robustness

> Interactive programs should include error-checking and mistake-correcting loops whenever possible. Nothing is more infuriating than a computer program that won't let a user change input she knows is wrong.

input error check program

```
procedure CheckInput (var Value : integer ;  Upper, Lower : integer ) ;
    {Gets and returns a Value between Lower and Upper.}
    begin
        repeat
            writeln ('Enter an integer from ', Lower :1, ' to ', Upper :1) ;
            readln (Value) ;
            if Value <Lower then
                writeln (Value :1, ' was too small.  Try again.')
                else if Value >Upper then
                    writeln (Value :1, ' was too large.  Try again.')
        until (Value>=Lower) and (Value<=Upper)
    end ;  {CheckInput }
```

The continued update of the exit condition shouldn't be taken for granted, particularly if you haven't done much programming. For example, this segment's exit condition will never be met, because the *boolean* expression (*Counter* = 100) is always *false—Counter* isn't changed in the loop.

infinite loops

```
Counter := 0;
repeat
    writeln (Counter)
until Counter =100;
```

Care must also be taken in stating *boolean* expressions. What's wrong with these exit conditions? Why are they probably in error?

```
     repeat
         SomeActions
a.   until true
b.   until false
c.   until abs (Counter) < 0
d.   until (Value>10) and (Value<=5)
e.   until (Value<=10) or (Value>=11)
```

All these exit conditions are either always *true* (*a, e*), or invariably *false* (*b, c, d*). There is no way any of them can be modified. Thus, the '*true*' loops will only take place once, and the '*false*' loops will repeat forever.

Since both **repeat** and **while** loops would work equally well in many applications, the particular choice of loops is often an essay question, best resolved by the programmer's judgement. Sometimes the ordinary English meanings of the reserved words best describe her intentions. 'Repeat' implies

repeat vs. **while**

that an action will take place at least once, whereas 'while' lets an element of doubt creep in—maybe the action won't take place at all—that accurately reflects the **while** statement's usage.

On the other hand, a **while** statement may be employed even if the loop's action is certain to occur. This is especially true when a **repeat** statement involves negated conditions. Placing the loop's condition in the first line makes the condition easier to state, and the program easier to read. This statement:

```
     repeat
         action
     until not A or not B;
```

is error-prone and hard to follow. A **while** loop makes the same statement more clearly:

```
     while A and B do
         action;
```

In the long run, common sense and clarity should be the programmer's guide.

Focus On
Programming:
Loop Basics

*sentinel, counter,
accumulator*

Although loops turn up in an extraordinary variety of applications, their structure follows characteristic patterns. Three basic concepts are frequently applied.

> A *sentinel* is a character or value used to mark the end of relevant input data. A *counter* variable keeps track of the number of values we've read. An *accumulator* keeps a running account (such as the sum) of values we've seen so far.

Any or all of these can be used to determine the appropriate moment for loop entry or exit. We'll look at a few examples, and see how problems can arise.

A simple first problem—computing an average—illustrates the interdependence of the three ideas. Program *DataAverage*, below, finds the average value of a sequence of positive numbers. Since it couldn't possibly be part of the program's data, a negative number is used to mark the end of input. The program's main loop counts and accumulates values until this sentinel is read.

*average until sentinel
program*

```pascal
program DataAverage (input, output);
    {Averages a series of numbers. -1 marks the end of data.}

const SENTINEL = -1;

var Value, Total, Average: real;
    Counter: integer;

begin
    Total := 0;
    Counter := 0;          {Initialization}
    Average := 0;
    read (Value);
    while Value<>SENTINEL do begin          {Process the data.}
        Total := Total +Value;
        Counter := Counter +1;
        read (Value)
    end; {while}
    if Counter =0
        then writeln ('No data entered.')
        else begin
            Average := Total /Counter;
            writeln ('The average of ', Counter:1, ' values is', Average)
        end {else}
end. {DataAverage}
```

↓   ↓   ↓   ↓   ↓

23.9   85.68   227E02   0.00863   75
93.44   71   14.7E-03   66   -1
The average of 9 values is 2.56833814777778E+03

Averaging numbers is a deceptively simple problem. What could have gone wrong with *DataAverage*? The sentinel might have been added to the running total. The first value could have been skipped inadvertently. An empty list might have gone undetected, leading to a divide-by-zero error. Although I won't digress now, the Chapter Notes present a sequence of buggy program segments that attempt to find averages, but err slightly in spotting the sentinel, or in maintaining the values of counters and accumulators.

graceful degradation
Note, incidentally, that if the data list is empty *DataAverage* prints an explicit message. This attention to detail could be quite important in a larger program, where an incorrect or unsupplied value could lead to wrong results, or even an inexplicable program crash. Explicit built-in error messages help a program to *degrade gracefully*, rather than failing catastrophically or invisibly.

Even when counters, sentinels, and accumulators are correct and applied without error, the discussion of loop basics must extend beyond the loop itself. If the *boolean* expression that states a loop's exit condition involves multiple conditions, we can find ourselves leaving a loop without knowing precisely why. Although the loop itself is correct, an error can develop further down the line. The problem crops up in a situation like this:

problem: find the letter 't'
Assume that you have as input to a program a sequence of 35 characters. Find the position of the first 't'—if there is one.

Pseudocode is brief and to the point:

refinement

repeat
    read a letter;
    count it
until we read a 't' or read 35 characters;
print the position of the 't';

The shaded exit condition is easy to implement with a *boolean* expression:

until (*Letter* = 't') **or** (*PositionCounter* = 35);

But what comes next? Although we have left the loop correctly, we're not sure why. We can't just claim that the 't' was found at position *PositionCounter*, because there might not have been a 't' at all. However, checking the value of *PositionCounter* and printing 'No t found' if it equals 35 might be wrong too—the 't' could be in the last position.

> Don't jump to a conclusion about why you left a multi-condition loop. Find out why the loop terminated before you act.

We complete the code above by checking the value of *Letter*. My sample input comes from the most famous 't' party of all.*

---

* The answer, of course, is that Edgar Allan Poe wrote on both.

t-finding program

```
program FindT (input, output);
   {Looks for a 't' in input.}
const LIMIT = 35;
var PositionCounter: integer;
    Letter: char;
begin
   PositionCounter := 0;
   repeat
       read (Letter);
       PositionCounter := PositionCounter + 1
   until (Letter = 't') or (PositionCounter = LIMIT);
   if (Letter = 't')
       then writeln ('t is in position ', PositionCounter:1)
       else writeln ('No t found.')
end.  {FindT}
```

↓   ↓   ↓   ↓   ↓

Why is a raven like a writing desk?
t is in position 26

A final basic example illustrates an alternative means of recording the reason for loop exit—using an auxiliary *boolean* 'found it!' variable. I've chosen a problem that lets the program's user rely on a clever searching algorithm (you'll get to implement it as a program in the Exercises).

problem: number
guessing

Write a program that picks a number in the range 1 through 100, and challenges a program user to guess it. Allow seven tries, and tell the user if she's too high or low.

A **for** loop would never do for this sort of problem—seven is the maximum number of tries, not the required number. Instead, we want to repeat a sequence of actions—allow a guess, then check it—until the game is either won or is over. In a first pseudocode refinement, we have:

first refinement

```
pick a random number;
repeat
    let the user guess;
    respond to the guess
until the guess is right or all the guesses are used up;
report on the game's outcome;
```

Note that when we leave the loop, we won't be sure of why we left. The user might have guessed correctly, or run out of guesses, or both. I'll check the value of an auxiliary *boolean* variable *Solved* before offering congratulations or condolences.

What kind of interaction will the program user require? Well, her guess will either be too high, too low, or exactly right. Since these possibilities are mutually exclusive, nested **if** statements can choose an appropriate response.

second refinement

```
pick a random number;
repeat
    let the user guess;
    if guess is high then give high error message
        else if guess is low then give low error message
            else if guess is right then Solved is true
until Solved or all the guesses are used up;
if Solved offer congratulations;
```

binary search

Why should seven guesses be sufficient to track down a number between 1 and 100? The key lies in the confirmation—high or low—of each try. In effect, each guess cuts the remaining pool of numbers in two—one half contains the number we want, and the other holds values that are too high or low and can be ignored. We may get lucky and hit the number earlier, but at worst only seven guesses will be required to narrow the pool down to a single value. This is a *binary search* strategy; we'll return to it when we discuss the array type.

random number generation

What about providing a random number? One algorithm, introduced by D. Lehmer in 1949 and called the *linear congruential* method, is to pick a starting number (called the *seed*), and subject it to this sequence of operations:

$$Seed := ((MULTIPLIER * Seed) + INCREMENT) \textbf{ mod } MODULUS;$$

(Values for the constants are given below.) The assignment gives *Seed* a value that is greater than or equal to 0, and is less than *MODULUS*. Dividing by *MODULUS* (using *real* division) reduces *Seed* to the range $0 \le Seed < 1$.

pseudo-random sequences

Repeating the assignment and extra division produces a *pseudo-random* sequence of numbers. The numbers are randomly distributed, but it's possible to predict what the series will be, and the sequence eventually repeats. In implementing a *Random* function, note that the *Seed* must be allowed to change on each call. It's passed as a **var** parameter (quite unusual for functions) so that a subsequent call of *Random* can differ.

```
function Random (var Seed : integer) : real;
    {Generates a pseudo-random number such that 0<=Random <1.}
    const MODULUS   = 65536;      {These are 'magic' numbers}
          MULTIPLIER = 25173;      {that produce a pseudo-random}
          INCREMENT  = 13849;      {sequence of numbers.}
    begin
        Seed := ((MULTIPLIER * Seed) + INCREMENT) mod MODULUS;
            {Pick an integer from 0 through MODULUS-1}
        Random := Seed / MODULUS
            {Adjust it to fall between (or including) 0, and 1.}
    end; {Random}
```

Now, any starting *Seed* value generates a particular sequence of numbers. Were *Seed* initialized to the same number for every run of a program containing *Random*, it would always return the same pseudo-random series. This is a lifesaver during debugging, because you know what numbers to expect. However, a game program isn't much fun if its random elements are the same for each play. My version of *NumberGuess* uses the admittedly lame method of asking the user to provide the starting seed. In real life, the problem is usually solved by calling a nonstandard function that returns a constantly changing *integer* value (like the time of day) to initialize a global *Seed* variable. Although the call makes a program nonstandard, it's really the best solution.

initializing the seed

```pascal
program NumberGuess (input, output);
    {Challenges a user to guess a number within 7 tries.}
const GUESSLIMIT = 7;
var Number, Guess, Count, Seed: integer;
    Solved: boolean;
function Random (var Seed: integer): real;
    {Generates a pseudo-random number such that 0<=Random <1.}
    const MODULUS = 65536;
          MULTIPLIER = 25173;
          INCREMENT = 13849;
    begin
        Seed := ((MULTIPLIER *Seed)+INCREMENT) mod MODULUS;
        Random := Seed /MODULUS
    end;  {Random}
begin
    writeln ('Play a guessing game.  Enter a number between 1 and 100.');
    readln (Seed);
    Number := 1 + trunc (100*(Random (Seed)));
    writeln ('Thanks.  Now, I''m thinking of a number from 1 through 100.');
    write ('You have ', GUESSLIMIT:1, ' tries to guess it.   ');
    Count := 0;
    Solved := false;
    repeat
        Count := Count +1;
        writeln ('Take a guess.');
        read (Guess);
        if Guess <Number
            then write ('Uh oh ... that number was too small.   ')
            else if Guess >Number
                then write ('Sorry, but that number was too big.    ')
                else Solved := true
    until Solved or (Count = GUESSLIMIT);
    if not Solved
        then writeln ('You lose!  The right number was ', Number:1)
        else writeln ('Congratulations!   ', Guess:1, ' was exactly right.')
end.  {NumberGuess}
```

number guess program

{output follows}

↓   ↓   ↓   ↓   ↓

Play a guessing game. Enter a number between 1 and 100.
91
Thanks. Now, I'm thinking of a number from 1 through 100.
You have 7 tries to guess it. Take a guess.
50
Sorry, but that number was too big. Take a guess.
25
Sorry, but that number was too big. Take a guess.
13
Uh oh ... that number was too small. Take a guess.
19
Sorry, but that number was too big. Take a guess.
16
Uh oh ... that number was too small. Take a guess.
18
Sorry, but that number was too big. Take a guess.
17
Congratulations! 17 was exactly right.

Three Outstanding Algorithms

I'll wrap up our discussion of iteration with three outstanding algorithms, developed over 2,000 years, that rely on loops in various forms. The first is attributed to Euclid (about 330–270 B.C.E.). Although best known for his contribution to geometry (and for his crack that even kings have to open the books and study: 'There is no royal road to geometry'), Euclid also formalized a method for finding two numbers' greatest common divisor, which has come to be known as *Euclid's algorithm* .

Euclid's algorithm

Euclid's algorithm is based on the insight that if one number is greater than another, their greatest common divisor is the same as the greatest common divisor of the smaller, and the larger minus the smaller. If we repeat this process, eventually the larger number equals the greatest common divisor, and the smaller number is zero. Note that this common divisor may be trivial, i.e. equal to 1.

Another way of picturing this is to call the greatest common divisor x. Then one number is Ax, and the other is Bx. By repeatedly subtracting the smaller from the larger (try setting A to 7 and B to 9), we eventually reduce one term to x itself, and the greatest common divisor is found.

Now, though you may have never thought of it in this way, the **mod** operator carries out precisely this kind of subtraction. We can pseudocode Euclid's algorithm as:

finding the GCD

```
repeat
    take one number mod the other;
    save the result, and the smaller number
until the smaller number equals 0;
{The larger number is now the original numbers' greatest common divisor.}
```

The pseudocode is easy to implement as function *GreatestCommonDivisor*, below. We'll be returning to use it later as part of this chapter's final example (finding prime factors).

GCD function

```
function GreatestCommonDivisor (Greater, Other: integer): integer;
    {Implements Euclid's algorithm to compute the GCD of its arguments.}
    var Remainder: integer;
    begin
        repeat
            Remainder := Greater mod Other;
            Greater := Other;
            Other := Remainder
        until Remainder = 0;
        GreatestCommonDivisor := Greater
    end; {GreatestCommonDivisor}
```

Before going on, let's implement a second historic algorithm—Sir Isaac Newton's method for finding square roots. His algorithm is:

Newton's method

Take a guess at the number's square root. The assignment:

$$Guess := ((Number / Guess) + Guess) / 2;$$

gives a number that is closer to being correct, no matter how wild the original guess was (as long as it wasn't 0).

Newton's method poses an interesting looping problem because of the unexpected exit condition its code requires. In purely mathematical terms, we can make the value of *Guess* more and more accurate by repeating the assignment indefinitely. However, we'll eventually surpass the precision of the computer's arithmetic, and continued guessing won't make the answer any more correct. Thus, the exit condition is met when there's no significant difference between successive guesses—when it's less than, say, 10E–09. (Incidentally, this method won't work well for numbers with very large square roots.)

first refinement

```
give NewGuess an initial value;
repeat
    OldGuess gets the value of NewGuess;
    compute the new value of NewGuess
until NoSignificantChange (OldGuess, NewGuess);
```

Note the pseudocoded *boolean* function call that states the exit condition.

Now, writing a program that implements Newton's algorithm isn't too challenging for us, so I'll make the problem more complicated:

Write a program that *tests* Newton's method by using it to find the square roots of various numbers. Exercise it by generating random test numbers, along with totally wild first guesses at their square roots. Count how many iterations Newton's method takes to arrive at the root, and compare its result to that of the standard function *sqrt*.

The pseudocode of function *SquareRoot* expands to:

> *pick a number to solve for*;
> *print the number*;
> *assign a wild first guess of its square root to NewGuess*;
> *print the guess*;
> **repeat**
>   *OldGuess gets the value of NewGuess*;
>   *compute the new value of NewGuess*;
>   *update the guess counter*
> **until** *NoSignificantChange (OldGuess, NewGuess)*;

I won't bother writing up a further refinement of a *TestNewton* program, since we've already worked on most of its components. Instead, let's try a program outline:

> **program** *TestNewton*;
> **const** *the starting seed, the number of trials we want,*
>   *and the upper limit on numbers and guesses*;
> **var** *the number we're examining, the seed, and a counter for trials*;
> **function** *RandomInteger--gets Seed and UpperLimit, returns an integer*;
> **function** *SquareRoot--gets Number, returns its square root*;
> **function** *NoSignificantChange--gets the two most recent guesses,*
>   *and returns true if they're very close*;
> **begin**
>   *initialize the seed*;
>   *label the program output*;
>   **for** *some number of trials*
>   *pick a Number*;
>   *print Number*;
>   *print SquareRoot (Number), sqrt (Number)*
> **end**.

The completed program is shown below. *RandomInteger* is a slightly modified version of function *Random*. It differs by returning an *integer* between 1 and an upper limit, rather than a *real* between 0 and 1.

```
program TestNewton (input, output);
   {Tests Newton's method of finding square roots.}
const STARTINGSEED = 187;
      NUMBEROFTRIALS = 10;
      UPPERLIMIT = 10000;
var Number, Seed, Counter: integer;
function RandomInteger (var Seed: integer; UPPERLIMIT: integer): integer;
   {Generates a pseudo-random integer from 1 through UPPERLIMIT.}
   const MODULUS = 65536;
         MULTIPLIER = 25173;
         INCREMENT = 13849;
   begin
      Seed := ((MULTIPLIER*Seed)+INCREMENT) mod MODULUS;
      RandomInteger := 1+trunc (UPPERLIMIT*(Seed/MODULUS))
   end; {RandomInteger}
function SquareRoot (Number: real): real;
   var OldGuess, NewGuess: real;
       GuessNumber: integer;
   function NoSignificantChange (Old, New: real): boolean;
      const EPSILON = 10E-09;
      begin
         NoSignificantChange := abs (Old-New)<EPSILON
      end; {NoSignificantChange}
   begin {SquareRoot}
      NewGuess := RandomInteger (Seed, UPPERLIMIT);
         {Take a wild first guess and print it.}
      write (trunc (NewGuess):15);
      GuessNumber := 0;
      repeat
         GuessNumber := GuessNumber +1;
         OldGuess := NewGuess;
         NewGuess := ((Number/OldGuess)+OldGuess)/2
      until NoSignificantChange (OldGuess, NewGuess);
      write (GuessNumber:8);
      SquareRoot := NewGuess
   end; {SquareRoot}
begin {TestNewton}
   Seed := STARTINGSEED;
   writeln ('Number':6, 'First Guess':15, 'Tries':8, 'Newton':12, 'sqrt':12);
   for Counter := 1 to NUMBEROFTRIALS do begin
      Number := RandomInteger (Seed, UPPERLIMIT);
      write (Number:6);
      writeln (SquareRoot (Number):12:5, sqrt (Number):12:5)
   end
end. {TestNewton}                                  {output follows}
```

Newton testing program

	↓	↓	↓	↓	↓
Number	First Guess	Tries		Newton	sqrt
398	9689	14		19.94994	19.94994
121	6579	14		11.00000	11.00000
5559	5521	11		74.55870	74.55870
6771	1498	9		82.28609	82.28609
7096	8394	12		84.23776	84.23776
6907	7754	12		83.10836	83.10836
7355	7527	12		85.76130	85.76130
4123	818	9		64.21059	64.21059
1177	4638	12		34.30743	34.30743
4513	8656	12		67.17887	67.17887

problem: finding prime factors

Our third outstanding algorithm isn't quite as historic than the others, but it is rather more interesting to program—especially since it involves elements of several of the other loop examples. John Pollard's 'rho' algorithm, introduced about a decade ago, can be used to find a number's prime factors, or smallest *integer* divisors. In essence, Pollard claimed that when a pseudo-random sequence was generated in a certain way, some of its values could usually be cajoled into sharing a prime factor—that could be found using Euclid's algorithm—with a given number.

a sort-of-random sequence

Sound interesting? Let's look at the algorithm for generating the sequence in detail. Suppose that we want to factor a number N. I'll say that a *Pollard number* called P begins as some small *seed* value—3 is suitable. Then, we can define a continuing series of Pollard numbers like this:

$$P_{i+1} \text{ is } (P_i^2 + Increment) \textbf{ mod } N;$$

the Pollard ´rho´ algorithm

In other words, the first Pollard number is 3. The next Pollard number equals the current Pollard, squared and plus an increment (which is usually a small prime number). This quantity is taken **mod** N, the number we want to factor. With a bit of thought you'll see that the Pollard sequence always yields numbers between 0 and $N-1$, since **mod** leaves the remainder of a division by N. This is one reason it's called the 'rho' algorithm—we can imagine the trail of numbers forming a loop that looks like the Greek letter ρ. Note the similarity between Pollard's rule, and the structure of a linear-congruential random number generator.

Suppose we compute a long sequence of Pollard numbers, and label them P_1, P_2, P_3, and so on. It turns out, for reasons that nobody really understands, that $(P_{2i}-P_i)$—the difference of the i th Pollard, and the $2*i$ th one—which I'll call Q, will eventually share a common factor with N. We'll actually wind up generating several terms of this Q sequence, but we'll usually get to the right one pretty fast.

Now we have two numbers—our starting N, and a Q that it may share a factor with. Stating the relations formally:

$P_1 := 3$; {use a seed as the first Pollard number}
$P_{i+1} := (P_i^2 + Increment)$ **mod** N; {successive Pollard numbers}
$Q_j := P_{2i} - P_i$; {Q may share a factor with N}

the shared factor is often prime

We know that when two numbers share at least one factor, the largest shared factor is called the greatest common divisor. What Pollard found, amazingly enough, was that when the greatest common divisor of N and Q was larger than one, it was usually a prime number. And, if it wasn't prime, reapplying his algorithm to this divisor—but starting with a new seed value or a different *Increment*—could eventually yield its prime factors.

Investigation of Pollard's algorithm showed that the occasional blind eye for non-prime factors could be sidestepped without too much difficulty. At times, a composite greatest common divisor will turn out to have been divisible by a very *small* prime, which can be divided out routinely. When a composite number with relatively *large* prime factors slips through, just one or two additional calls of the Pollard routine, but with different *Increment* values, usually takes care of the problem. Fancier versions of these basic tricks can be applied to make Pollard's algorithm extremely fast.

In my unsophisticated implementation, I just sift out the small primes 2, 3, and 5 before invoking the Pollard routine. Then, I use *Increment* values of 2, 3, and 5 on each proposed prime factor, to ensure that no large primes are missed. These checks let my program correctly factor numbers up to 100,000 with a single exception—80,551 (109 ∗ 739) is mistakenly returned as a prime.

Let's try proposing a pseudocode outline of a factoring program that uses Pollard's algorithm, and will correctly factor numbers 2 through 80,550. A first refinement is:

first refinement

get the number N;
sift out, and print, the 2, 3, and 5 factors;
while *N still has factors*
    compute a factor with Pollard, using 2 as the Increment;
    factor that factor with Pollard, using 3 as the Increment;
    factor that factor with Pollard, using 5 as the Increment;
    print the factor;
    remove the factor from N;

The step *compute a factor with Pollard* obviously needs further refinement. Recall that we want to generate a sequence of Pollard numbers until the difference between two particular Pollards share a factor with N. Fortunately, we don't have to save the entire sequence as we go along. If we initialize Pi and $P2i$ to some starting seed (like 3), then the statements:

a coding detail: computing Q values

{Get the next Q value.}
$Pi := (sqr(Pi) + Increment)$ **mod** N;
$P2i := (sqr(P2i) + Increment)$ **mod** N;
$P2i := (sqr(P2i) + Increment)$ **mod** N;
$Q := P2i - Pi$; {Eventually, this number shares a factor with N}

generate the P_i and P_{2i} squences. We can expand the pseudocode *compute a factor with Pollard* to:

finding a factor

initialize Pi and P2i to some seed;
repeat
    compute Q values
until Q *and* N *have a non-trivial (non-1) greatest common divisor*;

This expansion brings us to a final problem—finding the greatest common divisor of Q and N. Fortunately, we already know how to do this by applying Euclid's algorithm. My completed *FindFactors* program, below, has been tested for numbers up to 100,000, with the exception noted above.

In a different form, Pollard's algorithm has been used to factor huge numbers, some of which were previously conjectured to be prime, or whose factors were just not known. Probably the best-known of these are the *Fermat numbers* $2^{2^n} + 1$. In 1640, Pierre Fermat ventured the opinion that such numbers were always prime. A century later, Euler showed that Fermat 5 was composite, and now doubters even claim that all larger Fermat numbers have factors as well. In 1980, Pollard and Richard Brent gained admission to the Factorer's Hall of Fame by cracking Fermat 8—a 78-digit number—with the factor 1238926361552897.

prime factoring
program

program *FindFactors* (input, output);
    {Factors a number N with the Pollard 'rho' algorithm.}
var N, TrialFactor: integer;
procedure SiftOut (Divisor: integer; **var** N: integer);
    {Remove *Divisor* as a factor of *N*.}
    begin
        while (N **mod** Divisor) = 0 **do begin**
            N := N **div** Divisor;
            write (Divisor:1, ' ')
        end
    end; {SiftOut}
function GreatestCommonDivisor (Greatest, Others: integer): integer;
    {Uses Euclid's algorithm to compute the GCD of its arguments.}
    var Remainder: integer;
    begin
        repeat
            Remainder := Greatest **mod** Others;
            Greatest := Others;
            Others := Remainder
        until Remainder = 0;
        GreatestCommonDivisor := Greatest
    end; {GreatestCommonDivisor}

```
function NextFactor (Increment, N: integer): integer;
    {Implements Pollard's algorithm for guessing at a factor of N.}
    var Pi, P2i, Q, Temp: integer;
    begin
        Pi := 3;  {Initialize the sequences to a small number.}
        P2i := 3;
        repeat
            Pi := (sqr (Pi) + Increment) mod N;  {Generate the 'low' sequence.}
            P2i := (sqr (P2i) + Increment) mod N;
            P2i := (sqr (P2i) + Increment) mod N;  {Generate the 'high' sequence.}
            Q := P2i - Pi;  {We hope that their difference shares a factor with N.}
            Temp := GreatestCommonDivisor (abs (Q), N)
        until Temp <> 1;  {On exit, P-Q and N share a factor.}
        NextFactor := Temp
    end;  {NextFactor}
begin
    writeln ('Enter a number to be factored.  End the program with 0.');
    readln (N);
    while N > 0 do begin
        SiftOut (2, N);  {Get rid of the 'problem' factors 2, 3, and 5.}
        SiftOut (3, N);
        SiftOut (5, N);
        while N <> 1 do begin
            TrialFactor := NextFactor (2, N);  {Get a factor of N, then try ...}
            TrialFactor := NextFactor (3, TrialFactor);  {...to factor the factor.}
            TrialFactor := NextFactor (5, TrialFactor);
            N := N div TrialFactor;  {Remove the factor from N.}
            write (TrialFactor:1, ' ')
        end;
        writeln;
        readln (N)
    end
end.  {FindFactors}
```

↓   ↓   ↓   ↓   ↓

```
Enter a number to be factored.  End the program with 0.
9699690
2 3 5 7 17 11 13 19
80553
3 11 2441
687923478
2 3 3 11 11 315851
0
```

Text Processing: *eof* and *eoln* 5-2

WORK WITH CHARACTERS (AS OPPOSED to numbers) is called *text processing*—any sequence of characters forms text. This section introduces three concepts fundamental to text processing in Pascal—*lines* of text, *files* of lines, and a file *window* that holds the upcoming character.

Procedure *EchoOneLine*, below, gives us an idea of what text processing involves. The procedure reads in a line of text that contains an unknown number of characters one character at a time, and echoes each character as it goes along.

line-echoing procedure

```
procedure EchoOneLine;
    {Read and echo a single line of text.}
    var CurrentCharacter: char;
    begin
    while not eoln do begin        {While not at the end of line...}
        read (CurrentCharacter);        {...read and echo characters.}
        write (CurrentCharacter)
    end;
        writeln;        {Print a carriage return.}
        readln        {Dump the end-of-line character.}
    end; {EchoOneLine}
```

review of read and readln

discarding the line

EchoOneLine relies on the predefined function *eoln* to watch for the end of an input line. Our discussion begins, though, with a quick review of *readln* and *read*. *readln* finds the value of its parameter (or parameters), and then throws the rest of the line away in either case. Calling *readln* without any argument discards any values left on the current line of input. The next character read will be the first character of the next line.

The standard procedure *read*, in contrast, doesn't discard anything. When we use *read* to input *char* values, no character—not even a blank space—is ever thrown away. The next character read will be the next waiting value, no matter how long ago it had been entered.

the end-of-line

Now, for the convenience of both people and machines, text input in Pascal is divided into lines. A special nonprinting *control character*, which varies from system to system, usually marks the end of each line (and for the purpose of our discussion, we can assume that it's always done this way). Thus, every punched card represents a line of input in batch systems, and an end-of-line marker is generated whenever a card is read. In interactive systems, hitting the carriage return or new-line key sends the end-of-line character to the computer. When data files are stored in the computer, the end-of-line marker is usually hidden, and doesn't show up in a count of the number of characters the data file holds. But in any case . . .

the eoln function

A call of the *boolean* function *eoln* represents *true* if the character we're about to read is the end-of-line character (whether we can see it or not). Otherwise, *eoln* represents *false*.

what is the end-of-line?

The end-of-line character can be read. However, even though the end-of-line character has a special meaning to the computer, this cachet is lost once we read it as part of a Pascal program. Instead of printing as a carriage return, the end-of-line character is read and printed out as a blank space. A carriage return can only be generated from within a program by calling procedure *writeln*.

the next line

The character that follows an end-of-line character is the first character of the next line of input. But if we want to read from the next line, we must dispose of the end-of-line character first—either by reading the end-of-line, or by calling *readln*. Procedure *ReadOneLine*, below, uses the first approach. It reaches the end of the current line, then does one more *read* to get rid of the end-of-line. A call of *ReadOneLine* is equivalent to a call of the standard procedure *readln*, because it leaves us at the beginning of the next line.

imitating *readln*

```
procedure ReadOneLine;
    {Imitates the effect of readln.}
    var Character: char;
    begin
        while not eoln do read (Character);
        read (Character)
    end;   {ReadOneLine}
```

problem: echo a line of text

Let's expand *ReadOneLine* into a procedure that reads and echoes a full line of text, complete with carriage return (the end-of-line marker). In words, our algorithm is:

refinement

```
while it's not the end of the line
    read a character (using read);
    ready the character for printing (using write);
force printing of all output (by using writeln);
get ready for another line of input (by using readln);
```

To nobody's surprise, this turns out to be the starting example—procedure *EchoOneLine*.

So much for a single line of text. What about a series of lines, though? For all practical purposes, a *series* of lines is just as organized—complete with beginning and end—as the characters that form a *single* line. Computer scientists have developed a pleasant fiction to describe this line-by-line sequence of characters: As far as a Pascal program is concerned, its input comes from an imaginary entity called a *file*. Now, just as the end of each input line is marked by an end-of-line character, the end of the entire file is flagged with an end-of-file character.* It's used by the *end of file* function, *eof*.

---

* As with the end-of-line character, this may not be literally true. The end-of-file character may not actually be there as part of the file.

the *eof* function

> A call of *eof* causes the computer to inspect the very next input character, without otherwise disturbing it. If it's the end-of-file character, *eof* is *true* because we're at the end of the input file. If it's any other character, there must still be data in the file, and *eof* is *false*.

The *eof* function is necessary when we don't know how much input a program is going to receive, and when no explicit sentinel character marks the end of input. A general outline of programs that use *eof* to process *char* input is:

```
while not eof do begin
      get the data;
      process the data
end;    etc.
```

The internal processing of an *eof* loop need not be complicated. Perhaps the simplest example counts the number of lines in input:

counting lines

```
LineCount := 0;
while not eof do begin
      LineCount := LineCount + 1;
      readln          {Discard the current line.}
end;
```

Another easy code segment counts the number of characters in input:

counting characters

```
CharCount := 0;
while not eof do begin
      CharCount := CharCount + 1;
      read (Ch)          {Discard the current character.}
end;
```

However, we must realize that we're including any end-of-line characters in our count.

the basic text-processing program

Although we'll develop more specialized examples later, widespread applications of *eof* require it to be used in conjunction with *eoln*. Program *EchoText*, below, illustrates one of the most common models of text processing programs. It reads and echoes an entire input file one line at a time. In doing so, it maintains the line structure of its input—whenever *eoln* is *true*, a *writeln* prints a new carriage return.

EchoText is a very important and widely-used model. You should identify and understand:

1.   the outer loop that processes lines, while keeping an eye out for the end of the input file.

2.   the inner loop that processes characters, while watching for the end of the current line.

Note that the shaded portion is equivalent to procedure *EchoOneLine*.

file-echoing program

```
program EchoText (input, output);
    {Uses nested while loops to read and echo input text.}
var CurrentCharacter: char;
begin
    while not eof do begin
        while not eoln do begin
            read (CurrentCharacter);
            write (CurrentCharacter)
        end; {eoln while}
        writeln;
        readln
    end {eof while}
end. {EchoText}
```

Two special rules apply to the end-of-file character.

> A program cannot read the end-of-file character. Furthermore, when *eof* is *true*, *eoln* is undefined.

reading past *eof*

The end-of-file character can be heard, but not seen. Trying to read the end-of-file character (or even worse, trying to read *past* it), causes one of the quickest crashes in Pascal.

ATTEMPT TO READ PAST EOF

Thus, (**not** *eof*) is usually used as the *entry* condition of a **while** loop (as above), and not as the *exit* condition of a **repeat** loop.

text processing for robustness

Many programs that are not intended to process text still require the tools of text processing. Improving program robustness is a common motivation. For example, a program that expects numerical input is exceptionally sensitive to its environment. An inadvertent nonblank or non-digit character can cause a type clash, and program crash.

A basic form of run-time error checking helps prevent the problem. Since all input may be read as a sequence of *char* values, we can read a number's digits one at a time, then convert them into the number they represent (e.g. turn the sequence '1', '3', '7', into 137). Any non-digit characters that are encountered before the first digit can be skipped, and the first non-digit we run into afterward marks the number's end.

Simply reading an ordinary *integer* as a sequence of characters is a bit too easy for us, though, so I'll propose the following problem instead:

problem: hex conversion

In bases greater than 10, ordinary characters must appear within numbers. For example, the hexadecimal (base 16) system's digits are '0', '1', '2', '3', '4', '5', '6', '7', '8', '9', 'A', 'B', 'C', 'D', 'E', and 'F'. Write a program that reads and converts hexadecimal numbers to base 10 notation.

What are the basic steps of such a program? Obviously we have to read characters, one at a time, and assure ourselves that each character can appear in a legitimate hexadecimal number. As we go along, each valid character must be converted to its decimal equivalent. This is easy for the ordinary decimal digit characters—we compare the ordinal position of each digit to the position of the first digit, '0':

$$ConvertedToInteger := ord\ (InputCharacter) - ord\ (`0`);$$

The letters that serve as additional hex digit characters are compared to the first letter, 'A'. In addition, they require a correction factor, since they represent the decimal values 10 through 15:

$$ConvertedToInteger := ord\ ((InputCharacter) - ord\ (`A`))+10;$$

Once we feel confident about our ability to compute the decimal equivalents of individual hexadecimal digits, we can propose a first pseudocode refinement:

first refinement

> *find a digit;*
> *convert it into an integer;*
> *add it to the base (16) times the value of the digits read so far;*
> *keep reading and converting until we get to a non-digit;*

Note that the third step of the refinement maintains the relative positional values of the individual digits—the 'one' column, the 'sixteens' column, the 'two-fiftysixes' column, and so on.

As usual, we'll need a second refinement to express our algorithm in more procedural form.

second refinement

> **while** *there may be more values*
>   *initialize a variable Number to* 0;
>   **repeat**
>   *get each digit's decimal equivalent;*
>   *add the equivalent to* 16*Number;
>   *read in the next character*
>   **until** *we read a non-hex digit;*
>   *write the decimal equivalent;*

The completed program, shown below, implements the algorithm. It's worth studying the special techniques it employs (especially the use of the *ord* function), because the same methods will show up in many text processing programs and procedures. As you read it, note that the line-structure of input is ignored—the end-of-line serves as a space to separate numbers. What if there's more than one space between two hex values, though? Will program output be correct? Why?

```
program ConvertHex (input, output);
    {Converts hexadecimal numbers to base 10.}

const BASE = 16;

var Digit: char;
    Number, Decimal: integer;
    procedure GetDecimalEquivalent (Digit: char; var Decimal: integer);
        {Gives Decimal the base 10 equivalent of Digit.}
        begin
            if (Digit >='0') and (Digit <='9')
                then Decimal := ord (Digit)-ord ('0')
                else if (Digit >='A') and (Digit <='F')
                    then Decimal := (ord (Digit)-ord ('A'))+10
                    else Decimal := 0
        end; {GetDecimalEquivalent}

begin {ConvertHex}
    while not eof do begin
        Number := 0;
        read (Digit);
        write ('The decimal equivalent of hex ');
        repeat
            write (Digit);
            GetDecimalEquivalent (Digit, Decimal);
            Number := (BASE *Number)+Decimal;
            read (Digit)
        until ((Digit <'0') or (Digit >'9'))
            and ((Digit <'A') or (Digit >'F'));
        writeln (' is ', Number:1)
    end {while}
end. {ConvertHex}
```

hex conversion program

↓   ↓   ↓   ↓   ↓

A 10 1A
F00 ABCDEF
The decimal equivalent of hex A is 10
The decimal equivalent of hex 10 is 16
The decimal equivalent of hex 1A is 26
The decimal equivalent of hex F00 is 3840
The decimal equivalent of hex ABCDEF is 11259375

As a final point, suppose that we wanted to make *ConvertHex* even more bulletproof. We can avoid reading a number that's greater than *MAXINT* with a simple addition to the **repeat** statement's exit condition:

```
repeat
    . . .
until . . . or (Number > (MAXINT /BASE))
```

The File Window

Suppose that a line of input contains a series of non-digit characters, and then a number. Is there any way to skip past the non-digits so that we're about to read the number? It may seem unreasonable, but given the tools we know about so far, the job can't be done—we'll always end up going one character too far. Pascal comes to the rescue with a 'lookahead' mechanism for inspecting the upcoming character.

the file window

> The *file window* represents the first character that would be obtained in the next call of *read* or *readln*. The file window is denoted by the file's name followed by an up-arrow (↑) or circumflex (ˆ).

Thus, the character that is about to be read from ordinary *input* is called *input* ↑. (I'll always use the up-arrow in this text.) For our purposes, the file window is a read-only buffer variable. It can be inspected (i.e. compared or written out), but not changed by being assigned to. Other file window features are discussed in Chapter 9.

The hex-conversion example gives us the key to most file window applications. Use of the file window is appropriate when we want to stop *before* actually reading something, since this is often the key to writing modular code. For instance, suppose we know that a line of input contains a number hidden amongst a variety of non-digit characters. We want to skip characters up to, but not including, the start of the number. In pseudocode we have:

> **while** *we're not about to read a digit*
>   *read the next character*;

Our Pascal code uses the *input* file window. Assume the *char* variable *Ch*:

skipping leading non-digits

```
{Correct method of skipping leading non-digits.}
while (input↑<'0') or (input↑>'9') do
    read (Ch);
```

The alternative code segment shown below won't work because it goes too far. By the time we stop reading, we'll have already given *Ch* the first digit of the number.

```
{Incorrect method of skipping leading non-digits.}
read (Ch);
while (Ch <'0') or (ch >'9') do
    read (Ch);
```

Let's solve a problem faced by the implementor of every computer system.

problem: read reals

Write a program that reads a *real* value as a sequence of characters.

Reading *integer* values is relatively easy, because they contain only digits. *real* values, in contrast, invariably consist of digits intermixed with other valid characters—signs, a period, or the letter 'E' indicating a scale factor. A refinement would be:

decide if the number is positive or negative;
read the whole part;

refinement   **if** there's a fractional part **then** read it;
if there's a scale factor **then**
  decide if the scale factor is positive or negative;
  read the scale factor;
print the number;

It's clear that we are repeatedly faced with the dilemma of deciding what we are about to read before we can know what to do. Program *ReadReal*, below, uses the file window to 'look ahead' at the upcoming character. Note that *ReadReal*, like the Pascal system, will accept an *integer*, and represent it as a *real* value.

```
program ReadReal (input, output);
   {Read real input, character-by-character.}

var Whole, Scale, i: integer;
   Negative, Minus: boolean;
   Ch: char;
   Fraction, Place, TheReal: real;

begin
   Whole := 0;
   Fraction := 0.0;
   Scale := 0;
   Negative := input↑ = '−';
   if (input↑ = '+') or (input↑ = '−') then
       read (Ch);  {discard the sign if there is one}
   repeat  {read the whole portion}
       read (Ch);
       Whole := (10*Whole) + (ord (Ch) − ord('0'))
   until (input↑<'0') or (input↑>'9');
   if input↑ = '.' then begin  {look for the decimal part}
       read (Ch);
       Place := 0.1;
       repeat  {read the fractional portion}
           read (Ch);  {discard the decimal point}
           Fraction := Fraction + Place*(ord (Ch) − ord ('0'));
           Place := Place * 0.1
       until (input↑<'0') or (input↑>'9')
   end;  {Fraction-reading if.}              {program continues}
```

real-reading program

```
                {read the scale factor if there is one}
            if (input↑='e') or (input↑='E') then begin
                read (Ch);  {discard the scale-factor letter}
                Minus := input↑ = '-';  {the factor might be negative}
                if (input↑ = '+') or (input↑ = '-') then read (Ch);
                repeat  {read the scale factor}
                    read (Ch);
                    Scale := (10*Scale) + (ord (Ch) - ord ('0'))
                until (input↑<'0') or (input↑>'9')
            end;  {scale-factor reading if.}
            TheReal := Whole + Fraction;
        {Make corrections for negative whole part or scale factor.}
            if Negative then TheReal := TheReal * -1;
            if Minus
                then for i := 1 to Scale do TheReal := TheReal * 0.1
                else for i := 1 to Scale do TheReal := TheReal * 10.0;
            writeln (TheReal)
    end.  {ReadReal}
```

A Final Comment on Numbers

That Pascal was partially intended, in Wirth's words, to 'end the mystical belief in the segregation between scientific and commercial programming,' leads to conveniences that are sometimes rather inconvenient. The most easily observed examples involve numerical input. Suppose, for instance, that we want to read and echo *integer* input. Since blanks and end-of-lines are ignored except as value separators, this data-file-oriented program segment would seem to do the job:

```
    {incorrect program segment}
    while not eof do begin
        read (IntegerValue);
        writeln (IntegerValue)
    end;
```

Unfortunately, the program this segment appears in will crash as it tries to read past end of file! Since you are likely to write programs that analyze numerical data, it's crucial for you to understand why. The explanation involves the precise definitions of *read* and *readln*.

> If *read* or *readln* is given an *integer* or *real* variable as a parameter, it skips characters until it comes to a nonblank.

problems with reading
numbers

In other words, when the statement:

> *read (IntegerValue)* ;

is executed, the program jumps over spaces or end-of-lines, and reads the first nonblank value it finds (which, we hope, is an *integer*).

If we try to read another *integer* value, the process is repeated. The space or spaces that come before the next *integer* are skipped, and the *integer* is read in. Thus, after reading a numerical value, the computer is always about to read (and maybe ignore, if it's a space) a non-digit character.

Let's jump ahead to the end of the program's input data.

> By default, there is always an end-of-line character at the end of an input 'file' in Pascal.

the last end-of-line

Suppose we've just read what we (but not the computer) know is the program's last input number. The loop above asks itself:

> *Is this the end of the program's input?*

Then it answers:

> *No. There is at least one blank space left—the last end-of-line character. Perhaps there is more data.*

Since the program doesn't think that it's reached the end of the file, procedure *read* starts to repeat the **while** loop's action. It begins to skip spaces, looking for another *integer*. In the process, the program tries to read the end-of-file character, and it crashes.

There are two ways to avoid the problem of reading past end of file when numerical data is being input. One approach is to get input on a line-by-line basis using *readln*. The example below is correct if there are no extra blanks at the end of any input line.

a correct model for
number processing

```
{General-purpose outline for programs that read integer or real data.}
while not eof do begin
    while not eoln do begin
        read (IntegerValue);
        Process (IntegerValue);
    end;  {We've reached the end of a line.}
    readln  {Discard the rest of the line.}
end;
```

A second, more robust method is to define a procedure whose sole purpose is skipping blanks, like *SkipBlanks*, below.

procedure *SkipBlanks*;
    {Skips input blanks until *eof* or a nonblank.}
    var *Finished*: *boolean*;
        Ch: *char*;
    begin
      Finished := *false*;
      repeat
        if *eof* **then** *Finished* := *true*
            else if *input* ↑ = ' ' **then** *read* (*Ch*)
                    else *Finished* := *true*
      until *Finished*
  end; {*SkipBlanks*}

blank-skipping procedure

In practice, *SkipBlanks* is called like this:

{Another general-purpose outline for reading *integer* or *real* data.}
`SkipBlanks`;
while not *eof* **do begin**
  read (*IntegerValue*);
  Process (*IntegerValue*);
  `SkipBlanks`
end; {we've reached the end-of-file}

Chapter Notes 5-3

MOST OF THE BUGS ASSOCIATED WITH conditional loops are semantic. Since the compiler can't spot such bugs, they can only be found by program testing, or by visual inspection of the code itself. Now, reliance on testing is sometimes ill-advised, because it can lead programmers into an unnecessarily fatalistic state of mind.* In any case, a program test is only as reliable as the test data we provide, and our data may be insufficient.

Proving that entire programs are correct before they are even run (sometimes called *program verification*) is a task that requires a considerable amount of fasting and prayer. I'll discuss the idea of verification at length in Chapter 14. Still, it's fairly easy to become confident that a single loop statement will *usually* work by examining its *boundary conditions*—the exact circumstances of its first and last iterations.

boundary conditions

Entry: Can the entry condition be met? Have all its variables been initialized? Do we want a **repeat** loop or a **while** loop? Does the loop have to be conditional at all—might a **for** loop work?

---

* As a computer scientist named Graham once observed, "We build programs like the Wright brothers built planes. Build the whole thing, push it off a cliff, let it crash, and start all over again."

Exit: Can the exit condition be met? Is the entire loop action being repeated, or just its first statement? Are **and**s and **or**s being used correctly in the exit condition? Does some statement in the loop's action make it certain that the exit condition eventually *will* be met?

Off-by-one: Trace execution of the loop action through its first and final few iterations, step-by-step. Will all variables have their expected values when the loop is terminated? Is it possible that the loop takes place one time too often? Once too few?

Focusing on standard loop components—sentinels, accumulators, and counters—can help draw attention to some bugs. I'll state a problem for demonstration:

problem: find the
average

Write a code segment that finds the average value in a sequence of non-negative numbers. The sequence ends with a negative number.

Here's a first stab at encoding a solution. Can you spot the bug?

`adds sentinel' bug

```
Sum := 0;  {incorrect segment—adds the sentinel}
Count := 0;
repeat
    read (Number);
    Sum := Sum + Number;
    Count := Count + 1
until Number < 0;
if Count <>0 then Average := Sum /Count;
```

As the comment indicates, we add the sentinel by accident. The counter is 'correct,' but the accumulator stores an extra value.

Let's try again. This time, though, we'll try to be smarter—we'll read the first number before we enter the loop and add it to the accumulator.

`empty list' bug

```
read (Number);  {incorrect segment—won't detect an empty list}
Sum := 0;
Count := 0;
repeat
    Sum := Sum + Number;
    Count := Count + 1;
    read (Number)
until Number < 0;
if Count <>0 then Average := Sum /Count;
```

Well, we're getting a bit closer—but only if there are values to average. Suppose that the very first value entered is the sentinel. Not only will both the counter and the accumulator show incorrect values, but the sentinel won't even be seen in the right place. By the time we check for a negative value we'll have read the second input.

Let's go back to the drawing board. Our most obvious mistake was using a **repeat** loop, since entry to the loop wasn't even checked. We'll start from the beginning, using a **while** loop.

'initialization' bug

```
Sum := 0;  {incorrect segment—entry condition not initialized}
Count := 0;
while Number >= 0 do begin
    read (Number);
    Sum := Sum + Number;
    Count := Count + 1
end;
if Count <>0 then Average := Sum /Count;
```

We're still in hot water. Our quest for simplicity neglected to initialize *Number* before trying to enter the loop. A fix is easy, though:

'skipped value' bug

```
read (Number);  {incorrect segment—first value skipped, sentinel counted}
Sum := 0;
Count := 0;
while Number >= 0 do begin
    read (Number);
    Sum := Sum + Number;
    Count := Count + 1
end;
if Count <>0 then Average := Sum /Count;
```

It seems that we've really gone from the frying pan to the fire. Again, both the accumulator and counter will be off by one value—the first input will be skipped if the loop is non-empty. However, if the list isn't empty, the sentinel will be added and counted incorrectly. We need a fifth try:

correct at last!

```
read (Number);  {correct segment}
Sum := 0;
Count := 0;
while Number >= 0 do begin
    Sum := Sum + Number;
    Count := Count + 1;
    read (Number)
end;
if Count <>0 then Average := Sum /Count;
```

> Look before you loop. Don't make *any* assumptions about input, and always put the check before the action.

Successful models of loops that read and process input check it for validity before processing. In contrast, unsuccessful, incorrect versions process new items before making sure they're valid. The models to follow are:

> *get a data item*; {**while** version}
> **while** *the data is valid*
>   *process the data*;
>   *get more data*;

The **repeat** version only works if we're sure that input is available:

> *get a valid data item*; {**repeat** version}
> **repeat**
>   *process the data*;
>   *get more data*
> **until** *the data isn't valid*;

Let's move along to text-processing bugs. The important facts to remember are that *eof* and *eoln* are *true* when we are *about* to reach the end of the file or line, and neither before nor after. *eoln* causes problems in this regard when we read the end-of-line character itself. *eoln* is *false* at this point, because we're about to read the first character of the *next* line—even if there isn't any next line.

eof's problem is the opposite. If *eoln* is *true*, *eof* is *false*. Why? Because when *eoln* is *true*, we're about to read the end-of-line character—not the end-of-file character. There has to be a final *readln*—to get rid of this last end-of-line character—at the end of most text processing loops.

Unexpected encounters with the end-of-file tend to be unhappy experiences for the programmer. For instance, the program segment below prints every other line of a file—the first, third, fifth lines, etc. What would happen if the shaded **if** statement were omitted?

```
{correct way to print every other line}
while not eof  do begin
    while not eoln do begin
        read (Ch);
        write (Ch)
    end; {eoln}
    writeln; {print the current line}
    readln; {get rid of the end-of-line}
    if not eof then
        readln {skip the next line}
end; {eof}
```

Without the **if** check (in other words, just having the sequence *readln*; *readln*;) the code will work perfectly—but only if we have an even number of input lines. A odd number of lines causes a crash, though. *eof* will be *true* after the *readln* at the end of the third input line. An extra *readln* that tries to skip a non-existent fourth line will crash the program.

always check for *eof*

> Don't undermine the checks that are posted at the start of the loop. Check for *eof* or *eoln* whenever you read extra lines or characters inside the loop.

synchronization bugs

A final word concerns the text processing bugs known as *synchronization* errors. At some point, an off-by-one error enters the text processing loop and won't go away. A typical synchronization bug requires the user to enter an extra carriage return every now and then. This kind of bug is often found in highly interactive programs that obey many user commands.

What happens is this: Some commands are just one character or one line long. After reading the command, the programmer calls procedure *readln* to get rid of the end-of-line, so that the next command can be read eventually.

find the extra *readln*

Sometimes, though, a single command will require several characters or lines of input. The programmer may call a procedure that specializes in reading these multi-line commands—and which, for some reason, includes a *readln* of its own. This isn't at all unusual, since the more complicated procedure may have been written and tested in a driver program that required the *readln*.

Whatever the reason, we end up with two *readlns*—one in the procedure, and another back in the main program. Each one is just intended to flush the remnants of the current command line. The extra *readln* is usually not apparent until we expect a prompt for an additional command. The prompt doesn't appear until we impatiently hit the return key.

This kind of bug is hard to find because it seems to be somewhere that it isn't. The problem appears to lie with the current command since, after all, the previous command had worked perfectly well. Hopefully, an awareness of the problem will help you avoid it.

Important
to
Remember

- A **while** loop has an explicitly stated entry condition that must be met if the statement's action is to take place. A **repeat** loop has no entry condition. Therefore, a **repeat** statement's action will always take place at least once, but a **while** loop's action may not occur at all. If a loop is entered, the loop's action must help insure that the exit condition will eventually be met.

- A sequence of character input is called *text*. For all practical purposes, text is collected in files, and divided into lines. Each line ends with an end-of-line marker, read as a space, while every file ends with an end-of-file marker that cannot be read.

- Function *eoln* is *true* when the value about to be read is the end-of-line marker. Similarly, *eof* is true when the value about to be read is the end-of-file marker. When *eof* is *true*, *eoln* is undefined.

- When a file contains text, the end-of-file marker is always preceded by an end-of-line marker.

- The file window—the file's name followed by an up-arrow or circumflex—represents the value about to be read.

● A sentinel value is sometimes used to mark the end of input data relevant to a loop. A counter counts the number of values seen so far, while an accumulator sums them.

● When a loop can be left for more than one reason, don't jump to any conclusions. Add an **if** test to clarify the situation before acting.

● Off-by-one errors are the most common looping bug. Try to avoid them by mentally checking the boundary conditions under which a loop will be entered or exited.

● When possible, programs should degrade gracefully. They should give some idea of why the program fails, instead of simply failing abruptly, or producing incorrect results. Loops add to robustness by letting the user fix incorrect entries.

● Synchronization bugs can occur when an off-by-one error enters a text processing loop, and the computer's notion of its position on the current line starts to differ from the user's. Beware of unnecessary *readlns*.

Cross Reference

The **while** and **repeat** statements are quite similar—during the standardization debate, one expert even suggested that the **repeat** statement be done away with entirely! A less facetious suggestion, though, has actually been adopted in other languages (like Modula-2). It involves making the **while** statement 'self-bracketing,' like the **repeat**, by ending it with a reserved word like **endwhile**. See footnote 12, page A22, for the last word on this proposal.

● The **repeat** statement is defined in A22—A24. **while** follows in A24—A25.

● Textfile input and output are discussed at length in A47—A57. The discussion of input begins on A48, while output starts on A52. The discussion of input coercion, on A50, is particularly interesting.

● *eof* and *eoln* first introduced on A38. *eof* is described further on A128, while *eoln* is expanded on on A133.

● The file window, or buffer variable, is discussed on A127, although the explanation of file-handling primitives *get* and *put* is also interesting.

● Finally, *read* and *write* are formally described in A129—A130, while *readln* and *writeln* are dealt with in A132—A133.

Exercises

5-1   The great French mathematician Joseph-Louis Lagrange (1736-1813) wrote a friend the following note in 1768: 'I have been occupied these last few days in diversifying my studies a little with certain problems of Arithmetic, and I assure you I found many more difficulties than I had anticipated. Here is one, for example, at whose solution I arrived only with great trouble. Given any positive integer n which is not a square, to find a square integer x^2, such that $nx^2 + 1$ shall be a square.'

The problem Lagrange refers to—solving $ab^2 + 1 = c^2$, in *integers*, for non-prime a—is ancient. It turns out, for $2 \leq a \leq 50$, that most values of b that solve the equation are less than or equal to a. For example, if $a = 2$, b also equals 2, since $2*2^2 + 1 = 9$, a perfect square. Write a program that finds the values of a (there are between five and ten) for which a solution is not so easily found. Beware of searching for the missing solutions, though—some (like $a = 46$, for which $b = 3,588$ and $c = 592,192,225$, or $24,335^2$) will have a tendency to cause *integer* overflow.

5-2   The so-called *characteristic function*, often used to define set membership, is defined as 1 over a specified interval, and 0 outside this interval. In other words:

$$C(x,a,b) = \begin{matrix} 1 \text{ if } x \text{ is in the interval } (a,b) \text{ inclusive} \\ 0 \text{ if } x \text{ is outside the interval} \end{matrix}$$

By using the characteristic function, it's easy enough to decide if some x value belongs to the set of points that make up any particular interval, even though there are an infinite number of points in the interval.

Suppose, though, that we define an infinite set of such sets—the set of intervals j_1, j_2, j_3, and so on, where $j_k = (0, \frac{1}{2}^k)$, and k is a non-negative *integer* that goes to infinity. Write a program that determines, for a given *real* input value x, how many of the j_k sets contain x.

5-3   The least common multiple of two *integer* values is the smallest number they both factor; e.g. the least common multiple of 6 and 9 is 18. Recalling Euclid's *GCD* algorithm, we can say that:

$$least\ common\ multiple\ (a,b) = \frac{ab}{GCD\ (a,b)}$$

Write a program that computes the least common multiple of any two *integer* values.

5-4   A biologist doing research into pheromones, or chemical attractants, decides to drive a few of her bugs crazy. She places four bugs in the corners of a square test area, then douses each with a chemical that is sure to attract its right-hand neighbor. Driven by genetics, each bug starts walking counterclockwise toward its neighbor.

Now, each bug walks at the same speed. Before moving one of its little bug feet, the bug may change direction slightly so that it is heading directly toward its quarry. Write a program that answers these questions:

1)   Where do the bugs meet?

2)   How far has each bug walked, measured along its curved path, when they all finally collide?

5-5   An addict who likes cigarettes very much is willing to go to great lengths to supply her habit—even to the extent of rolling them from partly-smoked butts, and her inexhaustible supply of newspaper. Suppose that she begins with a carton of cigarettes (ten packages of twenty each). Assuming that she can roll one new cigarette from three butts, how many cigarettes will she be able to smoke in all? How many butts will be left over?

5-6   Monica Marin is trying to implement Newton's method of computing square roots. Unfortunately, all she remembers is that it involves making wild guesses. She uses the following algorithm: 'Well, suppose I want to find the square root of 44. I know that it's somewhere between 6 and 7. Suppose I generate n random numbers in that range, and see how many, when squared, are still less than 44. I bet that the square root equals:

$$6 + \frac{the\ number\ of\ low\ guesses}{the\ total\ number\ of\ guesses}$$

Implement Monica's method. Does it work? How may guesses does it take to arrive at each significant digit of the answer (i.e. to within 0.1, 0.01, 0.001, etc.)?

5-7   As promised, you now get the opportunity to write a program that takes the player's position in a number-guessing game (as described earlier in this chapter). Have the user think of a number between 1 and 100, then require the program to guess it within seven tries. Can you program a correct guess for a number between 1 and 1,000 in ten tries?

5-8   *Buffon's Needle* is a famous method, first presented by the Comte de Buffon in 1777, for estimating the value π. A needle of length l is dropped onto a wooden floor whose boards are exactly d apart. If the probability of the needle landing partially on a crack is called P, then $P = 2l/\pi d$, or π approaches $2l/Pd$ as the number of trials increases.

In 1812, Laplace extended Buffon's method to allow a grid of intersecting parallel lines. If the lines in one direction are a apart, and are b apart in the other, and the needle's length l is less than a or b, then:

$$P = \frac{2l(a+b)-l^2}{\pi ab}, \quad or \quad \pi = \frac{2l(a+b)-l^2}{Pab}$$

Write a program that simulates the dropping of the needle using Buffon's or Laplace's method. How many trials are needed to approximate π to within 5 decimal places? Does the length of the needle affect the speed at which either approach approximates π?

5-9   Two alternative methods of computing π are:

$$\frac{\pi}{4} = 1 - \frac{1}{3} + \frac{1}{5} - \frac{1}{7} + \cdots \qquad \text{(from Leibnitz)}$$

$$\frac{\pi}{4} = \frac{2}{3} \times \frac{4}{3} \times \frac{4}{5} \times \frac{6}{5} \times \frac{6}{7} \times \frac{8}{7} \times \cdots \qquad \text{(from Wallis)}$$

Which method—the sum of the series or the product of the series (or dropping needles)—approaches π most rapidly?

5-10   Consider Zeno's Paradox in the following form. An exhausted mountaineer is climbing Mount Everest. As she approaches the peak, the mountain becomes steeper, the air ever more rarified, and each step progressively more difficult. At one kilometer from the top, she makes the following mental deal with herself—each time she halves the remaining distance, she will rest for 10 minutes. Thus, she will rest after traveling an additional half-kilometer, then after the next quarter-kilometer, and so on.

Suppose, for the sake of making this problem more difficult, that the mountaineer takes one step per second. At first, a step is one 0.3 meters long, but after each rest break, it declines by ten percent. How long will she climb before she has rested more than she has walked? How long will it take for her to get to the point of taking a rest break after walking a single step? Can she reach the top from that point simply by falling down (or up)? How many steps and rest breaks will she have taken?

5-11   Finding the first derivative of a polynomial is a fairly straightforward mechanical process, however difficult it may seem in the first week of Calculus 1A. In general, if we have a power function $f(x) = x^n$, the equation of its first derivative is:

$$f'(x) = nx^{n-1}$$

The derivative of a longer polynomial is simply the sum of the derivative of its terms. Note that individual terms may include a *coefficient* or multiplier:

$$f(x) = 3x^4 + 5x^3 + 4x^2 + 1x^1 + 3x^0$$
$$f'(x) = 12x^3 + 15x^2 + 8x^1 + 1$$

Write a program that finds the equation of (but does not solve!) the first derivative of a polynomial. You may assume that input has this format:

1.   *eoln* follows the final term,

2.   all coefficients and exponents are single-digit numbers,

3.   all terms are positive,

4.   the final term will always have a zero exponent (which makes it a constant equal to the coefficient),

5   each exponent is preceded by a circumflex, e.g.: 4x^2

5-12   The *Newton-Raphson* method is an extremely powerful tool for finding a root of an equation, i.e. for finding an x such that $f(x) = 0$. For example, the roots of the equation:

$$f(x) = x^2 - 9$$

are 3 and −3. Remember that not all equations have roots (e.g. $f(x) = e^x$), some have only one, and some have an infinite number (e.g. $sin(x)$ has roots 0, $\pm\pi$, $\pm 2\pi$, ...).

The Newton-Raphson method requires that we calculate the first derivative of our function $f'(x)$, and take a guess x_0 as to its root. Then, iterate:

$$x_{i+1} = x_i - \frac{f(x_i)}{f'(x_i)}$$

until the difference between x_i and x_{i+1} is small *or* we decide that a root is not to be found (after, say, 20 iterations).

If you refer to the method of calculating square roots described earlier in Chapter 5, you're sure to notice some similarities. Suppose we want to find the square root of a. Present the equation as:

$$f(x) = x^2 - a$$

Since the derivative of $x^2 - a$ is $2x$, we iterate:

$$x_{i+1} = x_i - \frac{x_i^2 - a}{2x_i}$$

Write a program that extracts square roots by this method. Then modify the program to solve other problems; computing cube roots with:

$$f(x) = x^3 - a$$

or extracting natural logarithms by solving:

$$f(x) = e^x - a$$

5-13   An approach that is closely related to Newton's method of the last exercise lets us divide—using multiplication! For instance, suppose that we want to calculate the reciprocal of some number b, which would clearly seem to require division. We can state a function, below left, then use it to define the sequence on the right:

$$f(x) = \frac{1}{b} - x \qquad x_{i+1} = 2x_i - bx_i^2$$

Start with some wild first guess for x_0. We can solve for subsequent x values (and find the reciprocal of b) by iterating until the value of x barely changes from one computation to the next. This approach is called the *relaxation* method.

Use the relaxation method to write a program that performs division, without falling back on /, **div**, or **mod**. Let the user enter two reals x and y, then print out an approximation to the value x/y.

5-14   Continued fractions provide a way of mapping the set of all positive *real* numbers into the set of all subsets of positive *integers*. For instance, if x is *real*, and a_0, a_1 and so on are *integers* we can express x in an equation of the form:

$$x = a_0 + \cfrac{1}{a_1 + \cfrac{1}{a_2 + \cfrac{1}{a_3 + \cfrac{1}{a_4 + \cdots}}}}$$

It can be proven that every *real* can be represented like this.

Let's turn the problem around, though. Suppose we are given a particular set of values for a_0, a_1, a_2, and so on. How can we compute the *real* value x? It is tempting to propose the brute force approach of evaluating the fraction, term by term. However, the continued fraction may have infinitely many terms—a definite weakness to this approach.

Fortunately, there is an alternative approach. Define sequences P_n and Q_n such that:

$$P_{n+1} = a_n P_n + P_{n-1} \qquad\qquad Q_{n+1} = a_n Q_n + Q_{n-1}$$

and use as starting values $P_{-1} = 0$, $P_0 = 1$, $Q_{-1} = 1$, and $Q_0 = 0$. It turns out that, for some sequence of terms a_0 through a_k, the expression P_k/Q_k equals the computation of the continued fraction. Thus, if the fraction has finitely many terms (say, n terms), then x is rational and can be written as P_n/Q_n. If x is irrational, the continued fraction has an infinite number of terms, and:

$$x = \lim_{k \to \infty} \frac{P_k}{Q_k}$$

Suppose we let the fraction in question be denoted by:

$$[a_0, a_1, a_2, a_3, a_4, \cdots]$$

Armed with the theoretical considerations outlined above, write a program that evaluates various kinds of continued fractions. In particular, evaluate these examples:

1) $[1,1,1,1,\cdots]$ gives the Golden Ratio of antiquity. This is $\dfrac{1+\sqrt{5}}{2}$

2) $[1,2,2,2,\cdots]$ gives the square root of two.

3) $[2,1,2,1,1,4,1,1,6,1,1,8,\cdots]$ gives what?

5-15   Finding the terms of a continued fraction that describe a given positive *real* (as in the last exercise) is a qualitatively different problem from that of evaluating given elements. The idea is to generate, from an input *real* value x, a chain of *integers* that represent the a terms of:

$$x = a_0 + \cfrac{1}{a_1 + \cfrac{1}{a_2 + \cfrac{1}{a_3 + \cfrac{1}{a_4 + \cdots}}}}$$

The chain terminates if x is rational (can be expressed as the ratio of two *integers*). For instance, the fraction $0.8275862\ldots$, which happens to equal 24/29, can be expressed exactly as:

$$0.8275862\ldots = 0 + \cfrac{1}{1 + \cfrac{1}{4 + \cfrac{1}{1 + \cfrac{1}{4}}}}$$

One way to find proper a values is to compute the relations:

$$a_i = \lfloor x_i \rfloor \qquad \text{where } \lfloor x \rfloor = trunc\,(x)$$

$$x_{i+1} = \frac{1}{x_i - a_i}$$

where a_i is an *integer* that represents the current term, and x_0 is the original number.

Write a program that finds proper a terms for a given x. Test it on the irrational numbers:

$$e \qquad \frac{e+1}{e-1} \qquad \pi \qquad \sqrt{2}$$

Except for π, there should be a nice pattern to the chain of terms. (π's terms are 3 + [7, 15, 1, 292, 1, 1, 1, 2, 1, 3, 1, 14, 2, 1, 1, 2, 2, 2, 2, 1, 84, 2, 1, 1, 15, 3, 13,...].) For the others, how many terms can be found before evaluating the continued fraction they produce exceeds your computer's accuracy?

5-16   On the assumption that you are presently breezing through Physics 1A, let's model the travel of a cannonball. We will try to find the angle of fire that propels the cannonball for the greatest possible distance. Since the solution for a cannonball fired in a vacuum is trivial (it's 45°), I'll make the problem more interesting by introducing the resistance of a medium.

Let's define the following constants and variables:

θ:	variable launch angle with respect to horizontal
speed:	original cannon muzzle velocity, say 100 meters/sec
g:	constant acceleration of gravity, −9.8 meters/sec/sec
x, vx:	instantaneous horizontal position, velocity variables
y, vy:	instantaneous vertical position, velocity variables
time:	current time, starting with zero
dt:	constant small time increment, say 0.01 seconds

The laws of physics dictate the following equations for motion. Let's assume that the initial (x,y) position at time $t = 0$ is just $(0,0)$. Then:

$$v_x = speed\ \cos\theta, \qquad v_y = -speed\ \sin\theta$$

the new positions every dt increment are:

$$x\ position = x + v_x\, time, \qquad y\ position = y + v_y\, time$$

and finally, the change in velocity due to gravity (in the y direction), and drag (in both directions) are given by:

$$v_{x+1} = v_x - v_x^2\ drag\ constant$$
$$v_{y+1} = v_y + (g \times time) - v_y^2\ drag\ constant$$

Note that the effect of drag increases with speed.

Write a program that allows the user to enter a drag constant, then simulates the flight of a cannonball to find the best initial firing angle θ. The simulation should proceed until the projectile hits the ground (i.e., passes through $y = 0$). Some suitable drag constants are 10E–10 (air), 10E–6 (water), 10E–4 (salad oil). At what speed does the cannonball hit the ground in each case?

5-17   A *pretty printer* is a program that reads ragged student programs, and prints them using some readable standard for line breaks, indenting, and so on. Although full pretty printing is beyond us until we can use arrays to recognize reserved words, we can do a basic job just relying on particular symbols.

Write a program that reads a Pascal source program, then prints it while obeying these rules:

1.   A comment always begins on a new line, and code never appears on the same line as a comment.

2.   All comment lines are indented by five spaces.

3.   No comment line is more than 40 characters long, including indenting.

4.   A semicolon should always be followed by a carriage return, and marks the end of a line, except when it is located between parentheses (i.e. when it is part of a parameter declaration list).

5.   Blanks that come between a semicolon and a comment should be ignored.

5-18   An amusing and instructive problem associated with the great mathematician John von Neumann involves a fly, and two railroad engines. The trains are initially 100 miles apart, heading toward each other at 25 mph each. A fly that is initially on train A starts flying toward train B at 30 mph. At the moment of contact with the (moving) train B the fly immediately turns around and flies, again at 30 mph, toward train A. This continues until the trains collide and the fly meets its fate. The question is: what total distance does the fly fly?

Of course, this trick question has an easy solution method—calculate the time that elapses before the trains collide (two hours), then recognize that the fly will travel 60 miles in this period. Legend holds, though, that when von Neumann was posed this problem, he immediately provided the correct answer. The punch line comes wih his explanation of the method he used: he treated the fly's flight as a mathematical sequence, then summed the infinite series.

With a computer at our disposal, we can aspire to a fraction of von Neumann's ability. Naturally, I'll make the problem more difficult to compensate for our mechanical ally. Suppose the fly rests on each moving train for one minute before turning around. Moreover, let the left-hand train travel at 10 mph, while the right-hand train moves at 15 mph. If the fly starts on the left, how far will it fly before getting splattered?

Additional exercises that require recursion may be found following Chapter 16, starting on page 367.

6

New Types
and the **case**
Statement

This chapter concludes our discussion of simple values, and ways of choosing between actions. Section 6-1 describes *enumerated types*, which give type names to—and therefore, let variables represent—groups of values named and ordered by the programmer. We'll also see how to limit the range of values a variable can hold by defining *subrange types*—named subranges of a larger underlying type.

The **case** statement, discussed in 6-2, is a specialized form of the more commonly used **if**. The **case** statement allows a clear method of structuring choices between several exclusive alternatives—a problem that might otherwise require an awkward sequence of nested **if** statements. It becomes convenient when actions are associated with specific values instead of ranges; for instance, in evaluating letter grades. The **if** statement may suffice to decide if a grade is passing or failing (since these involve ranges of grades), but the **case** statement is better suited to making a special comment about the relative merits of any particular letter.

Finally, I'll introduce a new relational operator, **in**, that's used in establishing a value's set membership. Sets in general are further discussed in Chapter 10.

Enumerated and Subrange Types
6-1

IN THE FIRST COMPUTER LANGUAGES, EVERYTHING—commands, identifiers, values, etc.—had to be expressed in ones and zeros. As languages improved, the vocabulary of description expanded. Nevertheless, a fairly limited set of basic measures (usually just *real, integer*, and *char*) had to be employed to describe every value imaginable.

The real world, though, is filled with plenty of values that already have perfectly good names. This month might be January or July; today's weather could be sunny, cloudy, raining, or breezy. In Pascal, such groups of named values can be the basis of an *enumerated ordinal type* that's defined by the user. The first few lines of the Pascal program below introduce two new ordinal types, *Fruit* and *Vegetable*, that are defined in the shaded *type definition part* of *Menu*.

program *Menu* (*input, output*);
    {Demonstrates an enumerated type definition.}
type *Fruit* = (*banana, apple, orange, pear*);
    Vegetable = (*cabbage, leeks, beets, okra*);
var *Appetizer, Dessert*: *Fruit*;
    Entree: *Vegetable*;
begin   etc.

enumerated type syntax

The reserved word **type** introduces the type definition part. Each *type identifier* is followed by an equals sign and lists the type's value identifiers, or *constants*, within parentheses and separated by commas. In chart form:

enumerated type definition

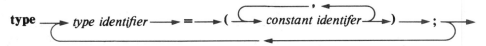

defining enumerations

The definitions and declarations from *Menu* allow assignments like:

Appetizer := *apple*;	{*Appetizer* gets the value *apple*.}
Dessert := *Appetizer*;	{*Dessert* is *apple* too.}
Entree := *leeks*;	{*Entree* is *leeks*.}
Entree := *cabbage*;	{Change *Entree* to *cabbage*.}

Appetizer or *Dessert* could not be assigned values of type *Vegetable*, since that would cause a type clash. Values or variables that have the same type can be compared:

    if *Appetizer* = *apple* **then**
        writeln ('An apple a day keeps the doctor away.');

pred, succ, ord

The predecessor function *pred* (*x*), successor function *succ* (*x*), and ordinal function *ord* (*x*) may all be given arguments of types enumerated by the programmer. Don't forget that the first ordinal number is 0, not 1. For the types defined above, we find that:

    ord (*apple*) is 1   {the second value of type *Fruit*}
    pred (*okra*) is *beets*
    succ (*orange*) is *pear*

When ordinal types are enumerated no value can belong to more than one type, since that would make type membership ambiguous. The definition below is illegal because the ordinal position of *Friday*, as well as its type, is unclear. Is it the last value of type *WeekDay*, or the first value of *WeekEnd*?

ambiguous type membership

    type *WeekDay* = (*Monday, Tuesday, Wednesday, Thursday, Friday*);
    WeekEnd = (*Friday, Saturday, Sunday*); {Illegal definition.}

ordinal constants
We can define constants of any ordinal type, but such definitions invariably occur within an enclosed subprogram. Why? Because the ordinal type must be defined before its constants can be used—but the type definition part comes before the constant definition part in the current block. Note that the constants of ordinal types aren't put in quotes, because that would make them text constants.

```
const FAVORITE = apple;        {A constant of type Fruit.}
      DAYOFF = Wednesday;      {A constant of type WeekDay.}
      BIRTHDAY = 'Monday';     {This is text—not a WeekDay value.}
```

external character
representation

> The constants of enumerated ordinal types cannot be read with *read* or *readln*, nor printed using *write* or *writeln*. They have no *external character representation*.

Aside from this exception, enumerated ordinals are used just like the standard ordinal values. For instance, enumerated values can be used to set the limits of a **for** statement, or (as we will soon see) in the constant list of a **case** statement.

scope of ordinals

Finally, the same scope rules apply to type and constant identifiers as to variable and subprogram identifiers. Once a type has been defined, its name, and the names of its constants, are known in all subprograms—unless they are locally redefined. However, the identifiers of types (and their constants) are usually preserved globally. Since they are often used for communication between different parts of a program, they're seldom redefined.

Subrange Types

We can restrict variables to representing *part* of the range of an ordinal type by defining another kind of ordinal type—an *ordinal subrange*. A subrange definition gives a type identifier to a particular segment of any standard or enumerated ordinal type.

```
type Day = (Monday, Tuesday, Wednesday,
                   Thursday, Friday, Saturday, Sunday);
     Weekday = Monday..Friday;         {Subrange of Day.}
     Weekend = Saturday..Sunday;       {Subrange of Day.}
     HoursInADay = 0..24;              {Subrange of integer.}
     CapitalLetters = 'A'..'Z';        {Subrange of char.}
var CardNight, SickDay: Weekday;
    SailingDay, GameDay: Weekend;
    HoursWorked: HoursInADay;
    FirstInitial, MiddleInitial: CapitalLetters;
```

Its syntax chart is:

ordinal subrange

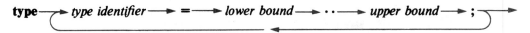

type ⟶ *type identifier* ⟶ = ⟶ *lower bound* ⟶ ·· ⟶ *upper bound* ⟶ ;

In the example above, a variable of type *Day* may represent any of the days, but *CardNight* (a variable of the *Weekday* subrange) can only represent one of the values *Monday* through *Friday*. Similarly, *HoursWorked* can only represent an *integer* value from 0 through 24—the values included in the ordinal subrange *HoursInADay*. Trying to assign it a value from outside this restricted range (say, −4 or 29) will cause a program crash.

limits of subranges

There is also a shorthand way to define subranges.

> The range of values a variable can represent may be specified when a variable is declared—but not when a parameter is declared.

```
type Day = (Monday, Tuesday, Wednesday,
                       Thursday, Friday, Saturday, Sunday);
```

shorthand subrange
declarations

```
var CardNight, SickDay: Monday..Friday;
    SailingDay, GameDay: Saturday..Sunday;
    HoursWorked: 0..24;
    FirstInitial, MiddleInitial: 'A'..'Z';
```

The variables declared with this shorthand are just like the variables in our last declaration, and represent the same limited range of values. User-defined constants can also be used to set the limits of a subrange, although variables, function calls, or other expressions may not be. The effect of this restriction is to prohibit any attempt to determine the bounds of a subrange during program execution.

On occasion, we may define subranges that are overlapping, similar, or even (apparently) the same. Understanding the differences between these subrange types is a confusing problem even for experienced programmers. For example:

```
type CapitalLetter = 'A'..'Z';
var FirstInitial, MiddleInitial: CapitalLetter;
    LastInitial: 'A'..'Z';
```

Are *FirstInitial* and *LastInitial* variables of the same type? A reasonable person, seeing that the subrange definitions are equivalent, would say yes. Unfortunately, Pascal draws a distinction between variables whose types are exactly *identical*, and those that are merely *compatible*. Only variables declared with the same type identifier are identical.

identical vs.
compatible types

In the case above, the types of *FirstInitial* and *MiddleInitial* are identical to each other, but not to *LastInitial*. We can still make an assignment between *FirstInitial* and *LastInitial* because they are compatible. Two variables are com-

underlying types

patible if they represent values of the same *underlying* type, even though they may be restricted to representing subranges of that type.

type *LowRange* = 1..5;
    MidRange = 1..10;
    HighRange = 6..20;

var *LowValue*: *LowRange*;
    MidValue: *MidRange*;
    HighValue: *HighRange*;
    AnyValue: integer;

LowValue, MidValue, HighValue, and *AnyValue* are clearly not of identical types, because they're all declared with different type identifiers. However, their underlying ordinal type (in this case, *integer*), determines type compatibility. Thus, the assignments:

MidValue := *LowValue*;
AnyValue := *LowValue*;

will always be legal, because *MidValue, LowValue*, and *AnyValue* all represent *integers*, and the subrange of *LowValue* falls within the subrange of *MidValue* (and is compatible with the *integer* range of *AnyValue*). However, this won't always be the case. These assignments:

LowValue := *MidValue*;
MidValue := *HighValue*;
HighValue := *AnyValue*;

may or may not be valid, depending on the values of *LowValue, MidValue, High-Value*, and *AnyValue* when the assignment actually takes place. If values are in the wrong subrange, a type clash will occur. Incidentally, checks on the plausibility of such assignments often aren't made until the program is run.

subrange parameters

    Is there any reason to define an ordinal subrange as a distinctly named type? Yes—we may have to use it to make declarations. When a value parameter, variable parameter, or function is created, its type must have a name. The shorthand method of specifying ordinal subranges can't be used.

    Moreover, procedure and function headings are type-checked very strictly. A variable parameter's type *must* be identical to its argument. Of all the variables declared above, only *LowValue* can be passed as an argument to procedure *DoesSomething*, below.

procedure *DoesSomething* (**var** *SmallNumber*: *LowRange*);

It's the only variable whose type is identical to the variable parameter *SmallNumber*.

    Since value parameters treat their arguments as values, they need not have identical types. As long as parameter and argument are type-compatible, a run-time error occurs only for an 'out-of-range' argument.

The result of a function may also be an enumerated or subrange value. For instance, *NextWorkingDay*, below, returns a value of type *Day*. Given an argument of type *Day*, it finds and represents the next working day.

enumerated typed function

```
function NextWorkingDay (Today: Day): Day;
    {Represents the next (sometimes first) value of Day.}
    const FIRSTDAY = Monday;
          LASTDAY = Friday;
    begin
        if (Today >=FIRSTDAY) and (Today <LASTDAY)
            then NextWorkingDay := succ (Today)
            else NextWorkingDay := FIRSTDAY
    end; {NextWorkingDay }
```

Let's consider a more complicated example that makes use of both enumerated and subrange types.

problem: employee payroll

Write a program that computes an employee's weekly pay, including benefits. Assume that we're paying time-and-a-half for Saturday, and double-time for Sunday work.

We'll read in the hours day by day, and make adjustments for overtime as we go along. In pseudocode our algorithm is:

first refinement

```
for each day of the week
    read in the number of hours worked
    make a weekend overtime bonus adjustment if necessary
```

We'll limit the variable that holds number of hours worked per day to a reasonable subrange of *integer*. A variable *Workday*, that take on values corresponding to the days of the week, lets us refine the pseudocode:

second refinement

```
for Workday := Monday to Sunday
    read in the number of hours worked
    make a weekend overtime bonus adjustment if necessary
```

How can we arrange for the Saturday and Sunday overtime rate? Why not use a nested sequence of mutually-exclusive **if** statements?

```
if Workday = Saturday
    then arrange for time-and-a-half
    else if Workday = Sunday
        then arrange for double-time
        else pay single-time
```

All that really remains is the definition of a new ordinal type:

data type definition

```
type Day = (Monday, Tuesday, Wednesday,
                    Thursday, Friday, Saturday, Sunday);
```

The addition of input, output, and a few calculations turn our pseudocode into program *Payroll*. Notice that *Payroll* is quite limited; it's practically a stub program that only handles one worker, at a single hourly wage and benefit rate. It only accepts full (i.e. *integer*) hours of work. It doesn't error-check input. Nonetheless, *Payroll* works, and can be upgraded later.

```
program Payroll (input, output);
     {Computes one employee's weekly payroll using enumerated types.}
const BENEFITRATE = 2.73;        {Benefits add $2.73/hour.}
     {Benefits are only paid on actual hours worked, not overtime.}
type Day = (Monday, Tuesday, Wednesday,
                         Thursday, Friday, Saturday, Sunday);
var Workday: Day;
    HourlyRate, TotalWages, HoursCredited, Benefits: real;
    HoursWorked: 0..10;
begin
    writeln ('Please enter the hourly wage rate.');
    readln (HourlyRate);
    TotalWages := 0.0;
    Benefits := 0.0;
    writeln ('Enter hours worked daily from Monday through Sunday.');
    for Workday := Monday to Sunday do begin
        read (HoursWorked);
        if Workday = Saturday
            then HoursCredited := 1.5*HoursWorked
            else if Workday = Sunday
                then HoursCredited := 2.0*HoursWorked
                else HoursCredited := HoursWorked;
        Benefits := Benefits + (HoursWorked*BENEFITRATE);
        TotalWages := TotalWages +(HoursCredited*HourlyRate)
    end; {for}
    TotalWages := TotalWages +Benefits;
    writeln ('Total wages for the week are $', TotalWages:2:2)
end. {Payroll}
```

employee payroll program

↓   ↓   ↓   ↓   ↓

Please enter the hourly wage rate.
9.37
Enter hours worked daily from Monday through Sunday.
8 8 6 9 10 0 4
Total wages for the week are $581.98

· ·

Q. Is this the beginning of a valid statement? Assume the definitions of program *Menu*.

if *Appetizer* <> *Entree* **then**   etc.

A. No, because comparing values of different types causes a type clash. We can no more compare *apple* and *leeks* (even for inequality) than we could 'S' and *true*.

Q. Is this a valid type declaration? Why or why not?

type *Letters* = ('A', 'B', 'C', 'D', 'E', 'F');

A. It's illegal. 'A', 'B', etc. are not identifiers—they're constant values of type *char*. The definition doesn't conform to Pascal syntax. We *could* use *A, B, C*, etc., as identifiers, but only if we omitted the single quote marks.

· ·

The **case** Statement 6-2

case demonstration program

PROGRAM *GRADECOMMENT*, BELOW, USES A **case** statement to take an action that depends on the value of *Score*. Although the program contains a variety of potential actions (including an empty statement), only one is executed.

```
program GradeComment (input, output);
    {Makes an appropriate comment about a user's grade.}
var Score : integer;
begin
    writeln ('What grade did you get?');
    readln (Score);
    case Score of
        0 : ; {Notice this empty statement}
        10 : writeln ('Exceptionally Good!');
        8, 9 : writeln ('Good!');
        5, 6, 7 : writeln ('Barely Passing!');
        3, 4 : writeln ('Flunking!');
        1, 2 : writeln ('Exceptionally Flunking!')
    end {the .case statement}
end. {GradeComment}
```

↓   ↓   ↓   ↓   ↓

What grade did you get?
2
Exceptionally Flunking!

The first line of the **case** statement contains an ordinal-valued *case expression*. Then comes a list of the **case** expression's potential values (the *case constant list*), and the proper action for each one. The reserved word **end** completes the statement. Its syntax chart is:

case statement

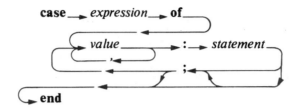

The **case** expression is frequently just a variable identifier, as in *GradeComment*. However, it may be any sort of expression, as long as it represents an ordinal value that appears in the case constant list. Naturally, all values given in the constant list must be of the same Pascal type as the **case** expression. Incidentally, in this context the word *constant* means that actual values (like 4 or ´D´) must be given. Expressions that represent values can't appear in the **case** constant list.

When the same action can be initiated by two or more possible values of the **case** expression, the constants are separated with commas. Most of the actions in *GradeComment* take advantage of this. As long as no constant calls for two different actions (that would be illegal), the order in which values are specified is irrelevant.

case expression

case constants .

give all values

Every potential value of the **case** expression must be specified in the **case** constant list. It's an error for the **case** expression to represent a value that is not given.

When some value of the **case** expression doesn't really require an action, the empty statement comes to the rescue, as it did for the constant value ´0´ in the example. More problematical is the possibility of the **case** expression attaining a value that has been entirely unanticipated. Some versions of Pascal (but not Standard Pascal) let the **case** statement include an **else** part to take care of these unexpected values. We can achieve the same effect in Standard Pascal by including an explicit **if** statement that can prevent entry, and provide an alternative action.

Let me digress for about a page to describe a convenient way of specifying a set of ordinal values. The Pascal relational operator **in** indicates whether or not a value is included in a larger group, or *set*, whose members can be defined as we wish. A number of other operations can be performed with sets, but we're not going to encounter them formally until Chapter 10.

the **in** operator

The relational operator **in** forms the following *boolean* expression:

value **in** [*a listed set of ordinal values*]

This expression represents *true* if *value* belongs to the specified set, and *false* if *value* isn't mentioned.

defining sets

It doesn't take much conceptual rewording to see that the constant list contains the *set* of values the **case** expression may legally assume. A set can be defined by listing its members, separated by commas, between *square brackets* : [ ] . All the members of a set must be of one ordinal type. For example, the set of integers from 0 to 9 is:

[0, 1, 2, 3, 4, 5, 6, 7, 8, 9]

whereas the set of *char* values (in quotes) that represent the digits is:

['0', '1', '2', '3', '4', '5', '6', '7', '8', '9']

set shorthand

If the members of a set are sequential ordinal values—*integers* in numerical order, or *char* values in the order of their collating sequence—we can simplify things a bit by using two periods between the first and last members, much as we would use an ellipsis in English. Two or more ordered sequences can also be shown in a single expression:

[0 .. 9]   ['A' .. 'Z']   ['0' .. '9']   ['a' .. 'z', 'A' .. 'Z']

The *Score* example might be rewritten with:

if (*Score* **in** [0 .. 10] **) then**
     case *Score* **of**   etc.

A **case** statement might require an error-checking **if** that only admits legal letter grades (note that 'E' is not included):

    if (*LetterGrade* **in** ['A' .. 'D', 'F']) **then**
        case *LetterGrade* **of**
            'A': *GPA* := 4.0 ;   etc.

or excludes non-vowels:

    if (*Letter* **in** ['a', 'e', 'i', 'o', 'u']) **then**
        case *Letter* **of**
            'i': *writeln* ('i before e except after c.') ;   etc.

two final points

Two small points end the discussion of sets. First, any representation of a value can be used in the set definition—it doesn't have to be one of the constants of the type.

    if (*Value* **in** [(*ErrorRange−Correction*) .. *HighBound*]) **then begin**
        etc. {Expressions can appear in the set definition.}

The second point is that in a set *non*-membership test, the entire *boolean* set expression is put in parentheses and preceded by the **not** operator.

> **if not** (*NextCharacter* **in** ['0' .. '9']) **then**
>   *writeln* ('You must enter a digit');

Focus on Programming: the **in** Operator

problem: odd/even counting

Let's consider a few examples that use the tools introduced in this chapter. The first demonstrates a typical application of both **case** and **in**.

Write a program that will determine how many odd, even, and zero digits there are in a sequence of input numbers. Count zeros as zeros, and as even numbers, but don't bother to count spaces or commas. There are 50 characters in all.

Clearly this will require a loop—we have to look at characters again and again. In pseudocode, we have:

first refinement

> **for** *the correct number of times*
>   *get an input value*;
>   **if** *it's* **in** *the set of values we're counting*
>   *count it properly*;
> *print the results*;

To *count it properly*, I'll pseudocode a **case** statement:

second refinement

> **case** *Current* **of**
>   *a zero*:   *add to the zero count*;
>   *add to the even count*;
>   *an odd number*:   *add to the odd count*;
>   *an even number*:   *add to the even count*;

Program *CountDigits* (on the next page), designed for data file use, solves our problem.

digit-counting
program

```
program CountDigits (input, output);
    {Count odd, even, and zero digits in input.}
const NUMBERINLIST = 50;
var ListCounter, Evens, Odds, Zeros: integer;
    Current: char;
procedure StoreCount (ThisChar: char;
                        var Ecount, Ocount, Zcount: integer);
    {Increments the proper total.}
    begin
        case ThisChar of
            '0':  begin
                    Zcount := Zcount+1;
                    Ecount := Ecount+1
                  end;  {counting the zero}
            '2', '4', '6', '8': Ecount := Ecount+1;
            '1', '3', '5', '7', '9': Ocount := Ocount+1;
        end {case}
    end; {StoreCount}
begin
    Evens := 0;
    Odds := 0;           {Initialize the 'total' variables}
    Zeros := 0;
    for ListCounter := 1 to NUMBERINLIST do begin
        read (Current);
        if Current in ['0'..'9'] then
            StoreCount (Current, Evens, Odds, Zeros)
    end; {for}
    write ('There are ', Zeros:1, ' zeros, ', Odds:1, ' odd ');
    writeln ('numbers, and ', Evens:1, ' even numbers.')
end.  {CountDigits}
```

↓   ↓   ↓   ↓   ↓

2,597 18 528 637 9,083,002 6 47,100 319 10 590,093
There are 8 zeros, 19 odd numbers, and 17 even numbers.

A second problem demonstrates some simple chemical reactions.

problem: chemical
reactions

Light metals show a particular affinity for forming compounds with both oxidizers and halogens. Write a program that lets a user enter appropriate ingredients, then reports the name and atomic weight of the resulting compound.

A refinement of the problem is hardly more than a simple restatement:

first refinement

have the user pick a light metal;
have the user pick an oxidizer or halogen;
compute the new atomic weight;
print the compound's name;

In expanding the pseudocode, we'll find an opportunity to showcase enumerated types, **case** statements, and **in**. First, to my knowledge, the elements are not one of the built-in ordinal types of any programming language, much to the dismay of chemistry students. Nevertheless, it's easy to enumerate an elemental type:

the underlaying data type

type *Element* = (*hydrogen, lithium, sodium, potassium, oxygen,*
                      sulfur, selenium, fluorine, chlorine, bromine, iodine);

The **case** statement comes into play any number of times. It is most convenient for allowing input and output of the enumerated type constants, which, you will recall, have no external character representations. For output, we can use a **case** statement to associate an appropriate output statement with each *Element*-type value.

        case *MyElement* **of** {print *MyElement's* value}
            hydrogen: *writeln* ('Hydrogen');
            lithium: *writeln* ('Lithium');
            ·.·   etc.

using a menu

For input, we can present the elements as a sequence of *menu* items, perhaps numbered according to their underlying ordinal positions. Instead of typing in the element's name, the program user chooses the proper number. Another **case** statement assigns *MyElement* the correct value.

some coding details

Nested **case** statements will be quite useful when a name depends not only on the element, but also its condition—are we working with pure bromine or a bromide? Recall our use of *state* variables in earlier examples. We can use the same technique here to specify whether an element has been combined in a reaction, or is still pure—all it takes is a type *States*, with values *Pure* and *Combined*.

Finally, set expressions will be needed when we want to discriminate between subgroups of the elements. For example:

        if *MyElement* **in** [*fluorine..iodine*] ...

forming the compounds

we know that *MyElement* is a halogen, and thus only one light metal atom will be required to form a compound. In contrast, the oxidizers [*oxygen..selenium*] will each require two light metal atoms for nature to take its course.

Since this is more of an 'observe these techniques' example than a problem in algorithm development, I won't bother with further refinements. However, you should note (in addition to the use of menus) the 'hardwired,' or built-in, table of atomic weights. The completed program is shown below.

chemical reaction
program

```
program MakeCompounds (input, output);
    {Makes a chemical compound, and reports its name and weight.}
type Element = (hydrogen, lithium, sodium, potassium, oxygen, sulfur,
                    selenium, fluorine, chlorine, bromine, iodine);
      States = (combined, pure);
var AnElement, TheMixer, TheLightMetal: Element;
procedure GetElement (var Item: Element);
    {Supports the menu in letting the user choose an element.}
    var Choice: integer;
    begin
        readln (Choice);
        case Choice of
            1: Item := hydrogen;
            2: Item := lithium;
            3: Item := sodium;
            4: Item := potassium;
            5: Item := oxygen;
            6: Item := sulfur;
            7: Item := selenium;
            8: Item := fluorine;
            9: Item := chlorine;
            10: Item := bromine;
            11: Item := iodine
        end
    end; {GetElement}
function Weight (Item: Element): real;
    {A 'hardwired' table of atomic weights.}
    begin
        case Item of
            hydrogen: Weight := 1.00797;
            lithium: Weight := 6.941;
            sodium: Weight := 22.9897;
            potassium: Weight := 39.0983;
            oxygen: Weight := 15.9994;
            sulfur: Weight := 32.064;
            selenium: Weight := 78.96;
            fluorine: Weight := 18.9984;
            chlorine: Weight := 35.453;
            bromine: Weight := 79.904;
            iodine: Weight := 126.9045;
        end
    end; {Weight}                                    {program continues}
```

```
procedure Print (MyElement: Element; State: States);
    {Prints MyElement in a manner that depends on its State.}
    begin
        if MyElement in [hydrogen .. potassium]
            then case MyElement of
                        hydrogen: write ('hydrogen ');
                        lithium: write ('lithium ');
                        sodium: write ('sodium ');
                        potassium: write ('potassium ')
                    end  {MyElement was a light metal.}
            else begin
                case MyElement of  {first, write the prefix ...}
                    oxygen: write ('ox');
                    sulfur: write ('sulf');
                    selenium: write ('selen');
                    fluorine: write ('fluor');
                    chlorine: write ('chlor');
                    bromine: write ('brom');
                    iodine: write ('iod')
                end;  {prefix case}
                case State of  {... then, print the suffix.}
                    pure: case MyElement of
                                oxygen: write ('ygen ');
                                sulfur: write ('ur ');
                                selenium: write ('ium ');
                                fluorine, chlorine, bromine, iodine: write ('ine ')
                            end;  {pure case}
                    combined: write ('ide ');
                end  {State case}
            end  {else part}
    end;  {Print}
procedure Report (LightMetal, Mixer: Element);
    {Decide what has been made, and compute and report its weight.}
    var MolecularWeight: real;
    begin
        if Mixer in [fluorine .. iodine]
            then MolecularWeight := Weight (Mixer) + Weight (LightMetal)
            else MolecularWeight := Weight (Mixer) + 2 * Weight (LightMetal);
        writeln ('You have made the compound');
        Print (LightMetal, pure);
        Print (Mixer, combined);
        writeln ('with molecular weight ', MolecularWeight:8:5)
    end;  {Report}
```

```
begin  {main program}
    writeln ('Pick a light metal.');
    write ('Light Metals are:  ');  {Prepare a menu of choices.}
    for AnElement := hydrogen to potassium do begin
        write ((ord (AnElement) + 1):1, ': ');
        Print (AnElement, pure)
    end;
    writeln;
    GetElement (TheLightMetal);
    writeln ('Pick an oxidizer or halogen.');
    write ('Oxidizers are:  ');
    for AnElement := oxygen to selenium do begin
        write ((ord (AnElement) + 1):1, ': ');
        Print (AnElement, pure)
    end;
    writeln;
    write ('Halogens are:  ');
    for AnElement := fluorine to iodine do begin
        write ((ord (AnElement) + 1):1, ': ');
        Print (AnElement, pure)
    end;
    writeln;
    GetElement (TheMixer);
    Report (TheLightMetal, TheMixer)
end.  {MakeCompounds}
```

↓   ↓   ↓   ↓   ↓

Pick a light metal.
Light Metals are: 1: hydrogen 2: lithium 3: sodium 4: potassium
1
Pick an oxidizer or halogen.
Oxidizers are: 5: oxygen 6: sulfur 7: selenium
Halogens are: 8: fluorine 9: chlorine 10: bromine 11: iodine
6
You have made the compound
hydrogen sulfide with molecular weight 34.07994

:·:

Self-Check   Q. Which of these values could be used in a **case** statement's constant list?
Questions
    a) Time   b) Year **div** 4   c) 5+2
    d) ord ('H')   e) 'B'   f) B
    g) 9   h) −4   i) true

A. The *integer* values 9 and −4 are valid, as is the *char* value ′B′. Answer *i*, *true*, is a *boolean* value, and may also be used. The remaining values—*Time, B, ord* (′H′), *Year* **div** 4, and 5+2—are identifiers or expressions, and may not be used.

Q. Is it possible for this to be a valid expression?

> *InputValue* **in** [−15 .. 25, ′f′ .. ′w′]

A. It couldn't possibly be a good *boolean* expression, because we've tried to define a set that contains two different types of values—*integer*, and *char*. The members of a set, and the value whose membership we're checking, must all belong to the same ordinal type.

:...:

Chapter Notes 6-3

SUPPOSE THAT A PROGRAM JUST WON'T SEEM to compile. Even though every **begin** has a matching **end**, the same compile-time error message keeps showing up:

"END" EXPECTED − − END OF PROGRAM NOT FOUND

> :..:
> :   Make sure your **case** statement ends with an **end**.   :
> :..:

Accidentally misplacing a semicolon within a **case** statement can be a calamity. Can you figure out what caused these error messages?

```
1 :  DOFIRSTTHING;
2 ;  DOSECONDTHING;
     MISSING "BEGIN"
↑UNDECLARED PROCEDURE "2"
↑"2" MAY NOT BE AN IDENTIFIER
```

The '2' is preceded and followed by semicolons—statement separators—so the compiler assumes that it is some kind of statement. However, 2 isn't a procedure call, and is an illegal identifier in any case.

missing **case** *constants*   Run-time errors occur when the **case** expression takes on a value that wasn't included, along with an appropriate action, in the constant list.

ABNORMAL TERMINATION − −
VALUE OF CASE EXPRESSION NOT IN CONSTANT LIST

Although this is an error in Standard Pascal, some implementations of Pascal don't deal so harshly with an unanticipated **case** expression value. They let the expression 'fall through' the **case** statement without causing a crash.

Now, when he designed Pascal, Wirth felt that the constant list was part of the **case** statement's documentation. Letting a program continue operation when the **case** expression had a value *not* specified might be misleading to a program reader. Thus, an unanticipated value was supposed to generate a run-time error to note an unexpected happening.

However, some Pascal implementors took a different view. They thought it was perfectly reasonable to expect the unexpected, and to provide a means of dealing with it less disastrous than a run-time crash. A simple approach was to ignore the offending **case** expression, as described above. Another innovation was the exception clause—a specific 'else' or 'otherwise' action to be taken if the value of the **case** variable could not be found.

case extensions

You should check your own Pascal system, see which philosophy its implementors adhered to, and then make your own decision: Is it better to write an absolutely standard program, sure to run on every system (even though it is very inflexible and prone to crashes), or to write your programs for a friendlier (although nonstandard) environment? Questions like this must usually be answered in every individual case—no hard and fast rules apply.

Let's move on to subranges. Variables should be declared as subrange types whenever practical, *particularly in large programs*. Since this calls for some changes in your programming habits, I'll try to justify the new dictum. Ordinal subranges are desirable for three reasons—self-documentation, program efficiency, and antibugging.

why use subranges?

1. Self-documentation. Knowing the range of values that a variable is going to represent, and saying so at the time of variable declaration, helps demonstrate that you have a firm grasp of what your program does.

documentation

It also helps another person who may be working on your program *get* an idea of appropriate values within a program. The declaration:

> *KilnTemperature*: *integer*;

says nothing, whereas:

> *KilnTemperature*: 400..1200;   {or, better yet...}
> *KilnTemperature*: 400..*MAXIMUMTEMPERATURE*;

is informative. Note that choosing to use the long or shorthand method of creating ordinal subranges is generally optional (except when needed for parameters).

2. Program efficiency. A variable declared to represent only a limited range of values can be dealt with (by the compiler) in a more economical manner than a variable that can represent *any* value of its type.

efficiency

This is really the least important reason. Under certain circumstances, though, a program may require so many variables that limiting the storage they require is a valid programming consideration.

3. Antibugging. Pascal's requirement that variables be of some particular type is a form of antibugging. Restricting the values that a variable may represent to a range of values we know it *should* have extends the protec-

antibugging

tion. We help assure ourselves (and the computer) that any operations we'll try to carry out will make sense.

Real life often places limits on the values that a variable can reasonably represent. A payroll program may 'work', but allow 37 deductions, or −2. A checker-playing program might devote a considerable amount of time looking for the ninth row of a checkerboard. A computer croupier could spin a computer roulette wheel, and decide the ball has landed on number 39—which doesn't exist.

These are all obviously bugs that should, and could, be spotted or prevented by the programmer. The most annoying aspect of bugs, though, is that you don't see them until it's too late. When a program announces that the sum of two and two is five, the programmer knows that something has gone wrong, and takes another look at her code. The results of a more complex program, however, are more likely to be taken for granted—even if some input datum or partial result hidden within the program is totally absurd.

the moral   Subrange types provide a constant check on variables and assure us that they have values appropriate to their application. They help prevent a very dangerous kind of program—one that appears to be reliable, but is not.

Important to Remember

- The **case** expression and values in the **case** constant list must all have the same ordinal Pascal type. The constant list must contain an action for every possible value of the **case** expression. Some implementations may allow a value that isn't in the **case** constant list to 'fall through' without ill effect, but this is a nonstandard extension.

- The constants of an enumerated ordinal type must be distinct. No enumerated type can share the same values.

- Enumerated type constants are considered to belong in the order they're defined in. This is reflected in use of the *pred, succ*, and *ord* functions. The numbering of enumerated ordinal values starts with zero. Subrange values must be in the same order as their underlying type.

- Enumerated ordinal type constants can't be input or output because they have no external character representations.

- Subrange types are useful because they help make programs self-documenting, and incorporate automatic run-time checks on variable values into programs. They may also contribute to efficiency.

- Two variables have the same, identical, type only if they're declared with the same type identifier. A variable parameter and its argument must have identical types. Assignments between two variables of the same, identical type will always be valid.

- Variables or values are compatible, as distinct from identical, if they have the same underlying type. The argument of a value parameter must have a compatible type. Assignments between compatible variables might not be valid, since they might represent (or be allowed to represent) different subranges of the underlying type.

Cross Reference

From the early implementors' point of view, the distinction between identical and compatible types was probably the most vexing in Pascal... and directions back to the discussion of assignment-compatibility on pages A10—A11 are certainly the most frequent cross reference! At any rate...

- The basic concepts of data typing and the simple types are discussed in A95—A100.

- Enumerated types are defined in A97—A99, and subranges continue in A99—A100.

- The fine points of type 'sameness' are discussed in A95—A96. This discussion, as it pertains to compatibility and assignment compatibility, is also found in A10—A11.

- The **case** statement is introduced in A20—A22.

- The **in** operator is introduced in the context of the relational operators in A45—A46. It's defined more explicitly on A124. The construction of simple set expressions is described on A123.

Exercises

6-1   Assume that a deck of cards is numbered 1 through 52. The first thirteen cards are spades, the second thirteen are hearts, the third thirteen are diamonds, and the last thirteen are clubs. Within each suit of thirteen, assume that the numbering corresponds to natural order, ace through king.

Write a program that generates a random number between 1 and 52, then prints the suit and value of the corresponding card. For example, if 16 is the random number, the output should be 3 of hearts. Have it generate and print a five-card hand. Determine either experimentally or mathematically about how long it takes for an illegal hand (one with two identical cards) to be dealt.

6-2   Write a program whose input is a date supplied as a month, day, and year, e.g. **7/29/53**.

1.   Print the day's number within the year, i.e. if the date supplied is **2/3/85**, the output should be be **34**. Don't forget that a leap year occurs every fourth year except if the year is divisible by 100, but not 400.

2.   Read a second date, and then calculate and print the number of days from one to the next (that is, including one but not the other).

6-3   Assuming input as above, write a program that prints the month and day in words. To save some trouble, assume that 1/1/87 (which falls on a Thursday) is the earliest possible day. Proper output for **1/2/87** would be: Friday, January 2, 1987.

6-4   Write a program that reads an *integer* value, then prints the 'word' equivalent. For example, for input **23567**, output should be:

Twenty three thousand five hundred sixty seven

Hint: As an easier warmup, write a program that might drive the electronic voice-box the phone company uses for automated directory assistance. For numbers of arbitrary length, start by by reading the number as a sequence of digits so you'll know its length.

6-5   Write a tiny Polish calculator. We want to be able to enter two numbers and an operand, e.g.:

2.34 5.92 *   or   −1.03 16 /

and have the correct operation performed. In Polish notation, if the input is:

  x   y   operation

where *x* and *y* are values, and *operation* is a single character, the more familiar order of evaluation is:

  x   operation   y

Have your calculator correctly handle +, −, *, /, and the *integer* operations **d** and **m** (for **div** and **mod**).

6-6   Two biology students are carrying out important scientific research on fleas. One student's job is to motivate the flea to jump (through use of a little electric flea prod), while the other student keeps tabs on its travel. The second student, unable to bear the sight of the suffering flea, resolves to write a program that will take over her job.

Write a program that tracks the flea as it hops around. Start at the origin *x, y* = (0,0) and print the current position after each hop. Each input should consist of a distance, and a direction. For example, input **2.3 nw** would mean 'move 2.3 units northwest.' The allowed directions should be:

  n   nw   w   sw   s   se   e   ne

6-7   Write a program that accepts an input *integer* and prints the correct representation in Roman Numeral form. Can you do the reverse as well?

6-8   Suppose that our universe contained just four fruits—say, lemons, oranges, watermelons, and bananas. Aside from making fruit salad rather dull, we would find that just two different questions—Is it round? Is it yellow?—could be used to determine a fruit uniquely.

However, not all questions have just two answers. Consider the questions that might describe an animal:

  diet = carnivorous, vegetarian, omnivorous
  size = humungous, regular, tiny
  hair = long, short, none

and so on. We will find that twenty-seven different animals can be uniquely identified through just three different questions. Write a program that does so. Please send your answer to the author.

6-9   A chessboard is empty except for a solitary white piece defined by a letter:

  p = pawn
  n = knight
  r = rook
  b = bishop
  q = queen
  k = king

Assume we number the board from 1 to 64 *lexicographically*, so that square 1 is at upper left and square 64 is at lower right, with numbers running as you read a printed page.

Write a program that asks for a piece's name and location, then prints a list of squares the piece may legally occupy on its next move. Assume, incidentally, that a pawn starts out on the row numbered 9 through 16.

6-10   A graphic artist taking her first computer class becomes convinced that the value π, $3.14159\ldots$, is really a secret code that describes a great work of art. She believes that each digit describes a different shade of gray, where 0 is blank and 9 is dark gray.

Unfortunately, even though she is sure that π has this wonderful property, she is uncertain as to how long each line of the picture is; i.e. how many digits 'wide' the picture is. Write a program that lets her try out different theories by entering a particular line length. Use a **case** statement to associate characters of progressively greater darkness or density with each digit (1 might be '.', while 9 is '#'.)

6-11   A mischievous bartender likes to fool her more tipsy customers by pouring drinks containing two different liquors, in equal quantities, into the serving glass.

Write a program that asks for two liquors from the list below, then prints the alcoholic content of the mixed drink. Assume that:

beer	4% alcohol
ale	7% alcohol
wine	12% alcohol
bourbon	40% alcohol
scotch	60% alcohol
rum	77% alcohol

The bartender is not exactly sober herself, so allow for the possibility that the two liquors be the same.

6-12   Even in this day of microchips, most people have seen component resistors. A simple resistor has three colored bands that code its resistance in ohms. The colors are:

0	black	5	green
1	brown	6	blue
2	red	7	violet
3	orange	8	gray
4	yellow	9	white

The formula for computing resistance is:

$$\text{Resistance in ohms} = (10(\text{1st band}) + (\text{2nd band})) \times 10^{\text{3rd band}}$$

For example, the coloring red, violet, yellow, on a resistor means that its resistance is 27×10^4, or 270,000 ohms. Write a program that lets you supply the first few letters of each of three colors (one per line), then tells you the correct resistance. If a color is ambiguous (e.g. only the letters **bl** were entered) print an error message.

6-13   The quadrants of a two-dimensional space—like a Cartesian coordinate system—are usually numbered I, II, III, IV, or just referred to as the 'upper left,' or 'lower right' quadrant.

The octants of three dimensional space can be dealt with in the same way, once an additional dimension—say, 'near' and 'far'—has been defined. Write a program that reads the x,y,z coordinates of a point in three-dimensional space, then by using a *sign* function:

$$sign(u) = -1 \text{ if } u < 0, \ 1 \text{ if } u > 0, \ 0 \text{ if } u = 0$$

and a **case** statement that involves the expression:

$$sign(x) + 2*sign(y) + 4*sign(z)$$

print an appropriate message, along the lines of The point lies in the far upper right octant. Be sure to print a special message if there is ambiguity as to octant, which happens if any coordinate is zero.

6-14   Return with me once again to New Mathico, where the moon sets on the y-axis, and most everything can be described by an equation.

As you know, New Mathico has various terrains, like the $f(x)=c$ Plains, the $\sin^2(x)$ Foothills, and the $\dfrac{2}{\pi}\sum\limits_{n=1}^{\infty}\dfrac{-1^{n+1}}{n}\sin\left[\dfrac{n\pi x}{L}\right]$ Range, better known as the Sawtooth Mountains. Not every horse runs equally well under all conditions; thus, the stable has the following sign posted prominently:

> New Mathico Stables / Traveling Speeds
> Plains: Pierre = Blaise = Rene / 2 = 3
> Foothills: Pierre^2 = Blaise = 4 × Rene = 4
> Mountains: e × Pierre = π × Blaise = $\sqrt{10}$ × Rene = 5

As you might imagine, figuring out what horse to take on any given day confuses even the most grizzled cowhands. Write a program that accepts as input the distance to be traveled over each terrain, and prints the name of the horse that will cover the entire distance most quickly. Hint: You will find that **case** statements come in handy for a travel-time function and a name-printing procedure.

6-15   Consider the scene in a closed-room, secret design session for the 1989 model of a big-name Detroit automobile. All around the conference table are engineers and executives trying to strike a balance between greed (which leads them to build the cheapest car possible) and fear (which pulls in the other direction, toward more reliable machines).

Now, the relation between the mean time between failures (MTBF) of a system and its subsystems can be described as:

$$\frac{1}{MTBF_{Total}} = \frac{1}{MTBF_{Sub1}} + \frac{1}{MTBF_{Sub2}} + \cdots + \frac{1}{MTBF_{Subn}}$$

and is correct if the failure of any subsystem dooms the entire car.

Suppose that the costs and MTBF's of various subsystems are:

Subsystem		MTBF	Manufacturing Cost
brakes	disc	4 years	$15.00
	drum	5 years	$25.00
engine	Wankel	3 years	$1,067.00
	conventional	6 years	$1,850.00
suspension	air	9 years	$430.00
	oil	7 years	$320.00
electrical	computer	2 years	$130.00
	standard	4 years	$40.00

Write a program that models each combination of subsystems (a quadruply-nested **for** loop will do nicely), and answers these questions:

1.   Which system is the cheapest?

2.   Which has the longest mean time between failures?

3.   Which system has the lowest cost per failure-free year?

Hint: Since an enumerated type value can't be printed directly, use a **case** statement to print its character equivalent.

6-16   The word *therein* is interesting because at least eleven words can be 'cut' from it without rearranging any letters—*the, here, in*, and so on.

Suppose we label the letters from 1 through 7. It turns out that a triply-nested **for** loop (calling on a **case** statement for actual printing) can be used to generate every possible subsequence of the letters in the word. How? What are the words?

6-17   There are twenty amino acids, and each one has one-letter and three-letter abbreviations. They are:

Alanine	Ala	A	Lysine	Lys	K
Arginine	Arg	R	Methionine	Met	M
Asparagine	Asn	N	Phenylalanine	Phe	F
Aspartic acid	Asp	D	Proline	Pro	P
Cysteine	Cys	C	Serine	Ser	S
Glutamine	Gln	Q	Threonine	Thr	T
Glutamic acid	Glu	E	Tryptophan	Trp	W
Glycene	Gly	G	Tyrosine	Tyr	Y
Histidine	His	H	Valine	Val	V
Isoleucine	Ile	I	Asn and/or Asp	Asx	B
Leucine	Leu	L	Gln and/or Glu	Glx	Z

1. Write a program that translates a sequence of proteins (supplied as a series of one-letter abbreviations) into the proper amino acids. Let the space character indicate a missing acid.

2. Write a program that uses nested **case** statements to translate three-letter abbreviations into either one-letter abbreviations, or the amino acids' full names.

As data, you might want to use these sequences, which give the first forty amino acids for human alpha hemoglobin and myoglobin:

alpha hemoglobin = **V LSPADKTNVKAAWGKVGAHAGEYGAEALERMFLSFPTT**
myoglobin = **G LSNGZWE VLNVWGKVEPNIAGHGEEVLIRLFKGHPET**

6-18   Suppose that we've made these definitions and declarations:

> **type** *Rainbow* = (*Infrared, Red, Orange, Yellow, Green, Blue, Violet, Ultraviolet*);
> *Spectrum* = *Infrared..Blue*;
> **var** *HotColors*: *Infrared..Green*;
> *Colors*: *Rainbow*;
> *CoolColors*: *Yellow..Ultraviolet*;

a) Which variables could be arguments to value parameters of type *Rainbow*?
b) Which variables could be arguments to value parameters of type *Spectrum*?
c) Which variables could be arguments to variable parameters of type *Spectrum*?
d) Which variables could be arguments to this value parameter:

> **procedure** *AnyProcedure* (*Hue*: *Infrared..Ultraviolet*);

7

The **array**
Type

They say that a topologist finds a doughnut and a coffee cup identical because each has the shape of a torus. I can just as reasonably describe a computer scientist as the sort of person who doesn't distinguish between a checkerboard and a topographical map—after all, each can be described with an array.

Chapter 7 officially introduces array-typed variables, although you should also read section 3-2 for a discussion of vector and matrix operations. My main focus will be on the close relationship between a program's data *types*, its data *structures*, and its algorithm. In the process, I'll consider a variety of specific methods for counting, searching, and string ('word' variable) manipulation. I'll close with a long program that will let you extend Pascal's ability to do multiplication. After reading Chapter 7, you may wish to check out section 16-2 for a discussion of recursive array programming techniques. Chapter 17 continues the discussion of searching.

Defining Array Types 7-1

STRUCTURED VARIABLE TYPES CAN STORE and represent one or more values that are simple, or are structured themselves. Structured types are defined along with ordinal types in a program's (or subprogram's) type definition part. The definition of an array-structured type tells the compiler three things:

elements, bounds, dimensions

1. What is the type of the array's *elements*—its stored values?

2. What is the array's *size*—how many elements will the array hold?

3. What are the array's exact *dimensions*—in what order will the elements be stored, and how will we refer to individual elements?

As with enumerated and subrange type definitions, the reserved word **type** always opens the type definition part. In outline form the definition and declaration of an array look like this:

array syntax

> **type** *array-type identifier* = **array** [*dimensions*] **of** *element-type identifier*;
>
> **var** *ArrayVariable identifier*: *array-type identifier*;

The syntax chart of an array type definition is given below. The significance of **packed** will be discussed when we deal with string types in a few pages.

array type

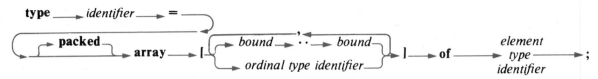

subscripts

Since an array variable holds more than one value, a *subscript* identifies the particular element that we want to access or modify:

ArrayVariable [*Subscript*] := *AnotherArray* [*AnotherSubscript*];

problem: statistical
smoothing

Two brief examples drawn from statistics will help illustrate the basic array ideas. First, consider *smoothing*, an averaging technique in which data points are influenced by neighboring values. Smoothed data is often used in financial computing to provide a 'moving average'—smoothing helps reduce daily aberations that might obscure longer-term trends. Thus, it's useful as a means of minimizing the effect of either incorrect or needlessly precise data. In pseudocode:

refinement

> **for** *each value*
>   *read it, and store it as an array element*;
> **for** *each element of the array*
>   *average its value with its neighbors' values*;
> **for** *each element of the array*
>   *print its stored value*;

Program *Smoother* smooths a year's worth of monthly data, stored in a twelve-element array of *real*. Note that the shaded loop, which computes the subscripts of the surrounding elements, is careful not to access *Year* [0] and *Year* [13], since they don't exist.

> Out-of-bound array references cannot, in general, be detected at compile-time. Any reference to an element whose subscript is outside the array's bounds will cause a program crash.

After reading *Smoother*, below, you might take a minute to figure out how to develop a procedure that would let the user specify a period longer than three months for the moving average.

program *Smoother* (*input*, *output*) ;
    {Compute three-month moving averages for a year's data.}
type *Monthly* = **array** [1..12] **of** *real* ;
var *Year* : *Monthly* ;
    i : *integer* ;

data smoothing
program·

begin
    writeln ('Please enter 12 monthly data points.') ;
    for *i* := 1 **to** 12 **do**   {get the data}
      read (*Year* [*i*]) ;
    for *i* := 2 **to** 11 **do**   {compute the averages}
      Year [*i*] := (*Year* [*i* −1] + *Year* [*i*] + *Year* [*i* +1]) / 3 ;
    writeln ('The three-month moving average is:') ;
    for *i* := 1 **to** 12 **do**   {print the results}
      write (*Year* [*i*]:4:1, ' ') ;
    writeln
end. {*Smoother*}

⬇   ⬇   ⬇   ⬇   ⬇

Please enter 12 monthly data points.
22.0 39.2 84.6 41.9 30.7 35.3 28.1 19.7 41.8 25.0 11.6 8.4
The three-month moving average is:
22.0 48.6 58.4 43.7 36.6 33.3 27.0 29.5 32.1 22.9 14.3   8.4

computing standard
deviation

A second example finds the mean and standard deviation of a similar array of data. Procedure *StatPak*, below, relies on the existance of a named type *Monthly* to allow the definition of the value parameter *Data*. We compute standard deviation according to the formula:

$$\text{standard deviation} = \sqrt{\frac{\sum_{i=1}^{n}(X_i - \bar{X})^2}{n-1}}, \quad \text{where } \bar{X} = \text{mean} = \frac{\sum_{i=1}^{n} X_i}{n}$$

procedure *StatPak* (*Data* : *Monthly* ; **var** *Mean*, *Deviation* : *real*) ;
    {Returns the mean and deviation of a *Monthly* -type array, as defined in *Smoother* .}
var *i* : *integer* ;
    Sum : *real* ;

standard deviation
procedure

begin
    Sum := 0.0 ;
    for *i* := 1 **to** 12 **do** {compute the mean}
      Sum := *Sum* + *Data* [*i*] ;
    Mean := *Sum* / 12 ;
    Sum := 0.0 ;
    for *i* := 1 **to** 12 **do** {compute the standard deviation}
      Sum := *Sum* + *sqr* (*Data* [*i*] − *Mean*) ;
    Deviation := *sqrt* (*Sum* / (12−1))
end ; {*StatPak*}

**Extending
Array
Definitions**

array bounds

Let's return to a more formal description of Pascal arrays. The array type *Monthly* had only one pair of *array bounds*, or limits, and was thus *one dimensional*. However, multidimensional arrays can be created by giving additional pairs of bounds, separated by commas. The bound values themselves must belong to an ordinal type (*real* is proscribed), and are often supplied as user-defined constants. Bound pairs are separated by two dots (..) that have the usual Pascal meaning of 'through and including.' The array type definition is completed by naming the ordinal, *real*, subrange, or structured type of its elements.

```
const LASTROW = 'Z';
      MAXIMUM = 20;
```

*sample array
definitions*

```
type Vegetables = (Leeks, Yams, Spuds, Okra, Artichokes);
     GroceryOrder = array [Leeks..Artichokes] of integer;
     DailyHelpings = array [Monday..Sunday, Leeks..Artichokes] of integer;
     ServingCosts = array ['A'..LASTROW,
                               1..MAXIMUM, Leeks..Artichokes] of real;
     SquareStatus = (Black, White, Empty);
     CheckerBoard = array [1..8, 1..8] of SquareStatus;
     FunnyCheckers = array [1..8, 1..8] of Vegetables;
```

The ability to make these wild combinations is one of the features that really characterizes Pascal, in contrast to older languages. Notice that the values of enumerated ordinal types can serve as array bounds.

*bounds must be
known values*

> However, bounds may *not* be supplied as variable identifiers, or other expressions that would have to be evaluated at run-time.

Thus, the size of an array is fixed when the array type is defined—before compilation. For convenience, an ordinal or subrange type identifier (except *integer*) can take the place of specific array bounds. The dimension thus stated has bounds equal to the first and last members of the type. This is especially handy for defining an array whose bounds are the first and last characters—very machine dependent—that is, nevertheless, still portable:

*type identifier as
bound*

```
type CharacterCount = array [char] of integer;
```

*assignment between
arrays*

Assignments can be made between two array variables with *identical* types. In effect, all corresponding elements are assigned simultaneously, so this method is frequently used to initialize arrays. A subtle point first made in the discussion of subrange types applies, though. In Pascal, two variables have identical types only if they're declared with the same type identifier. Two array-type variables that are exactly alike in every detail *except type name* are not identical, and one cannot be assigned to the other. Thus, these two definitions are equivalent from the viewpoint of data storage, but they define entirely different variable types for purposes of assignment:

$$\textbf{type } \textit{NumberOfHelpings1} = \textbf{array } [\textit{Tart..Mousse}] \textbf{ of } \textit{integer};$$
$$\textit{NumberOfHelpings2} = \textbf{array } [\textit{Desserts}] \textbf{ of } \textit{integer};$$

array subscripts

    As we've seen, individual elements are stored and retrieved by their location, given with subscript expressions. Naturally, each subscript must refer to a location that's within the array bounds, since the subscript of a non-existent location will cause an immediate program crash. If more than one subscript is required (for multi-dimensional arrays), separate the subscripts with commas.

random access

> Subscripts make the array a *random access* type, because we can immediately access any of its elements.

    It's crucial to make sure that subscripts are in the proper order. At best, misordered subscripts can cause compile or run-time errors (if they precipitate type or range problems), which is bad enough. However, experience will show you that an array reference whose subscripts are misorderd, but still legal, creates a bug that is quite difficult to track down.

    Extended array definitions can be complicated and confusing, but most ornate type definitions are built up step-by-step. As an example, let's follow the development of an array used to hold inventory figures. In its simplest expression, we are told of a store that contains a row of bins or cubbyholes, numbered 1 through 10, each filled with some amount of stock.

the inventory problem

$$\textbf{type } \textit{Inventory} = \textbf{array } [1..10] \textbf{ of } \textit{integer};$$
$$\textbf{var } \textit{Stock}: \textit{Inventory};$$

As sales or stock figures come in we can update the inventory, perhaps to show a sale of five units of item 3:

$$\textit{Stock}[3] := \textit{Stock}[3]-5; \quad \{\text{subtract 5 from } \textit{Stock}[3]\}$$

    Now, this system might be satisfactory if we were FORTRAN programmers in 1956, but we can do better with Pascal. As a first improvement, I'll use an enumerated type to name the inventoried products.

a better type definition

$$\textbf{type } \textit{Style} = (\textit{Flares, StraightLeg, BellBottom, BootCut, Leisure, Chinos});$$
$$\textit{Inventory} = \textbf{array } [\textit{Flares..Chinos}] \textbf{ of } \textit{integer};$$
$$\textbf{var } \textit{Stock}: \textit{Inventory};$$

    This change moves us rapidly into the '60s or '70s. But although our data type lets us name styles of pants, it hardly reflects the real world. For one thing, pants come in different waist sizes as well as styles. We need a second array dimension:

expanded definition

$$\textbf{type } \textit{Style} = (\textit{Flares, StraightLeg, BellBottom, BootCut, Leisure, Chinos});$$
$$\textit{WaistSize} = 25..48;$$
$$\textit{Inventory} = \textbf{array } [\textit{Flares..Chinos, 25..48}] \textbf{ of } \textit{integer};$$
$$\textbf{var } \textit{Stock}: \textit{Inventory};$$

Can the type definition be brought into the 80's? Yes—there is no reason to force a user to tailor her requirements to a programmer's convenience. Pants come in different lengths, and are manufactured from a variety of materials. I'll declare new types *Length* and *Material*, and add another two dimensions to the array.

further expansion of the definition

```
type Style = (Flares, StraightLeg, BellBottom, BootCut, Leisure, Chinos);
     WaistSize = 25..48;
     Length = (Short, Medium, Long);
     Material = (Denim, Corduroy, Polyester, Cotton);
     Inventory = array [Flares..Chinos, 25..48,
                        Short..Long, Denim..Cotton] of integer;
var Stock: Inventory;
```

abstracting information

Now, declaring third and fourth dimensions for the *Stock* variable was an important conceptual step. We're storing information about pants in the way we *perceive* it, instead of trying to mimic the appearance of pants on a shelf. A one-dimensional array is close to the original row of cubbyholes, but a four-dimensional better approximates the way we *think* about inventory. A four-dimensional show room cannot be constructed on a sales floor, but a type definition creates one within the computer. Finding the stock of boot-cut pants, size 34 medium, made of denim, requires a single statement:

```
writeln (Stock [BootCut, 34, Medium, Denim]);
```

We can quickly devise a function that represents the number of pairs of pants in all lengths and sizes, but of a particular style and material. Function *CountStyles*, below, travels through the array varying two subscripts (for the lengths and sizes) and keeping two subscripts (for the style and material) constant.

summing array elements

```
function CountStyles (TheStyle: Style; TheMaterial: Material;
                                       Stock: Inventory): integer;
   {Sums array elements.}
   var CurrentLength: Length;
       TotalCount: integer;
       CurrentSize: WaistSize;
   begin
      TotalCount := 0;
      for CurrentLength := Short to Long do
         for CurrentSize := 25 to 48 do
            TotalCount := TotalCount +
                   Stock [TheStyle, CurrentSize, CurrentLength, TheMaterial];
      CountStyles := TotalCount
   end; {CountStyles}
```

A program might include the statement:

> **if** *CountStyles* (*BootCut, Denim, Stock*)<(*OriginalOrder–ExpectedSales*) **then**
> *writeln* ('Sales of boot cut Denim pants are above expectations.') ;

I've discussed inventory for several pages without ever mentioning an algorithm. Nonetheless, as a problem it is substantially solved because of my choice of data type. Any operation I'm liable to want a program to perform— adding or diminishing stock, analyzing merchandise on hand, projecting sales or supplies—is easy to accomplish because of the four-dimensional array I've used to structure the data.

Focus on Data Structures

Indeed, this insight will change our programming focus entirely. Consider this equation, taken from the title of one of Niklaus Wirth's textbooks:

Algorithms + Data Structures = Programs

An algorithm is the sequence of steps a program takes; a data structure is a set of rules for storing and manipulating data. A program's algorithm relies on the statements a programming language allows, while its data structures are founded on the data types built into the language.

For six chapters, I've taken a lopsided view of Wirth's equation by concentrating on algorithms and the control of program actions. From now on, though, we'll devote more time to thinking about data type definitions, and their implications for data structures. I have three reasons:

1.   Many real-life programming problems don't really need to be solved, in the sense of finding unknown answers. Their difficulty lies in *implementation*—defining appropriate data types, and using them with comparatively simple arithmetic or input and output routines.

importance of data structures

2.   As the equation given above implies, there can be a trade-off between the complexity of an algorithm, and the data structures it uses. A sophisticated type definition can minimize the length and difficulty of a final program.

3.   The character of an entire program can be changed by slight modifications of a data structure. Thus, data type definitions are more important than their size in a program listing implies.

An algorithm that compensates for a too-simple data structure can become unnecessarily complex and detailed. This is one basis of objections to languages like BASIC and FORTRAN. Although their control statements are comparable to Pascal's, their general lack of abstract data types (they only have arrays) forces programmers to waste time explaining data in terms the language can handle.

In the remainder of this chapter we'll look at several kinds of problems that require array-based data structures. As you read, notice how algorithms and data structure designs take advantage of different array features—random access, the ability to store different types of values, the ease with which all array elements can be visited, different applications of subscripts, etc.

A first example investigates an interesting conjecture from number theory—that all perfect squares (and only perfect squares) have an odd number of divisors. Were we French majors eager to impress we'd probably demonstrate this with some impenetrable sequence of lemmas and theorems, but I think that (as computer scientists) we can find an elegant way to restate and solve the problem. Let me evoke a data structure often associated with arrays—an ordered row of bins or lockers.

problem: monitors and lockers

Imagine that a high-school hallway contains a long row of lockers, all closed, with one for each student. To teach civic responsibility, the school administration assigns each student in turn to hall monitor duty, charged with collaring truants, class-cutters, and the like.

To keep the monitors from getting into trouble themselves, the administration gives them this extra job: Each of the n monitors must go down the row of lockers, stopping at every nth locker. If it is open, it should be closed, and if it is closed, the locker should be opened. Write a program that simulates the activity of the monitors, then tells us which lockers remain open.

Thus, the first monitor opens every locker door. The second monitor closes the second, fourth, sixth, and so on. The third monitor closes the third, opens the sixth, closes the ninth, etc. Every door that has been visited an even number of times will be left open at the end of the exercise, and vice versa. Note that an array is not *required* to solve this problem. Nevertheless, the fanciful data structure I've presented (a row of lockers whose doors regularly open and close) is easily implemented with a one-dimensional array type.

At first glance the algorithm would seem to have something to do with prime numbers, and we'll see, in Chapter 10, a very similar example that actually does. A pseudocode description of each monitor's job is:

first refinement

> **for** *each of the lockers*
>   **if** *it's a locker she should deal with* **then**
>   *open or close the locker as appropriate* ;

With little thought, it won't be hard to write the **for** loop in a manner that avoids stopping at the in-between lockers the monitor doesn't worry about. A second refinement accounts for all of the monitors:

second refinement

> *initialize all the lockers* ;
> **for** *each of the hall monitors*
>   **for** *each of the lockers*
>   **if** *it's a locker she should deal with* **then**
>   *open or close the locker as appropriate* ;
>   *report on the results* ;

How shall we *report on the results*? Using an array to represent the series of lockers was an obvious choice of data type. But an array of what? *integer*? *boolean*? Why not use state variables as we did in the billiard table simulation of Chapter 4, and chemistry problem of Chapter 6, by defining a type whose values are *open* and *closed*?

the type definition

> **type** *State* = (*open, closed*);
> *LockerType* = **array** [1..*NUMBEROFLOCKERS*] **of** *State*;

The completed program is shown below. Does its output support the original conjecture about a number's divisors?

monitors and lockers program

```
program Lockers (input, output);
{Models the opening and closing of a series of NUMBEROFLOCKERS doors.}
const NUMBEROFLOCKERS = 400;
type State = (open, closed);
     LockerType = array [1..NUMBEROFLOCKERS] of State;
var Locker: LockerType;
    Counter, Monitor, LockerNumber: integer;
begin
    for Counter := 1 to NUMBEROFLOCKERS do
        Locker [Counter] := closed;  {Initialize the array of lockers.}
    for Monitor := 1 to NUMBEROFLOCKERS do
        for Counter := 1 to NUMBEROFLOCKERS div Monitor do begin
            LockerNumber := Monitor * Counter;  {Stop at every Nth locker...}
            if Locker [LockerNumber] = closed
                then Locker [LockerNumber] := open  {...and change its current state.}
                else Locker [LockerNumber] := closed
        end;
    writeln ('The lockers that remain open are: ');
    for Counter := 1 to NUMBEROFLOCKERS do
        if Locker [Counter] = open then
            write (Counter:1, ' ');
    writeln
end.  {Lockers}
```

↓   ↓   ↓   ↓   ↓

The lockers that remain open are:
1 4 9 16 25 36 49 64 81 100 121 144 169 196 225 256 289 324 361 400

Counting

The grunt work of counting and tabulating values is an application that often relies on arrays. I'll begin with a counting problem that's interesting because of the role subscripts play.

problem: count characters

Count the number of characters in a text sample. Print a table of the frequency of the lower-case letters.

An analysis like this is usually the first step in code-breaking programs. A starting pseudocode might be:

refinement

initialize counts;
while *there are characters to count*
    count each character;
    keep a running total;
for *every lower-case letter*
    print its relative frequency (*count/total*);

How can we use arrays to our advantage here? The last part of the pseudocode gives us a hint. Suppose that we had an array that stored *integers*, but used characters as its index values. We could initialize the array to zeros, then store the number of times 'a' appeared in *CountArray* ['a'], the number of times 'b' showed up in *CountArray* ['b'], etc. Each time we read a *Character*, we increment *CountArray* [*Character*] by one. Printing the count is just a matter of traversing the 'a'..'z' segment of the array.

Here's a type definition that will let us implement the pseudocode cleanly and easily:

type definition

type *CharacterArray* = **array** [*char*] **of** *integer*;

This creates an array type whose bounds are the first and last *char* values, whose elements are *integers*, and whose subscripts are the individual characters. With it, we can use the array element subscripted by a character to store the number of times that character appears as input. In program *CountTheCharacters*, on the next page, I've assumed the ASCII set of 128 characters.

```
      program CountTheCharacters (input, output);
        {Count input characters, print relative frequency of lower-case letters.}
      const NUMBEROFCHARACTERS = 128;
      type CharacterArray = array [char] of integer;
      var CountArray: CharacterArray;
        Character: char;
        Letters,                    {Letters counts lower-case letters.}
        Lines: integer;             {Lines counts lines for producing neat output.}
      begin
        for Character := chr (0) to chr (NUMBEROFCHARACTERS –1) do
          CountArray [Character] := 0;   {Initialize the array.}
        Letters := 0;
        while not eof do begin  {Count all the character frequencies.}
          read (Character);
          if Character in ['a'..'z'] then Letters := Letters +1;
          CountArray [Character] := CountArray [Character] +1
        end;  {while}
        Lines := 1;
        for Character := 'a' to 'z' do begin  {Print the output table.}
          write (Character, ' =');
          write ((CountArray [Character] / Letters)*100:6:2, '%    ');
          if (Lines mod  5) = 0 then writeln;
          Lines := Lines +1  {New-line every fifth write.}
        end;  {for}
        writeln
      end.  {CountTheCharacters}
```

character counting
program

I had *CountTheCharacters* analyze its own listing, and got this result:

a = 9.39%	b = 0.66%	c = 4.94%	d = 1.48%	e = 13.84%
f = 2.14%	g = 1.15%	h = 4.94%	i = 5.60%	j = 0.00%
k = 0.00%	l = 2.47%	m = 0.33%	n = 7.08%	o = 5.44%
p = 1.48%	q = 0.33%	r = 14.17%	s = 3.95%	t = 12.36%
u = 3.62%	v = 0.49%	w = 1.65%	x = 0.00%	y = 1.98%
z = 0.49%				

Chi-square Testing

Data collected in this manner can be put to some interesting applications. For example, the frequency with which letters appear—or better yet, of pairs or triples of letters—provides a characteristic 'signature' of a language that can be precise enough to allow probabilistic checks of spelling. More sophisticated frequency counts (say, of words) can be used to characterize an individual author's work, and help authenticate works of uncertain origin.

A numerical equivalent of these machinations involves seeking the mathematical signature of a sequence of numbers. The most intensively analysed sequences, by far, are those intended to produce random numbers. The random 'signature' is notoriously hard to define but, like some other hard-to-define qualities, we know it when see it. Which of these sequences of digits would you say is most random?

0000000000   0123456789   8971380146

The leftmost sequence hardly seems random at all—only one digit is represented. The center sequence has every digit, but it seems unrealistically neat. The right-hand sequence, oddly, comes off as the best bet, even though it's missing 2 and 5, and contains some regular clusters (89 and 01, 13 and 46).

Apparently, then, a balance between uniformity and irregularity is needed to confirm our intuitive notion of randomness. A statistical method used to authenticate this intuition is called the *chi-square* test. Assume that we have N outcomes of independent trials, observe O instances of a particular outcome i, yet expect E instances by a perfect distribution:

$$\chi \; square \; = \; X^2 \; = \; \sum_{i=1}^{N} \frac{(O_i - E_i)^2}{E_i}$$

In effect, the chi-square test measures the 'goodnes of fit' between prediction and observation. Tables of chi-square outcomes are arranged to show the likelihood of any particular result; a fit that is either too good *or* too bad will suffice to invalidate an outcome.

But I digress. Think back to the random number generator I declared in Chapter 5. We can use the chi-square test to investigate the randomness of its output in the following manner. Suppose that we generate single-digit numbers 0 through 9, then use pairs to form two-digit numbers. A two-dimensional array that is quite like the character-counting array of *CountTheCharacters* can keep track of the pairs:

type *NumberArray* = **array** [0..9, 0..9] **of** *integer*;

The number of observations is stored at each array intersection. Program *CountThePairs*, below, shows these counts, and reports the chi-square statistic, for 1,000 trials. Note the necessary use, in the shaded loop, of the temporary variables *a* and *b* to hold the array subscripts.

For the purposes of this sort of test, incidentally, a chi-square figure that equals the number of possible alternate outcomes, plus or minus the square root of twice that number (i.e. 99±14) can be considered reasonable. This figure should not decline with increasing sample size. If you have any interest in statistics or random numbers, you might want to consider what the result would be if the observed outcomes were too regular? Too irregular? You may want to copy this program and run it for a much larger sample. Does the chi-square figure decline? Why? What does this say about the true randomness of our linear congruential random number generator?

```
program ChiSquare (input, output);
    {Test the 'randomness' of function RandomInteger.}
const TRIALS = 1000;
type NumberArray = array [0..9, 0..9] of integer;
var Table: NumberArray;
    i,j,a,b: integer;
    Seed: integer;
    ChiSquare: real;
function RandomInteger (var Seed: integer): integer;
    {Generates a pseudo-random integer from 0 through UPPERLIMIT-1.}
    const MODULUS = 65536;
          MULTIPLIER = 25173;
          INCREMENT = 13849;
          UPPERLIMIT = 10;
    begin
        Seed := ((MULTIPLIER*Seed)+INCREMENT) mod MODULUS;
        RandomInteger := trunc (UPPERLIMIT* (Seed / MODULUS))
    end; {RandomInteger}
begin
    Seed := 99; {any number will do}
    for i := 0 to 9 do  {initialize the table}
        for j := 0 to 9 do
            Table [i,j] := 0;
    for i := 1 to TRIALS do begin
        a := RandomInteger (Seed);       {Why must we save the subscripts?}
        b := RandomInteger (Seed);
        Table [a,b] := Table [a,b] + 1
    end;
    ChiSquare := 0.0;
    writeln ('The outcome of ', TRIALS:1, ' trials is:');
    for i := 0 to 9 do begin  {print the table and compute chi-square}
        for j := 0 to 9 do begin
            write (Table [i,j]:4);
            ChiSquare := ChiSquare + (sqr (Table [i,j] – 10) / 10)
        end;
        writeln
    end;
    writeln ('Chi-square result is:   ', ChiSquare:5:2)
end. {ChiSquare}
```

randomness-testing
program

↓   ↓   ↓   ↓   ↓

The outcome of 1000 trials is:

```
13  17  13  13  11   7  14   7   9  10
11  11   6   9  15   7  10  12   7   9
14   7  14   8  10  12   7  10  11  10
11  11   9   8   8  11  10   5  15   6
11   8   8  11   5  11   9  14   7   8
12  11   6  14  13  19  10   7   6  13
18   7  11   9   9  10   9  10   9   7
14  11   7  14   9  16   8   8   7   8
 3  12   7   6  11  12  10  13   6   8
14  10  10   9   7   9  11   8  16   6
```

Chi-square result is: 92.60

Searching

If counting things is a major theme of programming, then searching for them is certainly one of the primary minor chords. Let's consider some of the standard techniques used in searching through arrays. For all examples, I'll use this definition:

basic definitions

```
type NumberArray = array [1..20] of integer;
var Numbers: NumberArray;
```

Our first searches will assume arrays that are *unordered*. Later, we'll see a variety of methods that can be used if we know that an array's values are in numerical or alphabetical order. Here's the first problem:

problem: find the
very first 7

Find the position of the first 7 stored in *Numbers*.

Once we've found the 7 we can stop searching. Our code, then, would seem to have a simple exit condition—we search *Current* elements, one by one, until *Numbers* [*Current*] equals 7. But what if no 7 is found? The *boolean* exit condition has to be a bit more complicated, as we see below. It's followed by an **if** statement that establishes exactly our reason for leaving the loop.

```
Found := false;
Current := 0;
while (Current < 20) and not Found do begin
    Current := Current + 1;
    Found := Numbers [Current] = 7
end;
if Found then
    writeln ('The 7 was in position', Current);
```

Let me change the problem slightly:

problem: find the
very last 7

Find the position of the last 7 stored in *Numbers*.

This change requires a different strategy, since we'll have to search the entire array. A **for** loop does the trick:

```
Position := 0;
for Current := 1 to 20 do
    if Numbers[Current] = 7 then
        Position := Current;
if Position <> 0 then
    writeln ('The last 7 was in position', Position);
```

Indeed, a clever reader might point out that we could have just started at the right end of the array! In any case . . .

When a list is unordered, inspection of each element from one end to the other is the only sure strategy for finding a value. However, when a list is ordered, there are many more effective approaches.

problem: is the value
present?

Suppose that *Numbers* is an ordered array of *integer* values. Is some given value stored in the array?

I'll write three different solutions to this simply stated problem. First, I'll encode a *linear search* that is similar to our search for the 7.

refinement

> **while** *we haven't seen a larger value*
> *move on to the next larger element*;

When you read the code below, decide what the value of *Location* is if the value *isn't* found.

a linear search
procedure

```
procedure Linear  (Value: integer; Numbers: NumberArray;
                                    var Position: integer);
    {Linear search for Value. Position will be 0 if it's not found.}
    var Location: integer;
        Located: boolean;
begin
    Location := 1;
    Located := false;
    while (Location < 20) and not Located do
        if Numbers[Location] >= Value
            then Located := true
            else Location := Location + 1;
    Located := Numbers[Location] = Value;
    if not Located then Position := 0
end; {Linear}
```

Note that this search can be simplified considerably if we're sure that the number we're looking for is actually present. A common solution is to store the sought number in the last element of the array; in effect, as a sentinel. If you plan on using this method, define the original array with one extra element from the beginning. Then, dispense with the auxiliary *boolean* variable, and simply search until you find the sentinel value.

using a sentinel

quadratic search

Now, the linear search we just used worked its way toward the sought value one element at a time. It's not hard to imagine that we could find the value a bit faster if we could take larger jumps. This is the basis of the *quadratic search* algorithm:

refinement

> *pick a good jump size*;
> **while** *the next jump won't take us too far*
>   *take the next jump*;
> **while** *single steps don't take us too far*
>   *implement an ordinary linear search*;
> *save the position if we've found the value*;

The square root of the total length of the array turns out to be a convenient size for the big jumps (hence the name of the search—quadratic means square). In the code below, we will assume that the number we seek is *Value*, and that the length of the array is *MAX*.

procedure *Quadratic* (*Value*: *integer*; *Numbers*: *NumberArray*;
                             var *Position*: *integer*);
  {Quadratic search for *Value*. *Position* will be 0 if it's not found.}

quadratic search procedure

var *Jump*: *integer*;
    TooFar, *Found*: *boolean*;
begin
  Jump := *round* (*sqrt* (*MAX* + 1));
  Position := 1;
  TooFar := *false*;
  {Jump until we get close.}
  while not *TooFar* **and** ((*Jump* + *Position*) <= *MAX*) **do**
    if *Numbers* [*Jump* + *Position*] > *Value*
      then *TooFar* := *true*
      else *Position* := *Position* + *Jump*;
  {Now, single step to the value.}
  Found := *false*;
  while (*Position* < *MAX*) **and not** *Found* **do**
    if *Numbers* [*Position*] >= *Value*
      then *Found* := *true*
      else *Position* := *Position* + 1;
  {Finally, store a zero if we didn't find *Value*.}
  Found := *Numbers* [*Position*] = *Value*;
  if not *Found* **then** *Position* := 0
end; {*Quadratic*}

Our final search method will not be given the analysis it deserves here, since I'll return to it later in a recursive implementation. It is the *binary search* algorithm, and is the fastest of the methods we've seen. While the quadratic search took jumps equal to the square root of the array's size, the binary search takes jumps up to half the size of the array.

binary search

Assuming, as we have been, that the array is ordered, we start by looking at the middle element. If it's too high, we look at the middle of the bottom half of the array, while if our guess is too low, we look at the middle of the top half. We repeat this step—'split the remainder'—until we find the value we want, or decide that it doesn't exist.

Binary search is the basic *divide and conquer* algorithm. In pseudocode, a first refinement of the binary search algorithm is:

first refinement

> **repeat**
>   compute a guess
> **until** *we find the value* **or** *decide to stop looking*;

How do we *compute a guess*? Well, we start by knowing the lower and upper bounds of the array, so adding them, then dividing by two, gives us a good starting 'middle.' The insight we need for computing successive middles is that, after each wrong guess, the old middle becomes the new lower or upper bound. In actual practice, we'll add or subtract 1 each time, since we've already checked the old middle. A second refinement is:

second refinement

> *get the lower and upper bounds*;
> **repeat**
>   *compute a middle*;
>   **if** *it's low*
>   **then** *make it (plus 1) be the new lower bound*
>   **else** *make it (minus 1) be the new upper bound*
> **until** *we find the number* **or** *decide to stop looking*;
> *decide why we left the loop*;

the bounds may cross

I've implemented the actual code as a function, on the next page. It returns the array position 0 if we can't find the value we're looking for. Note the ingenious method used to decide when we've looked long enough—the lower and upper bounds will cross.

procedure *Binary* (*Value* : *integer* ; *Numbers* : *NumberArray* ;
                var *Position* : *integer*) ;
{Binary search for *Value*. *Position* will be 0 if it's not found.}
   var *Midpoint, Left, Right* : *integer* ;

binary search function
   begin
      Left := 1 ;
      Right := *MAX* ;
      repeat
         Midpoint := (*Left* + *Right*) **div** 2 ;
         if *Value* < *Numbers* [*Midpoint*]
            then *Right* := *Midpoint* − 1
            else *Left* := *Midpoint* + 1
      until (*Value* = *Numbers* [*Midpoint*]) **or** (*Left* > *Right*) ;
      if *Value* = *Numbers* [*Midpoint*]
         then *Position* := *Midpoint*
         else *Position* := 0
   end ; {*Binary*}

Self-Check Questions

Q. The analysis of algorithms is discussed in Chapter 13. Nevertheless, I'll ask you now to guess, in the worst case, how long will each search method (linear, quadratic, and binary) take? In other words, about how many elements will have to be inspected to find the most hidden value, or a value that isn't there?

A. Since the linear search works one element at a time, its worst case search will be N for an N-element array. The quadratic search, at worst, will take square-root-of-N, less 1, big jumps, plus the same number of single steps. The worst case, then, is roughly twice the square root of N. The binary search algorithm has the best performance—only $log_2 N$ inspections in the worst case. In the best case, of course, the first inspection could be successful no matter what method we use.

String Types

The term *string* generally refers to any sequence of characters—usually a word or line. Dealing with strings is such a common computer application that many languages treat strings as basic data types, much like *real* or *integer*. Standard Pascal doesn't include the string as a built-in type, and it has been roundly criticized for this omission.

Nevertheless, even Standard Pascal lets us declare arrays that allow some convenience in dealing with strings. A string-type array definition is superficially like any other array definition, but it must obey these rules:

1. The array's elements must be of type *char*.

string rules   2.   The word **array** must be preceded by the word **packed**.

3.   The lower array bound must be 1.

In the example below, *Short* and *Long*, below, are string-type arrays.

> **type** *Short* = **packed array** [1..4] **of** *char*;
> *Long* = **packed array** [1..20] **of** *char*;
> **var** *Verb, Noun*: *Short*;
> *Phrase*: *Long*;

Technically, the reserved word **packed** may be applied to any type; it instructs the compiler to conserve space in allocating storage. In practice, most compilers do this automatically, and we will not concern ourselves with packed types other than strings.

String variables have all the properties of any other one-dimensional array variables, *plus*:

1.   A string variable can have a string constant (a sequence of characters between single quote marks) assigned to it all at once—not just one element at a time. The constant must have the same length as the variable.

string properties

2.   String variables can be output in their entirety—again, not just one element at a time.

3.   Strings can be compared (usually to determine alphabetical order) with the relational operators <, >, =, <=, >=, and <>.

string assignments   Property 1 makes the assignments below legal. Note that when the string constant has fewer characters than the variable has elements, blanks have to be added to the string constant to make the two lengths equal.

> *Verb* := 'Sing';   {assignment of string constant}
> *Noun* := *Verb*;   {assignment of identical array}
> *Phrase* := 'Rather short   ';   {note 8 added blanks}

Property 2 makes these output statements legal:

> *writeln* (*Verb, Noun*);
> *writeln* (*Phrase*);

SingSing
Rather short

string comparison   Property 3 allows comparison according to the computer's collating sequence. These words are in alphabetical order under three different systems:

> *English* .... Ant, art, ball, Bat
> *ASCII* .... Ant, Bat, art, ball
> *EBCDIC* .... art, ball, Ant, Bat

Strings can also be inspected one element at a time, just like all arrays. This is the method that *must* be used for string input—neither a *read* nor *readln* statement can read in an entire array at once.

program *StringInput* (*input, output*);
   {Demonstrates character-by-character string input.}
const *BLANK* = '   '; {15 blanks}
type *String* = **packed array** [1..15] **of** *char*;
var *Element*: *String*;
   i: *integer*;
begin
   writeln ('Please enter the name of your favorite element.');
   Element := *BLANK*; {initialize the array}
   i := 0;

```
   while (i < 15) and not eoln do begin
       i := i + 1;
       read (Element [i])
   end;
```

   writeln ('You don''t want to take too much ', *Element*)
end. {*StringInput*}

↓   ↓   ↓   ↓   ↓

Please enter the name of your favorite element.
Lithium
You don't want to take too much Lithium

Replacing the shaded **while** loop with a single input statement (like *readln* (*Element*)) would be illegal. I was careful to define *String* as a type long enough to hold any element (even the sneaky rare earth elements like Praseodymium, no. 59). Note that I began by initializing *Element* to all blanks. This precaution ensured that *Element* was fully defined even though my particular favorite is only seven characters long.

String variables are seldom used by themselves. The most frequently encountered applications involve arrays of strings, for example:

type *Word* = **packed array** [1..10] **of** *char*;
   WordList = **array** [1..100] **of** *Word*;
var *OneWord*: *Word*;
   WholeList: *WordList*;

The most difficult notion associated with this sort of definition involves accessing one element of one string stored in *WholeList*. Suppose we want to store 'B' as the fifth character of the twelfth word. The two methods shown below are equivalent in Standard Pascal:

string reading program

arrays of strings

WholeList [12] [5] := 'B';
WholeList [12, 5] := 'B';

elements of two-
dimensional arrays

However, in practice we'll usually write specialized procedures to take care of operations on single words, so the problem seldom arises. Let's develop an example.

problem: string
storage

Write a program that reads a list of as many as 100 names of up to 10 letters each. A blank line should end input. Then, let the user print a sublist of the names by providing starting and finishing names.

A pseudocode restatement of the problem gives us:

refinement

> **while** *there are more names* **and** *there's still room*
>   *load each name*;
> *read the output list boundary names*;
> *find the first one in the list*;
> **while** *we still haven't printed the last name*
>   *print each name*;

The solution is implemented as program *StoreNames*, below. Pay particular attention to its error checking, including the check for *eoln* and the word length in procedure *LoadOneName*. To what sorts of errors is the program still vulnerable?

```
program StoreNames  (input, output);
   {Maintains an array of strings.}
const BLANK = '          ';        {one Name's worth.}
type Name = packed array [1..10] of char;
     NameList = array [1..100] of Name;
var WholeList: NameList;            {the entire list of names}
    Start, Finish: Name;           {the bounds for name output}
    i: integer;                    {a loop counter variable}
procedure LoadOneName (var Current: Name);
   {Reads in the characters of one Name -type string.}
   var i: integer;
   begin
      Current := BLANK;
      i := 1;
      while not eoln and (i <= 10) do begin
         read (Current [i]);
         i := i + 1
      end;
      readln  {Get ready for the next line.}
   end;  {LoadOneName}
```

string storage
program

```
begin
    writeln  ('Enter names, one per line.  A blank line ends input.') ;
    i := 0 ;
    repeat  {get the list of names.}
        i := i + 1 ;
        LoadOneName  (WholeList [i])
    until  (WholeList [i] = BLANK)  or  (i = 100) ;
    writeln  ('Enter the first and last names you want back.') ;
    LoadOneName  (Start) ;
    LoadOneName  (Finish) ;
    i := 1 ;
    while WholeList [i] <> Start  do  {Find the first name ... }
        i := i + 1 ;
    writeln  (WholeList [i]) ;  { ... print it ... }
    repeat
        i := i + 1 ;  { ... and keep going until the last name.}
        writeln  (WholeList [i])
    until WholeList [i] = Finish
end.  {StoreNames }
```

Self-Check
Questions

Q. Suppose that program *StoreNames* contained this procedure declaration:

```
procedure Initialize (var Entire: NameList; Specific: Name);
    var i: integer ;
    begin
        for i := 1 to 100 do
            Entire [i] := Specific
    end ;  {Initialize }
```

Are any of these legal calls of *Initialize*? Why or why not?

> a) *Initialize (WholeList, Start)* ;
> b) *Initialize (Start, WholeList)* ;
> c) *Initialize (WholeList 'BLANKBLANK')* ;
> d) *Initialize (WholeList 'XYZ')* ;
> e) *Initialize (WholeList, WholeList [10])* ;

A. For a call of *Initialize* to be legal, the variable parameter *Entire* must have as an argument a variable of type *NameList*. The value parameter *Specific* has a weaker requirement—its argument need only be a value that could be assigned to *Specific*. Calls *a, c,* and *e* are legal (assuming that *Start* and *WholeList* [10] have been initialized themselves). Call *b* is illegal because its arguments are reversed. Call *d* is illegal because the argument 'XYZ' has only three letters, rather than the required ten.

Arrays of Arrays: Extended-Precision Arithmetic

Despite the speed of computers (or, more accurately, to maintain that speed), programming languages restrict the number of digits available for representing numbers. *integers* are severely limited, but the results of *integer* operations are guaranteed to be correct. *reals* are usually granted more digits, but at the potential expense of rounding errors in the course of computation.

Implementing procedures to handle arithmetic of long numbers is an programming problem that merges fancy data structuring techniques with an algorithm known to every second grader.

problem: long integer multiplication

Write a program that is capable of correctly multiplying two integers of arbitrary length. Show your work—neatness counts.

How do you multiply?

first refinement

> *get the first term* ;
> *get the second term* ;
> **for** *each digit of the second term*
>   *compute the partial product* ;
> *add all the partial products* ;
> *print the answer* ;

A one-dimensional array of *integer* is suitable for holding the digits of each term:

type definition

> **const** *MAX* = 40 ; {This can be any needed length.}
> **type** *Factor* = **array** [1..*MAX*] **of** *integer* ;

Although it is not strictly necessary, an array of *Factors* lets us 'show our work.' It creates a data structure not unlike the word list of program *StoreNames* .

> ·· . {type definition continues}
> *WorkPad* = **array** [1..*MAX*] **of** *Factor* ;

Why go to the trouble of defining two array types? After all, a single two-dimensional array type can also hold rows of figures. However, some of the details that were so hard to learn in second grade are going to return to haunt us. Consider this example of multiplication:

```
    9876
  x 987
  _____
   69132
  790080
 8888400
 _____
 9747612
```

Practically every line raises problems. The first two terms have to be read in, digit-by-digit. Then, the second term (987) must be indented to properly line up under the first term. In fact, both terms have to be indented, since the partial products stream off to the left. And how does that happen? The second and third partial products have to multiplied by an appropriate number of tens.

why an array of
factors?

> The fact that operations will have to be carried out on single lines make it advisable to define types that will let single lines be passed as parameters.

A second refinement might be:

second refinement

> *read and right-shift the first term*;
> *read and right-shift the second term*;
> **for** *each digit of the second term*
>   *compute a partial product*;
>   *left-shift it if necessary*;
>   *print it*;
> **for** *each partial product*
>   *add it to a running sum of terms*;
> *print the answer*;

A number of specialized subprograms are starting to appear:

> *ReadTerm* will get the initial terms from the user. Like *LoadOneName* (from the string example), it will have to watch out for an end-of-line that ends input—as well as a too-long entry that might end the program.

some useful modules

> *Shift* will shift a given term to the left or right if necessary.

> *Print* will print the stored values in a readable manner.

> *Add* will add terms—the partial products.

Are additional procedures or functions going to be required? Is it ever necessary to know the exact length of the numbers the program works with? What about error checking? You might also try to figure out how long *MAX* must be to allow terms of a given length.

a reading example

Instead of supplying yet another pseudocode refinement of the multiplication problem, I'll present program *LongMultiplication* as a 'reading' example, over the next few pages. I suggest that you develop refinements of some of the specialized subprograms given above before going through the actual program.

When you do read my code, think about how you might simplify *LongMultiplication*, or modify it to work with much longer numbers (or *reals*). Can you get rid of procedure *Add* by adding the columns of figures vertically? Can you add a procedure that does subtraction? Have fun (for a change) criticizing the work *I* slaved over!

```
program LongMultiplication (input, output);
   {Multiply two numbers, each up to MAX/2 digits long.}
const MAX = 40;
type Factor = array [1..MAX] of integer;
var Term1, Term2, Product: Factor;
procedure Shift (var Term: Factor; Start, Finish, Offset: integer);
   {Shift the number in the Term array, as needed.}
   var i: integer;
       Temp: Factor;
   begin
      for i := 1 to MAX do Temp[i] := 0;
      for i := Start to Finish do Temp[i+Offset] := Term[i];
      Term := Temp
   end; {Shift}
procedure ReadTerm (var Term: Factor);
   {Get the value of a term, one element at a time.}
   var Ch: char;
       i, Length: integer;
   begin
      i := 1;
      while not eoln and (i<= (MAX div 2)) do begin
         read (Ch);
         Term[i] := ord(Ch) - ord ('0');
         i := i + 1
      end; {We've read the number (or at least MAX/2 digits).}
      Length := i - 1;
      if not eoln then writeln ('Ignoring low-order digits.');
      readln; {Dump any remainder.}
      Shift (Term, 1, Length, MAX-Length)
   end; {ReadTerm}
function Length (Term: Factor): integer;
   {Find the length of the numerical (i.e. non-leading zero) part of Term.}
   var i: integer;
   begin
      i := 1;
      while (Term[i] = 0) and (i < MAX) do
         i := i + 1;
      if Term[i] = 0
         then Length := 0
         else Length := (MAX-i) + 1
   end; {Length}
```

```
procedure Times (Term: Factor; By: integer; var Product: Factor);
{Multiply Term by a single-digit number.}
var i, Temp, Carry: integer;
begin
    Carry := 0;
    for i := MAX downto Length (Term) do begin
        Temp := Carry + (Term [i] * By);
        Product [i] := Temp mod 10;
        Carry := Temp div 10
    end;
    Term [i –1] := Carry
end; {Times}
```

```
procedure Print (Term: Factor);
{Print Term, with spaces replacing leading zeros.}
var i: integer;
begin
    for i := 1 to MAX – Length (Term) do
        write (' ');
    for i := (MAX – Length (Term)) + 1 to MAX do
        write (Term [i]:1);
    writeln
end; {Print}
```

```
procedure Add (Term1, Term2: Factor; var Sum: Factor);
{Add two terms, digit by digit.}
var i, Carry: integer;
begin
    Carry := 0;
    for i := MAX downto 1 do begin
        Sum [i] := (Carry + Term1 [i] + Term2 [i]) mod 10;
        Carry := (Carry + Term1 [i] + Term2 [i]) div 10
    end
end; {Add}
```

```
procedure Multiply (Term1, Term2: Factor; var Product: Factor);
{Multiply Term1 by Term2. Print the partial products.}
type WorkPad = array [1..MAX] of Factor;
var Scratch: WorkPad;
    i: integer;
begin
    for i := 1 to Length (Term2) do begin
        Times (Term1, Term2 [(MAX–i)+1], Scratch [i]);
        Shift (Scratch [i], (MAX–Length (Scratch [i]))+1, MAX, 1–i);
        Print (Scratch [i])
    end;                                        {program continues}
```

```
                              {Add the partial products row-by-row.}
                          for i := 1 to Length (Term2) do
                              Add (Scratch [i], Product, Product)
                              {How would you add the digits column-by-column?}
                      end;  {Multiply}
              begin
                  ReadTerm (Term1);
                  ReadTerm (Term2);
                  Multiply (Term1, Term2, Product);
                  Print (Product)
              end.  {LongMultiplication}
```

↓   ↓   ↓   ↓   ↓

9999999999
12345679

                              89999999991
                             699999999930
                            5999999999400
                           49999999995000
                          399999999960000
                         2999999999700000
                        19999999998000000
                        99999999990000000
                        123456789987654321

Chapter Notes 7-2

CERTAIN BUGS INEVITABLY TURN UP during array processing. A classic problem that's been the subject of many articles involves searching an array for a value that might not be present. For example, suppose we define a variable *TheArray* as an **array** [1..20] **of** *integer*. The following program segment is intended to find the subscript of the stored value 0 (zero).

array searching bugs

```
{incorrect segment}
Counter := 1;
while TheArray [Counter]<>0 do
    Counter := Counter+1;
writeln ('A zero is stored at subscript ', Counter:1);
```

This code works perfectly if 0 is actually stored somewhere in *TheArray*. If it isn't, though, we'll eventually try to see if *TheArray* [21] equals 0, and the program will crash. A correct program segment would include a check to ensure that *Counter* never exceeds 20. What do you think of this version?

```
{incorrect segment}
Counter := 1;
while (Counter <20) and (TheArray [Counter]<>0) do
    Counter := Counter+1;
writeln ('A zero is stored at subscript ', Counter:1);
```

Suppose that *TheArray* still doesn't contain a zero, or holds a zero in element 20. In either case, the segment's output will be:

A zero is stored at subscript 20

As you can see, we've escaped the frying pan only to find ourselves in the fire. Another test has to be added to the end of the segment to make sure that we've really found the zero.

check after the loop

```
{correct segment}
Counter := 1;
while (Counter <20) and (TheArray [Counter]<>0) do
    Counter := Counter+1;
if TheArray [Counter]=0
    then writeln ('A zero is stored at subscript ', Counter:1)
    else writeln ('No zeros.');
```

Arrays of two or more dimensions are sometimes confusing. One common problem comes from using too many nested loops to inspect an array. two-dimensional bugs Suppose, for example, that we have a two-dimensional array and want to examine the values stored along one of its diagonals—*TheArray* [1,1], *TheArray* [2,2], etc. An intuitive, but incorrect, solution uses two **for** loops. Assume that we have an array whose dimensions are 1..*Last* and 1..*Last*.

```
{incorrect segment}
for Row := 1 to Last do
    for Column := 1 to Last do
        Examine (TheArray [Row, Column]);    etc.
```

This program calls *Examine* for *every* value stored in *TheArray*. A correct searching diagonals version requires only a single loop, regardless of the diagonal being searched. The 1,1, 2,2 3,3 ... diagonal is searched with:

```
{correct segment}
for Mark := 1 to Last do
    Examine (TheArray [Mark, Mark]);    etc.
```

Just for comparison, see how the opposite diagonal is searched:

```
{another correct segment}
for Mark := 1 to Last do
    Examine (TheArray [Mark, (Last–Mark)+1]);    etc.
```

Frequently we'll want to compare an array element to its neighbors. If we're at element i,j, we'll be looking at $i-1,j-1$; $i-1,j$; $i-1,j+1$; $i,j-1$; $i,j+1$; $i+1,j-1$; $i+1,j$; and $i+1,j+1$. There's nothing particularly difficult about cycling through an array to make the check for every i, j pair. However, not every element *has* a neighbor on every side! Trying to check the neighbors of an element on any side row or column will cause a subscript error.

> Think about the boundary conditions of searches, especially when you're dealing with border locations.

As always, when you're sure everything is right and the program still doesn't work, then one of the things you're sure of is wrong. This is particularly true when array subscripts are being computed. Now, an incorrect subscript won't always cause a program crash—it might just cause incorrect results. If a program performs strangely for inexplicable reasons, it's a good idea to use a statement or procedure that will provide a 'snapshot' of subscript values during execution.

```
{This output statement was added for debugging.}
writeln ('Subscripts before the call of DoSomething are: ',
          Computed (i), Margin /Border-1, Row *Column);
DoSomething (TheArray [Computed (i), Margin /Border-1, Row *Column]);
```

It's amazing how often this inspection solves the mystery. The use of snapshots and other embedded debugging tools is discussed at length in Chapter 12.

● The array is a random access type because array elements can be stored or inspected in any order. The size of an array (the number of elements it can hold) is determined by its dimensions. The bounds that set the dimensions can have any ordinal type. There's no limit on the number of dimensions an array can have, although the computer may restrict an array's total size.

● The bounds that set array dimensions must be given with actual values, known when the program is compiled (with the 'type name' exception given below). They can't be variables or expressions that aren't computed until the program is finally run. However, the name of an ordinal type can be used instead of actual values in giving an array dimension. It's as though the first and last values of the type itself were given.

● An array's elements can have any type, but all of an array's elements must have the same type. A 'complete array' assignment can be made between two array variables with the exact same type.

● A string type is a **packed array** of *char* values. It can only have one dimension, which must start at 1.

● Value parameters and variable parameters with structured types must be declared with type names. Their types can't be defined in the heading.

● String type array variables can be compared, and assigned to or printed all at once (rather than one element at a time). Values must still be read in element-by-element, though.

● The most common array bugs involve subscripts that are out of the range of the array's definition. Printing 'subscript snapshots' is a good debugging technique.

● Array-searching loops usually have multiple exit conditions, since the sought value may not be found. Be sure to check the reason for loop termination before assuming that you've found what you were looking for.

Cross Reference

● Structured types in general are defined on A101, while the array type in particular is discussed in A112—A121. The types of an array's subscripts and components are defined on A113, and A114 continues the discussion of subtle differences in the form of array type definitions.

● Indexed variables—individual array elements—are described in A114—A116.

● String types are described in A117—118. The definition of strings as constants is found in A65—A66, and the meaning of lexicographic ordering in comparing strings is found on A46.

● The transfer procedures *pack* and *unpack* are defined and explained in A119—A121. More general application of packing is introduced on A101.

Exercises

7-1   The generation of random numbers between two *integer* limits isn't very difficult, particularly if you use the code from Chapter 5. However, many applications require a sequence of numbers whose order is randomized, but whose distribution is perfectly uniform. You may recognize that a shuffled deck of playing cards fulfills both criteria.

Write a program that shuffles a sequence of contiguous values, say, the numbers from 1 to 100. Use a one-dimensional array of *integer* to represent the numbers. If you initialize each array element to its own subscript, there are several 'exchange' strategies that can be used to shuffle the array.

1.   (Using one array) Traverse the array, exchanging each element's value with the value of another element chosen at random.

2.   (Using two arrays) Fill a second array by choosing elements at random from the first, ordered array. However, after choosing an element from the first array, replace it with the first array's very last element (unless you happened to pick the last element), and reduce the length of the array by one. Thus, each subsequent choice will be made from an array that is one element shorter than its predecessor—as the first array shrinks, the second array grows.

7-2   An *anagram* is produced by rearranging the letters of one word or phrase to produce another. Write a program that determines if two sequences (of up to ten letters each) are anagrams. Test it on *cat/act*, and *scare/races/cares/acres*.

7-3   A *palindrome* is a series of letters that spell the same words both forward and backward, as Napolean's lament 'Able was I ere I saw Elba.' A *numerical palindrome* is a bit simpler—it's just a number that's the same front to back and back to front. 1234321 is a numerical palindrome; 123431 isn't.

Numerical palindromes can usually be generated from arbitrary *integers* with an easy algorithm: reverse the number, then sum the original number and its reversal. It may take many such steps, but a palindrome generally results: 561+165=726, 726+627=1,353, 1,353+3,531=4,884, which is palindromic. There are some notable exceptions to this—196 is the smallest—for which a palindrome *never* results, however.

Write a program that generates palindromic numbers up to fifty digits long. Announce the number of steps required, and be sure to check for, and halt before, overflow (just in case you try one of the 5,996 numbers below 100,000 that do not appear to be palindromic no matter how long you persist).

7-4   Two array initialization problems for those long, lonesome evenings. Suppose that you have two one-dimensional arrays (i.e. *n*-dimensional vectors) X and Y:

1.   *Vandermonde's* matrix is a two-dimensional array defined as $a_{i,j} = x_j^i$.

2.   *Cauchy's* matrix is a two-dimensional array defined as $a_{i,j} = \dfrac{1}{x_i + y_j}$.

Define suitable types and write procedures that initialize these arrays.

7-5   *Saddle points* appear, not on the backs of horses in New Mathico, but in three-dimensional graphs of functions. For example, the plot of the function $f(x,y) = y^2 - x^2$ (i.e. $z = y^2 - x^2$) shows this surface, below left:

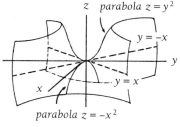

z *parabola* $z = y^2$

parabola $z = -x^2$

```
3 4 1 6 5 9
1 7 2 4 2 1
8 9 4 5 6 8
5 3 3 3 9 5
6 2 1 1 1 6
4·2 2 8 7 4
```

In array terms, a saddle point is found if the smallest element in a row and the largest element in a column occupy the same position (element 3,3 above right). Write a program that is able to locate a saddle point in an $n \times n$ square array. Can you search for a largest column element/smallest row element with the same code? (Hint: rotate the array.) Assume that there is only one saddle point in the array.

7-6   Most people know about the high probability that even relatively small groups contain at least one pair of people who share a birthday. But have you considered the following variation? Suppose that ten people write their names on slips of paper, then drop them in a hat. If all names are different, what is the likelihood, if each draws one slip, that nobody will pull his or her own name?

In theory, the chance that nobody will draw a match equals e^{-1}, or about 0.3. Indeed, even if everybody in New York (some seven million people), were to put their names into a hat, the result would be the same! Write a program that fills two thousand-element arrays with randomly-chosen numbers (between 1 and 1,000), then see how many numbers occupy the same position in each array on repeated trials. Is there any difference in simply checking to see if any element's contents equals its subscript?

7-7   Suppose we create an array that holds a relatively random sequence of characters, say:

A F K Z M L B Q R C J

We can test an individual's short-term memory by printing the characters, then scrolling them off the screen. (Depending on the speed of your system, either a **for** loop of *write-lns*, or a doubly-nested loop that prints lines of blanks, should do the scrolling job.) The test subject is asked to try to reenter the correct sequence.

Have your program test and report on these measures of recall:

1.   The number of letters entered that appeared somewhere in the list.

2.   The number of letters entered in their proper positions.

3.   An 'analog' score that smoothly penalizes out-of-position guesses. For each letter that is in the list, add 1 to the score if it's in the correct position, 1/2 if it's off by one, 1/3 if off by two, and so on.

Generate the sequence of characters by using a random number generator to pick numbers between *ord* ('A') and *ord* ('Z'). Extend the problem by generating progressively longer sequences of letters. Do your results agree with published studies that indicate that most people's short-term memories can hold seven, plus or minus two, values? Does presenting sequences of random length (rather than progressively longer) have any effect on the subject's ability to recall?

7-8   Come back once more to the high country of New Mathico, where most everything is described by an equation, and cattle ranchers have extraordinarily well-behaved animals that *always* follow the same path.

Hoping to capitalize on the back to nature movement, the New Mathico ranchers decide to build vacation homes on their cattle grazing range, particularly the prime area from 0 to $\pi/2$, ranging from the $f(x)=0$ River to the $f(x)=1$ irrigation ditch. What could be more bucolic, they reason, than waking up to 600 mooing head of cattle?

First, though, they must locate all the building sites that are not actually in the direct paths of the herds. The cattle that graze on this particular land are said to include the $y=\sin\frac{x}{4}$, $y=\sin 2x$, $y=\cos x$, $y=e^{-x}\sin x$, $y=\cos^2 x$, $y=.5^x$, and $y=x^2-x+.25$ herds (many of which are exceptionally difficult to brand).

Local zoning regulations require that 0.01 by 0.01 unit lots be allowed for each homesite (which would allow just over 157 riverfront homes, or some 15,707 potential sites total). How many building sites will actually be available?

7-9   A grape grower who had sampled her fermented wares found herself sitting in the middle of her vineyard. All around her were the stakes she had posted to support grape vines. She noticed that, although she was surrounded by a thicket of stakes, each visible stake blocked her view of stakes that were in a straight line further away. In her inebriated state it soon became quite important for her to discover just what fraction of the total number of stakes she could actually see.

Write a program that solves the grape grower's problem. Assume that the vintner sits at point 0,0 of a large coordinate plane, and that there is a stake located at each *integer*-valued coordinate. Thus, the stake at 1,1 can be seen, but 2,2, 3,3, and so on are blocked, and thus are invisible. We can assume that the stake's width is immaterial—a stake is only blocked if it falls on a line drawn from the origin past the first visible stake.

Hint: just mark the visible and invisible stakes in one quadrant of a large, square, field, with corners at $(0,1)$, $(0,n)$, (n,n), and $(1,n)$. Second hint: what don't the *x,y* coordinates of each visible stake have in common? Finally, you might want to compare your final answer to the value $\frac{6}{\pi^2}$.

7-10   I can remember when, in fourth grade or so, the one-to-one correspondence of the odd integers, and all the integers, was pointed out—with its resulting conclusion that the number of odd numbers was just as infinite as the number of numbers. Somehow, it didn't seem quite fair!

The integers get their revenge when we start to divide a line into closed segments (in a closed segment, the end points are not contained in the segment). Take a line, and mark a point in each half. In effect, were the line divided into two segments, each would contain a mark. Now, place a third mark so that each point is in a separate third of the line. Again, each segment has a mark. Can you place a fourth mark in such a way that, if we divide the line into four equal segments, each segment will contain only one mark?

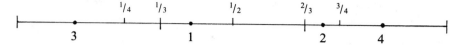

It turns out that no more than 17 marks can be placed, in order, while satisfying the segmenting rules. Note that the marks have to be placed one at a time—and that the segmenting rule must be satisfied at each step.

Using a long one-dimensional array to model the line, write a program that checks the placement of up to 10 marks. How many marks can you put down? You may want to have your program run the check backward, starting with multiple marks, then removing them one at a time.

7-11   An interesting problem from number theory involves the partitioning of *integer* values into sums (in a manner similar to the decomposition of *integers* into their factors). For example, 3 can be partitioned in three ways: 3, 1+2, and 1+1+1, while 5 can be partitioned in seven ways: 5, 4+1, 3+2, 3+1+1, 2+2+1, 2+1+1+1, and 1+1+1+1+1.

The game of *Bulgarian Solitaire* explores the partitioning of triangular numbers. A triangular number is the sum of the first n numbers for any given n. If you imagine setting row after row of bowling pins, the total number of pins required will always be triangular: 1, 3, 6, 10, 15, and so on. Triangular numbers can be generated with Gauss's formula for adding *integers*, $\frac{1}{2}n(n+1)$.

The rules are simple. Start with a triangular number of cards, then divide them into any number of piles. Then, take one card from each pile and place it on a new pile. What you will find, startlingly enough, is that no matter how the piles are originally ordered, or how many there are, you will eventually wind up with one pile of 1, one pile of 2, one pile of 3, etc.—just as though they were rows of bowling pins.

Write a program that lets you supply the starting 'piles' for a triangular number of cards, then plays Bulgarian Solitaire for you. How will you recognize the end of the game? As a safety valve, you may want to rely on the reasonable conjecture that the game will end within $n^2 - n$ steps.

7-12   DNA molecules are comprised of triples that consist of four different organic bases—adenine, cytosine, guanine, and thymine, usually abbreviated as A, C, G, and T. Although the entire molecule can be incredibly long, a single missing base can have catastrophic effects. For example, one particular rat gene associated with hereditary diabetes differs from the normal 1,000-base sequence by just one missing G residue:

normal sequence	GGA	AGC	GGA	GGC	CGC
diabetic sequence	GGA	AGC	GAG	GCC	GCT

The resulting *frame shift mutation* is apparent in the third triple.

The problem of spotting off-by-one errors of this sort has interesting applications in text processing as well; e.g. in comparing two files that differ by only one line. For now, though, just write a program that is able to find the location of a frame shift mutation in a DNA base sequence. Be sure to confirm that the molecules differ only by this one base, and do not diverge entirely at the point of departure.

7-13   Many maps include a table of distances between points. The table is basically a square two-dimensional array, subscripted on each axis by a list of cities, with each element showing a distance. The distance between a city and itself, of course, is zero.

Write a program that implements a table of distances between cities. Let a program user employ it to:

1.   Find the distance between any two cities.

2.   Find the cities closest to, and furthest from, any city.

3.   Find the total distance on a trip between any sequence of cities.

4.   Find out whether or not a journey between two cities can include a detour, to a third city, that will not extend the total trip length by more than x%. The user should only enter the first and final locations.

7-14   *Vector graphics* systems illuminate an essentially continuous line between arbitrarily located endpoints, while *raster display* systems build up images one *pixel*, or point, at a time. For various reasons raster systems are more popular, even though a great deal of work can go into deciding when and where to turn each pixel on.

Suppose we use a two-dimensional array to represent the pixels on a terminal screen. Each element is originally 'off,' but can be turned 'on' if a line passes through it. Write a program that decides which pixels to turn on to create a straight line between the origin (0,0) and an +X,+Y coordinate endpoint.

This problem is not quite as simple as it seems, if the lines are to look at all realistic, and if the amount of computation is to be kept to a minimum. An *integer digital differential analyzer* that follows the rules given below is useful. Assume that *slope* equals Y/X, *error* is initially zero, and the first pixel lit is 0,0:

1.   (*slope* ≤ 1, *error* <0) Turn on the pixel on the right of the last lit pixel, and add Y to *error*.

2.   (*slope* ≤ 1, *error* ≥ 0) Turn on the pixel located one up, one over, and add Y–X to *error*.

3.   (*slope* >1, *error* <0) Turn on the pixel located one up, one over, and add Y–X to *error*.

4.   (*slope* >1, *error* ≥ 0) Turn on the pixel located one up from the last lit pixel, and subtract X from *error*.

Note that the proper slope can be chosen without doing division. Can you devise a more general set of rules that allow any starting and ending x,y coordinates?

7-15   *Bresenham's circle algorithm* is a method of deciding which pixels should be lit in order to approximate a circle. Like the line-drawing algorithm described above, it attempts to minimize both computations and apparent irregularity. It relies on these characteristics of a circle:

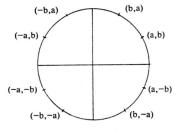
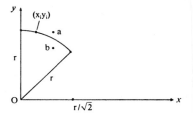

On the left, we see that a circle has an eight-fold symmetry. As a result, all computations of x,y points for half a quadrant can locate appropriate points in the others. On the right, we notice that as x values increase from 0 to $r\sqrt{2}$, each corresponding y value will either be the same, or decline by one. Two potential y choices are shown by a and b. A moment's reflection will reveal that both points are always on opposite sides of the circle, unless one actually touches it.

Suppose we define an *Error* function that represents the difference, positive or negative, between a point, and the ideal circle. According to Bresenham's algorithm, we should choose the *y* value that minimizes the difference between the plotted point's distance from 0,0, and the circle's radius. If *Error* (*point a*) + *Error* (*point b*) is greater than zero, plot the inner point, and otherwise plot the outer one. Write a program that implements his algorithm, and plots a circle for any radius 5 through some *MAX* .

7-16   Computer modeling can show that events that appear catastrophic at close range can be quite stable, and recur naturally in long-term cycles. For example, forest fires are usually viewed as disastrous, yet periodic, naturally occurring (e.g. by lightning) fires are an essential part of healthy forest ecology.

An interesting variation on the theme involves competition between species through *infestation* . For example, the spruce budworm is an unpleasant little beastie that defoliates balsam and spruce trees. Unfortunately for the budworm, these trees are replaced by beeches, which they find indigestable. The beeches, in turn, are eventually invaded and displaced by spruces and balsams, and the cycle starts again.

A simpler model of infestation can be set up with just three rules:

1.   An infested area becomes defoliated next year.

2.   A defoliated area becomes green next year.

3.   An infested site infects its neighbors to the north, south, east, and west next year, if they are currently green.

Write a program that tracks, and displays, a sequence of generations. Assuming a green forest to begin with, use a variety of patterns to initialize the model (at the center of the forest), including:

```
i i i i            g i g            d g d
d d d d            g d g            i g i
```

where **i** means infested, **g** means green, and **d** means defoliated. Note that when a focus, or center-point, of infestation is known, intentional defoliation can be used to break the cycle. Perhaps you should try to make your program run backwards as well!

7-17   The three Laws of Thermodynamics can be summarized as follows: 'You can't win; you can't break even; and you can't quit the game.' More seriously, the first law requires conservation of energy applied to heat, while the third deals with material properties at very low temperatures (and says that absolute zero can't be reached). The second law says that there is an inevitable, natural change in the distribution of energy from regions of high temperature to those of lower temperature. In other words, the *entropy* of the universe invariably tends to increase.

Entropy is determined by the formula $s = k \ln W$, where s is entropy, k is Boltzman's constant (which we can ignore here), and W gives the number of distinct ways a system can be rearranged—its potential chaos, so to speak. We can describe W with the combinatorial function. *Combo* (*n, p*)—the number of different combinations of n things taken p at a time—is $\frac{n!}{p!(n-p)!}$. (Note that since s is a logarithmic value, the factorials, which become extremely large, should just be computed by summing logarithms.) Boltzman was rather proud of devising this formula, and had it engraved on his tomb.

Implement a (somewhat) simplified model of the universe as a 400×400 array of elements that can be either hot, or cold. At first, only the 100 elements in one corner are hot—we will call this area *System 1* . However, over time, hot points, moving strictly at random, will seep out into the surrounding 1500 elements of *System 2* . Two hot points can't occupy the same area at once.

At first, both systems have very low entropy—neither a full system, nor an empty one, can be rearranged at all. As time progresses, though, the sum of the systems' entropy increases. Write a program that models the progress of our universe from low to

high total entropy. What is the maximum summed entropy of System 1 and System 2—
$lnW_{System1} + lnW_{System2}$? What are the relative numbers of hot points in each system at this
point? Will the entropy of the total system either increase further or decline?

7-18   The preceding problem should convince us of the overall tendency of heat to
flow from hot to cold. Laplace's equation:

$$\frac{\partial^2 T}{\partial x^2} + \frac{\partial^2 T}{\partial y^2} = 0$$

uses partial differential equations to make a quite simple statement about temperature
flow: the temperature at any given point is the average of the temperatures of the points
that surround it.

Suppose that a computer designer wants to model the temperatures surrounding a
chip in a solid plastic casing. We can picture the system as:

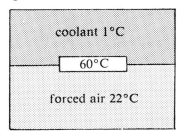

We can assume that the chip, coolant, and air temperatures will remain constant. Use a
52×52 array to model the casing, and treat the zeroth and fifty-first rows and columns as
the 'outer walls' of the system. Let the chip be located in the central 2×10 elements.

Write a program that finds the equilibrium temperature distribution of the plastic
casing by sweeping through the entire array (except for the walls) again and again, each
time setting each element's temperature to the average of its neighbors. Halt when no
element changes by more than 1°. What effect does your choice of initial temperature
for the plastic case have? What is the average temperature of the casing at equilibrium?
How might you display the temperature variations in the casing? (Hint: use a different
character for each 10° range.)

7-19   The regular rows and columns of atoms that form a crystaline structure can be
disrupted for a variety of reasons, not the least of which is the propensity of warm atoms
to wander about. This leads to two sorts of point defects—those caused by too many
atoms in one area, called *Frenkel* defects, and those caused by too few, known as
Schottky defects. In effect, we can view Frenkel defects as being caused by wandering
atoms, while Schottky defects are caused by wandering holes.

Write a program that initializes a two-dimensional array to hold alternating values
in each row and column, as though it were a checkerboard. Then, introduce random
point defects—both Frenkel defects (store the wrong kind of atom in an element) and
Schottky defects (remove an atom entirely). Finally, write procedures that can spot and
print the types, and locations, of defects in the array.

7-20   You've probably seen electron micrographs of incredibly twisted and tangled
strands of deoxyribonucleic acid, better known as DNA. But have you ever paused to
wonder about the statistical properties of the path a typical strand takes? In some sense,
the end of a strand simply takes a random walk, much like the random Brownian motion
of a gas molecule. However, the strand is limited by *steric hindrance*. In English, this
means (at the very least) that an effective model of a DNA molecule's path should not be
allowed to pass through itself.

The result of this restriction is that, while differential equations can be used to
analyze and mathematically simulate Brownian motion and other random walks, a *self-
avoiding* random walk must be simulated by computer.

Write a program that simulates 50 steps of *a*) a random walk, and *b*) a self-avoiding random walk. For convenience, assume that up to eight moves can be made from any point—a diagonal step takes the same amount of time as a vertical or horizontal one. Start in the center of a 101×101 (i.e. −50..50) array each trial. Run at least 100 trials of each walk, and plot a histogram of the final *x*-axis positions.

7-21   Write a program that lets two players play the game of *Nim*. One version of this game starts out with three rows of pebbles:

$$\circ \ \circ \ \circ \ \circ \ \circ \ \circ$$
$$\circ \ \circ \ \circ \ \circ \ \circ$$
$$\circ \ \circ \ \circ$$

On each turn a player may remove one or more pebbles, but can only take them from a single row. The winner is the player who removes the last pebble. Can you use binary arithmetic to figure out a winning strategy? The secret is in the columns!

For a harder problem, expand your program to let the computer play one side. Under what conditions can it always win? Can changing the number of rows or pebbles lead to a disadvantage?

7-22   Here are a few more problems that deal with computer graphics. First, let's consider *image enhancement*. We can assume that a picture is stored as a two-dimensional array of the *integer* values 1..128 that indicate light intensity, from black to white.

In general, techniques that try to bring more detail out of pictures attempt to increase the contrast between points. Let me propose three methods:

1.   *Renormalization*   In practice, most stored intensity values will fall into a relatively narrow central range, say 50—80. Renormalization spreads these values over the entire range available, even if the contrast of some of the outlying values is diminished.

2.   *Noise reduction*   Slight variations from one point to the next may simply be due to atmospheric disturbance, errors or roundoff in digitizing values, etc. Rounding each value to the nearest 5 or 10 diminishes resolution, but increases contrast, by reducing the number of different intensities shown.

3.   *Edge detection*   A relatively sharp difference in intensity between two adjacent points, especially if continued by their neighbors, often indicates an edge. Accentuating this difference by lightening the light points, and darkening the dark points, can make the edge appear more sharply.

These approaches may be combined, of course. The benefit of any particular method depends on application—a technique that sharpens a photograph of a license plate may not be appropriate for enhancing a blurry airport X-ray.

Write procedures that implement each method. Can they be combined? What problems may occur if any approach is carried too far?

7-23   Topographical maps are easily represented with two-dimensional arrays of *integer* or *real*-valued heights. However, the bird's-eye view they provide is sometimes difficult to appreciate after a day of lugging a 70-pound backpack.

1.   Write a program that locates *peaks*. We define a peak as any point that is higher than its eight neighbors.

2.   Write a program that locates *valleys*. A valley is any series of three points along a row or column that are lower than their twelve neighbors. (Can you deal with longer valleys as well?)

7-24   A considerable amount of computer work nowadays goes into creating three-dimensional graphical views from two-dimensional data. A standard problem involves generating an 'ant's-eye' side view from a bird's-eye top view, perhaps to simulate the effect that a new skyscraper will have on street-level scenery.

Consider the problem in just two dimensions. Suppose that you are looking toward the uptown horizon. The top of the nearest building is clearly visible. The top of the building behind it, though, can only be seen if:

$$arctan\left[\frac{height\ of\ closer\ building}{distance\ to\ closer\ building}\right] < arctan\left[\frac{height\ of\ further\ building}{distance\ to\ further\ building}\right]$$

Write a program that represents building heights (treated as points) in a two-dimensional array. Suppose a user wants to 'stroll,' from left to right, along any given row. Which buildings will be visible in each column to her left?

Additional exercises that use arrays and require recursion may be found following Chapter 16, starting on page 369.

8

The **record** Type

Ever since the Cro-Magnons introduced interior decoration to the Pleistocene epoch at Lascaux, people have been thinking up new methods of holding information. The **record** type is Pascal's second contribution to data storage. A record, like an array, holds more than one value and can be accessed at random. However, a record's *fields* can have different types and, unlike array elements, are referred to by individual names. We'll see how to define and use record types, and meet a new control statement, the **with** statement, used in accessing individual fields.

Our focus on programming joins records with arrays to create powerful new data structures. This combination is perhaps the most ubiquitous in programming; we combine the array's random access and ease of travel with the record's ability to hold values of different types. I'll show some basic methods of sorting array contents, and discuss lateral thinking approaches to more complicated type definitions. A brief closing note describes the sophisticated option of defining *record variants*. Although I include this section here for completeness, it's seldom necessary to use record variants in ordinary applications.

Defining Record Types 8-1

field list

THE DECLARATION OF A RECORD-TYPE variable begins with a definition of the record variable's type.

> The details of a record type are its *field list*, given between the reserved words **record** and **end**. A record's fields can be of any type—standard or user-defined, simple or structured.

We can draw a simplified chart of a record type's definition as shown below. It will be expanded after the discussion of record variants later.

record type (simple)

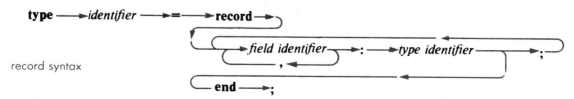

record syntax

For example, recall type *Factor*, defined in Chapter 7 to hold long positive *integer* values. Compare that to the definition of a record type used for representing extended-precision *real* values. It requires a variety of ordinal and structured types for its fields:

sample type definition

```
type Factor = array [1..MAX] of integer;
     Signs = (Plus, Minus);
     Number = record
             Sign: Signs;
             Term: Factor;
             ScaleFactor, DecimalPosition, Length: integer
     end; {Number}
var Term1, Term2, Product: Number;
```

Notice that the other structured types, and ordinal types and subranges, must be defined before they're used to provide the types of fields.

scope of fields

A special feature of field identifiers is their limited scope. The field identifiers of a given record have their own *name list* in the computer, and don't conflict with identifiers used elsewhere. A record, then could be defined to serve as the type of a field in another record—forming a nested record definition—without excessive concern about forming unique identifiers.

There are three ways to access the values stored in a record variable.

1.   Individual fields can be accessed with the 'period' notation (below).

2.   The complete record can be accessed in a single assignment statement—all the fields of one record variable can be assigned to the corresponding fields of another.

accessing fields

3.   The **with** statement lets us access fields without having to employ the period notation.

Let's define a record type to experiment with:

```
type CurrentConditions = (Clear, Cloudy, Raining);
     Weather = record
             Temperature: -25..125;
             Barometer: real;
             Present, Outlook: CurrentConditions
     end;
var Morning, Noon, Evening: Weather;
```

period notation

The series of assignments to *Morning*, below, use the 'period' notation. The record variable's identifier is followed by a period, and the name of a field.

```
Morning.Temperature := 73;
Morning.Barometer := 30.16;
Morning.Present := Cloudy;
Morning.Outlook := Raining;
```

complete record
assignment

If weather conditions are identical at midday, we can take a shortcut and assign all the *Weather* fields in one fell swoop, like this:

$\qquad$ *Noon* := *Morning* ;

This single assignment is equivalent to a sequence of field-by-field assignments. Every field of *Noon* gets the value of its counterpart in *Morning*. However, remember that complete record assignments can only be made between records of an *identical* type, declared with the same type name.

The third method of access to record-typed variables uses the **with** statement, whose sole purpose is convenience. When a record variable's identifier is given in the **with** statement (**with** *RecordName* **do**), its fields can be accessed directly during the statement's action. The period notation is not required.

the **with** statement

with statement

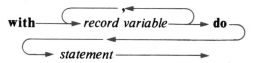

The **with** statement's action is almost invariably a compound statement (so that two or more fields can be accessed during the course of one action). The series of assignments below is equivalent to the last example:

using **with**

$\qquad$ **with** *Noon* **do begin**
$\qquad\qquad$ *Temperature* := 73 ;
$\qquad\qquad$ *Barometer* := 30.16 ;
$\qquad\qquad$ *Present* := *Cloudy* ;
$\qquad\qquad$ *Outlook* := *Raining*
$\qquad$ **end** ;

Similarly, this sequence:

$\qquad$ *writeln* (*Morning.Temperature*) ;
$\qquad$ *readln* (*Morning.Barometer*) ;

is the same as:

$\qquad$ **with** *Morning* **do begin**
$\qquad\qquad$ *writeln* (*Temperature*) ;
$\qquad\qquad$ *readln* (*Barometer*)
$\qquad$ **end** ;

How can we access a record that is a field of another record? Consider these definitions and declarations.

```
type PressureRecord = record
            Systolic, Diastolic :  50..200
        end ; {PressureRecord }
```
fields of fields
```
    PatientRecord = record
            Temperature : real ;
            BloodPressure : PressureRecord
        end ; {PatientRecord }
var Low, Normal, High : PressureRecord ;
    TodaysPatient : PatientRecord ;
```

A top-down approach is the key to taking apart structured variables. First, access the record, then, access any records contained in the record.

```
TodaysPatient.Temperature := 98.6 ;
TodaysPatient.BloodPressure.Systolic := 120 ;
TodaysPatient.BloodPressure.Diastolic := 90 ;
```

The **with** statement can be used to make dealing with nested records (like *TodaysPatient*) easier.

arguments to **with**

> The **with** statement can be given any number of record-structured variable identifiers as 'arguments.' This construct is equivalent to a series of nested **with** statements.

In other words, this **with** statement:

```
with Record1, Record2 do begin    etc.
```

is the exact semantic equivalent of:

```
with Record1 do
    with Record2 do begin    etc.
```

Similarly, both program segments below have the same effect. However, segment 2 uses **with** in a more sophisticated way by giving it two arguments.

```
with TodaysPatient do begin                {Segment 1}
    Temperature := 98.6 ;
    BloodPressure.Systolic := 120 ;
    BloodPressure.Diastolic := 90
end ;
with TodaysPatient, BloodPressure do begin       {Segment 2}
    Temperature := 98.6 ;
    Systolic := 120 ;
    Diastolic := 90
end ;
```

In some potential applications of the **with** statement, the scope of field identifiers must be taken into account. Suppose that a statement begins:

with *Low, Normal* **do begin**   etc. {Two *PressureRecord* variables.}

Within this **with** statement, is a mention of the identifier *Systolic* equivalent to *Low.Systolic*, or to *Normal.Systolic*?

scope of **with**

> The scope of nested records is similar to normal scope. The innermost record variable's field identifiers take precedence.

Thus, the last mentioned record variable's fields are accessed—*Systolic* really means *Normal.Systolic*. You can gather that, under certain circumstances, using a **with** statement may be inappropriate.

arrays of records

Once the idea of field access is firmly rooted in your mind, you'll appreciate that it doesn't really matter how deep a variable's structure is. Take a final example—the representation of a chessboard. The board itself can be a two-dimensional array. Each element, in turn, must tell us whether or not the square is occupied, the value of the piece (if any) on each square, and the owner of the piece. In the type definitions below, we first define ordinal types, then the record that uses them, and finally the array whose elements the records are.

chessboard type definition

```
type OwnerColor = (None, Black, White) ;
     PieceValues = (Empty, Pawn, Knight, Bishop, Rook, Queen, King) ;
     Squares = record
                 Occupied : boolean ;
                 Piece : PieceValues ;
                 Owner : OwnerColor
               end ;  {Squares definition}
     ChessBoard = array [1..8, 1..8] of Squares ;
var LastMove, CurrentMove : Squares ;
    Board : ChessBoard ;
```

Assume that a white pawn is stored in element 5,2 (its starting position). The statements below put a white pawn two rows up, on 5,4. Since *Board* [5,4] refers to an element that's an entire record, we must use record-access methods to get at a single field. Any of the examples shown below will do the job.

identical alternatives

```
Board [5,4] := Board [5,2] ;                    {1}

Board [5,4].Occupied := true ;
Board [5,4].Piece := Pawn ;                      {2}
Board [5,4].Owner := White ;

CurrentMove.Occupied := true ;
CurrentMove.Piece := Pawn ;
CurrentMove.Owner := White ;                     {3}
Board [5,4] := CurrentMove ;
```

```
with Board [5,4] do begin
        Occupied := true;                            {4}
        Piece := Pawn;
        Owner := White
    end;
```

You may note that I haven't emptied the square where the pawn used to be—right now it's in two places at once.

problem:
representing complex
numbers

A very natural application of records is the representation of complex numbers. Each complex number is presented as the sum or difference of a real part (that is, a mathematical real, and not a Pascal *real*), and an imaginary part, which is labeled i. For example, $5 + 2i$ and $2.5 - 4i$ are both complex numbers.

The imaginary part is actually a multiple of the mysterious square root of negative one. Although most textbooks consist of unremitting propaganda for the real numbers, their imaginary brethren help solve some relatively easy problems. The most familiar examples involve the quadratic equation, which on occasion (say, in solving $x^2 + x + 1 = 0$) require that the square roots of negative numbers be evaluated. However, complex numbers also find wide application in physics and engineering.

Once we allow the possiblity of complex numbers, can complex functions, complex integrals, and so on be far behind? And of what use are these without a plane—the complex plane, of course—to draw them on? Fortunately, all of these are beyond the scope of this book. I have, however, included a program that demonstrates some of the basic operations on complex numbers.

Program *ComplexMath*, below, is mainly intended to provide an example of record types as variables and parameters. As input I've given the cube roots of unity (the second factor is the square of the first). However, for your amusement, you may wish to use it to evaluate Euler's equality $e^{\pi i} + 1 = 0$, which uses the constants 0, 1, π, e, and i (of which π, e, and i were generally introduced as notation by Euler) in a single, economical equation.*

```
program ComplexMath (input, output);
    {Uses complex numbers to demonstrate some record operations.}
```

complex math
program

```
type Complex = record
                   real, imaginary: real;
               end;
var a, c, e: Complex;
procedure WritelnComplex (c: Complex);
    begin
        writeln (c.real, ' + ', c.imaginary, ' i')
    end;  {WritelnComplex}                          {program continues}
```

---

* 'Gentlemen, that [equation] is surely true, it is absolutely paradoxical; we cannot understand it, and we don't know what it means, but we have proved it, and therefore, we know it must be the truth.' B. Pierce.

```
procedure MultiplyComplex (a, b: Complex; var c: Complex);
    begin
        c.real := (a.real * b.real) - (a.imaginary * b.imaginary);
        c.imaginary := (a.real * b.imaginary) + (a.imaginary * b.real)
    end; {MultiplyComplex}
function Magnitude (a: Complex): real;
    begin
        Magnitude := sqrt (sqr (a.real) + sqr (a.imaginary))
    end; {Magnitude}
procedure DivideComplex (a, b: Complex; var c: Complex);
    procedure InvertComplex (var a: Complex);
        var SquaredLength: real;
        begin
            SquaredLength := sqr (Magnitude (a));
            a.real := a.real / SquaredLength;
            a.imaginary := -a.imaginary / SquaredLength
        end; {InvertComplex}
    begin
        InvertComplex (b);
        MultiplyComplex (a, b, c)
    end; {DivideComplex}
procedure ExpComplex (a: Complex; var z: Complex);
    begin
        with z do begin
            real := exp (a.real) * cos (a.imaginary);
            imaginary := exp (a.real) * sin (a.imaginary)
        end
    end; {ExpComplex}
begin
    write ('Enter two complex numbers ');
    writeln ('(a.real a.imaginary c.real c.imaginary):');
    readln (a.real, a.imaginary, c.real, c.imaginary);
    MultiplyComplex (a, c, e);
    write ('a*c = ');  WritelnComplex (e);
    DivideComplex (a, c, e);
    write ('a/c = ');  WritelnComplex (e);
    write ('|a| = ');  writeln (Magnitude (a));
    write ('|c| = ');  writeln (Magnitude (c));
    ExpComplex (a, e);
    write ('exp(a) = ');  WritelnComplex (e);
    ExpComplex (c, e);
    write ('exp(c) = ');  WritelnComplex (e)
end. {ComplexMath}
```

Enter two complex numbers (a.real a.imaginary c.real c.imaginary):
–0.5 +0.866 –0.5 –0.866
a∗c = 9.99956000000000e–01 + 0.00000000000000e+00 i
a/c = –4.99977999031957e–01 + –8.66038105676650e–01 i
|a| = 9.99977999757995e–01
|c| = 9.99977999757995e–01
exp(a) = 3.92958293038002e–01 + 4.62020801592420e–01 i
exp(c) = 3.92958293038002e–01 + –4.62020801592420e–01 i

Sorting

In Chapter 7 we wrote a program (*CountTheCharacters*) that determined the frequency of the appearance of lower-case letters in a text sample. Our program printed its results in alphabetical order. It's not unreasonable, though, to want our output printed in order of frequency, from the most used letter to the least. To get such a chart requires ordering the collected data.

Sorting data is one of the most thoroughly analyzed topics in computer science; people can write entire books about it, and I will also return to the subject later. For now, though, don't be intimidated, because some basic methods can work very well. A very obvious sorting routine known as a *selection sort* works like this:

Suppose that we have an array of *integer* values.

| 18 | 35 | 22 | 97 | 84 | 55 | 61 | 10 | 47 |

selection sort

Search through the array, find the largest value, and exchange it with the value stored in the first array location.

| 97 | 35 | 22 | 18 | 84 | 55 | 61 | 10 | 47 |

Next, find the second largest value in the array, and exchange it with the value stored in the second array location. This is identical to the first trip through the array, except that we don't look at the first value—we already know it's the largest. I've shaded the portion we're not inspecting.

| 97 | 84 | 22 | 18 | 35 | 55 | 61 | 10 | 47 |

Now, repeat the 'select and exchange' process, each time beginning the search one value further along the array. As we go along, we'll be building an ordered array of values (shaded). Eventually, we'll get all the way to the end of the array—which has to be the smallest stored value—and the array will be ordered.

| 97 | 84 | 61 | 18 | 35 | 55 | 22 | 10 | 47 |

| 97 | 84 | 61 | 55 | 35 | 18 | 22 | 10 | 47 |

| 97 | 84 | 61 | 55 | 47 | 18 | 22 | 10 | 35 |

| 97 | 84 | 61 | 55 | 47 | 35 | 22 | 10 | 18 |

| 97 | 84 | 61 | 55 | 47 | 35 | 22 | 18 | 10 |

A similar sorting algorithm is called *bubble sort*. This method usually requires fewer comparisons, but many more exchanges than the selection sort does. It tends to take more time to run than a selection sort. A bubble sort works like this:

Begin with the same array as before:

| 18 | 35 | 22 | 97 | 84 | 55 | 61 | 10 | 47 |

bubble sort   Compare the first value with the second. If the second is larger, exchange them.

| 35 | 18 | 22 | 97 | 84 | 55 | 61 | 10 | 47 |

Next, compare the second and third values, exchanging them if the third is larger.

| 35 | 22 | 18 | 97 | 84 | 55 | 61 | 10 | 47 |

Then compare (and possibly exchange) the third and fourth values, the fourth and fifth, etc. until you reach the end of the array. Note that the smallest stored value ends up stored in the last position (shaded).

| 35 | 22 | 97 | 84 | 55 | 61 | 18 | 47 | 10 |

Now, go back to the beginning of the array and start all over again. Work your way through the array comparing and exchanging values again. However, since the smallest value is already at the far right, you need not compare the final value.

| 35 | 97 | 84 | 55 | 61 | 22 | 47 | 18 | 10 |

Repeat the process of comparison and exchange without bothering the final *two* values.

| 97 | 84 | 55 | 61 | 35 | 47 | 22 | 18 | 10 |

As you can see, an ordered list is forming on the right. Continue the process of comparison and exchange, ignoring the last *three* values this time.

| 97 | 84 | 61 | 55 | 47 | 35 | 22 | 18 | 10 |

This particular array is already ordered. If it weren't, it *would* be when we got to the point of only comparing the first two values.

In a sense, the smallest values 'bubble' to the right side of the array.

Implementing these sorting algorithms will require a new data structure. Recall that we stored the values produced by *CountTheCharacters* in a one-dimensional array that was subscripted by letters, and stored *integer* values. Although such an array is easy enough to sort, the relationship between stored numbers and subscript characters can't be preserved. We'll wind up with an ordered array of numbers (the number of times each character appeared) but no idea of what characters they refer to.

Instead, we'll have to define an array whose elements store a character, and also the number of times that character has appeared. In other words, we'll need a one-dimensional array of records.

type definition

```
const ARRAYLIMIT = 26;
type CharData = record
                   TheCharacter: char;
                   Count: integer
               end; {CharData}
     RecordArray = array [1..ARRAYLIMIT] of CharData;
var OrderedArray: RecordArray;
```

Actually counting characters with this new data structure means we'll have to modify our counting algorithm. However, I'll save that problem for a rainy day and assume that an array variable named *OrderedArray*, of type *RecordArray*, already stores the number of times each letter appears in a text sample. For example, we'll assume that the value of *OrderedArray*[1].*TheCharacter* is 'a'. At the other end of the array, *OrderedArray*[26].*TheCharacter* is 'z'.

Since both the selection sort and bubble sort algorithms require many array values to be exchanged, procedure *Switch*, below, will come in handy. When called, it will be passed two array elements (of the record type *CharData*) as parameters.

element-switching
procedure

```
procedure Switch (var First, Second: CharData);
     {Exchanges the fields of two CharData records.}
     var Temporary: CharData;
begin
     Temporary := First;
     First := Second;
     Second := Temporary
end; {Switch}
```

As you read procedures *SelectionSort* and *BubbleSort*, below, bear in mind that each procedure rearranges records according to their *Count* fields. With slight modifications, they could be used to sort arrays of almost any type. The fact that we defined *ARRAYLIMIT* as a constant will make any conversion easier. As an aid in comparing the effects of each sort, I've kept count of the number of switches and comparisons each method requires. Assume the data of *CountTheCharacters*.

procedure *SelectionSort* (**var** *OrderedArray* : *RecordArray*) ;
   {Uses a selection sort algorithm to order an array of records.}

   var *First, Largest, Comparisons, Switches* : *integer* ;
      Current : 1..*ARRAYLIMIT* ;

selection sort procedure

   begin
      Comparisons := 0 ;
      Switches := 0 ;
      for *First* := 1 **to** *ARRAYLIMIT* −1 **do begin**
         Largest := *First* ;
         for *Current* := *First* **to** *ARRAYLIMIT* **do begin**
            Comparisons := *Comparisons*+1 ;
            if *OrderedArray* [*Current*].*Count*
                     >*OrderedArray* [*Largest*].*Count* **then**
               Largest := *Current*
         end ; {*Current* **for**}
         Switches := *Switches* +1 ;
         Switch (*OrderedArray* [*Largest*], *OrderedArray* [*First*])
      end ; {*First* **for**}
      writeln (*Comparisons* :2, ´ comparisons,   ´, *Switches* :2, ´ switches.´)
   end ; {*SelectionSort* }

↓   ↓   ↓   ↓   ↓

350 comparisons, 25 switches.

The difference between *SelectionSort* and *BubbleSort*, below, shows up in the number of comparisons and switches, and, more subtly, in the ordering they produce. Although both procedures correctly order the letters, the exact order of letters with the same frequency differs. This discrepancy doesn't cause any problems in this application, but it exemplifies the sort of detail we always have to be aware of. I'll return to this point—the distinction between stable and unstable sorting methods—in the exercises.

comparing the algorithms

```
procedure BubbleSort (var OrderedArray : RecordArray ) ;
    {Uses the bubble sort algorithm to order an array of records.}
    var Last : 2..ARRAYLIMIT ;
        Current : 1..ARRAYLIMIT ;
        Comparisons, Switches : integer ;
    begin
        Comparisons := 0 ;
        Switches := 0 ;
        for Last := ARRAYLIMIT downto 2 do
            for Current := 1 to Last –1 do begin
            Comparisons := Comparisons +1 ;
            if OrderedArray [Current].Count
                    <OrderedArray [Current +1].Count then begin
                Switches := Switches +1 ;
                Switch (OrderedArray [Current], OrderedArray [Current +1])
            end {if}
        end ;  {Current for}
        writeln (Comparisons :2, ' comparisons,   ', Switches :2, ' switches.')
    end ;  {BubbleSort }
```

bubble sort procedure

↓   ↓   ↓   ↓   ↓

325 comparisons, 132 switches.

Data Structuring: Arrays of Records

As noted, we will almost invariably find records being employed in conjunction with other data types; in particular, with arrays. Let's look at the definition of some of these relatively complicated types. As I go along, though, I'll continue to point out the distinction between Pascal definitions of data *types*, and algorithmic definitions of data *structures*. Recall once more that...

> A data *type* describes a particular kind of data. A data *structure* describes the way the data is stored.

data types, data
structures

As a data type, an array stores a sequence of values of one particular type. As a data structure, an array carries additional information related to the program's algorithm. For instance, the stored values may be in alphabetical or numerical order. They may bear some special relation to the array's subscripts. The array may just be used to keep track of when the values arrived.

An interesting class of data structuring problems can be broadly categorized as board or game-type problems. They generally call for arrays of records—arrays whose elements are structured themselves. For example:

A baseball game consists of nine innings.
A football game has four quarters.

A bowling match contains ten (sometimes eleven) frames.
A chessboard has 64 squares whose color and contents vary.
A Monopoly board has squares that represent properties, and usually include schedules of rents and buildings.
Computer games like Adventure, Hunt the Wumpus, and Rogue contain rooms filled with unknown objects, and connected in various ways.

Programming these games poses problems of keeping score, remembering positions, locating players, and the like. Do they require real algorithms? Well, although winning play might need some sort of algorithm, the programmer basically manages data by tracking scores and board positions.

> Data structures, rather than algorithms, are often the key to solving data-based problems. We can simplify a potential program with a data structure that makes it easy to do the arithmetic of scorekeeping, or the graphics of board positioning.

lateral thinking

Because the design of data types and structures is largely a mental exercise, a problem solving technique called *lateral thinking* can be put to good use. Lateral thinking is a name Edward DeBono invented to describe the process of repeatedly exploring and reconsidering possible solutions before committing ourselves to one particular method. For example, a lateral approach to digging for buried treasure would entail digging many shallow holes, instead of one hole that is very deep.

A lateral programmer might propose several potential data types before writing a program that relies on one of the alternatives. Experienced programmers can do this in their heads, but novices should sketch out some proposals on paper. For example, consider these two possible data type definitions for a program that scores a baseball game.

alternative data types

```
type Team = (Pirates, Mets, Astros, Giants, Yankees, Angels);
     Inning = (Top, Bottom);
     AtBats = record
                 TeamUp: Team;
                 Runs, Hits, Errors: integer
              end;
     Game = array [1..9, Top..Bottom] of AtBats;
```

```
type TeamName = packed array[1..15] of char;
     Inning = (Top, Bottom);
     Statistics = array [1..9] of integer;
     TeamStatistics = record
                 Name: TeamName;
                 Runs, Hits, Errors: Statistics
              end;
     Game = array [Top..Bottom] of TeamStatistics;
```

These data type definitions create two different ways of viewing and storing the exact same information. Choosing one over the other as the basis of our final data structure will depend on our ultimate application.

Programs that involve games (especially imaginary ones) can bring out the best in a programmer when it comes to design problems. Some game boards have an obvious representation—for instance, checkerboard games almost always call for a data type that is an **array** [1..8,1..8] of some record type. A board game like Monopoly, on the other hand, which appears to require a two-dimensional array, can be described as a single, long line of boxes—a one-dimensional array. Declaring a two-dimensional Monopoly board is unnecessary and slightly misleading because, aside from an occasional trip to Jail, the game moves in a straight line.

A game in which *nothing* moves in a straight line also calls for a one-dimensional array of records. *Hunt the Wumpus* is often found on interactive computer systems. Here's a description of a simple version.

You are in the cave of the Wumpus. The Wumpus likes you very much—especially for breakfast. To avoid being eaten, you must locate the Wumpus, and shoot it with your bow and arrow.

The Wumpus cave has 20 rooms, connected by narrow passageways. You can travel in any direction—North, South, East, or West—from one room to another. You also know the number of the room each passageway leads to. However, there are hazards to beware of. Some rooms contain bottomless pits, and others contain bats that will pick you up, and carry you to another room. One room contains the Wumpus. Entering a room that holds a pit or the Wumpus causes instant death. Fortunately, when you are one room away you can feel the breeze from a pit, hear the bats, or smell the Wumpus,

To win the game, you must shoot the Wumpus. When you shoot an arrow, it travels through three rooms—you can tell the arrow which tunnel to take as it passes through each room. Don't forget, though, that the tunnels often turn unexpectedly. You may end up shooting yourself. You have 5 arrows. Good luck.

A single refinement step is enough to state the rules of Hunt the Wumpus in an approximation of a Pascal program:

initialize the cave;
put the player in her first room;
if adjoining rooms have hazards, give warning;
repeat
    get the action—Move or Shoot?;
    case *Action* **of**
      Move: **begin**
          find out the direction;
          move;
          if adjoining rooms have hazards, give warning
      end;

problem: Hunt the Wumpus

refinement

Shoot: **begin**
     find out the arrow directions;
     shoot;
     update arrow count;
     is Player or Wumpus killed?
    end
   end {**case**}
  until (*Player is dead*) **or** (*Wumpus is dead*);

But does this pseudocode really help us write the final program? No. Our *real* problem is designing a data structure suitable for representing the Wumpus Cave.

 A good first step in this situation is to illustrate our data. The picture below has room numbers, contents (**B**at, **P**it, or **W**umpus), and connections between a number of the rooms.

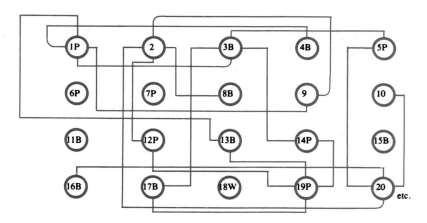

the Wumpus cave

Now we have to turn a data picture into a data type. How will the rooms be connected? As you can see, it's practically impossible to draw the cave *picture* in only two dimensions. At least three dimensions, and probably four, are needed to make rooms that seem to be right next to each other actually adjoin. But is a multi-dimensional array *type* needed to hold the cave of the Wumpus? Before you read on, stop for a moment and think about how you'd represent the entire group of rooms.

 The answer lies in considering the way we will use the stored data. Our main concern in playing is to know the contents of the current room, and the numbers of adjoining rooms. Suppose that we define *Rooms* as a record that holds just this information. We can draw a new and quite different picture of a room as a record with two fields. The *Contents* field represents any of the *Hazard* values. The second field is an array, subscripted by *Directions*, that contains *RoomNumbers* values.

a single room

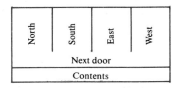

On the left, above, I've drawn a *Rooms* record in terms of its field and subscript names. The right-hand picture shows the values a typical *Rooms* record contains.

the entire cave

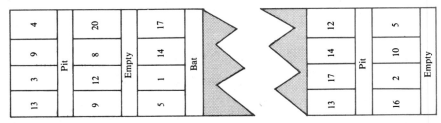

What about drawing the entire cave as a line of rooms? The map above contains the same information as the original picture. At this stage we can turn the drawing into a Pascal type definition.

> **const** *MAXIMUMNUMBEROFROOMS* = 20;
>
> **type** *Hazard* = (*Pit, Bat, Wumpus, Empty*);
>
>   *RoomNumbers* = 1..*MAXIMUMNUMBEROFROOMS*;
>
>   *Directions* = (*North, South, East, West*);
>
>   *PassageWays* = **array** [*North..West*] **of** *RoomNumbers*;
>
>   *Rooms* = **record**
>
>   *Contents*: *Hazard*;
>
>   *NextDoor*: *PassageWays*
>
>   **end**;
>
>   *Cave* = **array** [1..*MAXIMUMNUMBEROFROOMS*] **of** *Rooms*;
>
>   {We could have said '**array** [*RoomNumbers*] **of** *Rooms*.}
>
> **var** *WumpusCave*: *Cave*;
>
>   *CurrentRoomNumber*: *RoomNumbers*;

Wumpus type definition

Let's fill rooms 1 and 2 with data according to the map. For purposes of illustration, I'll use two different methods of access.

> *WumpusCave* [1].*Contents* := *Pit*; {Initialize Room 1.}
>
> *WumpusCave* [1].*NextDoor* [*North*] := 13;
>
> *WumpusCave* [1].*NextDoor* [*South*] := 3;
>
> *WumpusCave* [1].*NextDoor* [*East*] := 9;
>
> *WumpusCave* [1].*NextDoor* [*West*] := 4;

initializing the rooms

```
      with WumpusCave [2] do begin   {Initialize Room 2.}
         Contents := Empty;
         NextDoor [North] := 9;
         NextDoor [South] := 12;
         NextDoor [East] := 8;
         NextDoor [West] := 20
      end;
```

> One characteristic of a good data structure is to minimize the effort a pro-
> grammer must expend to examine data.

For example, at one stage of the game we must check neighboring rooms
to see if they contain hazards. Procedure *CheckForHazards*, below, does the job
quickly and neatly. Notice how the expression *NextDoor* [*Neighbor*] is used as an
array subscript.

inspecting a room

```
      procedure CheckForHazards (CurrentRoomNumber: RoomNumbers;
                                                WumpusCave: Cave);
         {Check out the neighbors of a Wumpus cave room.}
         var Neighbor: Direction;
      begin
         with WumpusCave [CurrentRoomNumber] do
            for Neighbor := North to West do
               case WumpusCave [NextDoor [Neighbor]].Contents of
                  Empty: ;
                  Bat: writeln ('I hear bats!');
                  Pit: writeln ('I feel a breeze!');
                  Wumpus: writeln ('I smell a Wumpus!')
               end {case}
      end; {CheckForHazards}
```

Is *CheckForHazards* perfect? Not really. One programmer might object
that it allows duplicated warnings, and that a clever player could figure out
which room contains what hazard. Another programmer might object to our
data structure, since the expression:

WumpusCave [*NextDoor* [*Neighbor*]].*Contents*

is unappealing on aesthetic grounds—it takes a concerted effort to understand it.
I tried to head off this objection by using a **with** statement and well-named variables.

One of the less visible features of *CheckForHazards* is its use of the
subrange *RoomNumbers* as the type of *CurrentRoomNumber*. This is a built-in
safety check on the value passed to *CurrentRoomNumber*, assuring us that the
room we're examining exists. It is precisely for such applications that ordinal
subranges were created.

I'll leave Hunt the Wumpus now. Although a program to play the game is fairly long, it is well within our abilities as programmers—given a suitable data structure.

Records with Variants

The records I've defined so far have each had a fixed contingent of fields. However, Wirth enhanced Pascal records by allowing the definition of *record variants*. When we use record variants, the effective number and type of fields in a single record may change during the course of a program. This means that two variables can be of an identical record type, yet have different numbers or types of fields.

I'll discuss record variants briefly. First I'll consider a record that has *only* a variant part, then I'll define a record with a fixed part *and* a variant part. Finally, I'll establish the syntax of record variants.

Let's begin with a data structuring problem that illustrates the need for record variants in the first place. Suppose that we're recording measurements that describe several four-sided figures. Each shape is defined by a different group of dimensions.

Shape	Required Dimensions
Square	Side
Rectangle	Length, Width
Rhomboid	Side, AcuteAngle
Trapezoid	Top, Bottom, Height
Parallelogram	Top, Side, ObtuseAngle

why do we need variants?

Now, we could easily define five different records—one for each shape. Or, it might be more convenient to define a single record with enough fields to record the dimensions of *any* of the shapes. However, both solutions have shortcomings. The first makes it difficult to define general-purpose subprograms, since each record type will require its own procedures and functions. The second solution is grossly inefficient, and a program that stored hundreds or thousands of such records might run into trouble.

shortcomings of records

Record variants come to the rescue. If you examine the list of shapes, it's easy to imagine a *WhatShape* field that could tell us which fields are actually required in the rest of the record, and which are superfluous.

the tag field

> The idea that the value of one field could or should determine the rest of the structure is the basis of record variants. One field is designated to be a *tag* or marker field—a field whose value tags or marks the proper group of *variant* fields.

Dimensions is redefined below as a record with variants. *WhatShape* is the tag field, and the record contains five groups of variant fields.

```
type Shape = (Square, Rectangle, Rhomboid, Trapezoid, Parallelogram);
     Dimensions = record
```

a record with variants

```
                        case WhatShape: Shape of        {The tag field}
                             Square: (Side1: real);
                             Rectangle: (Length, Width: real);
                             Rhomboid: (Side2: real; AcuteAngle: 0..360);
                             Trapezoid: (Top1, Bottom, Height: real);
                             Parallelogram: (Top2, Side3: real; ObtuseAngle: 0..360)
                        end; {Dimensions}
var FourSidedObject: Dimensions;
```

> Each variant's fields must be unique. No field identifier can appear in more than one group. The tag field, in contrast, is shared by each of the variant groups.

Until the tag field has a value, the remainder of the record variant's structure is undefined. At this point, we can only make an assignment to the tag field, *WhatShape*.

```
     FourSidedObject.WhatShape := Rectangle;
```

activating variants

Once *WhatShape* has been given a value, the fields associated with that value (given in parentheses in *Dimension's* definition above) are created. The assignment above activates a certain group of fields—in this case, *Length* and *Width*. As long as the value of *WhatShape* is *Rectangle*, these are the only fields that *FourSidedObject* will contain. We can make the assignments:

```
     FourSidedObject.Length := 4.3;
     FourSidedObject.Width := 7.5;
```

but an attempted assignment to a field in one of the other variant groups (say, *Top1* or *ObtuseAngle*) is an error—it does not exist.

What if the value of the tag field changes? If we now say that:

```
     FourSidedObject.WhatShape := Parallelogram;
```

we find ourselves able to access three new, but as yet undefined fields—*Top2, Side3* and *ObtuseAngle*. The former variant fields *Length* and *Width* simply don't exist any more—they've been deactivated and replaced. Thus, record variants act as an antibugging device, by restricting the assignments that can be made to a record variable.

advantages of
variants

A single record variant definition (like *Dimensions*) has other advantages over the five separate definitions we might have made. Suppose that we want to write a function that computes and represents the area of variable *FourSidedObject*. In function *Area*, below, a single variable of type *Dimensions* is passed as a parameter, then dissected within the routine. If we were using five different records, we'd have to write five different subprograms. But since *Dimensions* is defined as a record variant, just one declaration suffices.

function *Area (Object : Dimensions) : real ;*
{Computes an area that depends on an active variant.}

begin

using the active variant

```
        with Object do
            case WhatShape of
                Square : Area := sqr (Side1 ) ;
                Rectangle : Area := Length *Width ;
                Rhomboid : Area := sqr (Side2 )*sin (AcuteAngle) ;
                Trapezoid : Area := (Top1+Bottom)/2*Height) ;
                Parallelogram : Area := Top2 *Side3 *sin (ObtuseAngle)
            end {case}
    end ; {Area }
```

Notice how the **case** statement in *Area* parallels the construction of *Dimensions* variant part. Using a tag field as the **case** expression is quite common, and is why record variants are similar to **case** statements.

The variant parts of the *Dimensions* record were *disjoint*, which means that they only shared the tag field. However, Pascal lets us define records that share fields, and have variants as well.

fixed and variant parts

> A record definition may include a *fixed part* and a *variant part*. The fixed part *always* comes before the variant part, and only one variant part is allowed (although variants may be nested).

In the example below, the *Year*, *Fee*, and *ExpirationDate* fields form *Registration*'s fixed part. They, along with the tag field *VehicleType*, are shared by every variant.

```
type Model = (Motorcycle, Car, Truck ) ;
     Registration = record
                Year : 1915..1988 ;
                Fee : real ;
                ExpirationDate : 1987..1992 ;
                case VehicleType : model of
                    Motorcycle : (EngineSize : 50..1200) ;
                    Car : (Cylinders : 2..8 ; SmogRequired : boolean) ;
                    Truck : (Axles : 2..10 ; Weight, Tare : integer)
            end ; {Registration }
```

The current value of the tag field *VehicleType* determines which group of variant fields will be accessible. Other applications that require records with both fixed and variant fields include employment records, library records, medical records, and the like—any time some storage is specialized, and some general.

The syntax of a record with a variant part is, without doubt, the toughest in Pascal. By using the reserved word **case** in a misplaced moment of economy, Wirth managed to confuse nearly everybody. The reason is that the **case** of a record variant is only superficially similar to the **case** of a **case** statement. A record type's syntax chart is:

record type

The syntax of a field list is much harder to follow. If you read it carefully, you'll see that the field list is partially defined in terms of itself. Note that if a tag field selector value (or values) doesn't have any variant fields associated with it, an empty field list must be provided—*no* field names are put between the parentheses.

field list

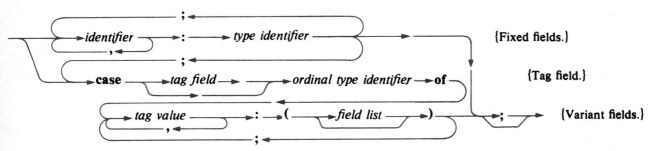

Chapter Notes 8-2

THE MOST COMMON ERROR IN DEFINING record types is to omit the **end** that marks the conclusion of the record definition. Imagine how a compiler might read this program segment:

> **type** *RealEstate* = **record**
> > *Street, Avenue* : *integer* ;
> > *Price* : *real* ;
>
> **var** *Apartment* : *char* ;

Since the end of the record definition isn't indicated, the compiler will probably think that **var** is one of *RealEstate's* fields, and print an error message that points out the futility of using reserved words as identifiers, along with a host of other presumed transgressions:

```
type RealEstate = record
                Street, Avenue: integer;
                Price: real;
        var Apartment: char;
        ↑RESERVED WORD "VAR" MAY NOT BE FIELD IDENTIFIER
            ↑MISSING COMMA
                    ↑MISPLACED COLON
                        ↑PROBABLE MISUSE OF IDENTIFIER "CHAR"
```

The fact that records and **with** statements have their own form of scope also causes confusion. This is a perfectly legal sequence of definitions and declarations:

```
type InnerRecord = record
                        AnyName: integer
                    end;
        OuterRecord = record
                        AnyName: boolean;
                        Inside: InnerRecord
                    end;
        var TestCase: OuterRecord;
            AnyName: char;    etc.
```

scope bugs   In the usual context of a program, the two *AnyName* fields will be distinct from each other, as well as from variable *AnyName*, because a reference to a field is usually prefaced by the name of the record-type variable it belongs to. The assignment below is to the *char* variable *AnyName*.

```
AnyName := 'R';
```

In the next example, the identifier *AnyName* refers to the *boolean* field of *TestCase*. The *integer AnyName* field of *Inside* must be referred to using the period notation, and the global variable *AnyName* cannot be accessed at all.

```
with TestCase do begin
    AnyName := true;
    Inside.AnyName := 5
end;
```

Giving two record names to the **with** statement further restricts the scope of the identifier *AnyName*. The *integer* field AnyName, of *Inside*, is accessed below. It's the most local because *Inside* is the last record named.

```
with TestCase, Inside do begin
    AnyName := 6
end;
```

An exceptionally sneaky bug can occur when we use a **with** statement to examine the record-type elements of an array. Suppose that we have an array of 100 elements, and want to examine the first element whose *Sum* field is nonzero (we're sure that one exists). Will this code work?

```
{incorrect segment}
Count := 1;
with TheArray [Count] do begin
    while Sum = 0 do Count := Count + 1;
        . . .
    manipulate other fields of TheArray [Count]
end;
```

No, it won't. Instead, if *TheArray* [1].*Sum* equals 0, the **while** loop will become an infinite loop.

> The specific record that a **with** statement has access to cannot be changed during the statement's action. It is determined when the statement is first entered.

The code above must be modified like this:

```
{correct segment}
Count := 1;
while TheArray [Count].Sum = 0 do
    Count := Count + 1;
with TheArray [Count] do begin
        . . .
    manipulate the TheArray [Count] fields
end;
```

The Pascal headaches caused by record variants extend far beyond their weird syntax. The discussion was less than candid (I lied) when I said that assigning a value to the tag field activated a particular group of variant fields. In reality, *all* of the record's fields are accessible *all* the time. Understanding why this spells trouble requires a bit of background in how values are stored. Usually, the computer provides a unique portion of its memory for the storage of each field and variable value. As you might imagine, values of different types require different amounts of storage. The illustration below shows how two distinct records might have space allocated for their fields.

	Rhomboid		Triangle		
Side	Acute Angle	Small Side	Middle Side	Big Side	

Now, let's imagine that instead of being separate records, the two groups above are variant parts of a single record. The compiler saves space by *overlaying* them—scheduling them for the *same* area in the computer's memory:

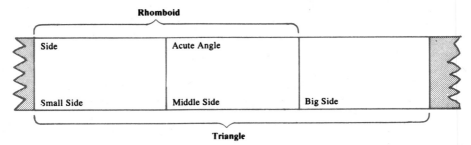

All is well and good as long as we only input and output values of one variant group. Trouble comes when we store values according to one scheme of occupancy, and then mistakenly try to read them according to the other. Although we get a value, it is gibberish. You would think that the compiler would prevent errors of this sort, but it doesn't because of a very specialized option of record variants I didn't shout about.

optional tag fields

> A tag field need not be specified for a record variant. However, a type identifier must still be given:
>
> **case** *TypeIdentifier* **of**   etc.
>
> The rest of the variant part's definition proceeds normally.

This feature is error-prone and rarely used. Since the tag field is optional, it can't be checked by the compiler. Thus, *you* should always declare a tag field, and check its value before trying to access fields of a variant part.

Important to Remember

● The **record** is a structured type that lets a variable store values of different types. A record's fields can be of any type, simple or structured. Fields can be assigned to individually using the 'period' notation or the **with** statement. Or, if two record variables have identical types, assignment can be made between all fields simultaneously.

● A record's fields must have different identifiers. However, different records can share the same identifiers—each record has its own name list. Field identifiers also don't conflict with identifiers defined elsewhere.

● A **with** statement can be given more than one record variable as an argument. This construction is equivalent to a series of nested **with** statements. The last-named (i.e. innermost) variable's fields take precedence.

- The specific record that a **with** statement has access to can't be changed during the statement's action. This rule is mainly of concern when we're looking at record-type elements of array variables.

- Lateral thinking is an approach to problem solving in which alternative strategies are explored before making any commitments.

Cross Reference

- The record type is discussed in A102—A112. The basic type definition is described in A102—A103, while the most common record usage is defined on A104.

- The **with** statement is defined in A105—A107.

- The discussion of records is expanded to include the notion of type unions on A107. The syntax of record variants follows in A108—A110. Finally, the rules that pertain to record variants are summarized in A111—A112.

- The dynamic allocation of record variants is discussed in A141—A142. This is relevant for some applications of pointer types.

8-1   A rather interesting exercise in array traversal involves finding the sequence of contiguous array elements that have the greatest sum. For example, given the array:

7   −8   7   6   −5   4   6   −1   −8   2

the contiguous sequence with the greatest sum runs from the third through seventh elements.

Write a program that reads up to fifty values, sums each subsequence, orders the ten largest sums, and prints the starting and ending points of the ten subsequences with the greatest sums. Cryptic hint: how do I know that there are $\frac{50(50 + 1)}{2}$ subsequences in all?

8-2   *Hailstone* numbers, like hailstones, go up and down but eventually reach the ground. We define each succeeding term in the hailstone sequence as equaling three times the previous term, plus 1, for odd-valued terms, and half the previous number for even hailstones. The hailstone sequence that starts with 3 is:

3, 10, 5, 16, 8, 4, 2, 1, 4, 2, ...

Any sequence that contains a 1, 2, or 4 is terminal, and is said to be the hailstone sequence's *ground state*.

Generate hailstone sequences for starting values of 1 through 1000. Which five numbers reach the largest values on the way to the ground state? Which five numbers take the longest to get there?

8-3   A sorting method is said to be *stable* if two equal keys maintain the same order in both unordered input and ordered output. The sort is *unstable* if it can change equal values. For example, if our starting data consists of counts of letters:

A(5)   B(7)   C(7)   D(6)

stable and unstable sorts are:

A(5)   D(6)   B(7)   C(7)   A(5)   D(6)   C(7)   B(7)
a stable sort   *an unstable sort*

Consider the procedures for selection sort and bubble sort that I wrote in 8-1. Are they stable or unstable? Can a stable implementation be made unstable, and vice versa?

8-4   Blood pressure is given by a pair of numbers—the systolic and diastolic pressures—in millimeters of mercury. Pulse pressure, in turn, is defined as the difference between the two.

Write a program that is able to:

1.   order blood pressure records by systolic, diastolic, or pulse pressures;

2.   print the *n* records with the highest pressures of a given type;

3.   print any records that appear on all three 'high pressure' lists.

Hint: use a single sorting routine by defining a *SortKey* field for each record. Don't forget to number (or somehow identify) individual records.

8-5   A fraction consists of a numerator and denominator. Write a program that reads an expression that contains plus or minus signs and numerator/denominator pairs, then:

1.   orders them by denominator;

2.   adds or subtracts, as appropriate, numerators of like denominators;

3.   prints the resulting expression.

For example, the input $+ \frac{2}{7} + \frac{3}{5} - \frac{1}{5} + \frac{3}{7} - \frac{1}{9}$ should yield $+ \frac{2}{5} + \frac{5}{7} - \frac{1}{9}$. Try your program by adding a *Farey Series*, devised by John Farey in 1816, of reduced fractions between 0 and 1, with denominator $\leq n$. The 7 series is:

$$\frac{1}{7} + \frac{1}{6} + \frac{1}{5} + \frac{1}{4} + \frac{2}{7} + \frac{1}{3} + \frac{2}{5} + \frac{3}{7} + \frac{1}{2} + \frac{4}{7} + \frac{3}{5} + \frac{2}{3} + \frac{5}{7} + \frac{3}{4} + \frac{4}{5} + \frac{5}{6} + \frac{6}{7}$$

(An interestingly difficult problem that I will raise, but not·pose, incidentally, is to write a program that produces a Farey series.)

8-6   After locating the waste dump as described in Chapter 4's exercises (maximizing the distance to five cities), the predictable occurs—a train carrying nuclear waste to the dump site derails. In the ensuing round of finger-pointing and recrimination, two facts become clear:

1.   in the absence of wind and rain, danger from the radioactive waste declines according to the inverse square of distance from the site, and

2.   the probability of a transport accident increases directly with the distance that must be traveled.

Write a program, that reads *x, y* coordinates (in a 100 × 100 plane) for five cities. Then, find the saddle-point that maximizes each city's distance from the viewpoint of reducing radiation exposure, but minimizes the distance that waste must travel on the way to the dump.

8-7   Use the binary search method described in Chapter 7 to implement a form of reverse telephone directory—one that is ordered by telephone number, rather than by the subscriber's name. Allow these operations:

1.   Add a name, number, and address.

2.   Look up a number, and print the name and address.

3.   Delete a subscriber.

8-8   Write a program that reads twenty *x, y* coordinate pairs, and sorts them:

1.   In order of increasing *x* values.

2.   In order of decreasing *y* values.

3.   In order of increasing distance from the origin.

Why might a mechanical pen plotter find this sorting useful? How difficult is it to sort the points in order of distance from an arbitrary point?

8-9   A *polygon* is a closed, many-sided figure. A regular polygon's sides are all the same length, while an irregular polygon's sides vary.

a regular polygon   *an irregular one*   *a possibility we'll ignore*

In either case, we can define a polygon as a collection of the end points of each side. If one segment's end point is always the same as one other segment's starting point, the polygon is closed, and if each segment has the same length, the polygon is regular. (We will assume that no two sides intersect except at their ends.) Write a program that reads up to twenty-five pairs of *integer*-valued *x, y* coordinates, and decides:

1.   if they form a polygon;

2.   what the polygon's perimeter is;

3.   if the polygon is regular (since *real* arithmetic will be used, assume that lengths within 1% are sufficiently identical).

For an easier version of this exercise, assume that the points are supplied in a regular progression, i.e. 'in order' around the polygon's perimeter. For a more difficult problem, let them be jumbled.

8-10   A problem that often arises in the design of VLSI (very large-scale integration) circuits is to determine whether or not two circuit wires inadvertently intersect. For all practical purposes, the lines are either vertical or horizontal. Each line can be described by a pair of endpoints—(4,7..4,12) is a vertical line, while (2,9..5,9) is horizontal.

A simple check of *x* and *y* coordinates can reveal if two lines intersect. Write a program that reads twenty pairs of coordinates, sorts them into horizontal and vertical lines, then determines which lines intersect.

8-11   A standard problem of computer graphics systems is the suppression of hidden surfaces—surfaces that are behind other surfaces, and should not be shown.

Write a program that lets a user specify the four corner locations of up to five rectangles (you can assume that two corners will never occupy the same location), along with their relative depths—which is closest, and which are further away. Print the visible portions of each rectangle by 'painting' each onto a two-dimensional array (using a different number for each rectangle), then printing the entire array. How difficult is it to change the relative depth of the rectangles? You may find that an auxiliary, one-dimensional 'depth chart' array comes in handy.

8-12   Yet another problem that involves computer graphics deals with the difficulty of using a mouse or joystick to draw lines that are perfectly aligned. This is often a requirement in design work, particularly in the design of integrated circuits, where space is at a premium.

A common technique is called *Manhattanizing*. Suppose we represent a drawing area as a two-dimensional array. A mouse is used to indicate the approximate starting and ending points of a line. A program then makes sure that all approximately vertical lines are in a single column, perhaps by slightly moving a start or end point.

Before Manhattanizing   *After Manhattanizing*

Write a program that lets a user supply (in lieu of a mouse) the starting and ending points of more than one horizontal or vertical line. Allow these Manhattanizing features:

1. *Fixed posting* Hold the upper and left-hand points fixed, relocate only lower and right-hand points.

2. *Two-point posting* Move both endpoints, if necessary, to an 'average' vertical or horizontal axis.

3. *Equidistant posting* Spread vertical and horizontal lines equally over the entire field.

8-13 Let's consider a diffusion problem that is bounded by a maximum level of absorption—for instance, the spread of oil from several different sources onto a standing body of water.

Suppose that a conveniently rectangular lake is 100 meters long and 50 meters across. If three different types of oil are dumped into the lake (at three different points), each will begin to spread evenly in all directions. However, when the oil slicks contact each other, they do not mix. Thus, the thickness of the oil layer within any particular slick at any particular point equals the average of the surrounding points *except that* a boundary with a different oil acts as an impenetrable edge.

Write a program that models the flow of oil across the surface of the lake. Assume that diffusion rates are equal, and the relative quantities of oil spilt are irrelevant. Where will the final boundaries between the slicks be? (Can you write a routine that represents a duck's attempt to remain in an unpolluted area?)

8-14 We usually think of computerized scheduling as an attempt to absolutely minimize usage of time or allocation of resources. In real life, though, such precision is impossible. Consider the problem of defining routes for garbage pickup. Two factors limit the length of each run: the garbage truck may get filled up, or it may be time to take a break. Suppose that we are given data of the following form:

block 1 weight 0.3 time 14
block 2 weight 0.1 time 8
⋱

Each block has two figures associated with it—the weight of its garbage, and the time it takes to pick it up. Naturally, blocks must be visited in order.

Write a program that can be used to schedule pickups, subject to these constraints:

Garbage constrained routes are limited by the capacity of the truck.

Time constrained routes are limited by the length of a shift.

A truck is assumed to be filled (or a shift ended) on the block prior to overflow (or overtime).

Your program should read data for an arbitrary number of blocks. Then, subject to maximum garbage and time constants supplied by the user, print the blocks on each garbage-constrained or time-constrained route. If you really want to help the dispatcher, order the list of time-constrained routes according to how full the truck is, and sort the list of garbage-constrained routes according to how long they take.

8-15   Anybody who has ever gone on vacation is familiar with the problem of *bin packing*—storing objects of varying sizes into a number of containers, or bins. There are actually many ways of picturing situations that involve bin packing—filling freight cars, stocking standard lengths of pipe, scheduling television commercials, buying assorted stamps from a vending machine, and so on—but the underlying problem is always the same: we want to store fixed-size values in the smallest possible number of fixed-size bins.

Packing and unpacking bins will eventually lead to the most effective solution, but the amount of work involved rapidly makes this approach infeasible. Two rote approaches that rely on simple rules are:

1.   *First fit increasing* loads the bins starting with the smallest items first.

2.   *First fit decreasing* loads bins starting with the largest items first.

Taking for granted that loads are ordered to begin with, write a program that implements and tests each method. Assume that we have twenty or more bins of capacity 100 each, and are given the following loads:

```
51   51   51   51   51   51
27   27   27   27   27   27
26   26   26   26   26   26
23   23   23   23   23   23
23   23   23   23   23   23
```

What are the contents of each bin after it is packed? Which strategy is better? Is either optimal? Can you devise a strategy for loads that arrive in random order? (It has been shown, incidentally, that first fit increasing requires no more than (17/10), plus 2, of the optimum packing, while first fit decreasing is no worse than (11/9), plus 4.)

8-16   Structural formulae are a handy way to describe the composition of simple, regular molecules. For example, the aliphatic hydrocarbons (the alkanes, or paraffins) are chained hydrogen/carbon sequences:

methane   *ethane*   *propane*   *butane*   *pentane*

This particular sequence continues with hexane, heptane, octane (and eventually becomes polyethylene).

Write a program that is able to recognize a molecule from this family. Assume that input is a two-dimensional array that contains a molecule—in any up, down, left or right orientation—based on the following record:

```
type direction = (up, down, right, left, none);
     links = array [1..4] of direction;
     atom = record
              name: char;
              bond: links
            end;
```

This problem is suitable for a two-person project—one person writes routines to 'plant' the molecule, while the other tries to identify it.

8-17   *Lewis notation*, also called electron dot notation, is a convenient means of representing structural chemical formulae involving elements of the first, second, and third rows of the periodic table (hydrogen through chlorine). These elements tend to form molecules that let each atom enjoy a full outer shell of eight valence electrons. An atom is shown by its chemical symbol, surrounded by up to eight dots that represent electrons:

```
       ..                                    ..              ..
  H : O :      H : O : H           : Cl : Cl :          H : F :
       ..               ..              ..              ..         ..
       H
```

| *water* | *chlorine molecule* | *hydrogen flouride* |

One atom's electrons will frequently be shown with an alternate symbol (×) to help distinguish their origin.

Write a program that builds Lewis diagrams. Hardwire the valence structure of hydrogen and the second and third row elements, then let the user specify two or more elements for bonding. Try your program on sodium chloride (NaCl), carbon dioxide (CO_2), and boron trichloride (BCl_3).

8-18   Geographic positions are given in degrees, minutes, and seconds of latitude and longitude. Since they are full circles of the Earth, latitude and longitude lines are broken into 360 degrees, where each degree has 60 minutes, and each minute has 60 seconds. Latitude lines are numbered from 0°, at the equator, through 90°, at each pole, which results in Northern and Southern (for their respective hemispheres) latitudes. Similarly, longitude lines begin with 0° at Greenwich, England, then increase toward both East and West until they reach 180° near Napier, New Zealand.

Now, although some variations may apply in the farm states, each fifteen-degree change in longitude usually implies a one-hour difference in standard time. Suppose that it is a clear Spring equinox. Write a program that reads three positions of latitude (North or South) and longitude (East or West), along with the time at Greenwich. What is the time at each location? Which location is likely to be coldest?

8-19   We can define the *information content* of a letter as its predictive potential for the letter that follows. Since 'q' is invariably followed by 'u,' for instance, we can say that 'q' has a high information content.

Write a program that reads the contents of a textfile, and creates a table of letter-pair frequencies. You should convert all letters to lower-case. Then, either:

1.   print the 100 most common letter pairs, in order (you'll find that keeping an array of records, where each record holds a letter pair and its count, is convenient), or,

2.   print, in declining order of information content, a list of letters. For this exercise, say that a letter that can be followed by many letters has a low information content, while a letter that can be followed by few of its fellows has a high information content. (You'll find it's convenient to order 26 records, where each record holds a letter, and the number of different letters that follow.) Can you suggest a method of ordering that doesn't automatically allocate a high information content to letters that appear infrequently?

9

The **file** Type

Ask most people to describe what worries them about computers in a single word, and that word is liable to be 'files.' With the aid of computers, it's possible to keep track of enormous amounts of information—or to pull out hidden facts from a mass of raw data. Credit history, police records, tax returns, school records, even the videotapes you rented last week are all on file in various computers.

The creation and use of files is the topic of Chapter 9. Starting with *textfiles*, the most familiar sort, I'll describe temporary, internal files, then show how to create permanent external files that exist between program executions. Then I'll look at more general applications of the **file** type, discuss some low-level details of file manipulation, and consider files of ordinal and structured types besides *char*. We'll see examples of a number of common file algorithms, along with a few uncommon ones that are useful for scientific programming.

Defining and Using Files 9-1

GARBO SPEAKS! LET'S SAVE HER FIRST SCREEN words for posterity in a file named *Garbo*.

```
program GarboSpeaks (Garbo, output);
    {Creates, and adds to, a textfile named Garbo.}
type text = file of char;
var Garbo: text;
begin
    rewrite (Garbo);
    writeln (Garbo, 'Gimme a viskey, and don'' be stingy.')
end.  {GarboSpeaks}
```

file components

> A *file*-type variable stores a sequence of any number of *component* values (except other files).

The syntax chart of a file-type definition is:

file type

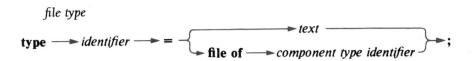

In comparison to other data types, files are interesting for two reasons. First, the number of components stored in a file isn't limited, except by the computer's memory. For all practical purposes, we can add additional components to a file indefinitely. Second, files can be made permanent. Unlike other program variables, which only exist for the life of a program, files can keep their contents after a program is finished.

file properties

I'll begin by concentrating on files of *char* values, called *textfiles*. To accommodate special treatment of such files, a structured type *text* is predefined in Pascal. Its definition, essentially the equivalent of:

type text

type *text* = **file of** *char*;

is a built-in part of every program (just like the definitions of the ordinal types *boolean* and *char*). The definition of type *text* in *GarboSpeaks* was redundant. (Actually, in some implementations, it is not exactly equivalent to a *text* definition—**file of** *char* may not include *eoln* values.)

program parameters

> To create a textfile, declare it as a variable of type *text*. If it is to be permanent, also name it as a *program parameter* in the program heading. Textfiles can go in place of, or in addition to, the normal program parameters *input* and *output*.

internal, external files

A permanent file is usually called an *external* file, while a temporary file is *internal*. In the example below, *Old* and *New* are external textfiles, while *Temp* is an internal textfile:

program *Example* (*Old, New*);
. . .
var *Old, New, Temp*: *text*;

Before we use a textfile, or any other file, it must be specially initialized. This is an unusual step that isn't applied to any other type of Pascal variable.

reset and rewrite

> Procedure *reset* prepares a file to be inspected or read, while procedure *rewrite* readies a file to be generated or written. Applying *rewrite* to a file removes any contents it may currently have.

Obviously, *input* and *output* are exempt from this rule, since the operating system takes care of initializing calls. It's important, though, to recognize that a file may only be in one state at a time—it's either being inspected (after a call of *reset*), or being generated (after a call of *rewrite*). Since a subsequent call of *rewrite* destroys the file's current contents, such calls should be made carefully.

The call of *reset* or *rewrite* is accompanied by the particular file's name in parentheses. From the brief program segment above we might have:

> *reset* (*Old*);   {Prepare to read *Old*.}
> *rewrite* (*New*);   {Prepare to write *New*.}

restrictions on file assignment

Two special restrictions apply to file-type variables, including textfiles. First, file variables can never be assigned to each other in their entirety, even if they have the same type. They must be copied, one component at a time. Second (and as a consequence of the first restriction), files must always be passed to subprograms as variable parameters. A file-type variable may not be defined as a value parameter.

Actually employing a textfile variable is very much like using ordinary *input* and *output*. When we're getting input from a textfile we'll want to be able to read values, to check for the file's end, to discard lines, or to check for the end of a line. Similarly, when we're sending output to a textfile we'll want to be able to print values and lines.

> Any of the procedures or functions used for ordinary input and output may be given a textfile identifier as a first argument. The subprogram then acts on that textfile.

textfile I/O

Naturally, we can only use the input-oriented subprograms with a textfile that has been *reset*, and the output-oriented procedures with a file that has been readied for output through a call of *rewrite*. For example:

> **while not** *eof* (*Old*) **do** ...   etc.
> **while not** *eoln* (*Old*) **do** ...   etc.
> *read* (*Old*, *First*, *Second*, *Third*);
> 　　{Read values for variables *First, Second*, and *Third* from file *Old*.}
> *write* (*New*, *Current*);
> 　　{Append the value of *Current* to file *New*.}
> *readln* (*Old*);
> 　　{Read past the current line of file *Old*.}
> *writeln* (*New*);
> 　　{Print the current line (or a blank line) in *New*.}

default I/O

The only reason that we haven't had to provide *input* and *output* as arguments to these subprograms is that *input* and *output* are the default textfiles. In other words:

eof	really means	*eof* (*input*)
read (*Ch*)	really means	*read* (*input*, *Ch*)
write (*Ch*)	really means	*write* (*output*, *Ch*)
writeln	really means	*writeln* (*output*)

Since the notion of lines only makes sense in reference to text, it's no surprise to find that *eoln, readln*, and *writeln* can only be applied to textfiles. Actually, it might even seem intuitively correct to assume that only *char* data could be read from files of type *text*. It's not, though—data of types *real* and *integer* can be read as well. When the computer expects to read such values, it automatically converts the sequence of characters into numbers of the appropriate type. A program can read an *integer* from, or write one to, a textfile as easily as a terminal.

We can take advantage of the file window in working with textfiles as well. If we had a textfile called *Temp*, and prepared it for reading with a call of *reset(Temp)*, then *Temp*↑ would represent the very first character in *Temp*. You may want to review section 5-2 for details on the file window.

the file window

Let's consider an example designed to exercise a few file handling skills. I won't try to dignify program *FileExercise* by claiming that it solves some sort of problem. Try to figure out what it does before you read its belated pseudocode.

textfile demonstration
program

```
program FileExercise (input, output, Data, Results);
   {Performs a few textfile manipulations.}
var Ch1, Ch2: char;
   Data, Results: text;
begin
   reset (Data);
   while input↑ = Data↑ do begin
      read (Ch1);
      read (Data, Ch2)
   end;
   rewrite (Results);
   while not eof do begin
      read (Ch1);
      write (Results, Ch1)
   end;
   while not eof (Data) do begin
      read (Data, Ch2);
      write (Ch2)
   end;
   writeln
end.  {FileExercise}
```

Program *FileExercise* is clearly just an excuse to use external files and the file window. First, it compares the contents of file *Data* with characters entered by the program user. As soon as a mismatch occurs, it sends the rest of the user's input to file *Results*. Finally, it prints the remainder of *Data* on the screen. In pseudocode, the program outline is:

its pseudocode

Ignore all input that matches file Data;
Save the rest of the user's input in file Results;
Print the rest of Data;

FileExercise dealt with its input stream relatively continuously. First we read data but ignored it, then we echoed input into file *Results*. Only after there wasn't any input left did we print the remaining contents of file *Data*.

Could we have taken these last steps in reverse? In other words, could we have printed *Data* before sending the rest of the user's input to *Results*? Yes. Data entered as input remains available even if we temporarily stop reading it, perhaps to deal with other files, or to produce output. The input stream is interruptable, but continuous.

Textfile Searches Insertions, and Comparisons

What are some advantages of textfile types over records and arrays? The most important feature is that the size of files is not predetermined. Although the bounds of an array or the fields of a record must be defined in advance, a file can grow almost indefinitely. When a program must store an unknown quantity of data, a file is the data type of choice.

Files allow permanent storage of program data. The success of programs that require substantial amounts of input is easily threatened by mistakes in data entry. As a defensive programming measure, data can be placed in a file, and a separate program or procedure written to error-check the file's contents. If the data is correct, the file can be reset and fed to the program proper. If it's incorrect, the program halts so that its data-file can be edited and fixed.

Files also have disadvantages in comparison to other types. Most important is that the information stored in a file cannot be accessed at random. Suppose that we want to read the last value stored in a file. Calling the *reset* procedure puts us at the file's beginning. We must read all the way through the file to reach the end—there's no way to jump there automatically. Similarly, how

can we easily compare the values on some particular line of two or more files? We have to *reset* and wade through each file (to the proper line) before making a comparison.

We're at a like disadvantage in writing files. The procedure *rewrite* puts us at the beginning of a blank file. Once *rewrite* has been called, we can only add data to the file's *end* (obviously, when a file is empty, its beginning and end are essentially the same). How could we possibly insert something at the beginning, or in the middle, of a file? Calling *rewrite* again erases all we've already written.

Naturally, there are shortcuts we can take to alleviate some of these problems. Since textfiles are divided into lines, we can jump from line to line (via *readln*) without bothering to peruse each line's contents. Let's solve the following problem of file *searching* (some problems that involve searching for strings are considered in Chapter 18):

Suppose that we have an ordered file of data on the elements, with one element described per line. Let the user enter an atomic number, then print the information found for that element.

The pseudocode program breakdown will have to include a check to make sure that a misinformed user doesn't go past the end of the *Elements* file:

> *get the atomic number*;
> *prepare to read Elements*;
> **while** *we're not at the line we want* **and not** *eof (Elements)*
>   *get the next line*;
>   *count the line*;
> **if** *there's a line for the element*
>   **then** *print it*
>   **else** *print an error message*;

Note that, when we leave the loop, we're not sure of why we left. Did we find the correct line number, or did we just run out of file? Did both happen at the same time? Indeed, did we enter the loop at all—perhaps the user entered the atomic number of one of the Klingon (or was it Romulan?) lighter-than-hydrogen elements. The shaded section of program *FindElements*, below, sees if we're on a proper line before it acts. The program will only print a line from *Elements* if we've reached an existing line number *AtomicNumber*.

refinement

line-counting program

```
program FindElements (input, output, Elements);
   {Finds and prints one line of textfile Elements.}
var Elements: text;
   AtomicNumber, CurrentLine: integer;
   NextCharacter: char;
begin
   writeln ('What atomic number would you like to learn about?');
   readln (AtomicNumber);
   CurrentLine := 1;
   reset (Elements);
   while (CurrentLine <AtomicNumber) and not eof (Elements) do begin
      readln (Elements);
      CurrentLine := CurrentLine +1
   end;
   if (CurrentLine <> AtomicNumber) or eof (Elements)
      then write ('The element you chose is not known to our science.')
      else while not eoln (Elements) do begin
            read (Elements, NextCharacter);
            write (NextCharacter)
      end; {we've printed a line}
   writeln
end. {FindElements}
```

↓   ↓   ↓   ↓   ↓

What atomic number would you like to learn about?
417
The element you chose is not known to our science.

Next, let's solve a problem that involves file *insertions*.

The word *concatenate* means to link together in a series or chain. For example, the concatenation of 'simple' and 'minded' is 'simpleminded'. Files are concatenated by being joined into a single longer file. Write a program that concatenates two files.

Concatenation—putting one file at the head of another—is just a special case of file insertion. We'll find that temporary internal files come in handy for such jobs. They're used as *buffers*, or temporary holding places, while editing

permanent external files. Internal files aren't included in the program heading since they, like ordinary program variables, don't exist before or after the program is run.

Suppose that we want to concatenate files *Beginning* and *Ending* into *Beginning*. *Beginning* will end up with its original contents followed by those of *Ending*. There is an almost overwhelming temptation to put the following pseudocode into effect.

> {incorrect pseudocode}
> *prepare to read Beginning*;
> *read it until eof (Beginning)*;
> *prepare to write Beginning*;
> *prepare to read Ending*;
> *add the contents of Ending to Beginning*;

However, we shall resist the temptation. Although the pseudocode reads to the end correctly, preparing to write *Beginning* will destroy its contents. To avoid this minor problem, we'll use *Temporary* as a transient, internal buffer file, and take the round-about route the pseudocode below suggests:

> {correct pseudocode}
> *prepare to write file Temporary*;
> *prepare to read Beginning*;
> *add the contents of Beginning to Temporary*;
> *prepare to read Ending*;
> *add the contents of Ending to Temporary*;
> *prepare to write Beginning*;
> *prepare to read Temporary*;
> *add the contents of Temporary to Beginning*;

Notice that the first and third concatenations are really just file copy moves, because we're concatenating an empty file to one that isn't empty. The implemented program is shown below.

```
program JoinFiles (Beginning, Ending, output);
   {Demonstrates file concatenation.}
var Beginning, Ending, TemporaryFile: text;
procedure Concatenate (var ToFile, FromFile: text);
   {Adds the contents of FromFile to the end of ToFile.}
   var CurrentCharacter: char;
   begin
      reset (FromFile);
      while not eof (FromFile) do begin
         while not eoln (FromFile) do begin
            read (FromFile, CurrentCharacter);
            write (ToFile, CurrentCharacter)
         end;
         readln (FromFile);
         writeln (ToFile)
      end
   end; {Concatenate}
begin
   rewrite (TemporaryFile);
   Concatenate (TemporaryFile, Beginning);
   Concatenate (TemporaryFile, Ending);
   rewrite (Beginning);
   Concatenate (Beginning, TemporaryFile)
end. {JoinFiles}
```

file concatenation
program

Procedure *Concatenate* is extremely powerful. For instance, suppose that the segment below was the statement part of *JoinFiles*, and that all files mentioned are validly declared. What is its effect?

```
begin
   reset (File1);      reset (File2);
   reset (File3);      reset (File4);
   rewrite (File0);
   Concatenate (File0, File1);     Concatenate (File0, File2);
   Concatenate (File0, File3);     Concatenate (File0, File4);
   rewrite (File4);
   Concatenate (File4, File0)
end.
```

multiple
concatenations

The program segment concatenates files *File1*, *File2*, *File3*, and *File4* into *File4*. In this case, *File0* serves as the temporary internal file.

Finally, let's look at a problem that involves file *comparison*.

problem: finding
common lines

We have three textfiles that contain names, one per line, in alphabetical order. We know that there is at least one name in common between the files. Find it.

This problem has historically been characterized as the 'Welfare Cheat' question; we imagine that we're given files that contain the names of welfare recipients in adjoining counties. However, we could just as easily call it the 'Cabinet Felon' problem, and have files that contain the names of Cabinet officers, indicted felons, and major contributors to the party in power.

Our first difficulty will be making the comparisons at all. Now, comparing two lines character-by-character isn't especially hard. This code will compare a line in *File1* to a line in *File2*:

a coding detail

```
{Travel along two lines until a mismatch or eoln .}
Ch1 := ' ';
Ch2 := ' ';
while not eoln (File1) and not eoln (File2) and (Ch1=Ch2) do begin
    read (File1, Ch1);
    read (File2, Ch2)
end;     etc.
```

But trouble starts when we leave the loop without a match. Suppose we decide that the first line of *File2* is lower, alphabetically, than the first line of *File1*. We should get the second line from *File2*, and compare it to the first line of *File1*.

But what do we make the new comparison between? We'll be at the beginning of the new line from *File2*, but in the middle of the current line of *File1*. They might be equal, but there's no way to back up to the beginning of the line to check. Worse yet, according to our problem, we have *three* files to contend with.

string buffers

Our solution will be to buffer the current line of each file in a particularly convenient manner—as a string. Recall that we can compare strings to each other in their entirety, using the relational operators. If a line of one file is 'low' in relation to the current lines of the other files, we get the next line from that file. In pseudocode:

refinement

```
prepare to read each file;
save the first line of each file as a string;
while all three lines aren't equal
    while the first file's line is lower than any other
        get the next line from the first file;
    while the second file's line is lower than any other
        get the next line from the second file;
    while the third file's line is lower than any other
        get the next line from the third file;
print the common line;
```

Program *FindTheCommonLine*, below, depends on the assumption that *First, Second*, and *Third* really do have a line in common. Increasing its robustness (to make it immune from crashes due to a missing common line) require checks for *eof*, rather than any basic change in the underlying algorithm.

```
program FindTheCommonLine  (First, Second, Third, output);
    {Find and print the common line in textfiles First, Second, and Third.}
const LINELENGTH = 80;
type String = packed array [1..80] of char;
var First, Second, Third: text;
    FirstLine, SecondLine, ThirdLine: String;
procedure GetTheNextLine  (var TheFile: text;  var TheLine: String);
    {Read a line of text up to LINELENGTH characters long.
     Advance to the next line of TheFile before leaving.}
    const BLANKLINE = '
    var Count: integer;
    begin
        TheLine := BLANKLINE;
        Count := 1;
        while (Count <=LINELENGTH) and not eoln (TheFile) do begin
            read (TheFile, TheLine [Count]);
            Count := Count + 1
        end;
        readln (TheFile)
    end; {GetTheNextLine}
begin
    reset (First);
    reset (Second);
    reset (Third);
    GetTheNextLine (First, FirstLine);
    GetTheNextLine (Second, SecondLine);
    GetTheNextLine (Third, ThirdLine);
    while (FirstLine <>SecondLine) or (FirstLine <>ThirdLine)
                        or (SecondLine <>ThirdLine) do begin
        while (FirstLine <SecondLine) or (FirstLine <ThirdLine) do
            GetTheNextLine (First, FirstLine);
        while (SecondLine <FirstLine) or (SecondLine <ThirdLine) do
            GetTheNextLine (Second, SecondLine);
        while (ThirdLine <FirstLine) or (ThirdLine <SecondLine) do
            GetTheNextLine (Third, ThirdLine)
    end; {outer while}
    writeln (FirstLine)
end. {FindTheCommonLine}
```

common line-finding
program

**Files of Simple
and
Structured Types**

Our introduction dealt solely with files of *char*. However, we can define and declare file variables that store values of *any* structured or simple type, except another file type. For example:

```
type Card = record
              ·· {Definition of Card's fields}
            end;
     CardFile = file of Card;
     Color = (red, blue, green, yellow);
     ColorFile = file of Color;
     NumberFile = file of real;
var Cards: CardFile;
    Numbers: NumberFile;
    Colors: ColorFile;
    OneCard: Card;
    OneNumber: real;
    OneColor: Color;
```

component types

As *text* is the only predefined file type, we have to explicitly define types *CardFile, NumberFile*, and *ColorFile*. The values stored in a file are the file's *components*, and their type is the file's *component type*. Except for components of type *char*, file components are stored according to the Pascal compiler's method of internal representation (which I'll explain soon), and usually cannot be read, printed, or created except with a Pascal program.

the file window

Access to files is handled by the standard (predefined) procedures *get* and *put*. Using these procedures requires something more than our current nodding acquaintance with the file window. Basically, the file window is a built-in variable that represents the component stored, or about to be stored, at the current file position—the component we're about to read or write. The file window's identifier is the name of the file, followed by an up-arrow (↑) or circumflex (^). (I'll always use the up-arrow.)

Every file access (even with *read* and *write*) uses the file window as a buffer, or intermediate storage place, between the computer and the actual file. To read a value from a file, we really 'get' the next value into the file window, and then read the file window. To write a value to a file, we assign the value to the file window, and then 'put' the window into the file.

procedure get

The procedure call *get* (*f*) assigns the next component of file *f* to the file window *f* ↑. Any current value of *f* ↑ is discarded.

As you might imagine, calling procedure *reset* implicitly involves a call of *get*. The call: *reset* (*FileName*); essentially tells the compiler:

> *go to the beginning of FileName;*
> *get* (*FileName*);

The file window *FileName*↑ now represents the first component of *FileName*.

Procedure *read* also uses *get*. The statement *read* (*f*, *X*) is equivalent to:

how *read* works

$$X := f ↑;$$
$$get\ (f);$$

Thus, the call *read* (*f*, *X*) gets the value of *X* from a file named *f*. The equivalent pair of statements first assign *X* the current value of the file window, then give the next value in file *f* to *f* ↑.

Finally, we can describe the effect of *readln* (*f*), where *f* is a textfile, as:

while not *eoln* (*f*) **do** *get* (*f*);
get (*f*);

The current line is discarded, and the file window is left at the beginning of the next line (or at *eof* if there isn't a next line).

Output to file variables uses the other file-access procedure, *put*.

procedure *put*

The procedure call *put* (*f*) adds the current value of *f* ↑ to the end of *f*.

Thus, *put* is always used after an assignment to the file window, and sometimes after a call of *rewrite*. The standard output procedure *write* also uses *put*. The call *write* (*f*, *X*) is the equivalent of:

how *write* works

$$f ↑ := X;$$
$$put\ (f);$$

The call of *write* adds the value of *X* to the file named *f*. The statements above assign the file window the value of *X*, then place this value at the end of file *f*.

limits on I/O

The standard procedures *write* and *read* can be used with files of any type, but if their file argument is not of type *text*, only one component argument may be given. Procedures *readln* and *writeln* may only be used with textfiles.

The statements *read* (*f*, *a*, *b*, *c*), *readln* (*f*), *write* (*g*, *a*, *b*, *c*), and *writeln* (*g*) are all illegal unless *f* and *g* are files of type *text*.

structured file components

A final word about the file window will end our discussion. As I said earlier, the file window represents a value of the file's component type (unless it's empty). If the component type is structured, the file window can be used to access stored values. For example, assume the following definitions and declarations:

type *StoredValues* = **array** [1..100] **of** *real*;
StoreFile = **file of** *StoredValues*;
var *Storage*: *StoreFile*;

Storage is a file that can hold many array components. Each array is capable of holding 100 elements. We'll access some elements of the fifth array stored in *Storage*. Naturally, we're assuming that *Storage* has at least five components.

*access through the
file window*

```
reset (Storage) ;  {Does the first get.}
for i := 1 to 4 do
    get (Storage) ;  {Go to the fifth array in Storage.}
Storage↑[10] := 9.39E02 ;
Storage↑[11] := Storage↑[11]+Storage↑[12] ;
writeln (Storage↑[23]:4:8) ;  {We can use format controls.}
```

Focus On Programming: Merging and Robustifying

Merging two files to form a third is a common programming task. Typically, we'll find ourselves dealing with files whose components are record types. A file might consist of student records, employment records, sales records, etc., but all that's really important is that one field of each record stores a name or number that can be used as the alphabetical or numerical basis for record ordering. File merging is similar to file concatenation (as discussed earlier) except that now we'll be interleaving individual file components, instead of joining the files end-to-end. I'll state our problem like this:

problem: file merging

> Imagine a record that contains a string-type *Name* field. Suppose that we have two files (call them *Old* and *Current*) whose components are these records. Assume that *Old* and *Current* are each in alphabetical order according to the *Name* fields. Merge them into file *Merged* while preserving this alphabetical order.

What will be involved? Imagine that you're merging two file cabinets by hand into a third (currently empty) cabinet. You open all the cabinets, and get the first record from each of the full ones. The alphabetically 'lower' of the two records goes into the third cabinet, and you pick up another record to replace it. The process of alphabetical comparison, moving, and replacing goes on until one of the original cabinets is empty. Then, since all the records in the remaining cabinet belong at the end of the large cabinet, and are in alphabetical order already, you move them into the large cabinet without making any comparisons.

A Pascal algorithm is much the same. We'll have to prepare *Old* and *Current* for reading, and *Merged* for writing. Then, we should see which file's first record's *Name* field is lower alphabetically. This record gets added to the *Merged* file. Naturally, we have to repeat this process until *Old* or *Current* is exhausted. In pseudocode we have:

refinement

> *prepare to write Merged* ;
> *get the first records from Old and Current* ;
> **while not** *the end of either Old or Current*
>   *add the lower record to Merged* ;
>   *get the next record from that file* ;
> *finally, add the non-empty file's remaining records to Merged* ;

A slight addition to the algorithm will be to have the procedure report on its activities. Without such a message, a merger of two empty files—probably a mistake—would be quite acceptable.

The **while** loop's action is easy to refine into Pascal. Let's assume that *Old's* present record is lowest.

a coding detail

```
OldCount := OldCount +1 ;
Merged ↑ := Old ↑ ;
if not eof (Old ) then get (Old )
put (Merged ) ;
```

The completed procedure is shown below. Note the **case** statement that takes the place of a possibly confusing nested **if** statement. It's perfectly acceptable here, even if it does only control two alternative actions.

file merging
procedure

```
procedure MergeRecords (var Old, Current, Merged : FileType ) ;
    {Merges Old and Current into Merged while preserving
     the alphabetical ordering of Name fields.}
  var OldCount, CurrentCount : integer ;
begin
    OldCount := 0 ;
    CurrentCount := 0 ;
    reset (Old ) ;
    reset (Current ) ;
    rewrite (Merged ) ;
       {Merge files until one of them is empty.}
    while not eof (Old ) and not eof (Current ) do begin
      case Old ↑.Name<Current ↑.Name of
         true : begin
                  OldCount := OldCount +1 ;
                  Merged ↑ := Old ↑ ;
                  get (Old )
                end ;
         false : begin
                  CurrentCount := CurrentCount +1 ;
                  Merged ↑ := Current ↑ ;
                  get (Current )
                end
      end ; {case}
      put (Merged )
    end ; {while}                                    {program continues}
```

```
{Flush the other file into Merged .}
while not eof (Old ) do begin
    Merged ↑ := Old ↑ ;
    OldCount := OldCount + 1 ;
    put (Merged ) ;
    get (Old )
end ;
while not eof (Current ) do begin
    Merged ↑ := Current ↑ ;
    CurrentCount := CurrentCount + 1 ;
    put (Merged ) ;
    get (Current )
end ;
writeln (OldCount +CurrentCount :1, ´ records were merged.´) ;
writeln (OldCount :1, ´ records from file Old.´) ;
writeln (CurrentCount :1, ´ records from file Current.´)
end ;  {MergeRecords }
```

A different sort of file manipulation problem—trimming the *outliers*, or uncommon data points—frequently arises in dealing with large files of experimental scientific data. For instance, the experimenter may want to establish the 'normal' characteristics of her data by deliberately discarding all values that fall outside the central region. Alternatively, it is not unusual to suspect that some data items may be inaccurate or invalid. They may have been incorrectly read or entered, or may just be so atypical that the experimenter wants to ignore them.

statistical outliers

Now, in some situations the problem of outlier detection is easy to cope with. For example, when gymnastics competitions are judged the highest and lowest scores—the outliers—are simply withheld from scoring. Unfortunately, outliers are not always so conveniently defined or discarded. This is particularly true when huge amounts of data have been gathered by electronic means.

A variety of numerical methods are available for statistically trimming or downweighting the outlying values (called *robustifying* the data). However, if we make the simple rule that, by definition, an outlier is the value that is furthest from the average value of the entire set of data, we can develop an interesting programming problem:

problem: removing outliers

Assume that you have a file of *real* values. Write a program that locates, removes, and saves, its outliers. Provide a means of specifying the percentage of starting values that should be removed.

Obviously, computing the file's average and finding the value furthest from that average hardly require the services of a computer. But if the file is long, or its percentage of outliers is high, the problem is ideal for computer solution. Consider this refinement:

prepare the Data file for inspection;
prepare the SavedOutliers file for the outliers;
count, sum, and compute the mean of, the values in Data;
while *we haven't removed enough of the outliers*
   find and remove an outlier;
recompute the mean;

first refinement

Thus, after removing each outlier, we recompute the mean, then go searching for the next outlier. The recomputation of the mean can be done mathematically (by subtracting the removed outlier and redividing), so this step won't require an extra trip through the file. In fact, with careful programming, we can combine the steps of searching for the current outlier we want removed, and finding the one that's next to go, into a single pass through the file.

using a state variable

The hard part of removing the current outlier derives from the possibility that it occurs more than once in the file. However, we can use the same 'state' variable technique employed in several previous examples—*AlreadyRemoved* will become *true* after we encounter, and remove, the first instance of the outlier we want to delete:

while *we haven't removed all the outliers*
  AlreadyRemoved := false;
  while *we go through the Data file*
    get the next number;
    if *it equals the current outlier* **and not** *AlreadyRemoved*
      then *don't save it in the Data file*;
      AlreadyRemoved := true
     else *see if it might be the next outlier*;
     do save it in Data in any case;

a coding refinement

Like as not, though, we won't program quite carefully enough, and will face the age-old problem of finding bugs. Note that both the *Data* and *SavedOutliers* files store *real* values, which means that we can't easily inspect them to check program operation. Indeed, the program won't necessarily have any input or output visible to the user at all.

embedded debugging statements

An *embedded debugging statement* is a statement, built into the program, that can be switched on and off by the programmer. When it is turned on, it provides diagnostic program output. When it is turned off, it's ignored during program operation.

What diagnostic output will the programmer need? A list of the starting values would be helpful, as well as continuing reports on the file's average, and the value being removed. For our purposes, an **if** statement does the trick:

if *DEBUGGING* **then**
  print diagnostic output;

The constant *DEBUGGING* is initialized to either *true* or *false*. I'll discuss the use of embedded debugging tools further in Chapter 12.

Program *OutLiers*, below, contains a number of nontrivial programming devices, and is well worth studying. You might want to consider what changes would be required to let it handle *text* files of *real* data, rather than *real* files. The final section of this chapter explains, among other things, why the **file of** *real* definition I've used is often preferable.

program *OutLiers* (*output, Data, SavedOutliers*);
    {Saves the *SIGNIFICANT* % values in *Data*, and stores the outliers in *SavedOutliers*.}
const *SIGNIFICANT* = 0.90;
       DEBUGGING = *false*; {Set to *true* for testing and debugging.}

outlier removal
program

type *Numbers* = **file of** *real*;
var *Data, SavedOutliers*: *Numbers*;
   Total, Mean, OutLier: *real*;
   DataCount, OriginalCount: *integer*;
   procedure *CountItems* (**var** *Data*: *Numbers*; **var** *Count*: *integer*;
                          var *Total*: *real*);
   {Counts data items and computes their sum.}
   var *Current*: *real*;
   begin
     Total := 0.0;
     Count := 0;
     reset (*Data*);
     while not *eof* (*Data*) **do begin**
       read (*Data, Current*);
       Total := *Total* + *Current*;
       Count := *Count* + 1;
       if *DEBUGGING* **then**
         writeln (*Current*) {Inspect *Data* if debugging.}
     end
   end; {*CountItems*}
   procedure *FindOutLier* (**var** *Data*: *Numbers*; *Mean*: *real*;
                       var *OutLier*: *real*);
   {Finds the value of the first outlier.}
   var *Current*: *real*;
   begin
     reset (*Data*);
     OutLier := *Mean*; {Initialize *OutLier* to a non-outlying value.}
     while not *eof* (*Data*) **do begin**
       read (*Data, Current*);
       if *abs* (*Current* − *Mean*) > *abs* (*OutLier* − *Mean*) **then**
         OutLier := *Current* {Find the *Current* furthest from the *Mean*.}
     end
   end; {*FindOutLier*}

```
procedure Sift (var Data: Numbers; var ToBeRemoved: real; Mean: real);
   {Remove the current outlier from Data, and look for the next one.}
   var TempData: Numbers;
       Current, NextToGo: real;
       AlreadyRemoved: boolean;  {In case ToBeRemoved isn't unique.}
   begin
       rewrite (TempData);
       reset (Data);
       NextToGo := Mean;  {Safely initialize the next potential outlier.}
       {First, put all the numbers except ToBeRemoved into TempData.}
       AlreadyRemoved := false;
       while not eof (Data) do begin
           read (Data, Current);
           if (Current = ToBeRemoved) and not AlreadyRemoved
               then AlreadyRemoved := true  {We don't save it.}
               else begin
                   write (TempData, Current);  {Save this value now . . .}
                   if abs (Current - Mean) > abs (NextToGo - Mean) then
                       NextToGo := Current  { . . . but it may be the next to go.}
               end
       end;
       ToBeRemoved := NextToGo;  {Save the new outlying value.}
       {Then, copy TempData (with the old outlier removed) back to Data.}
       reset (TempData);
       rewrite (Data);
       while not eof (TempData) do begin
           read (TempData, Current);
           write (Data, Current)
       end
   end;  {Sift}
begin  {OutLiers}
   CountItems (Data, OriginalCount, Total);
   Mean := Total / OriginalCount;    {Get the starting mean.}
   if DEBUGGING then
       writeln ('Mean: ', Mean:6:3, ', Count: ', OriginalCount:1, ', Total: ', Total:6:3);
   DataCount := OriginalCount;    {Save the starting sample size.}
   FindOutLier (Data, Mean, OutLier);    {Find the first outlier.}
   rewrite (SavedOutliers);    {Prepare to save the outliers.}
   repeat  {Finally, invoke the removal process until SIGNIFICANT% are gone.}
       Total := Total - OutLier;
       DataCount := DataCount - 1;
       Mean := Total / DataCount;  {Recompute the mean.}
       write (SavedOutliers, OutLier);
       if DEBUGGING then writeln ('New mean: ', Mean:6:3, ', Removing: ', OutLier:6:3);
       Sift (Data, OutLier, Mean) {Remove the outlier and locate the next.}
   until DataCount <= (OriginalCount * SIGNIFICANT)
end.  {OutLiers}
```

A Necessary Coda: Numbers in Textfiles

Since most scientific data processing involves files of *real* values, it's essential to understand some subtle points about internal representation. As you surely know, computer systems store values in a code of zeros and ones that is designed or chosen by the compiler writer. Pascal compilers are required to translate these internal representations into standard *external* representations (like ASCII or EBCDIC) for output of *char, boolean, real*, and *integer* values. If universal codes weren't available, each computer would need special keyboards, terminals, lineprinters, etc., that could understand the compiler's storage code.*

external character representations

Enumerated ordinal values and types are *not* required by Pascal to have external character representations. A compiler need not decode them into ordinary characters for input and output, or even allow them to be output in any form. Some compilers extend Pascal by giving character representations to ordinal data values—these compilers allow input and output of all ordinal values by automatically encoding and decoding them. Most compilers, though, aren't so generous. If you create a file of an enumerated type *Color* (with values *Red, Blue, Green*, etc.) and manage to inspect it using a text editor, chances are you'll find a meaningless (to us) file of binary or integer values.

real values provide a dramatic illustration. When they're input or output from *text* files (or the standard files *input* and *output*), they are given a character representation. However, when they're stored in a variable whose type is **file of** *real*, the internal, binary representation is used. Thus, while a *text* file of *real* values is readable (to a human), a *real* file of *reals* is not.

use of non-text files

Files with component types *real, integer*, and *boolean* are mainly used to increase speed and reduce size. Because values stored in such files need not be accessed and encoded or decoded individually, input and output of a program's data base can proceed quickly. Meanwhile, the compiler's coding system can store these types in an extremely compact manner—for example, it might store *false* and *true* as 0 and 1.

how read works

But let's get back to textfiles. The convenience of automatic conversion between *char* and internal representation of *real* and *integer* values causes a problem with end-of-file checks. Suppose that f is a textfile, and that *Data* is an *integer* or *real* variable. The statement *read (f, Data)* is equivalent to:

> **while** $f \uparrow = '$ $'$ **do**
>   *get* (f) ;
> *assign the next value to Data* ;

This means that blank spaces and new-lines are skipped before the numerical value is read. After the value is read, the file window $f \uparrow$ holds the character that immediately follows it.

> However, by default, there is always at least one blank at the end of every textfile.

---

* In fact, IBM has been accused of devising the EBCDIC code for this very reason.

There's no way to escape from this because the compiler is under strict instructions (from the Pascal Standard) to make sure that every textfile ends with an end-of-line.

What happens, then, if there are trailing blanks at the end of a file when we're trying to read a number—as there are sure to be? $f\uparrow$ is a blank, so *read* skips it, and any blanks that follow. In the process, it tries to *get* the end-of-file character, which causes a program crash. As a result, this convenient scheme for reading and processing data won't work:

problems with eof

```
while not eof (f) do begin          {Will crash trying to read past end-of-file.}
    read (f, Data);
    process (Data)
end;
```

Our problem is to write a procedure that skips blanks until a nonblank character is found, or until *eof (f)* is *true*. Although it has often been proposed as a solution, the program segment below won't work. Can you figure out why not?

```
while not eof (f) and (f ↑=' ') do
    get (f);          {This segment doesn't work either.}
```

> The file window is undefined when *eof* is *true*. It's an error to try to inspect it.

An error occurs when *eof (f)* is *true*, because $f\uparrow$ will be inspected when the expression is fully evaluated.

A correct procedure *SkipBlanks* is shown below. It uses nested **if** statements and an auxiliary variable to avoid the error of reading an undefined file window.

```
procedure SkipBlanks (var f: text);
    {Skips blanks until eof (f), or a nonblank is found.}
    var Finished: boolean;
    begin
        Finished := false;
        repeat
            if eof (f)
                then Finished := true
                else if f ↑=' ' then get (f)
                                 else Finished := true
        until Finished
    end;  {SkipBlanks}
```

*blank skipping
procedure*

SkipBlanks should be included in any program that reads *real* or *integer* values from a textfile. It's called prior to any invocation of procedure *read*:

model of *SkipBlanks*
use

```
{Model for reading and processing numerical values from textfiles.}
SkipBlanks (f);  {Skip leading blanks in case the file is empty.}
while not eof (f) do begin
    read (f, Data);
    process (Data);
    SkipBlanks (f)
end;
```

Note that *SkipBlanks* should not, and could not, be used when reading from a **file of** *integer* or **file of** *real*. Such files store numerical data only—blanks and end-of-lines don't exist.

Chapter Notes 9-2

EACH TYPE HAS ITS OWN QUIRKS. THREE common fatal errors that involve files are:

1. Attempting to inspect or read from a file that has not been *reset*.

2. Trying to generate or write to a file without first calling *rewrite*.

3. Reading past the end of a file.

confusing *reset* and
rewrite

The first two bugs are usually the result of oversight, or of inadvertently confusing *reset* and *rewrite*. Unfortunately, some errors of omission that are obvious to us aren't caught by the compiler, since they're syntactically correct. Although this program lacks a call of *rewrite*(*OutsideFile*), it compiles (and crashes) perfectly well.

```
program DoesntRewrite (OutsideFile, output);
var OutsideFile: text;
begin
    writeln (OutsideFile, 'Hi there!')
end.
            ↓      ↓      ↓      ↓      ↓

ABNORMAL TERMINATION – –
TEMP100937 NOT SET FOR WRITING
```

In some implementations, the run-time error message that's printed is of little help. In the example above, the computer printed its temporary, internal name for *OutsideFile*.

misplacing *reset* or
rewrite

A related error that's hard to find is a misplaced *reset* or *rewrite*. Remember that *reset* puts us at the beginning of a file so that we can inspect it. *rewrite* presents us with an empty file, ready for writing. What program mistakes do you think caused these complaints?

'I'm not sure I'm reading the right file—I keep getting the same piece of input.'

'My program creates a file all right, but when I print the file it only contains the last piece of data I entered.'

Both bugs are probably the result of putting a *rewrite* or *reset* inside a loop that was supposed to write or read a file. The call should have been made just prior to entering the loop action.

eoln bugs

The end-of-line function has always brought grief to Pascal programmers. What's wrong with the following bit of code? It's supposed to echo the contents of *Source* to *SavedOutput*. I'll tell you that *Source* has no leading blanks on any line.

```
while not eof (Source) do begin
    read (Source, CurrentCharacter) ;
    write (SavedOutput, CurrentCharacter) ;
    if eoln (Source) then
        writeln (SavedOutput)
end ;
```

↓   ↓   ↓   ↓   ↓

This little piggie went to market;
This little piggie stayed home.
This little piggie had roast beef,   *etc.*

The partial contents of *SavedOutput*, shown above, give a broad hint: the second and third lines are indented by one space. Since we forgot to get rid of the space at the end of each input line (with a *readln (Source)*, or even an extra *read (Source, CurrentCharacter)*), it showed up at the beginning of the next output line.

weird implementations

Another *eoln* problem is caused by an outlandish, illegal, and quite common extension of Pascal. Some nonstandard Pascal implementations automatically remove trailing blanks from the end of every line of text, while other systems *add* blanks to the end of text lines. If extra blanks appear at (or disappear from) the end of a text line, make sure that the system isn't responsible. This is one of the opportunities you'll get to blame a bug on the compiler, so enjoy it.

Attempting to read past the end of a file is a serious mistake. The next program segment is sure to fail, given the proper test input:

empty file bugs

```
reset (AnyFile) ;
repeat
    DoSomethingWith (AnyFile)
until eof (AnyFile) ;
```

An empty input file delivers the death blow, because *eof* (*AnyFile*) is *true* as soon as an empty file is reset.

> Check for end-of-file *before* working with any file.

Some of the most annoying file bugs are manifested by disappearing lines, and (for interactive programs) an inexplicable need to type extra carriage returns—I referred to these earlier as synchronization bugs. The root cause is often confusion about exactly what happens at the end of a line. The code below is supposed to read and partially print an input file, echoing the initial nonblank characters on each line. Try tracing through it by hand.

synchronization bugs

```
{Print leading nonblanks—contains a bug.}
while not eof do begin
    read (CurrentCharacter);
    while CurrentCharacter <> ' ' do begin
        write (CurrentCharacter);
        read (CurrentCharacter)
    end;
    readln;
    writeln
end;
```

If every line begins with nonblanks, and ends with blanks, everything works fine. Suppose, though, that there *are* no extraneous blanks at the end of a line. When the inner loop is exited the value of *CurrentCharacter* is ' '—it is the end-of-line character. What happens when the *readln* is executed? The next line is thrown away. If the program is being run interactively, the user has to enter an extra carriage return (or else there is no next line to get rid of).

Always make sure that textfile routines can handle these three special cases: blanks at the beginning of a line, blanks at the end of a line, and lines that are empty. The best antibugging technique is to print the file you're work-ing on *as* you work on it. Make sure that you can explain every blank space or empty line that shows up, as well as every full line that *doesn't* appear.

bug-prone special cases

Non-text files cause more trouble with syntax than semantics. The file window (the file's name followed by an up-arrow or circumflex) is, in effect, the name of a variable. Unfortunately, the up-arrow makes for unusual-looking identifiers. Suppose that we have a file of records. If each record has an array field, we might see these identifiers in a program:

non-text bugs

TheFile	{Name of the file.}
TheFile ↑	{The file window—the name of one record component.}
TheFile ↑.*TheArray*	{An entire array field.}
TheFile ↑.*TheArray* [10]	{One element of the array.}

Naturally, all assignments must involve values of an appropriate type.

> *TheFile* {can't be assigned to.}
> *TheFile* ↑ {may get a record of *TheFile's* component type.}
> *TheFile* ↑.*TheArray* {may get an array of *TheArray's* type.}
> *TheFile* ↑.*TheArray* [10] {may get any value of *TheArray's* element type.}

Important to Remember

• The **file** type creates variables that can store any number of component values of one type. Components may not be files, or include files. The file is a sequential access (as opposed to random access) type because file components must be inspected in sequence, starting at the file's beginning.

• The file window represents the currently accessible file component. It's the file variable's name followed by an up-arrow or circumflex.

• Program parameters are file names given in the program heading. They refer to external files that the program will inspect or add to. Except for the standard program parameters *input* and *output*, program parameters must be declared within the program as well.

• Procedure *rewrite* prepares a file for adding components: *rewrite* (*TheFile*). Any contents presently in the file are lost. Procedure *put* appends the value of the file window to the file: *put* (*TheFile*).

• Procedure *reset* prepares a file for inspection: *reset* (*TheFile*). The file window *TheFile* ↑ represents the first stored value. Procedure *get* advances the file window, so that it represents the file's next component: *get* (*TheFile*).

• The standard input and output-oriented procedures and functions (*read*, *readln*, *write*, *writeln*, *eof*, and *eoln*) can all be given a file-type variable as an initial argument. The subprograms then apply to that file, rather than to the default *input* or *output*. Naturally, *readln*, *writeln*, and *eoln* may only be given textfiles as arguments.

• Always, but always, check for *eof* before you try to get data from a file.

• Three last points. First, assignments can't be made between file variables. Second, file variables are either being generated or inspected—never both at the same time. Third, file variables can only be passed to variable parameters, and never to value parameters.

Cross Reference

• The file type in general is discussed in A125—A135. Textfiles, and in particular textfile input and output, are described in A47—A57, then again in A131—A134.

• A buffer-variable, which is the formal name for the file window, pops up in the discussion of variables on A71. The file window is discussed in more detail on A127.

- Restrictions on the use of files and buffer-variables as subprogram parameters are brought up in A81—A82. The use of files as program parameters is discussed in A130—A131.

- File components are defined in A125—A126. The primitives *get* and *put* are defined on A128; their use in defining *read* and *write* follows through A130.

- The textfile-oriented procedures *writeln, readln*, and *page* are described beginning on A132. Particular output formats are defined in A54—A57, while the coercion of input data is described on A50.

- Finally, *reset, rewrite*, and *eof*, and their relation to a file's generation or inspection state, are discussed in A127—A128.

Exercises

9-1 Write a program that reads a textfile, and determines the average length of its words. Ignore punctuation completely, and assume that one or more blanks separate each word. To make this dry exercise a bit more interesting, have your program print the length of each word in these samples:

1. 'How I want a drink, alcoholic of course, after the heavy chapters involving quantum mechanics.'

2. 'To express e, remember to memorize a sentence to simplify this.'

3. 'How I wish I could enumerate pi easily, since all these (censored) mnemonics prevent recalling any of pi's sequence more simply.'

4. 'In showing a painting to (probably) a critical or venomous lady, anger dominates. O, take guard, or she raves and shouts!'

9-2 *Run-length encoding* is a data compression technique that exploits repetition to shorten overall length. Any series of identical characters:

aaaaabbccccdddefg...

can be replaced by a marker (so that the source text can contain digit characters) and count. Here the marker is a backslash:

\5abb\4c\3defg . . .

Note that the replacements for '**a**' and '**c**' saved room, while '**d**' had no real effect, and '**b**' and '**e**' through '**g**' were untouched, since compressing them would have actually wasted space. Write programs that use run-length encoding to compress, and uncompress, a textfile.

9-3 How perfect is a perfect shuffle? Write a program that simulates the shuffling of a deck of cards. Start with an ordered list of cards (the numbers 1 through 52 will do). Split the file into left and right 'piles,' then interleave their contents element-by-element. What is the cards' order after 10 shuffles? 20? Where does the top card go? What effect does alternating the order of interleaving (i.e. does the left or right pile go first?) have?

9-4 An archeological survey team has taken advantage of laptop computers to carefully log findings in the field. As each new artifact is dug up, it is described, assigned a number and an approximate historical date, and so on. Each entry is placed at the end of the file, and is separated from the next entry by an empty blank line.

The survey team is mightily pleased with themselves when they return to civilization. Unfortunately, their homebound colleagues back in the lab complain. 'Who cares about all the Dr. Pepper bottles you dug up? We wanted the list in chronological order—from the oldest to the newest! Can't you reverse this file?'

Can you? Write a program that reverses the order of entries in the survey team's file. You can assume that each artifact's entry is no more than five lines (of eighty characters each) long.

9-5   Computer alphabets in general set aside a fixed number of binary digits, or bits, to represent each character. The number of bits allowed for each letter limits the size of the character set—a six-bit set can have at most 2^6, or 64, different characters, in effect numbered (in binary) from 000000 through 111111. Another way of looking at this is to recognize that, if a character is n bits long, a message that is m characters long will always require mn bits.

In most English text, though, some letters appear far more frequently than others. If we could figure out some way to separate the end of one character from the start of the next, we could use small binary numbers (like 0, or 1) to represent the frequent letters, and save the very long binary numbers (like 000000 and 111111) for letters that hardly appear at all. A technique called *Huffman coding* implements this idea, but relies on some techniques that are a bit too complicated to explain here to demarcate the end of each character.

Fortunately, we can cheat a little by using a *ternary*, or three-character, code. If we add any character as a third 'bit,' we can use it to mark the end of any simpler sequence. For instance, the Morse Code is a ternary code of dots, dashes, and spaces—the space is reserved for marking the end of each dot/dash-coded letter.

Write a program that creates a frequency table for a text sample, then encodes the text using Huffman's idea of coding frequent characters with short codes (thus, you'll read through the file twice). If, for example, the most frequent input letters turned out to be **e, s, t, r, a, h**, their codes might be 0, 1, 01, 10, 11, 001, and so on. The word 'esther' would be encoded as '0_1_01_001_0_10' (I've used '_' as the third bit character). Disregarding the separator, how many bits are required to store an 'average' character? How might you store the coding key at the beginning of the file (so that it can be decoded)?

9-6   A considerable amount of effort goes into protecting the integrity of digitized sound stored on compact discs. For example, imagine that discrete 'sound values' were simply stored in sequence:

17 15 91 68 52 84 ...

There is essentially no protection against loss of information here—a single lost bit destroys an entire value. Redundancy helps minimize the danger:

17 17 17 15 15 15 91 91 91 68 68 68 52 52 52 84 84 84 ...

Here, two complete numbers, plus part of a third, must be lost before an entire value is destroyed.

However, even the space allocated to storing three consecutive numbers is microscopic, so a tiny nick still causes problems. To further reduce the chance of error, redundancy is combined with a technique called *interleaving*—each triple is spread among its neighbors:

17 .. .. 15 17 .. 91 15 17 68 91 15 52 68 91 84 52 68 .. 84 52 .. .. 84 ...

(I've used each **..** as a space holder for unknown earlier or later values.) This approach is extremely fast to encode and decode. When they're interleaved like this, eight consecutive values, plus part of a ninth, must be lost to destroy a value. Various other techniques, incidentally, are used to help distinguish between a value that's correct, and one that's lost because of a changed bit.

Write a coder, and decoder, to implement redundant interleaving and deinterleaving. For fun, you might want to challenge a friend to destroy random parts of the encoded file (changing numbers to zeros), then see if you can reconstruct the original. Compact discs, incidentally, can withstand the destruction of as many as 14,000 consecutive bits—a hole can be drilled in the disc without losing a note!

9-7   A physics student who is holding down a full-time job finds that she does not have quite enough time to write a required term paper. She resorts to the time-honored expedient of copying a lengthy article from a musty back issue of the little known *Journal of the Royal Society of Physicists*. Naturally, she uses her personal computer to ease her efforts.

Unfortunately, about ten minutes before the paper is due, the student suddenly realizes that every figure has been supplied in old-fashioned British units. Convinced that her plagiarism will be discovered, she feverishly begins to convert furlongs per fortnight and the like to their SI equivalents.

Can you help (not that you would, of course)? Write a program that reads and echoes a text file, and makes appropriate conversions and substitutions. Assume that every numerical value in the file is followed by a unit name. Convert these units:

> 1 pound = 4.448 Newton
> 1 psi = 6895.0 Pascal
> 1 slug = 14.59 kilogram
> 1 foot = 0.3048 meter
> 1 quart = 0.9460 liter

9-8   A basic tool of data analysis is the *linear regression*, which defines a line that approximates the path followed by a sequence of data points. We can find the slope of the line that best follows n data values with:

$$slope = \frac{\sum xy - \dfrac{\sum x \sum y}{n}}{\sum x^2 - \dfrac{(\sum x)^2}{n}}$$

Note that only one pass through the file is necessary for this calculation. Along the way, we can also compute the average x and y values. Armed with this information, we can find the y-axis intercept easily. Once we have determined a linear regression, it can be used in a variety of applications, e.g. extrapolation, interpolation, and so on.

Suppose that a **file of** *real* contains x and y coordinate pairs. Write a program that computes a linear regression. What does its slope tell you about the relation between x and y values? Armed with the regression, travel through the file again and find the three points that have the greatest deviation from the regression line. If they are removed, do they significantly alter the values of the slope or intercept?

9-9   Natural phenomena are often difficult to analyze because a wide range of values may obscure an underlying pattern. For example, consider the measurement of ocean wave heights, which can range from a few centimeters to several meters—all within a single series of measurements. A human observer on the beach can estimate wave height fairly easily and accurately, though, because she ignores smaller waves. In formal terms, she focuses on the *significant wave height*—the height of, say, the tallest third of the waves. A computer, though, needs to have its data selectively filtered.

Write a program, similar to the example program *Outliers*, that analyzes the top third of the *real* values in a file. You may assume that all values fall between 0 and 5 meters, with 0.1 meter accuracy. However, the data file itself is of unknown length.

Answer these questions:

1.   How many waves were in the 2.3—2.4 meter interval?

2.   What was the range of the top-third waves?

3.   What was the average height of the top-third waves?

9-10   A *macro* is a brief, uniquely-identified sequence of characters that represents a longer text sequence. Macros are usually defined in a *macro file*—a brief macro name is followed by the macro's definition. A *macro preprocessor* spots macro names in input text, looks up their definitions in the macro file, then *expands* them as part of output.

Suppose that our macro file read:

```
\P
Whereas the party of the first part
\.
\D
the party of the second part
\.
```

Raw source text might be:

\P
, an unnamed plaintiff, and
\D
, defendant (the University of California, Berkeley) ...

Preprocessor output would be:

Whereas the party of the first part, an unnamed plaintiff, and the party
of the second part, defendant (the University of California, Berkeley) ...

Note that a macro call starts with a backslash, and appears on a line by itself. The macro definition begins similarly, and ends with a '\.' on a line by itself.

Write a program that allows the definition and use of one-letter macro names. Be sure to make your program relatively robust—it should at least be able to handle a macro that is called, but isn't defined. You need not allow recursively-defined macros—macros that contain other macros—but your program should be able to recognize attempts to define them.

9-11   A *shift* cipher encrypts plain text by shifting each character *n* characters to the right, **mod** the number of characters available (so that the last characters in the set can wrap around to the beginning again). For example, shifting the input **CAT** by 3 yields as output FDW, while shifting **XYZ** gives ABC. An obvious weakness of such ciphers is that they are easily cracked by brute force—a 26-character alphabet can only be encoded in 26 different ways.

Write a program that is somewhat more clever. Instead of using a fixed *n* shift, have a random number generator come up with a different *n* for each character. Assume that input comes from a file, and store the encrypted output in the same file. Let the program user enter a starting seed for the random number generator. Be sure to embed a switch in your program that lets it be used for decryption as well! How difficult is it to modify your program so that it can use a password instead of a numerical starting seed?

9-12   Practically everybody who is reading this text is familiar with the notion of *percentile ranking*, in which test-takers are given not only their raw scores, but also a number that indicates the percentage of test-takers whose performance they surpassed. Thus, the results of a test like the SAT or GRE let you know that your score was some value in the range 200—800, and that you placed in the *n*th percentile.

Write a program that reads a file of raw test scores, then prints the percentile ranking for one or more user-supplied raw scores. Somewhat counterintuitively, you should note that not every percentile will be represented. If more than 1% of the test-taking population achieves equally top-rank scores, nobody will lie in the 99 percentile bracket, a situation which sometimes occurs.

9-13   A fascinating branch of statistics is concerned with the development of *stopping rules* that help decision making. Suppose that we interview job candidates, and assign a relative value to each. Picking the best candidate is easy—if we can recall previous applicants. But perhaps each applicant has other job offers as well. What if a candidate must either be hired or turned down at the end of the interview? How can we choose the best possible applicant?

Suppose that there are four candidates. A *25% stopping rule* is:

'Evaluate, but don't hire, the first candidate. Then, hire the next applicant who's better than anybody you've seen so far.'

If we look at the 24 possible applicant sequences, this approach gives us the best candidate 46% (11/24) of the time, which is far better than a random choice (25%—1/4) would yield.

Write a program that generates randomly-ordered files of *integer* values 1 through 100, then investigates the effect of setting different stopping rules. What is the optimal value; i.e. how many applicants should be evaluated, but not hired, before invoking the 'next, best' rule? (Try checking the 20%—50% range.) How often will it lead to choosing the best candidate? What will the average rank of the hired applicant be? Suppose the number of applicants increases (say, to 1,000). Need we evaluate every remaining candidate to find a relatively high-ranking applicant, e.g. among the top 10?

9-14   Most schools require that even engineers spend a term or two studying a foreign language. Let's kill two birds with one stone by writing a drill program for verb conjugation.

Suppose that an unnamed foreign language (often used by the author on vacation) has three categories of regular verbs—those that end with *are*, those with *ere*, and those with *ire*. Their regular conjugations are:

infinitive	**compr***are*	**vend***ere*	**part***ire*
I	*–o*	*–o*	*–o*
you	*–i*	*–i*	*–i*
he, she, it	*–a*	*–e*	*–e*
we	*–iamo*	*–iamo*	*–iamo*
you (plural)	*–ate*	*–ete*	*–ite*
they	*–ano*	*–ono*	*–ono*

Create three files (one for each category) of English verbs and their foreign counterparts. Write a program that asks the user to conjugate a verb into a form chosen at random, e.g.:

        to drink   (you, plural)   Type 'return' for answer.

then prints the correct answer on request. Note that the files contain only the English and foreign-language verbs—the conjugation forms should be hardwired into your program.

9-15   Repetitive drill is an ideal problem for computer solution. The computer teacher—singleminded, purposeful, and utterly relentless—thinks nothing of asking questions, again and again, until you are as close to perfection as a mere human can be.

For simplicity, let's consider a drill problem with one-line questions and answers; say, states and their capital cities. A poor drill program simply travels through the entire list, then starts over again. A slightly more effective drill program will repeat only the questions that were answered incorrectly. The most effective drill program will return to incorrectly answered questions more frequently, but not exclusively, and not always in the same order.

One suggested algorithm for repetitive drill is:

1. Take a question from the head of the list.

2. If it's answered incorrectly, reinsert the question among the first n questions.

3. If it's answered correctly, put the question on the end of the list.

Write a program that implements this algorithm. How might you propose to set the value of n? (Suggestion: when a question is answered correctly, mark it, but reinsert it. When it's been answered correctly twice, put it on the end of the list, and decrement n.) For the purposes of this exercise, you can trust the user to confess if her answer was incorrect.

9-16 Suppose that we are given a computerized deck of playing cards, in a file called *PartialDeck*. The file begins:

Queen of Hearts Jack of Clubs Three of Spades

and continues until fifty-one cards have been named. Write a program that is able to determine which card is missing. (Hint: this program can be found in almost any well-written general introduction to Pascal programming.)

9-17 Personal computers have greatly increased the average person's ability to make spelling errors. To help alleviate this crisis, many word processors come equiped with on-line dictionaries for checking mistakes. However, most PC's have rather small memories, which can limit the effectiveness of straight dictionary lookups.

A different approach to checking spelling is to determine the relative frequency of letter conjunctions—e.g. three-letter triples—in correct English text. When unknown or very low frequency triples show up in sample text, they can be flagged as possible errors.

Write a pair of programs that use the triple frequency approach to check spelling. The first program should create a frequency database by counting triples in a large text sample known to be correct (perhaps your own computer's on-line dictionary). Note that, assuming only lower-case letters, there are 26^3 possible entries in this table, so I would suggest using a three-dimensional array subscripted by letters to create the table, but a **file of** *integer* (implicitly ordered *aaa, aab, ..., zzz*) to store it.

Then, write a second program that uses the frequency database to check a new text sample. As above, I suggest that you start by reading the database into an array-typed lookup table. Print the 50 words that have the highest liklihood of including spelling errors. How might you maintain, and use, a list of low-probability exceptions that are, nevertheless, correct?

9-18 *Computer-aided instruction* is a classroom assistant whose imminent arrival has been heralded for some time now. Let's try to speed things up with a computer-aided multiple-choice question tester. Write a program that lets an instructor prepare, and a student take, multiple-choice tests. The instructor's options should be:

1. Add a question: she should be prompted for the question, the correct answer, then alternate wrong answers.

2. Print the test: print the test, with questions numbered, and answers labled **a, b, c**, and so on. **a** is always the correct answer.

3. Delete a question: she should be prompted for the question's number.

The student's options are:

1. Take the test: the possible answers should be presented in random order, of course.

2. Confirm: the correct answer should be shown.

3. Review: as an alternative to immediately confirming, missed questions should be repeated.

The student's name and score (correct answers / questions) should be added to an external *Scores* file.

9-19   When more than one person works on a file, confusion reigns. The 'multiple-file-update' problem is particularly serious with program files, where side-effects or name changes buried deep in a program can have devastating effects elsewhere.

Many newer programming languages allow the creation of semi-independent *module* files that may be modified and compiled separately, and are not merged until actual program run-time. In this way, changes can be localized and identified; unfortunately, Pascal does not allow this convenience.

Write a program that takes a first step toward making Pascal better suited to a multi-programmer environment. Assume that a program consists of several separate files:

1. a *header* file that contains the program heading, and constant, type, and variable declarations;

2. *module* files that contain procedure or function declarations;

3. a *body* file that holds the main program's statement part.

The first line of each part should be the date that the file was last changed, given as a program comment, e.g. {**7-29-86**}.

Your program should be able to merge a header, three modules, and a body into a single external program file. However, it must print a warning if:

1. any file does not have a date listed in its first line;

2. the header and body files do not have the same date;

3. the header file has a more recent date than any module file.

Your program should also make a copy of the first two lines of each of the header, module, and body files, and embed them as comments at the head of the final program file.

9-20   A consumer reporting magazine has obtained a tape (equivalent to a Pascal textfile) that contains various statistics on automobiles. Each entry holds:

1. the manufacturer's name;

2. the vehicle's model name;

3. its price category (luxury, standard, compact);

4. its EPA estimated highway mileage;

5. its EPA estimated city mileage;

6. the cost of repairs after a 5MPH collision

An empty, blank line separates each entry.

Store this information in a file of appropriately defined records. Assume that all numerical values are *reals*. Write a program that:

1. lists all the cars in each price category;

2. finds and prints the best highway or city mileage in a given price category;

3. finds and prints the worst repair cost in each price category.

10

The **set** Type

For a short word, *set* certainly packs an awful lot of meaning. The Oxford English Dictionary devotes no less than twenty-two pages to *set*, and includes one hundred fifty-four definitions. Unfortunately, not one of the definitions given by the editors of the O.E.D. mentions Pascal. This is sad because Pascal was one of the first programming languages in the world to include a set type. It deserves some kind of recognition!

A Pascal set, like a real life set, is a collection of values that share some characteristic. In Pascal, that characteristic is their type. We'll see some set applications that are often solved with arrays instead (including the generation of prime numbers, and a revisit of the *monitor and locker* problem of Chapter 7), and a few that are peculiarly suited to the set type. The set type is interesting—it's possible to program for a long time without ever needing sets, but once you've used them they'll seem indispensable.

Defining Set Types 10-1

THE SET TYPE CREATES VARIABLES THAT CAN represent more than one value of a given ordinal type. The type definition of a set type contains the set type's identifier, the reserved words **set of**, and the type of the values the set will contain. This 'contents' type is called the set's *base type*. In chart form we have:

set type

type ⟶ *identifier* ⟶ = ⟶ **set of** ⟶ *base type identifier* ⟶ ;

set cardinality

> The maximum *cardinality* of a set type (the maximum number of values in its base type) is implementation defined—determined by the author of a system's Pascal compiler. It typically ranges from 64 to 2040 members.

Although we may have to severely limit the size of an ordinal type (as I do with *LowNumbers*, below), to make it a legal base type, compilers generally let sets be at least as large as the cardinality of type *char*. In this text, I'll assume that this definition is always valid:

type *TypeIdentifier* = **set of** *char*;

Once a set has been defined, we can declare set-typed variables.

type *CharacterSet* = **set of** *char*;
     Vitamins = (*A, B1, B2, B3, B6, B12, C, D, E*);
     NutritionType = **set of** *Vitamins*;
     LowNumbers = 1..12;
     GradesRepresented = **set of** *LowNumbers*;
var *InputCharacters, OutputCharacters: CharacterSet*;
    FruitVitamins, VegetableVitamins: NutritionType;
    Responses: GradesRepresented;

base types
The base type of *CharacterSet* is the predefined type *char*, the base type of *NutritionType* is the enumerated ordinal type *Vitamins*, and the base type of *GradesRepresented* is the subrange *LowNumbers*.

In set assignments, a set-valued expression is given to a set-typed variable. The expression may be another set-typed variable, or a list of individual set members supplied between square brackets. Don't forget that two dots (..) mean 'through and including':

    OutputCharacters := ['a'..'z', 'A'..'Z', '0'..'9'];
    FruitVitamins := [*A..B3, B12, C, E*];
    VegetableVitamins := *FruitVitamins*;
    InputCharacters := [*SomeCharacterValue*];
    OutputCharacters := [*chr* (74)];
    InputCharacters := *OutputCharacters*;
    Responses := [];

the empty set
The final assignment is unusual because it makes *Responses* an *empty set* —a set that contains no values at all. Such assignments are as necessary to sets as initializing assignments to 0 might be for *integer* or *real* variables. Note that *SomeSet* = [] is a reasonable *boolean* expression, *true* if *SomeSet* has no members and *false* otherwise.

set representation
If the value of *SomeCharacterValue* is 'B', and we assign it to *InputCharacters*, then the three expressions below are all equivalent ways of referring to a set whose base type is *char*, and whose only member is 'B':

    ['B']   [*SomeCharacterValue*]   *InputCharacters*

set order
A final point about set values is that they're *unordered*. Thus, these are equivalent representations of the same set:

    [*A..B3, C, E*]   [*E, A..B3, C*]

Set expressions can also be constructed with the *set operators* for union, difference, and intersection.

set union

> The *union* of two sets (or of two representations of Pascal sets) is a set that contains *all* the members of both sets. The regular addition sign (+) serves as the set union operator.

set difference

> The *difference* of two sets is a set that contains all the members of the first set that are not also members of the second set. The set difference operator is an ordinary minus sign (–).

set intersection

> The *intersection* of two sets is a set that contains all values that belong to both sets. The Pascal multiplication sign (*) is the set intersection operator.

In their simplest application, the set union and difference operators update the members of a set-structured variable. For instance, suppose that we want to inspect a text sample, and keep track of all lower-case letters that *do* appear, and all upper-case letters that *don't* appear.

set union/difference
program

```
program TrackTheLetters (input, output);
    {Use sets to find which letters appear in a text sample.}
type CharacterSet = set of char;
var Current: char;
    IncludedLetters, MissingLetters: CharacterSet;
begin
    IncludedLetters := [];
    MissingLetters := ['A'..'Z'];
    while not eof do begin
        read (Current);
        IncludedLetters := IncludedLetters +[Current];
        MissingLetters := MissingLetters–[Current]
    end;
    writeln ('Lower-case letters included were:');
    for Current := 'a' to 'z' do
        if Current in IncludedLetters then
            write (Current);
    writeln;
    writeln ('Upper-case letters not included were:');
    for Current := 'A' to 'Z' do
        if Current in MissingLetters then
            write (Current);
    writeln
end.  {TrackTheLetters}
```

↓   ↓   ↓   ↓   ↓

Pack My Box With Five Dozen Quick Brown Foxes
Lower-case letters included were:
acehiknorstuvwxyz
Upper-case letters not included were:
ACEGHIJKLNORSTUVXYZ

The program begins by initializing *IncludedLetters* (defined as a **set of** *char*) to the empty set. *MissingLetters* is initialized to the complete set of upper-case characters. Successive values of *Current* are read, then added to *IncludedLetters*, or removed from *MissingLetters*. When the loop is finished, *IncludedLetters* represents every character that's been read, while *MissingLetters* holds only those letters that haven't be read.

Some other set unions are:

more set unions

$$IncludedLetters := IncludedLetters + OutputCharacters;$$
$$IncludedLetters := IncludedLetters + OutputCharacters + ['D'..'T'];$$

Is this a reasonable and correct application of the set union operator?

$$InputCharacters := ['D'..'T'] + [CurrentCharacter] + ['9'];$$

Although the assignment is correct, it isn't reasonable. There's no need to use the set union operator, because we're not merging set-typed variables. The assignment below works just as well (note that *CurrentCharacter* may be '9' or in the range 'D'..'T'):

$$InputCharacters := ['D'..'T', CurrentCharacter, '9'];$$

set difference

Set difference gets a few more examples. Let's make these definitions:

type *Options* = (*ErrorRecovery, InputChecks, OutputChecks,*
                              Testing, LongMessages);
        OptionSet = **set of** *Options*;
var *AllOptions, TestOptions*: *OptionSet*;

A program might begin by initializing *AllOptions* and *TestOptions*:

AllOptions := [*ErrorRecovery..LongMessages*];
TestOptions := [*InputChecks, Testing*];

At this point, *AllOptions* contains every value of the ordinal type *Options*. We can reduce its membership by using the set difference operator:

AllOptions := *AllOptions − TestOptions*;
        {*AllOptions* now contains [*ErrorRecovery, OutputChecks, LongMessages*] }
AllOptions := *AllOptions − [ErrorRecovery..OutputChecks]*;
        {*AllOptions* now contains [*LongMessages*]}

difference of empty sets

What happens when we try to remove a value that's not included in a set variable? Nothing. Although the second of the assignments below is obviously fruitless, it's perfectly legal Pascal.

TestOptions := [];
TestOptions := *TestOptions − [InputChecks]*;

set intersection

Finally, let's consider intersection. If two sets don't contain any common values their intersection is, of course, the empty set. Assume that we've defined the months as an ordinal type. The value of this set expression:

$$[January..June, August] * [May..September]$$

is the set [May, June, August]. The intersection of [January..May] and [July..November] is the empty set [].

Sets are often used to record characteristics of some sort, and intersection can be used to find features shared by several different sets. For example, suppose that *OptionSet* is the set type defined earlier. If we declare some variables:

var *Luxury, Deluxe, Standard, Economy : OptionSet* ;

we can make the following assignment:

Luxury := Deluxe * Standard * Economy ;

The set variable *Luxury* holds the values (assuming that there are any) that belong to *all* of the other three sets. If there are no common elements *Luxury* equals [], the empty set.

Set operands can also be used with the ordinary relational operators, and with the set relational operator **in**, to form a variety of *boolean* expressions.

Sign	Operation	Example
=	set equality	*InputCharacters = OutputCharacters*
<>	set inequality	*Responses <> [1..4, 6..10]*
>=	set 'contains'	*Fruit >= [A, B2, C]*
<=	set 'is contained by'	*Luxury <= Standard*
in	set membership	'D' **in** *Included*

set relations (margin note beside the table)

The set operators let sets store data that might otherwise be kept in an array. For example, let's reconsider the Hunt the Wumpus problem of Chapter 8. I'll modify the problem slightly, so that instead of having tunnels that lead in each of four directions, each room can have *any* number of exit tunnels. In the solution I proposed then, each room of the cave was defined as a record with a *Contents* field (denoting any hazards in the room), and a *NextDoor* array-field to hold the numbers of neighboring rooms. What do you think about using this proposal instead?

return to the Wumpus Cave (margin note)

```
type RoomValues = 1..20 ;
     RoomInformation = set of RoomValues ;
     Cave = array [RoomValues] of RoomInformation ;
var PitRooms, BatRooms, WumpusRoom : RoomInformation ;
    CurrentRoom : RoomValues ;
    Neighbors : Cave ;
```

We've really changed our way of looking at the cave. In the new example, our central data structure is a set of possible room numbers—the *integer* values 1 through 20. Instead of putting hazards into each room of the cave, as we did before, we store the locations of each hazard in set variables:

```
PitRooms := [1, 5..7, 12, 14, 19];
BatRooms := [3, 4, 8, 11, 13, 15..17];
WumpusRoom := [18];
```

The cave itself has become an array of sets. Each set contains the numbers of the rooms that a given room is connected to. You'll probably find out the hard way that Pascal's economy in using square brackets with both arrays and sets can be confusing:

```
Neighbors [1] := [3, 4, 9, 13];
Neighbors [2] := [8, 9, 12, 20];
Neighbors [3] := [1, 5, 14, 17];
```

Suppose that we find ourselves in room number *CurrentRoom*. We can easily check for *any* hazard in the room with:

> **if** *CurrentRoom* **in** (*PitRooms*+*BatRooms*+*WumpusRoom*) **then**
> *writeln* ('Sorry, but you''re dead!');

Or, we can see if danger lurks in a neighboring room by determining if the *Neighbors* set has a non-empty intersection with one of the sets of hazards. To find bats, for example, use:

> **if** (*Neighbors*[*CurrentRoom*]∗*BatRooms*)<>[] **then**
> *writeln* ('I hear bats!');

Like array variables, set variables occasionally require special handling to accomplish relatively simple ends. For example, there's no automatic way to print either all the elements of an array variable (except for a string-type array), or all the members of a set variable. Suppose that we wanted to print out the numbers of the rooms containing bats.

set contents procedure

```
procedure PrintSetRooms (BatRooms : BatInformation);
    var Counter : RoomValues;  {1..20}
begin
    for Counter := 1 to MAXIMNUMBEROFROOMS do
        if Counter in BatRooms then
            writeln (Counter)
    end;  {PrintSetRooms}
```

We have to step through the set as though we were travelling through an array.

Programming With Sets

The usefulness of sets depends greatly on your application, and on the maximum cardinality allowed by the underlying Pascal implementation. Somewhat paradoxically, perhaps, large programs can often make do with rather small sets, while small programs will frequently require larger ones.

A typical large-program application of sets comes in the construction of a *lexical analyzer*. In the Appendix you'll see that in formal terms, Pascal programs consist of *tokens*—reserved words, identifiers, operators, and so on. The lexical analyzer, working on behalf of the compiler, reads the English language text of the program, and decides what category of token each word or symbol belongs to. If the tokens are internally defined as the constants of an enumerated ordinal type, then sets (with members of that *Token* type) can be used to easily describe the members of each category of tokens.

set applications

Although compilers are very large programs, most programming languages have relatively small numbers of tokens, and so require small sets. In contrast, the brief program below, which solves the Monitors and Lockers problem from Chapter 7, uses as large a set as it can. Recall that the problem involved a long row of *n* lockers, all initially closed, and an group of compulsive hall monitors. Each of the *n* monitors traveled down the row, opening or closing every *n*th locker to reverse its current state. I wrote this program to show that only perfect squares had an odd number of divisors.

problem: monitors
and lockers with sets

In Chapter 7 I used an array to represent the long row of lockers. Program *SetLockers*, in contrast, is built around this data type definition:

the underlying data
type

```
const NUMBEROFLOCKERS = 400;
type Numbers = 1..NUMBEROFLOCKERS;
     Lockers = set of Numbers;
var OpenLockers, MonitorSet, TempSet: Lockers;
```

Instead of beginning by initializing each array element to *Closed*, the set-based program starts with an *OpenLockers* set that doesn't contain any *Numbers*. Adding a value to *OpenLockers* is the same as opening a locker.

As each monitor comes along, she first decides what lockers she's going to look at—every second, or third, or fourth, and so on—and stores their numbers in *MonitorSet*. Then she considers the current contents of the *OpenLockers* set. Some of *OpenLockers*'s members may intersect hers, and should be removed, while, conversely, some of her members won't intersect *OpenLockers*'s and should be added. In pseudocode, we have:

```
initialize the OpenLockers to empty;
for each of the monitors
    generate a MonitorSet of lockers to look at;
    take the intersection of MonitorSet and OpenLockers from OpenLockers;
    add the difference of MonitorSet and the removed set to OpenLockers;
report on the results;
```

refinement

The completed program is shown below. Try to note and understand the sometimes confusing dual role of the '*' operator, used here for both multiplication and set intersection.

monitors and lockers
program, set version

```
program SetLockers (input, output);
   {Models the opening and closing of a set of NUMBEROFLOCKERS doors.}
const NUMBEROFLOCKERS = 400;
type Numbers = 1..NUMBEROFLOCKERS;
     Lockers = set of Numbers;
var OpenLockers, MonitorSet, TempSet: Lockers;
     Monitor, LockerNumber: integer;
begin
   OpenLockers := [];
   for Monitor := 1 to NUMBEROFLOCKERS do begin
     MonitorSet := [];
     for LockerNumber := 1 to NUMBEROFLOCKERS div Monitor do
          MonitorSet := MonitorSet + [Monitor * LockerNumber];
     TempSet := MonitorSet * OpenLockers;
     OpenLockers := OpenLockers - TempSet;
     OpenLockers := OpenLockers + (MonitorSet - TempSet)
   end;
   writeln ('The lockers that remain open are: ');
   for LockerNumber := 1 to NUMBEROFLOCKERS do
     if LockerNumber in OpenLockers then
          write (LockerNumber:1, ' ');
   writeln
end. {SetLockers}
```

↓   ↓   ↓   ↓   ↓

The lockers that remain open are:
1 4 9 16 25 36 49 64 81 100 121 144 169 196 225 256 289 324 361 400

An even more modest and unassuming program has been used with sets of
enormous size. It implements an algorithm that dates from before 200 B.C.E.—
Eratosthenes' sieve for prime numbers.

problem: sieve of
Eratosthenes

Begin with a sequence of numbers, 1 through n. Starting with 2, travel
through the sequence and remove every multiple (greater than one) of the
starting number. All the numbers that remain will be prime.

Ultimately this isn't a very effective way to find primes because of the
amount of computation involved. A more fruitful approach involves taking an
educated guess that some number is prime, then factoring it (or otherwise testing for primality) to see if you've guessed correctly. You might want to reconsider the cost of the sieve method after reading about the analysis of algorithms
in Chapter 13.

Nevertheless, the sieve of Eratosthenes can be implemented very elegantly
with sets. Consider the approach I've used below. We begin with a 'basket'
that contains every number from 1 through *SETLIMIT*. Then, we travel through
the basket removing multiples of each remaining number. In psuedocode:

first refinement

> *initialize the basket of numbers*;
> **for** *every Count from 2 through SETLIMIT*
>   **for** *every multiple of that Count*
>   *remove it from the basket*;
> *print the results*;

But (to anticipate the concerns of Chapter 13 for a moment), suppose that we use nested **for** loops as shown. Does the inner **for** always have to be invoked? No. Imagine that a given *Count* has already been removed from the basket. This means that one of its factors has already been removed—and with it, all of its multiples. We can revise the pseudocode as:

second refinement

> *initialize the basket of numbers*;
> **for** *every Count from 2 through SETLIMIT*
>   **if** *that Count is still in the basket* **then**
>   **for** *every multiple of that Count*
>   *remove it from the basket*;
> *print the results*;

The completed program is shown below. To make it a bit more interesting, I've computed the primes from 1 through 25,000, which took a few minutes of CPU time. Since primes make boring reading, only the last few numbers are printed.

sieve of Eratosthenes
program

```
program Sieve (input, output);
    {Implements the Sieve of Eratosthenes using sets.}
const SETLIMIT = 25000;  {Don't try this at home, kids!}
type Numbers = 1 .. SETLIMIT;
    NumberSet = set of Numbers;
var Basket: NumberSet;
    Count, Current: integer;
begin
    Basket := [1 .. SETLIMIT];
    for Count := 2 to SETLIMIT do
        if Count in Basket then
            for Current := 2 to SETLIMIT div Count do
                Basket := Basket - [Count * Current];
    writeln ('The higher primes we found were:');
    for Count := SETLIMIT - 100 to SETLIMIT do
        if Count in Basket then
            write (Count:1, ' ');
    writeln
end.  {Sieve}
```

↓   ↓   ↓   ↓   ↓

The higher primes we found were:
24907 24917 24919 24923 24943 24953 24967 24971 24977 24979 24989

Our final set application uses the more common **set of** *char* to compare the efficiency of two typewriter keyboards. The *QWERTY* keyboard is the current standard. Its letter keys are laid out like this:

```
Q W E R T Y U I O P
 A S D F G H J K L ; : space
 Z X C V B N M .
```

Unfortunately, few of the most frequently used letters (e, t, a, o, n, r, i, and s) appear on the center 'home' row—the row of keys that a typist's fingers normally rest on. As you might expect, continually jumping from one row to another slows and tires even the best typists.

Many new keyboard designs have been proposed. One of these is the *Maltron* keyboard, shown below. Since the most common characters are in the home row, fewer jumps are required while typing.

```
Q P Y C B V M U Z L
 A N I S F E D T H O R ; : . space
 J G W K X
```

problem: typewriter keyboards

Just how beneficial is the Maltron keyboard? Write a program that compares the number of jumps a text sample would require from QWERTY and Maltron typists.

A first refinement is:

first refinement

> *as long as there are characters to look at*
> >   *get the character;*
> >   *see if it's on the QWERTY or Maltron home row;*
> >   *see if it requires a jump from the QWERTY or Maltron home row;*
> *print conclusions;*

why use sets?

Set-typed variables are the data structure of choice, because we want to see if a particular value belongs to a group of values of the same type. If we define *CharacterSet* as a **set of** *char*, we can declare variables that represent the 'home' and 'others' characters of the keyboards above, as well as a *Valid* set-variable to help restrict the characters we consider.

What kind of conclusions should the program arrive at? Naturally we want to count the number of jumps that are made. However, this information isn't particularly helpful unless we know the total count of characters considered. The pseudocode below includes these refinements.

prepare the data file for reading;
initialize the set variables;
while not *the end of the input file*
    read the next character;
    if *it's in the set of valid characters*
        see if it's on the QWERTY or Maltron home row;
        see if it requires a jump from the QWERTY or Maltron home row;
        increment the Total count;
print the number of jumps for each keyboard, and the size of the sample;

second refinement

The completed program is shown below. As input, I gave it the complete text of this chapter (less typesetting commands).

typewriter keyboard program

```
program KeyBoards (DataFile, output);
    {Compares the jumps required by QWERTY and Maltron keyboards.}

type CharacterSet = set of char;

var DataFile: text;
    QWERTYHome, MaltronHome, QWERTYOthers,
                    MaltronOthers, Valid: CharacterSet;
    QWERTYJumps, MaltronJumps, Total: integer;
    Current: char;

begin
    Valid := ['a'..'z', 'A'..'Z', '.',';',',','.',' '];
    QWERTYHome := ['a','s','d','f','g','h','j','k','l',';','A',
                        'S','D','F','G','H','J','K','L',';',' '];
    MaltronHome := ['a','n','i','s','f','e','.','d','t','h','o','r',';',
                        'A','N','I','S','F','E','D','T','H','O','R','.',' '];
    QWERTYOthers := ['a'..'z', 'A'..'Z'] – QWERTYHome;
    MaltronOthers := ['a'..'z', 'A'..'Z'] – MaltronHome;
    QWERTYJumps := 0;
    MaltronJumps := 0;
    Total := 0;
    reset (DataFile);
    while not eof (DataFile) do begin
        read (DataFile, Current);
        if Current in Valid then begin
            Total := Total+1;
            if (Current in QWERTYOthers) then
                QWERTYJumps := QWERTYJumps+1;
            if (Current in MaltronOthers) then
                MaltronJumps := MaltronJumps+1
        end  {if}
    end;  {while}
    writeln ('Total number of input characters was ', Total:1, '.');
    writeln ('QWERTY keyboard required ', QWERTYJumps:1, ' jumps.');
    writeln ('Maltron keyboard required ', MaltronJumps:1, ' jumps.')
end.  {KeyBoards}                                    {output follows}
```

Total number of input characters was 28508.
QWERTY keyboard required 14543 jumps.
Maltron keyboard required 5157 jumps.

Q. Program *KeyBoards* treats its input as a stream of characters, without regard to its line structure. Does this cause any inaccuracy in *KeyBoards'* output?

A. Yes, because the carriage return at the end of each line is read, and recorded, as a space. Thus, the total of input characters considered is really too high, by the number of lines in the input sample.

• To represent a set, list its members between square brackets. A set-type variable doesn't need the brackets.

• The set operators + (union), – (difference), and * (intersection) must have set-type operands, and yield a set-typed result. The set relations, used to compare set operands, yield *boolean* values.

• The cardinality of a set is the number of values in its base type—the maximum number of values a set-type variable can represent. This maximum is set by each computer, but it's usually large enough to allow the set of characters.

• The empty set (shown with an empty set of square brackets: []) belongs to every set type.

• The set type in general is discussed in A121—A125. The set operators are first introduced in the discussion of simple expressions, in A44—A46.

• Set constructors, which represent set values, are defined on A122.

• Set assignments, and issues of compatibility, are described on A123. The set operators follow in A123—A124.

• Finally, the canonical-set-of-T is defined on A122. This is a formal way of associating types with particular set expressions.

10-1   Write a program that reads a text sample, and prints every word that contains all the vowels. If you have access to an on-line dictionary, use that as data. If not, try:

'If an authoritative argument for the augmentation of coeducational boar-dinghouses is to be communicated, dialogue to exhaustion is often necessary, since vexatious ultraconservatives take tenacious precautions against the refutation of their reputations. They consider sensible feed-back to be simultaneously sacrilegious and revolutionary since, after all, barefaced oneupmanship is an ostentatious form of persuasion.'

Can you modify your program to find two words (included) that contain the letters a, b, c, d, e, and f?

10-2   On a planet with D days, there is approximately a .5 chance that a group of $\sqrt{\dfrac{\pi D}{2}}$ natives will include at least two with the same birthday (or hatching day, or whatever they call it). On Earth, this works out to a group of twenty-four people.

Using a random number generator to pick birthdays, and a set to hold the birth-days already picked, write a program that tests this contention for Venusians (225-day year), humans (365-day year), and Jovians (11.68-year year—you may run into set-size limitations). Assume Earth-length days.

10-3   Write a program that reads three lines of text and prints:

1.   the vowels that appear on all three lines;

2.   the consonants that appear on the first two lines;

3.   the letters that appear on the first line.

10-4   A freshman programming student invents a simple way to shuffle a deck of cards—she defines a set of the *integer* values 1..52, then chooses a random number between 1 and 52. Each time she picks a number, she removes it from the set, and adds it to an array. Should she ever pick a number that has already been chosen, she simply picks again.

How long will it take her to deal two ten-card hands using this method? How long do you think it will take her to shuffle 52 cards?

10-5   A railroad company wishes to do away with hardwired signaling devices along its tracks, and replace them with microwave transmission devices. The plan is to put line-of-sight microwave transmitters on most track segments, and have them contact strategically-located ground-based satellite uplinks. Thus, the number of expensive satel-lite uplinks is minimized to the number required for visual contact with all track seg-ments.

A survey of the track yields good news and bad news. For all practical purposes, the track is as straight as an arrow. However, it undulates up and down. Although there are many relative high points along the track that are suitable for the satellite uplinks, there are also low-lying track segments that are hidden from uplinks located only two track segments away.

Suppose that you are given the survey results in the following format: for each track segment, there is a list of segments that are visible. Write a program that finds the smallest group of segments that are in visual contact with every segment of the track. Thus, you should check all pairs, then triples, etc. until at least one solution is found. Is a solution for some number of segments necessarily unique? Here is a sample input for twelve track segments:

1:(1,2) 2:(1,2,3) 3:(2,3,4,5) 4:(3,4,5) 5:(3,4,5,6) 6:(5,6,7,8,9) 7:(6,7,8) 8:(6,7,8,9) 9:(6,8,9,10,11) 10:(9,10,11) 11:(9,10,11,12) 12:(11,12)

In case you want to sketch this, the relative heights of the twelve points are 1, 4, 6, 4, 7, 7, 2, 5, 6, 3, 5, and 4.

10-6   A Pascal set is useful because of the operators defined for set expressions. Sets in general, though, are limited by a basic concept—that a set only contains one instance of a given member. Suppose we correct this deficiency by defining a *bag* as a set that can hold up to five instances of each value.

Write a program that uses an array of sets to implement a bag of the *integer* subset $1..25$. Write procedures that make use of the set operators to do bag addition, subtraction, and intersection.

10-7   For a text-oriented version of the bag problem, above, define a bag of characters. How many sets are required for the bag that contains this input sample (ignoring punctuation and capitalization)? What are the contents of each set?

> **Why jog exquisite bulk, fond crazy vamp,**
> **Daft buxom jonquil, zephyr's gawky vice?**
> **Guy fed by work, quiz Jove's xanthic lamp—**
> **Zow! Qualms by deja vu gyp fox-kin thrice.**

10-8   Yet another text-oriented bag problem. Two anagrams contain the exact same bag of letters (ignoring spaces and puncuation). Write a program that checks anagrams. As sample input, try:

> **multiple-word anagrams / plague raw mortal minds**
> **Donald Ervin Knuth / hunt, drink, and love / halt unkind vendor!**
> **Ronald Wilson Reagan / No, darlings—no ERA law.**

10-9   A group of twenty faculty members at an unnamed University have spent a year engaged in mutual backscratching. They have agreed that whenever one faculty member acknowledges (in print) the inspiration or encouragement of another, the second must return the favor.

Near the end of the year, the faculty gather to total up their accounts. Prof. A notes that she has thanked Profs. E, G, M, and N; Prof. B records that she has acknowledged Profs. A, G, and R, and so on. Clearly some accounts are unbalanced—although B has thanked A, A has not thanked B for something else.

Write a program that helps the faculty determine who owes whom. Assume that input consists of twenty sets (for Professors A through T) of names (A through T again). Hint: use an **array** ['A'..'T'] of appropriate sets.

10-10   Two engineers are comparing the merits of a number of building materials. They are having a difficult time of it because the tests are all equally important, and cannot be rank-ordered in any way. Worse yet, in any given test, each material either passed or failed.

Write a program that reads the results of ten tests on five materials. Create, for each material, a set of the tests it has passed. Write routines that determine:

1.   if any material has passed every test *all the others* have;

2.   if any material has passed all the tests that *any single other* has, plus at least one more;

3.   if any materials have passed none of the same tests;

4.   if any materials have identical test results.

10-11   A *lexical analyzer* is employed in the first phase of preparing a program for compilation. It scans through the characters and words that form a program, and tries to determine what kind of *token* each one is. (See page A3 for a brief explanation.)

Write a program that is able to recognize the tokens that appear in an assignment statement. Assume that:

1. *integers* are any sequence of digit characters;

2. *operators* are any of +, –, *, /;

3. *identifiers* are any sequence of letters;

4. *brackets* are (and),

5. *assignment* is :=.

Your program should echo, and print the type of, each token. For example, if input is '**Number** := **(52 + 3)**' your output should be:

```
Number  identifier
:=  assignment
(  bracket
52  integer
+  operator
3  integer
)  bracket
```

10-12 *Wheel of Misfortune* is one of the many television shows that would be available if I were in charge. The rules are simple: an equation is shown, with blank lights taking the place of the factors of each term. The players take turns calling out factors; any correct guesses are lit up. The first player to guess the contents of the equation wins.

For example, the equation 14 + 6 = 2 * 10 would initially be shown as:

☐☐ + ☐☐ = ☐ * ☐☐

After the guess '2' it would be:

2☐ + 2☐ = 2 * 2☐

A third guess of '5' would yield:

2☐ + 2☐ = 2 * 25

Unfortunately, a numerically-oriented Vanna White is not available. Write a program that takes her place.

10-13 Write a program that plays Tic-Tac-Toe. Number the boxes, then use one set to hold X choices, and another to hold the O's. Naturally, an array of sets should be used to hold, and check, winning positions.

11

The Pointer
Types

Chapter 11 introduces a new and rather unusual data type—the pointer. Pointer variables are unlike any we've encountered before. They're almost useless for storing values—they can't be written, read, or even compared except for equality—but they turn out to be incredibly useful as the building blocks of new data structures.

Section 11-1 explains pointer mechanics, and introduces some of the operations common in setting up linked structures. We'll see examples that range from maintaining lists to adding n-degree polynomials. Frankly, this chapter is hard because it has a lot of non-intuitive and un-obvious material— I've added more Self-Check questions to Chapter 11 than to the last few chapters combined. Skim through it quickly to get an idea of where the chapter leads, then reread it slowly for learning. Chapter 17 provides additional examples of pointer-based data structures. The regular closing material—debugging tips, cross reference, and exercises—are found there as well, beginning on page 395.

Basic Operations with Pointers 11-1

FOR A CHANGE I WON'T BEGIN WITH AN example. Instead, the next few pages will be a concentrated introduction to the concept and terminology of pointers, that you should plan to read twice. Our bottom-up introduction starts with the notion of a *storage location*—an area in memory that stores a value.

locations

A variable declaration makes the computer *allocate*, or set aside, a small portion of its memory as a storage location. When a Pascal program is directing computer operation, only the values of one particular type may be stored in a given location.* This is the basis of Pascal's strong type-checking—every location has a type associated with it.

allocation and access

Now, an assignment to a variable changes the value stored in 'its' location. For all practical purposes the variable identifier and its location are the same. Because of this, an assignment to an ordinary variable identifier is called a *direct access* of a location.

---

* This is not quite true. The location used to store a record variant can accommodate any of the variant groups—they are *overlaid* in a single location big enough for the largest group.

Pointer variables work a little differently, because a pointer is a variable that *references,* or points to, a storage location. The contents of the location can be inspected or changed *through* the pointer (called an *indirect* access) if we use

special notation. Without this notation, an assignment to a pointer-type variable changes the particular location the variable references, without affecting the contents of that location.

Let's look at a simple example. This definition:

> **type** *NumberPointer* = ↑*integer* ;

defines a pointer type. It is read '*NumberPointer* is a pointer to a location of type *integer* .'

> A *pointer* -type is defined as referencing (or pointing to) a location of a particular type (its *reference type*). An up-arrow (↑) or circumflex (^) precedes the name of the reference type.

The syntax chart of a pointer's type definition is:

> *pointer type*
>
> **type** ⟶ *identifier* ⟶ = ⟶ ↑ ⟶ *identifier* ⟶ ;

(In this text I'll always use the up-arrow.) The declaration of a pointer-type variable looks like any other variable declaration.

> **type** *NumberPointer* = ↑*integer* ;
> **var** *First, Second, Third* : *NumberPointer* ;

However, we can't assign specific *integer* values to *First, Second*, or *Third*. Instead, they will store the internal computer names associated with particular storage locations.

Like other variables, pointer variables are undefined when they're first declared. The particular location a pointer variable references must be *dynami-*

cally allocated with the standard procedure *new*. A location can be disposed of (for the computer to reallocate later, if necessary) with the standard procedure *dispose*. For example:

> *new* (*First*) ; {Allocate locations for *First* and *Second* to reference.}
> *new* (*Second*) ;

Space in computer memory can be freed for reallocation like this:

> *dispose* (*First*) ; {Free the location that *First* pointed to.}

First still exists, but it's undefined and doesn't reference any location. It's in the pristine condition it was in before the original call of *new* (*First*).

Pascal has a special provision for defining a pointer variable without giving it a location to reference.

Any pointer variable can be assigned the value **nil**:

First := **nil** ;

It is now called a *nil pointer*, and doesn't reference a location.

The advantage of a **nil** pointer over one that is simply undefined is that a pointer variable's **nil** /**not nil** status can be checked with a *boolean* expression.

{Determine if *First* references a storage location.}
if *First* = **nil**
    then *writeln* ('Warning! Nil pointer. Cannot be accessed.')
    else *writeln* ('This pointer accesses a stored value.')

The value **nil** is unusual in Pascal because it may be assigned to a pointer of *any* type. That's why **nil** is treated like a reserved word.

Our next step is to assign a value to, or inspect the value of, the location a pointer-type variable references.

assigning to locations

To assign a value to (or read a value from) the location referenced by a pointer variable, follow the pointer's identifier with an up-arrow or circumflex. The pointer must not be **nil**, because a **nil** pointer doesn't have a location.

For example:

First ↑ := 5 ;   {Assign 5 to the location *First* references.}
Second ↑ := *First* ↑ ;   {Assign 5 (the value *First* references) to *Second* ↑.}
writeln ('The value First accesses is', *First* ↑:2) ;
readln (*Second* ↑) ;   {Input a value to the location *Second* accesses.}

We also have to understand how to give a value to the pointer itself, in order to make it access a different location.

addresses

The value of a pointer is called an *address*. It is the computer's internal notation for a particular location in memory.

If we think of the computer's memory as being a very, very, long array, then an address is like an array subscript. A pointer's value (and thus, the address of the location the pointer references) can be changed in three ways:

1.   With procedure *new*. This gives it the address of a memory location whose contents are undefined.

changing addresses

2.   By assigning it the value **nil**, which gives it a null address.

3.   By assigning it the value of another pointer of the same type. Both pointers then hold the same address, and access the same location.

In the example below, we make *Second* and *Third* point to the same location by giving them the same address. Then, *Second* is changed to access the same location as *First*.

    Third := *Second*;   {These assignments change the locations that *Third*}
    Second := *First*;   {and *Second* access, but not the locations' contents.}

Note that the assignments can't be reversed.

    Second := *First*;
    Third := *Second*;

losing locations

After the second pair of assignments, *First, Second*, and *Third* all reference the same location, but the *integer* formerly referenced by *Second* has been cast adrift—the address of its location is lost. We cannot access it, and its storage area cannot be re-allocated by the computer.

How about printing the value of pointers? An address is an internal notation the computer uses for bookkeeping, and it has no external character representation.

using addresses

> The value of a pointer can't be printed or inspected. It can only be compared (for equality and inequality) to the value of another pointer-variable of the same type, or to **nil**.

    if (*First*<>**nil**) **and** (*Second*<>**nil**) **then**
      if *First* = *Second*
        then *writeln* ('First and Second reference the same location.')
        else *writeln* ('First and Second access different locations.');
      {*First*↑ and *Second*↑ might be the same anyway.}

pointers to structured types

Although pointers to ordinal values (like *integer*) are easy to understand, most pointers reference structured types. An especially common definition is a pointer to a record type that contains a pointer *of the same type* as one of its fields. For example:

    type *DataPointer* = ↑*DataLocation*;
        DataLocation = **record**
                      a, b, c: *integer*;
                      d, e, f: *char*;
                      Next: *DataPointer*
               end;
    var *CurrentRecord*: *DataPointer*;

order of pointer-type definitions

A peculiarity of definitions like this is that the pointer type is defined before the reference type—*DataPointer* is defined before *DataLocation*. Since *DataLocation* appears in the definition of *DataPointer*, we seem to have violated the 'define before you use' rule. However, reversing the definitions wouldn't help matters—if we did, we'd have to use *DataPointer* before *it* was defined. Pascal resolves this paradox by sidestepping it.

> In Pascal, pointer type definitions may precede the definitions of their reference types. However, the reverse is not true—a structure may not contain a field or component of a pointer type that has not yet been defined.

I'll summarize the new information presented so far.

1.   A pointer type is defined as pointing to a location of any type, using this format:

   type *PointerType* = ↑*ItsReferenceType* ;
   var *PointerVariable* : *PointerType* ;

summary of pointer facts

2.   The dynamic allocation procedure *new* gives a pointer-type variable a location in memory to reference or point to. Procedure *dispose* deallocates and frees this space.

3.   A pointer may be given an address value only by using *new*, or by assigning it the address value of a pointer of an identical type (which makes them both reference the same location). However, any pointer may be given the null value **nil**. A pointer's address value may not be printed or inspected; only compared to other pointer values for equality or inequality.

4.   The location that a pointer variable references can be accessed for assignment or inspection by following the variable's name with an up-arrow (or circumflex), e.g. *ThePointer* ↑.

5.   A pointer may be defined as referencing a type that has not yet been defined (but which will be defined further along in the type definition).

Self-Check Questions

Q. What's wrong with these statements? Assume that we're using pointers to *integer* storage locations.

   a) *First* := 5 ;
   b) *Second* ↑ := **nil** ;
   c) *writeln* (*Third*) ;
   d) *First* ↑ := *Second* + *Third* ;

A. *a*) This statement tries to assign 5 to *First* instead of assigning it to the location *First* references. It should be:

   First ↑ := 5 ;

b) The value **nil** may only be assigned to a pointer—not to the location the pointer accesses (unless it too is a pointer). The assignment should be:

   Second := **nil** ;

c) This output statement attempts to print the value represented by *Third*—which is just the address of a location within the computer—instead of printing the value stored at that location. It should be:

    writeln (*Third*↑);

d) This assignment tries to add two addresses instead of adding the values stored at each address. It should be written as:

    First↑ := *Second*↑ + *Third*↑;

Addresses may only be compared for equality, and are *never* used in arithmetic expressions.

The Linked Data Structures

Pointers to records are the most frequently defined pointer types. Such records invariably contain one or more pointer fields themselves, and therein lies their beauty: we can dynamically allocate a series of record locations, and tie them together with pointer fields. These are called *linked* structures because pointers form a chain of records.

Let's begin with an easy example that assumes the definition of *DataType*—we'll soon see that its particulars are not important.

a basic element

    type *ElementPointer* = ↑*Element*;
         Element = **record**
               Data: *DataType*;
               Next: *ElementPointer*
           end;
    var *FirstElement*: *ElementPointer*;

This puts us in position to *new* away to our heart's content:

    new (*FirstElement*);
    new (*FirstElement*↑.*Next*);
    new (*FirstElement*↑.*Next*↑.*Next*);
    new (*FirstElement*↑.*Next*↑.*Next*↑.*Next*);

linked lists

This particular linked structure is called a *list*. The individual records of a linked list are its *elements*.

A convenient visual notation is used for presenting linked structures. A box or circle represents a record location whose data fields can be labeled individually, or lumped together as 'data.' Each pointer's address—the location a pointer variable or field refers to—is shown with an arrow. The series of calls to *new*, above, resulted in this structure:

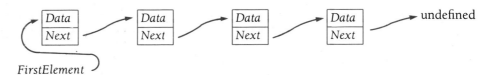

FirstElement

The combination of indirect access and ordinary record notation tends to make expressions long and incomprehensible.

accessing elements

FirstElement	{Represents an address}
FirstElement ↑	{The record at that address}
FirstElement ↑.*Data*	{One field of that record—a stored value.}
FirstElement ↑.*Next*	{Represents an address}
FirstElement ↑.*Next* ↑	{The record at that address}
FirstElement ↑.*Next* ↑.*Data*	{One field of that record—a stored value.}

Now, the illustrated list above shows one of the peculiarities of linked structures. Although the computer has allocated four different locations in memory, only a single identifier—*FirstElement*—is associated with them. This is a source of convenience and confusion. For instance, we can access the entire list through *FirstElement* to make the last record's *Next* field **nil** instead of merely undefined.

FirstElement ↑.*Next* ↑.*Next* ↑.*Next* ↑.*Next* := **nil** ;

At the same time, a misstep might cause us to lose contact with part of the list. The assignment below *advances* the pointer variable, so that it references the second record in the list.

FirstElement := *FirstElement* ↑.*Next* ;

Unfortunately, this leaves us with no way of accessing the very first list element.

auxiliary pointers

> Linked structures usually have several auxiliary pointers associated with them. These pointers act as place markers, maintaining contact with the beginning of a list, its end, our current position, etc.

Suppose that *FirstElement* points to the first link in a list, as in the illustration above. If we had an auxiliary pointer named *CurrentPosition*, and also of type *ElementPointer*, the assignment:

CurrentPosition := *FirstElement* ↑.*Next* ↑.*Next* ↑.*Next*

advancing the auxiliary pointer

would leave the list like this:

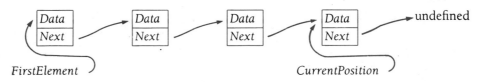

FirstElement   CurrentPosition

Clearly, the auxiliary pointer makes assignments to the last element of the list much easier to follow:

CurrentPosition ↑.*Data* := *Value* ;
CurrentPosition ↑.*Next* := **nil** ;

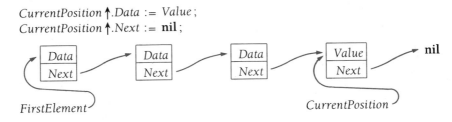

Self-Check
Questions

Q. What is the purpose and effect of these statements? Assume the situation of the last paragraph.

new (*CurrentPosition* ↑.*Next*) ;
CurrentPosition := *CurrentPosition* ↑.*Next* ;
CurrentPosition ↑.*Next* := **nil** ;

A. These statements extend the chain, but keep *CurrentPosition* pointing to the very last link. The result looks like this:

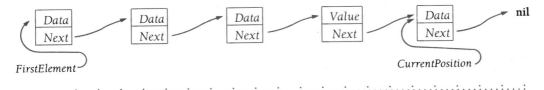

: · · : :

Operations
With Links

Like Tinker toys and Lego blocks, the individual elements of a linked structure may be attached to each other in a variety of patterns. However, certain basic operations (like connecting and disconnecting links) are required by most linked structures. In the self-check question above we saw how a linked list could be extended by connecting a new element to its end. The first statement:

new (*CurrentPosition* ↑.*Next*) ;

allocates a new location. *CurrentPosition* ↑.*Next* now references an undefined record, and the **nil** value is lost. The next statement:

CurrentPosition := *CurrentPosition* ↑.*Next* ;

is potentially the most confusing—it advances the current position pointer, moving it to the end of the list. The illustration below shows how the pointer is reconnected.

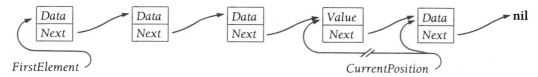

FirstElement   CurrentPosition

The third and final statement of the list extension makes the new list end **nil**.

$$CurrentPosition \uparrow .Next := \textbf{nil} \, ;$$

using **nil**

> In general, **nil** should always be used to mark the end of linked structures—a pointer should either have an address or be **nil**.

This makes list searching much easier. If *CurrentPosition* is pointing to a random element of a linked list, we can advance it to the list's end by searching for the **nil**-valued *Next* pointer—the last element.

while *CurrentPosition* ↑.*Next* **<> nil do**
 CurrentPosition := *CurrentPosition* ↑.*Next* ;

Let's write the code that creates a list in the first place. I'll pose the following problem:

problem: make a
linked list

> Read and save a sequence of positive numbers. Print the zero or negative number that ends the sequence, then echo the sequence in order.

I'll use an ordinary **while** loop to spot the sentinel, and a linked list to save the numbers. The pseudocode isn't too tough:

refinement

> *initialize the list* ;
> *read the first number* ;
> **while** *we're not at the sentinel yet*
> *add a new element to the list* ;
>   *read another number* ;
> *print the sentinel* ;
> **while** *we're not at the end of the linked list*
> *print the current value* ;
> *move to the next element* ;

The Pascal code is shown below. It illustrates some basic linked list methods, and you should be sure to understand it.

linked list program

```
program LinkAndEcho (input, output);
   {Store numbers in a linked list, then echo the sentinel and list.}
type ElementPointer = ↑Element;
     Element = record
                  Number: integer;
                  Next: ElementPointer
               end;
var FirstElement, CurrentElement: ElementPointer;
    TheNumber: integer;
begin
   {Initialize the list and its pointers.}
   new (FirstElement);
   FirstElement↑.Next := nil;
   CurrentElement := FirstElement;
   read (TheNumber);
   while TheNumber > 0 do begin
      {Add each number to the list, then add an element.}
      CurrentElement↑.Number := TheNumber;
      new (CurrentElement↑.Next);
      CurrentElement := CurrentElement↑.Next;
      CurrentElement↑.Next := nil;
      read (TheNumber)
   end ; {while}
   {Note that the current element doesn't store a value.}
   write (TheNumber);
   if CurrentElement<>FirstElement then begin
   {If they both point to the first element, there was no legal input.}
      CurrentElement := FirstElement;
      while CurrentElement↑.Next <>nil do begin
         write (CurrentElement↑.Number);
         CurrentElement := CurrentElement↑.Next
      end {while}
   end; {if}
   writeln
end. {LinkAndEcho}
```

↓		↓		↓		↓		↓		
12	**59**	**826**	**959**	**3**	**65**	**−84**	**444**			
	−84		12		59		826	959	3	65

element insertions

Suppose that we wanted to maintain the list in numerical order? We'd read in each new value, search through the list for its proper position, then insert it into the existing list. A single new element, referenced by the pointer *Temporary*, can be appended after the current pointer position with:

> *new* (*Temporary*) ;
> *Temporary* ↑.*Next* := *CurrentPointer* ↑.*Next* ;
> *CurrentPointer* ↑.*Next* := *Temporary* ;

Or, an existing element (referenced by *NewElement*) can be inserted *before* the current pointer position element with:

inserting before the
current pointer

> *new* (*Temporary*) ;
> *Temporary* ↑ := *CurrentPointer* ↑ ;
> *CurrentPointer* ↑.*Next* := *Temporary* ;
> *CurrentPointer* ↑.*Data* := *NewElement* ↑.*Data* ;
> *dispose* (*NewElement*) ;
> *NewElement* := *CurrentPointer* ;
> *CurrentPointer* := *CurrentPointer* ↑.*Next* ;

As you can see, I engaged in some sleight-of-hand, and didn't really insert the element referenced by *NewElement* into the list. Instead, I created a new, blank element:

> *new* (*Temporary*) ;

gave it the same *Data* and *Next* fields as *CurrentPointer* :

> *Temporary* ↑ := *CurrentPointer* ↑ ;

inserted it after *CurrentPointer* :

> *CurrentPointer* ↑.*Next* := *Temporary* ;

stored the new element's data in *CurrentPointer* :

> *CurrentPointer* ↑.*Data* := *NewElement* ↑.*Data* ;

disposed of the location no longer needed by the new element:

> *dispose* (*NewElement*) ;

arranged for *NewElement* to reference the list element that holds the new *Data* field:

> *NewElement* := *CurrentPointer* ;

and finally, advanced *CurrentPointer* :

> *CurrentPointer* := *CurrentPointer* ↑.*Next* ;

If you can follow that sequence, you shouldn't have any trouble with pointers. Here's an outline of the elements involved in the insertion—try filling in the pointers yourself.

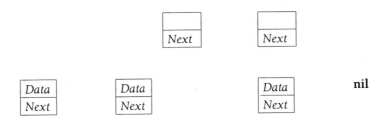

Having plenty of auxiliary pointers makes most list manipulations easier.
Suppose that we want to insert a new list between two elements of a currently
existing list. Two reconnections do the trick, and put the new list between the
elements referenced by *CurrentPosition* and *CurrentPosition↑.Next*.

list insertion

$$NewListEnd↑.Next := CurrentPosition↑.Next;$$
$$CurrentPosition↑.Next := NewListStart;$$

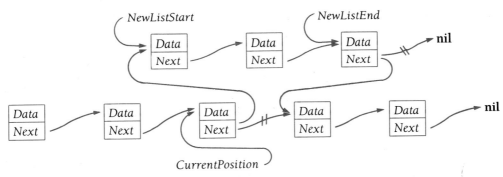

Auxiliary pointers are also useful for deleting one or more elements from a
list. As long as we don't let part of the list get away (if it does, it's impossible
to retrieve), list deletions take only a reconnection or two. Suppose this is the
situation.

element deletion

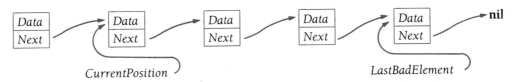

We can delete all elements from (not including) *CurrentPosition↑* through (and
including) *LastBadElement↑* with:

$$CurrentPosition↑.Next := LastBadElement↑.Next;$$

LastBadElement↑ will be retained in the new list if we do:

$$CurrentPosition↑.Next := LastBadElement;$$

Note that we haven't bothered to *dispose* of the elements we cut out.

Let's work out one last long problem that will use the techniques we've learned.

A *polynomial* is expressed as a series of *terms*:

$$a_n x^n + a_{n-1} x^{n-1} + \ldots + a_1 x^1 + a_0 x^0$$

The important features of each term are its *coefficient* (the *a's*) and its *degree* (the exponents). Write a program that adds two polynomials to form a third.

If two terms' degrees are identical, the coefficients are added, while a missing term's coefficient is assumed to be zero. Thus, since a coefficient may always be 0.0 (except in the *n*th term), not every term will be represented in an *n-degree* polynomial.

Now, if every term were always present, it would be tempting to use an **array** $[0..n]$ to hold the coefficients. This is convenient because each element's subscript is the same as its exponent. However, imagine a 1000-degree polynomial with only two terms; say, $x^{1000} + 1$. The array solution clearly is not going to be effective.

In contrast, the pointer solution almost seems to have been invented for representing polynomials. The type definition of a single term must look like this:

```
type TermPointer = ↑Term ;
     Term = record
              Degree: integer;
              Coefficient: real;
              Next: TermPointer
            end ;
```

We'll need three pointer variables to head three polynomials:

```
var First, Second, Third: TermPointer ;
```

Our solution will, figuratively, merge two polynomials into a third. Does this kind of problem ring any bells? It should, because we dealt with a similar situation in Chapter 9. Our problem then was to merge two files of records while preserving the alphabetical ordering of the records' *Name* fields. Now, in effect, we're merging records while preserving the order of their *Degree* fields (from greatest to least), with the additional complication of adding coefficients if any two terms have the same degree.

The barest pseudocode outline describes the main procedures we'll need:

```
get the First and Second polynomials ;
add First and Second to form Third ;
print the result ;
```

Getting the starting polynomials, and printing their sum, are essentially a solved problem, given our experience from program *LinkAndEcho*. I'll rely on a final, zero-exponent term to act as a sentinel and end each polynomial. The pseudocode for adding the polynomials is:

get the First and Second polynomials;
initialize a new polynomial linked list for Third;

second refinement

while *we still have terms left in either polynomial*
   if *Degree fields are equal, copy one term to the new list, adding coefficients*
   else if *the First exponent is higher, copy the term to the new polynomial*
   else *the Second exponent is higher, so copy the term to the new polynomial*;

do closing processing on the new polynomial;

The importance of the last step can't be overemphasized. Files have an end-of-file character added to them automatically, but the **nil** pointer that ends a linked listed must be added by hand. In reading the completed program, pay special attention to the *boolean* checks that determine the order of *Degree* fields, and set the main loop's exit condition.

polynomial addition
program

```
program Polynomials (input, output);
    {Uses linked lists to maintain and add two n-degree polynomials.}
type TermPointer = ↑Term;
    Term = record
                Degree: integer;
                Coefficient: real;
                Next: TermPointer
           end;
var First, Second, Third: TermPointer;
procedure MakeList (Head: TermPointer);
    {Read the coefficient and degree of each term.}
    var Temp: TermPointer;
    begin
        Temp := Head;
        writeln ('Please enter coefficients and degrees.');
        repeat
            read (Temp↑.Coefficient);
            read (Temp↑.Degree);
            if (Temp↑.Degree = 0)
                then Temp↑.Next := nil
                else new (Temp↑.Next);
            Temp := Temp↑.Next
        until Temp = nil;
        readln
    end;  {MakeList}
```

procedure *AddPolynomials* (*First, Second* : *TermPointer* ; **var** *Sum* : *TermPointer*) ;
{Create a linked list that adds the terms of two polynomials.}
var *SumCurrent* : *TermPointer* ; {An auxiliary pointer to the *Sum* list.}
   Finished : *boolean* ;
begin
   new (*Sum*) ; {We've been passed the pointer, not the list.}
   SumCurrent := *Sum* ; {*Sum* will stay at the list's head.}
   Finished := (*First* ↑.*Degree* = 0) **and** (*Second* ↑.*Degree* = 0) ;
   while not *Finished* **do begin**
      if *First* ↑.*Degree* = *Second* ↑.*Degree* **then begin** {equal exponents}
         SumCurrent ↑.*Degree* := *First* ↑.*Degree* ;
         SumCurrent ↑.*Coefficient* := *First* ↑.*Coefficient* + *Second* ↑.*Coefficient* ;
         First := *First* ↑.*Next* ;
         Second := *Second* ↑.*Next*
      end {the exponents were the same}
      else if (*First* ↑.*Degree* > *Second* ↑.*Degree*) **then begin**
         SumCurrent ↑.*Degree* := *First* ↑.*Degree* ;
         SumCurrent ↑.*Coefficient* := *First* ↑.*Coefficient* ;
         First := *First* ↑.*Next*
      end {the *First* list term comes first}
      else begin {*First* ↑.*Degree* was < *Second* ↑.*Degree* .}
         SumCurrent ↑.*Degree* := *Second* ↑.*Degree* ;
         SumCurrent ↑.*Coefficient* := *Second* ↑.*Coefficient* ;
         Second := *Second* ↑.*Next*
      end ; {the *Second* list term comes first}
      new (*SumCurrent* ↑.*Next*) ;
      SumCurrent := *SumCurrent* ↑.*Next* ;
      Finished := (*First* ↑.*Degree* = 0) **and** (*Second* ↑.*Degree* = 0)
   end ; {while}
   {Do the closing processing.}
   SumCurrent ↑.*Degree* := 0 ;
   SumCurrent ↑.*Coefficient* := *First* ↑.*Coefficient* + *Second* ↑.*Coefficient* ;
   SumCurrent ↑.*Next* := **nil**
end ; {*AddPolynomials*}

procedure *WriteList* (*Head* : *TermPointer*) ;
   {Print the sign, coefficient, and degree of each term.}
begin
   repeat
      if *Head* ↑.*Coefficient* > 0 **then**
         write (' + ') ; {A necessary detail for positive terms.}
      write (*Head* ↑.*Coefficient* :1:2, '↑', *Head* ↑.*Degree* :1, ' ') ;
      Head := *Head* ↑.*Next*
   until *Head* = **nil** ;
   writeln
end ; {*WriteList*}

```
begin {Polynomials}
    new (First);
    MakeList (First);   {Read each polynomial...}
    WriteList (First);  {...then echo it.}
    new (Second);
    MakeList (Second);
    WriteList (Second);
    AddPolynomials (First, Second, Third);
    writeln ('The sum of the polynomials is:');
    WriteList (Third)
end. {Polynomials}
```

↓   ↓   ↓   ↓   ↓

Please enter coefficients and degrees.

3.0   4   2.0   3   –1.0   1   10.0   0

+ 3.00↑4 + 2.00↑3 –1.00↑1 + 10.00↑0

Please enter coefficients and degrees.

4.5   1000   –1.0   4   2.0   3   –5.0   2   –2.0   0

+ 4.50↑1000 –1.00↑4 + 2.00↑3 –5.00↑2 –2.00↑0

The sum of the polynomials is:

+ 4.50↑1000 + 2.00↑4 + 4.00↑3 –5.00↑2 –1.00↑1 + 8.00↑0

Self-Check
Questions

Q. Suppose that we have a singly-linked list whose first element is accessed by two pointers—*CurrentPosition* and *PreviousPosition*. Assume that the last element of the list points to **nil**. What is the effect of this code?

```
while PreviousPosition <> nil do begin
    CurrentPosition := PreviousPosition↑.Next;
    dispose (PreviousPosition);
    PreviousPosition := CurrentPosition
end;
```

A. The code demonstrates a common *list-disposal* scheme. Each element of the list is disposed of in turn. After the segment, *PreviousPosition* and *CurrentPosition* are **nil**.

list disposal

More Link Operations

The basic linked list we've been using so far has an inconvenient shortcoming—it can only be traveled or inspected in one direction. An alteration in the type definition of *Element* solves this problem.

```
type ElementPointer = ↑Element;
     Element = record
                   Data: DataType;
                   Next, Previous: ElementPointer
               end;
```

doubly-linked lists

> A list that has backward as well as forward pointers is *doubly-linked*.

Inserting and deleting elements from doubly-linked lists is no more difficult than from singly-linked lists, as long as we remember to reconnect the links in both directions. Procedure *DoubleAppend*, below, puts a new, undefined element after the one accessed by *CurrentPosition*. Note that we have to re-do the links between the new element and *CurrentPosition*↑, and take care of the backward pointer of the element that follows the new one as well. Try to trace the procedure's operation without an illustration.

inserting new elements

```
procedure DoubleAppend (CurrentPosition: ElementPointer);
    var TemporaryPointer: ElementPointer;
begin
    new (TemporaryPointer);
    TemporaryPointer↑.Next := CurrentPosition↑.Next;
    CurrentPosition ↑.Next := TemporaryPointer;
    TemporaryPointer↑.Previous := CurrentPosition;
    TemporaryPointer↑.Next↑.Previous := TemporaryPointer
end;
```

The final assignment (to the backward pointer) is most confusing.

TemporaryPointer is a pointer.

TemporaryPointer↑ is the record it references.

TemporaryPointer↑.*Next* is a field of this record. However...

TemporaryPointer↑.*Next* is a pointer too. Therefore...

TemporaryPointer↑.*Next*↑ is a record;

TemporaryPointer↑.*Next*↑.*Previous* is a pointer field, as above.

The overall effect of the assignment is to make the element following the new element point back to the new one, instead of to the element referenced by *CurrentPosition*.

As we have seen, pointers may be passed as parameters. Soon it will seem obvious, but now I'll point out that...

pointers as
parameters

> When a pointer is passed as a variable parameter, its address may be changed, as well as the contents of the location at that address. When a pointer is passed as a value parameter, the contents of the location it references can be changed permanently. Changing the address of the value parameter is only a local assignment.

Thus, passing a pointer as a value parameter only partially inhibits our ability to reconfigure the structure it references.

. . . . . : . . . : . . . . : . . . . . : . . . . . . : . . . . . : . . . : . . . . : . . . : . . . : . . . :

Q. What is the output of this program? What conclusions can you draw about passing pointers as value parameters?

```
program RitesOfPassage (output);
    {Demonstrates some effects of passing a pointer as a value parameter.}
type ElementPointer = ↑Element;
    Element = record
                Data: char;
                Next: ElementPointer
            end;
var Current: ElementPointer;
procedure Change (Pointer: ElementPointer);
    begin
        Pointer↑.Data := 'C';          {Which of these}
        Pointer := Pointer↑.Next;      {are local assignments?}
        Pointer↑.Data := 'D'
    end;  {Change}
begin
    new (Current);
    Current↑.Data := 'A';
    new (Current↑.Next);
    Current↑.Next↑.Data := 'B';
    writeln (Current↑.Data, Current↑.Next↑.Data);
    Change (Current);
    writeln (Current↑.Data, Current↑.Next↑.Data)
end.  {RitesOfPassage}
```

A. RitesOfPassage illustrates some of the hazards of passing pointers. The output of the first writeln is 'AB', while the second yields 'CD'. During Change, alterations to Pointer are local, but changes within the location it references are global and permanent. The assignment:

Pointer := Pointer↑.Next;

is negated on return to the main program—Current again points to the start of the list. However, assignments to any fields of the record Pointer↑, and to other linked records are permanent—the Data fields of both records in the list are changed permanently. We could even have globally lengthened the list from within Change by adding this statement to the procedure:

new (Pointer↑.Next)

. . . . . : . . . : . . . . : . . . . : . . . . . : . . . . . . : . . . . : . . . . . . : . . . . : . . . . : . . . . :

Chapter Notes and exercises may be found following Chapter 17.

12

Defensive Programming

So far, I've assumed that most readers are somewhat familiar with computers and programming, so our introduction to Pascal has been swift. I must now beg you, though, to retain a bit of caution. Although it's tempting to say, with a sneer, that Pascal is merely a glorified version of the language used to program a hand calculator—or an easier version, actually, since we are not constrained to 99 statements—programming effectively will still require a certain degree of art and craft. This chapter summarizes some of the techniques that are useful to remember when programs begin to stretch beyond 99 steps.

BASIC programmers may be surprised to find that none of the methods I'll mention are intended to make programs run faster, or occupy less memory. Instead, they are the basis of *defensive* programming; trying to avoid problems by being aware of their potential for occurring. I'll begin with a look at some of the basic methods of avoiding confusion in coding, and then see how to build-in debugging tools. Next, I'll talk about program testing, and its shortcomings. I'll close with studies of two 'big' programming styles that rely, in different ways, on the development of modules—first as program *stubs*, and then as program *primitives*.

Basic Techniques 12-1

THERE'S NO RECIPE FOR A PERFECT program. A dollop of variables and a dash of comments are proper ingredients, but good programming (like good cooking) takes talent that doesn't come with the cookbook. Instructors at restaurant schools realize this, and begin their courses by teaching prospective chefs the Zen of boiling water or breaking eggs. As a programmer, I'll maintain the tradition by considering the many ways of naming a variable.

I'll start with the programming equivalent of making ice cubes—by writing a program that computes circumference. Only one algorithm really makes sense: get the diameter, use the circumference formula, and print the results.

Request information
Perform calculations
Print output

A working program is barely longer than the algorithm:

> **program** C (*input, output*); **var** *X,Y*: *real*;
> **begin** *readln* (X); Y := 3.14∗X; *writeln* (Y) **end**.

But simple as program C is, it's unacceptable because of poor style. The identifiers I've chosen, and the way the program is laid out, violate a basic precept of good programming—that a program should be as easy for a human being to read and understand as it is for a computer to execute.

Now, William Shakespeare ('A rose, by any other name, would smell as sweet') and Gertrude Stein ('A rose is a rose is a rose') didn't think names were especially important. Computers agree with them entirely, because as long as an identifier is formed in accordance with Pascal's syntax rules, anything goes. However, Abbott and Costello knew better, as their famous routine *Who's On First?* makes clear.* A name can carry a tremendous amount of information (or misinformation), and identifiers should be as meaningful as possible.

meaningful identifiers

For example, suppose that a program does a series of geometry calculations. We *could* have a variable declaration like:

> **var** *a, b, c, d, e, f, g*: *integer*;

But contrast that with:

> **var** *area, base, circumference, depth, elevation, frustum, girth*: *integer*;

The second set of identifiers is mnemonic. Every identifier is a memory aid that clarifies the purpose of each variable.

One might argue that it's easy to remember the meanings of shorthand variable names (like *a*, *b*, and *c*) in a brief program. Unfortunately, although computers never forget, people do. In time, you'll have occasion to dig up a program written weeks or months earlier, and try to rewrite it, or include it in a larger program. You may find to your dismay that convenient shorthands have turned into unbreakable codes.

expressions should be clear

Like variables, expressions are also documented by the way they're written. There is often more than one way to write a particular expression, or to choose between parentheses and operator precedence rules. The main rule of thumb to follow is that figuring out what an expression means (to say nothing of evaluating it) should not bring great anguish to someone who is reading your program.

A string of operations can sometimes be confusing or ambiguous, even though it accomplishes exactly what you intend. Compare:

> *PartialResult /CompleteData –Correction*
> {*vs.*}
> (*PartialResult /CompleteData*) – *Correction*

---

* Abbott describes the peculiar nicknames of a team of baseball players: Who's on first, What's on second, I Don't Know plays third, Why plays left field, Because is in center, and so on!

The first expression is correct, but unclear. The second is unambiguous. Write assignment statements and expressions that can be understood by human beings, and the computers will take care of themselves.

Once we discuss the naming of variables and expressions, can subprograms be far behind? Procedures and functions should be commented extensively. Mark the start of each subprogram declaration with a box that explains its purpose, as shown below.

commenting
subprograms

```
(*  *  *  *  *  *  *  *  *  *  *  *  *  *  *  *
 *            PROCEDURE REALIGN             *
 *  REALIGN IMPLEMENTS THE HOSPITAL RULE    *
 *  LIMIT REALIGNMENT ALGORITHM.  PARAMETERS *
 *  AFFECTED ARE:                           *
 *      DELTA, EPSILON:  INITIALIZED;       *
 *      PERMEABILITY:  UPDATED;             *
 *  FUNCTION AUDIT (SEE ABOVE) IS ALSO CALLED. *
 *  *  *  *  *  *  *  *  *  *  *  *  *  *  *  *)
```

Professionally produced code is usually commented like this. In addition to clarifying the action of each subprogram, comment boxes make individual procedures or functions easy to locate in a long program listing. In fact, you'll probably find that merely putting a few blank lines between each subprogram makes your code more understandable.

When a program is long and has many procedures it's a good idea to *precomment* them at the beginning of the program. Describe the program's action in terms of its procedure calls.

precommenting

```
(*  *  *  *  *  *  *  *  *  *  *  *  *  *  *  *
 *            PROGRAM SCRAMBLER             *
 *  THIS PROGRAM CAN BE USED TO ENCODE OR   *
 *  DECODE DOCUMENTS OR COMMUNICATIONS.  IT *
 *  CALLS PROCEDURES:                       *
 *      INSTRUCTIONS                        *
 *      CHOOSEOPTION                        *
 *      ENTERCODEKEY                        *
 *      ENCODE, DECODE  (ONE OPTION)        *
 *      PRINTRESULTS                        *
 *  ALL PROCEDURES ARE DESCRIBED BELOW.     *
 *  *  *  *  *  *  *  *  *  *  *  *  *  *  *  *)
```

In larger programs, the first page of comments can be crucial to keeping the software running. An outline like the one below contains all relevant information about the program and its history. This kind of comment is particularly necessary if the reader will go on to modify the code, as often *must* be done in the real world.

```
(*  *  *  *  *  *  *  *  *  *  *  *  *  *
 *        PROGRAM NAME               *
 *        AUTHOR(S)                  *
 *        DATES OF MODIFICATIONS     *
 *        PURPOSE OF PROGRAM         *
 *        DESCRIPTION OF ALGORITHM   *
 *        LIST OF PROCEDURES         *
 *        IMPLEMENTATION NOTES       *
 *  *  *  *  *  *  *  *  *  *  *  *  *  *)
```

program history

Active Antibugging

Samuel Johnson may or may not have been correct in his observation that remarriage is the triumph of hope over experience. Programming without planning for bugs, though, certainly demonstrates a failure to have learned from the past. Now, the techniques I've suggested so far can be described as a 'passive' defense system for programs. But labeling, commenting, and naming, no matter how good, will still not always prevent bugs. Let's look at some more active methods of defensive programming.

The first key to active antibugging involves opening a window into the program's operation, at run-time, by taking a picture of one or more variables. A *snapshot* procedure takes such a picture, by printing current variable values. Why would anybody want such a procedure?

The Golden Rule of Debugging

When you're sure that everything you're doing is right, and your program *still* doesn't work, one of the things you're sure of is wrong.

----

snapshot procedures

Frequently, a variable whose value you're certain of actually represents another value entirely. This holds true for experienced programmers as well as novices. Snapshot procedures should be used at the first sign of trouble; experienced programmers often build them into programs as a matter of course. Calls for snapshots can be spread liberally around a program during testing, and then turned into comments or edited out when the program is operational. For example, this sequence of procedure calls:

```
GetInputValues  (A, B, C, D, E);
PrintAllValues  (A, B, C, D, E);
ProcessData  (B, C, E);
PrintAllValues  (A, B, C, D, E);
PrepareOutput  (A, B, D);
PrintAllValues  (A, B, C, D, E);
```

is quickly modified when the program works:

```
GetInputValues  (A, B, C, D, E);
{  PrintAllValues  (A, B, C, D, E);  }
ProcessData  (B, C, E);
{  PrintAllValues  (A, B, C, D, E);  }
PrepareOutput  (A, B, D);
{  PrintAllValues  (A, B, C, D, E);  }
```

> Building debugging *writelns* and snapshot procedures into your programs is called *embedding* debugging code.

Why wait for a problem to develop? An obvious technique to follow in building-in debugging code is to use **if** statements and constants to switch parts of the program on and off:

```
const DEBUGGING = true;
```
     . . .
embedding debugging code

```
if DEBUGGING then begin
    writeln  ('Debugging point 7.');
    Print  (X,Y,Z);    etc.
```

In long programs, however, the use of **if** statements may not allow a fine enough control of diagnostic output. We may want to have a switch with intermediate positions, and not just the *boolean* equivalent of 'ON' and 'OFF.' A constant can be defined with a wider range of values, and used to control a **case** statement when convenient.

```
const DEBUGLEVEL = 3;
    {Available debugging levels:
        0:  all diagnostics off.
        1:  entry to procedures announced.
        2:  entry and exit of all subprograms announced.
        3:  parameters printed on entry to subprograms.
        4:  conditions printed at control statements.
        5:  special instructions followed.        }
```
debugging levels
                    . . .

```
case DEBUGLEVEL of
    1:  writeln  ('Welcome to procedure CheckInput');
    3:  writeln  ('CheckInput: Parameter Data: ', Data);
    5:    etc.
```

Another approach is to make debugging levels additive, so that every level implies all the actions of the lower levels as well. A sequence of nested **if** statements does the trick here:

```
                   if DEBUGLEVEL >= 1 then begin
                      writeln ('Welcome to procedure CheckInput') ;
                      if DEBUGLEVEL >= 2 then begin
additive debugging         writeln ('CheckInput: Parameter Data: ', Data) ;
           levels          if DEBUGLEVEL >= 3 then begin
                              {additional debugging levels}
                                 . .
                           end  {Level 3 debugging}
                        end  {Level 2 debugging}
                     end ;  {Level 1 debugging}
```

A final fillip to embedded debugging code is the *execution profile*. An execution profile is a count of the number of times each statement is executed, or the number of times every subprogram is called. This sort of information is use-

execution profiles   ful for improving the efficiency of programs, as well as for spotting runaway loops. An auxiliary counter variable can be inserted into a loop, and instructed to print during debugging runs (perhaps if a constant named *COUNTING* is *true*. For instance:

```
                  Iterations := 0 ;
auxiliary counters  while Looping do begin          {Loop 7}
                       . .     {the loop's action}
                       Iterations := Iterations + 1
                  end ;
                  if COUNTING then writeln ('Loop 7:', Iterations);
```

Similar variables can be used to count procedure or function calls. Some Pascal systems will have profilers built into their compilers, and can be told to spit out a profile after—or even while—running a program.

Testing

Clearly, at some point active antibugging spills over into being program testing. Now, I've probably never explained the difference between debugging and testing carefully enough.

> *Debugging* is what *you* do before you consider a program completed. *Testing* is what a program user does as she makes your program crash.

The programmer, faced with a particularly recalcitrant program, tends to think only of getting it to compile—if it works for a particular set of data, so much the better. This is debugging. But someone who must actually use (or grade the quality of) your program applies stiffer criteria. It doesn't matter much that the program compiles, since that's the bare minimum expectation. Nor is the user concerned with its operation under ideal conditions. Instead, she tries to find your program's limitations: to make it produce wrong results, or to crash. *That's* testing.

Thus, debugging tries to get rid of known bugs, while testing is an attempt to show that more bugs still exist. It's an unfortunate fact that both methods have severe limitations. The effectiveness of debugging depends largely on the diligence and experience of the programmer.

limits of testing

> Although program testing may show the *presence* of bugs, it can't guarantee their *absence*.

For instance, let's consider the problem of testing a random number generator. Can we test a *Random* function as easily as we tested function *Tan*, back in Chapter 2? Suppose we cleverly recognize that we can check the function by seeing if its result, on average, is 0.5. Ten thousand calls are easy to arrange:

```
Sum := 0.0;
for Count := 1 to 10000 do
    Sum := Sum + (Random (Seed)) ;
writeln (Sum / 10000);
```

But just how clever have we been? For all we know, the random function has produced many 0.4's, and just enough 0.9's to raise the average to 0.5 (or even just ten thousand 0.5's!).

problems with testing

How about inspecting the actual sequence of values, then? Well, although we might write a driver that prints the first ten or twenty numbers in the pseudo-random sequence it produces, such a small sample won't do us too much good. If we call the function repeatedly:

```
for Count := 1 to 10000 do
    writeln (Random (Seed)) ;
```

we're no better off. Nobody can inspect a list of ten thousand twenty-two digit *real* numbers and declare that they're randomly distributed.

Let's construct a test that combines our earlier tries. Suppose we modify the function call to produce a number in some reasonable *integer* range, say 1 through 10, then use an array to keep track of many calls. In program *TestRandom*, below, note that since *Random's* output currently falls between 0.000... and 0.999... we can multiply by 10, truncate, then add 1 to the result to normalize output into the range 1 through 10.

```
program TestRandom (input, output);
   {Checks the distribution of the Random function's output.}
const NUMBEROFTRIALS = 10000;
type Data = array [1..10] of integer;
var Counter, Seed, Temp: integer;
   TestBed: Data;
function Random (var Seed: integer): real;
   {Generates a pseudo-random number such that 0<=Random<1.}
   const MODULUS = 65536;
         MULTIPLIER = 25173;
         INCREMENT = 13849;
   begin
      Seed := ((MULTIPLIER*Seed)+INCREMENT) mod MODULUS;
      Random := Seed/MODULUS
   end; {Random}
begin
   for Counter := 1 to 10 do
      TestBed [Counter] := 0;
   writeln ('Please enter a seed.');
   readln (Seed);
   writeln ('Distribution of ', NUMBEROFTRIALS:1,' trials:');
   for Counter := 1 to NUMBEROFTRIALS do begin
      Temp := (1+trunc (10*Random (Seed)));
      TestBed [Temp] := TestBed [Temp] + 1
   end; {for}
   for Counter := 1 to 10 do
      write (Counter:3, '''s');
   writeln;
   for Counter := 1 to 10 do
      write (TestBed [Counter]:5);
   writeln
end. {TestRandom}
```

↓   ↓   ↓   ↓   ↓

Please enter a seed.
471
Distribution of 10000 trials:
   1's 2's 3's 4's 5's 6's 7's 8's 9's 10's
  1022 1057 1018 1015 991 1014 978 1007 917 981

    At this point can we safely say that *Random* doesn't contain any bugs? Not at all. Although a test has shown that none of the bugs we anticipated are present, it would be wishful thinking to hope that all bugs are absent. For

random function
testing program

instance, suppose that *Random's* output simply yielded a sequence close to 1, 2, 3...10 repeatedly. Our test shows a reasonable distribution of values, but says nothing about their predictability. You may want to refer to the discussion of chi-square testing in Chapter 7 for a more elaborate testing method. I'll talk more about testing when we discuss program correctness in Chapter 14.

Stub Programming

As programs get more complicated, testing and debugging alone may not be enough to produce reliable code. Instead, we have to write programs in a manner that will help insure that errors are caught or avoided. *Stub* programming is a method that allows for error and improvement.

> A *stub* program is a stripped-down, skeleton version of a final program. It doesn't implement details of the algorithm or fulfill all the job requirements. However, it does contain rough versions of all subprograms and their parameter lists. Furthermore, it can be compiled and run.

A stub program helps demonstrate that a program's structure is plausible. Its procedures and functions are primitive, unsophisticated versions of their final forms, but they allow limited use of the *entire* program. For example, if we were writing a payroll program, we might begin by developing a stub program that handles a fixed group of workers who each put in 50 hours per week, receive the same rate of pay, and declare the same number of dependents. Program *Payroll*, of Chapter 6, was basically such a stub.

dummy subprograms

The stub program approach is especially useful for beginning programmers, who are often forced to start working before they know enough Pascal to write the entire program. 'Dummy' procedures let novices get a head start on the program, without requiring implementation of the hard parts.

In developing a stub program, we start by writing a program's main modules. In the illustration below, *A, B,* and *C* demonstrate the major workings of a program, but they call dummy subprograms.

the stub approach

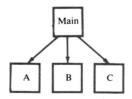

Next, the dummy procedures and functions—*M, N, O, P*—are expanded and debugged, but the program's smallest details still aren't implemented.

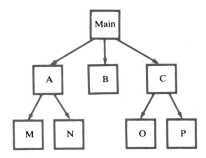

Eventually, the remaining subprograms—*X, Y, Z*—can be completed, and tested as they are added to the main program.

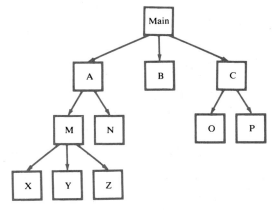

In practice, the first version of a stub program will contain many procedures that look like this:

procedure *TranslateCharacters* *(Old, New : char ; Distance : integer) ;*
{This procedure will take care of character translation—stub version.}
begin
    writeln ('In procedure TranslateCharacters. Arguments are') ;
    writeln ('Old: ', Old , ', New: ', New , ', Distance: ', Distance)*
end ;

stub procedures

The procedure does almost nothing for the action of the final program. However, it makes a considerable contribution to the final program's design.

    Another stub programming technique requires the generous use of comment brackets. We'd like to be able to have our high-level procedures ready to call lower-level code, even if the more detailed subprograms haven't even been written in the abbreviated form suggested above. 'Commenting out' segments of a **case** statement does the job:

```
                    ReadCommand  (Command) ;
                    case Command of
                      'A':  Add ;
                      'D':  Delete ;
                    {  'F':  Find ;
                       'S':  Skip ;
                       'T':  Translate ;
                       'V':  Verify  }
                    end ;
```

commenting-out code

The comment brackets can be moved, call-by-call, as the underlying procedures are actually written. In this segment, 'F', 'S', 'T', and 'V' will be written later.

top-down debugging

It's easy to appreciate that stub programming complements stepwise refinement. In fact, stub programs allow for something unexpected—*top-down debugging*.

> Stub programs let a large system be debugged and tested *as it is built*.

How can a program be tested or debugged before it's in operating shape? The dummy modules of stub programs can support rough runs on the computer. The proposed program can also be subjected to the intense scrutiny of your programming team—usually yourself and anybody else you can collar for ten minutes—in a *structured walkthrough*, or guided tour, of the partially completed program. It's an explanation *and defense* of the program's algorithm and implementation. I'm sure you've found that working on a program tends to create a mind set in the programmer that renders obvious mistakes invisible. Merely explaining a program aloud can give you a totally new view of it.

structured
walkthroughs

Top-down debugging of Pascal code has advantages too. To begin with, major program connections are tested first, which means that major bugs and shortcomings are detected early in the game. Furthermore, testing and debugging are distributed throughout the entire writing process. You're not forced to do all your program fixing just before the program is scheduled to be completed (which is invariably when the computer is least available). Finally, even if a program isn't completely finished by the due date it's a preliminary *working* version—and not just a useless mess of code.

Using Primitives

Stub programming is one approach to developing large programs, but it is not the only approach. I'll close this chapter with a long case study that employs a rather different programming methodology. I'll state the problem like this:

problem: text editing

Define a data type suitable for a text editing program. Create commands that would be useful for basic editing or formatting functions—centering, deleting text, moving or copying, etc.

A plain top-down approach to this problem seems reasonable. However, instead of dividing the editor into program stubs, and then writing the individual command modules one at a time, let's try a different technique: writing *primitives*.

primitives

A *primitive* procedure is a low-level, special-purpose subcommand that can be used by different program modules.

We'll use the primitives to implement the subtasks that our modules will ultimately require. We could call this a bottom-up approach to programming. We start out by writing and debugging a program's smallest subprograms—eventually they will be used elsewhere:

Then, the separate procedures and functions are incorporated into a subsystem of the main program:

bottom-up module
building

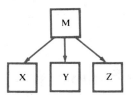

Finally, we put subsystems together to complete the program. This is the first time that they can be tested as a unit.

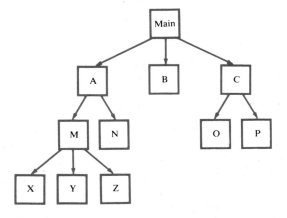

If we design primitives carefully, we'll find that each module is just a series of calls to primitive procedures. Had we adhered too religiously to stepwise refinement, we might have been misled into considerable duplicated effort.

Looking for, and writing, primitives is a useful approach in programs (like text editors) that have many similar commands. Instead of developing a series of nearly identical modules, we try to break each module down into underlying subcommands that may never be explicitly requested in the problem statement. An awareness of the potential of primitives is important as an alternative to strictly modular program development.

Our first programming consideration, though, is a data type definition. Suppose that we limit our editor to files *MAXLINES* lines long, with *MAXCHARS* characters allowed on each line. We'll keep the actual values low for now, so that we can print all our stored data on a single 'screen' during debugging.

data type limits

```
const MAXLINES = 20;
      MAXCHARS = 50;
```

It's pretty obvious that we'll want to represent our data as a two-dimensional array. However, we have two choices of how to do it. We can define a straightforward array:

```
type Sheet = array [1..MAXCHARS, 1..MAXLINES] of char;
var Whole: Sheet;
```

Or we can make the definition in a more roundabout way:

```
type Line = packed array [1..MAXCHARS] of char;
     Page = array [1..MAXLINES] of Line;
var Work: Page;
```

array of *char* vs. **array of** *Line*

What's the difference between these data types? They both define two-dimensional arrays, and each stores the same number of characters. We can use the same doubly nested **for** loop to travel through either, and, by changing the values of our constants, we can change the size of each array just as easily. Superficially, the two types are the same; at first glance, variable *Whole* and *Work* seem interchangable.

As a data structure, though, the *Page* type definition, used to define *Work*, will turn out to be considerably more convenient. Defining our type as a one-dimensional array of lines, instead of as a two-dimensional array of characters, lets us take advantage of Pascal string capabilities. We'll be thinking about our data in a line-oriented way (for printing, moving, copying, deleting, etc.). When each line is a string, we can print, move, copy, or delete the line in its entirety in a single stroke. If we have to work on a single line of the array, it can be passed as an argument to a procedure, without dragging the rest of the array along.

advantages of Page

But most important, it lets us define line-oriented primitives. Suppose that we have a two-dimensional array *Work* of type *Page*, above. Imagine some of the things we'd want to do to a single line:

delete part of the line;
delete its contents entirely;
center the line;
shift the line to obtain a ragged right or left margin;
number the line;

Now comes the hard part. Can we boil this group of possibilities down to
a handful of primitive? Well, the basic piece of information we need to know is
the length of the text portion on each line. Compare procedure *FindLength*,
below, to function *Length*, which found the length of a number in the long-
integer multiplication program of Chapter 7:

length-finding primitive

```
procedure FindLength (ThisLine: Line; var Length: integer);
    {Finds the 'useful' (non-blank) length of ThisLine.}
    var Position: integer;
    begin
        Position := MAXCHARS;  {the length of ThisLine}
        while (ThisLine[Position] = ' ') and (Position > 1) do
            Position := Position − 1
        if ThisLine[Position] <> ' '
            then Length := Position
            else Length := 0
    end;  {FindLength}
```

We'll also need to be able to delete individual characters on the line:

blanking primitive

```
procedure Blank (var ThisLine: Line; Start, Finish: integer);
    {Replace elements Start through Finish with blanks.}
    var Current: integer;
    begin
        for Current := Start to Finish do
            ThisLine[Current] := ' '
    end;  {Blank}
```

Finally, we'll need to be able to shift a sequence of characters within the
line. This wouldn't seem to be to hard, but a problem may arise if we're not
careful. We have to be sure that we don't move a character into an element
that we haven't yet moved, but nevertheless intend to move soon. For instance,
imagine shifting 'ABC ' one element to the right. We have to shift 'C', then
'B', then 'A'. If we move 'A' first, we'll screw up the rest of the move.

Procedure *ShiftRight*, below, takes care of the moving problem—but only if
we want to move characters to the right. As you read, try to figure out how I
might have written a procedure that shifts equally well both ways.

```
procedure ShiftRight (var ThisLine: Line; Start, Finish, Distance: integer);
   {Shift elements Start through Finish right by Distance.}
   var Current: integer;
   begin
      for Current := Finish downto Start do
         ThisLine [Current+Distance] := ThisLine [Current]
   end;   {ShiftRight}
```

shifting primitive

Now that we have three primitives at our disposal, it's not hard to implement the other commands we imagined. Assume that we're dealing with the *Current* line of the *Work* array. Deleting a line is taken care of with:

the delete command

     Blank (Work [Current], 1, MAXCHAR);

Shifting a line to the right takes a series of calls.

the right-adjust
command

     FindLength (Work [Current], Length);
     ShiftRight (Work [Current], 1, Length, MAXCHARS–Length);
     Blank (Work [Current], 1, MAXCHARS–Length);

Centering involves exactly the same sequence of primitives—only the arguments change:

the centering
command

     FindLength (Work [Current], Length);
     ShiftRight (Work [Current], 1, Length, (MAXCHARS–Length) **div** *2);*
     Blank (Work [Current], 1, (MAXCHARS–Length) **div** *2);*

Numbering a line will also involve calls of the primitives. We make sure that a number (say, two digits long, plus a blank) will fit, then make room for it. This code stops at the point of adding the number to the beginning of the line:

the numbering
command

     FindLength (Work [Current], Length);
     if *(MAXCHARS–Length)* >= 3 **then begin**
        ShiftRight (Work [Current], 1, Length, 3);
        Blank (Work [Current], 1, 3);
        {actually insert the number}
          ⋮
     end;

The same approach—thinking about the primitives that underly commands—pays off with two-dimensional problems. Assume that our array is filled with text from line 1 through 20, but that we want to remove lines 6 through 15 (a total of 10 lines). Stop for a moment, and try to describe the command *delete 6, 15* as a sequence of primitives.

Obviously we'll want to fill lines 6 through 15 with blank characters. But that's not enough for a text editor—we have to move lines 16 through 20 down into the breach. This move will actually take two steps. First, we'll copy line 16 to 6, 17 to 7, and so on. Then, we'll have to fill 16 through 20 with blanks.

deleting lines

If we don't take the last step, we'll have two copies of the last 5 lines of the array—lines 6 through 10 will be identical to 16 through 20.

How many primitives have we discovered? Two—a line blanking primitive, and one for shifting lines down. As a sequence of primitives, the delete command is:

the delete command

> *LineBlank (6, 15);*
> *ShiftDown lines 16 to 20 by 10 lines;*
> *LineBlank (16, 20);*

Draw a picture in the margin if you can't follow this sequence.

Why bother with the first *LineBlank*? Well, even though it's not really necessary (we could just *ShiftDown* over the lines we want to delete) it's useful as an antibugging technique. If we wanted to, we could print the contents of the data array after each step to make sure we were doing the right thing. If we imagine a call of a *Delete* procedure, complete with arguments, it might be:

> *Delete (Start, Finish, TotalLength);*

What about copying text? After the deletions above, we have information on lines 1 through 10. Suppose that we want to make an extra copy of lines 1 through 5 on the lines following line 7. We'll need to make room for the new lines (by shifting lines 8 through 10 up, out of harm's way), and then make the copies line by line. In primitive terms, we have:

the copy command

> *ShiftUp lines 8 through 10 by 5 lines;*
> *LineBlank (8, 12);*
> *Duplicate 1 through 5 into 8 through 12;*

The *ShiftUp* primitive is similar to our earlier *ShiftDown*, while *Duplicate* is really a brand new primitive. Were we to imagine a call of a *Copy* procedure, complete with arguments, it would look like this:

> *Copy (Start, Finish, AfterLine, TotalLength);*

How about moving lines? Let's move lines 4 through 7 to a new home following line 10. Assume that (after our previous set of moves) we have a total of 15 lines. We make room for lines 4 through 7, then copy them to their new home. Once the copy is completed, we delete the original lines 4 through 7. Finally, lines 7 on are moved down to fill the space vacated by the original 4 through 7. In terms of primitives, we have:

the move command

> *ShiftUp lines 11 though 15 by 4 lines;*
> *LineBlank (11, 14);*
> *Duplicate 4 through 7 into 11 through 14;*
> *LineBlank (4, 7);*
> *ShiftDown lines 8 through 19 by 4 lines;*
> *LineBlank (16, 19);*

Are you still with me? Again, some scribbling in the margin might help. Note that a move doesn't require any additional primitives. In fact, it's really the combination of two earlier commands:

> *Copy* (4, 7, 10, *TotalLength*);
> *Delete* (4, 7, *TotalLength*);

Since the number of lines of text stored in the array changes from call to call, we find that a *TotalLength* variable is passed each time. Were we to write the *Move* command as a procedure call, we'd have:

> *Move* (*Start, Finish, AfterLine, TotalLength*);

In conclusion, let me express some sympathy for the novice programmer. Stub programming and primitive programming are, at first, a bit like mathematical proof methods—easy to follow, but not so easy to think up! Rest assured that the experienced programmer's skill lies not in instantaneously sizing up a problem and knowing what method to use, but, rather in being flexible enough to experiment briefly with a variety of approaches.

13

Analysis of Algorithms

Introspection may or may not distinguish humans from the beasts, but it certainly separates the computer scientist from the hacker. What makes a program good? How can two programs that seem to achieve the exact same goals be compared? Can we ever say that a program, for all practical purposes, is as good as it is ever going to get?

This chapter focuses on the analysis of algorithms. We'll see methods for estimating the *running time* of particular algorithms, and get a feel for an algorithm's relative *efficiency*. I close with a cautionary tale on behalf of the occasional use of *brute force* algorithms despite their acknowledged inefficiency.

Why Analyze? 13-1

LET'S BEGIN TO CONSIDER ALGORITHMS and programs in a more abstract way. To start with, what's the difference between the two?

> An algorithm is a general method for solving some kind of problem. A program is an implementation of an algorithm; a particular algorithm put into practice.

Now, in our discussions so far we've generally talked about the 'goodness' of algorithms and programs in subjective phrases. A good program has been described in terms of certain characteristics—it does the job, or its output is well-labeled, or the program has good comments and is easy to understand.

However, we can form an entirely different basis of comparison between programs or algorithms by considering their relative *efficiency*.

efficiency

> In broad terms, efficiency is the measure of an algorithm's (or program's) impact on a computer. An algorithm or program is efficient if it accomplishes our goals with a minimal usage of computer resources.

Computers have only two basic resources at their disposal—*space* and *time*. This means that we can describe the impact of a program on a computer in two practical ways:

How much computer memory will the program require?
How long will the program take to execute?

Space is not of much concern to us right now. The programs we've developed thus far have had modest space requirements, and will continue so for a long time. Still, the notion that space can be a limiting factor is hardly foreign nowadays—almost every software ad (for spreadsheets, databases, etc.) states the minimum amount of memory needed to run the program.

Time is a more relevant consideration. By using a computer's built-in clock we can determine to the nearest milli- or microsecond how long it takes a program to execute. However, actual *running time* is a poor means for comparison between algorithms because it isn't universal. It will vary considerably depending on such unrelated factors as:

how well the algorithm was implemented in a computer language;
the speed of the computer the program is run on;
the compiler used to translate the program into executable form;
the computer's operating system;
other computer system loads.

As a result, actual running time measurements usually say more about the computer than about the algorithm. True running time measurements are generally employed for comparisons between computers, or between compilers for a particular language, or between different methods of coding a given algorithm.

How, then, do we compare algorithms? By getting an idea of the number of steps a program based on the algorithm will take.

> The running time of an algorithm is *proportional* to the number of steps it takes to carry the algorithm out.

This is a pretty reasonable notion. It says that, regardless of particular implementations, compilers, or computers, an algorithm that takes N steps to carry out will have a running time about twice that of an algorithm that only requires $N/2$ steps.

As you might imagine, it isn't necessary to figure out exactly how many steps an algorithm will require in order to get an idea of what its proportional running time will be. In fact, computers run so fast that a rough approximation is sufficient to characterize an algorithm. This approximation will usually be related to the amount of input the program expects, or the amount of output it will produce, or the 'size' of a value the algorithm's computations will be based on.

Let's compare two different algorithms for summing a sequence of numbers. The first is a simple iterative method, while the second uses the formula ascribed to Gauss. In pseudocode, our algorithms are:

two test algorithms

{A *summing* algorithm}
find out how long the sequence is;
initialize the running total to zero;
for *1 to the last number in the sequence*
   add the current number to a running total;
print the answer;

{*Gauss'* algorithm for adding }
find out how long the sequence is;
sum the series with Gauss' formula;
print the answer;

Now we'll actually implement the algorithms:

program *AddSeries* (*input, output*);
   {Add a sequence with a summing algorithm.}
var *N, Sum, Counter*: *integer*;
begin
   writeln ('This program will add the first N numbers. Enter N.');
   readln (*N*);
   Sum := 0;
   for *Counter* := 1 **to** *N* **do** *Sum* := *Sum* + *Counter*;
   writeln ('The grand total is ', *Sum*:1)
end. {*AddSeries*}

the summing algorithm

It's easy to count the statements that will be executed in *AddSeries*. There are two *writelns*, a single *readln*, an initializing assignment, and a loop that will execute N summing assignments. The total is $N+4$, or about N. For all practical purposes, if N doubles, then the running time of the program will double as well. We're in a position to say something about the summing algorithm itself.

> Since the running time of a program based on the summing algorithm will change by about the same amount that N changes, the algorithm is said to be *linear*, or directly proportional to N.

linear running time

Just how 'good' is the summing algorithm? Consider a program based on Gauss' algorithm:

Gauss' algorithm

program *Gauss* (*input, output*);
   {Implements Gauss' algorithm for summing a sequence.}
var *N, Sum*: *integer*;
begin
   writeln ('This program will add the first N numbers. Enter N.');
   readln (*N*);
   Sum := *round* ((*N*+1) * (*N*/2));
   writeln ('The grand total is ', *Sum*:1)
end. {*Gauss*}

Program *Gauss* has only 4 statements. A more practical way of stating this fact, though, is to say that Gauss' algorithm requires a constant number of statements *regardless* of the value of N.

constant running time

> An algorithm like Gauss' algorithm is said to have *constant* running time, since it doesn't vary with the value of N.

For any large value of N a constant algorithm (like Gauss) is clearly preferable to a linear algorithm (like the summing algorithm). Just how much better the algorithm is in practical terms will depend on the actual value of N. It's important to realize that comparing the statement counts of the programs themselves is quite misleading. It means almost nothing to say that program *Gauss* runs 104/4, or 26, times faster than *AddSeries* since this number will change with implementation, computer, and N itself. Describing the algorithm in terms of N is the only realistic basis of comparison.

N^2 running time

Just for fun, let's look at an algorithm that's much slower—an N^2 algorithm. Program *SumSubSeries*, below, implements a summing algorithm for adding subseries of numbers. Given a number N, it tells us the sums of the subsequences $1..1, 1..2, 1..3, \cdots, 1..N$.

subseries summing program

```
program SumSubSeries (input, output);
    {Sums all subsequences of a series of integers.}
var i, j, N, Sum, Total: integer;
begin
    writeln ('Enter the limit.');
    readln (N);
    Total := 0;
    for i := 1 to N do begin
        Sum := 0;
        for j := 1 to i do
            Sum := Sum + j;
        Total := Total + Sum
    end;
    writeln ('The sum of the subtotals is ', Total:1)
end. {SumSubSeries}
```

↓   ↓   ↓   ↓   ↓

Enter the limit.
12
The sum of the subtotals is 364

analyzing the algorithm

This algorithm is a little harder to analyze exactly. A quick inspection gives us the algorithm's main feature—it requires a loop within a loop. The outer loop will iterate N times. However, the outer loop includes more than one statement—there are two assignments, as well as an inner loop. The overall 'cost' of the outer loop, then, will be:

$$N * (2 + \text{the number of statements in the inner loop})$$

What about the inner loop? The first time it's entered only one statement will be executed. The second entry will execute two statements, then three, and so on. On the last run through the inner loop N statements will be executed. On average, about $N/2$ statements will be executed. The running time of our algorithm will be proportional to $N(2 + N/2)$, or about $N^2 + N$.

Big O Notation

As we noted earlier, we'll generally find a particular factor N—which is the number of characters that have to be inspected, the size of a file that must be sorted, etc.—that has primary influence over an algorithm's running time.

> *Big O*, or 'order of,' notation is used to express the running time of an algorithm in terms of N. For the purpose of big O notation, constant factors (constant multiples of, or additions to, N), or smaller terms involving N, are ignored.

Saying that an algorithm is $O(N)$ means that it takes on the order of N steps to complete. Similarly, an $O(N^2)$ algorithm will require about N^2 statements. We say 'about' and 'on the order of' because the number of steps may be multiplied by a constant, or have a factor added. Some typical big O values are:

$O(1)$ *Constant* time. The running time of the algorithm won't be affected by data, as in Gauss' algorithm. *Example*: Any algorithm that works by evaluating a formula.

$O(\log_2 N)$ *Logarithmic* time. Running time increases very slowly with N, since $\log_2 N$ only doubles when N is squared. For instance, $\log_2 1,000$ is 10, while $\log_2 1,000,000$ is just 20. *Example*: Binary search—the 'split the remainder' algorithm you follow when you look up a number in a telephone book N names long.

$O(N)$ *Linear* time. Running time is dependent on N; if N doubles, then running time doubles as well. *Example*: Searching through a list of length N, starting at one end.

typical Big O algorithms

$O(N \log_2 N)$ No special name. Usually implies that a linear algorithm invokes a $\log_2 N$ algorithm. Doesn't increase much faster than N alone. *Example*: Storing N numbers in a phone book in the first place.

$O(N^2)$ *Quadratic* time. Running time increases with the square of N; when N triples, its running time goes up nine times. *Example*: Sorting a list of N

elements by multiple passes, pulling out the largest one each time.

$O(N^3)$ *Cubic* time. When N is 1,000, N^3 is one billion. This time increases by eight whenever N doubles. *Example*: Matrix multiplication.

$O(2^n)$ *Exponential* time. If N is 10, running time is about 1,000; but doubling N (to 20) increases its running time to 1,000,000! Algorithms with exponential times are considered to be impractical. *Example*: Most brute-force code-breaking methods require exponential time algorithms.

Brute Force and Efficiency

Now that we have an idea of how to measure it, there is a strong temptation to worry about the efficiency of our programs. However, this tendency is largely misplaced. In terms of program *coding*, concern about the effect of minor variations in statement usage has all but disappeared. Believe it or not, programmers used to worry about such questions as which of these expressions:

$$a * (b + c) \qquad vs. \qquad (a * b) + (a * c)$$

would compile and execute more quickly. The answer varies from machine to machine, of course, and is practically irrelevant in any case. The few milliseconds that would be saved by knowing the correct answer are insignificant.

A more realistic approach to efficiency lies in recognizing that algorithm, not code, is the proper area of concern. An improved algorithm will pay off regardless of implementation, and the study of different algorithms is usually the content of the second or third computer science course.

Surprising as it may seem, though, we won't even always want to seek out the most efficient algorithm. Instead, we'll devise algorithms that use a time-honored method of problem solving know as *brute force*.

brute force

Solving a problem by brute force is not exactly what it sounds like—we don't write the problem on a piece of paper, then stomp on it until an answer crawls out. Instead, brute force implies that we repeat an unsophisticated solution step many, many times. The classic brute force solution was the Count of Monte Cristo's plot for his escape from the dungeons of the Chateau d'If.* Did he have a carefully planned route, split-second timing, and a diversion set up to distract the guards? No. Instead, he had a spoon, and fourteen years to spend in digging himself out. *That's* brute force.

Now, brute force tends to sound like a nasty method of solution, to be eschewed in favor of clever, elegant algorithms whenever possible. Although this is true in an abstract sort of way, real-life considerations make brute force methods a natural part of everybody's problem-solving repertoire. Suppose, for example, that you have to find out the number of distinct two-letter combinations that can be made with the letters a, b, c, d, and e (e.g. *ab, ac, ad*, etc.). Stop for a moment and figure out the answer.

* As related in *The Count of Monte Cristo* by Alexandre Dumas.

Of course there's a formula for figuring it out (there's always a formula), but what is it? 5 factorial divided by 2 factorial? 5 factorial over (5–2) factorial? 5 factorial minus 2 factorial? (Or does that have something to do with the formula for permutations?) In the time it takes to figure out the correct formula, we could write out every combination, count them up, and move on to bigger and better things.

Our example of a few pages back, *AddSeries*, performs the computer equivalent of 'writing down all the combinations.' Its linear running time algorithm is clearly less efficient than Gauss' formula even for small numbers, and it gets worse as the length of the sequence gets longer. Why, then, should we bother fooling around with inefficient, brute-force algorithms? I see three reasons.

advantages of brute
force

> Reason 1: Exploring a brute-force algorithm can lead to a better understanding of the problem.

There's a saying to the effect that you don't really understand a subject until you teach it. Why? Because teaching forces you to make a thorough, step-by-step analysis of the subject matter.

as thinking strategy

Brute force is a thinking strategy. It's used to *expand* a problem, to *separate* it into its constituent parts, to *simulate* the process a machine might use in solving it, to *exaggerate* the amount of repetition that may go into an algorithm, to *focus* attention on details of the problem or solution that might otherwise go unnoticed . . . the list could go on and on. Sometimes the best way to a clever solution lies in formulating a deliberately unclever answer, and then looking at it, and improving it.

> Reason 2: The real costs of a programming project are not always what they seem. Efficiency is a relative term.

ease of
implementation

The cost of computer time is only one factor in the price of a programming effort. Human costs—the time, effort, and wages of programmers—are usually greater than machine costs, and the gap is widening. This doesn't mean that grossly inefficient algorithms or quick and dirty programming methods should be tolerated. However, the savings that a more efficient method provides may be illusory. A brute-force algorithm is often the clearest and simplest way to do all or part of a job. A more efficient algorithm may exist, but it may not be cost-beneficial to discover it. Furthermore, an 'improved' algorithm might make the final program more complicated and difficult to understand.

> Reason 3: Brute-force algorithms tend to be adaptable. They are often easier to modify than more elegant, but more specialized, algorithms.

adaptability

Consider Gauss' algorithm. His formula is certainly efficient, but it's useless for solving other sum of the series problems. What about finding the sum of the squares of every number from 1 to 100? Or their cubes? Or their square roots? Our brute-force solution is a snap to adapt to solving these problems. Gauss' method is hopelessly narrow.

the moral

The real bottom-line of algorithms and programs, whether brute-force or elegant, is simple—*does it work*? In *The Psychology of Computer Programming*, Gerald Weinberg tells a story about a rescue programmer who was brought in to design a program to schedule the production of automobiles. The original programmer on the job was highly indignant over the rejection of his program, and complained that the new program was less than half as efficient as his discarded version. "However," retorted his relief, "my program works, and yours doesn't. If the program doesn't have to work, I can come up with an algorithm that runs twice as fast as yours!" Yes indeed!

14

Program
Correctness

The study of programming has always occupied an uneasy boundary between science and art. Somehow, it seems obvious that programming is a scientific pursuit. But although we can easily make sage observations about the characteristics of programs, we can seldom enunciate any underlying principles that will help us generate new ones. Where programming is concerned, computer science has had about as much relation to science as computer art has borne to art!

Nevertheless, it is only natural that, as scientists, we continue the search for a more formal basis of programming. A particularly interesting area of research is involved with attempting to define a language and method for reasoning about program *correctness*. This chapter introduces the notion of a program *proof*, and shows how mathematical modes of thinking have some use, but also some shortcomings, when they're applied to the writing of programs.

What is Correctness? 14-1

HOW DO WE SHOW THAT A PROGRAM works? A few weeks ago we might have given the obvious reply—*run it*. By now, though, we've probably learned to be a bit more cautious. We understand that, at best, running a program (and checking its results) shows that it works for a particular set of data. Making up a broader range of test data gives us a stronger feeling that the program will always work, but even testing is usually limited to ferreting out bugs whose symptoms we can imagine in advance.

Let's look at some of the methods used to gain assurance about the correctness, or reliability, of programs. Now, it's tempting to think that we can simply prove that any program will always work, just as we might prove that a mathematical theorem is correct. However, we'll find that confidence in the correctness of programs is much like confidence in the empirical correctness of engineering methods, rather than the more abstract notions of eternal correctness in mathematics.

What do I mean when I talk about developing confidence? Well, confidence lets us ride in airplanes, or cross bridges. We can't prove that a bridge won't ever fall down once it's in place, but we can feel certain enough about it to trust the bridge with our lives. A combination of tests join to give us this confidence. The bridge may follow the same design as other structures.

what is confidence?

We can build models for aerodynamic testing in a wind tunnel, and employ mathematical formulas for the design of structural members. We may even go so far as to stress randomly selected beams, cables, and the like to the point of destruction, in order to establish minimum strength levels.

Program tests are merged in the same manner to give us confidence in code. Some features are trusted because they've worked in similar programs, while others are allowed because the programmer and her peers believe that they will work. Parts of a program may have to undergo exhaustive testing by being run on carefully gathered real data, while for others, artificially manufactured data is good enough. Finally, some portions of the code may be so crucial that we have to try to prove, on paper, that they will always work.

Let's consider some of the less formal methods before we see what a program proof looks like. The first sort of testing most programs undergo can be called *bench testing*. The programmer explains her work to another programmer, or small group of programmers, in a structured walkthrough, or walking tour, of the code. This kind of examination is useful for two reasons. First, programmers less intimately involved with actual coding may spot conceptual errors that have escaped previous notice. Second, the discussion can lead to useful suggestions for tests that can be made at later stages of production.

Static analysis of the program is a step that's usually reserved for very large systems. Static analyzers are programs that examine the source code (e.g. the Pascal version) of a program without actually running it. They're able to spot certain kinds of errors that aren't always found by the compiler. One kind of error is the use of uninitialized variables in assignments, or as arguments to value parameters. A more interesting error that can be found through static analysis is the existence of unreachable code segments that won't ever be run, no matter what program input is.

Trace tools give us a window into program execution as the program runs. A simple kind of trace will print a message every time a subprogram is entered; arranging for a count and display of totals is barely more difficult. A trace tool might also keep track of changes in the value of a particular variable, or group of variables. In the hands of an expert, a trace is an invaluable tool for spotting potential errors in program design. As terminals with graphics capability become more widely available, we can expect to see trace tools become more widely available and exploited.

Finally, *data testing* is a method we should be quite familiar with. Builders of large systems often create *data generators*; programs that automatically produce data that has a set of characteristics specified by the programmer. The output of a data generator might be sophisticated data intended to make a program follow every possible execution path, or it might simply be a long, randomly-produced sequence of five-letter words. With huge amounts of test input available, it's no surprise to find programmers also creating automated tools for checking raw program output as well.

The methods we've mentioned here give only a rough overview of the kinds of tests that can be performed. To give you an idea of what a fertile field

bench testing

static analysis

trace tools

program testing is, consider a totally unexpected variation called *mutation testing*. In this approach, as exhaustive a set of test data as possible, with known results, is prepared. Next, programs are systematically mutated by having small errors introduced: a plus sign might be changed to a minus sign, or a constant might be increased by 1. The mutated program is then run on the original test data. If it works (i.e. it has the same results as the original program), we can conclude either that there is something very wrong with our original program, or that our test data is too weak to be useful. What an idea!

mutation testing

It's easy to imagine that a large program might require *all* of the different testing approaches described here to give us confidence that the program will really work. Even then, though, our faith in the program depends largely on its prospective application. We have greater faith in less important programs because we don't pay a high price for their failure. An interrupted video game may be annoying, but the manufacturer's desire to bring it to market will probably outweigh concern about some minor residual bugs. It's easy enough to refund the user's quarter if she's unlucky enough to find the bug the hard way.

limits on confidence

A program that controls a weapons system, on the other hand, is a different matter entirely. The recognition that no one test method is sufficient to guarantee that a program is correct and error-free is a cause for alarm, particularly when there is no way to undo a mistake. Indeed, there may not be *any* way to test such systems adequately.

Program Proofs

In recognition of the limits of program testing, computer scientists have tried to develop other methods of gaining confidence in programs.

> A *program proof* is a 'paper' analysis of a program that attempts to formally verify that the program will always produce a correct result.

In one sense, a program proof *is* like a mathematical proof. A mathematical proof tries to justify the correctness of a mathematical statement—a theorem. A program proof tries to give us the same sort of assurance about a sequence of code statements—a program.

However, there is also an important difference between the two kinds of proofs. A mathematical proof tries to show that following a certain sequence of steps will result in an irrefutable conclusion. A program proof, in contrast, tries to show that the conclusion reached by following a series of steps will always be correct. The mathematical sort of proof works well when we want to show that, in principle, an algorithm will work. However, proving an actual implementation—a completed program—requires a different sort of tack.

assertions

> The proof of a program is based on a series of *assertions* about the values of program variables and data.

An assertion is a statement that we expect to be true. Typically, we'll use *boolean* -valued expressions (like $a<>b$) to make assertions.

In general, we'll find that assertions come in pairs—there's an assertion right before a program action, then one immediately following it. We can think of the opening assertions as giving *preconditions*, while the closing assertions state *postconditions*. If you note that one statement's postcondition can be the next statement's precondition, you can begin to picture how program proofs are established. First, we make assertions about the effect of each statement:

preconditions,
postconditions

$\{assertion1\}$ *Statement1* ; $\{assertion2\}$
$\{assertion2\}$ *Statement2* ; $\{assertion3\}$
$\{assertion3\}$ *Statement3* ; $\{assertion4\}$

Then, by applying simple rules of logic, we can remove intermediate assertions:

$\{precondition\}$ *Statement1* ;
Statement2 ;
Statement3 ; $\{postcondition\}$

In practice, we usually work in the opposite manner, by starting with the outlying assertions, and attempting to develop assertions for parts of the program, then parts of those parts, etc.

Now, it's pretty easy to see how to make some kinds of assertions. Suppose that we want to divide A by B and save the result in C. The closing assertion is a check on the operation—our assertion that the answer is correct is $A = B*C$. However, if we want to be assured that we will survive the division we need an opening assertion as well—that B isn't 0. The sequence of assertions (in comment brackets) is:

verifying sequences

$\{B<>0\}$
$C := A/B;$
$\{A = B*C\}$

verifying loops

Looping statements are more interesting because assertions before and after the loop aren't sufficient to make a proof. Why not? Well, if the assertions are to actually prove anything, they must also establish that we arrive at the loop's end—that the loop isn't infinite!

variant and invariant
assertions

A loop's *invariant* assertion is a statement about the loop that is true both before and after each iteration of the loop. Its companion is a *variant* assertion whose truth will change between the loop's initial and final iterations. This is sometimes called the loop's *bound function* .

These two assertions serve complementary purposes in a loop proof. The invariant assertion makes a statement about the correctness of the loop's action, which is why it must always be true. The truth of the variant assertion, in contrast, is changed by the loop's action. It helps assure us that the loop will eventually be terminated, which is why it's also known as a bound function. The invariant assertion helps make sure that the loop doesn't do the *wrong* thing, while the variant assertion ensures that it does do the *right* thing.

For instance, suppose that we want to do *integer* division by repeated subtraction. The code segment below implements an algorithm most people learn in second or third grade:

```
Remainder := Dividend;
Quotient := 0;
while Remainder >= Divisor do begin
    Remainder := Remainder – Divisor;
    Quotient := Quotient + 1
end;
```

If this loop is correct, we should arrive at proper values for *Quotient* and *Remainder*. First, what's our invariant assertion? Well, both before and after each loop iteration there should be a special relationship between the dividend, divisor, quotient, and remainder:

$$\{Dividend = (Divisor*Quotient)+Remainder\}$$

Since *Dividend* isn't changed within the loop, we don't have to worry about monkey business that would require us to save *Dividend's* original value, and make our invariant more complicated. While the invariant relation is true, we can be confident that our loop, at the very least, isn't doing the wrong thing.

However, the invariant relation isn't enough. Suppose that the loop's action made no assignments to either *Quotient* or *Remainder*. Although the invariant assertion would still stay true, it wouldn't assure us that the loop would ever end. We need to state some sort of bound that is approached by the loop's action, but which can act as a threshold beyond which the loop won't venture.

The variant assertion:

$$\{Remainder >= Divisor, \text{ and } Remainder \text{ declines}\}$$

works for us. Its truth is potentially changed on each iteration of the loop—each time we change the value of *Remainder*. Eventually it becomes false; we pass the bound or threshold, and the loop is terminated. It is no accident that it forms the entry condition of the loop. Complete with assertions, the loop is:

```
Remainder := Dividend;
Quotient := 0;
{Dividend = (Divisor*Quotient)+Remainder}
while Remainder >= Divisor do begin
    Remainder := Remainder – Divisor;
    {Remainder >= Divisor, and Remainder declines}
    Quotient := Quotient + 1
    {Dividend = (Divisor*Quotient)+Remainder}
end;
```

As usual, I've made everything look easy by coming up with the correct answer on our first try. Let's consider a false proof, though. Suppose that we had chosen as our variant assertion the relation *Quotient <= Dividend*. We would still make progress toward loop termination, since we increment *Quotient* on each pass through the loop. Since it provides an upper bound on the loop, it's reasonable to think that the assertion is a good bound function.

Unfortunately, it's the *wrong* bound function. Before we reach the limit it sets, we'll have allowed the invariant assertion to become incorrect. Our attempted proof would fail, even though we set a threshold and approached it.

Difficulties In Proving Programs

The idea that we can prove that a program is correct is intensely appealing, since it would greatly increase our confidence in programs. True, verification seems complicated at first; but then again, so do mathematical proofs. Unfortunately, the promise of program proving has not been realized in as full a manner as was originally hoped. Let's investigate the reasons.

Two conditions have to be satisfied if we want a program proof to work. First, the action of a program statement can't undermine our assertions about what the statement will do. Although this notion seems obvious (we clearly wouldn't have a statement that directly contradicts an assertion), there are subtle difficulties that are easy to overlook. For instance, mathematical proofs don't have to worry about whether or not the axioms of mathematics will apply, but program proofs do. The machine code that takes care of computer arithmetic may never have been formally proven—and it may not always obey the rules!

correctness

Second, the assertions we make have to define the entire 'universe' of the program. Any necessary assertions that are left out cause gaping holes in the program proof that may not be detected until the program fails. For instance, suppose that a routine should sort three variables into increasing order. It's not enough to prove that the variables are in order when the routine ends. We can't ignore the possibility that the routine might have accidentally given all the variables the *same* value.

completeness

The need to satisfy these two conditions—correctness and completeness—make program proofs very difficult to develop.

In mathematical proofs, small errors will not necessarily have a negative impact on the proof as a whole. It may be that an individual step is incorrect or misstated. However, this sort of error won't always invalidate the overall goal of the proof—a fact can be true even if our explanation of it is faulty. Mathematical proofs usually fail because of larger conceptual errors.

For programs, though, the smallest step is vitally important to the conclusion of the program proof. The tiniest untested assumption about a data value in a program can suffice to undo an elaborate program proof.

limits of proofs

> More importantly, though, the knowledge that such errors can occur in proofs without being detected by expert computer scientists tends to undermine our confidence in the absolute reliability of program proofs at all.

Like a good trial attorney, we can cause a proof to collapse simply by demonstrating a reasonable doubt about its correctness. As a result, programs are actually proved only in a limited set of cases; and then only for relatively small program segments that are written with eventual proof in mind.

automated verification

Incidentally, you may be tempted to suggest that, since keeping track of small details is so important, program proving would be a perfect job for a computer. Why not write a program that could automatically check the correctness of a proof?

It's a good idea until you imagine what such a program's first job would be. Obviously we'd want to run it on itself. But what will we make of the answer? Suppose that the program announces that its own code is correct. Can we trust it? Worse yet (in a much more likely outcome) suppose that the automated verifier announces that its own code is *wrong*. Oh no! Back to the drawing board...

Even though few programs are formally verified, the techniques used to prove programs are widely applied as an aid to program development. In one aspect, the assertions that we might use to prove a program will turn up as detailed comments about the state of variables before and after a procedure or function call, or on the successful completion of a loop. Proof methods are also employed during the development of especially confusing program segments. In particular, ideas of loop invariants and bounding conditions are used to help assure ourselves that algorithms are correctly stated in the first place.

benefits of program proving

Another application of proof techniques is manifested by features built into programming languages. The availability of subrange types is a good example. A variable declared to have a subrange type is essentially a variable accompanied by an assertion—that is constantly checked—about the range of the variable's values. *Exception handling*—the specification of special notification procedures to be followed when errors are encountered—is another feature of recently developed programming languages.

Finally, programs can be written in a 'rough proof' form. You see, for many kinds of programs it almost seems easier to write the proof first, then tailor the code to fit the verification. In practice, when programs must be proved the development of proof and code usually go hand in hand. Even when the code is not intended to be exhaustively proved, writing code as though it will be verified can lead to less error-prone programs.

15

Software Engineering

Once a building has been erected and occupied it's not unreasonable to assume that major construction costs are a thing of the past. The construction of software, though, has not worked out quite this way. The original coding of a program accounts for a relatively small portion of its total lifetime cost. Time after time, organizations that depend on software have been stunned to find just how incomplete a 'finished' software product can be.

Chapter 15 describes the different stages of the software *life cycle*: analysis, specification, design, implementation, testing, and maintenance. Software life begins when problems are first being considered for computer solution, and doesn't end until the software has been discarded or completely replaced. Our discussion of software engineering will lay out some of the basic principles that have to be considered in designing and building successful software systems.

The Software Life Cycle 15-1

SOFTWARE ENGINEERING IS THE SCIENCE of the development of *software systems*—programs, large and small, that will be used to solve real problems. Like more traditional engineering endeavors, the study of software engineering is largely motivated by a desire to avoid repeating mistakes—mistakes that were only belatedly recognized as involving engineering at all. The opening paragraphs of a seminal text on software engineering (written barely a decade ago) describe the situation:

'No scene from prehistory is quite so vivid as that of the mortal struggles of great beasts in the tar pits. In the mind's eye one sees dinosaurs, mammoths, and sabertoothed tigers struggling against the grip of the tar. The fiercer the struggle, the more entangling the tar, and no beast is so strong or so skillful but that he ultimately sinks.

the tar pit

'Large-system programming has over the past decade been such a tar pit, and many great and powerful beasts have thrashed violently in it. Most have emerged with running systems—few have met goals, schedules, budgets. Large and small, massive or wiry, team after team has become entangled in the tar. No one thing seems to cause the difficulty—any particular paw can be pulled away. But the accumulation of simultaneous and interacting factors brings slower and slower motion. Everyone seems to have been surprised by the stickiness of the problem, and it is hard to discern the nature of it. But we must try to understand it if we are to solve it.'*

Dozens of software systems that have fallen into the tar pit Brooks describes. Sometimes the development effort is entirely unsuccessful; a satisfactory system isn't constructed. Other systems may be accepted by the end user, but be late, over budget, poorly suited to the intended application, or hamstrung by inefficient use of system resources. In either case, the programmer and user are equally dissatisfied with the end result.

The study of software engineering starts with the recognition that the development of software is a long-term process. It begins well before any program coding is done, and continues long after a program is thought to be finished. This continuing development process is known as the *software life cycle*. It can be divided into these distinct phases:

the software life cycle

1. *Analysis* of the problem.

2. *Specification* of the software's abilities.

3. *Design* of the software.

4. *Implementation* or coding.

5. *Testing* of the completed system.

6. *Maintenance* and evolution of the system.

Although our studies have focused mainly on coding, it is just one step in the process. As programs become larger and more complex, the earlier and later steps become increasingly important.

Analysis

Analysis of the problem is the first, and probably most difficult, step in the software life cycle. The real life problems faced by potential computer users are a far remove from the neatly prepared exercises presented in computer science textbooks. This is not because real life problems are any more difficult; indeed, the reverse is quite often the case. Instead, it is because customers and programmers often speak very different languages. As a result, simple problems can be misunderstood, or difficult ones understated.

The analysis phase tries to answer the question 'What should the software do?' in a manner that will be meaningful to the software designer. Simply saying that the software should 'keep our books,' or 'monitor our test equipment,' or 'give sample Pascal examinations' doesn't give much direction. Instead, the

* *The Mythical Man-Month*, by Frederick P. Brooks, Jr. Addison-Wesley Publishing Co., 1975. pg. 4.

analyst must work with the end user to answer many questions about the system. The system is pictured both as it is now, and as it may come to be:

- what will the system's input be? what output should the system produce?

- will these requirements change? how seriously? how often?

- what sort of people will use the system? can they be specially trained?

- will there be errors in input? in stored data? how should errors be fixed?

- what kind of equipment is available? what can be obtained?

- how fast should the system work? how reliable does it have to be?

- will the system grow? in what directions?

One current area of computer science research that's intended to help with the problems of analysis is *rapid software prototyping*. The idea of building prototypes, or test models, is common to many engineering disciplines. A prototype is a scaled-down model that can be examined and tested before any commitment is made to a final design. Prototyping is especially appropriate for software systems, since it helps facilitate communication between user and designer in the problem-analysis phase of program design.

Software prototyping relies on the idea that many software components—routines for input, output, data sorting—are more or less independent of the systems they're found in. These building blocks can be joined, with a minimum of new code, to rough out a prototype of the end-user's system. This working model can be used to help give the user an idea of a computer's capabilities, as well as to give the software analyst a feel for the users' needs. The user interface, or method the user employs to communicate with the program, is an area that's particularly suited for evaluation through prototyping.

Requirements Specification

The specification of a software system's requirements is a formal statement of its capabilities, capacities, and constraints. Whereas the analysis phase was intended to determine in general terms what the proposed system was supposed to do, the requirements specification states in detail what the finished system *will* do.

A requirements specification will be referred to throughout the entire software development process. It can act as the contract between programmer and end user, and is often the only point of contact between the two groups. If a feature or requirement isn't specified in the requirement, it's not liable to show up in the final product. The requirements specification will also generally be the standard against which the final system is tested.

Specification of software requirements is a more difficult task than it might appear to be at first glance. Consider the variety of areas that a specification has to define:

- It must state the specific abilities of the system—the commands that will be available to the user. These are the system's *functional requirements*.

- It has to specify the assumptions that will be made about the systems' input, users, response time, data—its operating environment.

details of the
specification

- It must define the system's limitations—how many users will there be, how much data need be handled, etc.

- It has to describe any special hardware requirements, or any restrictions imposed by hardware limitations.

- It must specify possible modifications to the system that have to be allowed for in the system's design.

- It should describe the nature and extent of documentation that are supposed to accompany the system. A preliminary users' manual may be required as well.

The functional specification is the most visible part of a requirements document. In small systems, stating functional requirements is a pretty straightforward task. A list of allowed commands may be all that is needed. In more complex systems, though, a list of commands may not be enough—we'll need a better mechanism for describing the big picture.

A variety of schemes have been developed to help in stating specifications. Most of them are elaborate charting systems; terms like *actigram*, *data-flow diagram*, and *Warnier diagram* abound. However, most specifications systems are built around a common theme: they describe a program in terms of its data—how it is stored and transferred, and what can be done with it in the process.

Once we begin to talk about data, programs can't be far away. Before we begin to code, though, we have to go through the design phase.

Design

software blueprint

The first two steps of the software life cycle determine *what* should be done. The design phase specifies *how* it should be done. The end result of the design phase is a *software blueprint* that can be implemented with a minimum of difficulty.

The importance of the design phase is probably the most underrated aspect of the software life cycle. Although it is inconceivable that one would embark on the construction of, say, a building without a detailed plan of action in hand, software projects are routinely undertaken with the barest minimum of advance planning.

How do we go about designing software, and how is a software design shown? *Structured design* has become a generic term for programming with an emphasis on modular design. Many of the design techniques we take for granted now were first formalized in a series of structured design texts and structured design

seminars put together by Larry Constantine and Ed Yourdon.* In particular, the emphasis on designing relatively independent program modules, whose inter-connections are specified in parameter lists, is characteristic of structured design. Many of the top-down programming techniques I've mentioned in past chapters, including stub programming, evolved naturally out of the desire to keep programs modular.

Flowcharting is the method originally used to make precise descriptions of a program's activity. A flowchart is a sequence of boxes, connected by arrows, that shows a program's flow of control. There is actually a government standard

flowcharts

for the shapes of boxes—a diamond indicates a decision, a parallelogram is input or output, and so on. Flowcharting is very popular in languages, like FOR-TRAN, in which programs can make sudden jumps to unexpected places.

Pseudocoding is quite familiar to us by now, and it seems like a self-evident idea. However, in the early 1970's, pseudocode was just an experimen-

pseudocode

tal alternative to flowcharting. A number of formalized pseudocoding systems were defined as *program design languages*, or PDL's. It's interesting to note that Pascal (which wasn't widely available at the time) and other recently designed languages incorporate many of the techniques they suggested.

Hierarchy and Input-Process-Output, or HIPO, charts are part of a typical

other formal systems

formal system for software design and specification (in this case, one developed by IBM). Although they were intended to be used as system documentation, these charts have also been found to be useful in system design. Hierarchy charts give a modular presentation of the work a program does, while input-process-output diagrams are more detailed pictures of the action of individual modules.

Regardless of the system used to design and specify code, the design phase has two goals. First, any ambiguities located in the requirements specification should be found and clarified. Second, there should be a detailed guide prepared for the next step—coding.

Coding

For most of the history of computing, coding the main program has been thought of as the programmer's main activity. Surprisingly, surveys consistently show that program coding occupies only about 20% of the time and effort involved in producing software systems. Nevertheless, carefully made specifications and designs are all for naught if they are not well-implemented.

The software engineer looks at the coding phase of programming in several different ways. First, there's the code itself. What language, or languages, should be used? How long should subprograms be? What rules should be followed for defining identifiers? How should the code be laid out? How efficient must it be? How detailed should comments be? Are any kinds of programming tricks forbidden?

* Such as *How to Manage Structured Programming*, by Ed Yourdon, YOURDON Inc. 1976 (and dedi-cated 'to my first, third, and fourth wives...').

Next, there's the programming staff. How can work be divided? What are the responsibilities of individual coders? How closely should programmers be supervised? How should proposals for coding be reviewed? How much communication should there be between programmers, and how can it be arranged? How can we estimate the difficulty of specific program segments?

Finally, there are the methods used to produce the code. What electronic tools are there for coding support? How are different versions of programs maintained? How should debugging or testing code be built into the software? Will different hardware—terminals, printers, interactive equipment—have any effect on programmer productivity?

Of all the phases of software development, coding is probably the least formalized. One reason is that the management of coding efforts has turned out to differ from other kinds of management in unexpected ways. A particularly instructive example comes from attempts to apply general notions of manpower to coding. Now, in most sorts of organized activity—drafting, or claims processing, or chopping wood—the volume of work accomplished grows in rough proportion to the amount of effort expended. As a consequence, doubling effort doubles results—or halves completion time, more or less.

the mythical man-month

The unanticipated results of applying this rule to programming gave Brooks the title of his book: *The Mythical Man-Month*. He found that most project managers treated software production just like other sorts of production. When a project fell behind schedule, they would add additional programmers. To their astonishment, they often found that adding help made matters worse! Extra programmers only made the project fall further behind schedule. Brooks characterized this experience rather cynically in Brooks' Law: *Adding manpower to a late software project makes it later*.

On close inspection we can recognize the two characteristics of software production that give the law its grain of truth. First, new staff must be trained. Even if they are expert programmers, the current project must be explained; they have to be brought up to speed in the project's goals, rules, coding strategies, etc. Second, they must communicate as they work, since a program's modules can never be made entirely independent of each other. A group of n people can meet in $n!/2(n-2)!$ different pairs; which means that doubling a group from three programmers to six increases the number of two-person meetings they can hold by a factor of *five*.

programming teams

A variety of solutions have helped improve the situation. Insistence on modular software design reduces the amount of communication needed between groups, and helps reduce the impact of delays in software production. A very effective approach suggested by Brooks and others is the creation of *programming teams*, in which outstanding 'superprogrammers' are given sufficient staff support to avoid unnecessary distractions. Such teams include a 'copilot' who helps the superprogrammer with design, a 'language lawyer' who specializes in knowing the ins and outs of a particular language or programming system, an 'editor' in charge of documentation, a 'program clerk' who can handle secretarial details that require technical expertise, etc.

Testing

The test phase of the software life cycle can involve as much time and effort as the coding phase. No matter how carefully a program is planned and coded, it will still contain bugs and imperfections. In addition, large software systems may not even be fully assembled until the test phase begins. A ship's maiden voyage is traditionally a shakedown cruise; a program's first run marks the start of the test period.

module testing

The test phase has several goals. Most obviously, we want to find bugs introduced during the coding process. The attempt to find this sort of bug relies on methodical testing of individual program modules. This is usually known as *module testing*. Many of the program testing techniques we've discussed elsewhere are employed in this phase.

integration testing

Next, modules are put together to form systems or subsystems. This is sometimes called *integration testing*, since we are integrating the activity of different modules. The bugs found during integration testing are generally due to design errors. These will typically involve the interface between separate modules. Code may have been implemented correctly, but programmers may have labored under false impressions of the input their particular modules could expect, or the output they were supposed to produce. If problems found in integration testing involve basic data storage methods they can be very serious, and involve a considerable amount of code rewriting.

acceptance testing

In the final testing step, the completed system is presented to its end users for *acceptance testing*. Well-managed software systems will usually work their way into this phase slowly by *alpha* and *beta* site testing. The system is distributed to a limited number of sites for feedback and refinement before it is presented for final validation and acceptance. Unfortunately, problems that come up in acceptance testing sometimes date back to the original analysis and specifications phases. The program does what is called for in the design, but the design itself may be incomplete or incorrect from the end user's point of view.

The testing scheme described here is, of course, a bottom-up approach. Since bottom-up approaches tend to hide early errors until late in the game, top-down approaches to system testing, like the stub programming methods described earlier, are becoming more popular. Some techniques mentioned earlier—particularly rapid software prototyping—will also help the situation.

Maintenance and Evolution

Software may outlive its usefulness, but it never wears out. Once an individual or organization has put effort into learning (or adapting to) a particular software system, there is a great tendency to prefer modification of existing software over the acquisition of new software. Even armed with this understanding, it will probably come as a great surprise to find that maintenance and modification of a program can cost two to four times as much as its original coding—or up to 80% of the costs contained in the entire software life cycle.

There are a number of motivations for modifying software once it is presumed to be complete. A first category involves *correction*. Although the

correction

rate at which bugs are found declines drastically, they usually appear throughout a software system's lifetime. Occasionally they will fall into the 'bug or feature?' column, especially when a user employs a poorly-documented or unintended command.

A second motivation for modification is the desire to improve the system's usefulness—*perfective* changes. Surprisingly, a successful system may require the most modifications, since it may be widely adopted in environments other than the one it was originally intended for. The addition of new features, or fine-tuning and improvement (perhaps by using new algorithms) of existing features are typical of this kind of modification and evolution.

perfection

A third category of modifications are sometimes called *adaptive* changes. These are mandated by changes in the system's operating environment. They may be caused by improvements in the hardware system, or by changes in external software the system relies on; for instance, a change in the computer's operating system.

adaptation

The understanding that maintenance accounts for such a large portion of software costs has been one of the prime motivating factors in the development of software engineering. Well-understood systems—say, automobiles—are designed with maintenance in mind. As a result, their construction is fairly modular, and points that need to be checked regularly are easily accessible.* Software is only recently developing this kind of self-awareness. The embedded debugging tools mentioned earlier are a perfect example of built-in aids for program maintenance.

One approach intended to improve the maintainability of systems involves the creation of *toolbox software*. A system is conceived of as being a collection of relatively independent tools, each with a specific task. The UNIX** operating system is typical of the toolbox approach. For instance, it doesn't contain a word-processing program, per se. Rather, it has separate programs (editors, formatters, printers, etc.) that a user can tie together to provide the function of a word-processor. Boxes of tools may produce larger systems, but they make it easier to improve specific tools as technology or understanding improves, or as needs change.

toolbox software

When adapted to the consumer market, toolbox systems generally appear as *integrated software* systems. In these systems, a single program is capable of a variety of functions. *Framework* and *Symphony* are two commercially available products that are typical of integrated systems. They each combine brand-name editors, spreadsheets, databases, etc. into a single program. However, integrated systems have been criticized for going too far—in attempting to create a single, easily-advertised product, the maintainability of the component parts is lost. At this point, the integrated systems have not fared well in the marketplace.

integrated software

---

* There are notable exceptions. Consider, for example, the Chevy Monza, which required that the engine be partly removed in order to change the spark plugs!
** UNIX is a registered footnote of Bell Laboratories.

16

Recursive Programming Methods

'There is always more than one way to skin a cat,' as the expression goes, and nowhere is this more true than in programming. But although we've spent many pages on the use of different control statements, and on the tradeoff between algorithms and data structures, there is still one unmentioned tool left in our bag of tricks—*recursion*.

A recursive subprogram calls itself. Now, this property alone might seem unremarkable, and indeed, hundreds of programming languages, from FORTRAN to BASIC, have thrived without allowing such references. We will see, though, that recursion adds enormous power to Pascal. It is as much a technique for structuring data as it is for structuring programs. We'll see recursion applied to simple and array types in this chapter, and deal with recursion and pointers in Chapter 17. This chapter also introduces the **forward** declaration of subprograms, necessary for mutually recursive calls.

Recursive Procedures and Functions 16-1

recursive sentence-reverse program

CONSIDER THIS DECEPTIVELY SIMPLE program:

```
program Reverse (input, output);
    {Recursively reads a sentence of input, and echoes it in reverse.}
procedure StackTheCharacters;
    var TheCharacter: char;
    begin
        read (TheCharacter);
        if (TheCharacter <> '.') then
            StackTheCharacters;              {A recursive call.}
        write (TheCharacter)
    end; {StackTheCharacters}
begin
    writeln ('Please enter a sentence.');
    StackTheCharacters;
    writeln
end. {Reverse}
```

Please enter a sentence.
This is not a palindrome.
emordnilap a ton si sihT

Program *Reverse* takes an ordinary sentence of text as input, and prints it out in reverse. It accomplishes this with a *recursive* procedure, *StackTheCharacters*.

recursion defined

> A procedure or function that calls itself is said to be *recursive*.

When *StackTheCharacters* is first invoked, a character is read as input to the local variable *TheCharacter*. Then (unless the first character was a period) *StackTheCharacters* is called again. Note that the final statement of the first call—*write (TheCharacter)*—is still pending. However, leaving uncompleted statements behind is nothing new; we do it almost every time we call a procedure or function. Sooner or later we'll get back to this output statement, and print the value of the first character.

recursive calls

Now let's look at the second call of *StackTheCharacters*. Once again, a new local variable (*TheCharacter*) is created, a new letter is read to give *TheCharacter* its value, and (assuming it wasn't a period), *StackTheCharacters* is called once more. Eventually, when the pending *write (TheCharacter)* is executed, the second character's value will be printed.

Since it's hard to visualize what happens in a series of identical procedure calls, computer scientists use a metaphor to help explain recursion.

the stack

> The variables and pending statements of a partially executed program or subprogram are said to go on a *stack* within the computer.

When we jump out of a subprogram (by calling another procedure or function) all currently active variables, along with any pending statements, are added to the stack. The number of times this can occur—the height of the stack—is only limited by the memory resources of the computer.

If we only look at the input statements executed during program *Reverse*, we'll see something like the series shown below. Although we keep creating local variables named *TheCharacter*, Pascal's scope rule (that the most local variable takes precedence) gives the current input value to the most recently created variable.

building the stack

```
read (TheCharacter);        {Reading in 'T'.}
  read (TheCharacter);        {Reading in 'h'.}
    read (TheCharacter);        {Reading in 'i'.}
      ⋱    {Intermediate calls...}
        read (TheCharacter);        {Reading in 'm'.}
          read (TheCharacter);        {Reading in 'e'.}
            read (TheCharacter);        {Reading in '.', the last call.}
```

The chain of calls to *StackTheCharacters* continues until we read the period that ends the sentence. At last we'll get past the **if** statement. We can finally complete the last invocation of *StackTheCharacters* by printing the character most recently read—the period. Since this particular invocation of *StackTheChar-acters* is finished, the program 'returns' to where it was when the procedure call was made—to the calling procedure, and eventually to the main program. In effect, the computer executes this series of statements:

undoing the stack

$$
\begin{array}{ll}
\textit{write (TheCharacter)} ; & \{\text{Printing out '.'.}\} \\
\textit{write (TheCharacter)} ; & \{\text{Printing out 'e'.}\} \\
\textit{write (TheCharacter)} ; & \{\text{Printing out 'm'.}\} \\
\quad \ddots \quad \{\text{Intermediate calls...}\} & \\
\textit{write (TheCharacter)} ; & \{\text{Printing out 'i'.}\} \\
\textit{write (TheCharacter)} ; & \{\text{Printing out 'h'.}\} \\
\textit{write (TheCharacter)} ; & \{\text{Printing out 'T'.}\} \\
\textit{writeln} & \{\text{This is the last statement in the main program.}\}
\end{array}
$$

Now, a stack is actually created in any series of procedure or function calls—the sequence need not be recursive. The stack can, and usually does, grow and shrink during the course of a program. However, it will always be empty when a program ends normally.*

Procedure *StackTheCharacters* is a good introduction to recursion because it lets you see how the stack is used in an obvious way. In *StackTheCharacters*, each time the recursive procedure was invoked, useful local variables and uncompleted statements were left on the stack. But now let's look at a related example that is also recursive, but that makes minimal usage of the stack.

Program *IntegerReverse*, below, leaves the minimum amount of business undone. All that each call of procedure *ReverseDigits* leaves behind is its final **end**. When the very last call is made (when (*TheNumber* **div** 10) equals zero), the entire stack of procedure calls can end without further ado.

recursive integer-reverse program

```
program IntegerReverse (input, output);
   {Recursively reverses the digits of an integer.}
var Number: integer;
procedure ReverseDigits (TheNumber: integer);
   begin
      write (TheNumber mod 10:1);
         {Output the rightmost digit in a one-space field.}
      if (TheNumber div 10) <> 0 then ReverseDigits (TheNumber div 10)
         {If there are more digits, strip off the rightmost one and pass the result.}
   end; {ReverseDigits}
```

* This simplified explanation of stacks helps explain how the computer keeps track of scope within a program. *All* identifiers defined in a subprogram are put on the stack when the subprogram is invoked. Then, when an identifier is used, the computer looks down the stack for the identifier's most recent definition or declaration. Although the stack may contain several different usages of a single name, the most recent definition is the first one found.

```
begin
    writeln ('Please enter a positive integer.');
    readln (Number);
    ReverseDigits (Number);
    writeln
end. {IntegerReverse}
```

↓   ↓   ↓   ↓   ↓

Please enter a positive integer.
789254
452987

....
end recursion   : This kind of recursion is called *end* or *tail* recursion. When the procedure
                  : makes its recursive call, no unfinished statements are left on the stack.
....

A procedure that uses end recursion is usually easy to write iteratively
(using a looping statement). For example:

```
procedure IterativeReverse (TheNumber: integer);
```
iterative reversing
procedure
```
    begin
        repeat
            write (TheNumber mod 10:1);
            TheNumber := TheNumber div 10
        until (TheNumber = 0)
    end;
```

::

Self-Check   Q. Is the procedure in *Print* recursive? Should it be? What does it do?
Questions
```
program Print (input, output);
procedure Echo;
    var TheCharacter: char;
    begin
        read (TheCharacter);
        write (TheCharacter);
        if TheCharacter <> '.' then Echo
    end; {Echo}
begin
    writeln ('Please enter a sentence.');
    Echo;
    writeln
end. {Print}
```

A. Procedure *Echo* offers another demonstration of end recursion. Although a stack is created, it doesn't contain any statements to be executed. The series of *TheCharacter* local variables is saved, but gets thrown away when the recursive calls end. The stack is created, but not used. A **while** loop would do the job perfectly well, because the program just echoes a line of input.

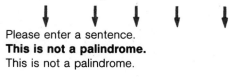

Please enter a sentence.
This is not a palindrome.
This is not a palindrome.

:..:

More Complicated Recursion

Our first two examples kept recursion simple by minimizing the numbers of statements and variables involved. The next recursive procedure will be the most complicated, even though it's just intended to help us play a game:

problem: towers of hanoi

The *Towers of Hanoi* game is played with three pegs, and a pile of disks of different sizes. We start with all the disks stacked on one peg, as shown:

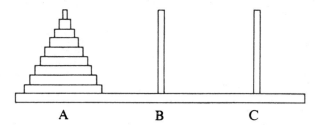

A   B   C

The object of the game is to move the entire stack from peg A to peg C, while obeying two rules:

the rules

1. Only one disk can be moved at a time.

2. A larger disk can never go on top of a smaller one.

Write a program that gives step-by-step instructions for moving a stack of height *n* from peg A to C.

The original version of this game was supposedly played as a religious rite with a set of three diamond needles and sixty-four golden disks. The end of the game was supposed to mark the end of the world.

the 1 or 2-disk problem

Let's try to get a handle on how the moves are made for stacks of various heights. Clearly a height of 1 is trivial—we move the disk directly from A to C.

What about a height of 2? We put the top disk out of the way—to B. Then the bottom disk goes to C, and the smaller disk from B to C.

the 3-disk problem

With a stack of height 3 it gets interesting. Let's suppose, though, that we restate the problem (as I'm liable to do when I'm up to something). Instead of moving 3 disks from A to C, let's move 2 disks from A to B—we already know how to move two disks from one peg to another. Next, move the third disk directly to C. Finally, make another two-disk move, from B to C. We've switched all three disks.

the 4-disk problem

How about starting with 4 disks? Once more, let's begin by restating the problem. Can we move 3 disks from A to B? Sure—it's essentially the same as moving them from A to C. Then we switch the fourth disk directly from A to C, and, finally, transfer 3 disks from B to C.

developing a recursive statement

As you can probably gather, I've insisted on restating the problem in a particular way each time so that we can develop a special insight. We begin to solve the Towers of Hanoi problem for a stack of height n by trying to solve it for a stack of height $n-1$. This solution must wait until we solve for $(n-1)-1$, and so on. Eventually we get to the trivial case of n equaling 1, and can begin to work our way back up.

induction

Almost without realizing it, we've used a high-priced method of thinking called *induction*. We start by solving a simple case of the Towers of Hanoi problem—a tower of height one or two. Then, we show that even if we start with a larger number, we can always work our way down to a problem that we know how to solve. This is the heart of what will become our recursive solution to the problem.

Now we're ready to make a recursive statement of our solution. To move n disks from peg A to peg C:

the recursive Hanoi algorithm

1. Move $n-1$ disks from A to B.

2. Move 1 disk from A to C.

3. Move $n-1$ disks from B to C.

In steps 1 and 3, of course, we will use the remaining peg as an auxiliary 'holding' peg.

In understanding program *Hanoi*, below, it may help to imagine that the three pegs are arranged in a circle rather than in a line. The particular pegs that *FromPeg*, *ToPeg*, and *UsingPeg* represent will change (they'll actually seem to rotate). However, we'll always eventually find ourselves fulfilling the second step of our algorithm, and announcing a particular move.

Towers of Hanoi
program

```
program Hanoi (input, output);
    {Recursively solves the Towers of Hanoi problem.  Moves disks from A to C.}
var Height: integer;

procedure Move (Height: integer;  FromPeg, ToPeg, UsingPeg: char);
    {Recursive procedure for determining moves.}
    begin
        if Height = 1
            then writeln ('Move a disk from ', FromPeg, ' to ', ToPeg)
            else begin
                Move (Height -1, FromPeg, UsingPeg, ToPeg);
                writeln ('Move a disk from ', FromPeg, ' to ', ToPeg);
                Move (Height -1, UsingPeg, ToPeg, FromPeg)
            end {else}
    end; {Move}

begin
    writeln ('How many disks are you going to start with?');
    readln (Height);
    Move (Height, 'A', 'C', 'B')
end. {Hanoi}
```

↓   ↓   ↓   ↓   ↓

```
How many disks are you going to start with?
4
Move a disk from A to B
Move a disk from A to C
Move a disk from B to C
Move a disk from A to B
Move a disk from C to A
Move a disk from C to B
Move a disk from A to B
Move a disk from A to C
Move a disk from B to C
Move a disk from B to A
Move a disk from C to A
Move a disk from B to C
Move a disk from A to B
Move a disk from A to C
Move a disk from B to C
```

Recursive Functions

Functions can be written recursively, just like procedures. Function *Sum*, below, uses a series of recursive calls to add a series of numbers from 1 to its argument *Limit*.

```
function Sum (Limit: integer): integer;
   {Recursively sums the series 1 through Limit.}
   begin
      if Limit<=1
         then Sum := Limit
         else Sum := Limit + Sum (Limit−1)
   end; {Sum}
```

recursive summing
function

A comparable iterative function would be:

```
function IterativeSum (Limit: integer): integer;
   {Iteratively sums the series 1 through Limit.}
   var TemporarySum: integer;
   begin
      TemporarySum := Limit;
      while Limit>1 do begin
         Limit := Limit−1;
         TemporarySum := Limit+TemporarySum
      end;
      IterativeSum := TemporarySum
   end; {IterativeSum}
```

iterative summing
function

However, both functions, if called in the same program, will produce the same results.

```
writeln (Sum (5), IterativeSum (5));
writeln (Sum (100), IterativeSum (100));
```

$$\downarrow \qquad \downarrow \qquad \downarrow \qquad \downarrow \qquad \downarrow$$

        15   15
        5050   5050

The stack produced by *Sum* is a bit peculiar because it contains a series of partially completed assignment statements.

stacking recursive
function calls

The general outline of *Sum* is typical of recursive functions—the recursive call occurs in the middle of an assignment statement. Thus, the stack serves to delay the evaluation of an expression.

Let's assume that *Sum* is called with 5 as its first *Limit* argument, as above. Remember that the **if** statement in function *Sum* looks like this:

```
if Limit<=1
   then Sum := Limit
   else Sum := Limit + Sum (Limit−1)
```

Here's the stack of partial assignments that's made in the sequence of calls:

$$Sum := 5 + Sum\ (5\text{--}1);\ \{first\}$$
$$Sum := 4 + Sum\ (4\text{--}1);\ \{second\}$$
$$Sum := 3 + Sum\ (3\text{--}1);\ \{third\}$$
$$Sum := 2 + Sum\ (2\text{--}1);\ \{fourth\}$$
$$Sum := 1;\ \{fifth\}$$

None of the stacked assignments can be completed until *Sum* gets a non-recursive value—the fifth assignment, which doesn't depend on calling *Sum* again. Let's follow the sequence of assignments as they're completed.

$$Sum := 1;\ \{fifth\}$$
$$Sum := 2 + 1;\ \{fourth\}$$
$$Sum := 3 + 3;\ \{third\}$$
$$Sum := 4 + 6;\ \{second\}$$
$$Sum := 5 + 10;\ \{first\}$$

the limit call

> The last of a series of recursive calls is the *limit* call. The circumstances that give rise to the limit call form the exit condition of the recursion.

infinite recursion

By our definition of the function, *Sum*'s limit call occurs when its argument is 1. An *infinite* recursion occurs if the exit condition can't be met, and the limit call is never made.

Once we understand how *Sum* is implemented recursively in Pascal, it's instructive to look at a recursive statement of its algorithm in English.

If *Limit* is 1 or less, the sum of 1 to *Limit* is *Limit*.

If *Limit* exceeds 1, the sum of 1 to *Limit* is *Limit*—plus the sum of 1 to *Limit*–1.

As you can see, this definition—like all recursive definitions—is essentially circular, since it's defined in terms of itself. If you're having trouble understanding recursion, take a deep breath and start again—it's well worth the effort.

Another definition that's easy to state recursively in English is that of the *n* th Fibonacci number:

problem: recursive Fibonacci definition

If *n* is 1 or 2, the *n* th Fibonacci number is 1.

If *n* is 3 or more, the *n* th Fibonacci number is the sum of the previous two.

To nobody's surprise, this algorithm works perfectly well when transliterated into Pascal.

```
program TestFibonacci (input, output);
    {Tests a function that recursively generates Fibonacci numbers.}
var Test1, Test2, Test3, Test4: integer;
```

recursive Fibonacci
program

```
function Fibonacci (Which: integer): integer;
    begin
        if (Which=1) or (Which=2)
            then Fibonacci := 1
            else Fibonacci := Fibonacci (Which −1) + Fibonacci (Which −2)
    end;   {Fibonacci}

begin
    writeln  ('Reading four test entries.');
    readln  (Test1, Test2, Test3, Test4);
    writeln  ('Fibonaccis', Test1:4, Test2:4, Test3:4, Test4:4, ' are:');
    write  (Fibonacci (Test1), Fibonacci (Test2));
    writeln  (Fibonacci (Test3), Fibonacci (Test4))
end.   {TestFibonacci}
```

↓   ↓   ↓   ↓   ↓

```
Reading four test entries.
1 7 15 25
Fibonaccis   1    7   15   25  are:
             1        13       610       75025
```

problem:
exponentiation

Our first two functions each used a single value parameter, but our third and final recursive function example will work with two value parameters. One will remain constant, while the other declines on each recursive call. Our problem is to raise some number X to the nth power, where n is an *integer*.

Defining a *Power* function in English is easy—'multiply X by itself n times.' However, this sounds like an invitation to a **for** loop. Before you read on, try to state a recursive algorithm.

Our recursive solution uses the same sort of thinking as our solution to the Towers of Hanoi problem—we give it in terms of a restatement:

the recursive
statement

If n equals 1, X to the n equals X.
If n is greater than 1, X to the n equals X times X to the $n-1$.

In reading the code of function *Power*, below, note the necessity of two value parameters. Each possible step of our recursive algorithm requires that we know the values of both X and n. However, as you can easily see in the algorithm, X remains constant while n declines steadily.

recursive power
function

```
function Power (X: real; n: integer): real;
    {Recursively calculates X ⁿ. Assume n >0.}
    begin
        if n = 1
            then Power := X
            else Power := X * Power (X, n −1)
    end;   {Power}
```

why use recursion?

Although I won't show it here, *Power* (like *Fibonacci*) can easily be implemented as an iterative function. In fact, every recursive procedure or function can be written in a non-recursive manner. Since recursion isn't absolutely necessary, why should it be used at all? The answer takes several tacks. In a few instances (such as reversing a string of characters of unknown length) recursion is the best way to solve the problem. Our main alternative is the impractical one of declaring enough variables to deal with every possible character sequence.

A more sophisticated reason for recursion will arise when we encounter recursive data structures in Chapter 17. Although we won't get into such data structures now, they also pose problems that are stated and solved recursively.

Finally, recursive solutions can be more elegant than their iterative counterparts. I'd hate to say that shortness is a virtue in itself, but recursive subprograms can often be written more briefly and clearly than iterative ones. When you become comfortable with recursion, and start to recognize 'standard' recursive algorithms, you'll appreciate the ease with which such algorithms can be put into programs.

. . . .

Self-Check
Questions

Q. What is the intention and effect of function *RawPower*, below? What restriction of *Power* does it remove?

```
function RawPower (X: real; n: integer): real;
    {Recursively calculates X ⁿ.  Assume ?}
    begin
        if n = 0
            then RawPower := 1
            else if n > 0
                then RawPower := RawPower (X, n−1)
                else RawPower := 1 / RawPower (X, −n)
    end; {RawPower}
```

A. *RawPower* is considerably more robust than *Power*. It is still a recursive procedure whose algorithm is nearly identical to *Power*'s. However, it can raise X to a power smaller than 1. In other words, n can be any *integer*, positive, negative, or zero.

Q. What is the largest number of times the innermost **else** will be entered, above?

A. At most, the call *RawPower* (X, −n) will occur once.

. . . .

forward References

In Chapter 2 we learned that once a procedure or function has been declared, its name has meaning in other parts of the program, including 1) the main program's statement part, 2) the statement part of the subprogram itself, and 3) the statement parts of subprograms declared after the procedure or function we're concerned with.

We're quite familiar with calls of the first sort, and we've just been looking at calls of the second kind. The third case calls for an example. Suppose that we make the following declarations:

```
program Main   (input, output);
    global declarations;
    procedure Early  (parameter list);
        local declarations
        begin
            statements
        end;
    procedure Late  (parameter list);
        local declarations;
        begin
            statements
        end;
    begin  {Main}
      ·.·          etc.
```

procedures calling procedures

Procedure *Early* can be called in procedure *Late*, or in the main program. Procedure *Late* can't be called in *Early*, though, because it hadn't been declared when *Early* was written.

Occasionally, the 'declare before you call' rule will seem to paint the programmer into a corner. Suppose that a procedure must call another procedure that hasn't been declared yet, but which will be declared by the end of the subprogram declarations. This can happen when procedure *A* calls procedure *B*, which, in turn, calls procedure *A* (sometimes called *mutual recursion*). We're in a fix—which declaration should come first? The forward declaration comes to the rescue.

mutual recursion

forward declarations

> A *forward declaration* tells the compiler that a subprogram identifier is valid, and may be used in a program before the actual subprogram declaration takes place.

how identifiers are validated

When a program is first compiled, the compiler scans (reads) the code from start to finish. As it goes along, it reads constant, variable, and subprogram declarations and creates an internal table of known identifiers. If the compiler encounters an identifier that hasn't been declared, it assumes that an error has been made. It jumps to the conclusion that the identifier won't *ever* be declared, and prints an error message.

The **forward** declaration puts the subprogram's name into the table of valid procedure and function identifiers. This doesn't mean that the subprogram need not be declared at all, or that the declaration can occur outside of the subprogram declaration part. A **forward** declaration is merely used to vary the order of declarations.

The complete subprogram heading, complete with parameter list, is followed by the word **forward**. Then, when the subprogram is actually declared, the parameter list is not repeated. **forward** is a statement, and should be preceded and followed by a semicolon.

procedure *Second* (**var** *M,N*: *integer*; *P*: *char*); **forward**;

 procedure *First* (*A,B*: *integer*; **var** *X*: *real*);
  local declarations
  begin
   statements;
   Second (*argument list*)   {Call procedure *Second*.}
    . . .

using **forward**

 end; {*First*}
 procedure *Second*;   {The parameter list is omitted.}
  local declarations
  begin
   statement part
  end; {*Second*}

Because a forward declaration may come well before the actual procedure or function declaration, it's usually a good idea to repeat the parameter list as a comment when the subprogram is finally declared.

 procedure *Second*; {var M,N: integer; P: char}
  local declarations   etc.

This is an excellent programming practice that adds documentation with almost no effort.

   Functions may be **forward**-declared too. The normal function heading, complete with parameter list and function type, is followed by the word **forward**. When the actual declaration of the function takes place, the parameter list and function type are omitted. For example:

function *DeclaredLater* (*Parameter*: *integer*): *char*; **forward**;

 procedure *CallManyFunctions* (*parameter list*);
  begin
   rest of the procedure declaration
   includes a call of DeclaredLater
  end;

 function *DeclaredLater*;
   {The parameter list and function type are omitted}
  begin
   rest of the function declaration
  end;

As usual, it's a good idea to include the parameter list and function type as a comment of the real function declaration.

function *DeclaredLater* {(Parameter: integer): char;}
     etc.

Why use **forward** declarations? As noted, we sometimes have to. However, even if they're not absolutely required (as with the procedures above, whose declarations could have simply been reversed), **forward** declarations can help make a program more readable. Sometimes it seems like a good idea to put the shortest, most easily understood procedures at the beginning, and **forward** declare a long, complicated routine they all call and use. It's equally plausible that we might want to do exactly the opposite, and start out with the hardest, least familiar procedure instead of burying it deep within the procedure declarations. Some programmers (and I don't advise this) **forward** declare *every* subprogram, to help keep track of the parameters each one expects to receive.

Recursive Array Programming 16-2

A LARGE NUMBER OF INTERESTING PROGRAMMING problems involve recursive array manipulation. The array is useful because it stores large amounts of data, while recursion is handy because it lets our manipulation of the data be described easily. In this section we'll look at problems that involve using recursion to inspect or modify the contents of an array.

The recursion we'll be using here differs from the examples presented in the last section in an interesting way. Then, we used recursion to solve problems that were stated 'one dimensionally,' so to speak. We would recursively progress along one particular path until we found the end of the sentence (or evaluated an expression, or reached the beginning or end of a series). Then, we'd tumble all the way back to the start of the sequence of recursive calls, and the program would be finished.

Now, though, we'll use recursion to allow algorithms that require movement in several 'dimensions,' some of which may be false starts, and others of which might help lead in the right direction.

backtracking algorithms

Backtracking algorithms involve a series of trial and error solutions. We travel toward a solution until we know we're heading in the wrong direction, then backtrack to where we think we took the incorrect turn. Then, we try again.

The children's game of 'Hot and Cold' uses a classic backtracking algorithm. One player takes guesses as to what the second player is thinking of. The second player tells the first if a guess is hot (close) or cold (far from the truth). Since in-between degrees of warmth are allowed (warmer, cooler, 'now you're practically boiling to death!' etc.), the first player is continually guessing and backtracking.

Backtracking algorithms are particularly suited to recursive programming methods. Each recursive call creates a context, or environment, associated with one step toward a solution. The sequence of steps that got us there is preserved in the series of recursive calls. Were we to look at the 'stack' of recursive calls, we'd generally find it growing and shrinking repeatedly as we search further toward—or back away from—potential solutions.

Maze Searching

Searching through a maze is an ideal problem for recursive solution. We'll state the problem like this:

problem: maze searching

Imagine that you are trapped in the center of a maze. Find all paths to the outside world.

We'll assume that the maze is given to us as a pattern of asterisks (marking walls) and blanks (marking potential paths). We'll always start in position 6,6. For example, this is a 12 by 12 maze, with our starting position (at 6,6) marked with a '!':

The maze

A false path

data type definition

First, let's agree on our representation of the maze. We can store the maze as a two-dimensional array of *char* that goes from 1 to *MAXCOL* horizontally, and from 1 to *MAXROW* vertically. When we initially read in our data, we'll put a * in each 'wall' location, and leave potential paths blank. As we search the maze, we'll mark each step with a '!'. We'll know that we're at an exit if we find ourselves on row 1 or *MAXROW*, or at column 1 or *MAXCOL*. Our Pascal type definition is:

      type *ArrayType* = **array** [1..*MAXROW*, 1..*MAXCOL*] **of** *char*;
      var *Maze*: *ArrayType*;

Now, how does one get out of a maze? Well, if you're Theseus, you trail a string behind you on the way in, then trace it back out again. Even if you don't have any string, a simple rule—stick to one wall, and always turn right—will eventually get you out of the maze.

Working with a computer, though, imposes certain limitations. Perhaps there's no Minotaur chasing us, but there's no string, either. Moreover, the path may be too narrow for a 'stick to a wall' rule. We may not be able to turn right, and if we reach a dead end, we'll have to back out (as shown in the right-hand illustration, above). We're more in the position of the monster than the hero!

Fortunately, the phrase 'back out' gives us a hint. Recall that one effect of recursive procedure calls is to create a stack of partially executed subprograms. Each one can have variables and pending statements associated with it. If each step down a path involves a recursive procedure call—building the stack—we can also imagine that exiting the sequence of procedure calls will back us out along our original path.

using the recursive stack

How can we state a maze searching method recursively? Let's try some inductive thinking as a warmup exercise. Suppose that we're one step away from an exit. Can we get to the door? Sure—just take one step in any direction. It may take several tries (once in each direction) but we'll certainly find the way out.

Suppose that we're two steps away. Can we get to the spot that's only one step away? For sure again, even though it may take us a few tries. Now comes the clever step—our inductive leap. What if we're N steps away? Can we get to be one step away? Of course. No matter what N starts at, we can always get to N−1. Since N keeps going down, it will eventually reach 2, and we'll be home free. No matter how many steps away we are, we can always get to a position we're sure we know how to solve.

using induction

Being clever was easy compared to our next task—stating the algorithm recursively:

first refinement

> *To search a maze (from the current spot)* . . .
> mark the current spot as part of the way out;
> **if** we're at the exit, print the maze
>   **else** *search a maze (from a new starting position)*;

I've added a new step to the mental warmup we worked on. Each time we call the *search a maze* procedure we mark our present position. The maze itself is passed as a value parameter to each call of the procedure. Note that the path of positions we've marked grows one step longer on each call. You can think of it as a snapshot of our current state—where we are, and how we got there.

The key to the algorithm is finding the new starting position. If we can—if there's no wall there—we'll *search a maze* starting one step to the left. Then, if we can, we'll *search a maze* starting one step up. Then we'll search to the right, and finally down, each time making sure that we're not running into a wall. The shaded section below corresponds to the **else** part shaded above:

To search a maze (from the current spot)...
mark the current spot as part of the way out;
if *we're at the exit, print the maze*

else if *we can, search a maze (starting one step left);*
       if *we can, search a maze (starting one step up);*
       if *we can, search a maze (starting one step right);*
       if *we can, search a maze (starting one step down).*

second refinement

Once more, the maze, with our current position marked on the pathway out, is passed as a value parameter to the *search a maze* procedure. In effect, we are always searching a maze that has already been partially searched. The computer maintains a stack of copies of the maze—one for each of the partially completed procedure calls. Each copy shows the path that led to that particular location. If we're at the exit, the current copy of the maze shows the way out.

If we don't get to an exit, nothing happens at all. Suppose we take a left turn into a dead end. Since we can't go left, forward, or right, that particular invocation of the procedure ends, and its copy of the maze (with an incorrect path out) is removed. The completed program is shown below.

```pascal
program ThreadTheMaze (input, output);
    {Recursively find and print all exit paths from a maze.}
const MAXROW = 12;
      MAXCOL = 12;
      POSSIBLEPATH = ' ';
      THEWAYOUT = '!';
type ArrayType = array [1..MAXROW, 1..MAXCOL] of char;
var Maze: ArrayType;
procedure StoreTheMaze (var Maze: ArrayType);
    {Reads in the maze.}
    var i, j: integer;
    begin
        for i := 1 to MAXROW do begin
            for j := 1 to MAXCOL do read (Maze [i, j]);
            readln
        end
    end; {StoreTheMaze}
procedure PrintTheMaze (Maze: ArrayType);
    {Print the maze contents, showing the exit path.}
    var i, j: integer;
    begin
        for i := 1 to MAXROW do begin
            for j := 1 to MAXCOL do write (Maze [i, j]);
            writeln
        end;
        writeln {Space between solutions.}
    end; {PrintTheMaze}
```

maze searching program

```
function AtAnExit (row, col : integer): boolean;
    {Tells whether or not we are on the border of the maze.}
begin
    AtAnExit := (row in [1, MAXROW]) or (col in [1, MAXCOL])
end;  {AtAnExit}

procedure ExploreTheMaze (Maze: ArrayType; Row, Col: integer);
    {Recursive procedure for searching the maze.}
begin
    Maze [Row, Col] := THEWAYOUT;
    if AtAnExit (Row, Col)
        then PrintTheMaze (Maze)
        else begin
            if Maze [Row-1, Col] = POSSIBLEPATH then
                ExploreTheMaze (Maze, Row-1, Col);
            if Maze [Row, Col+1] = POSSIBLEPATH then
                ExploreTheMaze (Maze, Row, Col+1);
            if Maze [Row+1, Col] = POSSIBLEPATH) then
                ExploreTheMaze (Maze, Row+1, Col);
            if Maze [Row, Col-1] = POSSIBLEPATH) then
                ExploreTheMaze (Maze, Row, Col-1)
        end {else}
end;  {ExploreTheMaze}
begin
    StoreTheMaze (Maze);
    ExploreTheMaze (Maze, 6, 6)  {We start in the center of the maze.}
end.  {ThreadTheMaze}
```

↓   ↓   ↓   ↓   ↓

```
*** *******        the input maze
***     *****
*** **  ****
***   *   ***
***** **  ***
***** **  ***
***** ******
*****    ****
****  *  ****
*   **  ****
* *     *****
* *********              {output follows}
```

```
*** !********
*** !    *****
*** !**   ****
*** ! ! !*    ***
***** !**  ***
***** !**  ***
*****  ******
*****      ****
****    *  ****
*      **  ****
*  *      *****
*  **********

***  ********
***      *****
*** **    ****
***     *   ***
***** **  ***
***** !**  ***
***** ! ******
***** ! ! !****
****    * !****
* ! ! !** ! !****
* ! * ! ! ! !*****
* !**********
```

The Eight Queens Problem

problem: eight queens

One of the best known examples of backtracking in programming is the *Eight Queens* problem. It's simply stated:

> A queen can move in any direction—vertically, horizontally, or diagonally—on a chessboard. Is it possible to place eight queens on a board so that no queen endangers another? How?

It turns out that the problem has many solutions. Gauss attacked the problem in 1850, but even he wasn't able to find all of them. How can we go about approaching it?

Let's imagine that we're trying to solve the eight queens problem by hand. We get a chessboard, and eight pieces to use as queens. Almost immediately we **working by hand** can realize that the board should be divided into eight columns. Since we can't have more than one queen in any column (because that would endanger her), we try placing one queen in each.

How many different ways can eight queens be put in eight columns? Since each queen can go to eight 'row' positions, the total number of different boards is 16,777,216 (8^8). An exhaustive search of this huge solution space **the solution space** might be a little too tedious even for a computer. Fortunately, it's not hard to see how to avoid checking most of them: As soon as we find a single bad row position, we'll stop looking at possible boards that incorporate that position. Let's look at an example.

Positioning the first queen is easy—she goes to the top of the first column. The second queen is a bit harder. The top row of the second column is out (that would put two queens on the same row), as is the second row (that would put two queens on the same diagonal). Our third try works, though, and we have two safely positioned queens. Note that, by not bothering to check any of the boards that start out with two queens in the top row or on the first diagonal, we avoid checking 524,288 ($2*8^6$) illegal positions. We've begun to limit our solution space very successfully.

limiting the solution space

Putting a queen in the third row isn't much harder. Again, the top position is out, since the first queen guards the top row. The third row is out because we've just put the second queen there. The second and fourth positions aren't any good either—diagonal problems with the second queen. We end up putting the third queen five rows down.

Let's jump ahead. The board on the left, below, shows the positions of the first five queens. Where will the sixth queen go? Stop for a second and try to figure out what to do next.

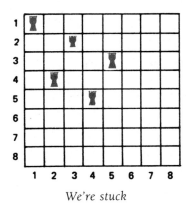

We're stuck

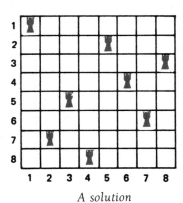

A solution

backtracking

Inspection will show that the sixth queen can't go anywhere without being taken by another queen. What do we do now? It's time for a second clever step—backtracking. We backtrack one step (by putting the fifth queen down a row), and try again.

An actual solution to the problem is shown, above, at the right. If you compare the solution to our starting position, you'll see that we've had to back up many times. The fifth queen isn't the only one that's been repositioned. In fact, only the very first queen is still in its original starting place.

Now, our mental exercise has given us two clues to a computer solution. First, we limit our solution space by ending one line of search whenever we reach a bad board. Second, we backtrack to a previous position whenever we get stuck at a dead end.

How far will we have to backtrack? Sometimes simply repositioning the queen in the previous column will suffice. We won't always be able to reposition, though, since a queen may eventually reach the eighth position in its column. If this happens we'll have to backtrack two or more columns, until we get to a queen that can be moved.

why use recursion?

As we've found earlier, the need for backtracking leads us toward a solution that uses a recursive stack. Although we may work on a single board (a global *Board* variable that's passed as a variable parameter) we stack our individual moves through a series of recursive calls. Each call represents one queen placement; but before the call ends, we'll pick the queen up, and return to a previous board layout.

Let's move on to the hard part of solving the Eight Queens problem—a recursive statement of the queen-positioning algorithm.

first refinement

> *to put a queen in column (N)...*
>   **repeat**
>   *try to put a queen in the current row*;
>   **if** *it worked, put a queen in column (N+1)*;
>   *remove the last queen we set down*;
>   *advance to the next row in this column*
>   **until** *we get to the eighth row*;

The shaded portion is our recursive call. Each call is temporarily suspended whenever we're able to legally place a queen. As a result, a long series of 'remove the queen and advance to the next row' statements remains stacked.

Let's look at a second refinement. This time, we'll deal with more of the bookkeeping details—when do we stop advancing? when do we have a solution? and so on.

second refinement

> *to put a queen in column (N)...*
>   **repeat**
>   **if** *the current row is safe* **then**
>   *place the queen*;
>   **if** *we're not in the eight column yet*
>   **then** *put a queen in column (N+1)*
>   **else** *print the board—we have a solution*;
>   *remove the queen*;
>   *advance to the next row in this column*
>   **until** *we get to the eighth row*

determining safe positions

Let's consider the shaded section of our second refinement. How do we know when a position is safe? It's easy enough to do this by eye—we just look down the row or diagonal for another queen—but how can we store the same information in a program? It's time for one of Martin Gardner's *Aha!* solutions. Clearly, we won't want to search the entire row or diagonal every time, so try to think of a simple means of putting an entire row or column off limits.

Well, let's suppose that we number the rows 1 through 8. It's not hard to imagine a *Safe* array of eight *boolean* values—each one representing an entire row—that's initially *true*, but can be set to *false* whenever we put a queen in the appropriate row. Aha!

Diagonals are a little bit tougher until we have a crucial insight. Imagine that each row, column position is an i, j coordinate. It turns out that every position in a given left-leaning diagonal has the same $i+j$ sum, while each position in a particular right-leaning diagonal has the same $i-j$ difference. How lucky for us! We can check any position's safety by looking at single elements from three arrays—one for the row, and one for each diagonal. (I assume that we'll never even try to put two queens in the same vertical column.)

The completed program is shown below. As you read it, try to imagine a sequence of recursive calls. It helps to start out in a deliberately bad position—stuck at the end of a column, say—that will require a sequence of backtrack steps. It is also an excellent exercise to try to state the program nonrecursively. The problem has 92 possible solutions, but I've only shown the first 3.

eight queens program

```
program EightQueens (input, output);
   {Recursive solution to the Eight Queens problem.}
type Play = array [1..8, 1..8] of boolean;
   RowCheck = array [1..8] of boolean;
   LeftDiagonalCheck = array [2..16] of boolean;
   RightDiagonalCheck = array [-7..7] of boolean;

var Board: Play;
   SafeRow: RowCheck;
   SafeLeftDiag: LeftDiagonalCheck;
   SafeRightDiag: RightDiagonalCheck;
   Row, Column, i: integer;

function Safe (Row, Col: integer; SafeRow: RowCheck;
               SafeLeftDiag: LeftDiagonalCheck;
               SafeRightDiag: RightDiagonalCheck): boolean;
   {true if a queen can be safely placed in the current position.}
begin
   Safe := SafeRow [Row] and SafeLeftDiag [Row+Col]
                          and SafeRightDiag [Row-Col]
end;  {Safe}

procedure Print (Board: Play);
   {Print the current board layout.}
var i,j: integer;
begin
   for i := 1 to 8 do begin
      for j := 1 to 8 do
         if Board [i,j] then write ('Q') else write ('*');
      writeln
   end;  {outer for}
   writeln  {Space between solutions.}
end;  {Print}
```

{program continues}

```
procedure TryColumn  (Column: integer; var Board: Play);
   {Recursive procedure for attempting queen placement.}
   var Row: integer;
   begin
      Row := 1;
      repeat
         if Safe  (Row, Column, SafeRow,
                          SafeLeftDiag, SafeRightDiag) then begin
            SafeRow [Row] := false;  {set the queen}
            SafeLeftDiag [Row+Column] := false;
            SafeRightDiag [Row−Column] := false;
            Board [Row, Column] := true;
            if Column < 8
               then TryColumn  (Column +1, Board)
               else Print  (Board);
            SafeRow [Row] := true;  {remove the queen}
            SafeLeftDiag [Row+Column] := true;
            SafeRightDiag [Row−Column] := true;
            Board [Row, Column] := false
         end;  {the row was safe}
         Row := Row  + 1;
      until Row > 8
   end;  {TryColumn }
begin
   for Row := 1 to 8 do SafeRow [Row] := true;  {initialize}
   for i := 2 to 16 do SafeLeftDiag [i] := true;
   for i := −7 to 7 do SafeRightDiag [i] := true;
   for Row := 1 to 8 do
      for Column := 1 to 8 do
         Board [Row,Column] := false;
   TryColumn (1, Board)  {make the first recursive call}
end.  {EightQueens }
```

```
      ↓       ↓       ↓       ↓       ↓
Q*******
******Q*
****Q***
*******Q
*Q******
***Q****
*****Q**
**Q*****
```

```
Q*******
******Q*
***Q****
****Q**
*******Q
*Q******
****Q***
**Q*****

Q*******
****Q**
*******Q
**Q*****
******Q*
***Q****
*Q******
****Q***
```

Exercises

Recursion involving loop equivalents

16-1   The basic stacking problems discussed in the text involved reading, and holding, a sequence of input characters. However, it's just as easy to recursively build a stack that holds the digits of a number. Write recursive procedures that:

1.   count the number of digits in a *integer*;

2.   print an *integer* with no leading blank spaces;

3.   print an *integer* with commas in appropriate places.

Hint: remember that n **mod** 10 yields the rightmost digit of n, and n **div** 10 effectively 'strips' the digit off.

16-2   The standard example of a recursive function (always, by law, accompanied by a note attesting to its impracticality), is the computation of factorials:

If n equals 0, then $n! = 1$

If n exceeds 0, then $n! = n \times (n-1)!$

Implement a recursive *Factorial* function. Can you think of a way to prevent *integer* overflow, or at least to spot it in advance?

16-3   The second ANSI standard example of recursion is Euclid's algorithm for computing two numbers' greatest common divisor, discussed in Chapter 5. The recursive statement of his algorithm is:

if q equals 0 then $GCD(p, q) = p$

if $q \neq 0$ then $GCD(p, q) = GCD(q, p \bmod q)$

Write a recursive version of Euclid's algorithm.

16-4   The third classic recursive function is *Ackermann's function*. It takes two *integer* arguments m and n. For initial m and n greater than zero, its definition is:

if $m = 0$ then *Ackermann* equals $n + 1$

if $n = 0$ then *Ackermann* equals *Ackermann* $(m-1, 1)$

if neither n nor $m = 0$ then *Ackermann* is *Ackermann* $(m-1,$ *Ackermann* $(m, n-1))$

Ackermann's function grows with amazing speed, and takes an astonishing number of calls (*Ackermann* (3,4) requires over 10,000 calls to be evaluated!). Implement it, and find the largest *m* and *n* values you can reasonably use as arguments.

16-5   Two ordered lists of numbers are to be merged. Unfortunately, one list is sorted from least to greatest, while the other is supplied from greatest to least. Write a program that uses recursion to merge the lists:

1.   from the smallest value to the largest;

2.   from the largest value to the smallest.

16-6   The idea of run-length encoding is discussed in the exercises for Chapter 9. Basically, any repeated sequence of any single character is replaced by a single instance, and the number of times it should appear. Thus, the input sequence:

aaaaabbccccdddefg...

might appear in output as:

\5abb\4c\3defg...

Note my use of the backslash \ as a marker character, so that digits can appear in the input. As you can see, the replacements for **a** and **c** saved space, while the **d** replacement had no effect, and **e**, **f**, and **g** weren't touched.

1.   Write a recursive procedure for run-length encoding.

2.   Write a recursive procedure that encodes runs of consecutive (e.g. **abcd**), rather than identical, characters in a similar manner.

16-7   Write a program that uses recursion to read an input sentence, and either:

1.   print every word that contains letters that are contiguous and identical (as in 'Miss Metteer, the excessively goodlooking bookkeeper of all cottonseed bills, was corrupted by a terra-cotta Cossack.'), or

2.   print every word that contains letters that are contiguous and consecutive (as in 'A stupid, laughing, crabcake deftly hijacked the first canopy.').

16-8   An *integer* is partitioned by being expressed as a sum of *integers* —4 can be partitioned as 4, 3+1, 2+1+1, and 1+1+1+1. I discussed an interesting application of partitions in the Bulgarian Solitaire exercise accompanying Chapter 7.

Finding partitions is a good problem for recursive solution as well. Write a program that prints all the partitions of an arbitrary *integer* value. It won't be too hard if you're able to come up with a recursive definition of partitioning.

16-9   When the order in which expressions are evaluated is controlled by parentheses, recursion lets subexpressions be stacked until they are required. For example, the expression below must be evaluated 'in parts' if it is to be evaluated correctly:

```
(2 * ((3 * 4) + (6 – 5)))
(2 * (12 + 1))
(2 * 13)
26
```

An implicit requirement of a recursive program for evaluating such expressions is that *mutual recursion* be employed. A single procedure cannot handle the simultaneous tasks of matching parentheses and evaluating subexpressions. Instead, two procedures are required. One procedure does the work of skipping parentheses, reading operations, and performing calculations, while the second either reads a value *or* calls the first procedure again (if the upcoming character is another opening parenthesis instead of a value).

In words, I can describe the two procedures like this:

to evaluate an expression
  skip a parenthesis;
  read a value;
  read the operator;
  read a value;
  skip a parenthesis;
  perform the operation;

to read a value
  if *the next character is an opening parenthesis*
    then *evaluate an expression*
    else *get the value*;

Write a program that evaluates expressions in the form given above. Assume that all input is correct, contains no spaces, and is fully parenthesized.

Recursion that requires array types

16-10   Write a function that recursively finds the product of the contents of a one-dimensional array of *MAX* elements. The code itself is very easy—the hard part is thinking up a recursive statement of the problem. Hint: the product equals the current element's value times the solution for the rest of the array.

16-11   Recall the continued fractions discussed in the exercises of Chapter 5. They let *real* values be mapped to to *integers* through equations of the form:

$$x = a_0 + \cfrac{1}{a_1 + \cfrac{1}{a_2 + \cfrac{1}{a_3 + \cfrac{1}{a_4 + \cdots}}}}$$

It can be proven that every *real* can be represented like this.

Suppose that a one-dimensional array holds the *integer*-valued a_i terms of a continued fraction. Write a recursive subprogram that evaluates the fraction. As test input, try:

    [1, 2, 2, 2, · · ·]   (square root of 2)
    [4, 1, 3, 1, 8, 1, 3, 1, 8 · · ·]   (square root of 23)
    [0, 3, 1, 2, 1, 1, 4]   (32/119)

16-12   Suppose you choose an arbitrary point on a two-dimensional grid. How many different paths lead to this point from the lower-left corner of the grid? Write a recursive program that finds out. Restrict travel to steps toward the upper or right-hand side of the grid. Hint: treat this as a maze searching problem.

16-13   *Flood filling* is a technique used by graphics programmers to color an arbitrary shape—i.e. to fill it with lit pixels. Suppose that we can rely on a function *Inside* (x,y) that lets us know if we are within the area we want to fill. The flood filling algorithm is:

to flood fill an area
  if *Inside* (x, y) **then**
    light the current pixel;
    flood fill x, y + 1;
    flood fill x, y − 1;
    flood fill x + 1, y;
    flood fill x − 1, y;

The initial *x, y* point is chosen at random.

Define a two-dimensional array of *on/off* pixels, and an *Inside* function that determines if any particular pixel is inside a simple shape (a circle or rectangle) 'drawn' on the array. Then, write a recursive flood fill procedure to turn all enclosed elements *on*.

16-14   A messy programmer eating a pizza pie at her terminal manages to splatter various ingredients over a two-dimensional array. Each spot covers one or more contiguous array elements. As pennance, she resolves to write a program that could count the number of splotches she had created.

Help her out by writing a recursive spot-counting program. Assume that your program's input will be a two-dimensional array of *integer*, with spots marked by 1's, and empty areas filled by 0's. Hint: travel through the array with ordinary loops, but whenever you encounter a spot—an area of 1's—use a recursive procedure to search (and re-number) it.

16-15   The discussion of Quicksort in Chapter 18 refers to, but does not describe, a related sorting method—*mergesort*. The idea is really quite simple: an unordered array is split in two, then the halves are split again and again until an array with just two elements is arrived at. This tiny segment (and, implicitly, every two-element segment) is sorted. Then, the sorted segments are merged into sorted segments of length four, eight, and so on until the entire array is sorted. A recursive statement of the algorithm is:

> to mergesort an array
>
> > **if** *the array has more than two elements*
> > > *mergesort the left half;*
> > > *mergesort the right half;*
> > > *merge the sorted left half and right half of the array;*

Naturally, programming a mergesort isn't so simple. To make your job a bit easier, assume that the unordered array has 256 elements. Good luck!

17

Advanced Applications of Pointer Types

The study of structures formed with pointer types is the province of typical second or third computer science courses. I'll jump the gun in this chapter, and present a brief overview of pointer-based data structures, including *queues, deques, stacks, graphs*, and *trees*. We'll also learn some of the operations and terminology associated with each, and see just how useful recursion can be. I close with a long example program that uses a variety of linked data structures.

Data Structures that Use Pointers 17-1

WE'VE ALREADY ENCOUNTERED LINKED AND doubly-linked lists. The illustration below shows a linked list with auxiliary pointers to its *head* and *tail*.

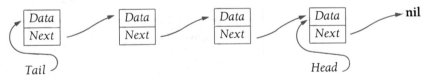

The type definition behind the structure is:

```
type ElementPointer = ↑ListElement;
     ListElement = record
                       Data: DataType;
                       Next: ElementPointer
                   end;
var Head, Tail: ElementPointer;
```

queues

A common application of singly-linked lists is the maintenance of *queues* (kews´). A programming queue is just like a queue that forms inside a bank or outside a movie theater. People (or data) are added to one end and taken from the other—the first in is always the first out. These rules make a queue a queue, and raise it above the level of an ordinary list.

> Data structures are characterized by the operations that can be performed on them, as well as by the way they're created.

adding to a queue

Although standing in line isn't an especially deep concept, there are some subtleties involved in setting up a queue as a data structure. Suppose that we're working on the basis of the illustration above. An obvious approach would be to add new items to the tail, on the left, and then remove them when they've worked their way up to the head of the queue at the right. Let's see if coding these operations causes any problems. Items are added with:

> *new (TemporaryPointer)* ;
> *TemporaryPointer* ↑.*Next* := *Tail* ;
> *Tail* := *TemporaryPointer* ;

On the other hand, taking an item from the head is pretty difficult, because the head pointer can't be moved backward. Some elaborate code is required.

queue deletion

> *TemporaryPointer* := *Tail* ;
>   {Start *TemporaryPointer* at the tail of the list.}
> **while** *TemporaryPointer* ↑.*Next* <> *Head* **do**
>   *TemporaryPointer* := *TemporaryPointer* ↑.*Next* ;
>   {This puts *TemporaryPointer* just before *Head*.}
> *Head* := *TemporaryPointer* ;
>   {Now both pointers reference the next-to-last element.}
> *TemporaryPointer* := *TemporaryPointer* ↑.*Next* ;
>   {*TemporaryPointer* points to the last element, and we can remove it.}
> *Head* ↑.*Next* := **nil** ;

A queue doesn't really have to cause this much trouble. We can use a technique called *visual thinking* to get some other (and perhaps better) ideas about how to set one up.

visual thinking

> Visual thinking involves imagining the resolution of a problem in visual, and not algorithmic, terms.

In other words, a visual thinker might try to imagine that she can see a program working (and then try to figure out how or why it works), instead of first trying to come up with its algorithm.

The most famous example of visual thinking is probably that of the chemist Friedrich Kekule, who literally dreamed up the ring-shaped structure of benzene in a vivid reverie in which he saw that a snake biting its own tail could represent a series of linked atoms.* However, the visual approach to problem solving is thoroughly engrained in ordinary thinking. We *look* at problems and *see* their solutions. A bug is due to *oversight*. Wise people are *seers* with great *insight*. We could go on (and McLuhan has in *The Medium is the Massage*).

---

* Remember this when I bring up circular lists, below.

Visual thinking is particularly applicable to linked structures because the way that elements are connected (and not the type definition of each element) primarily characterizes a structure. We can radically change a queue representation without altering the basic *ListElement* definition at all. Just imagine a line of people (or list elements) moving from left to right, as above. This time, though, let's have each person point to the person *behind* instead of ahead.

Believe it or not, reversing the pointers will transform our linked list into a convenient representation of a queue. A new element is added with:

> *new* (*Tail*↑.*Next*);
> *Tail* := *Tail*↑.*Next*;
> *Tail*↑.*Next* := **nil**;

Elements are removed in a similar manner.

> *TemporaryPointer* := *Head*;
> **if** *Head*↑.*Next* <> **nil then** *Head* := *Head*↑.*Next*;

Now, let's suppose that we want to make a structure similar to a queue, but which relaxes the restrictions on additions and deletions. Although elements will continue to move from the tail to the head, we'll reserve the right to cut into line—even at the head—in order to give some items extra priority. The name *deque* (dek), or double-ended queue, usually describes such a structure. Bearing in mind the difficulty we just had with a single-ended queue, can you propose an approach to implementing a deque?

Well, our problem with an ordinary queue was due to the 'directionality' of pointers in a linked list. We can travel and make connections in one direction, but not in the other. Using a doubly-linked list to implement the deque solves the problem. No matter where we are in the deque, we can make insertions or deletions before, after, or at the current element.

> **type** *TwoElementPointer* = ↑*StackElement*;
> *StackElement* = **record**
>   *Data*: *DataType*;
>   *Next, Last*: *TwoElementPointer*
>   **end**;
> **var** *Head, Tail, ListPointer*: *TwoElementPointer*;

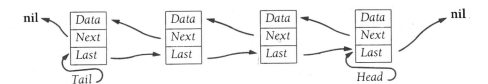

How about another variation? Nothing in the definition of *ListElement* says that we have to create lists with heads *or* tails. A *circular* list has no beginning or end—the last element points to the first. A circular list with only one element is interesting, and perfectly legal.

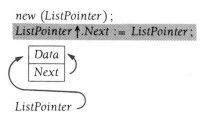

new (ListPointer);
ListPointer↑.Next := ListPointer;

circular lists

Although some applications specifically require circular data structures, many circular lists are generated because a single 'current position' pointer can act as both a head and tail pointer. This circular list implements a queue:

circular queues

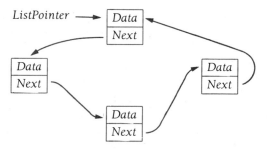

ListPointer points to the end of the queue. A new element is put on the queue with:

new (TemporaryPointer);
TemporaryPointer↑.Next := ListPointer↑.Next;
ListPointer↑.Next := TemporaryPointer;
ListPointer := ListPointer↑.Next;

The element that's been on the queue the longest is removed with:

TemporaryPointer := ListPointer↑.Next;
    {Point *TemporaryPointer* at the oldest element.}
ListPointer↑.Next := ListPointer↑.Next↑.Next;
    {Relink the list around it.}

Stacks

Another variation on the usage of lists produces a *stack* structure. Stacks are last in, first out structures—the most recently added element is the first to be taken off. Thus, a stack has a *top*, instead of a head or tail. New elements are *pushed* onto the stack, while old ones are *popped* off. This terminology comes from the most popular image of stacks—the spring-loaded stack of trays in a cafeteria.

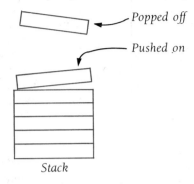

Stack

Implementing stacks requires a simple renaming of the basic linking and unlinking operations, as well as a design decision akin to the choice we made for a queue—should the pointers go up or down the stack? In procedures *Push* and *Pop*, below, we've stayed with our basic, single-pointer, *ListElement* data structure. Each new element points to the current stack, which means that the pointers go down.

Procedure *Push* puts a new element (referenced by *NewElement*) on top of the stack, then advances *Top* there as well. Only *Top* need be passed as a variable parameter.

adding to a stack

```
procedure Push (NewElement: ElementPointer; var Top: ElementPointer);
    {Pushes NewElement on top of a stack.}
    begin
        NewElement↑.Next := Top;
        Top := NewElement
    end; {Push}
```

Pop points *PoppedElement* at the top element of the stack, then moves *Top* down by one element. Because both pointers are permanently changed, they're both passed as variable parameters.

taking from a stack

```
procedure Pop (var PoppedElement, Top: ElementPointer);
    {Pops PoppedElement from a stack.}
    begin
        PoppedElement := Top;
        Top := Top↑.Next;
        PoppedElement↑.Next := nil
    end; {Pop}
```

A popped element should be isolated from the rest of the stack. Although setting *PoppedElement's* pointer field to **nil** isn't essential, doing so helps prevent inadvertent errors in another part of the program.

If we didn't set its *Next* field to **nil**, *PoppedElement* could still be used to access and change the entire stack.

What are stacks and queues used for? Queues are essential when, by accident or design, data can't be relied on to arrive in an orderly fashion. For example, programs that run timeshared computers (which are used simultaneously by several users) use queues to keep track of each user's input. In effect, the computer executes commands at one end of the queue while adding new commands to the other end as they come in. A deque can be used to give commands varying priority by inserting them *within* the queue.

Queues are also useful for simulating real-life processes. Suppose that we run a ticket counter, and want to decide if each window should have its own line, or if a single line should feed all the windows. The nature of the problem—customers arriving at irregular intervals, and being served after varying waits—calls for a queue representation.

Stacks tend to have more specialized, computer-oriented applications, and are less representative of real-life phenomena. For example, many kinds of *reversals* use stacks—you may recall our recursive use of the computer's stack in reversing a sentence of input (section 16-1). Arithmetic expressions often take advantage of stacks as well—the order of operators and operands on a stack does away with the need for parentheses.

For example, here is the pseudocode of a stack-oriented expression evaluator:

> **while** *we're still reading the expression*
>   *read a term* ;
>   **if** *it's an operand, push it on the stack* ;
>   **else if** *it's an operator*
>   *pop the two most recent terms from the stack* ;
>   *operate on them* ;
>   *push the result on the stack* ;
> *pop the top term from the stack* ;
> *print it* ;

For a bit of mental challenge, you might want to think about implementing this algorithm with an explicit stack constructed from pointers and elements. Then, try to figure out how you'd implement it using the computer's stack (through a series of recursive procedure or function calls) instead.

Graphs

A more liberal application of pointers between individual elements leads to a more complicated pointer structure called a *graph* .

> I'll broadly define a *graph* as a pointer structure whose elements are not required to be in linear order.

The picture of the Cave of the Wumpus was a graph, as is this diagram of distances between cities.

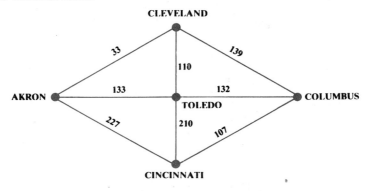

A much simpler graph can be used to represent a *sparse matrix*. Now, since *matrix* is a rough synonym for a two-dimensional array, a sparse matrix is an array whose component values are almost all identical. As a result, only the non-identical elements are interesting and worth storing. For example, suppose that we want to hold some of the data connected with running a university. *Oh! Pascal! U.* has 100 courses and 10,000 students. How can we keep track of what classes each student is taking, and of which students are in each class?

sparse matrix

A reasonable first proposal would be to use a two-dimensional array, with course numbers providing one subscript, and student identification numbers the other. An element is filled in with:

>   *Enrollment* [*Course, Student*] := *Taken* ;

However, even though such an array would be quite large—one million elements—most of its stored values would be the same—**not** *Taken*. If each student were taking four classes, the array would only be 4% filled. *Enrollment* is clearly a sparse matrix.

Representing the enrollment data with pointers is a much better approach. We want an interlaced network of two sorts of lists—lists of the courses each student is taking, and lists of the students enrolled in each course. The illustration below shows how it's done, and demonstrates some new techniques. To begin with, enrollment data is stored in a record with the following structure:

the underlying data type

>   **type** *String* = **packed array** [1..20] **of** *char* ;
>   *CoursePointer* = ↑*EnrollmentData* ;
>   *EnrollmentData* = **record**
>   *Course, Student* : *String* ;
>   *NextCourse, NextStudent* : *CoursePointer*
>   **end** ;

A single record is simultaneously a 'students in this course' and 'courses of this student' element. The structure is like that of a doubly-linked list, except that the links are rotated 90° (instead of 180°) to each other.

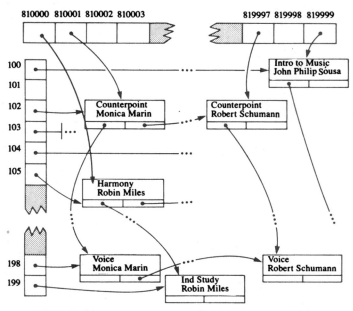

The start of each list is set up in a clever manner. Although we could easily have linked lists of course and student numbers, defining two arrays of type *CoursePointer* takes advantage of the random-access feature of arrays. This lets us find a particular student or course list quickly. The type definition moves along with:

```
{type definition continued}
    CourseNumbers = 100..199;
    StudentNumbers = 810000..819999;        {Class of '81.}
    CourseArray = array [CourseNumbers] of CoursePointer;
    StudentArray = array [StudentNumbers] of CoursePointer;
```

Suppose we want to print the names of all students taking course *Too-Crowded*. No sooner said than done.

using the sparse matrix

```
procedure PrintStudentNames (TooCrowded:  CourseNumbers;
                                  Enrollment:  CourseArray);
{Prints the names of all students in course TooCrowded.}
    var Temporary: CoursePointer;
begin
    writeln ('Students enrolled in course ', TooCrowded:1, ' are:');
    Temporary := Enrollment [TooCrowded];      {Go to the list head.}
    while Temporary <> nil do begin      {While there are still records,}
        writeln (Temporary↑.Student);       {print the stored name, and}
        Temporary := Temporary↑.NextStudent      {advance the pointer.}
    end
end;  {PrintStudentNames}
```

Self-Check
Questions

Q. Would this code be equivalent to the shaded program segment above? Why or why not?

```
TemporaryPointer := Enrollment [TooCrowded];
repeat
    writeln (Temporary↑.Student);
    Temporary := Temporary↑.NextStudent
until Temporary = nil;
```

A. The code is fine—if any students are taking the class. If nobody has enrolled in course *TooCrowded*, the program crashes attempting to output the *Student* field of a **nil** pointer.

Binary Trees

Of all the data structures that can be represented with pointers, *trees* are probably the niftiest. A *node* at the top of the tree points the way to zero or more different nodes. Each of these, in turn, points to another group of distinct nodes. We can draw a general tree as:

a general tree

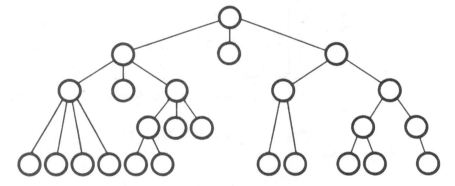

If you look carefully a whole forest is visible—each labeled node points to one or more sub-trees. Now, it's essential that each sub-tree consist of *distinct* nodes—no two sub-trees can share a node. This restriction makes trees *recursively defined* pointer structures. Any tree can be defined as being an element that's linked to one or more trees, or to nothing.

tree terminology

The *root* of a tree is its first (topmost) node. The nodes that each element points to are its *children*; it is the *parent*. Finally, a node that has no children is called a *leaf*.

Limiting each node to a maximum of two children (i.e. to two potential sub-trees) creates a *binary* (two-part) tree, which is a structure we'll explore in

binary trees

detail. The definition of a binary-node type is much like that of a doubly-linked list element. Only the identifiers have been changed to protect the confused.

a binary tree element

```
type NodePointer = ↑Node;
     Node = record
               Data: DataType;
               LeftChild, RightChild: NodePointer
            end;
```

Since trees are recursively defined, recursive subprograms are convenient for tree structure operations. These usually involve searching trees, or adding additional nodes. We can describe the recursive steps of one tree-searching algorithm in English. (Assume that *CurrentNode* starts by referencing the root.)

To Search a Tree...

recursive tree-searching algorithm

1. If *CurrentNode's* left child isn't **nil**, point *CurrentNode* at the left child and search the tree.

2. If *CurrentNode's* right child isn't **nil**, point *CurrentNode* at the right child and search the tree.

3. Print the value stored in the current node.

In practice, each time we return to action 1 (the equivalent of making a recursive procedure call) the values associated with the current node will be saved, along with any pending actions.

> Using recursion allows backtracking without backward pointers.

The tree-searching algorithm is implemented in the recursive procedure *InspectTree*.

binary tree inspection procedure

```
procedure InspectTree (CurrentNode: NodePointer);
   {Visit every node of a binary tree.}
   begin
      if CurrentNode↑.LeftChild <> nil then
         InspectTree (CurrentNode↑.LeftChild);
      if CurrentNode↑.RightChild <> nil then
         InspectTree (CurrentNode↑.RightChild);
      writeln (CurrentNode↑.Data)
   end; {InspectTree}
```

The effect of *InspectTree* can be described as:

Go down the tree as far as possible, trying to go left, but going right if necessary. Print this node's value. Back up one node, then go down the tree again, following the same strategy—left if possible, right if necessary—until you come to a dead end, or a node you've already visited.

Inspect this node, then repeat the search process. When there are no more nodes to search—each child has been visited already—the root has been found, and the entire tree has been inspected.

If you have difficulty imagining the operation of a recursive procedure, stepping through an example on a small tree may help. Looking at the boundary cases of a large tree is also useful.

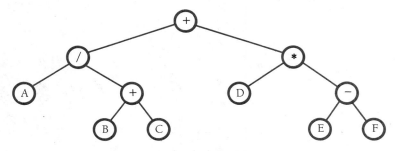

postorder (RPN) search

Suppose we use *InspectTree* to search the binary tree above. Its nodes will be searched in the following order, called *postorder*. *Postfix* and *Reverse Polish* (or *RPN*) are other names for this particular notation.

$$A \ B \ C + / \ D \ E \ F - * +$$

If you own a stack-type calculator you'll recognize this as an arithmetic expression, equivalent to $A / (B+C) + D*(E-F)$. In postorder search, a node's subtrees are inspected before the node itself is. As a result, the root is looked at last.

Suppose that I reorder the three statements of *InspectTree* like this:

{First variation.}
writeln (CurrentNode↑.Data);
if *CurrentNode↑.LeftChild* <> **nil then** *InspectTree (CurrentNode↑.LeftChild)* ;
if *CurrentNode↑.RightChild* <> **nil then** *InspectTree (CurrentNode↑.RightChild)*

{Second variation.}
if *CurrentNode↑.LeftChild* <> **nil then** *InspectTree (CurrentNode↑.LeftChild)* ;
writeln (CurrentNode↑.Data);
if *CurrentNode↑.RightChild* <> **nil then** *InspectTree (CurrentNode↑.RightChild)*

preorder search

Both variations work perfectly well, and change only the order in which nodes are visited. The first yields a *preorder* search—first a node is inspected, and then its sub-trees. Applying the preorder algorithm to the tree above will give us: $+ / A + B C * D - E F$

inorder search

The second modification produces an *inorder* search. The left sub-tree is searched, then the node, and finally the right sub-tree. The search path followed is: $A / B + C + D * E - F$

Programming Binary Trees

The applications of binary trees are unexpectedly diverse. Consider the tree below. Can you guess what it represents?

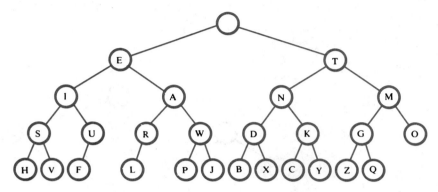

Perhaps the type definition of each node will help.

```
type NextCodeNode = ↑CodeNode;
     CodeNode = record
                     Letter: char;
                     Dot, Dash: NextCodeNode
                end;
var Root: NextCodeNode;
```

A procedure that uses the tree gives away the secret:

morse code decoding
procedure

```
procedure Decode (RootPointer: NextCodeNode; var DataFile: text);
     {Decodes Morse Code input. Each full letter must be followed by a blank.}
     var CurrentPointer: NextCodeNode;
         InputCharacter: char;
     begin
         reset (DataFile);
         CurrentPointer := RootPointer;
         while not eof (DataFile) do begin
             read (DataFile, InputCharacter);
             case InputCharacter of
                 '.' : CurrentPointer := CurrentPointer↑.Dot;
                 '-' : CurrentPointer := CurrentPointer↑.Dash;
                 ' ' : begin
                           write (CurrentPointer↑.Letter);
                           CurrentPointer := RootPointer
                       end
             end {case}
         end; {while}
         writeln (CurrentPointer↑.Letter)
     end;  {Decode}
```

```
.__. ._ _._. _._   __ _.__   _... ___ _.._
._. .. _ .... .._. .. ._ .   _.. ___ __.. . _.
._.. .. __._ ._. ___ ._ .___ .._ __. ...
```

PACK MY BOX WITH FIVE DOZEN LIQUOR JUGS

As you can probably gather, the tree represents the Morse code. Procedure *Decode*, above, uses the code tree to translate a file of Morse into the letters it stands for. Its parameters are *RootPointer*, which points to the root of the stored code-tree, and *DataFile*, a *text* file of dots, dashes, and spaces. Since we never backtrack (and don't need a stack) *Decode* wasn't written recursively. However, we do have to maintain a pointer to the root of the code tree, to start all over again for each new letter.

Morse can be stored in a binary tree because the dot/dash code is essentially a series of yes/no questions. Surprisingly, most data can be stored and retrieved using binary trees. An interactive computer game called *Animal* is a good example. The computer plays by trying to guess the name of an animal the player imagines. Although an animal may have many characteristics, considering only one at a time—Is the animal furry? Does it have horns?—reduces its description to a string of binary (two-way) choices. Some sample output from an *Animal* run will help you picture its operation.

binary tree applications

Think of an animal.
Does it have fur? Answer yes or no.
no
Does it have tusks?
yes
Does it have big ears?
no
Is it a rhino?   *etc.*

The *Animal* program relies on two kinds of stored data—characteristics, and (ultimately) the names of animals. The most crucial set of facts—the relationship between characteristic and name—is contained in the binary tree that *holds* the information. The program begins at the tree's root and asks the question stored as a string in that node. Whether the left or right node is visited next visited depends on the answer—sometimes a further question is required (and the process starts again), and sometimes we reach a leaf or final node (and with it, the name of an animal).

Incidentally, the *Animal* program learns as it plays. If it reaches a leaf and guesses wrong, the following transaction takes place.

I guessed wrong. What animal were you thinking of?
a wild boar
Type in an additional question I should have asked.

Does it have bad breath?
Is the correct answer yes or no?
yes   *etc.*

Internally, a new node is added to the stored data structure, along with the
implication that rhinos don't have bad breath.

embedding information

A subtle aspect of understanding tree structures is recognizing the relation
between the way data is stored and the way that it's retrieved again. This is
especially true when a hand-drawn representation of a tree's stored data doesn't
(at first glance) show its order or purpose. Consider this tree.

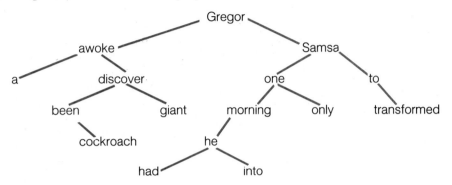

The tree stores the words of this sentence:

**Gregor Samsa awoke one morning only to discover he had been
transformed into a giant cockroach**

in alphabetical order (disregarding capitalization). The first word, 'Gregor', goes
to the root of the tree. The second word follows the first alphabetically, so it's
stored in the right child. The third word precedes the first alphabetically, so it
goes into the left-hand node. The fourth word, 'one', comes after the first, but
before the second. It goes to the root's right child's left child. The final resting
place of each word is determined by traveling down the tree, turning left or
right, or making a new node as necessary.

As you might imagine, we can recursively describe the ordering algorithm.

To Build an Alphabetically Ordered Tree...

1.   If the current node is **nil**, store the new word there and stop.

2.   If the new word precedes the word in the current node, point to the left
      child and build an alphabetically ordered tree.

binary tree building

3.   If the new word follows the word in the current node, point to the right
      child and build an alphabetically ordered tree.

4.   If the new word is the same as the word in the current node, stop.

In procedure *AddAWord*, below, the final **else** (which represents step 4) isn't necessary, and could be omitted. I've just included it to show you how to touch all the bases.

binary tree building
procedure

```
type String = packed array [1..15] of char;
     WordPointer = ↑WordStorage;
     WordStorage = record
                         Word: String;
                         Before, After: WordPointer
                   end;
  ·· .    {Other definitions and declarations.}
procedure AddAWord (var Current: WordPointer; NewWord: String);
     {Adds the string NewWord to an alphabetically ordered binary tree.}
     begin
         if Current =nil
             then begin
                 new (Current);
                 Current↑.Word := NewWord;
                 Current↑.Before := nil;
                 Current↑.After := nil
             end
             else if NewWord <Current↑.Word
                     then AddAWord (Current↑.Before, NewWord)
                 else if NewWord >Current↑.Word
                         then AddAWord (Current↑.After, NewWord)
                     else {The word is a duplicate—NewWord=Current↑.Word.}
     end; {AddAWord}
```

AddAWord is probably the most complicated recursive procedure we'll have to deal with. Note that *AddAWord* is an end recursion—the stack isn't used to store values or pending statements. It could easily be written iteratively.

It will come as a welcome surprise to find that a job that seems complicated (like printing the contents of a tree in alphabetical order), is really pretty easy. It takes an inorder traversal—one of the possible variations on procedure *InspectTree*, which we wrote a few pages back to search an expression tree. The output of *PrintInOrder*, below, assumes that *CurrentWord* currently references the root of the Gregor Samsa awoke... tree. (I broke the output into two lines myself.)

binary tree inspection
procedure

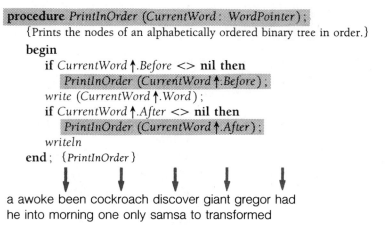

```
procedure PrintInOrder (CurrentWord: WordPointer);
    {Prints the nodes of an alphabetically ordered binary tree in order.}
    begin
        if CurrentWord↑.Before <> nil then
            PrintInOrder (CurrentWord↑.Before);
        write (CurrentWord↑.Word);
        if CurrentWord↑.After <> nil then
            PrintInOrder (CurrentWord↑.After);
        writeln
    end; {PrintInOrder}
```

a awoke been cockroach discover giant gregor had
he into morning one only samsa to transformed

As a closing note, I'll point out that not all structures produced by *AddA-Word* will look quite so tree-like. Consider the trees produced by these input sentences:

a big cat did everything

zesty young xylophones wed violins

A quick perusal shows that the sample sentences are in alphabetical and reverse-alphabetical order. They produce *degenerate* trees—trees that can't be distinguished from ordinary lists.

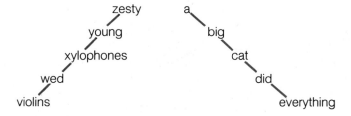

Focus On
Programming:
KWIC

I'll end the discussion of pointers with a long example program. It uses some of the linked structures we've just met, and helps demonstrate how simple ideas and techniques can be joined to form long and useful programs. The problem is:

problem: KWIC

> Write a program that reads a list of words of interest (keywords), then searches a source file for those words. Each keyword should be printed in its context, e.g. with the four words that come before it and after it.

This is an on-line form of a *KWIC—Key Word In Context*—program. A first appraisal of the problem presents an unremarkable program outline.

first refinement

Get the keywords;
Read in the source file one word at a time;
If the current word is a keyword, print it in context;

What should we do with the keywords as they're read in? It's not much trouble to store them in a variety of ways—array, file, linked list, etc. However, step three—*If the current word is a keyword...*—means that we'll want to be able to search through the stored keywords very quickly.

> As we've often found, the choice of an algorithm is intimately tied to the design of a data structure.

It turns out that if keywords are read in at random, then alphabetically ordering them in a binary tree helps minimize the time required to confirm or deny that a given word is present. As a result, 'Get the keywords' is, more or less, procedure *AddAWord* (from the last section). We get the keywords by constructing an alphabetically ordered binary tree.

The last part of the last step—*print it in context*—presents a more serious problem. Should we look up each word as it's read in, then somehow back up the source file to get the words that came immediately before? Unfortunately, if you know Pascal, you know that we can't back up—we have to reread the entire file. What we really need is a small buffer of some sort that holds the current nine words, and lets us look up the central one. That way, if the central word is in the tree of keywords, we already have the words surrounding it. Any ideas?

choosing data
structures

The word *buffer* should be a giveaway. A buffer is a queue—the whole point of a buffer is to provide a temporary holding place for data while maintaining its order. In fact, we can represent the queue with a circular list (sometimes called a *ring* buffer). As each new word comes in, it replaces the oldest word in the queue and the 'oldest word' pointer is advanced one place. The current central word (the one we're going to look up) can be accessed with an auxiliary pointer.

ring buffers

Using a ring buffer isn't entirely a bed of roses. We have to establish a context for the first word by pretending to read blank words when initializing the queue. Similarly, pretending to input four blanks at the end of the source file maintains a context through the very last word. This is a small detail, but it's big enough to stump many programmers.

In a second refinement our algorithm becomes:

second refinement

Get the keyword file ready;
Build an alphabetically ordered binary tree;
Get the source file ready;
Initialize a buffer;
Using the buffer, inspect the source file and print its keywords in context;
Inspect the words left in the buffer;

Now, when we begin to write our program, we'll have to address some global concerns that might not seem too urgent, but which could cause trouble. For instance, several of the values the program relies upon may require modification. They should be defined as constants: the length of the longest word, a blank word of that length, and the exact size of a 'context.'

robustness

What about error checking? This means user's errors as well as run-time errors—our program should at least ensure that the keyword and source files aren't blank. A harder sort of robustness involves errors that aren't mistakes at all. Is 'Important' the same word as 'important'? Is a word followed by punctuation identical to the same word followed by a space? Most people would say yes, and a well-written program should agree.

Let's try a third refinement of the *KWIC* algorithm.

get the keyword file ready;
get the source file ready;
if *neither of the files is empty*

third refinement

    then   {Make the binary tree of keywords.}
      initialize the tree by creating a root;
      repeat
        get the next word from the keyword file;
        add it to the binary tree of keywords
      until *there aren't any keywords left*;
      initialize the ring buffer with blanks, and the first few source words;
      repeat   {Look for the keywords in the source file.}
        get the next word from the source file;
        add it to the ring buffer;
        if *the buffer's center word is found in the keyword file* **then**
          print the contents of the ring buffer
      until *there aren't any source words left*;
      Flush the buffer—take care of the words remaining in the buffer;
    else *Give abnormal termination messages—one of the files was empty*

How can we flush (empty) the buffer without losing the last words it stores? I'll do just what I said a few paragraphs back—add four blank words to the buffer. A jump ahead to a deeper refinement level points the way.

a coding detail

for *the first half of the buffer*
    add a blank to the end of the buffer;
    if *the center word in the buffer is a keyword* **then**
      print the whole buffer;

An issue that I won't deal with (but which you'll be stuck with in your own programs), is a writing schedule. Sometimes, contradictory programming techniques must be applied at different levels. For example, it's a good idea to

stub programming

omit many refinements and write a program as complicated as *KWIC* in the form of a stub program. A detail as important as searching for the last few words of the source file is, in the final analysis, just a detail. You shouldn't let it delay production of a partially working version.

My final pseudocode version of *KWIC*, below, leaves out some refinements I brought up earlier—it doesn't implement upper- to lower-case conversions, or ignore punctuation. Its main purpose is to give names to the program's main procedures, and to help identify the parameters each one will require.

final refinement

> *Get file KeyWords ready*;
> *Get file Source ready*;
> **if** *neither of the files is empty*
>   **then**   {Make the binary tree.}
>   *Root* := **nil**;
>   **repeat**
>   *InputString* (*KeyWords, TheWord*);
>   *AddAWord* (*Root, TheWord*)
>   **until** *eof* (*Keywords*);
>   *InitializeTheBuffer* (*Source, Center, Tail*);
>   **repeat**   {Look for the keywords.}
>   *InputString* (*Source, TheWord*);
>   *AddItToTheBuffer* (*Tail, Center, TheWord*);
>   **if** *ItIsAKeyWord* (*Root, Center↑.Word*) **then**
>   *PrintTheContext* (*Tail*);
>   **until** *eof* (*Source*)
>   *FlushTheBuffer* (*Root, Tail, Center*)
>   **else** *Give abnormal termination messages.*

> No matter what programming method you use to develop a program as large as *KWIC*, you shouldn't be afraid of trying to perfect one or more procedures in dummy 'driver' programs.

debugging

If, for example, you're uncertain about your ability to build a binary tree, you should probably write a quick program that builds and traverses binary trees—even if you're using a stub programming approach. A complete tree traversal—which isn't necessarily required in the *KWIC* program—takes only a few lines of code and will confirm that your *AddAWord* procedure was correctly implemented. We've installed an *InspectTheTree* procedure in our *KWIC* that's called only if a global constant called *DEBUGGING* is set to *true*.

testing

Program testing is equally important. By now you should be sophisticated enough to realize that experienced programmers usually find program bugs or shortcomings *not* because they're sharp enough to pick out errors on sight, but by understanding that certain kinds of program input are usually overlooked by novices. Empty keyword or source files shouldn't cause a program crash; neither should blank lines or punctuation. Most potential problems are easy to fix—the hard part is anticipating them.

The actual program is shown over the next few pages. The contents of file *Source* are shown as the program's input. Since *DEBUGGING* is set to *true*, the contents of the alphabetized *KeyWords* tree are shown as well.

program *KWIC* (*KeyWords, Source, output*);
    {Prints all *KeyWords* that appear in *Source* in their context.}

const *DEBUGGING* = *true*; {If *true*, the *KeyWords* tree is printed.}
    MAXIMUMWORDLENGTH = 20; {Length of the longest string.}
    BLANKWORD = ´   ´; {*MAXIMUMWORDLENGTH* spaces.}
    SIZEOFCONTEXT = 9; {Must be an odd number.}

KWIC program

type *String* = **packed array** [1..*MAXIMUMWORDLENGTH*] **of** *char*;
        {Binary tree node definitions.}
    NodePointer = ↑*Node*;
    Node = **record**
            Word: *String*;
            Before, After: *NodePointer*
        end;
        {Circular list (ring buffer) element definitions.}
    ElementPointer = ↑*Element*;
    Element = **record**
            Word: *String*;
            Next: *ElementPointer*
        end;

var *KeyWords,*   {File of words we're checking for.}
    Source: *text*;   {The file we're checking through.}
    Root: *NodePointer*;   {Accesses the root of the keyword tree.}
    Tail,   {Accesses the oldest element in the buffer.}
    Center: *ElementPointer*;   {Accesses the 'current' buffer element.}
    TheWord: *String*;

procedure *SkipBlanks* (**var** *FromFile*: *text*);
    {Skips leading or trailing blank spaces, including new-lines.}
    var *Finished*: *boolean*;
    begin
        Finished := *false*;
        repeat
            if *eof* (*FromFile*)
                then *Finished* := *true*
                else if *FromFile* ↑ = ´ ´
                    then *get* (*FromFile*)
                    else *Finished* := *true*
        until *Finished*
    end; {*SkipBlanks*}

```
procedure InputString (var FromFile: text; var Word: String);
        {WARNING! Breaks words over MAXIMUMWORDLENGTH characters long.}
        {This version does not modify upper-case letters or punctuation.}
    var Counter: integer;
    begin
        Word := BLANKWORD;
        Counter := 1;
        while (FromFile↑<>' ') and
                (Counter <=MAXIMUMWORDLENGTH) do begin
            {Code to convert upper-case to lower-case and remove
             punctuation will go here at next program refinement.}
            Word [Counter] := FromFile↑;
            get (FromFile);
            Counter := Counter +1
        end;
        SkipBlanks (FromFile)
    end; {InputString}
procedure OutputString (Word: String);
        {Prints the leading nonblank portion of each String array.}
    var Counter: integer;
        Finished: boolean;
    begin
        Counter := 1;
        repeat
            Finished := (Word [Counter]=' ');
            if not Finished then write (Word [Counter]);
            Counter := Counter +1
        until (Counter >MAXIMUMWORDLENGTH) or Finished
    end; {OutputString}
procedure AddAWord (var Current: NodePointer; NewWord: String);
        {Recursively creates an alphabetically-ordered binary tree.}
    begin
        if Current =nil
            then begin
                new (Current);
                Current↑.Word := NewWord;
                Current↑.Before := nil;
                Current↑.After := nil
            end
            else if NewWord<Current↑.Word
                then AddAWord (Current↑.Before, NewWord)
                else if NewWord>Current↑.Word
                    then AddAWord (Current↑.After, NewWord)
    end; {AddAWord}                                        {program continues}
```

```
procedure InspectTheTree (CurrentNode : NodePointer);
        {A recursive debugging procedure that does an inorder search of the binary tree
        of keywords.  Only called if the global constant DEBUGGING is true.}
    begin
        if CurrentNode↑.Before <> nil then InspectTheTree (CurrentNode↑.Before);
        writeln (CurrentNode↑.Word);
        if CurrentNode↑.After <> nil then InspectTheTree (CurrentNode↑.After)
    end; {InspectTheTree}

procedure InitializeTheBuffer (var Source : text; var Tail, Center : ElementPointer);
{Creates a ring buffer SIZEOFCONTEXT elements long.  Elements older than and
 including Center are initialized as blanks; the rest of the buffer is filled from Source.}
    var TemporaryPointer : ElementPointer;
        Counter : integer;
    begin
        new (TemporaryPointer);
        Tail := TemporaryPointer;          {Locate the oldest element.}
        for Counter := 1 to (SIZEOFCONTEXT div 2) do begin
            TemporaryPointer↑.Word := BLANKWORD;
            new (TemporaryPointer↑.Next);
            TemporaryPointer := TemporaryPointer↑.Next
        end;
        Center := TemporaryPointer;        {Locate the central 'working' element.}
        for Counter := 1 to (SIZEOFCONTEXT div 2) do begin
            new (TemporaryPointer↑.Next);
            TemporaryPointer := TemporaryPointer↑.Next;
            InputString (Source, TemporaryPointer↑.Word)
        end;
        TemporaryPointer↑.Next := Tail          {Make the list circular.}
    end; {InitializeTheBuffer}

procedure AddItToTheBuffer (var Tail, Center : ElementPointer; TheWord : String);
        {Replaces the oldest word in the buffer with the one just input.
         Advances the tail and 'current' pointers.}
    begin
        Tail↑.Word := TheWord;
        Tail := Tail↑.Next;
        Center := Center↑.Next
    end; {AddItToTheBuffer}
```

```
function ItIsAKeyWord (CurrentNode: NodePointer; TheWord: String): boolean;
    {Search the binary tree for a particular word.}
var ItsFound: boolean;
begin
    ItsFound := false;
    repeat
        if TheWord<CurrentNode↑.Word
            then CurrentNode := CurrentNode↑.Before
            else if TheWord>CurrentNode↑.Word
                then CurrentNode := CurrentNode↑.After
                else ItsFound := true
    until (CurrentNode=nil) or ItsFound;
    ItIsAKeyWord := ItsFound
end; {ItIsAKeyWord}

procedure PrintTheContext (Tail: ElementPointer);
    {Prints each word in the buffer (spacing between), then new-lines.}
var TemporaryPointer: ElementPointer;
begin
    TemporaryPointer := Tail;
    repeat
        OutputString (TemporaryPointer↑.Word);
        write (' ');
        TemporaryPointer := TemporaryPointer↑.Next
    until TemporaryPointer = Tail;
    writeln
end; {PrintTheContext}

procedure FlushTheBuffer (Root: NodePointer; var Tail, Center: ElementPointer);
    {Inspects the words remaining in the buffer.}
var Counter: integer;
begin
    for Counter := 1 to (SIZEOFCONTEXT div 2) do begin
        AddItToTheBuffer (Tail, Center, BLANKWORD);
        if ItIsAKeyWord (Root, Center↑.Word) then PrintTheContext (Tail)
    end
end; {FlushTheBuffer}                                    {program continues}
```

```
begin  {KWIC}
  reset (KeyWords);
  SkipBlanks (KeyWords);
  reset (Source);
  SkipBlanks (Source);
  if not eof (KeyWords) and not eof (Source)
    then begin        {KWIC action.}
            {Set up the tree of keywords.}
         Root := nil;
         repeat
           InputString (KeyWords, TheWord);
           AddAWord (Root, TheWord)
         until eof (KeyWords);
         if DEBUGGING then InspectTheTree (Root);
            {Set up the buffer and search for words.}
         InitializeTheBuffer (Source, Tail, Center);
         repeat
           InputString (Source, TheWord);
           AddItToTheBuffer (Tail, Center, TheWord);
           if ItIsAKeyWord (Root, Center↑.Word) then
             PrintTheContext (Tail)
         until eof (Source);
         FlushTheBuffer (Root, Tail, Center)
       end  {KWIC then action}
    else begin        {Abnormal termination messages.}
         if eof (KeyWords) then
           writeln ('Abnormal program termination.  KeyWord file empty.');
         if eof (Source) then
           writeln ('Abnormal program termination.  Source file empty.')
       end  {else action}
end.  {KWIC}
```

here is a kwic test file that is designed to check special cases of kwic operation. It includes blank lines,

punctuation, and has key words at both the beginning and

end of the file. however, it doesn't include capital letters. the keyword file also contains blank lines. end

blank
end
file
here
it
lines
that
    here is a kwic test
is a kwic test file that is designed to
a kwic test file that is designed to check
kwic operation. It includes blank lines, punctuation, and has
both the beginning and end of the file. however,
of the file. however, it doesn't include capital letters.
capital letters. the keyword file also contains blank lines.
keyword file also contains blank lines. end
also contains blank lines. end

Chapter Notes 17-2

THE WAY TO UNDERSTAND POINTERS, LIKE the way to Carnegie Hall, is practice, practice, practice. Although pointers aren't an exceptionally hard abstraction, many little rules must be followed when they're used. As a result, not everyone who understands a linked structure can implement it in Pascal. With pointers, we always have to insist on the highest degree of learning—not 'Do I understand it?' but rather, 'Can I duplicate it on a closed-book exam?'

The difference between an undefined pointer and a pointer that references an undefined location causes many run-time errors. Suppose that we have these definitions:

```
type ElementPointer = ↑Element;
     Element = record
                    A, B: integer;
                    NextElement: ElementPointer
              end;
     var CurrentPosition: ElementPointer;
```

At the start of a program, *CurrentPosition* is undefined (although many Pascal compilers initialize pointer-type variables to **nil**).

> Whether or not *CurrentPosition* has been initialized to **nil**, it does *not* reference a location.

undefined pointer bugs

Programmers usually make the mistake of assuming that *CurrentPosition* references a record of type *Element* whose fields are undefined. Unfortunately, trying to make an assignment results in a run-time crash.

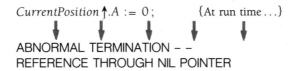

$CurrentPosition \uparrow .A := 0;$ {At run time...}

ABNORMAL TERMINATION – –
REFERENCE THROUGH NIL POINTER

Before a reference can be made through any pointer variable, a location must be allocated (using procedure *new*).

$new\ (CurrentPosition)\ ;$

Now *CurrentPosition* references a record whose fields are undefined.

infinite loop bugs

Two varieties of infinite loops are caused by pointers. The first occurs when dynamic allocation runs wild.

```
new (SomeRecord) ;
repeat
    new (SomeRecord ↑.Next) ;
    SomeRecord := SomeRecord ↑.Next
until false          etc.
```

overallocation

This program segment generates a never-ending list. When the computer runs out of new locations to allocate, the program may crash with:

ABNORMAL TERMINATION – – HEAP OVERFLOW

> Pointer locations are said to be allocated from a *heap* of unused locations in memory.

Heap overflow* crashes are no more serious than 'statement limit exceeded' crashes. They can also occur (rarely) in programs that dynamically allocate many locations without ever using *dispose* to allow reallocation.

endless searches

The second kind of infinite loop results from an endless search, usually through a circular list, for a location or pointer value that isn't there. The fail-safe of running past the end of an array simply doesn't exist. The examples below show **while** loops that are reasonable if and only if we're certain to find pointer *SoughtPosition* or value *SoughtData*.

while *CurrentPosition* <> *SoughtPosition* **do**
    $CurrentPosition := CurrentPosition \uparrow .Next$ etc.

while *CurrentPosition* ↑.*Data* <> *SoughtData* **do**
    $CurrentPosition := CurrentPosition \uparrow .Next$ etc.

Saving an extra pointer to the starting position and making an additional *boolean* check can be an invaluable antibugging device.

* Some systems call these *stack overflows*. We'll see why at the end of this section.

Start := *CurrentPosition* ;
while *(CurrentPosition <>SoughtPosition)*
       and *(CurrentPosition↑.Next <>Start)* **do**
    CurrentPosition := *CurrentPosition↑.Next*   etc.

Of course, we're still not in the best of all possible positions—we don't know if we left the loop because we found the location we were looking for, or because we made a complete circuit. Fortunately, that's a minor problem an extra **if** statement can straighten out.

As you might imagine, there are many bugs associated with pointer structures, rather than with pointer types per se. We've just discussed some of the difficulties of using circular lists. Stacks have one very common bug.

stack bugs

> Don't try to pop elements from an empty stack.

A simple check for *TopPointer* =**nil** helps sidestep this problem.

Queues and other structures that use lists also tend to generate boundary errors. When writing procedures that manipulate such structures, it's usually a good idea to remember special (but inevitable) cases. Will the procedure work...

list bugs

    . . . at the beginning of a list?
    . . . at the end of a list?
    . . . if the list is empty?
    . . . if the procedure makes the list empty?

It's easy to make boundary mistakes. For example, the following code is supposed to print a list's contents. Can you spot the bug it contains?

```
CurrentPosition := HeadPointer ;
while CurrentPosition↑.Next <> nil do begin
    writeln (CurrentPosition↑.Word) ;
    CurrentPosition := CurrentPosition↑.Next
end ;
```

check boundary
conditions

It really holds two bugs. What if the list is empty, and *HeadPointer* is **nil**? The *boolean* expression causes a run-time crash—we're trying to reference the *Next* field of a **nil** pointer. However, a non-empty list has troubles as well. What's the last *Word* field printed? Is it the last element of the list? No—it's the next-to-last. We've made an off-by-one error.

Another common boundary error occurs during list searches. The following bit of code is intended to search a list for a particular *Data* field. I've tried to avoid the error, cited above, of trying to reference the *Next* field of a **nil** pointer.

while *(CurrentPosition<>**nil**)*
       and *(CurrentPosition↑.Data<>SoughtData)* **do**
    CurrentPosition := *CurrentPosition↑.Next* ;

Unfortunately, I've forgotten that *boolean* expressions are fully evaluated. When *CurrentPosition* is **nil**, it's clear that the **while** loop's entry condition won't be met. Nonetheless, the second part of the condition (*CurrentPosition↑.Data<>SoughtData*) is still tested. The program crashes making a reference through a **nil** pointer.

A general problem associated with linked structures is the inadvertent loss of individual pointers.

don't lose locations

> It *is* possible to lose locations. When a location *or chain of locations* is lost there's no way to find it again.

A chain of pointers isn't like a ball of string—if the end gets lost, it's really gone. In most operations that involve list insertions or deletion, the order of statements is crucial. Remember that, in making a deletion from a list, pointers must detour around the unnecessary element or elements *before* the deletion takes place.

By their nature, pointers partially deprive the programmer of one of the best debugging tools—the snapshot of current program conditions. The value of a pointer is either **nil**, or the address of a location in memory, and neither value can be printed out.

print the data structure

What we need are procedures that display the contents of a pointer structure. It should be no trouble to pull such routines from Chapter 11. A list is printed with:

```
CurrentPosition := FirstPointer ;
while CurrentPosition <>nil do begin
    writeln (CurrentPosition↑.Word) ;
    CurrentPosition := CurrentPosition↑.Next
end ;
```

Although binary trees can be terrifying, they're easy to search recursively. Here's the code for an *inorder* search of a binary tree.

```
procedure SearchTree (CurrentNode : NodePointer) ;
    begin
        if CurrentNode↑.Before <> nil then
            SearchTree (CurrentNode↑.Before) ;
        Inspect (CurrentNode) ;
        if CurrentNode↑.After <> nil then
            SearchTree (CurrentNode↑.After)
    end ;
```

> When in doubt, print the contents of your data structure.

A quick look at a common implementation of pointers may help you understand potential bugs. For all practical purposes, we can imagine that a computer's memory is an extremely long array, like this one:

2.535E-14	'D' 'O' 'U' 'G'			FALSE TRUE TRUE TRUE TRUE TRUE FALSE TRUE FALSE FALSE FALSE TRUE FALSE TRUE FALSE TRUE TRUE FALSE TRUE FALSE FALSE FALSE FALSE FALSE	2701 694
0	1	2	65533	65534	65535

The array's element type is usually called a *word*. It's a basic memory location, usually capable of storing a single *real*, a handful of *char* values, or as many as five or six dozen *boolean* values. (Obviously, a group of two or more words would be required to store larger, structured value types.) The memory array's length is huge—in the tens of thousands.

The value of a pointer variable is essentially a subscript of this large array. As a result, trying to reference a pointer that is undefined (or whose value is **nil**) is much like using an out-of-range array subscript. However, instead of getting a 'subscript out of range' error message, we get a 'reference through **nil** pointer' message.

In terms of the illustration above, the computer's stack is allocated from the left-hand portion of the memory array, while the heap comes from the right-hand side. A run-time error occurs when the stack and heap collide, which is why an error message may refer to a stack overflow, and not a heap overflow.

The last antibugging comment I'll make involves auxiliary pointers. Very often, bugs are caused because programmers are needlessly stingy when it comes to declaring auxiliary pointers. In the end they have to play musical chairs with the values of the pointers that *are* available. When one pointer serves two purposes, bugs tend to happen.

> Extra pointers are cheap—use them.

● A pointer is defined as a type that references, or points to, values of another type. The definition of a pointer type may precede the definition of the type it references.

● A pointer variable represents the value stored in a memory location. Pointers can only be compared, for equality or inequality, to each other or to **nil**. The value of a pointer can't be inspected directly.

● A pointer variable is given a value in three ways. It's given a new location with *new*, or can have the current value of another pointer (of the same type) assigned to it, or can be assigned the value **nil**. The *dispose* procedure removes the pointer variable's value.

● The value a pointer variable references (as opposed to the value it represents) can be accessed, for inspection or assignment, using special notation—the name of the pointer variable followed by an up-arrow or circumflex.

● A linked list is a sequence of elements (invariably records) that are connected by pointers. A doubly-linked list has pointers connecting in both directions.

● A variety of data structures can be constructed by imposing rules on a simple linked list. In a queue, elements are added to one end, and taken from the other. A deque allows additions or deletions from either end. In a stack, the most recently added element is the first element removed.

● The tree is a recursively defined data structure. Each node of a tree points to one or more distinct sub-trees. In a binary tree, a node can only have two sub-nodes (its children). The topmost node is called the tree's root, while nodes that don't have any children are called leaves.

● A binary tree can be searched in a number of different ways, including preorder (node, then sub-trees), inorder (left sub-tree, node, then right sub-tree), and postorder (sub-trees, then higher nodes).

● Losing track of the end of a list or tree is one of the most common pointer-type bugs. Use auxiliary pointers to avoid this problem. Be sure to initialize pointers to **nil** to avoid running past the end of a list or tree.

● When you're dealing with linked structures, the first procedure you write should be a snapshot procedure that prints the data structure's contents.

Cross Reference

● Pointers are discussed in A136-A142. Pointer domain-types, which define the objects pointers can reference, are dealt with on A136.

● Formally, a pointer variable is called an identified-variable, described on A71 and A139. Identifying-values, which I've called addresses so far, are defined on A137.

● **nil**, and **nil**-valued pointers are discussed on A137.

● The dynamic allocation procedures *new* and *dispose* are defined in A137-A138. They are applied to record variants in A141-A142.

Exercises

17-1   Write a program that prints a list in reverse order by:

1.   stacking its elements, then popping them; or,

2.   recursively traversing the list, then printing values on the return path.

17-2   'The only good stack is an empty stack' is an expression that is often heard in mathematical programming. This thought is especially applicable to parentheses and brackets—a solitary delimiter is invariably up to no good.

Write a program that reads an expression and stacks the delimiters {, [, and (. As their matching counterparts },], and) appear, they should be popped. Your program should detect two error conditions—unpaired delimiters (like {5/[3+7]), and misordered delimiters (like {5/[3+7}–2])—and announce which delimiter was expected. All operands and operators should be ignored.

17-3   Suppose that three linked lists are each internally ordered, from least to greatest. Write a procedure that merges them to form a fourth list that is ordered from greatest to least.

17-4   Write a subprogram that implements the *boolean* relations =, <>, >=, <=, >, and < for two polynomials of arbitrary degree *a*) symbolically (with values for coefficients and exponents only) and *b*) with values for the variables as well.

17-5   Modify the polynomial addition program of Chapter 11 to multiply two polynomials, e.g.:

$$(x^5 + 3x^3 - x) \times (2x^9 - 6x^4 + 7x) =$$
$$(2x^{14} + 6x^{12} - 2x^{10} - 6x^9 - 18x^7 + 7x^6 + 6x^5 + 21x^4 - 7x^2)$$

For a rather more difficult problem allow two variables, e.g.:

$$(2x^4 + x^3y + 4x^2y^2 + 3xy^3 + y^4) \times (3x^2 - xy + y^2) =$$
$$(6x^6 + x^5y + 13x^4y^2 + 6x^3y^3 + 4x^2y^4 + 2xy^5 + y^6)$$

17-6   Write a *boolean* -valued subprogram that is passed pointers to the roots of two trees, and lets you know (depending on your level of ambition) if:

1.   they are *similar*, which means that their structure of left and right subtrees are identical.

2.   they are *equivalent*, which means that they are similar and also hold the same information.

17-7   A *memo procedure* helps define a data structure intended to minimize unnecessary recomputation. A linked list holds the arguments, and results, of calls to an arbitrary function. Whenever the function is computed, the memo procedure first checks this list to see if the result is already known. If it is, the result is returned; if not, the new result is computed and added to the list.

Write a program that computes values of the hailstone sequence (exercises, Chapter 8), while relying on a memo procedure. You will recall that each odd term is tripled and incremented by one, while every even term is divided by two, until the ground state of 1, 2, 4 . . . is reached. Can you modify your program to investigate the properties of negative hailstones (*n* is negative, even terms are divided by 2 and odd terms are tripled and decremented by 1)?

17-8   Recall that a *leaf* of a binary tree is a node that has no children. Are the leaves of a binary tree listed in the same relative order by preorder, postorder, and inorder searches, as defined in Chapter 17? Write a program that searches a tree using each of the search paths, saves the 'output' of each search in a linked list, then compares the order of leaves in each list. (Hint: Start by creating an ordered list of leaves only.)

17-9   The *internal path length* of a tree is defined to be the sum of the number of paths to each and every node. By definition, counting starts just above the root. The distance to the root is 1, the distance to each of the root's children is 2, each child's children have path lengths of 3, and so on.

path length 17   path length 9

Write a subprogram that is passed a pointer to the root of a tree, and returns its internal path length.

17-10   Many chemical substances have more than one molecular form, although each form shares the same atomic formula. These *isomers* can have surprisingly different physical properties, due to geometrical rearrangement of chemical bonds. A simple example of this is found in *optical* isomerism. Two substances that have the same formula and internal bonds, but are mirror images of each other, are optical isomers. They are identical except in the manner they reflect polarized light.

As a problem simpler than writing a isomer-analysis problem, write a procedure that creates a mirror-image of a binary tree. In the mirror image, left subtrees will become right subtrees, and so on. How difficult is it to show that two trees are identical except for being reflections?

17-11   Although I described the definition of the elements of a doubly-linked list, I didn't develop the operations that go along with a deque, or double-ended queue structure. We can imagine that a deque is really like two stacks implemented back-to-back. In contrast to a stack, which only lets us push or pop from the top, a deque lets us push elements on to, or pop elements off of, either end.

Write procedures to maintain a deque, and allow pushing or popping from either end. How might you use the deque to model deposits and withdrawals from a joint checking account?

17-12   Most computer systems use various kinds of *buffers*, or temporary holding places, to minimize the amount of work required of the CPU. Buffers are like semi-autonomous worker bees; they can do simple tasks that do not require any appreciable computation.

In one common application, buffers do the grunt work of holding a line of characters until the user hits the return key. Suppose that a line is a maximum of 128 characters long. A buffer should:

1.   let additional characters be added to the end of the line, up to the maximum;

2.   let the user backspace to delete single characters;

3.   let the user 'rubout' or delete the entire line;

4.   let the user end the line with a carriage return or equivalent.

Implement a line buffer, using a deque as the underlying data structure. Note that this is an input-restricted deque, since values can only be added on the user's side, and not on the system side.

17-13   A fascinating theorem from analysis states that, given any sequence of n distinct numbers, a *monotonic* (either increasing or decreasing), but not necessarily contiguous, subsequence of at least length $n^{1/2}$ can be made from its elements. For example, the 9-term sequence:

$$2, \quad -1, \quad 3, \quad -7, \quad -4, \quad 9, \quad -10, \quad 0, \quad 8$$

contains the monotonic subsequences **2,3,9** and **-1,-7,-10**, both of length $9^{1/2}$.

Write a program that reads an input sequence of any length n, then finds and prints a monotonic subsequence of at least length $n^{1/2}$.

17-14   Assignment of computer memory to running processes is the basic *dynamic storage allocation* problem. It is somewhat similar to the bin packing problem discussed in the exercises accompanying Chapter 8, but with two crucial differences. First, we must allocate memory as jobs arrive, and thus cannot predict the amount of resources required. Second, our work is never finished. Jobs are periodically completed and relinquish their hold on memory that can then be reassigned.

Modeling the performance of memory allocation schemes is a fascinating problem. Although in reality computer memory is very much like a long array, it is convenient to represent it as a linked list of 'free' and 'occupied' areas. Memory is initially a single element labeled 'free' with a very large *Size* field. As each new job arrives, an additional 'taken' element, with its size, is added to the list at the expense of the 'free' element.

The allocation problem becomes interesting when we let jobs release memory. Free space is no longer found only at the end of the list. Instead, the list holds interspersed segments of open memory and used memory. How do we decide where to place a new job? Two simple strategies, similar to those employed in packing bins, are *first fit*—stick the new job in the first area that's big enough, and *best fit*—put the new job in the smallest open area that will do.

Write procedures capable of modeling each strategy. They should be able to:

1.   search a linked list for the first 'free' element with *Size* equal to or greater than some required n,

2.   search for the 'free' element with *Size* closest to, but not less than, n,

3.   recognize, and merge, contiguous 'free' elements.

Hint: you may want to consider keeping an auxiliary list of pointers to 'free' elements.

17-15   An interesting problem proposed by R. Hamming is to print a list, in numerical order and with no duplicates, of numbers that have no prime factors other than 2, 3, or 5. The appropriate sequence begins $2, 3, 4, 5, 6, 8, 9, 10, 12, 15, 16, 18, 20\ldots$ Each term is a number of the form $2^i 3^j 5^k$, for all non-negative integer i, j, k values.

One approach to solving this problem involves the repeated creation and merger of lists. Suppose we start with a $List_{final}$, empty to begin with, of all the terms of the answer. A $List_{temp}$, initially 2, 3, 5, contains some, but not all, of the terms that go into a $List_{final}$. Finally, we can begin to generate a $List_{2terms}$, a $List_{3terms}$, and a $List_{5terms}$ by multiplying the current contents of $List_{temp}$ by 2, 3, and 5.

Now we have a *final* list, a *temp* list, and three *term* lists. The final list grows by being merged with the current temp list. The temp list, in turn, is replaced by the merger of the three term lists. New term lists are generated by multiplying the new temp list by 2, 3, and 5.

Write a program that carries out all this list generation and merging. How do you know how much of the final list can be safely printed at any point?

17-16   The *Traveling Salesman* problem is the best-known of a class of problems known as *scheduling* problems. A salesman must travel a circular route between a number of cities, visiting each one, and ending up at the starting point. What path should he take to minimize the total distance traveled? Unfortunately for the salesman, there is no known way to find the optimal route short of a brute-force trial of every possible solution (although there are programming approaches that help nip ineffective trials in the bud).

Let me present a simplified version of the problem. Suppose that the shortest known route between a number of points is:

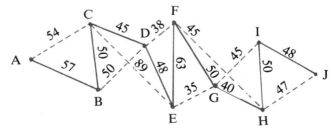

A new salesman, lazier than the others, suspects that reversing the order in which two particular cities are visited will shorten the route. For example, an *A, C, B, D* trip might be faster than the *A, B, C, D* route. Write a program that uses pointers to represent the current route, and solve the problem.

18

Introduction to Algorithms

Term after term, there seems to be room in the last weeks of the introductory programming course for harder topics. Obviously, students are getting smarter! In anticipation of a continuation of this trend, I've included a survey of some harder material. We'll cover three topics joined by one theme—the desire to find things.

Sorting is probably the most-studied subject in computer science. We'll revisit the sorting algorithms we met earlier, and learn about the aptly named *Quicksort* algorithm. *Searching*, our second topic, is closely related to sorting, since arranging data in the proper way can make it easier to find what we're looking for. We'll look at two searching algorithms—*binary* search, and *hashing*. *String matching* is our final topic. Sometimes data (like the words in this book) is stored in a manner that appears to be totally random, but that actually contains a great deal of meaning. How can we find one word, or sequence of words? We'll look at some methods of finding strings, and see how earlier techniques can be used in surprising ways.

Sorting, Searching, Matching 18-1

WE HAVE ALREADY SEEN THREE ELEMENTARY sorting methods—selection sort, insertion sort, and bubble sort. Let's reprise their algorithms, in each case sorting an array of *integers* from the least value to the greatest. This simplifies the general sorting problem, in which we have an array of records that we want sorted according to the value of a single field. For convenience, we'll assume the existence of a procedure *Switch* that can exchange the values of two elements of the array we're sorting.

Our first algorithm is selection sort. In a selection sort, we find the smallest array element and exchange it with the array's first element, then find the second smallest element and exchange it with the array's second element, etc. In pseudocode, we have:

selection sort

> **for** *every 'first' element in the array*
> > *find the largest element in the array*;
> > *exchange it with the 'first' element*;

The elements to the left of the current 'first' element are always in order, while the 'first' and its right-hand neighbors are random. The outer loop is entered N times, since we have to consider N subarrays. Within the inner loop, we must travel from one end to the other looking for smallest remaining value. This trip takes N steps the first time, $N-1$ the second, $N-2$ the third, etc. On average, it requires $N/2$ steps. Since we ignore constants in big O notation, we'll say that the time required for the algorithm to sort N elements is $O(N^2)$. The code for selection sort is:

analyzing selection sort

```
procedure SelectionSort (var Data : TheArrayType);
    {Sorts array Data using selection sort.}
    var First, Current, Least : integer;
    begin
        for First := 1 to ARRAYLIMIT – 1 do begin
            Least := First; {Take a guess that this is the least value.}
            for Current := First +1 to ARRAYLIMIT do
                if Data [Current] < Data [Least] then Least := Current;
                {Look for a smaller value in the remainder of the array.}
            Switch (Data [Least], Data [First])
        end
    end; {SelectionSort}
```

selection sort procedure

Insertion sort is the second of the simple sorting methods. Now, selection sort kept the array to the left of the current 'first' element sorted. It repeatedly added the smallest remaining element (on the right) to the end of a sorted section (on the left). Insertion sort also keeps the section on the left sorted. However, it takes elements from the right as they come. In contrast to selection sort, it doesn't look for the *smallest* element on the right. Instead, it takes the next element, whatever it is, and inserts it into the proper position on the left. We take a new element from the right, then travel toward the left looking for its correct position. In pseudocode, we have:

insertion sort

for *every 'newest' element remaining in the array*
    remove it from the array;
    while *we haven't found a smaller element among elements Newest–1 . . 1*
        slide elements to the right one at a time;
    insert the 'newest' element;

insertion sort pseudocode

It's easier to picture this if you imagine that the array is already sorted—except for the very last, rightmost element. We remove the last element, then slide its left-hand neighbor to the right. Does the saved element belong in the new 'hole?' If not, slide another element over from the left and check again. Eventually, we make a hole whose left neighbor is smaller than the saved element, and whose right-hand neighbor is bigger. To make sure that we *will* find a smaller element before running off the left end of the array, the data array is defined with one extra element—a 'zeroth' element that's initialized to a very small number.

This algorithm is also an $O(N^2)$ sorting method. However, we can notice an important difference from selection sort—the *average* time required for insertion sort will probably be less. Indeed, if the list is already nearly sorted, it will approach linear, or $O(N)$ time. For selection sort, in contrast, all elements had to be searched repeatedly regardless of their original order. The code of insertion sort is:

```
procedure InsertionSort (var Data : TheArrayType);
    {Sorts array Data using selection sort.}
    {Assume that Data runs from 0..ARRAYLIMIT}
    var TheNewValue, NewestPos, CurrentPos : integer;
    begin
        Data [0] := −MAXINT;
        for NewestPos := 2 to ARRAYLIMIT do begin
            TheNewValue := Data [NewestPos];
            CurrentPos := NewestPos;
            while Data [CurrentPos−1] > TheNewValue do begin
                Data [CurrentPos] := Data [CurrentPos−1];
                CurrentPos := CurrentPos − 1
            end;
            Data [CurrentPos] := TheNewValue
        end
    end;  {InsertionSort}
```

Bubble sort was our third method. To use this algorithm we travel through the entire array, starting from the far right, exchanging adjacent elements if they are out of order. At the end of one pass the smallest element has traveled all the way to the left. The second pass can start from the second element, the third from the third element, etc. By starting each pass on the right, we build an ordered array on the left.

We can imagine that bubble sort combines the techniques of selection sort and insertion sort. Like selection sort, we are repeatedly making exchanges of elements, but like insertion sort, we are sometime inserting elements into the midst of a list that is already ordered. Bubble sort is also an $O(N^2)$ algorithm. Its analysis is like that of selection sort. The outer loop takes N steps, and the inner loop ranges from 1 to N steps, for an average of $N/2$.

These three methods are all $O(N^2)$ algorithms in the worst case. They share certain characteristics that give a clue to their cost. In each algorithm, we travel down the array, one element at a time, for an outer loop of cost N. For each element, we have to deal with the remainder of the array one element at a time, either looking for a proper element, or looking for the current element's position, again at an average cost of $N/2$.

Note, though, that I said *worst* case. There is a branch of computer science devoted to ignoring Murphy's Law, and estimating the *expected* performance of algorithms. We'll take a closer look at this concept after our next topic—Quicksort.

Quicksort

The algorithms we've seen so far have been stated iteratively, which has made them easy to understand. One of the best sorting algorithms is almost invariably given recursively. It's called *Quicksort*, and was devised by C.A.R. Hoare, who also invented the **case** statement (a question that will probably never appear in *Trivial Pursuit*). At worst, Quicksort is also an $O(N^2)$ algorithm, but in practice, its running time is usually proportional to $N \log_2 N$. Let's reinvent it, and see how and why it works.

The algorithms we've looked at so far have always concentrated on methodically working from one end of an array to the other. Let's try a

divide and conquer

different approach this time—*divide and conquer*. Suppose that we put all the 'big' numbers in one half of the array, and all the 'small' numbers in the other half. Then, once we have the array neatly divided, we'll take each half, and do the exact same thing. Eventually, we'll get down to subarrays of length one or two, and the array will be sorted.

Sounds easy, doesn't it? Let's follow one of the stored values. Suppose that the very smallest value (call it *a*) starts out at the far right end of the array—the place where the biggest value is supposed to be:

We'll take this small value and put it into the left-hand half of the array:

Were we to check the left half—and split *it* in two—we'd move the *a* again:

Eventually, the *a* will get to its proper position at the start of the array:

How long did it take the *a* to get to its final resting place? Each time we moved it halfway home. As a general rule about divide and conquer methods...

> An algorithm that works by splitting the remainder in two will take about $\log_2 N$ steps.

Our rule is true because $\log_2 N$ is the maximum number of times we can divide N by 2—$\log_2 N$ of 4 is 2, $\log_2 N$ of 8 is 3, $\log_2 N$ of 32 is 5, etc.

Our algorithm requires that we repeatedly move the *a* into the proper half of the remainder of the array. If the original array is N elements long, $\log_2 N$ steps are required. Since the array has N elements to begin with, we'll have to repeat our basic algorithm N times to sort the entire array. The overall running time of our algorithm, then, will be proportional to N times $\log_2 N$, which is written as $O(N \log_2 N)$.

Now, our algorithm looks good on paper, but we've relied on magic too often to implement it as a program. How do we know what 'big' and 'small' numbers are? How do we know which half of the array to put any given number in? What do we do with the number that was already stored in the element we so cavalierly took over?

This was the problem Hoare faced. Stop reading for a moment and try to imagine how he solved it.

discovering Quicksort

Hoare's solution was very clever. He began by picking a number at random from the array. This lucky value, he claimed, could be considered to be the dividing point between 'big' and 'small.' Then, he searched the left side of the array for a bigger or equal value, and the right side of the array for a smaller value. These values, he said correctly, were in the wrong sides of the array, so he switched them. He started the searches from the ends, going toward the middle, so that eventually the two searches would meet.

One last insight remained. Where would the starting number be when the two searches finished? It would be in its final resting place in the sorted array. As a result, he could ignore this 'middle' value when he repeated the whole process on the left and right sides of the array.

Let's work on the array below. Our wild guess will be that the middle value (3, here) divides the 'big' and 'small' numbers:

9   1   5   7   3   6   4   2   8

a Quicksort example

We exchange the first number greater than or equal to 3 (working from the left) with the first number less than or equal to 3 (working from the right):

2   1   5   7   3   6   4   9   8

Now we repeat the step. It is the 3 itself that gets moved this time:

2   1   3   7   5   6   4   9   8

Our left and right searches meet at this point. Note that the 3 is in the correct position for the final sorted array. Each side is unordered, but all the 'small' numbers are on the left, while the 'big' ones are on the right.

What are the differences between Hoare's Quicksort algorithm, and the algorithm we started out with? Our original method relied on neatly dividing the array in half each time, so we know that it's an $N \log_2 N$ algorithm. We were able to do this because we assumed that we would magically know the median value stored in each array segment.

Since Hoare didn't rely on magic, Quicksort might pick a very non-median value to be the basis of the left/right separation of values. In fact, if we somehow pick the very worst value each time—the highest or lowest value in each segment—Quicksort turns out to be an N^2 Slowsort! Fortunately, this would require very bad luck indeed. On the average, we will pick a reasonably median number by chance (even though we were a little bit unlucky in our example, above). Since we'll be roughly splitting the subarrays in half each time, we can expect Quicksort to be an $N \log_2 N$ algorithm.

It's interesting to note that Hoare might have taken an entirely different tack. The Quicksort algorithm roughly organizes the array before splitting it in

merge sort

half. However, the opposite approach (splitting, then organizing) is also effective. Suppose that we divide the original array in half, then in half again, and so on, until we have an array of length two. This array can be sorted easily. Then, two ordered arrays of length two can be merged, then two arrays of length four, etc. This is the basis of the recursive algorithm called *merge sort*, which is discussed briefly in the Chapter 16 exercises.

The final Quicksort algorithm can be described recursively like this:

recursive refinement

> *to sort an array by Quicksort ..*
>> *pick some starting element value from the array;*
>> *exchange equal or larger elements (working from the left) with*
>>> *equal or smaller elements (working from the right);*
>> **if** *it's longer than one element,* sort the left-hand array by Quicksort;
>> **if** *it's longer than one element,* sort the right-hand array by Quicksort;

Let's look at the shaded section more closely. Suppose we begin by picking, as our starting element, some *StarterValue*. We expand the pseudocode above to:

second refinement

> **repeat**
>> *working from Start to Finish, try to find an element with*
>>> *value* >= *to StarterValue:*
>> *working from Finish to Start, try to find an element with*
>>> *value* <= *to StarterValue;*
>> *switch these two elements;*
>> *move left one, and right one, so that we don't check*
>>> *the elements we just exchanged*
> **until** *left and right pass;*

After each sorting run, the element that holds *StarterValue* is in its final position—elements to the left are smaller, while elements to the right are larger.

Can you see why the algorithm is stated recursively? Our intention is to 'sort of sort' the array into two sections. Then, we'll sort of sort one of those sections, then one of the new subsections, etc. We can keep track of the *Start* and *Finish* that delimit each subsection by having them declared as value parameters associated with a particular instance of the recursive call.

How do we choose our starting value? As we've formulated the algorithm, we pick the value of the element in the middle of the array segment we're sorting, with:

StarterValue := Data [*(Start+Finish)* **div** 2)];

What information does each call of the Quicksort procedure need? It must have the subscripts of the left and right ends of the array being sorted. The array itself is passed as a **var** parameter, which means that only a single copy of the array ever exists. The completed procedure is shown below:

procedure Quicksort (Start, Finish: integer; **var** Data: TheArrayType);
　{Recursively sort array Data, with bounds Start and Finish, using Quicksort}
　var StarterValue, Left, Right, Temp: integer;
　begin
　　Left := Start;
　　Right := Finish;
　　StarterValue := Data [(Start+Finish) **div** 2];　{Pick a starter.}
　　repeat
　　　while Data [Left] < StarterValue **do**
　　　　Left := Left + 1;　{Find a bigger value on the left.}
　　　while StarterValue < Data [Right] **do**
　　　　Right := Right − 1;　{Find a smaller value on the right.}
　　　if Left <= Right **then begin**　{If we haven't gone too far...}
　　　　Temp := Data [Left];　{...switch them.}
　　　　Data [Left] := Data [Right];
　　　　Data [Right] := Temp;
　　　　Left := Left + 1;
　　　　Right := Right − 1
　　　end　{**then**}
　　until Right <= Left;
　　if Start < Right **then** Quicksort (Start, Right, Data);
　　if Left < Finish **then** Quicksort (Left, Finish, Data)
　end;　{Quicksort}

quicksort procedure

The procedure's first call is:

　Quicksort (1, ARRAYLIMIT, Data);

Earlier I mentioned that the worst-case performance of an algorithm was not the only measure of its suitability. Thinking only in terms of worst-case performance can be misleading, because a particular algorithm's worst case might be very unlikely to occur. A more Panglossian body of computer science research is devoted to calculating an algorithm's *expected* performance, or the behavior it is likely to exhibit most of the time.

performance of algorithms

When sorting algorithms are compared by expected performance, Quicksort dominates the field. Even though the algorithm's worst case make it no better than the much maligned bubble sort, it is the method of choice for most sorting jobs.

The sorting methods described here are known as *in-place* algorithms because they do not require additional computer memory for the sort. As a result, any of the methods could be used to sort enormously large arrays—even arrays that came close to the computer's memory limit.* Naturally, very large

in-place sorting

* This is not true for special cases of Quicksort that require close to N recursive calls. However, simple modifications can be made to the algorithm so that there will be no more than $\log_2 N$ recursive calls.

sorting jobs would probably call for Quicksort. If the array is known to be in close to correct order, though, insertion sort might be used. On occasion, one method will be used to partially sort an array, with another algorithm called to finish the job.

Searching

Now, for some jobs, a sorted array is all we need. For instance, many applications require alphabetically sorted lists. Imagine that a program is supposed to print a dictionary, or the telephone book, or even the index of this text. We start out with a data base, or pool, of values, then we sort the values. Once the values—our names or numbers—are in order, all that's left is printing. The hard computation of the program is finished.

sorting vs. searching

Sometimes, though, the existence of a sorted list can be taken for granted. Instead of *sorting* values, we'll be interested in *finding* individual names or words with a minimum of trouble. Now, how long does it take to find something in a array? Well, the obvious algorithm is:

> **repeat**
>   *look at an array element*
> **until** *we find what we're looking for*;

How long will it take, on average, to an element this way? Suppose that the array contains N elements. Our algorithm takes $O(N)$ steps, since the value of N controls the number of elements we inspect. In the worst case, we'll have to look at all N elements, but on average, inspecting $N/2$ will suffice.

Incidentally, it's interesting to note that sorting the array will only improve our expected performance if the value we're looking for is liable to be absent. In a sorted array, we can cut off the search as soon as we've gone past the position we expect the value to belong in, but an unordered array must be searched all the way to the end.

searching binary trees

It turns out that we already know a much faster way to find things. Recall the discussion of binary search trees in Chapter 17. Suppose that we have our values stored in an ordered binary tree instead of an array. Let's assume that it's an exceptionally neat tree (called a *balanced* binary tree) in which most nodes have the same number of left and right descendants. In this case, finding a value takes $O(\log_2 N)$ steps, even in the worst case (where the node we want is way at the bottom). You should try sketching this out on paper to convince yourself that a value can really be found so quickly.

tree disadvantages

Binary trees look like sure winners on paper (since an $O(\log_2 N)$ search is much faster than an $O(N)$ search), but other considerations may rule out their use. In particular, storing links means that they tend to use considerably more memory than array-based storage methods, and, depending on the values stored, may not be well-balanced without a considerable amount of juggling.

Fortunately, there are some very fast methods we can use to find values in plain old-fashioned arrays. We'll look at two. The first, binary search, relies on an array that is sorted, and will let us find a value in $O(\log_2 N)$ time. Since we've already seen the algorithm (in Chapter 7) I'll make binary search interesting by implementing it recursively. The second search method, hashing, is both a means for storing values, and for finding them again. Incredibly, hashing lets us find a value in constant time—the length of the search doesn't depend on N at all. Let's see how they work.

Binary Search

How do you find a number in a phone book? Open it to the middle, and decide if the number is in the lower or upper half of the book. Then, decide which half of the half it's in, then which half of that half, and so on. As a recursively stated solution, *finding a number* is:

> *to find a number in a phone book . . .*
>   *decide which half of the book the number is in ;*
> *find a number in a phone book ;*

dividing the solution space

Once again we return to the the divide and conquer method of problem solving. Note that we aren't so much conquering the problem as wearing it down. We repeatedly divide its solution space until finding the correct solution is trivial. How long will it take? If our solution space is N numbers, then a divide and conquer search takes, at most, $\log_2 N$ steps:

Number	$\log_2$ of that number (approx.)
10	3
100	7
1,000	10
10,000	13
10,000	17
1,000,000	20
15,000,000	24
30,000,000	25

logs grow very slowly

According to this table, if New York, Tokyo, and Buenos Aires all shared a single telephone book, a quick-fingered operator would only have to check 25 numbers *at most* before finding the one we want.

Let's apply the binary search idea to finding a number in an array. We've already written code to do this iteratively, so our problem will be coming up with a recursive solution to the problem. A first refinement sheds more heat than light:

first refinement

> *to find an element by binary search . . .*
>   *split the array in half ;*
> *find an element by binary search ;*

Perhaps a reprise of the iterative pseudocode will help:

get the lower and upper bounds;
repeat
    compute a middle;
    if *it's low*
        then *make it (plus 1) be the new lower bound*
        else *make it (minus 1) be the new upper bound*
until *we find the number* **or** *decide to stop looking*;
decide why we left the loop;

iterative binary search pseudocode

The shaded sections give us our clue. Suppose that we implement the algorithm as a function. We *get the bounds* as arguments of a call; we can make new bounds simply by changing those arguments. Let's have a second try at a recursive pseudocode:

second recursive refinement

to find an element by binary search (left and right bounds) ...
    check the middle element;
    if *we've found it, or have searched the whole array*
        then *make the proper assignment to the function*
        else *find an element by binary search (with new bounds)*;

The completed recursive function is shown below. I'm assuming that the array being searched is of type *NumberArray*, with *integer* elements from 1 through *MAX*. A call of *BinarySearch* would be something like:

    Position := *BinarySearch* (*Sought, TheArray,* 1, *MAX*);

As before, I'll use a value of 0 to indicate that the sought number could not be found.

recursive binary search function

```
function BinarySearch (Value: integer; Numbers: NumberArray;
                                       Left, Right: integer): integer;
{Recursive binary search for Value. Returns 0 if it's not found.}
var Midpoint: integer;
begin
    Midpoint := (Left + Right) div 2;
    if Left > Right
        then BinarySearch := 0
        else if Value = Numbers[Midpoint]
            then BinarySearch := Midpoint
            else if Value < Numbers[Midpoint]
                then BinarySearch :=
                        BinarySearch (Value, Numbers, Left, Midpoint−1)
            else if Value > Numbers[Midpoint] then
                BinarySearch :=
                        BinarySearch (Value, Numbers, Midpoint+1, Right)
end; {BinarySearch}
```

Q. Each time function *BinarySearch* is called, a value parameter copy of the array is created. Can we know how much memory will be required to store all the copies of the array? Will this ever be a problem? What could we do about it?

A. A value parameter will require as much memory as its argument. Fortunately, the function will be called, at most, $\log_2 MAX$ times. That number, times the size of the array, is the largest amount of memory that will be required. If this is a problem, passing the array as a variable parameter avoids the issue. Only one copy of the array will be extant.

Hashing

We can conclude that when an array of items is sorted, we can employ some pretty clever techniques for finding any particular item. Can we come up with an even better approach? Well, the binary search does about as well as we can expect for an array in 'relative' (e.g. least to greatest) order. To improve on binary search, we'll keep the idea of having the array sorted to begin with, but try to expand our notion of what *sorted to begin with* means.

hashing algorithms

Hashing algorithms compute the location of a particular array element. A hashing algorithm is used both *a*) for originally arranging the array, and *b*) to see if a particular value is present.

Suppose that we sort the values stored in an array according to some consistent rule or formula. We can apply the same rule or formula twice. First, we use it to see where each value is supposed to be stored. Once we've arranged the array according to our method, we apply the same rule or formula in order to *find* a value. We pretend that we're going to *store* the value, then look to see if it's already there.

It's clear that not every rule or formula will give us suitable results. For instance, if our rule is *stick it on the end of the array*, we won't gain any advantage over a simple linear search—the rule is too simple. Since it doesn't take any special characteristic of the value into account, it's not repeatable. However, if our rule is too complicated—*stick it in the proper relative position in the array*—we won't net any gain either.

the hash table

In practice, a good *hash function* will distribute values uniformly throughout a waiting array (called the *hash table*). It will use some unchanging characteristic of the value itself, along with some simple arithmetic, to determine where the value should go.

For example, suppose that we were storing a maximum of one hundred numbers, known to lie in the range 1 through 1,000. We *might* create an array of a thousand elements, and use the actual value as the proper hash table position. This would be wasteful, though, since nine hundred elements will remain unused. Instead, we'd probably declare an array of one hundred elements, and divide each incoming number by 10 to determine its position. This rule—divide by 10, and round up—is our hash function.

It's not hard to imagine a hash function that we could use to distribute string values. Suppose that we want to store one hundred words. If we treat the first two letters as a base 26 number, we'll get a number between 0 (for 'aa') and 675 (for 'zz'). If we **mod** by 100, then add one, we'll have devised a hash function that gives us a hash table position between 1 and 100.

Now, if a hash function were perfect, it would automatically put every incoming value into a different spot in the hash table. Unfortunately, hash functions tend to be imperfect. Unless we make the hash table excessively large, two or more different values will eventually be sent to the same spot. This is called a *collision*. Every program that uses hashing will have some rule for *collision resolution*—for determining where the value should go if the first choice location is occupied. Stop reading for a moment, and try to think of a rule for resolving collisions.

Programmers take three main approaches. The first is called *probing*. It's simple—stick the value in the next spot. If that's occupied, go one more. If we reach the end of the array, the **mod** operator will let us wrap back to the start of the hash table. Probing is easy to implement, but has the unfortunate side effect of causing problems for values that haven't arrived yet. A new value's proper space may have been taken to resolve an earlier collision, so we've really just robbed Peter to pay Paul. In fact, we'll find that collisions tend to *cluster*, and only make the problem worse.

The second approach to collision resolution is harder to implement, but it avoids the clustering problem. It's called *chaining*. Instead of storing the values themselves in the hash table, we make each table entry the head of a linked list. We store incoming values by adding them to the appropriate linked list. If there's ever a collision, we add a new element to the linked list associated with the particular hash value. Some lists will probably be longer than others (and slow down searches later), but no hash value will interfere with others.

A third means of collision resolution is probably the neatest. We just rehash, generally using a slightly different hash function. This method is called *double hashing*. This method also avoids problems with clustering, and is a little easier to deal with than chaining algorithms.

Hashing, like sorting, is interesting for discussion because there's no 'best' method. Although considerations of efficiency have not weighed heavily on us in this text, tradeoffs between the two computer resources—space, and time—usually determine how and why we choose to implement particular algorithms. If space isn't an issue, we can achieve rapid hashing by declaring extremely large hash tables, ensuring that collisions will seldom occur. If time isn't an issue, we can declare a minimally-sized hash table, and expect to have to resolve collisions.

hash table collisions

probing

chaining

double hashing

tradeoffs in hashing

In practice, we generally find that optimum results are achieved with a table that's one-and-a-half to two times as large as the number of values that are to be stored. Optimum, in this case, means that time requirements get much worse as we occupy less space, but don't improve greatly when we use a larger hash table.

Let's consider some basic hashing code. In each case, I'll assume that we're storing records in an array that's been defined like this:

type definition

```
const LIMIT = 199;

type Data = record
              TheInformation: ItsType;
              Key: integer  {this is the search key}
            end;
     HashTable = array [0..LIMIT] of Data;
```

The *HashTable* array index starts with 0 in order to make some calculations further along that involve **mod** easier.

the search key

> The value a hash is based on is called the *search key*. This key is eventually used as the argument of the hash function.

I'll begin by looking at the simplest method of storing a single value:

problem: hashing

> Imagine that we have a hundred records with non-zero *integer* keys, as above. Write a hash function (and related routines) for implementing a hash table.

We can start by initializing the *HashTable*-type variable. If we set each *Key* field to zero, we can easily spot an element that hasn't been used for storage yet.

hash table initialization procedure

```
procedure InitializeTable (var Table: HashTable);
   {Initialize the Key fields of the table elements.}
   var i: integer;
   begin
      for i := 1 to LIMIT do
         Table [i].Key := 0
   end;  {InitializeTable}
```

Next, I'll write a routine for inserting an element into the table. Procedure *Insert* using a basic probing algorithm. If the table entry the hash function calls for (element *Position*) is occupied, *Insert* advances to the next location. However, I don't simply increment *Position*. Instead, I increment, and **mod** the sum by the length of the table. This guarantees that we will wrap back to the beginning when we reach the table's end.

```
       procedure Insert  (Position : integer ;  Element : Data ;
                                          var Table : HashTable ) ;
```
hash table insertion
procedure
```
       {Insert Element into Table, at or near Position.}
       begin
          while Table [Position ].Key <> 0 do
             Position := (Position + 1) mod LIMIT ;
          Table [Position ] := Element
       end ;  {Insert }
```

A function that locates an element follows a similar model. We start knowing the *Position* that the element should occupy, based on its key value. The search continues until we find a like key, or until we find a zero-valued key that indicates that the element we're seeking isn't present. If the element isn't found, the function returns a *Position* of *MAXINT*. This time, note that I've taken the trouble of making sure that we don't wind up in an endless loop, searching a full table for a key that isn't there.

```
       function Search  (Position : integer ;  Element : Data ;
                                          Table : HashTable ) : integer ;
```
hash table search
function
```
       {Search for Element.Key. Returns MAXINT if not found.}
       var Count : integer ;
       begin
          Count := 0 ;
          while (Table [Position ].Key <> Element.Key )
                      and (Table [Position ].Key <> 0)
                              and (Count <= LIMIT ) do begin
             Position := (Position + 1) mod LIMIT ;
             Count := Count + 1
          end ;
          if Table [Position ].Key = Element.Key
             then Search := Position
             else Search := MAXINT
       end ;  {Search }
```

Finally, let's get to the most interesting part—the hash function. Now, we can write a trivial function like this:

```
       function EasyHash  (Key : integer ) : integer ;
```
first hash function
```
       {Find the proper table entry for Key.}
       begin
          EasyHash := Key mod Limit
       end ;  {EasyHash }
```

No matter what the *Key* value is, *EasyHash* will return a hash table position between 0 and *LIMIT*. But can you spot the flaw that makes it a poor hash function? To give you a better feel for the problem, imagine that the *Key* value is derived from a name or English word using the method, described earlier, of pretending that the letters represent digits in base 26.

     EasyHash's weakness lies not with the arithmetic of the function, but with the tendency of names and words to cluster around particular values. In person, for all we know, Mary A. Smith may party hearty, while dull Mary B. Smith takes *Condensed Pascal* along on dates. To *EasyHash*, though, the keys Smith, Mary A., and Smith, Mary B. will undoubtedly wind up with the same hash table entry.

     A quick look at the dictionary will convince you that the clustering problem isn't limited to Smiths and Joneses. The problem we face, then, is to take keys that are very similar, and somehow transform them into hash table positions that are quite different. Stop for a minute and try to think of a method.

     Well, one approach is to devise algorithms that avoid characterizing the key by the first few letters of the word. For instance, we might 'add' the first letters to the last letters, or reverse the string, or only consider the middle letters. All these methods have been used, and can be quite successful.

     A quite different approach provides the basis of more modern hashing algorithms. Instead of trying to create a random number of sorts by jumbling the letter, why not assume that the number *is* random to begin with? Then, use it as the seed of a random number generator! The next number in the generator's pseudo-random sequence (**mod** the length of the hash table, of course) will be the proper hash table position.

     The advantage of this method is that, while two keys may be very close to each other numerically, their positions (and hence, the numbers each is followed by) in a pseudo-random sequence are liable to be far apart. Function *RandomHash*, below, employs a random number generator function similar to the one we wrote earlier. As mentioned then, the *Key* value is used as the seed.

```
function RandomHash (Key: integer): integer;
    {Choose a random table entry based on Key.}
    const MODULUS  = 65536;
          MULTIPLIER = 25173;
          INCREMENT = 13849;
    begin
        Key := ((MULTIPLIER*Key)+INCREMENT) mod MODULUS;
        RandomHash := Key mod LIMIT
    end;  {RandomHash}
```

A test of *RandomHash* with some sample keys shows that an effective distribution can be obtained even when the keys are very close together.

```
for Seed := 1 to 5 do
    write (Seed:6, ': ', RandomHash (Seed):3);
writeln;
for Seed := 10001 to 10005 do
    write (Seed:6, ': ', RandomHash (Seed):3);
writeln;
```

1:	18	2:	117	3:	151	4:	51	5:	85
10001:	73	10002:	107	10003:	7	10004:	106	10005:	140

As an exercise, you might want to try plotting the output of *RandomHash* for longer runs of close keys—you'll find that, for this particular random number function, some interesting patterns of close calls and collisions develop. How can they be avoided or mitigated?

String Matching

Text editors provide most people's introduction to computing. I think it's only appropriate, then, to close by considering some of the algorithms that make computerized text editors so impressive. In particular, I'll look at the methods text editors use to find individual words in text.

> *String matching* algorithms are used to located a particular subsequence of characters in a much longer file or array.

For our purposes I'll assume that we're always trying to find a string that's located in an array. Does it matter if the array is one or two-dimensional? In most cases, the answer is no. Suppose that we have an algorithm for finding a string in a one-dimensional array of type *Line*. We can usually search a two-dimensional **array of** *Line* by repeating the basic algorithm again and again.

If the string we're looking for contains a blank, matters become more complicated. In ordinary English text, the end of a line implies a space between two words. Fortunately, modifying a *Line*-based algorithm only requires simple arithmetic. Suppose we keep a running count of characters. We can calculate the location *of* the current line with:

$$(TotalCount \textbf{ div } length\ of\ one\ line)+1$$

and figure out our exact position *on* the current line with:

$$TotalCount \textbf{ mod } length\ of\ one\ line$$

To keep matters relatively comprehensible, I'll only deal with the one-dimensional case. Let's assume these definitions:

basic definitions

```
type Source = array [1..MAX] of char;
     String = array [1..LENGTH] of char;
```

I haven't defined either of these as formal string types because we're not going to exploit the special capabilities of Pascal strings. I'll state our problem like this:

problem: string matching

Assume that an array of type *Source* is filled with characters. Write a procedure or function that tries to find a string *Pattern*, and returns its starting position in the *Source* array.

the brute force
approach

The most obvious tack to follow is the direct brute force approach. First, compare the first elements of the source and pattern, then the next two, and so on. Eventually we'll either reach a mismatch (and can start a new set of comparisons one element further further along in the source), or we'll have matched every element, and can announce success. In pseudocode, we have:

refinement

```
initialize the element counters;
repeat
    compare two elements;
    if they match
        then increment the element counters
        else reinitialize the element counters
until we're done;
```

A few parts of this refinement look suspiciously easy. For instance, the *element counters* keep track of which element of the source and pattern we're comparing. When they're first initialized, each counter will equal one—the very first element of each array. How will they be reinitialized if we find a mismatch?

Well, suppose that *PatPos* gives our current position in the pattern array when a mismatch occurs. Let *SorPos* hold the current position in the source array. If we subtract *PatPos* from *SorPos*, then add one, we'll be back to where we started from. Naturally, *PatPos* itself gets set back to one—the start of the pattern array.

We can expand the *reinitialize the element counters* pseudocode as shown below. As you read, try to decide why *SorPos* has a 'correction' increment of two, rather than one? Also, is the order of assignments important?

second refinement

$$SorPos := (SorPos - PatPos) + 2;$$
$$PatPos := 1;$$

The correction factor of two is needed because we don't want to be back where we started from. Rather, we want to be one element further along. The order of the assignments are crucial, since the first assignment uses the original value of *PatPos*.

The **until** *we're done* part of our first refinement also seems to have been tossed off a bit casually. When are we finished? Well, my plan to increment the counters as long as elements keep matching gives us a clue. We'll be finished when *SorPos* exceeds *MAX* (the pattern wasn't there) or when *PatPos* is greater than *LENGTH* (we've found it). A final **if** check lets us know exactly why we left the loop.

The completed code of our brute force algorithm is shown below. Note that the function returns *MAXINT* if the pattern isn't matched.

```
function StringMatch (Pattern : String; SorText : Source) : integer;
   {Brute force pattern-matcher.  Returns MAXINT for no match.}
   var PatPos, SorPos : integer;
   begin
      PatPos := 1;
      SorPos := 1;
      repeat
         if Pattern [PatPos] = SorText [SorPos]
            then begin
               SorPos := SorPos + 1;
               PatPos := PatPos + 1
            end {then}
            else begin
               SorPos := (SorPos - PatPos) + 2;
               PatPos := 1
            end {else}
      until (PatPos > LENGTH) or (SorPos > MAX);
      if PatPos > LENGTH
         then StringMatch := SorPos - LENGTH
         else StringMatch := MAXINT
   end; {StringMatch}
```

brute-force string-matching procedure

Self-Check Questions

Q. Suppose that the *Pattern* string were longer than the *SorText* source. Would *String-Match* still work?

A. Yes. We'd leave the loop because of the **until** exit checks.

Q. What is the worst-case performance of the brute force algorithm? What kind of pattern and source would cause this performance?

A. Suppose there are M elements in the source, and N elements in the pattern. As we travel along the source array, each source element takes a turn at being the first element of a potential match. How many comparisons are associated with each potential match? In the worst of all possible worlds, we'll repeatedly have mismatches on the very last character of the pattern. Thus, the worst case performance of the algorithm is $O(MN)$. There are M (actually $M-N+1$) possible patterns to match, times the N (actually $N-1$) comparisons it takes to establish a mismatch. We assume that *Pattern* is very small compared to the source.

In practice, of course, we'll find mismatches much sooner. The worst possible case would be a source consisting of all zeros, and a pattern of zeros followed by a 1.

Q. In the worst case described above, how long is the pattern in relation to the source?

A. Disregarding the small corrections, the number of element comparisons is $(M-N)*N$, or $MN-N^2$. Using calculus, we can determine that the number of comparisons peaks when $M-2N$ equals zero, or when the pattern is about half as long as the source.

Getting Clever: Matching Meets Hashing

An improved pattern matching algorithm (like improved algorithms for sorting and hashing), is computer science's better mousetrap, if not its Fountain of Youth. The last decade or so has seen an explosion of new approaches to finding patterns quickly. Let's look at some of the more successful methods of finding a pattern in a larger source text.

To begin with, can we improve the performance of our brute force algorithm, function *StringMatch*? As we saw above, the worst case comes when a mismatch doesn't occur until the last character of the pattern. If our source and pattern follow the 'worst case form' of a **000...0** source, and a **000...1** pattern, we can make an obvious improvement by checking the last character immediately after we check the first.

tweaking algorithms

This strategy drastically betters the performance of the absolutely worst case, since we won't waste time checking long potential matches that don't fail until the final test. However, it can't be counted as a genuine improvement to our underlying brute force algorithm. What if the pattern we're searching for is **000...10**? Just about any special case improvement we can think of can be confounded by a simple counterexample. We've just *tweaked* the algorithm—fine-tuned it without making a real change.

A more fruitful approach was developed in the mid 1970's when researchers considered the problem from a different point of view. What kinds of patterns cause problems that lead to worst-case performance, they asked? Their conclusion was that complicated patterns, like English words, tend not to be especially difficult to match—not because matches came easily, but because *mismatches* showed up right away.

As a simple example, imagine that we're looking up a word in a dictionary. For the vast majority of the search we'll have mismatches on the very first character. Once the first character matches, we'll have many mismatches on the second. But only in a relatively few cases will we have to compare most of the characters of a word. It may take a long time to, say, distinguish a *lightning rod* from a *lightning bug*, but overall, the varieties of lightning are comparatively limited. For the non-difficult patterns, then, the expected search time will usually be proportional to $M+N$—the length of the source plus the pattern.

Now let's consider the uncomplicated patterns, like **000...1**, that cause problems. Since even English words are liable to be stored in a binary code, such patterns are not at all unusual. Working independently or in pairs, half a dozen computer scientists had the same clever insight about uncomplicated patterns—*they are repetitious*. As a result, they realized that it might not be necessary to start comparing from the beginning whenever a mismatch was found.

Let's look at an example. Imagine, as source, this repeated sequence:

0101010101 . . .

and, as a pattern, a similar sequence with an exception:

010100

How can we use repetition to speed our search? Suppose that we start to compare the source and pattern, character by character. For five characters all goes well. The sixth is a mismatch—the zero in the pattern doesn't match the one in the source. But must we go back to the first character of the pattern, and compare it to the *second* character of the source? Not if we recognize that we can 'slide' the pattern to the right. The search picks up by comparing the fifth character of the pattern to the seventh character of the source.

I'm not going to go into detail here, but the underlying idea isn't complicated. By carefully analyzing the pattern in advance, we can get an idea of how far we must back up in the event of a mismatch. The simpler and more repetitive the pattern and source are, the more effective this approach becomes. There are different aspects to these algorithms (some require backing up in the source, others limit backup to the pattern), but in general, they reduce the number of steps in finding the string to $M+N$ or less.

other approaches

An entirely different solution to the string-matching problem comes from accepting the fact that computers are just pretty bad at comparing strings. Determining whether or not two sequences of characters (of arbitrary length) are identical has always involved a laborious series of character-by-character comparisons.

Now, if numerical comparisons were as slow as string comparisons, computing as we know it would grind exceeding slow. Fortunately, numbers can be compared very quickly because of one-step operations that are built into the computer hardware. The arithmetic/logic unit, which we discussed way back in the Introduction, can compare two reasonably large (e.g. *MAXINT*-sized) numbers in a single operation.

In developing a quite different approach to the string-finding problem, Richard Karp and M.O. Rabin took advantage of the computer's speed in comparing numbers. They used tools similar to those we explored a few pages ago to develop an algorithm whose performance equals that of the methods described above, and which is a little easier to understand and implement.

Their algorithm, published just eight years ago, employs a typically unexpected insight. Now, when we're actually hashing values, we store each value and hope to avoid collisions. Using the Rabin-Karp approach to finding strings, though, we throw the values away—except for the pattern's hash value—and hope that we *have* a collision. If a collision occurs we have a potential match; and if our hash function is really good, the match is almost certain.

The importance of the Rabin-Karp algorithm derives from the technique it uses to avoid collisions due to non-matches.* However, it's not hard to see how the basic algorithm works. We assume that the pattern and source both consist of digits of a base B numbering system, where B is the number of different letters used. The pattern, then, is just a number written in base B. We start by counting the number of characters in the pattern. Then we pick a hash function and hash the pattern.

* In effect, it chooses a hash function at run-time so that a 'malicious' user can't intentionally design a source or pattern that will cause non-match collisions.

Now, there are two ways to accomplish the hashing. The most obvious method would be to convert the entire pattern from base B into decimal notation, then hash the whole thing at once. However, we can also use an alternative method—hash one character at a time *during* the conversion into decimal. The pseudocode algorithm is:

hashing the pattern

> *initialize a running total to zero*;
> **for** *each 'digit' of the pattern*
> > *convert the digit to base* 10;
> > *hash it*;
> > *add the hashed value to the original base times the running total*;

There are two advantages to taking the digit-by-digit route. First, we're able to keep numbers relatively small. Were we to try hashing the entire pattern at once, we might run into *integer*-overflow problems, especially if the random-number-like function we use for hashing employs large primes.

hashing the source

The second advantage comes when we start to hash the source text. Suppose that there are eight letters in the pattern. We'll begin by hashing the first eight letters of the source, and comparing it to the pattern hash. If it doesn't match, we 'subtract' the portion of the source hash due to the first letter, then 'add' a new component to the source hash—the hash of the ninth letter. If the hashes still don't match, we subtract the second letter's hash, and add the tenth's, and so on. In pseudocode:

Rabin-Karp pseudocode

> *hash the eight digits of the pattern*;
> *hash the first eight digits of the source*;
> *initialize Counter to* 8;
> **while** *the source hash and pattern hash aren't equal*
> > > **and** *Counter is less than the source length*
> > *increment Counter*;
> > *reduce SourceHash by the hash of TheSource*[*Counter* −8];
> > *increase SourceHash by the hash of TheSource*[*Counter*];

Although the initial hashes take time proportional to the length of the pattern (call that M), travel through the source text (length N) takes place in $O(N)$ steps.

Preface

*'The abuse of truth ought to be as much pun-
ished as the introduction of falsehood.'*
Blaise Pascal, *Pensées*

The purpose of this manual [here supplied as an appendix to *Condensed Pascal*, but with the original page numbering] is to provide a correct, comprehensive, and comprehensible reference for Pascal. Although the official 1983 Standard promulgated by the International Standards Organization (ISO) is 'correct' by definition, the precision and terseness required by a formal standard makes it quite difficult to understand. This book is aimed at students and implementors with merely human powers of understanding, and only a modest capacity for fasting and prayer in the search for the syntax or semantics of a *domain-type* or *variant-selector*.

As far as possible, I have introduced and retained the technical terms of the Standard. I recognize that many readers will use this manual as an adjunct to the Standard, and I intend to help them understand it as well as the language it defines. After the ISO went to the trouble of writing that:

> 'The activation of a procedure or function shall be the activation of the block of its procedure-block or function-block, respectively, and shall be designated within the activation containing the procedure or function, and all activations that that containing activation is within.'

I cannot, in good conscience, fail to use the term 'activation' early and often.[1] I have tried, though, to use it a bit more clearly.

Besides presenting the facts, this manual illustrates some of the reasoning behind them. In explaining the Standard, I've tried to point out some of the ambiguities and insecurities it addresses. Where necessary, I've also traced the development of potentially confusing—or apparently arbitrary—restrictions and requirements.

Why is there a new Standard? What was wrong with the *Report* [J&W] released by Kathleen Jensen and Niklaus Wirth in 1974? In short, the *Report*, despite its long tenure as a de facto standard, became a victim of its own success in popularizing Pascal. Before we begin to look at the new Standard, let's review some of Pascal's history.

Unlike Pascal, many languages developed during the 1960's tended to be more elaborate versions of existing languages. PL/I, for instance, was an unabashed amalgam of FORTRAN, ALGOL, and COBOL. Unfortunately, increased

---

[1] To be fair I should point out that the ALGOL 68 definition includes such terms as *notion, metanotion, paranotion, protonotion,* and *hypernotion*.

power often brought excessive complexity to definition and implementation. This led to poorly understood languages, widespread subsetting, and a subsequent lack of program portability. Pascal represented a retrenchment toward simpler ideas of programming language design, and a move away from the notion that complexity was equivalent to, or necessary for, flexibility and power.

Wirth's description of his discovery of the 'simplicity' that came to characterize Pascal is almost poetic:

> 'The more the ALGOL compiler project neared completion, the more vanished order and clarity of purpose. It was then that I clearly felt the distinct yearning for simplicity for the first time.' [Wirth74]

Appropriately, he had modest ambitions for his new language. Wirth wanted:

1.   To devise a language suited for teaching programming as a systematic discipline, with fundamental concepts clearly and naturally reflected by the language.

2.   To define a language that could be reliably and efficiently implemented on then available computers.

As long as Pascal was limited to these ends, minor ambiguities in its definition caused neither users nor implementors any loss of sleep. But to everyone's surprise—since no major commercial concern or political entity had a vested interest in the new language's success—Pascal became enormously popular during the mid 1970's. It was broadly adopted as an instructional language, usually at the expense of FORTRAN (see [SIGCSE80]).[2] Pascal was also used as a development language, and ballyhooed as a productivity 'discovery' in many business environments. A slightly extended version of the language was implemented on a number of microcomputers. Eventually Pascal caught the fancy of the press as being an ultimate programming language, and the bandwagon was really under way. Every manufacturer felt compelled to offer a Pascal processor, and every publisher had to have a Pascal text on its list. The grey areas in Wirth's standard became too important to ignore.

Early on, ISO TC97/SC5/WG4 (the ISO's Pascal committee) decided that its task was to clarify Wirth's definition, even though many writers from Wirth on down had pointed out various shortcomings in the language itself. But as Welsh, Sneeringer, and Hoare conclude in their discussion of the ambiguities and insecurities found in Pascal:

> 'Because of the very success of Pascal, which greatly exceeded the expections of its author, the standards by which we judge such languages have also risen. It is grossly unfair to judge an engineering project by standards which have been proved attainable only by the success of the project itself....' [Welsh77]

Although most Pascal implementors had followed, more or less, the same course in bringing up their versions of Pascal, a language extensions meeting in

---

[2] However, the FORTRAN 77 standard has certainly been influenced by Pascal. This brings to mind the saying that, although nobody knows what the most generally used language of the 1990's will look like, it will certainly be called FORTRAN.

1978 showed that there was a wild divergence in people's notions of how Pascal could, and should, be extended.[3] However, many manufacturers—the main force in most standards organizations—felt a great need for an official unextended Standard Pascal (even if it was not the best of all possible Pascals), reasoning that an imperfect standard (now) is better than uncertain progress toward a more perfect standard (later). Besides, as Lecarme and Desjardins note in their comments on Pascal:

> '[The] creation of an endless list of constructs is clearly not the right direction to follow for the development of better programming languages. The most unfortunate attempt in this direction is that of PL/I, and even its most irreclaimable addicts and most enthusiastic eulogists always seem to find more constructs to incorporate in it.' [Lecarme75]

The standardization process lasted about three years. Lines were soon drawn between two distinct camps, which we can characterize, perhaps somewhat unfairly, as being composed of *Scholars* and *Salesmen*. The Scholars felt an urgent need for a precise, unambiguous Standard. To a certain extent they were motivated by the desire to define Pascal in a manner that, in theory, anyway, would allow program verification, or proofs that a program would actually do its intended job.[4] At the same time, they were simply rankled by obvious inconsistencies in the Standard. The Scholars were always ready to point out examples of Pascal processors that had misinterpreted [J&W] with a resultant loss of reliability or portability.

The Salesmen gathered in the other group. They felt, with some reason, that in the majority of unclear situations one interpretation was obviously *the right thing*, and that their employers (usually commercial interests who presumably had the right stuff) did not need a Standard that split hairs quite so finely. For their part, the Salesmen always stood ready to point out examples in the Standard that were too incomprehensible to be interpreted at all.

The British Standards Institute (BSI), as the national sponsoring body of the new Pascal Standard, was caught in the middle. As soon as a draft proposal came out, it would be attacked on one hand by those who felt that it was vague and needed more detail, and on the other by those who felt that large sections could be excised with no corresponding loss of accuracy. Few people were surprised to see this note accompanying the responses to the second Draft proposal:

> 'The sponsor [Tony Addyman] is fed up with people who complain about the wording of the draft, and expect him or someone else to find a solution for them to criticise next time.' [Addyman81]

---

[3] University of California, San Diego, Workshop on Systems Programming Extensions to Pascal, July 1978.
[4] An early attempt along these lines was [Hoare73b]. His (with Wirth) axiomatic definition of Pascal was intended to provide, among other things, an axiomatic basis for formal proofs of properties of programs.

The final draft of the ISO Standard describes a language that is almost identical to Wirth's Pascal. It is a far more precise description, though, that contains 160 BNF productions, compared to the 107 defined in [J&W]. It includes more simple, useful examples than [J&W], but it often harder to follow because it addresses many issues of little consequence to the average programmer in considerably greater detail than any earlier Pascal standard. The new Standard is ordered in a somewhat unnatural manner that conforms to ISO rules.

The single unanticipated extension incorporated in the ISO Pascal Standard provides *conformant array parameters*. Since there was rather less than universal agreement on the exact specification of this extension (discussed in section A9-5), the ISO Standard provides for two versions of the language, dubbed Levels 0 (regular Pascal) and 1 (regular plus conformant arrays).

As a matter of fact (but not of law), the Pascal approved by the American National Standards Institute (ANSI) and the Institute of Electrical and Electronics Engineers (ANSI/IEEE770X3.97-1983) is equivalent to Level 0 ISO Pascal. Although this manual describes the complete ISO Standard (ISO dp7185), all discussion of Level 1 features is confined to section A9-5.

A1

Pascal Processors and Programs

The Pascal Standard is a set of rules that defines what a legal Pascal *program* is, and explains what a *processor* —a mechanism that prepares for execution, and runs such programs—is expected to do. A processor may be an interpreter, a compiler, or any other system (complete with computer) that can run programs. The standard doesn't specify how programs will get from paper to computer, what the minimum capacity of any processor is, or how a processor is activated by its users.

There are three loopholes in the picture of a precise and perfect Pascal brought to mind by the phrase 'set of rules.' First, certain features of a Pascal processor are *implementation-defined*. Though they may differ between processors, they always exist. The largest valid *integer* is a good example of an implementation-defined value. Second, there are some features that are *implementation-dependent*. A processor may have its own version of such features (like additional directives), or may omit them entirely.

directives A86-A87

The third loophole is the most difficult. The word *error* has a very specific meaning within the Standard: It is a *violation* of a requirement of the Standard that a conforming processor may leave undetected.[1] Errors are violations that are caused by program data (or by implementation-defined features), whose detection might require simulated program execution. Processors are supposed to detect as many errors as possible, or risk being thought of as 'not of the highest quality.' However, it should be noted that some kinds of errors are not mistakes as such, or might be quite difficult to detect. Errors are collected in Appendix B.

Errors must be dealt with in at least one of these four ways:

1) The processor's documentation must admit that certain classes of errors won't be detected.

2) The processor itself must announce that certain classes of errors won't be detected.

3) If the processor detects the error when the program is being prepared for execution, it must report it.

4) If the processor detects the error at run-time, it must report it, and halt program execution.

A program that complies with the Standard may rely on specific implementation-*defined* features or values, but can't require a particular interpre-

---

[1] Thus, errors are discouraged, but violations are expressly prohibited.

tation of implementation-*dependent* features. Similarly, a processor that complies with the Standard may accept programs that use language *extensions*. The extensions must be documented, though, and a processor may not require their use. Moreover, it must be able to treat the use of extensions (and implementation-dependent features) as though they were errors.

Some people find it disturbing that a program can produce dissimilar results when run on different complying processors. Obviously, such a program relies on some implementation-defined value or feature (but *not* an extension); an example is a program that prints the maximum valid *integer* value. Thus, a legal Pascal program may rely on implementation-defined values even if this keeps the program from being portable. In practice, most programmers rely on good programming style to avoid creating problems with portability.

Although Pascal implementations generally favor one-pass compilation, it is not required of any processor. Indeed, it has never been an explicit requirement, although the fact that the original implementation of Pascal was a one-pass compiler (for the CDC 6000 series of computers [Wirth71]) certainly helped convince people that Pascal could be implemented efficiently. Subsequent modifications of Pascal, however, have tended to favor changes that are amenable to one-pass compiling.

A1-1 Basic Notation

Our first step is to agree on a notation for showing proper Pascal. The *Backus-Naur Formalism*, called *BNF* for short, uses *meta-symbols* to help define the *meta-identifiers* we use to describe Pascal.[2] A BNF *production* (a meta-identifier and its definition) precisely specifies a language's *syntax*, the relative positioning of the symbols that make up a program. Every production is ultimately reduced to *terminal* symbols that are not defined further. Terminal symbols are the characters, words, and signs that Pascal programs are written with. Pascal's complete BNF is collected in Appendix C.

Note that BNF productions don't explain the semantics, or effect, of a programming language's features. Nor can a BNF, no matter how lengthy, completely demonstrate what a valid Pascal program is. A program can conform perfectly to Pascal's BNF without having a prayer of running successfully on a computer.

The meta-symbols we'll use have been somewhat modified in the years since Backus first came up with them, and are sometimes called an *Extended* BNF, or EBNF. The main modifications let iterative constructs replace recursive ones.

---

[2] Meta means 'beyond'; meta-symbols describe other symbols.

Meta-Symbol	Meaning
=	is defined to be
>	has as an alternative definition[3]
|	alternatively
(*this* | *that*)	grouping; either of *this* or *that*
[*something*]	0 or 1 instance of *something*
{ *something* }	0 or more instances of *something*
' **xyz** '	the terminal symbol **xyz**
	end of the BNF production

A1-2 Tokens

The smallest individual units of a program written in any language are called *tokens*. Pascal's tokens are divided into several categories. First are the *special-symbols*. Dipping our feet into the BNF, we have:

$$\begin{aligned}
special\text{-}symbol = \ & \text{`+'} \mid \text{`--'} \mid \text{`*'} \mid \text{`/'} \mid \text{`='} \mid \text{`<'} \mid \text{`>'} \mid \text{`['} \mid \text{`]'} \\
& \mid \text{`.'} \mid \text{`,'} \mid \text{`:'} \mid \text{`;'} \mid \text{`↑'} \mid \text{`('} \mid \text{`)'} \\
& \mid \text{`<>'} \mid \text{`<='} \mid \text{`>='} \mid \text{`:='} \mid \text{`..'} \mid word\text{-}symbol \ .
\end{aligned}$$

Some of these tokens can be recognized as mathematical symbols, and others are borrowed from ordinary English punctuation. The tokens in the third row are interesting because each consists of two or more characters. However, like the *word-symbols* (the second class of tokens), each one is thought of as a single symbol.

$$\begin{aligned}
word\text{-}symbol = \ & \textbf{`program'} \mid \textbf{`label'} \mid \textbf{`const'} \mid \textbf{`type'} \mid \textbf{`procedure'} \mid \textbf{`function'} \\
& \mid \textbf{`var'} \mid \textbf{`begin'} \mid \textbf{`end'} \mid \textbf{`div'} \mid \textbf{`mod'} \mid \textbf{`and'} \mid \textbf{`not'} \mid \textbf{`or'} \mid \textbf{`in'} \\
& \mid \textbf{`array'} \mid \textbf{`file'} \mid \textbf{`record'} \mid \textbf{`set'} \mid \textbf{`packed'} \mid \textbf{`case'} \mid \textbf{`of'} \\
& \mid \textbf{`for'} \mid \textbf{`to'} \mid \textbf{`downto'} \mid \textbf{`do'} \mid \textbf{`if'} \mid \textbf{`then'} \mid \textbf{`else'} \\
& \mid \textbf{`repeat'} \mid \textbf{`until'} \mid \textbf{`while'} \mid \textbf{`with'} \mid \textbf{`goto'} \mid \textbf{`nil'} \ .
\end{aligned}$$

Word-symbols are printed in bold face throughout this manual to distinguish them as Pascal *reserved words*, or *keywords*. Like the special-symbols they are all terminal symbols, since they're given between quote marks. They may not be redefined within a program.

A third group of tokens is the *identifiers*. They may be of any length, and all of an identifier's characters are significant. This slightly extends [J&W], which allowed 'very long' identifiers, but only promised to differentiate between identifiers on the basis of their first eight characters.

$$identifier = letter \ \{ \ letter \mid digit \ \} \ .$$

This production says that an identifier is a *letter* followed by zero or more additional letters or *digits*. Naturally, we must define these new meta-identifiers.

---

[3] The symbol '>' was added to the BNF so that productions referring to Level 1 Pascal can be shown as 'alternative' BNFs. This device lets all syntactic references to conformant arrays be isolated in a few sections of the Standard (section A9-5 in this book).

letter = 'a' | 'b' | 'c' | 'd' | 'e' | 'f' | 'g' | 'h' | 'i' | 'j' | 'k' | 'l'
        | 'm' | 'n' | 'o' | 'p' | 'q' | 'r' | 's' | 't' | 'u' | 'v' | 'w' | 'x' | 'y' | 'z' .
digit = '0' | '1' | '2' | '3' | '4' | '5' | '6' | '7' | '8' | '9' .

Every Pascal processor is required to recognize a character set that, with the exceptions given below, contains the special-symbols, letters, and digits just defined. This set of characters constitutes a ***reference representation*** for Pascal programs. Exceptions are allowed because of differences between the character sets used by different manufacturers and national standards organizations. The following substitutions can be made. Naturally, variations in font or typeface are irrelevant.

strings A117-A119

1) Upper-case letters may replace lower-case letters (except within strings). Here are three equivalent representations of the word-symbol **program**, and of the identifier *Initialized*:

program	**PROGRAM**	**PrOgRaM**
initialized	*INITIALIZED*	*iNiTiAlIzEd*

2) ***Alternative symbols*** may replace certain special-symbols:[4]

Reference Symbol	Alternative Symbol
^	@ or ↑
{	(*
}	*)
[	(.
]	.)

comments A6-A7

Since these alternatives are equivalent to the reference symbols, a comment, say, could begin with '{' and end with '*)'.

Since the implications of BNF productions are not always obvious at first (or twenty-seventh) glance, *syntax charts* (sometimes called *railroad charts*) have become popular as visual representations of the same information.[5] We can show an identifier as:

identifier

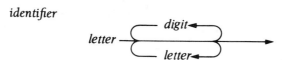

Following the arrows leads to the same restrictions as the BNF. The shortest legal identifier is a single letter. Longer identifiers may contain any sequence of letters and digits as long as the identifier starts with a letter.

These identifiers are illegal, because they don't conform to the BNF, or because they are syntactically identical to word-symbols:

---

[4] Throughout this book I use the alternative symbol ↑ in place of ^ because ↑ is much more readable in this typeface.

[5] *Caveat emptor*: Syntax charts are sometimes slightly simplified (which is one reason they're useful). The BNF alone can serve as the final arbiter of syntax.

Gia_Carangi   a.out   Program   3rdTestRun

A fourth class of token is the numbers. Their BNF productions should be read slowly and carefully if you want to learn to appreciate the subtlety inherent in BNF definitions. First come the signed and unsigned numbers:

signed-number = signed-integer | signed-real .
unsigned-number = unsigned-integer | unsigned-real .

integer A32-A33 In the definition of an *integer*, below, note the apparently unnecessary definition of a digit-sequence.

digit-sequence = digit { digit } .
unsigned-integer = digit-sequence .
sign = '+' | '−' .
signed-integer = [sign] unsigned-integer .

Example of *integers*:

285   −19   +055

real A31-A32 The digit-sequence shows up again as part of a *real* number's definition. The terminal symbol 'e' that precedes a scale-factor means 'times ten to the power.'

unsigned-real = unsigned-integer '.' fractional-part ['e' scale-factor]
| ⌐unsigned-integer 'e' scale-factor .
fractional-part = digit-sequence .
scale-factor = signed-integer .
signed-real = [sign] unsigned-real .

Example of signed and unsigned *reals*:

823.9   1e−3   9.3725e+027   −0.79

The definition means that, in the *real* value 1234.5678, '1234' is an unsigned-integer, but '5678' is merely a digit-sequence. Hairs are being split here because the size of an unsigned-integer falls in the range bounded by (and including) 0 and the implementation-defined constant *maxint* (the maximum legal *integer* value). A digit-sequence, in contrast, has no such restriction.

Equivalent syntax charts for *integer* and *real* values lose some of the fine distinctions of the BNF, but are a bit easier to follow.

signed-integer

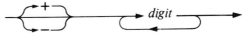

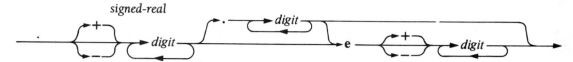

signed-real

The fifth category of tokens also uses the digit-sequence defined above. *Labels* (used with the **goto** statement) were unsigned-integers in [J&W]. Now, they're digit-sequences:

goto *A13-A15*

> *label = digit-sequence .*

that are neither numbers nor character-strings (see below). Instead, they're just sequences of digits that, according to their apparent integral values, must fall into the range 0—9999.

The sixth variety of token is the *character-string*, commonly referred to as a *string*. Although strings are most frequently encountered as program output, they'll come up again in conjunction with the string-types.

string types A117-A119

> *character-string = '" string-element { string-element } '" .*
> *string-element = apostrophe-image | string-character .*
> *apostrophe-image = '" .*
> *string-character = one-of-a-set-of-implementation-defined-characters .*

Like the numbers we defined earlier, character-strings represent values of a particular Pascal type. A one-character string denotes a value of the *char*-type, while every longer string denotes a value of a string-type. There is no null string in Pascal; the string '' is illegal (although '''' is valid).

char A34-A35

> 'These are all strings.'
> '−937.815e+03'
> '0   0'
> ';' {This string is of type *char*}

The occasional need to quote the quote leads to the peculiarly named *apostrophe-image*, which is just a doubled single-quote mark:

> *writeln* ('I can''t dance, don''t ask me!')

directives A86-A87

A seventh kind of token is called a *directive*, defined as:

> *directive = letter { letter | digit } .*

forward *A86-A87*

forward is the only directive required by the Standard. However, additional implementation-dependent directives may be provided—a directive that indicates external compilation is a likely candidate. The word 'directive' implies that the Pascal processor is being addressed at a higher level than usual. For instance, **forward** informs the processor that a Pascal program is being defined in an unusual, but syntactically correct, order.

The eighth and last token, the *comment*, is merely an honorary token, since its only semantic effect is to separate other tokens. A comment doesn't even have an official BNF, but we can describe it as:

$$comment = \text{`\{'} \ any\text{-}number\text{-}of\text{-}characters\text{-}or\text{-}lines \ \text{`\}'} \ .$$

with the understanding that an extra right brace may not appear within the comment. This rule keeps comments from enclosing other comments.

{This is a comment.}

{ This is longer,
and it is also
a comment.   }

Comments are ignored by a Pascal processor (except as token separators). Nevertheless, they should be included in every program to provide documentation for program readers. Comments may appear within individual lines of code, which lets documentation flow more smoothly in Pascal than in languages (like FORTRAN and COBOL) that require an entire line for each comment.

alternative symbols A4   The alternative symbols '(*' and '*)' are allowed as substitutes for '{' and '}'. Thus, '{ ... *)' is a legal comment, but this is certainly not recommended as a regular commenting style. All alternatives are syntactically equivalent, which means that comments can't be nested. This is often inconvenient because segments of code that contain comments can't be 'commented out' in their entirety. In practice, many implementations treat the two forms of comment as being separate but equal, to allow nesting. Such processors do not conform to the Standard, though, and programs they accept might not run elsewhere.

Token separators are important because they make Pascal programs 'free-form.' The separators—comments, empty lines, spaces (and tabs, implicitly), and the separation of lines—can all be used to make programs more readable. Pascal's spacing requirement is that at least one token separator appear between *program heading A130*   identifiers, word-symbols, and unsigned-numbers. This program heading:

program{Here's a comment.}*Pascal* (*output*);

is as legal as this one:

program   *Pascal*   (
output
)
;

However, separators may not occur between the characters of any token. This expression is legal:

WordCount <>1000

but this one is invalid:

WordCount <{not equal}>1000

The purpose of most useful programs is to take actions that carry out algorithms. Pascal's actions are *statements*. They fall into two categories: *simple*, and *structured*.

Simple statements are unconditional, noniterative actions (or on occasion, inactions). The most common simple statement is *assignment*. *Procedure calls* are also simple statements, even though a call may invoke a long series of statements of any kind. The **goto** is a simple statement, as is a syntactic peculiarity called an *empty* statement.

Structured statements, sometimes called *control structures* or *control statements*, are used to monitor other actions. There are two sorts of structured statements—*iterative* statements, and *conditional* statements.

boolean expressions
A33-A34

Iterative statements repeatedly execute an action. Two of these (**repeat** and **while**) use conditions phrased as *boolean*-valued expressions to limit the number of times the action is repeated. The third iterative statement (the **for** statement) specifies a fixed number of repetitions.

Two conditional statements choose between actions. The **if** statement uses a *boolean* condition to decide whether or not a statement (or which of two alternative statements) should be executed. The **case** statement decides among several alternatives; it picks one action to be executed from a variety of options.

The two final structured statements are less easily characterized. A *compound* statement groups a sequence of statements into a single syntactic action by bracketing them between the reserved words **begin** and **end**. The **with** statement is really only an honorary structured statement. It allows a simplified

records A102-A112

notation for accessing record-type variables, and is discussed along with them in section A11-1.

labels A6, A13-A15

The BNF of a statement lets it be prefixed with a label. Although any statement may be labeled, restrictions on using **goto** statements and labels are discussed in section A2-3.

> *statement* = [*label* ':'] (*simple-statement* | *structured-statement*) .
> *simple-statement* = *empty-statement* | *assignment-statement*
> | *procedure-statement* | *goto-statement* .
> *structured-statement* = *compound-statement* | *conditional-statement*
> | *repetitive-statement* | *with-statement* .
> *conditional-statement* = *if-statement* | *case-statement* .
> *repetitive-statement* = *repeat-statement* | *while-statement* | *for-statement* .

A semicolon (;) serves as a *statement separator*. It is *not* a statement terminator (as it is in some other languages). Thus, a semicolon isn't ever the last terminal symbol in a statement's BNF. However, semicolons *are* used to terminate program parts, definitions, headings, etc.—they play a different syntactic role in such cases.

A2-1 Assignment Statements

about expressions A39-A43
about variables A67-A71

The *assignment statement* attributes the value of an expression to a simple or structured variable, or to a function defined by the programmer:

$$assignment\text{-}statement = (\ variable\text{-}access\ |\ function\text{-}identifier\ )\ ':='\ expression\ .$$

For example:

Solved := *Solution* <64;	{assignment to *boolean* variable}
Matrix [*i,j*] := 1;	{assignment to array component}
output ↑ := *chr* (73);	{assignment to file buffer variable}
Position.x := 3.917;	{assignment to record field}
Factorial := *Factorial* (*n* −1);	{recursive assignment to function *Factorial* }
Current := **nil**;	{assignment to pointer variable}

special-symbols A3

The heart of any assignment statement is the *assignment operator* ':='. Since it's a special-symbol, spaces or other separators may not appear between the colon and equals sign. Kathleen Jensen tells an interesting story about the origin of the symbol Pascal uses for assignment.

'Traditionally, a beginning programmer is usually confused by one of the first statements he is bound to come across:

$$x = x + 1$$

Now, any first-year algebra student knows this is wrong; hence, entering the world of computers is equated with entering another dimension, one where his previous skills of abstraction must be phased out and a new 'logic' learned.' [Jensen79]

Wirth's solution (taken from ALGOL 60) was to use an assignment operator that could not be confused with the relational operator. The operator is usually verbalized as 'gets,' so we can informally describe an assignment statement as:

a variable (or function)   *gets*   a value

The order of accessing the variable (on the left) and evaluating the expression (on the right) is implementation-dependent. As a result, the effect of weird assignments like:

$$x := x + f(x);$$
$$A[x] := f(x)$$

where the call $f(x)$ modifies x, may vary between processors. Once a variable is accessed, a single reference to it is established for the entire assignment.

Assignments to function-identifiers (like the recursive assignment to *Factorial*, above) are discussed in section A9-2. Explanations of the other assignments accompany the discussions of variables and individual types.

A2-1.1 Assignment Compatibility

The basic law of assignments in Pascal is that the types of a variable and its prospective value be *assignment compatible*. Assignment compatibility relies, in part, on the rules for *compatibility* given below. Both sets of rules will be referred to several times in the coming sections. Types *T1* and *T2* are compatible if any of these statements are true:

Compatibility Rules

1)   *T1* and *T2* are the same type.

ordinal types A97-A100
subrange types A99-A100

2)   Ordinal type *T1* is a subrange of *T2* (or vice versa), or both of them are subranges of the same host ordinal type.

base types A122-A123
packed types A101

3)   Set types *T1* and *T2* are compatible if their ordinal base types are compatible, and if either both of them, or neither of them, are packed.

string types A117-A119

4)   *T1* and *T2* are string types with the same number of components.

A variable of type *T1* is assignment compatible with (and may be assigned a value of) type *T2* if any of these statements are true:

Assignment Compatibility Rules

file types A125-A135

1)   *T1* and *T2* are the same type, but not a file-type (or a type with file components).

2)   *T1* is *real* and *T2* is *integer*.

3)   *T1* and *T2* are compatible ordinal types (as described above), and the value with type *T2* falls in the range of *T1*. (It's an error[1] if the types are compatible, but the value of type *T2* is out of the range of type *T1*.)

4)   *T1* and *T2* are compatible set-types, and all the members of the value of type *T2* belong to the base type of *T1*. (It's an error if any member doesn't.)

5)   *T1* and *T2* are compatible string types.

[1] Don't forget the special meaning of *error* in the Standard—it is a violation that may go undetected. See section A1.

structured types A101

The assignment compatibility rules are easier to follow if we look at their underlying intent. Rule 1 of assignment compatibility should be thought of as applying to structured types. Two types are the *same* if their definitions can be traced back to a common *type-identifier*.[2] In the following example, types *T1*, *T2*, and *T3* are the same type, because they have effectively been defined with the same type identifier:

type

...

    T1 = *SomeTypeIdentifier* ;
    T2 = *SomeTypeIdentifier* ;
    T3 = *T2* ;

new-types A95-A96

This means that Pascal does *not* follow a strict rule of **name** equivalence of types. If it did, types *T1, T2, T3* and *SomeTypeIdentifier* would all be different. At the same time, **structural** type equivalence isn't followed either. Two new-type definitions are not the same even if the objects they describe are letter-for-letter identical. Also note that, because of rule 1, two file-type variables are never assignment compatible.

integer A32-A33
real A31-A32

Rule 2 lets *integers* be assigned to *real* variables. Since values of type *integer* can generally be exactly represented as *reals*, such assignments should not cause alarm in either program or processor. Of course, the *integer* value will henceforth be represented, and retrieved, as a *real*.

Rule 3 relates to ordinal types. In Pascal, a subrange of any ordinal type can be given a unique type-identifier, but individual values still retain the cachet of their underlying 'host' type. Since an out-of-range assignment under rule 3 might not be detectable until run-time, it is an error rather than a violation. However, it's hard to imagine a processor that would deliberately subvert the programmer's use of a subrange by ignoring the error.

Rule 4 makes a roughly parallel case for assignment between set types. In a sense, set types enjoy structural equivalence, because the compatibility of underlying base-types, rather than the syntax of a set-type's definition, determines assignment compatibility. As before, an assignment that should be invalid because a member of *T2* falls out of the range of *T1* is an error—it might not be detectable at compile-time. Again, it's unlikely that a processor would fail to detect such an error, and possibly halt program execution.

Finally, rule 5 codifies the special status of string types in Pascal. They, too, are assignment compatible if they're structurally equivalent—if each has the same number of *char* component values.

---

[2] A *new-type*, which is a type description (rather than an identifier), creates a type that is not the same as any other type. See section A9.

A2-2 Procedure Statements

about procedures
A73-A75

In Pascal, any sequence of algorithmic steps can be written as a **procedure**, which is a named subprogram or subroutine. This has advantages for programming as a systematic discipline, and for efficient program execution.

A **procedure -statement**, generally called a *call*, invokes execution of a procedure. The procedure-block—all the definitions, declarations, and statements

activations A63-A64

that constitute the procedure—is activated, its constants are defined and variables allocated, its identifiers are given meaning, and its actions take place. After the procedure has run normally, the statement that follows the call is executed.

When a procedure has *formal parameters*[3] declared in its heading, a call must include a list of *actual parameters* (or *arguments*), between parentheses, that are separated by commas and correspond to the formals by type and position. Since calls of the required I/O procedures obey less stringent rules, the BNF of a **procedure -parameter -list** allows for their special syntax, as well as for the **actual -parameter -list** of ordinary procedure calls.

$$procedure\text{-}statement = procedure\text{-}identifier\ (\ [\ actual\text{-}parameter\text{-}list\ ]$$
$$|\ read\text{-}parameter\text{-}list$$
$$|\ readln\text{-}parameter\text{-}list$$
$$|\ write\text{-}parameter\text{-}list$$
$$|\ writeln\text{-}parameter\text{-}list\ )\ .$$

$$procedure\text{-}identifier = identifier\ .$$
$$actual\text{-}parameter\text{-}list = `(`\ actual\text{-}parameter\ \{\ `,`\ actual\text{-}parameter\ \}\ `)`\ .$$
$$actual\text{-}parameter = expression\ |\ variable\text{-}access$$
$$|\ procedure\text{-}identifier\ |\ function\text{-}identifier\ .$$

The *read, readln, write*, and *writeln* parameter lists are all discussed in sections A5 and A11-4. Parameter-lists and procedures are discussed in more detail in section A9.

Some typical procedure statements are:

GiveInstructions;
MainBody;
PostScore;
Switch (First, Second);
Order (abs (Correction), round (Deviation));
Tabulate (1.7, 'X', Prime)

Note that in many cases the actual-parameter-list gives no hint of whether it's composed of expressions or variable, procedure, or function identifiers. Mark well the advice:

'If you have a procedure call with ten parameters, you probably missed some.' [SIGPLAN82]

[3] These are identifiers, used within the procedure, that rename the arguments of a call. See section A9-3.

The order of evaluation, accessing, and binding of the actual parameters is implementation-dependent. The Standard recognizes that agreement on a 'proper' order is impossible—who can say if left-to-right is any better, worse, or more natural than right-to-left? An arbitrary imposition of one order is sure to be unfair, and is liable to be ignored.

A2-3 **goto** Statements

The **goto** allows an unstructured branch to a statement marked by a label. Typically, its use in Pascal is actively discouraged. The **goto** statement's BNF is:

> *goto-statement* = 'goto' *label* .

blocks A58-A59   Labels are declared in a *label-declaration-part*, at the beginning of any program or subprogram block. Every label is required to prefix a single statement in that block, as explained below.

> *label-declaration-part* = ['**label**' *label* { ',' *label* } ';'] .
> *label* = *digit-sequence* .
> *digit-sequence* = *digit* { *digit* } .

In chart form we have:

label-declaration-part

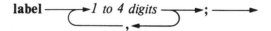

regions A59-A63   The region of a label is the block it is declared in, which includes all blocks *within* that block. A **goto** statement may refer to a label from anywhere within the label's region.[4] However, the Standard specifically requires that every label *prefix*, or go before, a single statement in the block that immediately contains its declaration—the block the label is declared in, but *not* any other block within that block. A label prefixes a statement by appearing before it, as allowed in the BNF of a statement:

> *statement* = [*label* ':'] (*simple-statement* | *structured-statement*) .

Syntactically, a label may prefix any statement. However, a **goto** can only jump to certain statements, and it's useless to label others. A **goto** statement can only cause a jump to:

1)   The statement that contains the **goto** (a special case of 2).

2)   Another statement in the statement-sequence that the **goto** is part of, or a statement in a statement-sequence that contains the **goto**'s statement-sequence.

---

[4] Unless the label is redeclared, which removes the enclosed region from the original label's *scope*. See section A6-2.

3)   Another statement in any block that contains the **goto**, as long as that statement isn't part of the action of a structured statement (aside from the compound statement that forms a block's statement part).

We can informally rephrase condition 3 by saying that the labeled statement must be at the outermost level of nesting in the statement part it appears in. Naturally, when a **goto** causes a jump to a calling subprogram, the called subprogram is immediately terminated, as are any intermediate subprograms involved in the call.[5]

The BNF of a statement-sequence is shown below. Notice the use of a semicolon as a statement separator:

> *statement-sequence* = *statement* { ';' *statement* } .

A label is distinguished by its apparent integral value, which must fall in the range 0 through 9999. Thus, 1 and 0001 denote the same label. Remember that a label is a label—it is not an identifier, string, or *integer*. In consequence, labels cannot be passed as parameters, stored, or modified; expressions can't be used to denote labels; and computed **goto**s, whose effect depends on the dynamic history of a program, are barred. This prohibition adds greatly to the readability and reliability of Pascal programs.

An example of a legal **goto** is:

```
procedure LegalGoto;
label 1;
     · ·.  {Other definitions and declarations}
begin
  1: readln (Data);
  while Data <Limit
    do begin
       Process (Data);
       if ErrorCode then goto 1
    end
```

In *LegalGoto* the labeled statement—*readln (Data)*—is another statement in the statement-sequence that contains the **goto**. An illegal formulation of the same segment of code is:

```
{Illegal example}
if DataIsReady
  then goto 1
  else repeat
     PromptAndRead (Data);
     1: Process (Data)
  until Finished
```

---

[5] For example, suppose a label is declared and employed in subprogram *A*. If *A* calls *B*, and *B* calls *C*, and *C* contains a **goto** back to a label in the body of *A*, then *B* and *C* are both terminated. See the discussion of activations in section A6-3.

This violates the rules because *Process* (*Data*) is contained by a statement in the **goto**'s statement-sequence.

In Pascal programs, the **goto** is most appropriate when an algorithm must be terminated in midstream. For instance, suppose that a subprogram detects data that renders continued processing pointless. A **goto** to the program's final **end** will halt the entire program:

> **program** *EscapeExample* (*input, output*);
> **label** 1;
>   ·.·
> **procedure** *Fail*;
>   ·.·
>   **begin**
>   ·.·
>   **goto** 1; {terminate processing}
>   ·.·
>   **end**;
> **begin** {*EscapeExample*}
>   ·.·
>   1: **end**.

Remember that labeled statements are executed whether or not they are arrived at via a **goto**. If program *EscapeExample*, above, ended like this:

>   ·.·
>   1: *writeln* ('Abnormal termination')
> **end**.

the message 'Abnormal termination' would print every time the program ended.

A2-4 Empty Statements

The BNF of the *empty* statement is hard to misinterpret:

> *empty-statement* = .

Don't be mislead by the period, which just marks the end of the definition, because an empty statement is not even a blank space. In an unnerving moment of clarity you may even realize that, despite the best of intentions, your programs are full of them.

An empty statement is a null action. An empty statement is usually noticed when it constitutes the action of a structured statement. For example, this construct is legal, even though the **else** portion is superfluous:

> **if** *InputIsValid* **then** *ProcessData*
>   **else**;
> *NextStatement*

The statement below is also legal, even though it is liable to confuse the casual program reader:

> **if** *InputIsValid* **then** {empty statement}
>   **else** *PromptForNewInput*

case *statement A20-A22*

In some circumstances, though, an empty statement is practically mandatory. For instance, the **case** statement, which executes an action that depends on the value of a *case-index*, is required (on pain of error) to have an action for the current case-index value. If one or more potential values have no actions to instigate, the empty statement comes to the rescue with a null action:

> **case** *Operator* **of**
>   *plus* : *x* := *x* +*y* ;
>   *minus* : *x* := *x* −*y* ;
>   *times* : *x* := *x* ∗*y* ;
>   *divide, modulo* :   {empty statement}
> **end**

Although empty statements are invisible, they're generally found in the vicinity of semicolons. As a result, misplaced semicolons can cause serious semantic errors. For instance:

> **if** *Condition* **then** ; {Notice the statement separator.}
>   *Action*

The segment above is syntactically correct. However, if *Condition* is *true*, then an empty statement (rather than *Action*) is executed. *Action* will always be executed, regardless of *Condition's* value.

A2-5 Compound Statements

A structured statement controls the execution of an action. Unfortunately, an *action* is a human concept that may require more than one Pascal statement. The *compound-statement* groups several statements in a way that, for syntactic purposes, turns them into a single statement.[6] Its BNF is:

> *compound-statement* = '**begin**' *statement-sequence* '**end**' .
> *statement-sequence* = *statement* { ';' *statement* } .

In chart form:

> *compound statement*

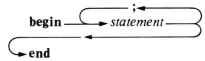

---

[6] In fact, the statement-part of a program or subprogram is written as a compound statement.

In effect, the **begin** and **end** of a compound statement are statement brackets.[7] A compound statement that contains one statement:

>   **begin** *Statement* **end**

is semantically equivalent to the statement alone:[8]

>   *Statement*

The action of the following compound statement exchanges the values of x and y. No semicolon statement-separator is required before the **end**.

>   **begin**
> $Temp := x$;
> $x := y$;
> $y := Temp$
>   **end**

As a matter of programming style, though, the last statement of a compound statement is often followed by a semicolon, even though it adds a superfluous empty statement (between the semicolon and the **end**). This practice helps prevent syntax violations that can occur when new statements are added. For example, suppose that the *writeln* below was added during debugging:

>   {Illegal example}
>   **begin**
> $Temp := x$;
> $x := y$;
> $y := Temp$ {Missing statement separator.}
>   *writeln* $(x, y, Temp)$
>   **end**

A new bug has inadvertently been introduced because the *writeln* isn't separated from the assignment to y.

A2-6 **if** Statements

The **if** statement is actually two statements in one.

>   *if-statement* = '**if**' *boolean-expression* '**then**' *statement* [*else-part*] .
>   *else-part* = '**else**' *statement* .

A syntax chart makes the BNF easier to see:

---

[7] Some languages, notably C, cleverly use braces ({ and }) as brackets, instead.

[8] ...except that if *Statement* is an **if** statement (see below), putting it in a compound statement disassociates it from a following **else** part.

if statement

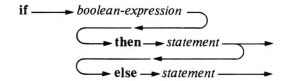

A brief **if** statement might control an assignment:

> **if** *Argument* >=0
>   **then** *Argument* := *sqrt* (*Argument*);
> *NextStatement*

boolean expressions
A33-A34

The *boolean* expression *Argument* >=0 is evaluated. If it is *true*, the assignment is made. Otherwise, the assignment is skipped. In either case, the next statement executed is *NextStatement*.

An **if** statement with an **else** portion provides an alternative action. (We'll see below that an **else** is always the alternative of the nearest prior **then** in the current statement-sequence, as long as there are no intermediate statements.[9])

> **if** *Argument* >=0
>   **then** *Argument* := *sqrt* (*Argument*)
>   **else** *writeln* ('No roots for negative numbers.');
> *NextStatement*

If the *boolean* condition (*Argument* >=0) is met the assignment is executed, otherwise the *writeln* procedure is called. One, and only one, of the alternative actions will be executed. Again, *NextStatement* is the next statement executed no matter what happens.

> **program** *FindSmallest* (*input, output*);
>   {Finds and prints the smallest of three input *integers*.}
> **var** *a, b, c, Smallest*: *integer*;
> **begin**
>   *writeln* ('Enter three integers.');
>   *readln* (*a,b,c*);
>   **if** (*a*<=*b*) **and** (*a*<=*c*)
>   **then** *Smallest* := *a*
>   **else if** (*b*<=*a*) **and** (*b*<=*c*)
>   **then** *Smallest* := *b*
>   **else** *Smallest* := *c*;
>   *writeln* ('The smallest number was ', *Smallest*)
> **end**.

[9] This point is obscured in the Standard by being stated in reverse: 'An if-statement without an else part shall not be immediately followed by the token **else**.' [6.8.3.4]

Notice the position of semicolon statement-separators in the examples. Were a semicolon to appear adjacent to a **then** or **else**, it would almost certainly be in error. A semicolon immediately after a **then** or an **else**:

> **if** *B1* **then** ; *S1*
> **if** *B2* **then** *S2* **else** ; *S3*

means that the **if** statement controls an empty statement. Although this is syntactically legal, it is usually semantically undesirable. A semicolon before an **else**:

> **if** *B1* **then** *S1* ; **else** *S2* ;

leaves the **else** dangling. It appears to be a misplaced word-symbol.

Structured statements may be *nested*, which means that the actions they control can be structured statements too. When an **if** statement's action is another **if** statement, an **else** portion is the alternative of the nearest prior **if** (as long as there haven't been any extraneous intermediate statements). For example:

> **if** *Sleepy*
>   **then** **if** *Grumpy*
>   **then** *writeln* ('Sleepy and Grumpy.')
>   **else** *writeln* ('Sleepy but not Grumpy.')
>   **else** *writeln* ('Not Sleepy, and who knows about Grumpy?')

This prose addendum to the **if** statement's BNF is needed because, in formal terms, it is *ambiguous*. This means that the BNF alone isn't sufficient to define the association of nested **if** statements.[10]

If it becomes necessary to change the normal association of **then** and **else** parts, the compound statement comes to the rescue by putting the closest **then** part in a different statement sequence.

> **if** *Sleepy*
>   **then** **begin**
>   **if** *Grumpy*
>   **then** *writeln* ('Sleepy and grumpy.')
>   **end** **else** *writeln* ('Not Sleepy, and who knows about Grumpy?')

Although indenting statements has absolutely no effect on program semantics—the processor couldn't care less—most programmers use indentation to clarify the association of statements. Try to trace the effect of this poorly-indented program segment:

---

[10] It could be defined in an unambiguous way, but that would really complicate the BNF. See the Dragon Book [Aho77], section 4.3, for a brief discussion of this issue.

>   **if** *Numerator* =0 **then if**
>   *Denominator* =0
>   **then** *writeln* ('Indefinite') **else**
>   *writeln* ('Infinite') **else** *writeln*
>   (*Numerator /Denominator*)

The sequence of **if** statements shown below is also prone to error:

>   **if** *B1* **then** *S1* ;
>   **if** *B2* **then** *S2* ;
>   **if** *B3* **then** *S3* ;
>   ⋱
>   **if** *Bn* **then** *Sn*

Suppose that the conditions $B1 \cdots Bn$ are mutually exclusive; i.e., that only one of them is supposed to be met. What happens if a statement S_i has the effect of altering the outcome of condition B_{i+m}, for $m \geq 1$? More than one of the supposedly alternative actions may be taken.

   An additional problem is that (for exclusive alternatives) the scheme shown above is quite inefficient, since all remaining *boolean* conditions will have to be evaluated regardless of which is *true*. A better model uses a nested structure, since any remaining statements can be short-circuited—skipped entirely.

>   **if** *B1* **then** *S1*
>   **else if** *B2* **then** *S2*
>   **else if** *B3* **then** *S3*
>   ⋱
>   **else if** *Bn* **then** *Sn*

A2-7 **case** Statements

ordinal types A97-A100

The **case** statement uses an ordinal-valued expression to determine which of a sequence of alternative statements should be executed. In the BNF below, the expression is called the *case -index*, and values it may have are *case -constants*. A list of case-constants, and the action they invoke, are together called a *case - list -element*.

>   *case-statement* = 'case' *case-index* 'of'
>   *case-list-element* { ';' *case-list-element* } [';'] 'end' .
>   *case-index* = *expression* .
>   *case-list-element* = *case-constant-list* ':' *statement* .
>   *case-constant-list* = *case-constant* { ',' *case-constant* } .
>   *case-constant* = *constant* .
>   *constant* = [*sign*] (*unsigned-number* | *constant-identifier*) | *character-string* .

labels A6, A13-A15   Case-constants are not the same as labels, although their appearance may be identical. A syntax chart is a particular relief in unraveling the BNF.

case statement

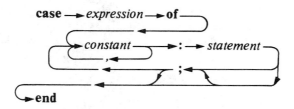

about constants
A65-A66, A98
enumerated types
A97-A99   The word 'constant,' as applied to a case-constant, refers to a token or identifier that is permanently designated (like a number) or defined (like a defined constant, or a constant of an enumerated type) to denote a specific value. If the constant is a character-string, it must have length one (which makes it a constant of type *char*).

For example, *false* and *true* are the constants of type *boolean*, while 1 and 2 are *integer* constants. In contrast, a declared variable, or another expression that might represent *any* value, isn't a constant. This **case** statement simulates the effect of an **if** statement with an **else** clause:

```
case Age >=18 of
    true: writeln ('Old enough to vote.');
    false: writeln ('Not old enough to vote.')
end
```

A more typical application might be:

```
program ElectionDetection (input, output);
        {Keep track of American national elections.}
var Year: integer;
begin
    readln (Year);
    case Year mod 4 of
        0: writeln ('Presidential and Congressional elections.');
        1: writeln ('Voted last year.');
        2: writeln ('Elections for Congress only.');
        3: writeln ('Vote next year.')
    end
end.
```

empty statements
A15-A16   If a case-constant doesn't require an action, the empty statement lets it appear without any inadvertent effect, as shown in the discussion of empty statements.

A small number of rules flesh out the **case** statement's syntax.

1) The case-index must be an expression of an ordinal type—it cannot be *real*-valued. The expression is evaluated when the **case** statement is executed.

2) A **case** statement's case-constant-lists have to be disjoint, because letting one value appear in more than one list would make the statement ambiguous. Naturally, all case-constants must be of the same ordinal type as the case-index.

about errors
A1, A149-A152

3) It is an error if the case-index's value does not appear as a case-constant.

Rule 3 is a step up from [J&W], which said:

'...if no such label [case-constant] is listed, the effect is undefined.'

Error status recognizes that some implementors let a case-index whose value doesn't appear in a case-constant-list 'fall through', as though an empty statement had been specified. The error compromise is far less stringent than a proposed requirement that *all* possible values of the case-index appear in constant-lists, or, at the very least, that the *current* value appear.[11]

The **case** statement was devised by C.A.R. Hoare, who made this hopeful comment about its utility:

'[The **case** statement] was my first programming language invention, of which I am still most proud, since it appears to bear no trace of compensating disadvantage.' [Hoare73]

A2-8 **repeat** Statements

The **repeat** statement is the only structured statement that never requires a compound statement to delineate its action, since the **repeat** and **until** serve perfectly well as brackets.[12] Its syntax isn't too troublesome:

repeat-statement = '**repeat**' *statement-sequence* '**until**' *boolean-expression* .
statement-sequence = *statement* { ';' *statement* } .

In chart form, we have:

---

[11] Imagine the problems the first proposal would cause for a case-index of type *integer*! Actually, many implementors have extended Pascal to give the **case** statement an **otherwise** clause that is executed if the case-index value is not found in a constant-list. This approach has become the first formally proposed ANSI extension.

[12] There has been an ongoing debate over the necessity of compound statements in languages like Pascal, since all structured statements could easily require word-symbols as statement terminators; e.g., **while** . . . **endwhile**, or **do** . . . **od**, or even **do** . . . **ob** (since **ob** is a more thorough reversal of **do** than **od** is). See [Harel80].

repeat statement

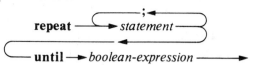

The **repeat** statement is used for *conditional iteration*. An action is executed, then a *boolean* expression is evaluated. If it is *true*, the **repeat** statement is terminated and the next program statement (if there is one) is executed. If the expression is *false*, the **repeat** statement's action is executed again.

```
program CountDigits (input, output);
      {Counts digits by repeated division.}
var InputNumber, NumberOfDigits : integer;
begin
   NumberOfDigits := 0;
   writeln ('Enter an integer.');
   readln (InputNumber);
   write (InputNumber);
   repeat
     InputNumber := InputNumber div 10;
     NumberOfDigits := NumberOfDigits + 1
   until InputNumber =0;
   writeln (' has', NumberOfDigits, ' digits.')
end.
```

A **repeat** statement whose *boolean* **exit condition** is never met is said (disparagingly) to be an **infinite** loop.

```
{An infinite loop.}
repeat
   writeln ('More fun than catching flies with one finger.')
until 1=2
```

Notice that since this bug has perfectly legal Pascal syntax, it can seldom be caught in advance by a Pascal processor. The lesson to be inferred is that a loop's action should contain a statement that ensures that the exit condition will eventually be met.

Since the **repeat** statement's *boolean* expression is only evaluated after the statement's action is completed, the exact point at which the expression becomes *true* is irrelevant; there is no notion of a loop-and-a-half in Pascal. **goto** *A13-A15* However, the **goto** statement *can* provide an exceptional exit from (and termination of) a **repeat** structure. Under normal circumstances, though, a **repeat** statement's action will always be executed at least one time.[13]

A2-9 **while** Statements

The **while** statement also provides for conditional repetition. Its BNF is similar to the **repeat**, except that the *boolean* expression provides an *entry condition*; it is evaluated before the statement's action is executed, instead of afterward. Thus, the **while** statement's action may not be executed at all.

> *while-statement* = '**while**' *boolean-expression* '**do**' *statement* .

Its chart equivalent is:

while statement

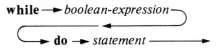

For example:

```
program AverageInput (input, output);
        {Average a sequence of integers that terminates with –999.}
var Current, Count, Sum : integer ;
begin
   Count := 0;
   Sum := 0;
   read (Current);
   while Current <>–999
      do begin
        Sum := Sum + Current ;
        Count := Count +1;
        read (Current)
      end ;
   if Count =0
      then writeln ('No input')
      else writeln ('Average is ', Sum /Count)
end.
```

We can duplicate the effect of a **while** statement with **if** and **repeat** statements. For instance:

---

[13] *Normal circumstances* means that most folks don't use **goto**s to jump from structured statements.

>   **if** *Condition*
>   **then repeat**
>   *Action*
>   **until not** *Condition*

is an unnecessarily complicated semantic equivalent of:

>   **while** *Condition*
>   **do** *Action*

The **while** statement is another danger-zone for extra semicolons. This innocent segment:

>   {An infinite loop}
>   **while** *Condition* **do** ;
>   **begin**
>   *S1* ;
>   *S2*
>   **end**

creates an infinite loop (if *Condition* is *true*) because of the semicolon—and implied empty statement—that follows the word-symbol **do**.

evaluating expressions
A39-A41

textfiles A131-A134

Although expressions are not *required* to be fully evaluated in Pascal, the programmer must proceed as though they always are. The two incorrect schemes below, which rely on partial evaluation, are typical sources of bugs in **while** statements.

>   {Incorrect way to skip blanks in a textfile.}
>   **while not** *eof* **and** (*input*↑=´ ´)
>   **do** *get* (*input*)
>   {Since every textfile ends with an end-of-line, this
>   model may attempt to inspect *input*↑ when *eof* is *true*.
>   A correct version is found in section A5-1.}

>   {Incorrect search of twenty-component array.}
>   *i* := 1;
>   **while** (*i* <=20) **and** (*Vector* [*i*]<>*Sought*)
>   **do** *i* := *i* +1
>   {May attempt to inspect *Vector* [21] if *Sought* isn't found.}

It has been pointed out that the **repeat** and **while** statements are dreadfully similar. One expert even suggested that **repeat** be dropped from the language entirely! His argument was that, in contrast to **while**, the **repeat** statement tends to cause programming errors. Interestingly, the exclusion was proposed as an *extension*—the word-symbols **repeat** and **until** were to be added to the set of acceptable identifiers. The proposal has not been greeted with enthusiasm.

A2-10 **for** Statements

The **for** statement provides *definite* iteration—it repeats an action a specifically determined number of times.

> *for-statement* = '**for**' *control-variable* ':=' *initial-value*
>   ('**to**' | '**downto**') *final-value* '**do**' *statement* .
> *control-variable* = *entire-variable* .
> *entire-variable* = *variable-identifier* .
> *initial-value* = *expression* .
> *final-value* = *expression* .

The visual equivalent of the **for** statement's BNF is:

for statement

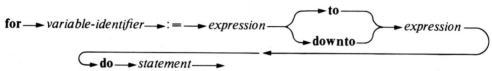

ordinal types A97-A100

       The **for** statement's lengthy syntax may obscure its best feature—it can be used to 'count' iterations in any ordinal type:

> **for** *Letter* := '9' **downto** '0'   {*Letter* is of type *char*}
>   **do** *writeln* (*Letter*);

> **for** *i* := 1 **to** 5   {*i* is of type *integer*}
>   **do** *Sum* := *Sum* + 2*i* ;

> **for** *ErrorCondition* := *Thrashing* **to** *Deadlocked*
>   **do** *Testfor* (*ErrorCondition*)
>   {*Thrashing* and *Deadlocked* are ordinal values with
>   the same type as the variable *ErrorCondition* .}

The control variable is subject to several restrictions:

variable declarations A67-A69

formal parameters A79

1)   A **for** statement's control variable must be declared in the variable declaration part of the program or subprogram that immediately contains it. It may not be a formal parameter, or a relatively global variable.

2)   The control variable must have an ordinal type. It may not be of type *real*.

entire-variables A70

structured types A101

pointers A136-A142

3)   The control variable must be an *entire-variable*, which means that it cannot be a component of a structured variable, or a variable accessed through a pointer.

4)   After a **for** statement is executed, its control variable is undefined—unless the statement has terminated abnormally (because of a **goto**).

blocks A58-A59

5)   The control variable may not be *threatened* (see below) within the **for** statement's action, or in any subprogram defined in the same block as the **for** statement.

The final rule effectively prohibits assignments to the control variable.[14] However, the rule turned out to be surprisingly difficult to put into the Standard. In his original description of Pascal, Wirth said:

> 'The repeated statement *S* must alter neither the value of the control variable nor the final value.' [Wirth71]

[J&W] relaxed the rule a bit by requiring that the expression representing the final value be evaluated only once:

> '[The control variable alone] must not be altered by the **for** statement.' [J&W]

In the first BSI Draft 'must' had been softened to:

> 'An error is caused if the control variable is assigned to by the repeated statement or altered by any procedure or function activated by the repeated statement.' [BSI79]

'Error' had roughly the same meaning then as it does now—it is a violation that is not required to be detected. The first ISO draft went back to the stricter limitation, saying:

> 'Assigning references to the control variable shall not occur with the repeated statement.' [ISO80]

An 'assigning reference' was defined in a way that virtually precluded any change in the value of the control variable (and would have required data flow analysis to detect a change). A slightly reworded version of the same restriction appeared in the second ISO draft. [ISO80]

At this point, members of various Standards Committees pointed out that it could be prohibitively expensive to police assignments to control variables within subprograms called by a **for** statement—especially if such subprograms were processed under some future arrangement for external compilation. What assigning reference to a control variable *V* can be spotted easily?

1)   An ordinary assignment to *V*.

variable parameters
A81-A83

2)   Passing *V* as a variable-parameter to a subprogram.

3)   A call of *read* or *readln* with *V* as a parameter.

4)   The use of *V* as the control variable of another **for** statement.

---

[14] One motivation for such a rule is that allowing assignments (that might change the number of iterations) would undermine the 'internal documentation' implied by the choice of a **for** (rather than a **while** or **repeat**).

These four statements are said to *threaten* the control variable. A threatening statement may not appear within the **for** statement, or within any procedure or function declared in the block the **for** statement is used in.

The *initial-value* and *final-value* determine the number of times a **for** statement iterates. This number may be 0. Assuming that i is an *integer* variable, neither $S1$ nor $S2$, below, will be executed:

> **for** $i := 11$ **to** 10 **do** $S1$;
> **for** $i := 10$ **downto** 11 **do** $S2$

$S3$ and $S4$ will each be executed exactly once:

> **for** $i := 10$ **to** 10 **do** $S3$;
> **for** $i := 11$ **downto** 11 **do** $S4$

Two rules apply to the initial-values' and final-values' types.

assignment compatibility
A10-A11

compatibility A10-A11

1) If the **for** statement's statement is executed, the types of the initial-value and final-value must be *assignment compatible* with the control variable.

2) If the **for** statement's statement is *not* executed, the types of the initial-value and final-value are only required to be *compatible* with the control variable.

Two ordinal types are compatible if they are the same type, or if one is a subrange of the other, or if both are subranges of the same host type.[15]

In effect, the control variable is a *read-only* variable that may be inspected, but not altered. The Standard is unexpectedly coy on the subject of the control variable's current value *during* the **for** statement's execution. It simply says that:

> '...a progression of values is attributed to a variable that is designated the control variable of the **for** statement.' [6.8.3.9]

Fortunately, an equivalent code example makes it clear that processors must do the right thing—the control variable equals the initial-value throughout the first iteration, and is incremented (or decremented) by 1 (or its ordinal equivalent) on successive iterations.

The expressions that provide the initial-value and final-value are only evaluated once, when the **for** statement is first entered. Although the **for** statement's action may change the actual values of these expressions, the modification has no effect on the number of times the **for** statement's action is

---

[15] Suppose that the type of i restricts it to values in the *integer* subrange 1..10. This is a legal **for** statement:

> **for** $i := 12$ **to** 11 **do** S

because the statement's action is never invoked. This statement:

> **for** $i := 1$ **to** 11 **do** S

is illegal, since its action is invoked, and 11 isn't assignment compatible with i.

executed. The segment below will print 'Le plus ca change...' three times.

```
a := 1;
b := 3;
for Counter := a to b
   do begin
      writeln ('Le plus ca change...');
      a := -2000;  {These assignments have no}
      b := 2001    {effect on the for statement.}
   end
```

Ordinary Data and Required Functions

The definition of a vocabulary for describing values, or **data**, is part of the creation of any programming language. In Pascal, four ordered sets of values—the required *simple types*—form the basic data vocabulary. Although other simple types may be defined (as *enumerated* types), only values of the required simple types may pass through the standard I/O channels. This section briefly describes required simple types, and the operators and required functions associated with them. Expressions, and the role operators play in forming them, are covered in more detail in section A4.

enumerated types
A97-A99

A3-1 Required Simple Types

Because the values they describe form a convenient common ground between humans and computers, the simple type identifiers *real, integer, boolean*, and *char* are required to be recognized by every Pascal processor, which means that they're **predefined** type identifiers.[1] The phrase 'simple type' is a meta-identifier that replaces the less precise [J&W] term 'scalar type.'

> *simple-type = ordinal-type | real-type-identifier .*
> *ordinal-type = new-ordinal-type | ordinal-type-identifier .*

Each simple type is an ordered group of values. Type *real* is different from all the others because it is not **enumerable**, which means that its values cannot be numbered.[2] *Real* values in Pascal have to be thought of as being close approximations to the reals of mathematics. Although they're ordered—1.0 is obviously less than 1.1—the representation and accuracy of reals in computers varies so much that the notion of a standard 'next' real is meaningless.

ordinal types A97-A100

Ordinal types are more well-behaved (with the exception of implementation-defined aspects of type *char*). Their values can be numbered starting with zero (except for *integer*) and manipulated with the exact same results on every Pascal processor. The BNF of *ordinal-type*, above, implies the required ordinal type identifiers *integer, boolean*, and *char*, and lets new ordinal types be defined by the programmer.

---

[1] Technically, the required identifiers may be redefined. Doing so is not the right thing, though, and you deserve what you get. Only one other type is predefined—the file type *text* (see section A11-4).
[2] '*real*' is the required real-type-identifier mentioned in the BNF. However, synonyms for *real* (as well as for the other required type identifiers) can be defined. See section A10-1.

A3-1.1 *real*

There are limits to the accuracy with which mathematical reals are represented within computers, as well as bounds on their magnitude; thus type *real* is an implementation-defined subset of the real numbers.

The BNF for constants of type *real* allows both positive and negative values. It relies in part on the syntax of signed and unsigned *integers*, and *digit-sequences*, discussed in the next section.

$$signed\text{-}real = [\ sign\ ]\ unsigned\text{-}real\ .$$
$$unsigned\text{-}real = unsigned\text{-}integer\ `.'\ fractional\text{-}part\ [\ `e'\ scale\text{-}factor\ ]$$
$$|\ unsigned\text{-}integer\ `e'\ scale\text{-}factor\ .$$
$$fractional\text{-}part = digit\text{-}sequence\ .$$
$$scale\text{-}factor = signed\text{-}integer\ .$$

The allowed magnitude of the scale factor is implementation-defined. A syntax chart simplifies the BNF:

signed-real

Remember that '**e**' is a synonym for 'times ten to the power of' a stated scale factor. Unless a *real* includes a scale factor, it must contain a decimal point, with at last one digit (even a zero) on each side of the decimal. Some legal *real* values are:

187.4   −0.2   45e−003   −1.4497e−19

Illegal *reals*:

e25   10.   .7391

There are four *real* operators. A **result** value is always *real* if:

1)   both **operands** are *real*, or

2)   one operand is *real*, and the other is *integer*, or

3)   both operands are *integer*, but the *real* division operator (/) is used.[3]

Operator	*Operation*
+	addition
−	subtraction
*	multiplication
/	division

In *real* division, it is an error for the divisor (the denominator of a fraction) to be zero. The results of all legal *real* operations are approximations

---

[3] This means that *integer* operands are sometimes *coerced* into being *reals*; i.e., they are temporarily treated as values of type *real*.

whose accuracy is implementation-defined, but are presumably close to the corresponding mathematical results. Just *how* close they are has been a matter of contention since computers were invented. (Does (10/3)∗3 equal 10 or 9.999...?)

A3-1.2 *integer*

Values of type *integer* are whole numbers. Like *real*, type *integer* specifies a subset—there is a 'maximum' *integer* value given by the required constant-identifier *maxint*. Every whole number in the closed interval −*maxint*..*maxint* is an *integer*.

The *integer* requires a relievingly short BNF:

> *signed-integer* = [*sign*] *unsigned-integer* .
> *unsigned-integer* = *digit-sequence* .
> *digit-sequence* = *digit* { *digit* } .
> *sign* = '+' | '−' .

An equivalent syntax chart is:

signed-integer

Since *integer* is an ordinal type, it is enumerable. Each *integer* numbers its own ordinal position.

The *integer* arithmetic operators given below require *integer* operands. A *real* that appears to have an integral value (like 10e2) won't do.

Operator	Operation
+	addition
−	subtraction
∗	multiplication
div	*integer* division (fractional remainder is ignored)
mod	modulo (the remainder of an *integer* division)

expressions A39-A41 An expression that involves *integer* values is required to be correctly evaluated if its operands, and intermediate and final results, fall within the range −*maxint* through *maxint*.

Suppose, though, that one or both operands, or a partial or final result, of an *integer* expression happens to fall outside the range −*maxint* through *maxint*. In this circumstance, it is an error (rather than a violation) if the expression is not evaluated according to the rules of ordinary integer arithmetic.[4]

---

[4] The classic problem is determining the result of the expression *maxint* + 1. It might be evaluated as −*maxint* (on one's-complement machines), or as −*maxint* −1 (on two's-complement computers), or it might be detected as a violation and halt program execution.

The **div** and **mod** operators require a few comments.

abs function A36

1) i **div** j represents a value such that:

$$abs(i) - abs(j) < abs((i \text{ div } j)*j) <= abs(i)$$

The value is zero if $abs(i)$ is less than $abs(j)$. If it isn't zero, the value is positive if i and j have the same sign, and negative if i and j have different signs.

2)   The value of i **mod** j is the value of $i - (k*j)$ for an *integer* value k, such that $0 <= (i \text{ mod } j) < j$.

3)   The expression i **div** j is an error if j is zero.

4)   The expression i **mod** j is an error if j is zero or negative.

Note that **div** and **mod** do not necessarily give a consistent quotient and remainder. Only for $i >= 0$ and $j > 0$ (a restriction not mentioned in [J&W]) does:

$$((i \text{ div } j)*j) + (i \text{ mod } j) = i$$

A3-1.3 *boolean*

Type *boolean* (named after George Boole, the originator of logical calculus) has only two members—the logical values whose required identifiers are *false* and *true* (and have ordinal numbers zero and one). The *boolean* values establish conditions for some of the structured statements. Three operators take exclusively *boolean* operands:

ordinal numbers A37
structured statements A8

Operator	Operation
not	logical negation
or	logical disjunction
and	logical conjunction

Assume (for the sake of tradition) that p and q are *boolean*-valued operands. Then:

not q	means *true* if q is *false*, and *false* otherwise.
p **or** q	means *true* if either p or q is *true*, or if both are.
p **and** q	means *true* if both p and q are *true*, and *false* otherwise.

We can express the same information with these *truth tables*.

not *true* is *false*
not *false* is *true*

true **and** *true* is *true*	*true* **or** *true* is *true*
true **and** *false* is *false*	*true* **or** *false* is *true*
false **and** *true* is *false*	*false* **or** *true* is *true*
false **and** *false* is *false*	*false* **or** *false* is *false*

relational operators
A45-A46

The relational operators also yield *boolean* results. Since the ordinal numbers of *false* and *true* are zero and one (which means that *false* <*true*), we can construct three more logical operators. If, as above, we let p and q represent *boolean* values, then:

$p <= q$	implication	$(p \Rightarrow q)$
$p = q$	equivalence	$(p \equiv q)$
$p <> q$	exclusive **or**	$(p$ **and not** $q)$ **or** $(q$ **and not** $p)$

Several relationships come in handy for simplifying *boolean* expressions. The *distributive* laws are:

$(p$ **or** $r)$ **and** $(q$ **or** $r)$ equals $(p$ **and** $q)$ **or** r
$(p$ **and** $r)$ **or** $(q$ **and** $r)$ equals $(p$ **or** $q)$ **and** r

De Morgan's laws serve a similar purpose:

$(\textbf{not}\ p)$ **and** $(\textbf{not}\ q)$ equals   **not** $(p$ **or** $q)$
$(\textbf{not}\ p)$ **or** $(\textbf{not}\ q)$ equals   **not** $(p$ **and** $q)$

A3-1.4 char

Like the *integer* type, *char* specifies an implementation-defined subset; but of the set of characters. There are many different kinds of characters (upper- and lower-case letters, digits, punctuation marks, etc.) and not all of them are required to be visible (the non-printing ones are usually called **control** charac-

chr A37

ters, and are summoned up with the *chr* function).

There are a number of 'standard' character sets, whose members vary because of manufacturers' machine limitations (like the 64-character CDC set), or because of a perceived commercial advantage in introducing a new set. Even character sets that are accepted and employed internationally (like the ISO character set) allow national variants so that, where possible, natural languages will not be discriminated against. But no matter what character set a processor accepts, the individual characters go in an order that preserves these relationships:

1)   The characters that represent the digits 0 through 9 must be numerically

ord function A36

ordered and contiguous. Thus:

$ord\,('1')-ord\,('0') = 1$

2)   The characters that represent the upper-case letters A through Z—if they are available—must be alphabetically ordered, but not necessarily contiguous. Thus:

$ord\,('B')-ord\,('A') >= 1$

3)   The characters that represent the lower-case letters a through z—again, if they are available—also must be alphabetically ordered, but not necessarily contiguous. Again:

$ord\,('b')-ord\,('a') >= 1.$

Although the characters each set contains are defined by its respective standard, their ordering is implementation-defined (except as constrained by the rules given above). This order is called the character set's *collating sequence*. The collating sequence is the basis of any comparison between *char* values. As a result, the relations ´a´<´b´, ´a´<>´b´, and ´b´>´a´ are always *true*, but ´A´<´b´ and ´a´<´B´ are implementation-dependent.[5]

When characters are used as *char* data values within a program, they must be enclosed between single quote marks. This indicates that they're being employed as **constants** (members) of type *char*, and that any other meaning they might have as symbols, identifiers, or constants of another type should be ignored. For example:

> ´4´ is the *char* value 4, and not the *integer* 4.
> ´*´ is the character *, and not the multiplication symbol *.

The single quote *char*-value is a special case. It is defined as an **apostrophe**-*image*, like this:

> *apostrophe-image* = ´ ´´´ ´ .

When it is used as a constant of type *char*, the apostrophe-image must still be enclosed within single quotes. This statement prints a single quote character:

> *writeln* (´´´´)

There is no null string in Pascal.

A3-2 Required Functions

about functions A76-A78

A Pascal function computes and returns a value of a simple type. Several functions must be predefined in every implementation, and are called *required functions*. Every processor may recognize additional functions (like clock or random-number functions), but they may not be required.

Functions are predefined in Pascal (and in most programming languages) for a variety of reasons. First, they rescue the programmer from the death of a thousand cuts—the necessity of writing the code of frequently required computations (like the trigonometric and logarithmic functions). Second, it's usually assumed that particularly accurate (and efficient) versions of these algorithms will be implemented. Finally, certain required functions act as magical windows into a program or implementation. They do not necessarily obey the restrictions placed on programmer-defined functions.

---

[5] Incidentally, in the ASCII character set the letters of both the upper-case and lower-case character sets are contiguous. In the EBCDIC set, neither case is. In all circumstances, of course, the letters are in alphabetical order.

The required functions are grouped in the categories *arithmetic*, *transfer*, *ordinal*, and *boolean*. I've used the following terminology in their explanations: a function f is given an argument (usually called x). The value represented by $f(x)$ is the result of evaluating the function call. You'll notice that the type of the function's result frequently differs from the type of its argument.

A3-2.1 Arithmetic Functions

Except as noted, the arithmetic functions may be given either *integer* or *real* arguments. Their result types are shown.

sqr (x) Computes the value x^2 (or $x*x$). The result is of the same type as x. It is an error if this value doesn't exist.

sqrt (x) Determines the square root of x. Its result is a non-negative *real*. It is an error if x is negative.

abs (x) Computes the absolute value of x ($|x|$). The result is of the same type as x.

sin (x), *cos* (x) These functions represent the sine and cosine of x, respectively, where x is given in radians. The result is always *real*.

arctan (x) Computes the principal value of the inverse trigonometric function arctangent. The *real* result is in radians.[6]

exp (x) The exponential function; computes e to the power x. The result is of type *real*.

ln (x) Computes the *real* natural logarithm of x. It is an error for x to be less than or equal to zero.[7]

A3-2.2 Transfer Functions

A few of Pascal's required functions do not have common mathematical counterparts. The **transfer** functions are used for *real* coercion; they represent their *real* arguments as *integers*. For both functions below, it is an error if the result is not in the *integers* (i.e. the range *−maxint..maxint*).

trunc (x) The truncating function takes a *real* argument and returns its *integer* portion; i.e. the greatest *integer* less than or equal to x for $x \geq 0$, and the least *integer* greater than or equal to x for $x < 0$.

> *trunc* (2.5) represents 2
> *trunc* (−2.5) represents −2
> *trunc* (2.5074e2) represents 250

---

[6] The other trigonometric functions can be built up in terms of these three. For example, tangent=sine/cosine, secant=1/cosine, etc. Incidentally, the Standard doesn't prescribe this but *arctan* is usually evaluated over the range $[-\pi/2, \pi/2]$.

[7] Although it may not be the most efficient method, the *ln* and *exp* functions are easily used to perform exponentiation. For example, b to the power x can be expressed as $exp(x*ln(b))$.

round (x) Represents x rounded to the nearest *integer* according to this rule: if x is greater than or equal to zero, then *round* (x) equals *trunc* (x + 0.5), and if x is less than zero, then *round* (x) equals *trunc* (x − 0.5).

> *round* (2.5) represents 3
> *round* (−2.5) represents −3
> *round* (2.5074e2) represents 251

A3-2.3 Ordinal Functions

The ordinal types (the simple types other than *real*) are enumerable, which means that their values can be numbered, in order, starting with 0.[8] This suggests a need for functions that describe the ordering relationship between different values of a given type.

ord (x) The **ordinal position** function takes an argument of any ordinal type, and returns as a result the ordinal number of that value within that type. For example, *ord* (*true*) is 1, since type *boolean* is defined as (*false, true*).

succ (x) The *successor* function takes an argument of any ordinal type, and returns the type's next value—the value whose ordinal number is one greater. It is an error if no next value exists.

> *succ* (9) represents 10
> *succ* ('8') is '9'
> *succ* ('9') is implementation-defined, and may be an error
> *succ* (*true*) is an error
> *succ* (*maxint*) is an error

pred (x) The **predecessor** function is the inverse of *succ* . Its result is the value that immediately precedes the ordinal argument x —the value whose ordinal number is one less. Again, it is an error if no such value exists.

> *pred* (9) represents 8
> *pred* ('9') represents '8'
> *pred* (*succ* ('R')) represents 'R'
> *pred* (*false*) is an error
> *pred* (*chr* (9)) is implementation-defined
> *pred* ('a') is implementation-defined, and may be an error

chr (x) The *chr* function takes an *integer* argument. It returns the *char* value whose ordinal number equals x, if such a character exists. It is an error otherwise.

---

[8] Except *integer* , where each number describes its own ordinal position.

When considered in terms of type *char*, *ord* and *chr* are inverse functions—what one does, the other can undo. Thus:

$$chr\,(ord\,(\text{'R'}))\ \text{represents 'R'}$$

A3-2.4 *boolean* Functions

The three final required functions have *boolean*-valued results. The first (*odd*) is easily described, but the others (*eoln* and *eof*) are explained in further detail in section A11-4.

odd (*x*) The *odd* function takes an *integer* argument. Its *boolean* result is *true* if *x* is odd (more precisely, if (*abs* (*x*) **mod** 2) equals 1), and *false* otherwise.

buffer variables A127

eoln (*f*) The end-of-line function has the value *true* if the file buffer variable *f* ↑ is positioned at the end of a line in the textfile *f*, and is *false* otherwise. It is an error to call *eoln* (*f*) if *f* is undefined, or if *eof* (*f*) is *true*. If an argument textfile (like *f*) is not specified, *eoln* applies to the required file *input*.

input A131-A132

eof (*f*) The end-of-file function has the value *true* only if the current file buffer variable *f* ↑ is positioned at the last component of the file *f*, or if *f* is empty. The call *eof* (*f*) is an error if *f* is undefined. If no file argument is given, *eof* applies to file *input*.

Simple Expressions

In Pascal, as in algebra, any given value can be shown in a variety of ways. The representation of a value is called an *expression*. All of these are expressions, even though not all of them contain operators, or even identifiers:[1]

    10
    sqrt (7)
    ord ('K')+7
    p **and** q
    (17*(−5)) **mod** Quotient
    Matrix [10,27]
    Box.Bin [3]−IntegerFile ↑

The explanation of expressions is an explanation of *operators* and *operands*, and of the order in which they are *evaluated*. A trivial expression like (10) is easily evaluated, and (1+1) isn't much harder. However, the ambiguity that can arise in more complex expressions (does 10−3*2 equal 4 or 14?) must be resolved by a scheme of **operator precedence**. Expressions are evaluated according these rules:

1)   The *boolean* operator **not** has the highest precedence.

2)   The *multiplying* operators *, /, **div**, **mod**, and **and** are employed next.[2]

3)   The *adding* operators +, −, and **or** have lower precedence.

4)   The *relational* operators =, <>, <, >, <=, >=, and **in** have the least precedence.

Parentheses can be used to circumvent the operator precedence rules. For example:

    2*3−4 equals 2, but ... 2*(3−4) equals −2

In the absence of parentheses, a sequence of two or more operators of equal precedence is **left associative**. This means, for example, that 3−2−1 is the semantic equivalent of (3−2)−1.

The order of operand evaluation of a *dyadic* operator (an operator that requires two operands) is implementation-dependent. This is an important qualification, because it means the operands may be evaluated from left to right

---

[1] The expressions we'll deal with in this section all represent simple values. However, expressions can represent structured values as well.

[2] The notion of precedence cuts across type lines—the *real* operator /, *integer* operator **div**, *boolean* operator **and**, and set operator * are all multiplying operators.

(in textual order), from right to left, simultaneously, or they might not both be evaluated.

The last possibility can occur when evaluating one operand is enough to give a value to the whole expression. For instance, the expression $0*x$ need not be fully evaluated, since it always equals 0 (unless x isn't a number). A more likely case of truncated evaluation would involve the *boolean* operators **and** and **or** . This statement relies on truncated evaluation:

> **if** $(x <> 0)$ **and** $(i / x > Limit)$
> **then** *CallProcedure*

Some processors, recognizing that the entire expression is *false* if x equals zero (because both operands of **and** must be *true* for the entire expression to be *true*), can execute this statement without trouble (since the *boolean* expression is *not* fully evaluated).[3] Processors that do full evaluation, on the other hand, will try to find the value of i / x —an error if x equals 0.0.

The punch line is that when portability is a concern, making the order of evaluation implementation-dependent loosens requirements for processors without really relaxing them for programs. Although some processors may choose to partially evaluate certain expressions, the fact that other processors fully evaluate *all* expressions makes it necessary, in practical terms, to program as though this were always the case.[4]

A4-1 BNF of Expressions

A fairly complicated sequence of BNF productions codifies the scheme of operator precedence described above. First, we have to categorize some special-symbols and word-symbols:

> *multiplying-operator* = '*' | '/' | '**div**' | '**mod**' | '**and**' .
> *adding-operator* = '+' | '−' | '**or**' .
> *relational-operator* = '=' | '<>' | '<' | '>' | '<=' | '>=' | '**in**' .

These productions establish distinct levels of precedence, given from second-highest (multiplying operators) to lowest (relational operators). The first and highest level is occupied by the **not** operator.

The meta-identifiers *multiplying-operator* and *adding-operator* are phrases of convenience that are only marginally related to multiplication and addition. For example, '*' might be the *real* multiplication operator, the *integer* multiplication operator, or the set intersection operator, depending on the types of its

---

[3] Assuming that they evaluate expressions in textual order.
[4] In contrast to Pascal, a language like C specifically requires that evaluation proceed from left to right, and that the evaluation of *boolean* expressions cease when the result is known.

operands. The meaning of such operators is said to be *context-dependent*.

The BNF of an expression is set up in a clever way that associates each level of the operator hierarchy with a particular breed of subexpression. The more 'irreducible' a subexpression is, the higher is the precedence of any operators its BNF allows. A *factor*, which can include the **not** operator, is the most elemental expression. A *term* may be a factor, or it can be two or more factors joined by a multiplying operator. A *simple-expression*, in turn, can be a term (which implies that it might even be a mere factor), or it can be formed from (possibly signed) terms and adding operators. Finally, an honest-to-goodness *expression* may be a simple-expression, or a term, or a factor, or any pair of these along with a relational operator.[5]

> *expression* = *simple-expression* [*relational-operator simple-expression*] .
> *simple-expression* = [*sign*] *term* { *adding-operator term* } .
> *term* = *factor* { *multiplying-operator factor* } .
> *factor* > *variable-access* | *unsigned-constant* | *function-designator* | *set-constructor*
> | '(' *expression* ')' | '**not**' *factor* .

Notice a neat trick in the definition of *factor*. When an expression is enclosed in parentheses, it reverts to the humble status of a factor. Because the definition of an expression is *recursive*—circular, because it relies on its own definition—the length of expressions is not limited.[6]

Tracing the BNF of a factor requires some legwork. '(' *expression* ')' and **not** *factor* are self-referencing, and don't add much light. A *function-designator* is a function call—a function's identifier, along with any arguments that are required. *Set-constructors* denote set-type values, and are discussed in section A11-3. An *unsigned-constant* is:

about functions A76-A78

> *unsigned-constant* = *unsigned-number* | *character-string* | *constant-identifier* | '**nil**' .
> *unsigned-number* = *unsigned-integer* | *unsigned-real* .

An *unsigned-number* is a value of type *integer* or *real* that's shown with actual numbers (e.g. 739 or 1.093). A *character-string* is a string-type value—a sequence of two or more characters between single-quote marks (like 'Patti'). *Constant-identifier* has a double meaning. It is either a declared constant, or one value of an ordinal type. The final unsigned-constant, **nil**, is a word-symbol that belongs to a pointer-type determined by context.

strings A117-A119

*about constants
A65-A66, A98*

pointer types A136-A142

---

[5] Pascal's BNF for expressions, simple-expressions, etc., is interesting because it attempts to clarify a *semantic* issue (the precedence of operators) with a *syntactic* tool (the BNF). However, the parse tree produced by following the BNF correctly reflects the precedence of operators in Pascal expressions. A simpler BNF (say, *expression* = *factor* { *operator factor* } .) would produce almost no useful information.

[6] Also note that since *factor* is defined with a '>', it has an alternative BNF—a factor may also be a conformant array parameter's *bound-identifier*. See section A9-5.

The *variable-access* BNF takes us further afield:

variable-access = entire-variable | component-variable | identified-variable | buffer-variable .

A variable-access is a name that denotes a variable. We'll see in section A8-2 that this isn't necessarily an identifier—variables may require 'manufactured' names, or may even be anonymous.

It is an error for an undefined variable-access to appear in an expression. In this situation error status is granted largely because it is so difficult to determine whether or not a variable has been initialized.

We can develop the syntax chart of an expression like this:

factor

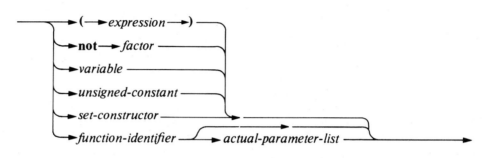

term

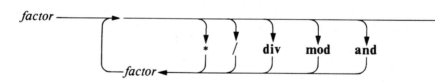

simple-expression

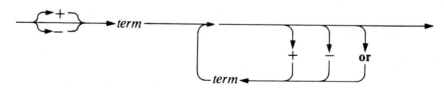

expression

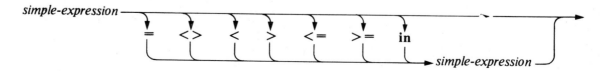

Some examples are:

factors

> 5
> [1..10, 20..30]
> *Scale* [7]
> **not** $(x = 5)$
> *maxint*

terms

> 5∗10
> $(2-n)/z$
> (*First* <*Second*) **and not** *Finished*

simple-expressions

> **not** $(x = 5)$ **or** (*First* <*Second*) **and not** *Finished*
> 2+2
> *Scale* [7]

expressions

> $p <= q$
> *input*↑ **in** ['A'..'Z']

A4-2 Operators

As noted before, the four levels of operator precedence are:

not						*greatest*
div	**mod**	**and**	∗	/		
or	+	–				
in	=	<>	<	>	<=	>=	*least*

The arithmetic operators were discussed in section A3-1 as they related to values of type *real* and *integer*. The actions of the *monadic*—one-operand—arithmetic operators are summarized in Table 1, and those of the *dyadic*—two-operand—arithmetic operators are given in Table 2. Some symbols (like '+', '–', and '∗') serve double or even triple duty.

Table 1. Monadic Arithmetic Operators

operator	operation	type of operand	type of result
+	identity	*integer*	*integer*
		real	*real*
–	sign inversion	*integer*	*integer*
		real	*real*

operator	operation	type of operands	type of result
		Table 2. Dyadic Arithmetic Operators	
+	addition	*integer* or *real*	*integer* if both operands are *integer*, otherwise *real*
–	subtraction	*integer* or *real*	
*	multiplication	*integer* or *real*	
/	division	*integer* or *real*	*real*
div	truncated division	*integer*	*integer*
mod	modulo	*integer*	*integer*

Table 3 shows the *boolean* operators. Recall that the relational operators also have *boolean* result values.

operator	operation	type of operands	type of result
		Table 3. Boolean Operators	
not	negation	*boolean*	*boolean*
or	disjunction	*boolean*	*boolean*
and	conjunction	*boolean*	*boolean*

The set operators are given in Table 4. They are discussed in detail in section A11-3, as is the mysterious phrase 'canonical set-of-*T* type.'

operator	operation	type of operands	type of result
		Table 4. Set Operators	
+	set union	any canonical set-of-*T* type	same as the operands
–	set difference		
*	set intersection		

An operator that is noticeable by its absence from Pascal is exponentiation. Wirth deliberately omitted an exponentiation operator on the grounds that it would complicate the processor with no corresponding gain in program efficiency. An exponentiation operator has been proposed as a nonstandard extension.

A4-2.1 Relational Operators

The **relational** operators of Table 5 take a variety of operands, but always yield *boolean* result values.

	Table 5. Relational Operators	
operator	*type of operands*	*type of result*
= <>	any simple, pointer, or string type, or a canonical set-of-*T* type	*boolean*
< >	any simple or string type	*boolean*
<= >=	any simple or string type, or a canonical set-of-*T* type	*boolean*
in	left operand: any ordinal type *T* right operand: a canonical set-of-*T* type	*boolean*

special symbols A3

Some of the relational operators that require a single symbol in mathematical notation are constructed from two characters in Pascal. They're still special-symbols, though, and may not be split by spaces or other separators.

Pascal	Math	English
<>	$\neq$	not equal
<=	$\leq$	less than or equal
>=	$\geq$	greater than or equal

compatible types A10-A11

With various restrictions, different relational operators (besides **in**) can compare values of any compatible simple type, pointer type, string type, or set type. Because of the implicit coercion of *integer* values into *reals*, values of these two types may be compared. Comparisons between other ordinal-type values are based on the ordering of values in the definition of the type. Thus, an expression like ('a'<'A') might be either *false* or *true*, depending on the ordering of the implementation-defined *char* type. The expression ('a'<5) is a violation, since 'a' and 5 are values of different types.

Since *boolean* expressions represent values of the ordinal type *boolean*—whose values are *false, true*—they can be used as operands of the relational operators. Suppose, as usual, that *p* and *q* are *boolean* expressions. Then:

Expression	Meaning
p =*q*	equivalence
p <>*q*	exclusive or
p <=*q*	*p* implies *q*

Under no circumstances can the relational operators be used as they are in ordinary mathematics. For example, the mathematical expression:

$$5 < x \le 10$$

is interpreted as $(5<x)<=10$, which is a violation in Pascal (it compares *boolean* to *integer*). It is rewritten correctly as:

$$(5<x) \textbf{ and } (x<=10)$$

strings A117-A119   The relational operators can also compare string-type values if, and only if, each string has the same number of characters, which makes the strings compatible. The comparison is **lexicographic**, which is a formal way of saying alphabetical. The distinction is lost on an expression like:

$$\text{'cat'} < \text{'dog'}$$

which is obviously *true*, but is necessary to evaluate expressions like:

$$\text{'@\&\#!?!!'} >= \text{'+-<>\%\~('}$$

Lexicographic ordering is determined by the order of the collating sequence of the constants of the implementation-defined type *char*.

set types A121-A125   The use of relational operators with set-type operands is somewhat different, since set values aren't ordered. Suppose that u and v are simple-expressions of some set type. Then:

Expression	Meaning
$u = v$	every element of u and v is identical
$u <> v$	at least one element of u and v differs
$u <= v$	every element of u is in v
$u >= v$	every element of v is in u

The **in** operator creates an expression that is *true* if a given ordinal value is an element of a set of values of a compatible ordinal type. The **in** operator's right operand is a set-type value, and its left operand is an ordinal value. The expression:

$$\textit{Letter } \textbf{in} \; [\text{'A'} .. \text{'F'}, \textit{Pass} .. \textit{Fail}]$$

is valid if *Letter, Pass*, and *Fail* all belong to a type compatible with *char* (e.g., a subrange or renaming of *char*). Relational expressions that involve set operands are discussed further in section A11-3.

about pointers A136-A142   Finally, pointers may be compared to each other, or to the pointer value **nil**. Only the equality ($=$) and inequality ($<>$) operators may be used—there is no way to determine the relative ordering of two pointers.

Textfile Input and Output[1]

To most program users, the only salient feature of a language definition is its specification for the input of data, and the output of results. The average nonprogrammer would probably be hard-pressed to distinguish between a computer and the peripheral hardware it uses to communicate with humans.

We can divide most of the hardware into two categories. *Input devices* route information into a running program. There are many such devices— teletype keyboards, punched card readers, magnetic or paper tape readers, light pens, videoterminal keyboards. If they're suitably fitted with analog-to-digital converters, then gauges, sensors, thermometers, detectors, meters, and measuring devices of every description can also be input devices. Even a radio that relays a rocket guidance computer's flight instructions is an input device.

Output devices display the partial or final results of a running program. Videoterminal screens, lineprinters, paper tape and card punches, teletype platens and keys, typesetting machines, graphics terminals—even radio transmitters—are all output devices. Note that many pieces of equipment we usually think of as being a single device (like a videoterminal and its keyboard), are actually two entirely independent devices in a single box.

Since there are great differences between many input and output devices, the idea that a Pascal Standard should or could require particular devices is silly. Instead, the Standard requires that every processor have so-called 'standard' input and output devices that have the characteristics of *textfiles*, and that these devices should provide 'legible input and output.'[2]

For now, it's sufficient to say that the standard input and output devices both use the same character set for communication with programs—the implementation-defined group of characters that forms the required type *char*. Their application within a program is signaled by the appearance of the required identifiers *input* and *output* as program parameters, e.g.:

---

[1] This section is not intended to supplant the discussion of file types, but to provide a reasonable explanation of textfile I/O to readers who are totally unfamiliar with the intricacies of files in Pascal. Aside from the description of output format, it is recapitulated in more formal terms in section A11-4.

[2] A file of the required type *text* is a textfile. Such files have the characteristics of the type **file of** *char*, i.e. of file structures with *char*-valued components. However, special functions and procedures (*eoln, readln, writeln*, and *page*) are defined for textfiles alone.

program *Foo (input, output)*;

although neither must appear if it is not used within the program.

Four required procedures maintain contact between a program and its operating environment. To a certain extent they depend on input and output devices to recognize *lines* of data. The basic input procedure *read* gets values for its argument variables, while a corresponding output procedure named *write* arranges to print its argument values. The second input procedure, *readln* ('read line'), can be used to discard partial or full input lines, as well as to read values à la *read*. Similarly, a second output procedure called *writeln* ('write line') controls the production of distinct lines of output, as well as printing like *write*.

Although many of the devices we mentioned earlier don't deal with lines as such, many computers benefit from the **buffering** that line structure allows. Input or output data can be collected, and transmitted, in more efficient packages than a required character-by-character update would allow.

Another convenience implemented by Pascal's I/O mechanism is the conversion of *real, integer*, and, for output only, *boolean* values, between a binary internal representation and the *char* representation needed by textfiles. For example, a program that is attempting to read in the value of a *real*-type variable recognizes the special sequence of *char*-type digits and characters that denotes *real* values, and automatically converts it to its *real* equivalent. Similarly, *real* values can be output (as a sequence of characters) in either floating-point or fixed-point decimal notation.

Remember that automatic conversion to *char* representation is only enjoyed by values of the required simple types. Since enumerated ordinal types have no external character representation they can neither be read from a Pascal program's standard input, nor written to its standard output.[3]

enumerated types A97-A99
external representation A48

A5-1 Input

parameter lists A79

The required procedures *read* and *readln* allow program input. Although *read* and *readln* are procedure identifiers, the BNFs of their parameter lists are different from those for ordinary parameter-lists:

read-parameter-list = '(' [*file-variable* ','] *variable-access* { ',' *variable-access* } ')' .
readln-parameter-list = ['(' (*file-variable* | *variable-access*) { ',' *variable-access* } ')'] .

Notice that the readln-parameter-list is optional—*readln* need not be given any arguments. The BNF productions are a bit easier to follow in these charts, which show the syntax of legal calls of *read* and *readln*.

---

[3] However, allowing an external character representation for enumerated ordinal values has been frequently proposed (and sometimes implemented) as a nonstandard extension to Pascal. Note that type *boolean* is, in effect, one enumeration for which such an output conversion exists.

read call

readln call

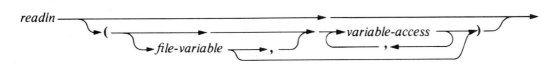

about files A125-A135

The call *read* (*f, V*) reads a value for variable *V* from file *f*. At least one variable-access (like *V*) must be specified, but a file-variable argument (like *f*) need not be given. If none is supplied, the value is read from the required file *input*.[4]

The call *readln* (*f, V*) also reads a value for variable *V* from file *f*, which must be a textfile. If a file-variable isn't supplied, input again comes from the required file *input*. However, a variable-access argument need not be given.

end-of-line A132

readln differs from *read* in the following manner: When a call of *readln* is completed, any values remaining on the current input line (including the end-of-line) are discarded. The next value read will be the first value on the next line of file *f* (or *input*). If no variable-access is supplied as an argument to *readln*, the current line of input will be discarded (even if it only contains an end-of-line).

A call of *read*, in contrast, does not affect any values left on the current input line. The next value to be read will be the value that immediately follows the last value obtained during the current call of *read*.

Now, when *read* or *readln* obtains a value or values for its argument variable or variables, the line structure of file *f* (or *input*, if *f* isn't named) is ignored. As a result, input data may be spread over two or more lines without ill effect.

1) If *integer* or *real* data are being input, the end-of-line (as well as all blank spaces) serves as a value separator.

2) If *char* values are being read, the end-of-line 'character' is read as a blank space.

Both *read* and *readln* may be given more than one variable-access argument. The call:

$$read\ (f,\ V1,\ V2,\ \cdots,\ Vn)$$

[4] Reading from files in general is discussed in section A11-4.

is equivalent to the sequence:

> **begin** *read (f, V1)*; *read (f, V2)*; $\cdots$; *read (f, Vn)* **end**

Similarly, the call:

> *readln (f, V1, V2, $\cdots$, Vn)*

can be duplicated as:[5]

> **begin** *read (f, V1)*; *read (f, V2)*; $\cdots$; *read (f, Vn)*; *readln (f)* **end**

A5-1.1 Coercion of Input Data

textfiles A131-A134

All data obtained from the required file *input*, or from any other textfile, is of type *char*. As a result, reading in values for *char*-type variables doesn't require any special handling by the processor.

Getting the value of an *integer* variable needs more consideration. The processor first skips over blank spaces and end-of-lines, because when they're not being read as *char* values they just serve as value separators. Then it reads

signed integer A5

the longest sequence of characters that forms a signed *integer*. The first nondigit encountered (after a possible leading sign character) marks the end of the *integer*. This nondigit will be the first character inspected by a subsequent call of *read* or *readln*.

Input of *real* values is handled the same way. First, blanks and end-of-lines are skipped. Then, the longest sequence of characters that forms a

signed numbers A5

signed-number is read in, 'converted,' and attributed to *read* or *readln's* variable-access argument Why look for a signed-number, rather than a signed-*real*? Because an *integer* value, as well as a *real* value, can be read into a *real* variable.

What if the first nonblank (or non-end-of-line) encountered during an attempted *integer* or *real* read isn't a sign character or a digit? This would make the *read* (or *readln*) unable to read a numerical value for its argument. The Standard specifically states that this is an error, rather than a violation. Similarly, it is an error, rather than a violation, if a number isn't assignment compatible with the variable it is being attributed to. The motivation for making these errors is that they can't be detected until run-time. They are very likely to be detected as violations, though, and halt execution.

A5-1.2 Dealing with the end-of-line

The following program scheme is used for reading *real* or *integer* data from a textfile *f* that (aside from spaces or end-of-lines used as value separators) does not contain extraneous nonnumerical characters. It relies heavily on details introduced in the discussion of file types in section A11-4.

[5] As a result (and speaking as a Salesman) calls of the form *readln (i, A[i])* do the right thing.

```
{Process a file of integer or real values.}
SkipBlanks (f);
while not eof (f)
    do begin
        read (f, Data);
        Process (Data);
        SkipBlanks (f)
    end
```

where the declaration of *SkipBlanks* is:

```
procedure SkipBlanks (var f: text);
        {Skips blanks until eof (f), or a nonblank is found.}
    var Finished: boolean;
    begin
        Finished := false;
        repeat
            if eof (f) then Finished := true
                        else if f ↑=' ' then get (f)
                                        else Finished := true
        until Finished
    end;  {SkipBlanks}
```

Note that the widely used formulation shown below (and orginally proposed in [J&W]) contains an error—it will eventually attempt to inspect the (undefined) file buffer variable when *eof* is *true*.[6]

```
procedure BadSkipBlanks (var f: text);
        {Incorrect way to skip blanks.}
    begin
        while (f ↑=' ') and not eof (f)
            do get (f)
    end;
```

As I mentioned earlier, when *char* values are read from a textfile, the end-of-line is treated as though it were an ordinary space. Thus, if *C1*, *C2*, etc., are *char* variables, the call:

```
read (C1, C2, C3, C4, C5)
```

when given this input:

```
go<newline>
toot  your<newline>
horn.<newline>
```

---

[6] This is because every textfile ends with at least one end-of-line. Thus, *eof* is not *true* immediately after the final number has been read. Frankly, this is a very confusing point—the incorrect [J&W] procedure (renamed *BadSkipBlanks*) that appeared in their second edition was *itself* a correction of an incorrect model given in the first edition!

will read these letters:

'g'   'o'   ' '   't'   'o'

The end-of-line (shown as <*newline*>) was attributed to *C3* as a blank space. The letter about to be read (by another call of *read* or *readln*) is the second 'o' of toot.

Suppose, instead, that we make the call:

readln (C1, C2, C3, C4, C5)

The assignment of values to *C1, C2*, and the others will be the same as they were before. However, the final effect of *readln* is to discard the remainder of the second input line. The character about to be read after the call is the 'h' that starts 'horn.'

Procedure *readln* provides a simpler scheme (that doesn't require a procedure like *SkipBlanks*) for reading unknown quantities of *real, integer*, or *char* input from a textfile *f*—if we know the number, and types, of the data values on each line:

    {Process a file of *real, integer*, or *char* data.}
    while not *eof (f)*
      do begin
        readln (f, V1, ··· , Vn);
        Process (V1, ··· , Vn)
      end

read and *readln* are described in terms of more primitive procedures in section A11-4.

A5-2 Output

It is a rare program that does not have output. Even programs that check the validity of data (or of Pascal processors) and are mainly intended to warn of violations or errors should (and usually do) issue a positive validation if no mistakes are found. A result that says 'All O.K.' is, somehow, much more reassuring than no output at all.

strings A117-A119

Output to textfiles (including the standard output) is restricted to values of the required simple types (*real, integer, char*, and *boolean*), and of the string-types. These values are all said to have **external character representations**; they are automatically 'converted' to, and output in terms of, an implementation-defined character set. Although the required output procedures *write* and *writeln* don't have BNF descriptions (after all, they're just identifiers), their parameter-lists do:

write-parameter-list = '(' [*file-variable* ','] *write-parameter* { ',' *write-parameter* } ')' .
writeln-parameter-list = ['(' (*file-variable* | *write-parameter*) { ',' *write-parameter* } ')'] .
write-parameter = *expression* [':' *expression* [':' *expression*]] .

The optional portions of a write-parameter are used to specify output format. As usual, a chart of valid calls of *write* and *writeln* clarifies matters.

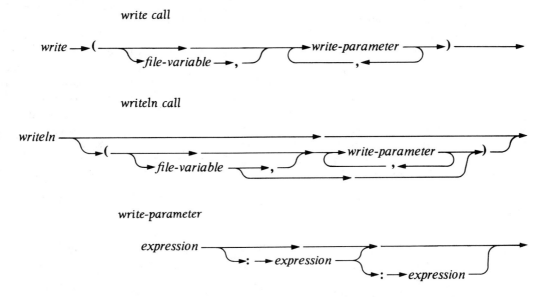

write call

writeln call

write-parameter

Although a file-variable may be named specifically (it must be a textfile for *writeln*), we'll assume throughout this section that no file is given, which means that the call of *write* or *writeln* applies to the required file *output*.

output A131-A132

write collects (or possibly prints) partial output lines, while *writeln* appends an end-of-line component to the partially collected line (which includes any write-parameters that accompanied the *writeln* call). In practical terms, *write* can often be assumed to *buffer* its output—hold it temporarily—while *writeln* actually causes the printing of a complete line of output.[7] Thus, the segment:

end-of-line A132

> *write* ('Enter data');
> *read* (Data)

may halt for input without ever printing the prompt! The *write* should be replaced by a *writeln*.

---

[7] The tidy scheme I describe pours well, but it may lack a certain syrup. Although *writeln* does, and *write* does not, append an end-of-line to each line, the actual time of output of a *write* or *writeln* can vary widely between implementations. It is possible for the output of both to be entirely unbuffered (and printed immediately), or be buffered in blocks of some convenient size (and not printed until the buffer is full). A more subtle variation uses block buffering, but flushes the buffer whenever *input* is inspected (perhaps with a *read* or *readln*).

I chose the simple model (where *writeln* prints and *write* doesn't) because it conforms to the Standard, it is often implemented, and it clearly motivates the different rationales behind *write* and *writeln*.

A call of *writeln*, with no arguments for output, ejects any current partial line (the result of previous calls of *write*) by appending an end-of-line to it. Incidentally, this is the only way an end-of-line can be generated. If there isn't a partial line pending, and if there aren't any write-parameters, the *writeln* call prints a blank line—a line whose only component is the end-of-line.

Readers familiar with interactive videoterminals will realize that the buffer scheme causes a slight problem. Many applications require the cursor to remain at the end of the current output line. If output is buffered, though, it may not appear until a call of *writeln* moves the cursor to the next line. Fortunately, the Standard doesn't require *write* to buffer its partial lines—partial lines may be printed while they're being collected. If their processors work this way, authors of (possibly nonportable) menu programs can heave a sigh of relief.

As the BNF and charts show, both *write* and *writeln* can be given a series of expression write-parameters for output. The statement:

write (V1, V2, ··· , Vn)

is equivalent to:

begin *write* (V1); *write* (V2); ··· ; *write* (Vn) **end**

Similarly, the call:

writeln (V1, V2, ··· , Vn)

can be duplicated as:

begin *write* (V1); *write* (V2); ··· ; *write* (Vn); *writeln* **end**

A5-2.1 Output Formats

To help produce neat columns or tables, all printed output is treated as though it is right-aligned in a Procrustean *field* of blank spaces. If the field is larger than the output value, blank spaces are added to the value's left (except in floating-point *real* output). In most cases, if the field is too small, characters may be lopped from the value's right end until it fits. The actual field width may be specified like this:

e :*TotalWidth*

where *e* is an *integer, real, char, boolean*, or string-type expression. *TotalWidth* is an expression that represents a positive *integer* amount. It is an error for *TotalWidth* to be less than 1. (We will also see that a *real* expression may be given an additional *FractionalDigits* parameter that allows fixed-point notation.)

Default field widths are implementation-defined for *integer, real*, and *boolean*-type values, and are prescribed for *char* and string-type values. The default field width is applied unless a colon and *TotalWidth* value follow the output expression.

Char-type expressions, by default, are printed in a field of one space, which means that no blanks appear on either side. If the *char* expression is followed by a colon, and a value for *TotalWidth*, the character is preceded by *TotalWidth*–1 spaces when it is printed. Assume that $c1:='a'$, $c2:='b'$, and $c3:='c'$. A blank space is shown for examples in this section as '_'.[8]

writeln $(c1:1,\ c2:2,\ c3:3,\ 'A':4,\ 'B':5,\ 'C':6)$

a_b__c___A____B_____C

Integer expressions are a bit more complicated. The default field width of an *integer* is implementation-defined (but is often the number of digits in *maxint*, plus one for a sign). All the digits of an *integer*-valued expression (preceded by a minus sign if it is negative) are printed, even if a *TotalWidth* argument is smaller than necessary. If *TotalWidth* exceeds the number of digits in the expression (plus one if it's negative), the extra spaces precede the expression when it's printed.[9] Assume that $e1$, below, equals 22:

writeln $(e1:1,\ -e1:1,\ e1:5,\ e1:9,\ 5:1,\ 66:1,\ 777:1)$

22–22___22_____22566777

Boolean-valued expressions can also be output (although the *boolean* constants *false* and *true* can't be read in). The *boolean* expression is evaluated, and the character-string 'false' or 'true', as appropriate, is printed. The case (upper or lower) of each letter is implementation-defined, as is the default field width. The minimum number of characters is not printed if a *TotalWidth* value is too small—the rules pertaining to character-strings (below) are followed in such cases. As usual, extra spaces go to the left. Assume that $b1$ equals *true*:

writeln $(b1,\ 1=2,\ 1=1,\ false:1,\ true:10)$

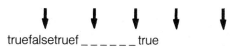

truefalsetruef_____true

---

[8] By the way, the write-parameter ' ':*n* represents a sequence of *n* blanks—it's a blank that's right-aligned in a field of *n* blanks.
[9] By the way, if an expression equals zero, it has one digit.

Character-strings and all other string-types (as well as values of type *boolean*) follow a special rule that lets them be truncated during output. The default field width for an *n*-character string is, naturally, *n* spaces. If a *TotalWidth* field specification is greater than *n*, then *TotalWidth–n* blanks are printed before the string. If, however, *TotalWidth* is less than *n*, only the first *TotalWidth* characters of the string are printed. As a result, characters may be missing from the right end of a string.

writeln ('Short,':2, 'although':5, 'getting':7, 'longer':10, ' ':5, *true*:3)

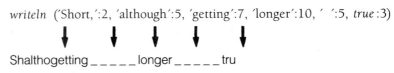

Shalthogetting _ _ _ _ _ longer _ _ _ _ _ tru

Output of *real*-type values is most complicated, because the value's format (fixed- or floating-point) can be specified. If *e* is a *real*-valued expression, then it may take two forms as a write-parameter:

$$e:TotalWidth \qquad\qquad e:TotalWidth:FractionalDigits$$

The left-hand format is used for floating-point *real* output; the right-hand option provides fixed-point output.

In floating-point representation, a *real* value *e* is written with a single non-zero digit to the left of the decimal point.[10] It takes this form:

1)   A minus sign (–) if *e* is less than 0, otherwise a blank space.

2)   The first non-zero digit of *e*.

3)   A period (.).

4)   Enough digits of *e* to fill out the *TotalWidth* field, leaving room for 5, 6, and 7, below.

5)   Either 'e' or 'E', the implementation-defined exponent character.

6)   The sign of the exponent (either '+' or '–').

7)   The exponent itself. The number of digits in the exponent is implementation-defined. If the exponent has fewer than this number of digits, it is preceded by one or more zeros.

Requirement 4 is slightly confusing. The default field width (i.e., the default value of *TotalWidth*) is usually chosen so that all significant digits of *e* are printed. However, a *TotalWidth* of any size may be specified. As a result, a large *TotalWidth* may result in spurious least-significant digits. Unlike other types of output, additional blanks do not precede the floating-point representation of *e*.

Fixed-point notation lets the programmer specify the number of digits that are to follow the decimal point. A write-parameter of the form:

$$e:TotalWidth:FractionalDigits$$

---

[10] In effect, the decimal always 'floats' to that position. Since a floating-point *real* is expressed as a power of ten, its exponent's value can change to make up for any change in magnitude.

is printed as:

1) *TotalWidth* – *MinimumCharacters* (defined below) blank spaces, if *TotalWidth* >= *MinimumCharacters*.

2) A minus sign (–) if *e* is less than 0.

3) The integer, or 'whole,' portion of *e*

4) A period (.).

5) *FractionalDigits* of the fractional portion of *e*.

where *MinimumCharacters* is *FractionalDigits*, plus the number of digits in *e's* integer portion, plus 1 (for the decimal place). If *e* is less than zero, increase *MinimumCharacters* by 1 (for the minus sign.). At least *MinimumCharacters* are always printed.

A6

Blocks, Scope, and Activations

The rules that relate to *blocks*, their *activation*, and the *scope* of the identifiers they contain, form one of the most impenetrable sections of the Standard. Primarily of interest to implementors, these rules attempt to pin down some aspects of Pascal that were ignored or assumed in [J&W].

The rules of scope and activations are probably difficult because they deal with broad program semantics, rather than with the syntax of individual structures or statements. Such rules are so basic to any programming language that their implications may not be obvious at first.

Unfortunately for programmers looking for clarification, many of the issues these rules address involve *pathological* program examples unlikely to be written by anybody but the most deranged syntax lawyers.[1] However (speaking as a Scholar), such programs need to be well-defined regardless of how unlikely they are to appear. It's best to plan ahead; as Lecarme and Desjardins point out:

'... you cannot prevent the user from writing silly programs, unless you prevent him from writing any program at all.' [Lecarme75]

A6-1 Blocks

Pascal is a **block-structured** language. A Pascal program can be seen as a collection of segments, called *blocks*, in which definitions and declarations are made, and program actions specified. The BNF involved is:

> *program* = *program-heading* ';' *program-block* '.' .
> *program-block* = *block* .
> *block* = *label-declaration-part*
>   *constant-definition-part*
>   *type-definition-part*
>   *variable-declaration-part*
>   *procedure-and-function-declaration-part*
>   *statement-part* .

---

[1] This term was added to the English language during the intense discussion of the ALGOL 60 standard. The debaters were first called (in a not unfriendly tone) ALGOL syntax lawyers, but eventually came to be known as ALGOL theologians.

program

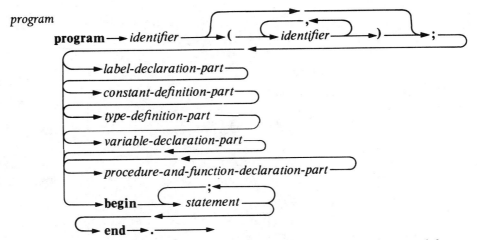

A program's first block is called the *program-block*, while procedures and functions consist (aside from their headings) of *procedure-blocks* and *function-blocks*, respectively. Since every block includes its own procedure and function declaration part, blocks can be *nested*—any block can contain other blocks. The maximum depth of such nesting is not specified by the Standard, but is often limited by a processor.

The BNF of a block's parts shows that (aside from the statement-part) they are all optional—each part's syntax is given between square brackets. Each part is analyzed in detail elsewhere.

label-declaration-part = ['**label**' *label* { ',' *label* } ';'] .
constant-definition-part = ['**const**' *constant-definition* ';' { *constant-definition* ';' }] .
type-definition-part = ['**type**' *type-definition* ';' { *type-definition* ';' }] .
variable-declaration-part = ['**var**' *variable-declaration* ';' { *variable-declaration* ';' }] .
procedure-and-function-declaration-part = { (*procedure-declaration* | *function-declaration*) ';' } .
statement-part = *compound-statement* .

labels A6, A13-A15   There is a special requirement that every label prefix a single statement in the statement-part of the block it is defined in. This is discussed along with the **goto** statement in section A2-3.

A6-2 Scope

For our purposes, blocks are important because they include the *defining-points* of labels, and constant, type, variable, procedure, and function identifiers. A block (and any blocks it contains) constitutes the *region* in which a label or identifier can retain its original meaning. This means that an identifier or label defined in the *program-block* (the block of the main program) will be recognized in any procedure or function declared within the program-block, as well as within any subprograms declared within those subprograms. Figure 1 shows the regions associated with defining points in several nested blocks. Notice that a region can contain other regions.

```
program A
procedure B
   procedure D
      begin {D}
        ...
      end; {D}
   begin {B}
     ...
   end; {B}
procedure C
   procedure E
      begin {E}
        ...
      end; {E}
   procedure F
      begin {F}
        ...
      end; {F}
   begin {C}
     ...
   end; {C}
begin {A}
  ...
end {A}
```

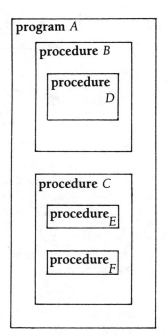

Figure 1

Identifiers and labels defined in:	Their region is blocks:
program A	A, B, C, D, E, F
procedure B	A, B, C, D, E, F
procedure C	B, D
procedure D	C, E, F
procedure E	E
procedure F	F

Although a region is the largest possible area of a program in which a given identifier or label can keep its original connotation, the identifier's or label's *scope*, or true range of meaning, can be limited by an intentional or inadvertent redefinition. Figure 2 shows the effect of redefining the identifier X in several nested regions. Even though the region of each definition corresponds to figure 1, the scope of any X (i.e., to which constant, type, variable, etc., does X refer?) limits its effective meaning.

program *X*

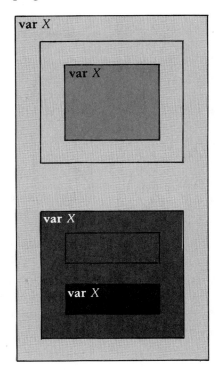

Figure 2

Shading shows the scope of an identifier *X* when it is redefined in a nested region.

Thus, an identifier's scope may be smaller than its region, but it is never larger. Identifiers or labels defined in the program-block are called *global*, while identifiers or labels created in nested blocks are said to be *local* to their defining blocks. However, identifiers and labels are often referred to as being relatively local or global.

A locally defined or declared type, value (like a constant or enumerated value), variable (like a variable, value-parameter, or variable-parameter), or subroutine (a function or procedure) is said to take *precedence* to an identifier used by a type, value, variable, or subroutine that has a relatively global defining point. Relatively global meanings of the name are ignored—the most local application takes precedence. This makes subprograms modular, in the sense that the programmer usually need not worry about reusing relatively global identifiers. Be aware, though, that reusing an identifier can make it impossible to refer to a relatively global type, value, variable, or subroutine.[2]

---

[2] An interesting example of this can be found in the discussion of enumerated types in section A10-1.

Under most circumstances regions can be characterized as blocks (as in Figures 1 and 2). However, there are situations (discussed elsewhere) in which a region can be smaller.[3] Although every identifier or label may be redefined, the new defining point must occur in a different region. In other words, an identifier may be redefined within an enclosed block, or a 'parallel' block, but it can't be defined twice in a single block (unless the redefinition occurs in a record definition).

records A102-A112

about pointers A136-A142

As you might expect, an identifier can't be used before it is defined. (The sole exception to this rule allows the mutually recursive definitions of pointers and their domain types, as described in section A12.) As a result, the scope of an identifier is also restricted by the exact location of its defining point. This program segment is illegal even though *Sixes* has the same region (the program-block) as *Boxcars*:

```
{illegal example}
program Dicey (ouput);
const Sixes  = Boxcars;
      Boxcars = 12;
  ...    etc.
```

An identifier is recognized within an enclosed region, though. The segment below is correct, since *Sixes* is defined in an 'outer' region (the program-block) before it appears within procedure *Enclosed*:

```
{legal example}
program Dicey (ouput);
const Sixes = 12;
procedure Enclosed;
  const Boxcars = Sixes;
   ...   etc.
```

The act of defining an identifier removes its entire region from the scope of a like-named, but relatively global, identifier. As a result, one cannot define an identifier, then use *and* redefine it in an enclosed block. The rewritten segment below is illegal:

```
{illegal example}
program Dicey (ouput);
const Sixes = 12;
procedure Enclosed;
  const Boxcars = Sixes;
        Sixes = 6;
   ...   etc.
```

[3] Record type definitions set up enclosed regions, and **with** statements create regions for their durations. See section A11-1.

Required identifiers that denote required constants, types, procedures, or functions (like *maxint, integer, new,* or *sqrt*) are treated as though they're defined in a region that encloses the entire program. This means that they have their predefined meanings throughout the whole program, but can be redefined if necessary.

input, output A131-A132

The required textfiles *input* and *output*, in contrast, are treated as though they were defined *within* the program—their appearance as program parameters serves as a defining point. In consequence, they may not be redefined in the program block if they are given as program parameters.[4]

This program segment is illegal because it attempts to define an identifier twice in the current region—a program-block, procedure-block, or function-block:

```
{illegal example}
var A : integer;
procedure A ;
     ·.    etc.
```

In contrast, the redefinition below is quite all right:

```
{legal example}
program A (output);
     ·.
procedure A ;
     var A : integer;
        ·.    etc.
```

The program-identifier A (the program's name) has no meaning within the program, since its region effectively contains that of the program-block (which means that it can be redefined there). In turn, the defining-point of variable A is in a region contained by the region procedure A is defined in. The 'inner' region is simply removed from the scope of procedure A. A could not call itself recursively, nor could it be defined as a function.

recursive calls A75, A78

A6-3 Activations

The possible effects of region and scope on identifiers or labels is academic until the blocks they're defined in are *activated*. The program-block is activated when the program is run, while procedure-blocks and function-blocks are activated when their associated procedures or functions are called.

---

[4] Of course, redefining *input, output,* or any of the required identifiers is usually not a bright idea. Note that redefining the identifiers *input* and *output* does not change the effect of procedures or functions that default to the required textfiles *input* and *output*—these files exist independently of their identifiers.

totally undefined A67

goto *A13-A15*

When a block is activated, its local variables are allocated, and are totally undefined.[5] If the block is a function-block, the result of that function is also totally undefined. As noted before, the region the block defines (and any regions it contains) is removed from the scope of any relatively global identifiers that are locally redefined.

A block's activation lasts while the actions given in its statement-part (the block's algorithm) are being executed. After the last statement is executed, the activation is terminated. Only a **goto** statement can cause an early termination, by indicating that execution is to continue in a block that encloses the current block.[6] Note that a **goto** cannot cause a new activation; it can only end the current activation, or end activations that contain (led to) the current activation.

Once a block has been activated, the procedures or functions declared within it can be called. When a subprogram is called (at its *activation-point*) further processing of statements is temporarily suspended while the subprogram is activated, and executed. However, the calling block's variables remain allocated, and other procedures and functions whose scope includes the calling (and called) block can be invoked themselves.

When a block's activation is terminated, the variables it contains can be assumed to be deallocated. Pascal has no form of 'own' variables—local variables that are not deallocated at the block's termination (and thus, would not need to be reinitialized when that block is activated again).[7] (Relatively) global variables must be employed if (relatively) permanent allocation is desired. This is unfortunate, because it tends to make Pascal programs less modular than they might be.

[5] Program parameters—external files—are not necessarily totally undefined. See section A11-4.
[6] This will turn out to be the block in which the label was defined. See section A2-3.
[7] Although FORTRAN, C, and quite a number of other languages do.

Constant Definitions

Programmer-defined constants provide alternative names—identifiers—for values. It's important to remember that the word 'constant' has several applications in the context of Pascal. This section discusses constants that are defined by the programmer for the explicit purpose of acting as synonyms for other values.

enumerated types A97-A99
strings A117-A119

However, we sometimes also refer to the constants of enumerated types, string-type constants, and the constants of the required simple types (see the discussion of *tokens* in section A1-2).

Programmer-defined constants are often used to document the usage of implementation-defined values, and to help increase program portability. They're also valuable for setting, and implicitly documenting, program-specific limits. For example:

```
const LineLength = 80;
      PageLength = 66;
       . . .

type Page = array [1..LineLength , 1..PageLength] of char ;
```

A7-1 Constant Definition Part

A constant definition supplies an identifier as a synonym for a value. Zero or more constants can be defined in the *constant -definition -part* :

constant-definition-part = ['**const**' *constant-definition* ';' { *constant-definition* ';' }] .
constant-definition = *identifier* '=' *constant* .
constant = [*sign*] (*unsigned-number* | *constant-identifier*) | *character-string* .
constant-identifier = *identifier* .

The chart equivalent is:

constant-definition-part

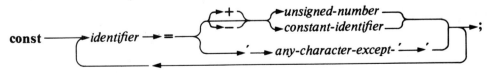

Although the BNF can't specify this restriction, if a sign is used any constant-identifier that follows it must denote a *real* or *integer* value. For example:

         const *LowNumber* = −*maxint*;
               pi = 3.1415926;
               MinusPi = −*pi*;
               InitialLetter = ′a′;
               FinalLetter = ′z′;
               TrueLove = ′Patti′;

maxint A32   Only one constant—*maxint*—is required to be predefined in Pascal.

1)   Even though the appearance of an identifier in a constant definition serves
     as its defining point for a block's region, the constant can't appear as the
     'value' of its own definition.

2)   A variable or other expression may not provide the value of the constant.

These definitions are illegal:

         {illegal definitions}
         const *A* = −*A*; {Definition is self-referencing.}
               LowerLimit = *Bound*; {Illegal if *Bound* is a variable.}
               Deuce = 1+1; {Expressions aren't allowed.}

A character-string was defined as a token way back in section A1-2.

         character-string = ′″ *string-element* { *string-element* } ′″ .
         string-element = *apostrophe-image* | *string-character* .

String types are the only structured constants. Allowing other structured constants has often been proposed as an extension to Pascal, but is not included in
the Standard.

A8

Variables

Variables are easily characterized as locations in the computer's memory that store and represent values. There is no default initialization (assignment of starting values) to Pascal variables. When a variable is first allocated it is *undefined*. If it's a structured variable, it is said to be *totally undefined*, which means that all its components are undefined.

structured types A101

Three ideas characterize variables in Pascal.

1)   Every variable has one particular type, and can only store values of that type.[1]

Unlike FORTRAN and PL/I, Pascal has no default typing of variables. A type must be explicitly associated with any variable when it is declared, and this type cannot be changed.[2]

formal parameters A79

2)   Each variable must be declared in a variable declaration part or formal parameter list before it is used.

This stands in contrast to languages that allow variable declarations in the 'block' of a compound statement (like ALGOL), or even let variables be declared implicitly by being used (like BASIC or APL).

dynamic allocation A137-A138

3)   The lifetime of a variable (except for a dynamically allocated variable) is restricted by its declaration point.

activations A63-A64

Because Pascal has a block structure, no declared variable is allocated until the block it's declared in is *activated*, or entered. *Local* variables, declared within procedures and functions, are only allocated during the activation of their subprograms. As a result, a subprogram's variables must be reinitialized on every call of the subprogram. In contrast, *global* variables exist for the entire run of the program.

A8-1 The Variable Declaration Part

blocks A58-A59
type definitions A95-A96

Variables can be declared in the block of any program, procedure, or function. The **variable declaration part** comes immediately after the type definition part, and right before the subprogram declarations. Since the BNF below is enclosed within square brackets, it is optional—a block doesn't have to include variable declarations.

---

[1] Precise restrictions are detailed in the discussion of assignment compatibility in section A2-1.
[2] Record variants, however, do their best to get around this rule. See section A11-1.

variable-declaration-part = ['**var**' variable-declaration ';' { variable-declaration ';' }] .
variable-declaration = identifier-list ':' type-denoter .
identifier-list = identifier { ',' identifier } .
type-denoter = type-identifier | new-type .
type-identifier = identifier .

The word-symbol **var** opens the variable declaration part, and may be followed by one or more variable declarations. The names that appear in the

regions A59-A63

identifier-list are variable identifiers whose region is the block the declaration appears in. If a like identifier has been defined in a relatively global region, the current region is removed from the relatively global identifier's scope—the identifier loses its relatively global meaning. We can simplify the BNF with a chart:

variable-declaration-part

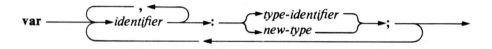

The type-denoter specifies the type of value—simple, structured, or pointer—the variable will represent. If the type-denoter is an identifier, we can safely assume that it is a required type identifier (*real, integer, boolean, real*, or

text A131

text), or was defined in a prior type definition part. For instance:

    type *Color* = {rest of *Color* definition}
          Matrix = {rest of *Matrix* definition}
          ShortInteger = {rest of *ShortInteger* definition}

    var *Channel* : *integer* ;
          BattingAverage, Temperature, ConversionFactor : *real* ;
          Data, Results : *text* ;
          Station : *integer* ;
          Shade : *Color* ;
          Maze, Labyrinth : *Matrix* ;
          Limited : *ShortInteger* ;

A type-denoter may also be a *new-type*, whose BNF is:

    new-type = new-ordinal-type | new-structured-type | new-pointer-type .

This BNF is pursued further when type definitions are discussed in section A10. A new-type establishes the type of a variable through a description of its structure or subrange, rather than with an explicitly defined and named type. Such a

type definitions A95-A96

description would be equally at home in a type definition. For example:

```
var LowerCase : set of 'a'..'z';
    Position : record
                  Latitude, Longitude : real
               end ;
    Board : array [1..8, 1..8] of boolean ;
    YearsToGettysburg : 0..86;
```

Using a new-type as a type-denoter lets the intermediate step of defining a type be skipped—the variable is given an **anonymous**, or unnamed, type. However, since Pascal does not adhere to a strict structural equivalence of types, the shortcut can cause problems. For example, these two variables are not assignment compatible. They belong to entirely different types, and assignments cannot not be made between them:

assignment compatibility
A10-A11

```
var a : record
           x,y,z : real
        end ;
    b : record
           x,y,z : real
        end ;
```

A second reason for explicitly defining types (and then using type identifiers in variable declarations) is that the types of functions, value-parameters, and variable-parameters must all be given with type identifiers, and cannot be described with new-types. Variable a or b, above, could not be passed, say, as a variable-parameter, since an actual variable-parameter must always be of the same type as its corresponding formal parameters.[3]

about parameters
A79-A87

If a and b were both defined at the same point the definition would probably be:

```
var a,b : record
             x,y,z : real
          end ;
```

This gives them the same (anonymous) type, and makes them assignment compatible. However, if a and b were declared in different blocks, they would have to be declared with type-identifiers, rather than as new-types, to be assignment compatible.

A8-2 Kinds and Categories of Variables

Ordinary variable declarations allocate variables, and associate identifiers with them. However, we must clearly distinguish between *variables* and *identifiers*. Although an identifier may refer to a variable—to a storage location—it is not synonymous with the variable itself. A variable may have more than one name, or it may not be named at all.

[3] Nor could they be passed as value-parameters—the actual and formal parameters still have to be assignment compatible.

A somewhat more confusing fact is that storage locations may be subdivided. As a result, a variable may contain variables itself. Such variables are said to be *structured*.[4] In contrast, a variable that doesn't contain variables is a *simple* variable. The declaration of structured variables can often be seen as a convenient way of allocating simple variables without going through the drudgery of naming each one.

structured types A101

Variables can be allocated or renamed in other places besides a variable declaration.

value-parameters A80-A81

1) Value-parameters allocate and name local variables.

variable-parameters A81-A83

2) Variable-parameters rename relatively global variables.

3) The dynamic allocation procedure *new* allocates anonymous variables at run-time.

(Although function declarations allocate and name storage locations, these are not, strictly speaking, variables.)

A declared variable, value-parameter, or variable-parameter has an identifier that names it. This identifier is known as an *entire-variable* because it refers to an entire variable—not just to a single component (or subvariable). The components of a structured variable don't have identifiers, though, and must generally be accessed using names 'manufactured' with the entire-variable's identifier. A variable's name is called a *variable-access*, of which an entire-variable is just a special case.

variable-access = entire-variable | component-variable | identified-variable | buffer-variable .
entire-variable = variable-identifier .
variable-identifier = identifier .

for statement A26-A29

The only context that entire-variables appear in involves the **for** statement, whose control variable must be an entire-variable.

Although all the structured variables are usually said to have components, a *component-variable* is a name that denotes one component of an array or record:

component-variable = indexed-variable | field-designator .

about arrays A112-A119

An *indexed-variable* denotes one component of an array variable. Notice in the BNF that an array-type variable is itself a variable-access. This indirectly confirms that the components of structured variables may be structured too.

indexed-variable = array-variable '[' index-expression { ',' index-expression } ']' .
array-variable = variable-access .
index-expression = expression .

[4] Although set-type variables are usually lumped with the structured variables, and have a discernible internal structure, they do not contain component variables.

about records A102-A112

A *field-designator* denotes a single component (a *field*) of a record variable. Under most circumstances, the field is denoted by the record's name, a period, and the field's identifier. However, within the purview of a **with** statement the field-identifier alone names the component.

with statements
A105-A107

field-designator = record-variable '.' field-specifier | field-designator-identifier .
record-variable = variable-access .
field-specifier = field-identifier .
field-identifier = identifier .

about files A125-A135

A *buffer-variable* denotes one component of a file-type variable.

buffer-variable = file-variable '↑' .
file-variable = variable-access .

The definition of a file-variable as a variable-access is not wholly accurate, because files may not have file-type components. Since a file's components are anonymous (they all share the same name—the buffer variable), only one component of a given file can be referred to at any time. Finally, files are peculiar variables because a file can be in different 'states' that affect the accessability of its buffer variable.

The final category of variable-accesses are *identified-variables* .

identified-variable = pointer-variable '↑' .
pointer-variable = variable-access .

about new A137, A141
about pointers A136-A142

Identified-variables name *dynamically allocated* variables. Such variables are not declared at all. Instead, a call, at run-time, of the required procedure *new* allocates an anonymous variable that is referenced by the pointer-type variable that serves as *new's* argument. The variable remains allocated until it is disposed of with a call to the required procedure *dispose* .

Subprograms and Parameters

Procedures and functions are named subprograms that carry out part of a program's algorithm. Although subprograms have been implemented in nearly every high-level language, Pascal programs tend to rely on them to an exceptional extent.

Subprograms benefit most aspects of Pascal usage and implementation. At the machine level, subprograms help minimize processor-time, and reduce the amount of memory a program requires. The *object* (machine language) code of a procedure or function need only be stored a single time, even if the algorithm it represents is invoked more than once. Any memory that is required for locally declared variables must be allocated only when the subprogram is activated, and can be freed when the activation is complete.

activations A63-A64

Subprograms make programs easier to write. A solution step that's required at more than one stage of an algorithm can be written as a *procedure*, then invoked with a procedure call as necessary. A computation that must be repeated (with different arguments) can be written as a *function*, because a function call is an expression that represents the value the function computes.

Subprograms make their most significant contribution in the areas of problem solving and programming methodology. They go a long way toward fulfilling Wirth's promise that Pascal would be:

'...a language suitable to teach programming as a systematic discipline....'[1]

In the last few years it has become generally accepted that programming instruction should promote the use of computers for problem solving in general, and not be limited to teaching the syntax of a particular computer language, or methods for coding specific algorithms. A problem solving technique called *stepwise refinement* is a particularly successful approach. A problem is broken down into its subproblems by being repeatedly restated in a *pseudocode* that (in Pascal classes, at least) becomes progressively more Pascal-like. This step-by-step refinement results in partial algorithms that are easy to encode.

A special advantage of stepwise refinement is that the partial algorithms it produces are often precise specifications for subprograms. Pseudocode descriptions of algorithmic steps that appear during stepwise refinement usually wind up being implemented as individual procedures or functions.

[1] [J&W] page 133.

A9-1 Procedures

Procedures are declared in the (optional) procedure and function declaration part of any block.

procedure-and-function-declaration-part = { (*procedure-declaration* | *function-declaration*) ';' } .

Procedures and functions are the last items declared in a block, which makes sense because procedures and functions frequently require the constants, types, and variables defined earlier. The BNF of a *procedure-declaration* looks complicated:

> *procedure-declaration* = *procedure-heading* ';' *directive*
> | *procedure-identification* ';' *procedure-block*
> | *procedure-heading* ';' *procedure-block* .

But under most circumstances a procedure declaration consists of a procedure heading and its block:[2]

> *procedure-heading* = '**procedure**' *identifier* [*formal-parameter-list*] .
> *procedure-block* = *block* .

regions A59-A63

recursion A75, A78

The region of the procedure's identifier is the block the procedure is defined in, along with any blocks the procedure encloses. Since this includes the block of the procedure itself, recursive procedure calls are allowed—a procedure can call itself. Syntactically, the block of a procedure is identical to that of a program:

> *block* = *label-declaration-part*
> *constant-definition-part*
> *type-definition-part*
> *variable-declaration-part*
> *procedure-and-function-declaration-part*
> *statement-part* .

scope A59-A63

A procedure block, like a program block, may contain label declarations, and the definitions and declarations of local constants, types, variables, etc. The region of these identifiers is the block of the procedure, as well as any block(s) the procedure contains. The region is removed from the scope of any likenamed, relatively global identifier.

about parameters
A79-A87

Besides naming the procedure, the heading lists its *formal parameters*. There are four varieties:

value-parameters
A80-A81

1) *Value-parameters* are similar to variables declared within a procedure, but differ because value-parameters are initialized during the procedure call. An access or modification of a value-parameter has no effect on the actual parameter expression that provided the initializing value.

---

[2] The remainder of the BNF is required when directives (in particular, the required directive **forward**) are used. Directives, which relate to both procedures and functions, are discussed in section A9-4.

2)   *Variable-parameters* are local aliases, or synonyms, for variables declared outside the procedure. An assignment to a variable-parameter is equivalent to an assignment to its actual parameter (which must be a variable).

3,4) A *procedural-parameter* is a local alias for a procedure declared outside the current procedure. A *functional-parameter* is an alias for a function declared outside the current procedure.

A9-1.1 Procedure Calls

A procedure is invoked by being *called* in a procedure statement:

procedure-statement = *procedure-identifier* ([*actual-parameter-list*]
                                              | *read-parameter-list*
                                              | *readln-parameter-list*
                                              | *write-parameter-list*
                                              | *writeln-parameter-list*) .

The BNF of a procedure's parameter list defines parameter lists for calls of the required procedures *read, readln, write*, and *writeln* (which don't interest us now), as well as for the **actual -parameter -list** of arguments that can accompany an ordinary procedure call.

actual-parameter-list = '(' *actual-parameter* { ',' *actual-parameter* } ')' .
actual-parameter = *expression* | *variable-access*
                   | *procedure-identifier* | *function-identifier* .

The **binding**, or correspondence, of actual and formal parameters is established by position. If the first two formal parameters in a procedure heading are, say, a variable-parameter and a value-parameter, then the first two actual parameters of a procedure call must be a variable-access and an expression, in that order. There must always be exactly one actual parameter for each formal parameter.

The exact order of evaluation, accessing, and binding of actual parameters is implementation-dependent. Since the expression that is the argument of a value-parameter is evaluated at the time of the procedure call, it is an error for it to be an undefined variable. However, since the variable-access that is the argument of a variable-parameter isn't evaluated, it *may* be totally undefined without error.

A brief example program demonstrates the use of value-parameters and variable-parameters. Additional examples accompany the discussion of parameters in section A9-3.

```
program Example (output);
        {Demonstrates local and global scope.}
var i, j, k: integer;
procedure Demonstrate (i: integer;  var j: integer);
    var k: integer;  {i and k are local variables, distinct from globals.}
    begin
      k := 1;
      writeln (i, j, k);
      i := 2*i;        j := 2*j;
      writeln (i, j, k)
    end;
begin
    i := 3;        j := 5;        k := 7;
    writeln (i, j, k);
    Demonstrate (i, j);
    writeln (i, j, k)
end.
```

↓	↓	↓	↓	↓
3	5	7		
3	5	1		
6	10	1		
3	10	7		

Notice that the local variables i and k, declared within Demonstrate, are distinct from the variables i and k declared in the program block. The rules by which the region of a procedure is removed from the scope of a program or subprogram that contains it were discussed in section A6-2.

A recursive subprogram calls itself. For example, program Reverse uses the recursive procedure Stack to echo, in reverse order, the characters on one line of input:

```
program Reverse (input, output);
        {Demonstrates a sequence of recursive procedure calls.}
procedure Stack;
    var Character: char;
    begin
      read (Character);
      if not eoln then Stack;
      write (Character)
    end;
begin
    Stack;
    writeln
end.
```

↓	↓	↓	↓	↓

This is not a palindrome.
emordnilap a ton si sihT

A9-2 Functions

A function is a subprogram that is invoked during the evaluation of an expression. A function *returns*, or represents, a value of any simple or pointer-type.[1] Technically, a function-designator is a *factor*, one of a class of expressions that also includes variable-accesses and unsigned constants. It's not too inaccurate to think of a function as an expression that computes its own value.

factor A41-A42

Function -declarations mingle with procedure declarations in the procedure and function declaration part of any block. The BNF is complicated by the possibility of directives:

directives A86-A87

> *function-declaration = function-heading ';' directive*
> *| function-identification ';' function-block*
> *| function-heading ';' function-block .*

But when a directive is not used, the function's declaration consists of its heading and block. The heading is like that of a procedure, except that the function's **result type** must be specified. In the BNF below, notice that a function's result type must be given with a type-identifier, and may *not* be a new-type. This means that the type of a function cannot be defined on the spot. Instead, it must have been defined (in a type definition) prior to the function's declaration.

new-types A95-A96

> *function-heading = 'function' identifier [formal-parameter-list] ':' result-type .*
> *result-type = simple-type-identifier | pointer-type-identifier .*
> *function-block = block .*

The BNF of a block was given in 6-1. Formal-parameter-lists are discussed in 9-3. Some example function headings are:

> **function** Greatest (First, Second, Third : real): real ;
> **function** IsPrime (Arg : integer): boolean ;
> **function** LastElement (CurrentPosition : PointerType): PointerType ;

Although a function may have parameters of any sort, the intended purpose of a function is to represent a *single* value of a simple or pointer type—not to modify its arguments. Thus, variable-parameters rarely appear in a function's formal-parameter-list.[2]

---

[1] However, a pointer-valued function can't be used to access a dynamically allocated variable. An honest-to-goodness pointer variable is required to construct an *identified-variable*. See section A12.
[2] We'll see a common exception—a function that computes and represents a random number. The seed is usually passed as the argument of a variable-parameter, and modified within the function.

A function is invoked by the appearance of a *function-designator*, which calls the function, and represents its value as an expression. The function-designator's region is the block it is defined in, as well as any blocks contained by the function itself. Thus, a function can call itself; recursive function calls are legal.

> *function-designator = function-identifier [actual-parameter-list] .*
> *function-identifier = identifier .*

Within the block of the function, the function-identifier alone (without a parameter list) serves a different purpose. It represents a storage location, whose type is the function's result-type, that may only be assigned to.[3] The value assigned must be assignment-compatible with the result-type of the function. This application was anticipated in the BNF of an assignment statement:

> *assignment-statement = (variable-access | function-identifier) ':=' expression .*

Every function must contain at least one assignment to its identifier. But since this assignment won't necessarily be executed, the Standard makes it an error for a function to be undefined on the completion of its activation.

Some example function declarations are:

> **function** *Tan   (Angle: real): real*;
>   {Returns the tangent of its argument.}
>   **begin**
>   *Tan := sin (Angle)/cos (Angle)*
>   **end**;
>
> **function** *Even   (Number: integer): boolean*;
>   {Returns *true* if its argument is an even number.}
>   **begin**
>   *Even := (Number* **mod** 2) = 0
>   {We could have just said *Even :=* **not** *odd (Number).*}
>   **end**;

A function's block, like that of a procedure, may contain local definitions and declarations of labels, constants, types, etc. Their region is the block of the function, and of any subprograms defined within the function. This region is removed from the scope of any relatively global identifiers with the same names.

Although it is rare, functions may have formal variable-parameters. Function *Random*, below, demonstrates one application.

---

[3] Of course, a function that has no formal parameters may confuse novice program readers, since its function-designator will be indistinguishable from its function-identifier. Some languages (like C) avoid this problem by requiring that the function-designator have an empty parameter list (e.g., *foo()*); Pascal does not.

```
function Random (var Seed : integer): real;
        {Returns a pseudo-random number such that 0<=Random (Seed)<1.}
    const Modulus = 65536;
          Multiplier = 25173;
          Increment = 13849;
    begin
        Seed := ((Multiplier *Seed)+Increment) mod Modulus;
        Random := Seed /Modulus
    end;
```

side-effects A79 The fact that functions (which can serve as actual parameters) can have variable-parameters (as well as out-and-out side-effects) is one reason that the phrase:

'The order of evaluation, accessing, and binding of the actual-parameters shall be implementation-dependent.'

appears several times in the Standard. Suppose that this procedure call occurs in a program:

```
Inspect (Random (Seed), Seed)
```

A cursory reading of function *Random*, above, confirms that it modifies the value of *Seed*. But in the call of procedure *Inspect*, is the variable *Seed* evaluated before or after the call of *Random*? Is the modified or unchanged value of *Seed* passed?

The answer is implementation-defined. Inasmuch as natural (i.e., human) languages are read from right to left, left to right, and even top to bottom, it is difficult to argue convincingly that evaluating actual parameters from left to right is necessarily the right thing. It is up to the programmer to devise an alternative formulation that sidesteps implementation dependencies, e.g.:

```
Temporary := Random (Seed);
Inspect (Temporary, Seed)
```

As stated earlier, recursive function calls are permitted in Pascal:

```
function GreatestCommonDenominator (i,j : integer): integer;
        {Returns the greatest common denominator of i and j.}
    begin
      if i<j
        then GreatestCommonDenominator :=
                        GreatestCommonDenominator (j, i)
        else if j =0
          then GreatestCommonDenominator := i
          else GreatestCommonDenominator :=
                        GreatestCommonDenominator (j, i mod j)
    end;
```

A9-3 Parameters[6]

Procedure and function calls frequently require arguments whose number and type don't change, but whose names or values vary from one call to the next. *Formal parameters* provide a way to rename the variables, expressions, procedures, or functions that serve as subprogram arguments. Parameter declarations give local identifiers to arguments (and possibly allocate new variables) for the duration of a procedure or function call.

   The mechanism of parameters is virtually required when procedures or functions are written independently of the programs they are used in, and relatively global identifiers are unknown. Parameters also help increase program reliability by promoting *modularity*. Assignments to relatively global variables from within subprograms, called *side-effects*, tend to reduce the reliability of code by making its effect harder to verify. A subprogram's parameter list serves as an easily checked table of the connections between a procedure or function and its environment.

A9-3.1 Formal Parameter Lists

Procedure and function declarations begin with a heading that names the subprogram (and its result type, if it's a function), and provides the defining point for a list of the subprogram's *formal parameters*.[7]

formal-parameter-list = '(' *formal-parameter-section* { ';' *formal-parameter-section* } ')' .
formal-parameter-section > *value-parameter-specification*
                | *variable-parameter-specification*
                | *procedural-parameter-specification*
                | *functional-parameter-specification* .
value-parameter-specification = *identifier-list* ':' *type-identifier* .
variable-parameter-specification = '**var**' *identifier-list* ':' *type-identifier* .
procedural-parameter-specification = *procedure-heading* .
functional-parameter-specification = *function-heading* .

   Formal parameters are identifiers that, within the subprogram, denote (or are initialized by) the *actual parameters*, or arguments, that accompany a subprogram call. Depending on the specification of its corresponding formal parameter, an actual-parameter may be a variable, an expression (of which a variable is just a special case), or a subprogram.

---

[6] Conformant array parameters (which are confined to Level 1 Pascal) are discussed in section A9-5.
[7] The alternative formulation of a formal-parameter-section (defined with a '>') is given in section A9-5.

A9-3.2 Value-Parameters

A *value-parameter* is, in effect, a local variable whose initial value is supplied by an actual parameter. Its BNF is:

> value-parameter-specification = identifier-list ':' type-identifier .
> identifier-list = identifier { ',' identifier } .

Although all the value-parameters listed in a single value-parameter specification are of the same type, not all the value-parameters of a given type need be declared in the same value-parameter specification. The parameter lists of procedures *Together* and *Separate*, below, declare the same number and types of value-parameters. We will see, though, that these parameter lists are not *congruous*. *Together* contains only one formal parameter specification, while *Separate* has three.

congruous lists A85

> **procedure** *Together* (x,y,z: integer);
> **procedure** *Separate* (x: integer; y: integer; z: integer);
> **procedure** *Compare* (First, Second: TheirType);

Unlike an ordinary variable, a value-parameter is not undefined when it is allocated. Instead, the value-parameter's corresponding actual parameter—its argument—is evaluated when the subprogram is called. When the subprogram's block is first activated, this value is attributed (assigned) to the value-parameter. Assignments to a value-parameter have no effect on the actual parameter, even if the actual parameter happens to denote a variable. For example:

```
program Test (output);
    {Demonstrates value-parameters.}
var x, y: integer;
procedure NoEffect (x, y: integer);
    begin
      x := y;       y := 0;
      writeln (x, y)
    end;
begin
    x := 1;       y := 2;
    writeln (x, y);
    NoEffect (x, y);
    writeln (x, y)
end.
```

```
1      2
2      0
1      2
```

In more formal terms, a value-parameter specification is the defining point of a value-parameter whose region is its formal-parameter-list, as well as the defining point of an *associated* variable-identifier whose region is the subprogram's block. What does this mean in practice? Well, although a subprogram and a formal parameter may have the same identifier:

> **procedure** *Legal* (*Legal*: *integer*);

because the procedure and parameter are defined in different regions, a formal parameter's identifier may not be redefined in the subprogram's block:

```
{illegal example}
procedure Foo (Bar: integer);
    const Foo = 5;   {A legal definition.}
            Bar = 3;   {An illegal definition—Bar is already defined in this block.}
    ·.·   etc.
```

assignment compatibility
A10-A11

1)   The actual-parameter that corresponds to a value-parameter can be any expression that is *assignment compatible* with the value-parameter.

2)   As a result, file-type variables (or structured variables with file-type components) cannot be passed as value-parameters. They must be passed as variable-parameters, discussed below.

3)   The argument expression is evaluated at the time of the subprogram call, although the exact order of evaluating, accessing, and binding of a given call's arguments is implementation-dependent.

A9-3.3 Variable-Parameters

A *variable-parameter* (sometimes called a 'var parameter' for short) is a renaming of, or local alias for, its actual parameter. Its syntax is:

> *variable-parameter-specification* = 'var' *identifier-list* ':' *type-identifier* .
> *identifier-list* = *identifier* { ',' *identifier* } .

variable declarations
A67-A69

This syntax is almost identical to that of an ordinary variable declaration, with two important exceptions.

1)   The word-symbol **var** must be repeated with each additional type of variable-parameter.

2)   The type of the variable-parameters being declared must be given with a *type-identifier*—the name of a previously defined type.

new-types A95-A96

Thus, a new-type description cannot appear in a parameter list.

Not every variable-parameter of a given type need be declared in a single variable-parameter specification. The headings shown below declare the same number and type of variable-parameters.

> **procedure** *Close* (**var** *a,b,c*: *real*);
> **procedure** *Far* (**var** *a*: *real*; **var** *b*: *real*; **var** *c*: *real*);

variable-access A70
about packing
A101, A119-A121

The actual parameter that corresponds to a variable-parameter *must* be a variable-access. It must denote a variable (or, implicitly, a component of a variable that is not packed). It can't merely represent a value, such as a constant or function call.

There are four restrictions on variables passed to variable-parameters.

same types A95-A96

1)   The actual parameter must possess the same type as its formal parameter.[8]

record variants
A107-A112

2)   The actual parameter may not denote a field that is the selector of a record's variant part.

packed types A101

3)   An actual parameter may not denote a component of a packed variable (although a variable passed as a parameter *may* be packed).

buffer variables A127

4)   If a file buffer variable $f\uparrow$ is passed as the argument of a variable-parameter, it is an error to modify the value of the file f.[9]

A variable-parameter (rather than a value-parameter) is usually defined if the actual parameter is going to be modified within a subprogram. However, situations arise that make it desirable to pass data to a variable-parameter even if it is not going to be altered. When a large array is passed by value, for instance, the value-parameter may require a considerable amount of space, and the attribution of actual to formal parameter may be time consuming. The problem is avoided by passing the relatively global variable to a variable-parameter—a low-overhead operation. Although the protection of a value-parameter is lost, the documentation and modularity advantages of parameters in general are retained.

In formal terms, a variable-parameter specification is the defining point of a variable-parameter whose region is its formal parameter list, as well as the defining point of an 'associated' variable identifier whose region is the subprogram's block.

However, no new variable is allocated. Instead, the formal variable-parameter (or, if you prefer, its associated variable-identifier) denotes the variable that is passed as an actual parameter. Any assignment to the variable-parameter is equivalent to an assignment to the actual parameter. Given this procedure:

```
procedure Double (var Parameter : integer);
   begin
      Parameter := Parameter * 2
   end ;
```

the procedure call *Double* (x) is equivalent to the assignment $x := x*2$.

---

[8] In contrast to a value-parameter, which is only required to be assignment compatible with its actual parameter.
[9] This rule is intended to avoid the sticky situation that might result if, for instance, $f\uparrow$ is passed as a variable-parameter to a procedure that resets f as a side-effect!

The actual-parameter is accessed when the subprogram is called (although the exact order in which actual-parameters are accessed is implementation dependent). In consequence, if the variable-access is an indexed-variable, changing the index does not affect the component that has already been passed as a parameter. Changing the value of i within the block of some procedure *Modify* will *not* cause the component passed in this call of *Modify* to change:

indexed variables
A70, A115-A117

     Modify (Matrix [i])

Although the variable-parameter is an alias for a relatively global variable, the relatively global name is still validly defined (unless it is redefined within the subprogram). Suppose we define this procedure:

     procedure *DoubleAndAddOne* (**var** *Parameter* : *integer*);
       begin
         Parameter := *Parameter* * 2;
         x := *x* + 1
       end ;

The call

     DoubleAndAddOne (*x*)

is equivalent to this pair of statements:

     x := *x* * 2;
     x := *x* + 1

Although [J&W] implied that the actual parameters of variable-parameters must denote *distinct* variables, the current Standard makes no such restriction.

A9-3.4 Procedural-Parameters and Functional-Parameters

Just as a variable may be renamed within subprograms through a variable-parameter-specification, a procedure can be given a local alias with a *procedural -parameter -specification* .

     procedural-parameter-specification = procedure-heading .
     procedure-heading = '**procedure**' identifier [formal-parameter-list] .

Functions (and their parameters) may also be declared as formal parameters in a *functional -parameter -specification* .

     functional-parameter-specification = function-heading .
     function-heading = '**function**' identifier [formal-parameter-list] ':' result-type .

Functional-parameters are much like procedural-parameters, except for the requirement that a functional-parameter's result type must appear as part of its declaration. For the remainder of this section I'll just refer to 'procedural/functional'-parameters and specifications when I mean 'procedural-parameters or functional-parameters,' etc.

The identifiers that denote the formal parameters of the procedural/functional parameters have no meaning or application. In the example below, the value-parameter x (of function f) never appears again.

```
procedure Bisect (function f (x: real): real;
                         LowBound, HighBound: real;
                         var Result: real);
          {Finds a zero of f (x). Assume f (LowBound)<0 and f (HighBound)>0.}
    const Epsilon = 1e–10;
    var MidPoint: real;
    begin
       MidPoint := LowBound;
       while abs (LowBound –HighBound) > Epsilon *abs (LowBound)
          do begin
            MidPoint := (LowBound +HighBound)/2;
            if f (MidPoint)<0
               then LowBound := MidPoint
               else HighBound := MidPoint
          end;
       Result := MidPoint
    end;
```

When procedures or functions are passed as parameters, they are not accompanied by their own actual parameters. For instance, in this call a function named ProductionFunction is the actual parameter of f:

```
Bisect (ProductionFunction, –5, 5, Answer)
```

The fact that a procedural/functional-parameter definition is accompanied by its own formal parameter list (which may include the declarations of any other kinds of formal parameters) is a change in Pascal, since [J&W] only allowed value-parameters. Thus, procedure Bisect, above (which requires a variable-parameter), could itself be passed as a procedural parameter. A more elementary example is:

```
procedure Demo (procedure Show (var x: integer));
    var y: integer;
      ...
    begin
      ...
       Show (y);
      ...
    end;  {Demo}
```

When a parameter list contains a parameter list (as the parameter list of *Show* is contained by the parameter list of *Demo*), the 'internal' list establishes a new region in relation to the rest of the parameter list. The defining points found within this region have an extremely limited scope. For example:

> **procedure** *Outer* (**var** *Outer*: *boolean*;
>   **procedure** *Inner* (*Outer, Inner, Change*: *real*);
>   *Change*: *integer*);

The parameter list of procedure *Outer* is in one region (which lets *Outer* appear legally as a variable-parameter of type *boolean*). The *boolean* identifier *Outer*, procedure identifier *Inner*, and *integer* identifier *Change* must all be different, since they share the same defining region. However, *Change, Inner*, and *Outer* can all show up again within the parameter list of procedure *Inner*—it is a new and separate region. They are just 'dummy' identifiers; all (relatively) global meanings of *Change, Inner*, and *Outer* are preserved.

function designators A77

A more formal explanation might not hurt. A procedural/functional-parameter-specification is the defining point of a procedural/functional-parameter whose region is its formal-parameter-list, as well as the defining point of a procedure identifier or function-designator for the block it is a parameter of. However, the identifiers 'declared' in the formal parameter list of a procedural/functional-parameter-specification are not associated with any block. Their region (and with it, their scope) is limited to the formal parameter list they appear in.

The actual parameter that corresponds to a formal procedural/functional-parameter must obey certain rules. First of all, it must have been defined within the program, which means that it *cannot* be a required (predefined) procedure or function.[10] Second, the actual parameter (a procedure or function) and the formal parameter (a procedural/functional-parameter) must have **congruous** formal parameter lists. Remember that a formal parameter list consists of one or more formal parameter specifications. To be congruous, each specification must:

1)   contain the same number of parameters of the *same* type if they are value-parameter-specifications; or

2)   contain the same number of parameters of the *same* type if they are variable-parameter-specifications; or

3)   be procedural-parameter-specifications with congruous formal parameter lists; or

4)   be functional-parameter-specifications with congruous formal parameter lists *as well as* the same result type.

---

[10] ...probably because the formal parameters of required procedures and functions will not necessarily be able to meet the second rule.

Finally, each parameter list must contain the same number of formal parameter specifications. The two parameter lists shown below are not congruous, even though they declare the same number and type of formal parameters. The first parameter list contains only one formal parameter specification, while the second has three:

$(x,y,z: integer)$
$(x: integer; y: integer; z: integer)$

A9-4 The **forward** Directive

There are special circumstances in which the block of a procedure or function cannot appear in its usual place (immediately following the heading). For example, the subprogram might have been externally compiled, or be located in another file. The notion of *directives* was introduced into the Standard to provide a means of dealing with these situations. A directive follows the subprogram heading in place of its block, and acts as a special instruction to the Pascal processor. The BNF of a directive is:

directive = letter { letter | digit } .

The BNFs of both procedures and functions refer to directives:

procedure-declaration = procedure-heading ';' directive
| procedure-identification ';' procedure-block
| procedure-heading ';' procedure-block .
function-declaration = function-heading ';' directive
| function-identification ';' function-block
| function-heading ';' function-block .

When a directive is used, it follows the subprogram heading—the subprogram's name, parameter list (and type, if it's a function). Thus, the directive takes the place of the subprogram's block.

Only one directive is required in Pascal—**forward**. It makes a *forward-reference* whenever a procedure or function identifier must appear in advance of its declaration. This situation is usually brought about by mutually recursive subprograms, which are subprograms that call each other.[11] However, there are times when a programmer wants to have a particular procedure or function heading appear early in the text of a program for its effect on program documentation, even if it calls subprograms declared later on.

Forward references are made like this: When the procedure or function heading first appears, it is followed by the directive **forward**. When the text of

---

[11] Suppose that A is declared first. How can a call to B appear within A? B hasn't been declared. Yet declaring B first is no solution if B must contain a call of A.

the block finally shows up, it is preceded by a *procedure -identification* or *function -identification*—the variety and name of the subprogram.

> *procedure-identification* = '**procedure**' *procedure-identifier* .
> *function-identification* = '**function**' *function-identifier* .

The parameter list (and type, if it's a function) is not repeated. For example:

```
program References (output);
   ·· {Definitions and declarations.}
procedure Early (a, b, c: char); forward;
procedure Late (x, y, z: char; i, j: integer);
      ·· {Definitions and declarations.}
   begin {Late}
      ·· {Late's statement part contains a call of Early.}
   end; {Late}
procedure Early;  {Parameter list is not repeated.}
      ·· {Definitions and declarations.}
   begin {Early}
      ··
   end; {Early}
begin  {References}
   ··
end. {References}
```

A9-5 Conformant Array Parameters (Level 1 Pascal Only)

Probably the most vocally reported shortcoming in [J&W] Pascal was its lack of *dynamic*, or variable-length, array types. It was impossible to define an array whose length depends in any way on program data. As a result, general-purpose array-handling procedures could not be written; often a severe shortcoming in non-instructional applications.

The omission was not accidental. Wirth felt that a processor should have full knowledge of program characteristics when the program was prepared for execution. This information lets the processor generate appropriate and efficient instructions for handling such features as packing and unpacking.

> 'The whole advantage of this scheme, however, immediately vanishes, if, for example, we introduce so-called dynamic arrays, that is, if we allow information about the actual dimensions of an array to be withheld from the compiler....This not only impairs the efficiency of the code, but—more importantly—destroys the whole scheme of storage economy [i.e. packing]....A capable language designer must not only be able to select appropriate features, but must also be able to foresee all effects of their being used in combination.' [Wirth74]

Of course, one need not agree with Wirth's assessment. B. Kernighan has said that:

'This botch [no dynamic arrays] is the biggest single problem with Pascal. I believe that if it could be fixed, the language would be an order of magnitude more useful.' [Kernighan81]

while A.N. Habermann maintains:

'The true reason for not incorporating dynamic arrays in Pascal is probably the fact that variable subranges can hardly be treated as a type.' [Habermann73]

And, in fact, the necessity of providing secure type checking has been a major obstacle to incorporating them into the language.

Originally, the ISO standardization effort did not intend to deal with the issue of dynamic arrays, leaving it for specification as an 'official' extension to the language. However, several member countries protested so vociferously that a number of draft proposals for allowing the definition of formal array-type parameters (whose lengths would depend on the actual parameters of the sub-program call) were made.

Most of these proposals fell apart (generally in the area of providing type security) when subjected to the intense scrutiny of twenty member countries' Pascal experts. The surviving proposal does not allow true dynamic arrays. Instead, it creates a new class of array-type parameters whose arguments may have nearly arbitrary dimensions.

Unfortunately (or fortunately, if you prefer), the new proposal did not meet with universal approbation. A compromise was hammered out—there would be two 'levels' of Pascal, one incorporating the proposal, and the other not.[12]

In brief, a formal *conformant array parameter* includes read-only *bound identifiers* as part of its definition. They set the bounds, or lower and upper limits, of the conformant array parameter's index (dimension size). The conformant array parameter's actual parameter may be any array that is *conformable* with the formal parameter. Conformant array parameters may be either value-parameters or variable-parameters, and they may be packed. For example:

```
procedure Sum  (var Total: real;
                      Vector: array [Lower..Upper: integer] of real);
    var i: integer;
    begin
      Total := 0.0;
      for i := Lower to Upper
        do Total := Total + Vector[i]
    end;
```

[12] Predictably, this caused problems as well. 'Numbering [the levels] 0 and 1 is a barbarism in the English language.... Levels 1 and 2 would be far preferable.' thundered the Australians [X3J9/81-98], who *really* preferred Standard Pascal and Extended Pascal. Addyman's reply: 'One is then left with the problem of choosing two designations which are not derogatory. One could choose Red Pascal and Green Pascal, perhaps, but not extended, subset, or other emotive terms.' [Addyman81]

Procedure *Sum* sums the components of an array. Its array-valued actual parameter may be any array whose components are *real*, and whose single index is *integer*, or an *integer* subrange. Within *Sum*, the bound identifiers *Lower* and *Upper* play their typical role as the initial-value and final-value of a **for** statement. Given these declarations:

> **var** *Short* : **array** [1..2] **of** *real* ;
>   *Long* : **array** [−*maxint*..*maxint*] **of** *real* ;
>   *Answer* : *real* ;

both calls below are correct:

> *Sum* (*Answer*, *Short*);
> *Sum* (*Answer*, *Long*)

A9-5.1 Conformant Array Parameter Syntax

The formal explanation of conformant array parameters begins with the alternative formulation of a *formal -parameter -section* .

formal-parameter-section > *conformant-array-parameter-specification* .
conformant-array-parameter-specification = *value-conformant-array-specification*
                        | *variable-conformant-array-specification* .
value-conformant-array-specification = *identifier-list* ':' *conformant-array-schema* .
variable-conformant-array-specification = '**var**' *identifier-list* ':' *conformant-array-schema* .

A value-conformant-array, like a value-parameter, creates a local copy of its actual parameter. Modifying a value-conformant-array has no effect on the actual parameter. A variable-conformant-array, in contrast, is like a variable-parameter—it is a local renaming of its argument. Thus, changing a variable-conformant-array also changes its actual parameter.

In either case, when an identifier appears in the identifier-list of a conformant array parameter specification, it becomes defined as a parameter whose region is the formal parameter list that immediately contains it, and as a variable identifier whose region is the block of the subprogram it is a parameter of. In addition:

regions A59-A63

1) All the formal parameters in any particular identifier-list share the same (unnamed) type.

new-types A95-A96

2) This type (like a *new-type*) is distinct from any other type. Thus, two or more absolutely identical conformant array specifications define formal parameters with different types.

string types A117-A119

3) A formal conformant array parameter cannot be a string type, because its type isn't denoted by an *array-type* (as defined in section A11-2).[13]

[13] This restriction denies formal conformant array parameters the special privileges associated with string types. Although the syntax of a packed-conformant-array-schema (below) is similar to the syntax of a string type array, it is not the same. A string may be a parameter of such a schema, though.

4)   If the identifier-list of a single conformant array specification defines more than one *formal* parameter, then all its *actual* parameters must have the same type.

same types A95-A96

For example, suppose we have the heading:

procedure *P* (*A,B*: **array** [*i..j*: *T1*] **of** *T2*;
$\qquad\qquad$ *C,D*: **array** [*m..n*: *T1*] **of** *T2*);

Variables *A* and *B* have the same type, and thus are assignment compatible. The same is true for *C* and *D*. However, the type of *A* and *B* is distinct from the type of *C* and *D*, and assignments may *not* be made between them. Finally, according to rule 4, both actual parameters of *A* and *B* (and both actual parameters of *C* and *D*) must have the same type.

assignment compatibility
A10-A11

A *conformant-array-schema* (which I'll just refer to as a *schema*) serves as the 'type definition' of a conformant array parameter. A schema may be packed or not, just like an ordinary array type definition. However, the Standard restricts any packed schema to a single index (because of implementation considerations).

packing A101, A119-A121

conformant-array-schema = packed-conformant-array-schema
$\qquad\qquad\qquad$ | *unpacked-conformant-array-schema* .
packed-conformant-array-schema = 'packed' 'array' '[' *index-type-specification* ']'
$\qquad\qquad\qquad$ 'of' *type-identifier* .
unpacked-conformant-array-schema = 'array' '[' *index-type-specification*
$\qquad\qquad\qquad$ { ';' *index-type-specification* } ']'
$\qquad\qquad\qquad\qquad$ 'of' (*type-identifier* | *conformant-array-schema*) .

Notice that an unpacked schema doesn't necessarily close with a type identifier. But if it *does*, that type is the schema's *fixed component type*.

The definition of an unpacked schema is recursive. This can lead to lengthy definitions, in which one schema immediately contains another, which in turn contains a third, etc. For instance:

array [*index-type-specification*] **of array** [*index-type-specification*] **of**   etc.

To simplify matters, an equivalent shorthand form is allowed. The sequence '] **of array** [' is replaced by a semicolon; e.g.:

array [*index-type-specification*; *index-type-specification*; …] **of**   etc.

We finish the BNF of conformant array parameters with their **bound identifiers**.

index-type-specification = identifier '..' *identifier* ':' *ordinal-type-identifier* .
bound-identifier = identifier .
factor > bound-identifier .

Bound identifiers denote the lower and upper limits of the *index-type* required in an array type definition:

array types A112-A119

$$array\text{-}type = \text{`array'} \text{`['} \; index\text{-}type \; \{ \; \text{`,'} \; index\text{-}type \; \} \; \text{`]'} \; \text{`of'} \; component\text{-}type \; .$$
$$index\text{-}type = ordinal\text{-}type \; .$$

One can intuitively appreciate the close tie between an array's index-type, and a schema's index-type-specification.

1)   If an *n*-dimensional array can be thought of as having *n* index-types, then the *i*th index-type is said to *correspond* to a schema's *i*th index-type-specification.

2)   The first bound identifier denotes the smallest value of its corresponding index-type, and the second bound identifier denotes that index-type's largest value.

3)   The type of a pair of bound identifiers is the same as the type of its corresponding index-type.[14]

The region of bound identifiers is the formal parameter list that immediately contains their specification, as well as the block of the procedure or function whose heading their specification appears in. Bound identifiers are neither variables nor constants, which means that they cannot be assigned to; nor can they be used in constant or type definitions. Nevertheless, a bound identifier denotes a value. It is classed as a factor, and also provides an alternative BNF for factor.

factor A41-A42

A9-5.2 Conformability

The types of a conformant array parameter and its argument must *conform*.[15] Suppose that we have the 'givens' listed below. They are named in a peculiar manner because we are being required to treat potentially *n*-dimensional arrays as though they were just one-dimensional. We can get away with this because the full and shorthand forms of array (and conformant array) type definitions are equivalent. This odd starting position lets us state the rules for conformability recursively (a mixed blessing if there ever was one). Suppose that

1)   *T1* is an array-type with a single index-type.

2)   *T2* is the type of the bound identifiers of a conformant array parameter that immediately contains a single index-type-specification.

A value of type *T1* conforms with a conformant array parameter if *all* four statements below are true. (Note the slight hedge in requirement 2.)

compatible types A10-A11

1)   The index-type of *T1* is compatible with *T2*.

2) .   The smallest and largest values of the index-type of *T1* lie in the closed interval given by *T2*. It is an error if the smallest or largest value falls outside the interval.

[14] Which may often be a subrange of the type of their ordinal-type-identifier.
[15] Additional restrictions are placed on value-conformant-arrays.

fixed component type
A90

3) The component-type of *T1* (i.e., the type of the array's components) is the same as the conformant array parameter's fixed component type, *or*

the component-type of *T1* conforms to the conformant array parameter's conformant-array-schema.[16]

4) Both *T1* and the conformant array parameter are either packed or not packed.

Requirement 3 is recursive, which makes everything seem very complicated. In effect, we compare the conformant array parameter's index-type-specification to its argument's corresponding index-type. If types match all down the line, the two conform.

A9-5.3 Additional Restrictions on Variable-Conformant-Array-Parameters

variable-access A70
activations A63-A64

packing A101, A119-A121

A variable-conformant-array-parameter, like an ordinary variable-parameter, is a local renaming of a relatively global argument. The actual parameter (which is a variable-access) is accessed prior to the activation of the block it is an argument of. This access is maintained for the entire activation of the block. As usual, the actual parameter may not be a component of a packed variable. However, a conformant array parameter can serve as the argument of a variable-conformant-array-parameter as long as it *conforms*, as described above.

```
procedure VectorAddition (var X,Y,Z : array [Least..Greatest : Limits] of real);
    var Counter : Limits ;
    begin
        for Counter := Least to Greatest
            do X [Counter] := Y [Counter] + Z [Counter]
    end ;
```

In procedure *VectorAddition*, *Y* and *Z* are defined as variable-conformant-arrays (for reasons described below) so that their actual parameters may be conformant array parameters themselves.

A9-5.4 Value-Conformant-Array-Parameters

Value-conformant-array-parameters are considerably more restricted, for reasons that have to do with the implementation of value-parameters in general. In effect, a value-conformant-array is a local variable that is initialized by its actual parameter. Modifying the formal parameter has no effect on the actual parameter.

strings A117-A119

The actual parameter is an expression: in this case, it is either a variable-access or a string constant. It may *not* be a conformant array parameter.

---

[16] Recall that an unpacked schema doesn't necessarily end with the specification of a type identifier (the schema's fixed component type).

Clearly, there are circumstances that may require some modification of usual programming conventions. Parameters *used* as value-conformant-arrays may have to be *defined* as variable-conformant-arrays (just so that their arguments can be conformant arrays). See program *VectorAddition*, above, for an example.

There are two situations in which a conformant array parameter may be *part* of a value-conformant-array's actual parameter.[17]

1)   The conformant array parameter can be used to help denote an *indexed-variable* (a representation of one array component) that serves as the actual parameter. The indexed-variable's type (that is, the type of the component it represents) must be the same as the value-conformant-array's fixed component type.

2)   The conformant array parameter can appear as an argument to a function call that in turn helps denote an indexed-variable (as above). Again, the indexed-variable's type must be the same as the value-conformant-array's fixed component type.

For example (on the next page):

---

[17] The Standard puts it this way:

   'If the actual-parameter contains an occurrence of a conformant-array-parameter then for each occurrence of the conformant-array-parameter contained by the actual-parameter, either *a*) the occurrence of the conformant-array-parameter shall be contained by the function-designator contained by the actual-parameter, or *b*) the occurrence of the conformant-array-parameter shall be contained by an indexed-variable contained by the actual-parameter, such that the type possessed by that indexed-variable is the fixed-component-type of the conformant-array-parameter.' [6.6.3.7.2]

Such sentences have been thought to provide an existence proof for the undesirability of conformant array parameters.

```
program Shell (input, output);
type Ray = array ['A'..'Z'] of integer;
var Arc: array [1..10] of Ray;
   ···

procedure Inner (B: array [l..m: char] of integer);
  begin
     ···

  end; {Inner}
   ···

procedure Outer (A: array [i..j: integer] of Ray);
   var B: array ['A'..'Z'] of Ray;
       K: integer;
   begin {Outer}
      ···

     Inner (A[i +1]);  {Example of case 1.}
     Inner (B[chr (A[K])]);  {Example of case 2.}
        {Assume that 'A' ≤ chr (A[K]) ≤ 'Z'.}
        ···

   end; {Outer}
    ···

begin {Shell}
   ···

Outer (Arc);
   ···

end. {Shell}
```

Disallowing conformant array arguments to value-conformant-arrays ensures that a subprogram's *activation record* can have a fixed size.[18] This restriction simply makes it easier to develop Pascal processors, and isn't required by any insurmountable limitation inherent to computers.

The Standard goes so far as to specify a particular method for implementing value-conformant-arrays. Suppose that an expression E is passed to a value-conformant-array A. The value of E is attributed to an 'auxiliary variable' X (that is created by the processor, and does not otherwise exist in the program) before the activation of A's block. Naturally, the type of X is the same as the type of E.

Within A's block, the value-conformant-array A (and its associated variable identifier) refers to the auxiliary variable X for the entire activation. Since there is a ban on passing conformant array parameters to value-conformant-arrays, the types of E and X will always be known at compile-time, and all activation records can be of a fixed size.

---

[18] We can think of an activation record as being the minimum set of data associated with a subprogram call (prior to the execution of its algorithm). This includes the names, types, and sizes of its parameters and local variables.

A10

Data Typing and Simple Types

The variety of data types available in Pascal, coupled with the programmer's freedom to define new types, has been a prime reason for the language's success. The notion of type serves several purposes. It can be the basis of automatic checks that improve program consistency and reliability, if not correctness. Type definitions also give the Pascal processor enough information to choose efficient storage representations for variables. But most important, types—especially structured types—allow data structuring methods that simplify programming tasks. It is largely for this reason that in Pascal:

'...fundamental concepts [are] clearly and naturally reflected by the language. [1]
[J&W]

Although Pascal provides a rich variety of data typing and structuring techniques, it stops short of defining an exhaustive set of operators to go with them.[2] This must be seen as a compromise in Pascal's design—the programmer is allowed a mix of data types, but must often declare special procedures and functions (but not operators) to manipulate them. The advantage of this compromise is that Pascal is kept to a reasonable size; its disadvantage is that Pascal may not have the 'industrial strength' required for highly specific applications.[3]

There are three categories of types in Pascal—*simple, structured*, and *pointer*. Types are described and named in **type** *definitions*, then these names are used in variable, parameter, or function declarations.

> *type-definition-part* = ['**type**' *type-definition* ';' { *type-definition* ';' }] .
> *type-definition* = *identifier* '=' *type-denoter* .
> *type-denoter* = *type-identifier* | *new-type* .
> *new-type* = *new-ordinal-type* | *new-structured-type* | *new-pointer-type* .

By definition, a **new**-*type* is a type that is distinct from all other types. Consequently, the BNF above allows an inference about the 'equivalence' of types in Pascal. Two named types are the **same** if, and only if, they derive from the same type identifier. Suppose that *T1* is a type identifier:

---

[1] Well, to be fair, A.N. Habermann claims that:

> 'The most unsatisfactory aspect of the Pascal language is the artificial unification of subranges, types, and structures.' [Habermann73]

[2] For instance, APL includes an extensive set of operators for array manipulation, while FORTRAN allows operations on complex numbers. Pascal has neither.

[3] The natural solution to this problem—let the programmer define operators and/or operations—surfaced in the late 1970's in languages like CLU and Ada.

type
. . .
T2=T1;
T3=T2;

Types *T1*, *T2*, and *T3* are all the same type. If *T2* or *T3* were defined with a new-type—even if it were character-for-character identical to the definition of *T1*—it would denote a different type.

Type sameness becomes an important issue on two occasions: for determining the validity of assignments, and when arranging for subprogram parameter declarations and arguments. Variables *V1* and *V2* must have the *same* type when:

1)   They are both records, and *V1* is being assigned to *V2*.

2)   They are both arrays—but not string types—and *V1* is being assigned to *V2*.

3)   *V1* is a variable-parameter, and *V2* is its argument.

A general chart of a type definition part in Pascal is:

type-definition-part

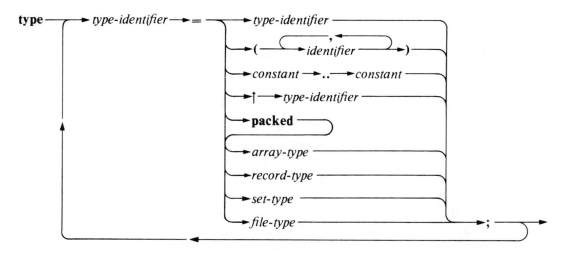

A10-1 Simple Types

A simple type is a collection of elementary, indivisible data items. The simple types are divided into two categories—*real* and *ordinal*.

simple-type = ordinal-type | real-type-identifier .

The *real* type is required in Pascal. Its values are an implementation-defined subset of the real numbers, as described in section A3-1. Synonyms for *real* can be defined:

type *Precision* = *real* ;

Type *Precision* is the same type as *real*. Subranges of *real* can't be defined, and there is no concept of double-precision *real*'s in Pascal.

Ordinal-*types* are characterized by being enumerable. Values of an ordinal type can be numbered, and compared for equality and relative position.

> *ordinal-type* = *new-ordinal-type* | *ordinal-type-identifier* .
> *ordinal-type-identifier* = *type-identifier* .

The three required ordinal type-identifiers *integer,* *boolean,* and *char,* are described in section A3-1. An ordinal type that is defined with the identifier of an existing ordinal type becomes a synonym for that type. For example:

> **type** *Natural* = *integer* ;
> *Number* = *Natural* ;

Natural, Number, and *integer* all denote the same type.

Although the required simple types are deemed sufficient for ordinary input and output of program data, additional types can be created by defining new categories of values, or by restricting existing ones. Such definitions are called **new** **-ordinal** **-types** .

> *new-ordinal-type* = *enumerated-type* | *subrange-type* .

new-ordinal-type

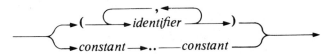

A10-1.2 Enumerated Ordinal Types

An *enumerated* -*type* is a group of values that are named and ordered by the programmer.

> *enumerated-type* = '(' *identifier-list* ')' .
> *identifier-list* = *identifier* { ',' *identifier* } .

For example:

> **type** *Color* = (*Red, Green, Blue, Orange*);
> *PinStatus* = (*Low, High*);
> *Interrupts* = (*Stop, Kill, Wait, Trap, Pipe, Bus, Child*);

The order of enumerated values is textual. If *Red* precedes *Blue* in the definition of *Color*, then *Red* is less than *Blue*. Counting of ordinal positions begins with zero—in the definition of type *Interrupts*, *Stop* is in the 'zeroth' ordinal position, while *ord* (*Kill*) is 1.

The identifiers that name the values of an enumerated type are that type's *constants* just as 'A', 'B', 'C', etc., are the constants of type *char*. However, the constants of enumerated types (unlike constants of the required types) don't have external character representations, and can't be read or written to or from textfiles—in particular, from the standard input and output.

textfiles A131-A134

If the values of enumerated ordinal types can't be read as input, or printed, what good are these types? In small programs, enumerated types often provide the values of 'state' variables that control program actions. Enumerated types are also found in larger programs, where they name collections of abstract values: potential error conditions, job classifications, device names, marital status, employment categories, etc. All these divisions *could* be represented as numbers (à la FORTRAN),[4] but that can cause awful confusion in nontrivial programs. Letting new types be enumerated as needed makes a major contribution to the *transparency* of Pascal programs.

An identifier that denotes a constant of an ordinal type may not be redefined within the current block. As a result, it can't be used as a constant of another ordinal type. These definitions are illegal:

```
{illegal example}
type Odds = (1, 3, 5, 7, 9);
     Deficiency = (Pellegra, Rickets, Scurvy);
     Illness = (Rickets, Yaws, Beriberi);
  var Beriberi: integer;
```

because the constants of *Odds* are predefined as *integers*, because the identifier *Rickets* appears in two different enumerated type definitions, and because *Beriberi* is simultaneously defined as a constant and declared as an identifier.

However, the identifier of an enumerated-type constant *may* be redefined in an enclosed block without affecting its host type.

```
program Test (output);
     ···
type Color = (Red, Green, Blue, Orange);
     ···
procedure Trial;
   var Green: integer;
       Hue: Color;
     ···     etc.
```

In the example above, the redefinition of *Green* has no effect on the enumerated type *Color* except that the identifier *Green* now refers to a variable of type *integer*, rather than a constant of type *Color*.

---

[4] In fact, this is how processors usually deal with enumerated types; but it is the processor's job, not the programmer's.

This has some unexpected effects. For instance, the statement below may appear within *Trial*:

for *Hue* := *Red* **to** *Orange* **do** *writeln* ('Hi.')

because it does not contain any applied occurrences, or appearances, of *Green* as a constant. In contrast, this statment:

for *Hue* := *Green* **to** *Orange* **do** *writeln* ('Hi.')

is illegal, because the *integer* variable denoted by *Green* is not assignment compatible with the *Color*-type control variable *Hue*. The *Color* constant *Green* still exists, but it can no longer be referred to by name.

A10-1.1 Subrange Types

The division of values into types is, by itself, of major importance for reliable programming. In Pascal, though, individual ordinal types can be further refined through the definition of **subrange** types. A subrange type consists of a contiguous group of values that nominally belong to the subrange's **host** type.[5] A variable of a subrange type has the characteristics of a variable of its host type, except that it is an error to assign the variable a value that does not fall into the proper subrange.

subrange-type = *constant* '..' *constant* .

The constants that delimit the subrange must both belong to the same host type, naturally, and the lower bound must be less than or equal to the subrange's upper bound. Partially relying on earlier examples, we have:

type
```
   . . .
   Positive  =  1..maxint;      {host type integer}
   TwoBits   =  -25..25;
   Index     =  0..50;
   Primary   =  Red..Blue;      {host type Color}
   ShortButLegal  =  'A'..'A';    {host type char}
   Characters  =  'a'..'z';
```

Subranges of type *real* may not be defined, because all subranges must belong to ordinal types.

The attraction of subrange types is their contribution to programming methodology, although it is reasonable to suppose that a processor might use the information in a subrange definition to tailor efficient storage for variables of that type.[6] Since it is an error to assign a variable of a subrange type a value that does not fall in the subrange, it is possible to give variables restrictive

---

[5] Often called the *underlying type*.
[6] The fact that a variable of type *Index* requires only six bits might become important if it were allocated in the tens of thousands—say, as an array component.

invariant properties—in effect, assertions about current conditions are associated with the use of subrange variables, rather than with statements inserted at specific program points.

An ultimate check on the propriety of assignments is made at run-time via the type mechanism.[7] However, the (usually) fatal nature of a failed test makes it incumbent on the programmer to provide careful checks for improper assignments.

Note that it's an *error*, rather than a *violation*, to assign a variable a value that falls outside its subrange (although it is, of course, a violation to assign it a value of a different host type). This would seem to compromise the security offered by subrange types, because properly documented processors can choose to ignore errors! Error status is granted because potentially incorrect assignments can't always be detected at compile-time without inspecting program data, or knowing some implementation-dependent features of a processor.

Consider this situation:

> **type** *LowRange* = 1..5;
> *MidRange* = 1..10;
> *HighRange* = 6..20;
> **var** *LowValue*: *LowRange*;
> *MidValue*: *MidRange*;
> *HighValue*: *HighRange*;

Although an assignment like:

> *LowValue* := *HighValue*

assignment compatibility
A10-A11

will always be an error according to the rules of assignment compatibility, the assignments:

> *LowValue* := *MidValue*;
> *HighValue* := *MidValue*

may or may not be valid, depending on the current value of *MidValue*. If there is an error, though, any self-respecting processor should detect it at run-time.

Subranges also increase the transparency and self-documentation of programs. Declarations like:

> **var** *Dependents*: 0..15;
> *KilnTemperature*: 0..*MaximumSafeTemperature*;

obviously contain more useful information than:

> **var** *Dependents, KilnTemperature*: *integer*;

---

[7] Not always, unfortunately. Some processors have a run-time mode that turns such checks off. This mode may even be the default.

A11

Structured Types

The simple data types allow the creation of variables that represent single values. Structured types, in contrast, provide the template needed for *structured variables* that can store more than one value. Since structured types may be built from structured types themselves, a wide variety of types can be defined in Pascal.

A structured type is not a data structure, although they're often confused. A data structure—a stack, a list, a tree—is a means of organizing data that has certain rules for adding, deleting, or finding data associated with it. It's generally possible to create a given data structure using a variety of structured types.

A structured type—a record, set, file, or array—is a building block whose characteristics (the operations that can be performed with it, or on it, in Pascal) make putting together a given data structure easier or more difficult. Each structured type has features that make it more or less attractive for any given application.

Any of Pascal's four basic structured types may be designated as being *packed*, which tells the processor to economize storage requirements for variables with that type.

> *structured-type* = *new-structured-type* | *structured-type-identifier* .
> *new-structured-type* = ['**packed**'] *unpacked-structured-type* .
> *unpacked-structured-type* = *array-type* | *record-type* | *set-type* | *file-type* .

By definition, a new-structured-type is distinct from any other new type; it is not the 'same' as another new-structured-type. This definition of 'newness' precludes structural equivalence of structured types.

Defining a type as **packed** will often increase the time or space required for accesses of, or operations on, variables of that type. Packing is transparent to the user, but the programmer should remember that:

string types A117-A119 1) A packed array of *char* whose index begins with 1 is a string-type.[1]

2) A packed set type is not compatible (and therefore, not assignment compatible) with a set type that is not packed.

3) Components of packed variables may not be the actual parameters of variable-parameters. (They may appear in calls of *new, read,* or *readln*, though.)

pack, unpack A119-A121 4) The required transfer procedures *pack* and *unpack* are only used in conjunction with packed array types.

[1] String-type variables can be written to textfiles, and, under certain circumstances, may be the operands of the relational operators.

A11-1 The Record Type

Of the four elementary structured types, the *record* is probably the most ubiquitous in Pascal. Pascal owes a debt to COBOL here, since that language first introduced the record as a data structure. Wirth was quite aware of this:

'The introduction of record and file structures should make it possible to solve commercial type problems with Pascal.... This should help erase the mystical belief in the segregation between scientific and commercial programming methods.' [Wirth70]

Although records seldom appear as individually declared variables, they frequently act as components of array and file types, and help make the creation of linked data structures possible. To help set a firm foundation for the other types, we'll look at the record structure first.

A record structure consists of any number of *fields*. Unlike the components of arrays or files, fields have individual identifiers. However, a single record may include fields of different types (whereas all the components of an array or file must belong to a single type). A record's fields are named in a *field list*. A preliminary BNF for a record-type definition is:[2]

    record-type = '**record**' field-list '**end**' .
    field-list = [(fixed-part [';' variant-part] | variant-part) [';']] .

record variants
A107-A112

The BNF of a field-list is quite complicated (because of record *variants*), so for the time being, I'll limit discussion to records that only have *fixed parts*. Such records (i.e., with fixed parts only) always have the same number and type of fields.[3] A fixed part is essentially a list of field-identifiers and their types.

    fixed-part = record-section { ';' record-section } .
    record-section = identifier-list ':' type-denoter .
    identifier-list = identifier { ',' identifier } .
    type-denoter = type-identifier | new-type .

I'll draw the chart of a *record with fixed-part only* as:

record with fixed-part only

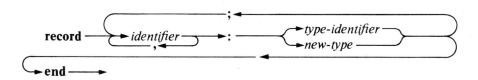

---

[2] The full BNF accompanies the discussion of records with variant parts.
[3] In effect, a *variant* part specifies alternative fixed parts. If a record type has a variant part, its structure (its number and type of fields) can be modified at run-time.

For example:

type
   ··.
     Coordinates = **record**
               x,y : *real*
            end ;
     Apartment = **record**
               Floor : *integer* ;
               Letter : *char* ;
               Wing : (*North, South, East, West*)
            end ;
  var *Position, Location* : *Coordinates* ;
     ToLet, ForLease : *Apartment* ;
     Building : **array** [1..100] **of** *Apartment* ;
     Workers : **array** [1..1000] **of record**
             Name : **record**
                   LastName, FirstName : **packed array** [1..15] **of** *char*
                 end ;
             Married : *boolean* ;
             Age : *Positive* ; {Assume *Positive* is an integer subrange.}
             Job : *Classification* ; {Assume *Classification* is an enumerated type.}
             HireDate : 1960..1990
         end ;

regions A59-A63   The defining points of field identifiers occur in a region that is distinct from the rest of the type definition part. Although field identifiers must be unique within a given record definition, they do not conflict with identifiers used outside the current record's definition.[4]

An enclosed record definition establishes a new defining region. This is a legal series of definitions:

       type *a* = *real* ;
           b = *boolean* ;
           c = **record**
               a : **record**
                   a, b : *char*
               end ;
               b : *integer*
           end ;

Identifiers used in record *c* don't conflict with identifiers used in either record *a*, or the rest of the type definition part.

---

[4] Thus, the definition: **type** *A*=**record** *A* : *char* **end**   is legal.

A11-1.1 Record Variables and Field-Designators

Assignments may be made between two record variables that are assignment
compatible. For record types, assignment compatibility means that both variables must have the *same* type. The entire-variables *ToLet* and *ForLease* are
assignment compatible with each other, as well as with the components of the
array variable *Building*.

entire-variables A70

```
ToLet := ForLease;
Building [1] := ToLet;
Building [2] := Building [1]
```

In an assignment between record variables, each field of the left-hand
variable is assigned the value of the corresponding field of the right-hand variable. Such an assignment is an error if any field of the record variable on the
right is undefined.

Individual fields may be accessed as well. A *field-designator* is usually
constructed from the record-variable's identifier, a period, and an individual
field's identifier.[5]

> *field-designator = record-variable '.' field-specifier | field-designator-identifier* .

A field-designator is a variable-access that may be assigned to, passed as a
parameter, etc.[6]

```
readln (Position.x, Position.y);
ToLet.Floor := 2;
ToLet.Letter := 'K';
ToLet.Wing := East;
ToLet.Floor := ForLease.Floor
```

If a field-designator is a component of another structured variable, or if it
denotes a structured object, a variable-access may get a bit longer:

```
Workers [1].Name.LastName := 'Carangi          ';
Workers [1].Name.FirstName := 'Gia              ';
Workers [1].Married := false;
Workers [1].Age := 24;
Workers [1].Job := Model;
Workers [1].HireDate := 1982
```

The relational operators may not be applied to record-type operands.
Two records can only be compared for equality field-by-field:

---

[5] Within the purview of a **with** structure (below) the field's identifier alone is a field-designator-
identifier.

[6] The only substantive difference between an entire-variable and a field-designator is that a field-
designator can't serve as a **for** statement's control variable.

{See if two records' fields are equivalent.}
if (*ToLet.Floor=ForLease.Floor*)
    and (*ToLet.Letter=ForLease.Letter*)
        and (*ToLet.Wing=ForLease.Wing*)
then *writeln* ('ToLet and ForLease are equal.')
else *writeln* ('ToLet and ForLease are not equal.')

A11-1.2 The **with** Statement

In practice, we'll often want to access several of a record's fields in a single sequence of statements. When a record variable's name is long or unwieldy, the **with** statement allows a convenient shorthand.

> *with-statement* = '**with**' *record-variable-list* '**do**' *statement* .
> *record-variable-list* = *record-variable* { ',' *record-variable* } .
> *record-variable* = *variable-access* .

Its chart equivalent is:

with statement

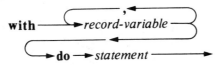

regions A59-A63 Formally speaking, the record-variable-list is the defining point of a *field-designator-identifier* (whose region is the **with** statement's statement), for every field of the record.

> *field-designator-identifier* = *identifier* .

After a record variable appears in a **with** statement's record-variable-list, its field names denote fields for the remainder of the **with** statement's action. Fields can be referred to without being preceded by the record variable's name and a period. For example:

> **with** *ForLease* **do begin**
>   *Floor* := 2;
>   *Letter* := 'K';
>   *Wing* := *East*
> **end**

Within a **with** statement, then, there are two ways to access a given field. The assignments below are identical:

> **with** *ToLet* **do begin**
>   *Floor* := 1;
>   *ToLet.Floor* := 1
> **end**

The BNF of a record-variable-list allows more than one record variable. A statement of the form:

   with *V1, V2,* ··· *, Vn* **do** *S1*

is equivalent to the sequence of nested statements:

   with *V1* **do**
    with *V2* **do**
      ···
       with *Vn* **do** *S1*

If *V1*, *V2*, etc., do not share any field identifiers, then the nesting of regions implied above doesn't cause any problems. But why bother with such an obvious example? Let's get right to the most pathological case—a list of variables that have the exact same record type. For example, let's look at:

   with *ToLet, ForLease* **do** *S1*

which is equivalent to:

   with *ToLet* **do**
    with *ForLease* **do** *S1*

The outer **with** statement is the defining point for a group of field-designator-identifiers whose region—their maximum potential range of meaning—includes the nested **with** statement, as well as *S1*. But the inner **with** statement is also a defining point. Thus, its region is removed from the scope (or *actual* range of meaning) of the field-designator-identifiers defined in the outer **with** statement. As a result, these statements are equivalent:

   with *ToLet, ForLease* **do** *Floor* := 3;
   ForLease.Floor := 3

The field-designator-identifier *Floor* does not access the *Floor* field of *ToLet*. Individual fields of *ToLet* must be referred to the longhand way:

   with *ToLet, ForLease* **do begin**
    Floor := 3;
    ToLet.Floor := 3
   end

The Standard modifies a rather arbitrary restriction mentioned in [J&W]. According to the Standard, when a **with** statement is entered any record variable given is accessed *before* the **with**-statement's action is executed. Furthermore, this access establishes a reference to the record variable for the entire duration of the **with** statement. This is important when the record variable is itself a component of another variable. For example:

> **with** *ArrayOfRecords* [i] **do begin**
>   i := i + 1;
>   ... etc.

The assignment to *i*, which was simply forbidden in [J&W], does *not* cause a different record to be accessed.

A11-1.3 Type Unions With Variant Parts

The record structure is a *type union* that makes three distinct contributions to data typing in Pascal.

1)   A record is a *heterogeneous* structure, because its fields can have different types.[7]

   This is the feature we've taken advantage of so far. Although a record's fields may have had different types, the record's true structure was fixed at compile-time. Every variable of a given record type has had the same number and type of fields.

2)   A record structure lets variables of different types (and disjoint lifetimes) be *overlaid*.

   In this section we'll see how to define a record that consists of alternative groups of fields that share a single fixed field called the *tag* field. The tag field's value, at run-time, determines which of the alternative groups is active. In this application, a record is known as a *discriminated type-union*. It is a union, or merger, of several different record types. We can discriminate, or distinguish, a record's current structure through the value of its tag field.

3)   Although it is nominally an error, and will undermine program portability, records allow a certain way of getting around Pascal's type rules.

   A record can be defined (and even serve) as an overlaid type (as above). However, it need not be given a tag field. This makes it a *free type-union*. There is no way to determine such a record's structure at run-time.[8] If the error mentioned above is not detected by a processor, a value can be stored as though it belonged to one type, then retrieved as a value of another type entirely.[9]

---

[7] In contrast, a structure like an array or file is *homogeneous* —every component must be of the same type.

[8] This is the method used by the C programming language. In C, a record is either entirely fixed, or is a free type-union.

[9] For instance, Pascal does not allow a pointer variable's actual value to be inspected. If, however, it is stored in a record as a pointer, then later read as an *integer*, Pascal's restriction can be sidestepped.

The records we've seen so far have only had fixed parts. We can use records as discriminated or free type-unions by defining one or more *variant - parts* in addition to, or in place of, fixed parts. The exact syntax used to define the variant part makes it a discriminated or free type-union.

> *record-type* = '**record**' *field-list* '**end**' .
> *field-list* = [(*fixed-part* [';' *variant-part*] | *variant-part*) [';']] .

fixed-parts A102   The fixed-part has already been introduced as:

> *fixed-part* = *record-section* { ';' *record-section* } .
> *record-section* = *identifier-list* ':' *type-denoter* .
> *identifier-list* = *identifier* { ',' *identifier* } .
> *type-denoter* = *type-identifier* | *new-type* .

A variant-part superficially resembles a **case** statement. The form of the *variant -selector*, below, determines whether the variant part is a discriminated or free type-union. If a tag-field is given, it is discriminated; if no tag-field is specified, it is a free union. In either case a previously defined ordinal type must be specified as the *tag -type*. Inasmuch as the tag-field is optional, 'tag-type' is an unfortunately misleading name—'case-constant-type' might get the idea across more clearly.

> *variant-part* = '**case**' *variant-selector* '**of**' *variant* { ';' *variant* } .
> *variant-selector* = [*tag-field* ':'] *tag-type* .
> *tag-field* = *identifier* .
> *tag-type* = *ordinal-type-identifier* .

new-types A95-A96   Note that the tag-type must be a type identifier. Unlike the type of an ordinary field, it cannot be given as a new-type.

One or more constants of the tag-type must **correspond** to each variant group of fields by appearing in a *case-constant-list*. Each case-constant-list must contain unique identifiers, and the field names used in each field-list must also be distinct.

> *variant* = *case-constant-list* ':' '(' *field-list* ')' .
> *case-constant-list* = *case-constant* { ',' *case-constant* } .
> *case-constant* = *constant* .

It is an error if any value of the tag-type cannot be found in a case-constant-list.[10] Fortunately, the field-list associated with a case-constant-list may be *empty*—remember that its entire BNF is given between square brackets. In chart form:

---

[10] Which means that, for all practical purposes, type *integer* won't ever appear as a tag-type (although a subrange may be appropriate). Incidentally, error status, in this case, was a bitterly debated question.

record-type

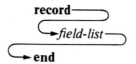

field-list

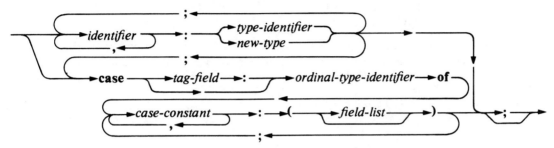

Examples will make this a lot clearer. First, a record that is a discriminated type-union. Aside from the tag field (*Figure*) there are no fixed fields.

> **type** *Shape* = (*Circle, Square, Triangle, Point*);
>   *Dimensions* = **record**
>   **case** *Figure* : *Shape* **of**
>   *Circle* : (*Diameter* : *real*);
>   *Square* : (*Side* : *real*);
>   *Point* : ();
>   *Triangle* : (*Side1* : *real*; *Angle1, Angle2* : 0..360)
>   **end** ;
> **var** *Object* : *Dimensions* ;

1)   The variant-selector *Figure* : *Shape* serves as the defining point of a field named *Figure* .

2)   Although the case-constant *Point* has no fields associated with it, it corresponds to an empty field list (avoiding an error).[11]

3)   The field identifiers defined in each variant are distinct from any other field identifiers defined elsewhere within the same record.

That's why the first field in the field-list corresponding to *Triangle* is called *Side1* —the identifier *Side* had already been taken.

---

[11] You might notice that requiring an empty pair of parentheses is somewhat inconsistent, since a subprogram call without parameters does *not* require an 'empty' parameter list. Welcome to life in the big city.

It's not hard to take advantage of the parallel construction of discriminated type-unions and **case** structures. This **case** statement determines the currently active (see below) variant of *Object*, and takes an appropriate action:

```
case Object.Figure of
    Circle: readln (Object.Diameter);
    Square: readln (Object.Side);
    Point:  ;  {Notice that parentheses aren't needed (or allowed) here.}
    Triangle: readln (Object.Side1, Object.Angle1, Object.Angle2)
end
```

Once an assignment to the tag field *Figure* has been made, the field list corresponding to the value of *Figure* is said to be *active*.[12] A field list that is not active is totally undefined. Suppose that we have made these assignments:

```
with Object do begin
    Figure := Triangle;
    Side1 := 23.5;
    Angle1 := 45;
    Angle2 := 22
end
```

Were we to then make the assignment:

```
Object.Figure := Circle
```

the *Object.Diameter* field would be undefined.

1)   It is an error to reference a field of a variant part that is not currently active.

2)   It is an error to pass the tag field of a variant-part as the argument of a variable-parameter.

variable parameters
A81-A83

Notice that rule 1 places a constraint on the order of assignments. The pair:

```
Object.Figure := Circle;
Object.Diameter := 5.0
```

is legal, but the reversed assignment is not:

```
{illegal example}
Object.Diameter := 5.0;
Object.Figure := Circle
```

[12] The importance of 'activation' varies. In some languages (like Modula and Ada) it is a violation to access an 'unactivated' field. A less strict language (like Pascal) treats such an access as an error. This opens the door to the type 'change' mentioned a few pages back.

A free type-union can be defined like this:

```
type Flavor = (Chocolate, Vanilla, Strawberry);
     Cone = record
                case Flavor of
                    Chocolate: (Cocoa, Thickness: integer);
                    Vanilla: (VanillaBeans: integer; Available: boolean);
                    Strawberry: (Berries: integer)
                end;
var Dessert: Cone;
```

Some assignments are shown below. In effect, the processor automatically activates the correct variant part after an assignment.[13]

```
Dessert.Cocoa := 100;  {Chocolate variant active, all others undefined.}
Dessert.Thickness := 3;
Dessert.Berries := −40  {Strawberry variant active, all others undefined.}
```

Notice that the tag-type (*Flavor*) serves no purpose except to help document the record definition. As far as any application of *Dessert* is concerned (such as in the assignments above), the definition below is equivalent to the earlier one:

```
type Flavor = 1..6;
     Cone = record
                case Flavor of
                    1,2: (Cocoa, Thickness: integer);
                    3: (VanillaBeans: integer; Available: boolean);
                    4: (Berries: integer);
                    5,6: ()
                end;
```

It's useful to summarize some of the rules that pertain to record variants.

1) All field identifiers must be unique within the current record definition, regardless of variants. They may be reused within a nested record definition.

2) The case-constant-list of every variant must contain at least one constant of the tag-type. Case-constant-lists may not share any constants.

3) It is an error if any constant of the tag-type does not appear in a case-constant-list. However, the field list it corresponds to may be empty (shown by empty parentheses).

4) When a variant is not active, its fields are totally-undefined.

---

[13] However, it might not check the currently active variant before an inspection, and may let an inactive variant be inspected. This is an error, of course.

5)   It is an error to access any field of a variant that is not active.

6)   The tag field of a variant part may not be the actual parameter of a variable-parameter.

Additional restrictions are discussed along with procedures *new* and *dispose* in section A12.

A11-1.4 Final Comments

Pascal's approach to type unions should be viewed in historical perspective. Allowing fixed fields only would be a great inconvenience in a strongly typed language like Pascal. It would often be necessary to define many more fields than are ultimately needed in a single record type, wasting storage space and programmer time.

Type-unions imply that the alternative groups of fields will be overlaid in memory. Since only one group is activated at any time, all the groups can share the same area in memory. However, the tag fields of discriminated unions can be expensive—not only because of the space they take, but because of the necessity (in a rigidly discriminated type-union) of performing a run-time check on the tag field's value before allowing a given field to be accessed (i.e., to see if that field currently 'exists').

Free type unions blithely ignore run-time checks entirely. This is useful for storing a value as an object of one type, then retrieving it as though it were a value of another type. Motivations for permitting this subterfuge include garbage collection, inspecting pointer values, and exploiting various internal representations. Unfortunately, most people agree that making this hack available to the user (and not restricting it to the processor) jeopardizes program stability, reliability, and portability, and is exactly the kind of trick that strong typing is supposed to prevent. A high quality processor will detect the trick (after all, it's an error) and disallow it.

A11-2 The **array** Type

The importance of arrays in programming varies from language to language. In APL, arrays—as the sole data type—are paramount. Similarly, in FORTRAN, arrays are the only structured type. The Pascal programmer, in contrast, requires less willing suspension of disbelief to form data structures from data types. Since sets, records, linked data structures, etc., can all be implemented transparently and conveniently through other building blocks, arrays are relegated to a lesser role. The array is *a* data type, rather than *the* data type.

In Pascal, the array type defines a structure that contains *components*, or elements, of any simple, structured, or pointer type. The number of com-

about files A125-A135

ponents is fixed at compile-time by the number of constants of its *index*.[14]
Arrays, like records (but unlike files) are *random-access* structures, because a
component's position doesn't affect run-time overhead in retrieving the data it
stores. An array-type's BNF is:

> *array-type* = '**array**' '[' *index-type* { ',' *index-type* } ']' '**of**' *component-type* .
> *index-type* = *ordinal-type* .
> *ordinal-type* = *new-ordinal-type* | *ordinal-type-identifier* .

In chart form:

array-type

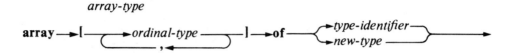

ordinal types A97-A100

The *index-type* can be any ordinal type. But an important point about
index-types is that they are, after all, types. When we say:

> **array** [1..100]   *etc.*

we are defining an ordinal subrange, and not merely naming the array's bounds.
Thus, the BNF of a subrange-type must be adhered to, and expressions may *not*
appear as subrange bounds.

> *subrange-type* = *constant* '..' *constant* .

The *component-type* of an array may be any type, except the type of the
array itself! The component-type can be a previously defined type-identifier, or
a new-type described on the spot.

> *component-type* = *type-denoter* .
> *type-denoter* = *type-identifier* | *new-type* .

The maximum number of components and index-types is not specified by
the Standard. Some example definitions and declarations are (on the next
page):

---

[14] This also holds true for arrays declared as formal parameters.

```
const
    LineLength  = 80;
    PageLength  = 66;
```

```
type
    LetterCount = array [char] of 0..2000;
    Page = packed array [1..LineLength, 1..PageLength] of char;
    Board = array [1..8, 1..8] of record
                                    Piece: (Pawn, Rook, Knight, Bishop,
                                            Queen, King, Empty);
                                    Owner: (Black, White, None)
                                  end;
    LargeSet = packed array [1..10000] of boolean;
    Color = (Red, Blue, Green);
    Palette = array [Color] of Color;
```

```
var
    Verb, Noun: packed array [1..15] of char;
    Sample, Standard: LetterCount;
    Book: array [1..500] of Page;
    Chess: Board;
    Touched, Visited: LargeSet;
    DisplayHues: Palette;
```

Notice that more than one index-type may be specified. An array with *n* index-types is said to be **n -dimensional**.[15] Technically, the specification of additional index-types is a shorthand for a sequence of component type-denoters. The definition:

```
    array [char] of array [1..10] of array [Color] of real;
```

(where *Color* is an ordinal type) may be equivalently stated as any of:

```
    array [char] of array [1..10, Color] of real;
    array [char, 1..10] of array [Color] of real;
    array [char, 1..10, Color] of real;
```

about packing
A101, A119-A121

Although the four types described above are interchangeable, each one, in effect, has a different sequence of components. The shorthand form is packed if each of the 'component sequence' forms is packed; similarly, if the shorthand form is packed, then so are the component sequences. For instance, these are equivalent descriptions of a single type:

```
    packed array [1..10, 1..10] of char;
    packed array [1..10] of packed array [1..10] of char;
```

---

[15] Incidentally, two-dimensional arrays are generally implemented in row-major order—*A* [i,j] in Pascal is *A* [j,i] in FORTRAN.

In contrast, the definitions below are different. Neither could be obtained using a shorthand form:

> **array** [1..10] **of packed array** [1..10] **of** *char*;
> **packed array** [1..10] **of array** [1..10] **of** *char*;

A11-2.1 Arrays and Indexed-Variables

assignment compatibility
A10-A11

string types A117-A119

An array variable can be accessed in its entirety, or one component at a time. Assignments may be made between any two array variables that are assignment compatible. Usually, this means that they must be of the same type—declared with the same type-denoter. However, *string-type* variables (and constants) are assignment compatible as long as they have the same number of components. The effect of an assignment between two array-type variables is to assign the value of every component of one to its counterpart in the other. Thus, if *Touched* and *Visited* are variables of type *LargeSet* (as defined above), the assignment:

> *Touched* := *Visited*

is equivalent to the statement below (assuming the *integer* variable *i*). Naturally, it is an error in either case if any component of the right-hand array is undefined.

> **for** *i* := 1 **to** 10000
>   **do** *Touched* [i] := *Visited* [i]

component-variables A70

Array variables, like record variables, are called *component-variables*. An individual component of an array is denoted by an **indexed -variable**, which consists of the array variable's name, and the **subscript**, or location, of a particular component.

> *indexed-variable* = *array-variable* '[' *index-expression* { ',' *index-expression* } ']' .
> *array-variable* = *variable-access* .
> *index-expression* = *expression* .

Some typical array accesses are shown below. Note that an index-expression may be computed.

> **for** *i* := 1 **to** 15 **do** *read* (*Verb* [i]);
> *Simple* ['A'] := 0;
> *Book* [213] := *Book* [214];
> *Chess* [1,4].*Piece* := *Queen*;
> *Chess* [1,2+2].*Owner* := *White*;
> *DisplayHues* [Red] := *Blue*

The type of the index-expression must be assignment compatible with the index-type. Nominally, this means that the index-expression must fall within the closed interval of the index-type. A careful reading of the assignment compatibility rules, though, reveals that it is an *error*, rather than a violation, for the index-expression's value to fall outside the proper range (as long as it still has the proper host type). Error status is granted to range errors because the value of the index-expression can't always be determined at compile-time. However, it is not likely that a processor will fail to detect such an error—and cease program execution—at run-time.[16]

The program fragment below shows the classic situation for generating range errors. Assume that we are searching through *TheArray* for the component that contains *SoughtNumber*.

```
var TheArray: array [1..20] of integer;
    i, SoughtNumber: integer;
    . . .
    i := 1;
    while (i <= 20) and (TheArray[i] <> SoughtNumber)
    do i := i+1
```

Suppose that *SoughtNumber* is never found. On the last loop iteration the expression (i <=20) will be *false*, which means that the **while** will not be entered again. Unfortunately, *boolean* expressions in Pascal may be fully evaluated. When a fully-evaluating processor attempts to deal with (*TheArray*[i]<>*SoughtNumber*), a range error will occur, and the program may halt if it is detected.

Arrays of arrays require a special mention. Suppose that we make these definitions and declarations:[17]

```
type Vector = array [1..10] of integer;
     Matrix = array [-5..5] of Vector;
var Slot: Vector;
    Grid: Matrix;
```

full evaluation A39-A40

The smallest indivisible component of *Grid* is a variable of type *integer*, which we can refer to like this:

   Grid [0] [5]

For convenience, an abbreviated form can be used, in which '] [' is replaced by ','. This indexed-variable refers to the same component.

   Grid [0,5]

The substitution may be made whenever an array variable is itself an indexed-variable.

[16] Some processors, however, do have a runtime-checks-off mode. If this mode is the default, watch out.
[17] The two-step definition lets us declare variables—including parameters—of type *Vector*. If *Matrix* were simply defined as two-dimensional array, it would be impossible to make assignments to its one-dimensional components—they have anonymous types, and are only assignment compatible with each other.

We can also access any of the array-type components of *Grid*. For example:

> *Grid* [3] := *Slot*

Note that the possibilities for 'slicing' a two-dimensional array are limited by the array's definition. In the assignment above, *Grid* [3] is a variable of type *Vector*. There is no way we could 'slice' *Grid* along its second dimension instead.

A11-2.2 String Types

Sequences of *char* values, or **strings**, are grudgingly admitted as a type in Pascal.[18] String-type values are unusual for three reasons:

1)   Their assignment compatibility is determined by structure.

2)   String constants are the only structured constants.

3)   String-type variables (or constants) may be output to textfiles in their entirety.

character strings A6

A constant of a string-type is called a *character-string*. It is a sequence of characters (the string's *components*) between single quote marks, with the exception that a character-string only one character long denotes a *char*-type value:

> *character-string = '" string-element { string-element } '" .*
> *string-element = apostrophe-image | string-character .*
> *apostrophe-image = '"' .*
> *string-character = one-of-a-set-of-implementation-defined-characters .*

Recall that an *apostrophe-image*, or doubled single-quote, lets a single-quote mark be included in a string. Strings may be defined as constants:

> **const** *Name* = 'Patti';
> *Blanks* = '   ';

By definition, a packed array whose component type is *char* is a string-type if its index-type is an *integer* subrange that begins with 1, and has a length of 2 or more. For example:

> *Length* = 1..10;
> *alpha* = **packed array** [*Length*] **of** *char*;
> *beta* = **packed array** [1..10] **of** *char*;
> *Name* = **array** [1..3] **of** *alpha*; {*Name's* components are strings.}

---

[18] Nevertheless, there is no required type-identifier '*String*.' One of the main differences between UCSD Pascal and Standard Pascal is that the former includes standard string types and a number of mechanisms for dealing with them. The addition of such string extensions to Standard Pascal was intensely debated, but was rejected. It has, however, been proposed as a 'standard' extension.

Some illegal examples are:

```
{illegal examples}
ReallyChar = packed array [1..1] of char;  {too short}
BadWord = array [1..10] of char;  {not packed}
NotAString = packed array [0..20] of char;  {index-type must begin with 1.}
NotAStringType = packed array [1..10] of 'A'..'Z';  {component type must
                                                     denote char.}
```

Two string types are assignment compatible (and also compatible) if they both have the same number of components. Thus, variables of types *alpha* and *beta* are assignment compatible. Assuming *alpha* variable *Good* and *beta* variable *Bad* these are legal assignments:

```
Good := 'Programmer';
Bad := 'Hacks     ';
Good := Bad
```

Notice that it is necessary to pad the string 'Hacks' with five blanks to make it assignment compatible with *Bad*.

lexicographic order A46

The relational operators are defined for string operands, and yield *boolean* results.[19] String values are compared according to their lexicographic ordering. Formally, if *String1* and *String2* are compatible string-types, then:

1) *String1* equals *String2* if, and only if, for all i in $[1..n]$, $String1[i] = String2[i]$.

2) *String1* is less than *String2* if, and only if, there exists a p in $[1..n]$ such that for all i in $[1..p-1]$, $String1[i]$ equals $String2[i]$, and also, $String1[p]$ is less than $String2[p]$.

The ordering of any two characters is determined by their ordinal values in the required type *char*. As a result, although the expression 'cat'<'dog' will always be *true*, the value of the expression 'cat'<'CAT' (to say nothing of '22cats'<'cats22') will vary between processors.

write, writeln A52-A54, A129-134

enumerated types A97-A99

Strings may be output to textfiles using *write* and *writeln*. Exact specifications of output fields are given in section A5-2. A particularly handy application of this feature simulates the output of enumerated ordinal type constants. For example:

```
type WeekDays = (Monday, Tuesday, Wednesday, Thursday, Friday);
     Words = packed array [1..9] of char;
     WeekDayStrings = packed array [WeekDays] of Words;
var Today: WeekDays;
    DayName: WeekDayStrings;
```

---

[19] The Standard states that when a value of a string type (in this case, a variable or defined constant) is compared to a character-string, their components are compared from left to right.

After suitably initializing *DayName*:

> *DayName* [*Monday*] := 'Monday   ';
> *DayName* [*Tuesday*] := 'Tuesday   ';
>   ⋱
> *DayName* [*Friday*] := 'Friday   '

we can print the current value of *Today* with:

> *writeln*   ('Today is ', *DayName* [*Today*])

A11-2.3 The Transfer Procedures *pack* and *unpack*

packing A101, A119-A121
Although any structured type may be designated **packed**, the feature is usually taken advantage of in the definition of array types. One motivation lies in the privileges associated with string-types, as discussed above. However, an exceptionally stupid processor may not recognize that these two arrays:

> **array** [1..10000] **of** *real*
> **array** [1..10000] **of** *boolean*

have vastly different storage requirements. Packing the second is intended to minimize the space allotted to it, although it may increase the time required to access a single component.

Designating an array as packed has no effect on its components if they are structured. The components of:

> **packed array** [*Number*] **of** *Components*

will only be packed if *Components* has itself been defined as a packed structured type. If *Components* is, in fact, packed, then these array descriptions are equivalent:

> **packed array** [*Quantity, Count*] **of** *Components*
> **packed array** [*Quantity*] **of packed array** [*Count*] **of** *Components*

Although designating an array as packed can make it expensive to access individual array components, the programmer is not necessarily forced to sacrifice speed for space. The array can be unpacked, and its components assigned to a variable of a similar—but not **packed**—array type. After its components are inspected or modified as necessary, the original array may be repacked. The required *transfer procedures* *unpack* and *pack* do the job.[20] Suppose we make these assumptions:

1)   *Vunpacked* is a variable whose type can be stated as: **array** [*T1*] **of** *Components*.

---

[20] We assume that, beyond some cutoff point, the entire array can be unpacked, and then repacked, more efficiently than individual components; and that *unpack* and *pack* are implemented in this efficient manner.

2)   *Vpacked* is a variable with the same component type, but possibly a different (perhaps smaller) index-type: **packed array** [*T2*] **of** *Components* .

3)   The smallest and largest values of *T2* are *Lower* and *Upper* .

4)   Variable *k* has type *T1* .

5)   Variable *j* has type *T2* .

6)   *StartingSubscript* is an expression whose value is assignment compatible with *T1* .

The procedure call *unpack* (*Vpacked*, *Vunpacked*, *StartingSubscript*), as defined in terms of other statements, means:

```
begin
  k := StartingSubscript ;
  for j := Lower to Upper
    do begin
      Vunpacked [k] := Vpacked [j ];
      if j<>Upper then k := succ (k )
    end
end
```

unpack attempts to assign every component of *Vpacked* to a counterpart in *Vunpacked* , starting with *Vunpacked* [*StartingSubscript*]. In consequence, it is an error for any component of *Vpacked* to be undefined. If *Vunpacked* runs out of room, the program will almost undoubtedly halt when it detects the erroneous assignment:

$$k := succ (k)$$

host types A99   Note that *T1* and *T2* may have different host types.[21]
Procedure *pack* reverses the process. The call *pack* (*Vunpacked*, *Starting-Subscript*, *Vpacked*), as defined in terms of other statements, is equivalent to:

```
begin
  k := StartingSubscript ;
  for j := Lower to Upper
    do begin
      Vpacked [j ] := Vunpacked [k ];
      if j<>Upper then k := succ (k )
    end
end
```

As above, if we attempt to pack a segment of *Vunpacked* that is smaller than *Vpacked* , a run-time error will occur because of the assignment:

---

[21] Such subtleties were not specified by [J&W], which implied that *T1* and *T2* had to be *integer* subranges.

$$k := succ(k)$$

It is also an error to try to access any undefined component of *Vunpacked*.

In summary, packed arrays must be packed and unpacked in their entirety. A packed array may be unpacked into, or packed from, any contiguous section of an unpacked array. It is an error if this section holds fewer components than the packed array. String constants cannot appear in calls of either *pack* or *unpack*.

A11-3 The Set Type

Pascal's set types allow the declaration of variables that can represent a set, or group, of values of any ordinal type.[1] The BNF of a set type is:

> *set-type* = 'set' 'of' *base-type* .
> *base-type* = *ordinal-type* .

In chart form:

set-type

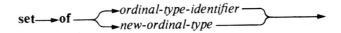

For example:

> **type** *Characters* = **set of** *char*;
>   *Things* = (*a,b,c*);
>   *ThingSet* = **set of** *Things*;
>   *Seasons* = **set of** (*Spring, Summer, Fall, Winter*);
> **var** *Year*: *Seasons*;
>   *Included, Excluded*: *Characters*;
>   *SmallPrimes, TrialNumbers*: **packed set of** 1..29;
>   *Conditions*: **set of** (*Testing, Running, ErrorFree, Ready, Active*);

The size of allowable set types is implementation-defined, and there is no required minimum value. Historically the maximum set size has been equal to the implementation's word size—which frequently made the type **set of** *char* illegal—but many current implementations allow vastly larger sets.[2]

---

[1] Pascal's sets are said to have **members**, in contrast to the *components* of the other structured types (and also, unfortunately, in contrast to the *elements* of real-life sets).
[2] At this writing, I believe the winner is the Storage Technology implementation, which constrains set definitions by the size of available memory. Famous losers (which don't allow the type **set of** *char*) are too numerous to mention. There was, incidentally, a good deal of wrangling over this issue, and a very early draft of the Standard did require **set of** *char*.

Formally, a set type defines the *powerset* of an ordinal type, called the set's **base type**. Even though a base type may contain many subsets, every subset (including the empty set) has the powerset's type. The total number of subsets is called the *cardinality* of the powerset. If the base type of any set type has b values, then the cardinality of its powerset is 2 to the b power.[3]

A11-3.1 Set Constructors

The constants of set types are denoted by *set-constructors*. Like set-type variables, set-constructors are factors, and may be used to build longer set-type expressions. A set-constructor is a list of set members given between square brackets:

factor A41-A42

> set-constructor = '[' [member-designator { ',' member-designator }] ']' .
> member-designator = expression { '..' expression } .

ordinal types A97-A100

A member-designator is either a value of an ordinal type, or two such values (separated by a '..') that designates the range the two values delimit. Some example set-constructors are:

> [ ]   [Spring]   [Spring..Winter]   ['a'..'z', 'A'..'Z']
> [1,3,5,7,9]   [1, 3..5, 10..15]   [';',',','.',':']   [sqr (3)+5]

The *empty* set, shown by an empty pair of square brackets: [ ], is a constant of every set type. The empty set is also designated by an empty closed interval; e.g., [3..1]. Note that [3..1] (whose type is explicitly given by the expression it contains) isn't necessarily equivalent to [ ] (whose type is determined by context). Thus, given the declaration:

> **var** Letters : **set of** char ;

this assignment is legal:

> Letters := [ ]

but the assignment below is illegal:

> Letters := [3..1]

Now, how is the type of a set-constructor or other set-type expression determined? In Pascal, every expression of a set type is said to be a value of the *canonical set-of-T*, where T is an ordinal type. Consequently, expressions like [1,2,3] and [3..1] are values of the canonical set of *integer*. The canonical set is a device that is helpful in other descriptions of set expressions.

---

[3] For example, since the base-type of *ThingSet* (*Things*) has three values, we expect, and find, eight (2^3) possible set-values of type *ThingSet*:

> [ ]   [a]   [b]   [c]   [a,b]   [a,c]   [b,c]   [a,b,c]

A11-3.2 Set Assignments and Expressions

Some sample assignments to set-type variables are:

> *Year* := [*Spring..Winter*];
> *Included* := ['a'..'z'];
> *Excluded* := *Included*;
> *SmallPrimes* := [ ];
> *Conditions* := [*Testing, Ready*]

For the purposes of compatibility, the set types are treated similarly to strings and ordinal types, in the sense that values are inspected more closely than type names. Two set types *T1* and *T2* are *compatible* if:

1)   They have compatible base-types;[4] and

2)   either both are packed types, or neither is packed.

A set value of type *T1* is *assignment compatible* with a type *T2* if:

1)   They are compatible set types, and all the members of the value of type *T2* are also members of the base type of *T1*; except that

2)   it is an *error* if *T1* and *T2* are compatible, but a member of the value of type *T2* is *not* in the base type of *T1*.[5]

A set-valued expression must be assignment compatible with the set-type variable it is being assigned to. A set-valued actual parameter must be compatible with its formal parameter. Regardless of their base types, two sets cannot be assignment compatible if one is packed and the other is not.

A11-3.3 Expressions That Use Sets

As data structures, sets are easy to implement with arrays: the type definition **array** [*Season*] **of** boolean defines a structure that can be allocated as cheaply and easily as the set type **set of** *Season*.

However, the operators associated with set operands can make sets the data *type* of choice. The operators are:

Set Operators

Operator	Name	Precedence Category
*	set intersection	multiplying-operator
+	set union	adding-operator
−	set difference	adding-operator

In all cases, both operands must have the same canonical set-of-*T* type, and either both or neither must be packed. The result has the same canonical set-

[4] The base types are compatible if *T1* is a subrange of *T2*, or vice versa, or both are subranges of the same host type.

[5] It's an error, rather than a violation, solely because a check cannot necessarily be made until run-time. It's the kind of error that almost every processor will detect, and halt for.

of-*T* type as the operands. The *intersection* of sets *a* and *b* (*a*∗*b*) is the set whose members are currently in both *a* and *b*. The *union* of the same sets (*a* +*b*) is the set of members formed by merging *a* and *b*. Finally, the *difference* of the sets (*a* –*b*) is the set of *a's* members that are not also in *b*.

$$[1..5, 7] * [4, 6, 8] \quad \text{is} \quad [4] \cdot$$
$$[1..5, 7] + [4, 6, 8] \quad \text{is} \quad [1..8]$$
$$[1..5, 7] - [4, 6, 8] \quad \text{is} \quad [1..3, 5, 7]$$

Several relational operators may also be applied to set operand(s), and yield *boolean* -valued results. Again, either both operands or neither must be packed.

Relational Operators

Operator	Name	Precedence Category
=	set equality	relational-operator
<>	set inequality	,,
<=	'included in'	,,
>=	'includes'	,,
in	set inclusion	,,

For all operators besides **in**, both operands must have the same canonical set-of-*T* type.

1)   *a*=*b* is *true* if all members of both *a* and *b* are identical.

2)   *a*<>*b* is *true* if any member of *a* cannot be found in *b*, or vice versa.

3)   *a*<=*b* is *true* if every member of *a* is also a member of *b*.

4)   *a*>=*b* is *true* if every member of *b* is found in *a*.

5)   *V* **in** *S* is *true* if the ordinal value *V* is a member of set *S*.

The final relational operator, **in**, requires a left operand of any ordinal type *T1*, and a right operand of the canonical set-of-*T1*.

Set expressions usually provide a clean, obvious, and efficient method of stating relationships. For example:

  if *SpecialSymbol* **in** [';', ':', ',', '.']
   then *HandlePunctuation* etc.

  repeat
    ⋰
  until ([*Running, Ready*] <= *Conditions*) etc.

Naturally, they also describe sets of data:

```
program FindMissingLetters (input, output);
      {Finds capital letters not included in a text sample.}
type CharacterSet = set of char;
var Current: char;
    MissingLetters: CharacterSet;
begin
  MissingLetters := ['A'..'Z'];
  while not eof
    do begin
      read (Current);
      MissingLetters := MissingLetters −[Current]
    end;
  for Current := 'A' to 'Z'
    do if Current in MissingLetters then write (Current);
  writeln
end.
```

A11-4 The File Type

The structured types described so far have shared an important restriction—the number (as well as the type) of components each structure holds has been part of its definition. *File* types, in contrast, are not limited to storing any particular number of components. The 'size' of a file-type variable may change during program execution.

A second crucial difference between files and all other types is that file-type variables may exist independently of any program. This means that:

1) Programs can access external data files that were allocated *before* program execution.

2) Programs can make storage allocations that persist *after* program execution.

The BNF of the file type is:

> *file-type* = '**file**' '**of**' *component-type* .
> *component-type* = *type-denoter* .

> *file-type*

```
file → of ── ⟨ → ordinal-type-identifier ──── ⟩ ────→
              → new-ordinal-type ────────
```

The components of a file may belong to any simple, structured, or pointer type, with these exceptions:

1)   File components may not be file types themselves.

2)   File components can't be structured types that contain file-type components.

Some legal definitions and declarations are:

> **type** *Date* = **file of** *real*;
>   *DataFile* = **file of array** [1..10] **of** *integer*;
>   *Lines* = **array** [1..10] **of file of** *char*;
>   *Employees* = **file of record**
>   ⋱   *description of record fields*
>   **end**;
>
> **var** *Calendar*: *Date*;
>   *Vectors*: *DataFile*;
>   *Course*: *Lines*;
>   *Payroll*: *Employees*;
>   *NewInput*: *text*;

text A131

The required identifier *text* denotes a predefined type similar to **file of** *char*, and is discussed later on. An *illegal* definition is:

> {illegal definition}
> *PersonData* = **array** [(*Job, Family, Study*)] **of** *text*;
> *SuperFile* = **file of** *PersonData*; {*PersonData* has file components.}

Unlike all other variables, which may be inspected or modified at any time, active file variables must be in one of two states: either being *generated* — written to—or *inspected* —read from. A file may not be in both states at once. Another restriction is that files may not be the actual parameters of value-parameters.[6] They must be passed to variable-parameters instead.

variable-parameters
A81-A83

Files are *sequential-access* structures, in contrast to *random-access* structures like records and arrays. When a file is being generated, new components are always added to the file's end. A file that is being inspected must be searched in the order that its components were added. The search for an individual file component must start at the file's beginning, and go all the way through, component by component, until the sought component is found.

File variables are atypical for Pascal because of the extent to which they reflect underlying computer systems. Space for file variables is often allocated on comparatively slow secondary storage devices (which, for all practical purposes, enables files to grow without limit). To avoid slowing down the processor (by requiring it to deal with these devices) implementations generally allocate intermediate buffers that are large enough for efficient update of, or by, secondary storage.

---

[6] A value-parameter's actual parameter must be assignment compatible with it, and file-types are never assignment compatible. See section A2-1.

Since secondary storage devices and intermediate buffers are wholly dependent on implementation, Pascal deals with files consistently by introducing a *buffer variable* that represents a single file component. The buffer variable is automatically allocated in conjunction with a file variable's declaration; every file has a buffer variable associated with it. It is denoted by the file-variable's name and an up-arrow or circumflex.[7]

$$buffer\text{-}variable = file\text{-}variable \text{ '}\uparrow\text{'} .$$
$$file\text{-}variable = variable\text{-}access .$$

The buffer variable acts as a window that contains (or more accurately, can allow access of) the 'current' file component. In effect, the programmer manipulates a file's buffer variable (possibly using procedures *get* or *put*) to inspect or add to the file itself. The exact point at which changes in a buffer variable are reflected in secondary storage is implementation-defined (which lets implementors take advantage of the aforementioned intermediate buffers). It is an error to change the value of a file when a reference to its buffer exists.

get, put A128

Since a file variable's components are anonymous (they don't have individual identifiers) the buffer variable serves as the name of the currently accessible file component. As a result, the buffer variable's type is the component-type of the file. For a file of type *text*, the buffer variable has type *char*. Some typical accesses are:

```
Calendar ↑ := 1.30;
writeln (Calendar ↑);
for i := 1 to 10 do Vectors ↑[i] := 0;
Course [1]↑ := 'H';
Payroll ↑.Field := Info;
read (NewInput ↑)
```

A11-4.1 The File Handling Procedures

When a file variable is first declared, it is undefined—neither in the state of inspection nor generation—and its buffer variable is totally undefined. Four required procedures are sufficient to put the file into an active state, and then manipulate the file's buffer variable to inspect or alter the file.

rewrite (f) The procedure statement *rewrite (f)* puts file *f* in the generation state. Any current contents are lost—the file becomes **empty** (but defined), while the buffer variable *f* ↑ becomes totally undefined.

reset (f) The procedure statement *reset (f)* puts file *f* in the inspection state. It is an error if *f* is undefined before the call of *reset*; however, *f* may have been empty. After the call of *reset*, the buffer variable *f* ↑

---

[7] I'll always use the up-arrow (an ISO national variant) because it's more readable in this typeface.

represents the first file component, *except that* if the file is empty, the buffer variable is totally undefined.

textfiles A131-A134   In the special case of f as a textfile, *reset* (f) requires, if f is nonempty, that its last component be an end-of-line. Thus, a textfile may not contain a partial last line; in effect, a call of *reset* adds an end-of-line component if necessary.

put (f) The procedure statement *put* (f) appends the buffer variable $f \uparrow$ to file f. It is an error if f isn't being generated, if $f \uparrow$ is undefined, or if $f \uparrow$ isn't put on the end of the file. After the *put*, the buffer variable becomes totally undefined, but the file stays in the 'generation' state. Note that the buffer variable's current value is not added to a file until it has been *put* there.

get (f) The procedure statement *get* (f) causes the buffer variable $f \uparrow$ to represent file f's next component. It is an error if the file is not in the inspection state, or if there isn't any 'next' component; i.e. if *eof* (f), discussed below, is *true*. If the second error occurs, the buffer variable becomes totally undefined.

We can see that avoiding some errors requires knowledge about whether a file is empty to begin with, or whether the buffer variable currently represents the file's last component. A *boolean* **end-of-file** function provides this knowledge.

eof (f) The function call *eof* (f) yields the value *true* if the file is empty beyond the component that $f \uparrow$ currently represents, or if f is empty. It is an error to call *eof* (f) if f is undefined.

input A131-A132   If the function is called without an actual parameter list (e.g. *eof*), it
eoln A38, A133   applies to the required textfile *input*. An additional file-oriented function called *eoln* applies only to textfiles, and is discussed later.

The program fragment below demonstrates a common model of file usage. Note that there is an implicit call of *get* (*Data*) when *Data* is reset.

```
{Inspect and modify components of Data (with procedure
 Process), and store the modified components in Results.}
var Data, Results: file of FileComponent;
    OneComponent: FileComponent;
    ...
 reset (Data);  {prepare to inspect Data}
 rewrite (Results);  {prepare to generate Results}
 while not eof (Data)
   do begin
       Process (Data↑, OneComponent);
       Results↑ := OneComponent;  {define the Results buffer variable}
       put (Results);  {append Results↑ to Results}
       get (Data)  {advance the buffer variable Data↑}
     end
```

It's important to realize that this alternative formulation:

```
      . . .
      reset (Data);
      rewrite (Results);
      repeat
          Process (Data↑, OneComponent);
          Results↑ := OneComponent;
          put (Results);
          get (Data)
      until eof (Data)
```

is incorrect if *Data* is an empty file. The access of its buffer variable will be an error, as will the attempted *get*.

A11-4.2 *read and write*

Although procedures *get* and *put* are sufficient for inspecting or updating individual file components, they are not necessarily convenient. In practice, one usually advances the buffer variable immediately after inspecting or assigning it. For instance, if data items are considered to belong in triples, then one of the following fragments is needed to assign (or record) a given triple to (or from) variables *V1*, *V2*, and *V3*.

```
{Get V1, V2, V3}                    {Save V1, V2, V3}
reset (Data);                       rewrite (Results);
V1 := Data↑;                        Results↑ := V1;
get (Data);                         put (Results);
V2 := Data↑;                        Results↑ := V2;
get (Data);                         put (Results);
V3 := Data↑;                        Results↑ := V3;
get (Data)                          put (Results)
```

The required procedures *read* and *write* simplify this job by combining the two steps, like this:[8]

```
{Get V1, V2, V3}                    {Save V1, V2, V3}
reset (Data);                       rewrite (Results);
read (Data, V1, V2, V3)             write (Results, V1, V2, V3)
```

There is a dual advantage to using *read* and *write*: the primitive operations *get* and *put* are concealed, as is any monkeying around with the file buffer variable.

variable-access A70   The procedure call *read* (*f*,*V*), where *f* is a file variable and *V* is a variable-access, establishes a reference to *f* for the remainder of the statement's execution.

---

[8] In the following discussion, we assume that file *f* is *not* a textfile. *read* and *write* are defined slightly differently for textfiles; also, two additional procedures (*readln* and *writeln*) are predefined for textfiles.

read (*f*,*V*) is equivalent to **begin** $V := f \uparrow$; *get* (*f*) **end**

Note that the file buffer now serves as a *lookahead* variable. It contains the component that will be assigned in the process of the next *read*.

The procedure call *write* (*f*,*E*), where *f* is a file variable and *E* is an expression, also establishes a reference to *f* for the rest of the call.

write (*f*,*E*) is equivalent to **begin** $f \uparrow := E$; *put* (*f*) **end**

In both cases, the file *f* may be of *any* type, which either extends or clarifies [J&W], which seemed to allow only textfiles.

Both *read* and *write* allow multiple arguments, and imply a repeated sequence of assignments and calls. The call *read* (*f*, *V1*, $\cdots$, *Vn*) is equivalent to the sequence:

begin *read* (*f*, *V1*); $\cdots$; *read* (*f*, *Vn*) **end**

Similarly, *write* (*f*, *E1*, $\cdots$, *En*) is equivalent to the sequence:

begin *write* (*f*, *E1*); $\cdots$; *write* (*f*, *En*) **end**

Once again, for both *read* and *write*, a single reference to file *f* exists through the entire procedure call. For example, suppose we make this declaration:

var *A*: **array** [1..10] **of file of** *integer*;
      i, a, b: *integer*;

During the whole peculiar call of *read* shown below, only a single component of *A* will be accessed.

read (*A*[*i*], *i, a, i, b*)

Incidentally, all assertions about, and implementation-defined aspects of, the procedures *get* and *put* apply, since for all practical purposes they are used by *read* and *write*. In a call of *read* that applies to a file *f*, it's an error if each value obtained isn't assignment compatible with *f*'s buffer variable, or if the buffer variable is undefined immediately before the call. Similarly, in a call of *write*, it's an error if the type of any expression being written isn't assignment compatible with the file's buffer.

A11-4.3 External Files: Program Parameters

An *external* file exists independently of any program activation. It may contain input data, or be a depository for program results. Such files are named in the program's *heading* as *program parameters*.

program-heading = '**program**' *identifier* ['(' *program-parameters* ')'] .
program-parameters = *identifier-list* .
identifier-list = *identifier* { ',' *identifier* } .

defining points A59-A60

If an identifier (besides *input* or *output*) appears as a program parameter, it must have a defining point as a variable-identifier for the region of the program block. (In English, this means that it must be declared as a variable in the main program.) Technically, the identifiers are not required to be declared as files—if they aren't, their binding to external entities is implementation-dependent.[9] If they *are* declared as files, which is the usual case, then their binding is implementation-defined. All program parameter identifiers must be distinct.

After appearing in the program heading, external files are declared and treated just like ordinary file types. Program *Duplicate*, below, copies the contents of file *Old* into file *New*.

```
program Duplicate (Old, New);
   {Copy file Old to the external file New}
type DataType = {Definition of DataType.}
   . .
var Old, New: file of DataType;
    Temp: DataType;
begin
   reset (Old);
   rewrite (New);
   while not eof (Old)
      do begin
         read (Old, Temp);
         write (New, Temp)
      end
end.
```

A11-4.4 Textfiles

The required file-type *text* is the only predefined structured type. Files of type *text* are called *textfiles*. Type *text* is superficially like the type **file of** *char*, in that it defines a file type with *char* components.[10] All required procedures and functions that are applicable to variables with type **file of** *char* may also be applied to textfiles. However, additional procedures and functions are required (*readln, writeln, page*, and *eoln*) that may only be used with textfiles.

The most important textfiles are *input* and *output*, which are both predefined. *input* and *output* generally represent the processor's standard input/output mechanism—the *input* 'file' may be a keyboard or card reader, while *output* is usually a CRT screen or lineprinter.

[9] Typically, this will allow particular I/O devices to be named as program parameters.
[10] The two types were identical in [J&W].

1)   Although either must appear as a program parameter if used within a pro-
     gram, neither *input* nor *output* may have a further defining point within
     the program block.

2)   If either appears as a program parameter, an implicit call of *reset* (*input*) or
     rewrite (*output*) is made before the first access of either the textfile, or its
     buffer variable.[11]

3)   The effect of any further call of procedures *reset* and *rewrite*, as applied to
     input or *output*, is implementation-defined.

I/O devices A47

Textfiles, like files in general, are structured in the sense that they are
sequences of components—in this case, of *char* values. However, textfiles are
also divided into **lines**, to help the line-orientation of most I/O devices and
textfile applications. A special value called the **end-of-line component** marks
the end of every line (including the last line) of every textfile. Although the
end-of-line is required to be indistinguishable from a blank space (except as perceived by *eoln, readln*, and *reset*), its actual representation is implementation-
dependent.[12]

Three required procedures, and one required function, are predefined to
enable certain textfile prerogatives. In all cases below, the file *f* must be a
textfile.

writeln (*f*)   The procedure call *writeln* (*f*) appends an end-of-line to file *f* (ter-
             minating any partial line being produced with *write*). It is an error
             if *f* is undefined. After the call, *f* ↑ is totally undefined, and *f*
             remains in the 'generation' state. Note that a line may consist solely
             of the end-of-line. *writeln* applies to *output* if no file is named.[13]

readln (*f*)   The procedure call *readln* (*f*) positions the file buffer variable just
             past the current line's end-of-line—at the first character of the next
             line. In effect, it skips over the current line. Applies to *input* if no
             file is named. The call *readln* (*f*) is equivalent to:

             begin while not *eoln* (*f*) **do** *get* (*f*); *get* (*f*) **end**

             which makes it an error to call *readln* (*f*) if *eof* (*f*) is *true*.

page (*f*)   The procedure call *page* (*f*) is equivalent to *writeln* (*f*) except that it
             also has an implementation-defined effect—further text written to *f*

---

[11] [J&W] implied that the *reset* of file *input* had to occur before program statement execution,
which meant (in interactive systems) that actual input had to begin before it was prompted for!
Under the present standard, the implicit *get* (*input*) is usually delayed until the first *read* or *readln*.
(This is traditionally known as *lazy I/O*.)

[12] Typically, the end-of-line is one or more control characters (like the line feed and carriage return
characters). However, some systems treat each line as a record with an associated 'length' value—
physically, there is no end-of-line component.

[13] An implicit call of *writeln* may be made prior to program termination for every textfile being generated, since the predefined procedure *reset* requires every nonempty textfile to end with an end-
of-line.

will appear on a new physical page if the textfile is being printed on a suitable output device.[14] However, *page* is not required to modify the file, because the effect of inspecting a textfile to which *page* has been applied is implementation-dependent. *page* applies to *output* if no file is named.

eoln (f)   The function call *eoln* (f) is *true* if the buffer variable $f\uparrow$ is the end-of-line. It is an error if f is undefined, or if *eof*(f) is *true*. *eoln* applies to *input* if no file is named.

Although the file primitives *get* and *put* may be applied to textfiles, procedures *read*, *write*, *readln* and *writeln* are generally used instead. When applied to textfiles, the latter four procedures share an attractive feature—they automatically coerce a sequence of *char* values to *integer* or *real* (for *read* and *readln*) or vice versa (for *write* and *writeln*).[15]

I/O coercion A48, A50

When applied to textfiles, the parameter lists of *read*, *readln*, *write*, and *writeln* have specific BNFs:

write-parameter-list = '(' [*file-variable* ','] *write-parameter* { ',' *write-parameter* } ')' .
writeln-parameter-list = ['(' (*file-variable* | *write-parameter*) { ',' *write-parameter* } ')'] .
write-parameter = *expression* [':' *expression* [':' *expression*]] .
read-parameter-list = '(' [*file-variable* ','] *variable-access* { ',' *variable-access* } ')' .
readln-parameter-list = ['(' (*file-variable* | *variable-access*) { ',' *variable-access* } ')'] .

A variable-access, as used in the BNF of a read- or readln-parameter-list, is not a variable-parameter. As a result, it may be a component of a packed structure, and the buffer variable's value need only be assignment compatible with it.

packing A101, A119-A121

If the file-variable argument of *write* or *writeln* is omitted, the procedure applies to the required textfile *output*. Similarly, if the file-variable argument of *read* or *readln* is omitted, the procedure applies to the required textfile *input*.

The exact meaning of the *write-parameter* syntax was discussed in detail in section A5-2; it suffices for now to say that it allows the printing of *char*, *real*, *integer*, and *boolean* values, as well as specification of field width, or floating/fixed-point representation. The call *writeln* (f, E1, $\cdots$, En) is equivalent to:

   begin *write* (f, E1, $\cdots$, En); *writeln* (f) **end**

A statement of the form *readln* (f, V1, $\cdots$, Vn) is equivalent to:

   begin *read* (f, V1, $\cdots$, Vn); *readln* (f) **end**

In consequence, it is easy, deliberately or inadvertently, to discard data that remains on an input line.

---

[14] If there is no partial line, there is no implicit *writeln*.
[15] Note that the buffer variable of a textfile is always of type *char*. It's generally reserved for use as a lookahead.

The effect of *write* (*f,E*) on interactive files is a matter for special consideration. Although the call is equivalent to:

begin $f \uparrow := E$; *put* (*f*) **end**

the observant reader will remember that the exact time a *put* is reflected in the physical file is implementation-defined. In some implementations the *put* takes place immediately; others delay a sequence of *puts* until an arbitrary output buffer is filled; others buffer *puts* until a *read* or *readln* is encountered; still others buffer *puts* until procedure *writeln* (or *page*) is called. Since a *writeln* almost invariably acts as a line-feed, this means that interactive applications programmers may not be able to position a cursor or print head at the end of a line of output.

A11-4.5 Comments

The precise definition of file types has brought grief to programmers and implementors from the beginning. In a 1975 paper that reviewed his experience with Pascal, Wirth titled one section '*An Important Concept and a Persistent Source of Problems: Files,*' and admitted that:

> '...some inherent difficulties became evident only after extended usage.' [Wirth75]

The roots of the problem lie in the poorly understood relationship between programs and I/O devices in general. These devices are not easily abstracted as data types; a cantankerous lineprinter can make a mess of a well-pedigreed file abstraction. As a result, Pascal's file types labor under a double burden. They're intended to describe not only malleable locations in memory, but actual storage devices as well. Unfortunately, what appears to be a fine solution for a certain class of devices may fail miserably for others.

The best example involves the widely documented problem of implementing interactive Pascal programs according to [J&W]. The original Pascal implementation was a compiler for the CDC 6000 series of *batch-oriented* computers. Now, if batch programs have one distinguishing feature, it is that all data associated with the required file *input* is available at the start of program execution. As a result, the initializing call *reset* (*input*) can be performed without difficulty—there is a component available for the buffer variable.

Interactive files are less amenable to being reset. A typical program begins:

```
begin
    writeln ('Enter data');
    readln (Data);
        ...     etc.
```

Under [J&W] the user was required to enter at least one character *before* the prompt. Since this was obviously impractical, a host of 'solutions' appeared in the pages of *SIGPLAN Notices* and other journals. Proposals (which, in general, were actually implemented—with horrible results for program portability) included initializing *input*↑ to end-of-line, creating a new class of interactive files, adding new required functions, and the ultimate winner, lazy I/O.

lazy I/O A132

I mention this only to illustrate the basic law of Standards—*if it doesn't work, it won't stay standard very long.*

Pointer Types

A variable of a pointer type is used to *reference*, or indirectly access, a variable of the pointer's **domain -type**.

> *pointer-type* = *new-pointer-type* | *pointer-type-identifier* .
> *new-pointer-type* = '↑' *domain-type* .
> *domain-type* = *type-identifier* .

Either a circumflex or up-arrow (an ISO national variant) can be used in conjunction with pointer types and variables. I use the up-arrow because it's more readable in print.

   For all practical purposes, a pointer-type can't be defined within the definition of its domain-type. However, a pointer type may be defined *in advance* of its domain-type, as long as the domain-type is defined in the same type definition part. Some legal definitions and declarations are:

```
type IntegerPointer = ↑integer;
     NodePointer = ↑Node;
     Node = record
               Data: integer;
               Lchild, Rchild: NodePointer
            end;
     MoreBuckets = ↑Buckets;
     Buckets = record
                  ·. {details of data fields}
                  OverFlow: MoreBuckets
               end;
     HashTable = array [1..100] of MoreBuckets;
     TypeOfGarbage = (IntPtr, NodePtr, MorBkts);
     AdditionalGarbage = ↑Garbage;
     Garbage = record
                  MoreGarbage: AdditionalGarbage;
                  case TypeOfGarbage of
                     IntPtr: (NewIntPtr: IntegerPointer);
                     NodePtr: (NewNodePtr: NodePointer);
                     MorBkts: (NewMorBkts: MoreBuckets)
               end;

 var Head, Tail, Current, Auxiliary: NodePointer;
     Symbols: HashTable;
     NewSymbol: MoreBuckets;
     Free: AdditionalGarbage;
```

Certain self-referencing definitions are legal:

type *2* = **array** [1..100] **of** ↑*T1* ;
      T2 = ↑*T2* ;

but are so peculiar that it is doubtful if they are ever made. Another legal, but unlikely, definition is:

type *Element* = **record**
            Info : *char* ;
            Newer : ↑*Element*
       end ;

Although the definition of *Element* is legal, field *Newer* has an anonymous type. This means that it's impossible to declare an auxiliary pointer variable or function with the same type as *Newer* .

A12-1 Pointer Variables

Any discussion of pointer variables must first distinguish between the pointer, and the variable referenced by the pointer. A pointer variable can be initialized or modified in one of three ways:

1)   It can be assigned the *nil -value* , which is denoted by the token **nil** . A *nil -pointer* does not reference a variable.

2)   It can be given a unique *identifying -value* , which serves as the address of a variable of the pointer's domain-type.

3)   It can be assigned the value of another pointer of the same type. Either it will become **nil** , or it will acquire the same identifying-value—and thus reference the same variable—as the other pointer.

tokens A3-A6

empty sets A122

      The nil-value is kind of peculiar. First, although it denotes a value, **nil** is a token, and not an identifier. This means that **nil** may not be redefined. Second, the exact type of **nil** depends on its context. In the same way that the empty set ([]) is a member of every set type, **nil** is effectively a member of every pointer type.

relational operators
A45-A46

      Under no circumstances can the value of a pointer be printed, used in an arithmetic expression, or otherwise inspected. Pointers of compatible types (i.e., with the same type) may, however, be compared to each other or to **nil** with the relational operators '=' and '<>'.

      A pointer is given a unique identifying value by using the required procedure *new* to **dynamically allocate** a new variable.

new (p)   The procedure call *new (p)*, where *p* is a variable-access of any pointer type, creates a totally undefined variable of *p's* domain type. *p* is said to *reference* this variable.

The new variable is unusual because it is anonymous, and is dynamically allocated. It remains allocated for the duration of program execution, even if it's created within a subprogram.[1] As a result, if it is necessary to reclaim the storage used by a referenced variable, another procedure call is required. The action that is absolutely required of *dispose* is limited:

dispose (*q*)   The procedure call *dispose* (*q*), where *q* is a variable or function of any pointer type, serves to disassociate the variable referenced by *q* from any pointer.[2] It is an error to *dispose* of a variable that is currently being accessed, or to attempt to *dispose* of an undefined or nil-valued pointer.

The first *dispose* error might occur in a situation like this:

> {illegal example}
> **with** *p* ↑ **do begin**
>   · · ·
>   *dispose* (*p*)   {This call is illegal because *p* is being accessed.}
> **end**

In most implementations a call of *dispose* (*q*) is assumed to free the memory occupied by the variable referenced by *q*. Whether or not this memory is actually released, it becomes an error to attempt to access the variable through *q*, or through any other pointer (since they have become undefined). Error status here is intended to resolve the problem of 'dangling' references to dynamically allocated variables.[3]

The effect of *new* and *dispose* in regard to records with variants is discussed later in this section. Some examples of ordinary assignments, allocations, and disposals are:

> *Head* := **nil**;
> *Tail* := **nil**;
> *new* (*Current*);
> *Tail* := *Current*;
> *dispose* (*Tail*);   {*Current* and *Tail* are both undefined now.}
> **for** *i* := 1 **to** 100 **do** *new* (*Symbols* [*i*])

---

[1] However, a locally declared variable (i.e., one that is not dynamically allocated) that happens to have a pointer type is allocated and deallocated just like any other local variable.

[2] This is truly one of the most obscure entries in the Standard, which says that the call 'shall remove the identifying-value denoted by the expression *q* from the pointer-type of *q*.' In English, this means that any pointer that previously referenced the variable becomes undefined, and that the variable itself becomes inaccessible.

[3] Suppose that several pointers reference a single dynamically allocated variable. If a call of a *dispose*-like procedure only made its single argument pointer undefined, then the remaining pointers would be 'dangling' references to the variable—they would still reference it. Unfortunately, finding every pointer that references a given variable causes nightmares for implementors. In consequence, the 'error' frequently goes undetected.

A12-1.1 Identified Variables

Since dynamically allocated variables don't have identifiers, they are anonymous, and must be referred to by manufactured names. A dynamically allocated variable is denoted by an *identified-variable*.

> *identified-variable* = *pointer-variable* '↑' .
> *pointer-variable* = *variable-access* .

It is an error if the pointer-variable used to form an identified-variable is either **nil** or undefined.

Now, although a function's result-type may be a pointer type, a function call can't be used to construct an identified-variable. As shown in the BNF, a pointer variable must be a variable-access (which a function call isn't). For example, suppose that the declaration of function *ListEnd* begins with:

> **function** *ListEnd* (P: *NodePointer*): *NodePointer*;
>   etc.

ListEnd is a function that returns a pointer type, so the call *ListEnd* (*Current*) represents a pointer to a dynamically allocated variable. The assignment:

> {illegal example}
> *Tail* ↑.*Data* := *ListEnd* (*Current*) ↑.*Data*

is incorrect, because it tries to use a function call in constructing an identified variable. An auxiliary variable must be assigned the function's value (as a pointer) to access the variable the pointer references:

> *Auxiliary* := *ListEnd* (*Current*);
> *Tail* ↑.*Data* := *Auxiliary* ↑.*Data*

Although an identified variable may have any type, in most applications it has a record type that contains at least one field that is a pointer to another record of the same type. For instance:

> **type** *ElementPointer* = ↑*Element*;
>   *Element* = **record**
>   *Data*: *integer*;
>   *Left, Right*: *ElementPointer*
>   **end**;
> **var** *Current, Saved*: *ElementPointer*;

Since variables of type *Element* contain pointers to other variables of type *Element*, they can be used to form a variety of **linked** data structures: lists, queues, trees, stacks, etc. Individual elements of most linked structures are practically identical (data fields, and one or more pointer fields that provide links to other elements).

Linked structures are characterized by the operations that can be performed on them. A singly-linked list that might serve as a queue is implemented with:

new (Saved); {Allocate the first list element or link.}
Saved↑.Left := **nil**; {Make the *Left* field a nil pointer.}
Saved↑.Right := **nil**; {Make the *Right* field a nil pointer.}
Current := *Saved*; {Point *Current* at the first element.}
read (Current↑.Data); {Store data in the current link.}
new (Current↑.Right); {Allocate a new link.}
Current := *Current↑.Right*; {Advance the *Current* pointer.}
Current↑.Left := **nil**; {Make the *Left* field a nil pointer.}
Current↑.Right := **nil**; {Make the *Right* field a nil pointer.}
read (Current↑.Data); {Store data in the current link.}
  ··.   etc.

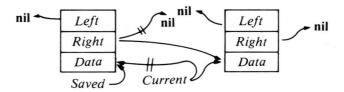

Notice that although the *Right* fields are used as links, the *Left* fields are set to **nil**. If the application demanded it, we could easily create a doubly-linked list:

  ··.
new (Current↑.Right); {Allocate a new link.}
Current↑.Right↑.Left := *Current*; {Point the new link backward.}
Current := *Current↑.Right*; {Advance the *Current* pointer.}
  ··.   etc.

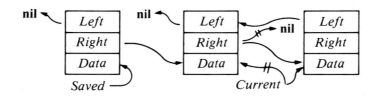

As noted earlier, the relational operands = and <> may be given pointer type operands. Either list created above can be searched for a specific value, starting with the first element and searching toward the right, with:

Current := *Saved*;
if *Current* <> **nil then** {make sure the list is nonempty}
    while (*Current↑.Data* <>*SoughtData*) **and** (*Current↑.Right* <>**nil**)
      do *Current* := *Current↑.Right*

Notice that an additional check must be made on termination to see if the sought element has actually been located—the list might empty, or just not contain the desired element. An alternative formulation:

> $Current := Saved$;
> **if** $Current <>$ **nil then** {make sure the list is nonempty}
>   **while** $(Current\uparrow.Data <> SoughtData)$ **and** $(Current <> $**nil**$)$
>   **do** $Current := Current\uparrow.Right$

contains a potential error. Suppose that the sought data is not contained in the list. We will find ourselves in the awkward position of inspecting the *Data* field of a **nil** pointer. Remember that, to help ensure portability, *boolean* expressions should be assumed to be fully evaluated.

A12-1.2 Dynamic Allocation of Variants

record variants
A107-A112

Variant forms of *new* and *dispose* let records with variant parts be allocated and deallocated more efficiently.

Recall that one purpose of record variants is to let variables with disjoint lifetimes be overlaid in memory. The amount of space such a record requires will be at least the size of its largest variant. Suppose, though, that we want to allocate a 'small' variant. The alternative form of *new* described below allows (but does not require) a processor to allocate the minimum amount of space required.

case constants A20-A22

$new(p, C1, \cdots, Cn)$ The procedure call $new(p, C1, \cdots, Cn)$ creates a totally undefined variable of p's domain type, which p references. p is a pointer variable-access, while $C1, \cdots, Cn$ are case-constants (not variables or other expressions) that apply to variants nested at increasingly deep levels of the record.

1)   The dynamically allocated variable has nested variants that correspond to the case-constants $C1, \cdots, Cn$.

2)   These variants should not be changed, because it is an error if a variant that was not specified becomes active (unless it's at a deeper level of nesting than Cn).

3)   One case-constant for every potential variant in the range $C1, \cdots, Cn$ must be specified. A variant not given must be at a deeper level of nesting than Cn.

4)   It is an error if a variable created using the second form of *new* is accessed by the identified-variable of the variable-access of a factor, of an assignment-statement, or of an actual-parameter. In English, this means that the variable can't appear in an assignment, or as an actual parameter (although its individual fields may).

5)   If, as above, a variable is created using the second form of *new*, it is an error to deallocate it using the first (short) form of *dispose*.

Once we have specified a given set of variant parts, we are stuck with it. Rule 2 makes it an error to try to activate a different variant.

The required procedure *dispose* also has an alternative form.

dispose (*p*, *K1*, ··· ,*Km*)   The procedure call *dispose* (*p*, *K1*, ··· ,*Km*) makes the dynamically allocated variable referenced by *p* inaccessible by any pointer variable.

1)   *K1*, ··· ,*Km* are case-constants that apply to variants nested at increasingly deep levels of the variable.

2)   It is an error if the variable was created by a call *new* (*p*, *K1*, ··· ,*Kn*) and *n* isn't equal to *m* , or if any of the variants are different.

3)   It is an error if the pointer variable *p* is **nil** or undefined.

Thus, an application of *dispose* must parallel that of *new*. A variable allocated with the variant form must be disposed of in the same manner.

We close with some famous last words from C.A.R. Hoare:

> '[Pointers] are like jumps, leading wildly from one part of a data structure to another. Their introduction into high-level languages has been a step backward from which we may never recover.' [Hoare73]

The problems of concern above involve possible confusion between a pointer's value (an address), and the value of the variable located at that address, as well as the potential for 'spaghetti' data structures. Fortunately, the restrictions Pascal places on pointers—the prohibition against reading, writing, or assigning pointers as *integers*—along with the specification of procedure *dispose*, help obviate most of these concerns.

Collected Errors

As noted in section 1, an error is a violation of the Standard that a conforming processor may leave undetected. However, each processor's documentation must specify the manner in which errors—particularly undetected errors—are dealt with. The errors contained in this appendix serve as a checklist for potentially non-portable program features. They are numbered only for convenience, since there are no 'official' error numbers. Page numbers in brackets refer to the original discussion of each error.

Array Types and Packing

1. It is an error if the value of any subscript of an indexed-variable isn't assignment-compatible with its corresponding index-type. [A115]

2. In a call of the form *pack* (*Vunpacked*, *StartingSubscript*, *Vpacked*), it is an error if the ordinal-typed actual parameter (*StartingSubscript*) isn't assignment compatible with the index-type of the not-packed array parameter (*Vunpacked*). [A120]

3. In a call of the form *pack* (*Vunpacked*, *StartingSubscript*, *Vpacked*), it is an error to access any undefined component of *Vunpacked*. [A121]

4. In a call of the form *pack* (*Vunpacked*, *StartingSubscript*, *Vpacked*), it is an error to exceed the index-type of *Vunpacked*. [A120]

5. In a call of the form *unpack* (*Vpacked*, *Vunpacked*, *StartingSubscript*), it is an error if the ordinal-typed actual parameter (*StartingSubscript*) isn't assignment compatible with the index-type of the not-packed array parameter (*Vunpacked*). [A120]

6. In a call of the form *unpack* (*Vpacked*, *Vunpacked*, *StartingSubscript*), it is an error for any component of *Vpacked* to be undefined. [A120]

7. In a call of the form *unpack* (*Vpacked*, *Vunpacked*, *StartingSubscript*), it is an error to exceed the index-type of *Vunpacked*. [A120]

Record Types

8. It is an error to access or reference any component of a record variant that is not active. [A110]

9. It is an error if any constant of the tag-type of a variant-part does not appear in a case-constant-list. [A108]

10. It is an error to pass the tag-field of a variant-part as the argument of a variable-parameter. [A110]

11. It is an error if a record that has been dynamically allocated through a call of the form *new (p, C1,···,Cn)* is accessed by the identified-variable of the variable-access of a factor, of an assignment statement, or of an actual parameter. [A141]

File Types, Input, and Output

12. It is an error to change the value of a file variable f when a reference to its buffer variable $f\uparrow$ exists. [A82, A128]

13. It is an error if, immediately prior to a call of *put, write, writeln*, or *page*, the file affected is not in the 'generation' state. [A128]

14. It is an error if, immediately prior to a call of *put, write, writeln*, or *page*, the file affected is undefined. [A128]

15. It is an error if, immediately prior to a call of *put, write, writeln*, or *page*, the file affected is not at end-of-file. [A128]

16. It is an error if the buffer variable is undefined immediately prior to any use of *put*. [A128]

17. It is an error if the affected file is undefined immediately prior to any use of *reset*. [A127]

18. It is an error if, immediately prior to a use of *get* or *read*, the file affected is not in the 'inspection' state. [A128]

19. It is an error if, immediately prior to a use of *get* or *read*, the file affected is undefined. [A128]

20. It is an error if, immediately prior to a use of *get* or *read*, the affected file is at end-of-file. [A128]

21. It is an error if, in a call of *read*, the type of the variable-access isn't assignment compatible with the type of the value read (and represented by the affected file's buffer-variable). [A130]

22. It is an error if, in a call of *write*, the type of the expression isn't assignment compatible with the type of the affected file's buffer-variable. [A130]

23. In a call of the form *eof* (f), it is an error for f to be undefined. [A128]

24. In any call of the form *eoln* (f), it is an error for f to be undefined. [A133]

25. In any call of the form *eoln* (f), it is an error for *eof* (f) to be *true*. [A133]

26. When reading an *integer* from a textfile, it is an error if the input sequence (after any leading blanks or end-of-lines are skipped) does not form a signed-integer. [A50]

27. When an *integer* is read from a textfile, it is an error if it isn't assignment compatible with the variable-access it is being attributed to. [A50]

28. When reading a number from a textfile, it is an error if the input sequence (after any leading blanks or end-of-lines are skipped) does not form a signed-number. [A50]

29. It is an error if the appropriate buffer variable is undefined immediately prior to any use of *read*. [A130]

30. In writing to a textfile, it is an error if the value of *TotalWidth* or *Fractional-Digits*, if used, is less than one. [A54]

Pointer Types

31. It is an error to try to access a variable through a **nil**-valued pointer. [A139]

32. It is an error to try to access a variable through an undefined pointer. [A139]

Dynamic Allocation

33. It is an error to try to *dispose* of a dynamically-allocated variable when a reference to it exists. [A138]

34. When a record with a variant part is dynamically allocated through a call of the form *new*(*p, C1,···,Cn*) it is an error to activate a variant that was not specified (unless it's at a deeper level than *Cn*). [A142]

35. It is an error to use the short form of *dispose* (e.g., *dispose*(*p*)) to deallocate a variable that was allocated using the long form (e.g., *new*(*p, C1,···,Cn*)). [A141]

36. When a record with a variant part has been dynamically allocated through a call of the form *new*(*p, C1,···,Cn*), it is an error to specify a different number of variants in a call of *dispose*. [A142]

37. When a record with a variant part has been dynamically allocated through a call of the form *new*(*p, C1,···,Cn*), it is an error to specify a different sequence of variants in a call of *dispose*. [A142]

38. It is an error to call *dispose* with a **nil**-valued pointer argument. [A138]

39. It is an error to call *dispose* with an undefined pointer argument. [A138]

Required Functions and Arithmetic

40. For a call of the *sqr* function, it is an error if the result is not in the range −*maxint*..*maxint*. [A36]

41. In a call of the form *ln*(*x*), it is an error for *x* to be less than or equal to zero. [A36]

42. In a call of the form *sqrt*(*x*), it is an error for *x* to be negative. [A36]

43. For a call of the *trunc* function, it is an error if the result is not in the range *–maxint..maxint*. [A36]

44. For a call of the *round* function, it is an error if the result is not in the range *–maxint..maxint*. [A36]

45. For a call of the *chr* function, it is an error if the result does not exist. [A37]

46. For a call of the *succ* function, it is an error if the result does not exist. [A37]

47. For a call of the *pred* function, it is an error if the result does not exist. [A37]

48. In a term of the form x/y, it is an error for y to equal zero. [A31]

49. In a term of the form i **div** j, it is an error for j to equal zero. [A33]

50. In a term of the form i **mod** j, it is an error if j is zero or negative. [A33]

51. It is an error if any *integer* arithmetic operation, or function whose result type is *integer*, is not computed according to the mathematical rules for integer arithmetic. [A32]

Parameters

52. It is an error if an ordinal-typed value-parameter and its actual-parameter aren't assignment compatible. [A81]

53. It is an error if a set-typed value-parameter and its actual-parameter aren't assignment compatible. [A81]

Miscellaneous

54. It is an error for a variable-access contained by an expression to be undefined. [A42]

55. It is an error for the result of a function call to be undefined. [A77]

56. It is an error if a value and the ordinal-typed variable or function-designator it is assigned to aren't assignment compatible. [A10, A77]

57. It is an error if a set-typed variable, and the value assigned to it, are not assignment compatible. [A10]

58. On entry to a case-statement, it is an error if the value of the case-index does not appear in a case-constant-list. [A22]

59. If a for-statement is executed, it is an error if the types of the control-variable and the initial-value aren't assignment compatible. [A28]

60. If a for-statement is executed, it is an error if the types of the control-variable and the final-value aren't assignment compatible. [A28]

actual-parameter = *expression* | *variable-access*
              | *procedure-identifier* | *function-identifier* .

actual-parameter-list = '(' *actual-parameter* { ',' *actual-parameter* } ')' .

adding-operator = '+' | '−' | '**or**' .

apostrophe-image = ' " ' .

array-type = '**array**' '[' *index-type* { ',' *index-type* } ']' '**of**' *component-type* .

array-variable = *variable-access* .

assignment-statement = (*variable-access* | *function-identifier*) ':=' *expression* .

base-type = *ordinal-type* .

block = *label-declaration-part*
        constant-definition-part
           type-definition-part
              variable-declaration-part
                  procedure-and-function-declaration-part
                    statement-part .

boolean-expression = *expression* .

bound-identifier = *identifier* .

buffer-variable = *file-variable* '↑' .

case-constant = *constant* .

case-constant-list = *case-constant* { ',' *case-constant* } .

case-index = *expression* .

case-list-element = *case-constant-list* ':' *statement* .

case-statement = '**case**' *case-index* '**of**'
        case-list-element { ';' *case-list-element* } [';'] '**end**' .

character-string = ' " ' *string-element* { *string-element* } ' " ' .

component-type = *type-denoter* .

component-variable = *indexed-variable* | *field-designator* .

compound-statement = '**begin**' *statement-sequence* '**end**' .

conditional-statement = *if-statement* | *case-statement* .

conformant-array-parameter-specification = *value-conformant-array-specification*
                                   | *variable-conformant-array-specification* .

conformant-array-schema = packed-conformant-array-schema
                          | unpacked-conformant-array-schema .

constant = [sign] (unsigned-number | constant-identifier) | character-string .

constant-definition = identifier '=' constant .

*constant-definition-part = ['**const**' constant-definition ';' { constant-definition ';' }] .*

constant-identifier = identifier .

control-variable = entire-variable .

digit = '0' | '1' | '2' | '3' | '4' | '5' | '6' | '7' | '8' | '9' .

digit-sequence = digit { digit } .

directive = letter { letter | digit } .

domain-type = type-identifier .

*else-part = '**else**' statement .*

empty-statement = .

entire-variable = variable-identifier .

enumerated-type = '(' identifier-list ')' .

expression = simple-expression [relational-operator simple-expression] .

factor > variable-access | unsigned-constant | function-designator | set-constructor
        *| '(' expression ')' | '**not**' factor .*

factor > bound-identifier .

field-designator = record-variable '.' field-specifier | field-designator-identifier .

field-designator-identifier = identifier .

field-identifier = identifier .

field-list = [(fixed-part [';' variant-part] | variant-part) [';']] .

field-specifier = field-identifier .

*file-type = '**file**' '**of**' component-type .*

file-variable = variable-access .

final-value = expression .

fixed-part = record-section { ';' record-section } .

*for-statement = '**for**' control-variable ':=' initial-value*
              *('**to**' | '**downto**') final-value '**do**' statement .*

formal-parameter-list = '(' formal-parameter-section { ';' formal-parameter-section } ')' .

formal-parameter-section > value-parameter-specification
                          | variable-parameter-specification
                          | procedural-parameter-specification
                          | functional-parameter-specification .

formal-parameter-section > *conformant-array-parameter-specification* .

fractional-part = *digit-sequence* .

function-block = *block* .

function-declaration = *function-heading* ';' *directive*
       | *function-identification* ';' *function-block*
         | *function-heading* ';' *function-block* .

function-designator = *function-identifier* [*actual-parameter-list*] .

function-heading = '**function**' *identifier* [*formal-parameter-list*] ':' *result-type* .

function-identification = '**function**' *function-identifier* .

function-identifier = *identifier* .

functional-parameter-specification = *function-heading* .

goto-statement = '**goto**' *label* .

identified-variable = *pointer-variable* '↑' .

identifier = *letter* { *letter* | *digit* } .

identifier-list = *identifier* { ',' *identifier* } .

if-statement = '**if**' *boolean-expression* '**then**' *statement* [*else-part*] .

index-expression = *expression* .

index-type = *ordinal-type* .

index-type-specification = *identifier* '..' *identifier* ':' *ordinal-type-identifier* .

indexed-variable = *array-variable* '[' *index-expression* { ',' *index-expression* } ']' .

initial-value = *expression* .

label = *digit-sequence* .

label-declaration-part = ['**label**' *label* { ',' *label* } ';'] .

letter = '**a**' | '**b**' | '**c**' | '**d**' | '**e**' | '**f**' | '**g**' | '**h**' | '**i**' | '**j**' | '**k**' | '**l**'
       | '**m**' | '**n**' | '**o**' | '**p**' | '**q**' | '**r**' | '**s**' | '**t**' | '**u**' | '**v**' | '**w**' | '**x**' | '**y**' | '**z**' .

member-designator = *expression* { '..' *expression* } .

multiplying-operator = '∗' | '/' | '**div**' | '**mod**' | '**and**' .

new-ordinal-type = *enumerated-type* | *subrange-type* .

new-pointer-type = '↑' *domain-type* .

new-structured-type = ['**packed**'] *unpacked-structured-type* .

new-type = *new-ordinal-type* | *new-structured-type* | *new-pointer-type* .

ordinal-type = *new-ordinal-type* | *ordinal-type-identifier* .

ordinal-type-identifier = *type-identifier* .

packed-conformant-array-schema = '**packed**' '**array**' '[' *index-type-specification* ']'
         '**of**' *type-identifier* .

pointer-type = *new-pointer-type* | *pointer-type-identifier* .

pointer-type-identifier = *type-identifier* .

pointer-variable = *variable-access* .

procedural-parameter-specification = *procedure-heading* .

procedure-and-function-declaration-part =
         { (*procedure-declaration* | *function-declaration*) ';' } .

procedure-block = *block* .

procedure-declaration = *procedure-heading* ';' *directive*
         | *procedure-identification* ';' *procedure-block*
         | *procedure-heading* ';' *procedure-block* .

procedure-heading = '**procedure**' *identifier* [*formal-parameter-list*] .

procedure-identification = '**procedure**' *procedure-identifier* .

procedure-identifier = *identifier* .

procedure-statement = *procedure-identifier* ([*actual-parameter-list*]
         | *read-parameter-list*
         | *readln-parameter-list*
         | *write-parameter-list*
         | *writeln-parameter-list*) .

program = *program-heading* ';' *program-block* '.' .

program-block = *block* .

program-heading = '**program**' *identifier* ['(' *program-parameters* ')'] .

program-parameters = *identifier-list* .

read-parameter-list = '(' [*file-variable* ','] *variable-access* { ',' *variable-access* } ')' .

readln-parameter-list = ['(' (*file-variable* | *variable-access*) { ',' *variable-access* } ')'] .

real-type-identifier = *type-identifier* .

record-section = *identifier-list* ':' *type-denoter* .

record-type = '**record**' *field-list* '**end**' .

record-variable = *variable-access* .

record-variable-list = *record-variable* { ',' *record-variable* } .

relational-operator = '=' | '<>' | '<' | '>' | '<=' | '>=' | '**in**' .

repeat-statement = '**repeat**' *statement-sequence* '**until**' *boolean-expresion* .

repetitive-statement = *repeat-statement* | *while-statement* | *for-statement* .

result-type = *simple-type-identifier* | *pointer-type-identifier* .

scale-factor = *signed-integer* .

set-constructor = '[' [*member-designator* { ',' *member-designator* }] ']' .

set-type = '**set**' '**of**' *base-type* .

sign = '+' | '−' .

signed-integer = [*sign*] *unsigned-integer* .

signed-number = *signed-integer* | *signed-real* .

signed-real = [*sign*] *unsigned-real* .

simple-expression = [*sign*] *term* { *adding-operator* *term* } .

simple-statement = *empty-statement* | *assignment-statement*
         | *procedure-statement* | *goto-statement* .

simple-type = *ordinal-type* | *real-type-identifier* .

simple-type-identifier = *type-identifier* .

special-symbol = '+' | '−' | '*' | '/' | '=' | '<' | '>' | '[' | ']'
        | '.' | ';' | ':' | ';' | '↑' | '(' | ')'
        | '<>' | '<=' | '>=' | ':=' | '..' | *word-symbol* .

statement = [*label* ':'] (*simple-statement* | *structured-statement*) .

statement-part = *compound-statement* .

statement-sequence = *statement* { ';' *statement* } .

string-character = *one-of-a-set-of-implementation-defined-characters* .

string-element = *apostrophe-image* | *string-character* .

structured-statement = *compound-statement* | *conditional-statement*
         | *repetitive-statement* | *with-statement* .

structured-type = *new-structured-type* | *structured-type-identifier* .

structured-type-identifier = *type-identifier* .

subrange-type = *constant* '..' *constant* .

tag-field = *identifier* .

tag-type = *ordinal-type-identifier* .

term = *factor* { *multiplying-operator* *factor* } .

type-definition = *identifier* '=' *type-denoter* .

type-definition-part = [**'type'** *type-definition* ';' { *type-definition* ';' }] .

type-denoter = *type-identifier* | *new-type* .

type-identifier = *identifier* .

unpacked-conformant-array-schema = **'array'** '[' *index-type-specification*
           { ';' *index-type-specification* } ']'
            'of' (*type-identifier* | *conformant-array-schema*) .

unpacked-structured-type = *array-type* | *record-type* | *set-type* | *file-type* .

unsigned-constant = *unsigned-number* | *character-string* | *constant-identifier* | **'nil'** .

unsigned-integer = *digit-sequence* .

unsigned-number = *unsigned-integer* | *unsigned-real* .

unsigned-real = *unsigned-integer* '.' *fractional-part* ['e' *scale-factor*]
                  | *unsigned-integer* 'e' *scale-factor* .

value-conformant-array-specification = *identifier-list* ':' *conformant-array-schema* .

value-parameter-specification = *identifier-list* ':' *type-identifier* .

variable-access = *entire-variable* | *component-variable* | *identified-variable* | *buffer-variable* .

variable-conformant-array-specification = '**var**' *identifier-list* ':' *conformant-arrary-schema* .

variable-declaration = *identifier-list* ':' *type-denoter* .

variable-declaration-part = ['**var**' *variable-declaration* ';' { *variable-declaration* ';' }] .

variable-identifier = *identifier* .

variable-parameter-specification = '**var**' *identifier-list* ':' *type-identifier* .

variant = *case-constant-list* ':' '(' *field-list* ')' .

variant-part = '**case**' *variant-selector* '**of**' *variant* { ';' *variant* } .

variant-selector = [*tag-field* ':'] *tag-type* .

while-statement = '**while**' *boolean-expression* '**do**' *statement* .

with-statement = '**with**' *record-variable-list* '**do**' *statement* .

word-symbol = '**program**' | '**label**' | '**const**' | '**type**' | '**procedure**' |'**function**'
          | '**var**' | '**begin**' | '**end**' | '**div**' | '**mod**' | '**and**' | '**not**' | '**or**' | '**in**'
          | '**array**' | '**file**' | '**record**' | '**set**' | '**packed**' | '**case**' | '**of**'
          | '**for**' | '**to**' | '**downto**' | '**do**' | '**if**' | '**then**' | '**else**'
          | '**repeat**' | '**until**' | '**while**' | '**with**' | '**goto**' | '**nil**' .

write-parameter = *expression* [':' *expression* [':' *expression*]] .

write-parameter-list = '(' [*file-variable* ','] *write-parameter* { ',' *write-parameter* } ')' .

writeln-parameter-list = ['(' (*file-variable* | *write-parameter*) { ',' *write-parameter* } ')'] .

Index to BNF

Collected Syntax Charts

array-type

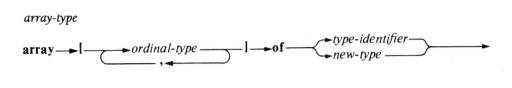

case statement

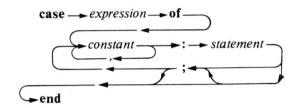

compound statement

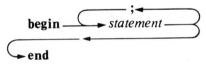

constant-definition-part

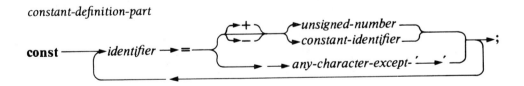

expression

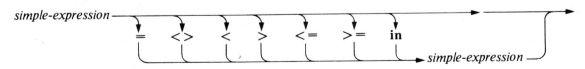

factor

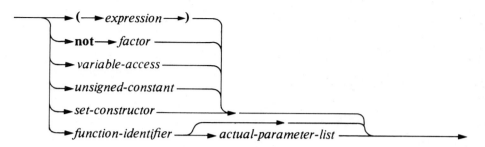

field-list

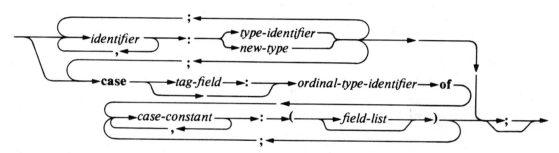

file-type

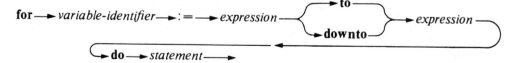

for statement

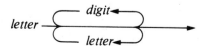

identifier

if statement

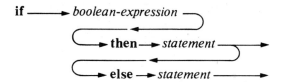

label-declaration-part

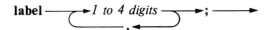

new-ordinal-type

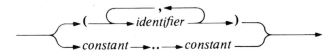

program

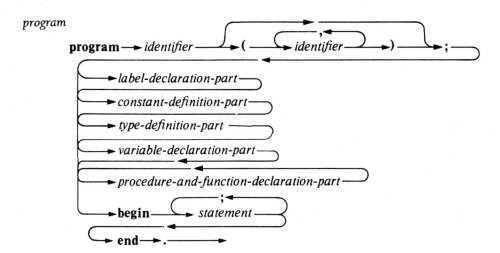

read call

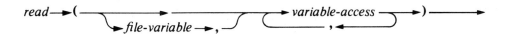

readln call

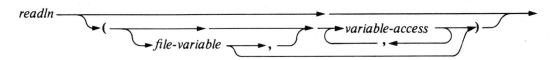

record with fixed-part only

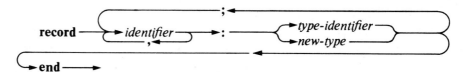

record-type

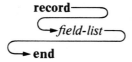

repeat statement

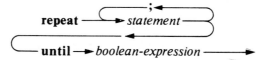

set-type

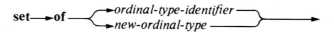

signed-integer

signed-real

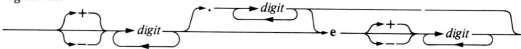

simple-expression

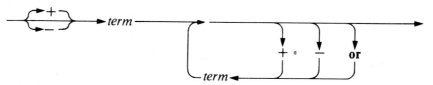

term

type-definition-part

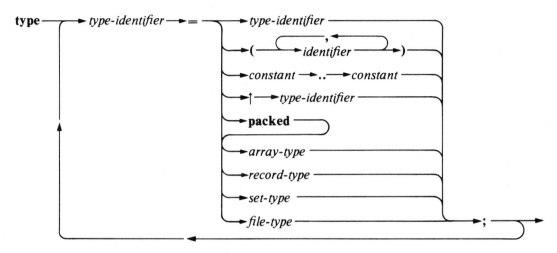

variable-declaration-part

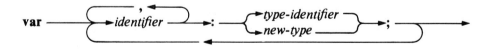

while statement

while ⟶ *boolean-expression*

⟶ do ⟶ *statement* ⟶

with statement

write call

write-parameter

writeln call

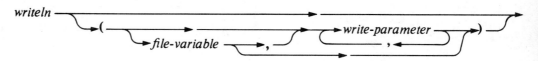

References

[Addyman81]   *Responses to Comments on the Second Draft Proposal*, A. Addyman, ISO/TC97/SC5/WG4 N11 August 1981.

[Aho77]   *Principles of Compiler Design*, A. Aho and J. Ullman, copyright 1977 Bell Telephone Laboratories. Published by Addison-Wesley.

[BSI79]   *Working Draft of Standard Pascal by the BSI DPS/13/14 Working Group*, Pascal News, Vol. 14, January 1979.

[Habermann73]   *Critical Comments on the Programming Language Pascal*, A.N. Habermann, Acta Informatica, Vol. 3, No.1, 1973, pp. 47-57. Copyright 1973 Springer-Verlag.

[Harel80]   *do Considered od Considered Odder than do Considered ob*, D. Harel. SIGPLAN Notices, Vol. 15, No. 4, April 1980.

[Hoare73]   *Hints on Programming Language Design*, C.A.R. Hoare, Stanford University Technical Report No. CS-73-403, December 1973.

[Hoare73b]   *An Axiomatic Definition of the Programming Language Pascal*, C.A.R. Hoare and N. Wirth, Acta Informatica, Vol. 2, No. 4, 1973, pp. 335-355. Copyright 1973 Springer-Verlag.

[ISO80]   *First DP 7185—Specification for the Computer Programming Language Pascal*, May 1980.

[ISO80]   *Second DP 7185—Specification for the Computer Programming Language Pascal*, December 1980

[Jensen79]   *Why Pascal?*, K. Jensen, EDU Twenty-five, Fall 1979. Copyright 1979 Digital Equipment Corporation.

[J&W]   *Pascal User Manual and Report*, K. Jensen and N. Wirth, Second Edition. Copyright 1974 Springer Verlag.

[Kernighan81]   *Why Pascal Is Not My Favorite Programming Language*, B.W. Kernighan, Computing Science Technical Report No. 100, Bell Labs, July 18, 1981.

[Lecarme75]   *More Comments on the Programming Language Pascal*, O. Lecarme and P. Desjardins, Acta Informatica, Vol. 4, No.3, 1975, pp. 231-243. Copyright 1975 Springer-Verlag.

[SIGCSE80]   *Programming Languages for Service Courses and Courses for C.S. Majors*, SIGCSE Bulletin, Vol. 12, No.4, December 1980.

[SIGPLAN82]   *Epigrams on Programming*, Alan J. Perlis, SIGPLAN Notices, Vol. 17, No. 9, September 1982.

[Welsh77]   *Ambiguities and Insecurities in Pascal*, J. Welsh, W.J. Sneeringer, and C.A.R. Hoare, Software—Practice and Experience, Vol. 7, 1977, pp. 685-696. Copyright 1977 John Wiley & Sons, Ltd.

[Wirth71]   *The Programming Language Pascal*, N. Wirth, Acta Informatica, Vol. 1, No.1, 1971, pp. 35-63. Copyright 1971 Springer-Verlag.

[Wirth74]   *On the Design of Programming Languages*, N. Wirth, Information Processing 74, pp. 386-393. Copyright 1974 North Holland Publishing Company.

[Wirth75]   *An Assessment of the Programming Language Pascal*, N. Wirth. IEEE Transactions On Software Engineering, Vol. SE-1, No. 2, June, 1975.

[X3J9/81-98]   *Summary of Voting on the Specification for the Computer Programming Language Pascal*, May 8, 1981.

Index to Example Programs

Chapter 8   The **record** Type

Chapter 9   The **file** Type

Chapter 10   The **set** Type

Chapter 11   The Pointer Types

Chapter 12   Defensive Programming

Index

Note: All entries from the *Reference* section (numbered consistently with *Standard Pascal User Reference Manual*) are printed in a sans serif font. This has led to some duplication of entries and headings (*abs* / *abs*, **and** / **and**, assignment / assignment), but it does make finding formal references much easier.

Model Program

```
program SoTypical (input, output);                              {heading}

const   LIMIT = 10;                                             {integer constant}
        POUNDSIGN = '#';                                        {char constant}
        AMORCITA = 'Ilana';                                     {string constant}

type    Hues = (Red, Blue, Green, Orange, Violet);             {enumerated ordinal type}
        Shades = Blue..Orange;                                  {subrange}
        SmallNumbers = 1..10;                                   {subrange}
        String = packed array [1..LIMIT] of char;              {string}
        Class = record
                    Name: String;
                    Units: integer;
                    Grade: char
                end;                                            {record-type}
        Grades = array [SmallNumbers] of Class;                {array type}
        ColorCount = array [1..10, 'A'..'Z'] of Hues;          {array type}
        ClassFile = file of Class;                             {file type}
        Pastels = set of Shades;                                {set type}
        NextWord = ↑ Sentence;                                  {pointer}
        Sentence = record                                       {dynamically allocable record}
                    CurrentWord: String;
                    ComingWord: NextWord
                end;

var     High, Low, Counter: integer;                            {integer}
        First, Last: char;                                      {char}
        Height, Weight: real;                                   {real}
        Testing, DeBugging: boolean;                            {boolean}
        Colors: Hues;                                           {enumerated type}
        Shorts: SmallNumbers;                                   {subrange}
        Name: String;                                           {string}
        OneCourse: Class;                                       {record}
        Curriculum: Grades;                                     {array}
        ColorSquares: ColorCount;                               {array}
        Schedule: ClassFile;                                    {file}
        Source, Results: text;                                  {textfile}
        Crayons: Pastals;                                       {set}
        List, Pointer: NextWord;                                {pointer}

procedure VeryBusy (Incoming: integer; var Outgoing: integer);      {procedure declaration}
    {A procedure with value and variable parameters.}
    var Local: integer;
    begin
        readln (Local);
        Outgoing := Incoming * Local
    end;   {VeryBusy}
```